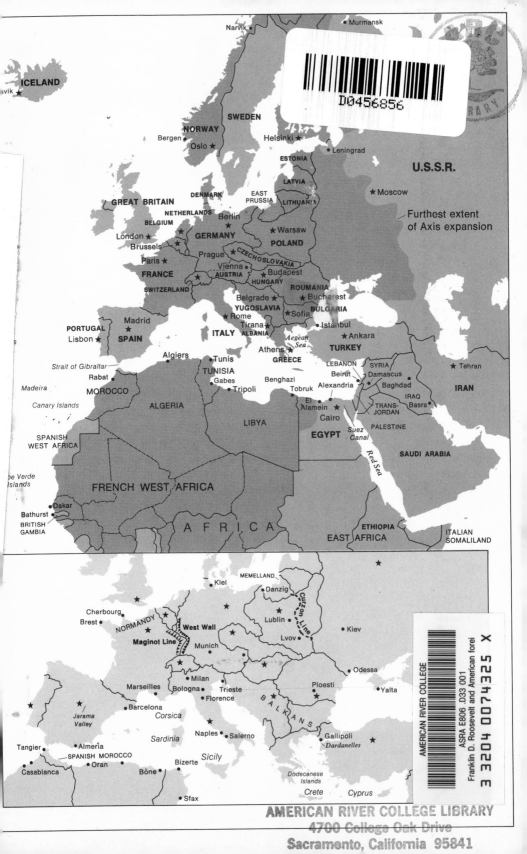

Franklin D. Roosevelt
and American Foreign Policy, 1932–1945

Franklin D. Roosevelt and American Foreign Policy, 1932-1945

ROBERT DALLEK

New York
OXFORD UNIVERSITY PRESS
1979

Copyright © 1979 by Oxford University Press, Inc.

Library of Congress Cataloging in Publication Data
Dallek, Robert.
    Franklin D. Roosevelt and American Foreign
    Policy, 1932–1945
    Bibliography: p.
    Includes index.
    1.   United States—Foreign relations—1933–1945.
2.   Roosevelt, Franklin Delano, Pres. U. S., 1882–1945.
I.   Title.
E806.D33   327.73   78-7910
ISBN 0-19-502457-5

Printed in the United States of America

FOR MATTHEW AND REBECCA

PREFACE

THIS BOOK HAS two general purposes: to meet the need for a comprehensive one-volume study of Franklin Roosevelt's foreign policy, and to wrestle anew with the many intriguing questions about that subject.

The nineteen seventies have been a good time to reconsider FDR's direction of foreign affairs. The appearance of a large and generally excellent specialized literature and the availability of almost the entire American and British record on foreign relations in the thirties and the forties allowed me to reappraise and revise significant parts of the Roosevelt story, particularly on the war years. The London Economic Conference of 1933, the Spanish Civil War, the Quarantine Address, Munich, the Welles Mission of 1940, the Atlantic Conference of 1941, American participation in the war, wartime policy toward Russia and China, the origins of the Unconditional Surrender doctrine, Trusteeships, the Morgenthau Plan, and the Atomic Bomb are some of the principal subjects on which I think Roosevelt's intentions have not been fully understood.

Roosevelt's actions, as many others have observed, are not easy to explain. Rexford G. Tugwell, one of his advisers and biographers, has written, "[He] deliberately concealed the processes of his mind. He would rather have posterity believe that for him everything was always plain and easy . . . than ever to admit to any agony of indecision . . . any misgiving about mistakes." ". . . You are one of the most difficult men to work with that I have ever known," Secretary of the Interior Harold Ickes once told FDR. "Because I get too hard at times?" the President asked. "No," Ickes answered, because ". . . you won't talk frankly even with people who are loyal to you. . . . You keep your cards close up against your belly. You never put them on the table."

I make no claim to some special technique for deciphering Roosevelt's motives. My method has been to reconstruct as fully as possible the context in which he acted. Following Roosevelt in this way gives one the feeling of peering into a kaleidoscope in which a shifting array of pressures moved him from one position to another: his own ideas, domestic considerations, and foreign events, either individually or in various combinations, determined Roosevelt's behavior in foreign affairs. The challenge in explaining FDR is to determine which of these forces influenced him at any given time. Some of my answers will undoubtedly stir debate. That would be all to the good. Roosevelt's presidency is among the most important in American history and deserves continuing scrutiny. It will remain a continuing source of interest and instruction to the nation.

A number of people and institutions have aided me in my work on this book. Professor Lawrence W. Levine of the University of California, Berkeley, provided me with a detailed and challenging critique of the full manuscript. I am particularly indebted to him for persuading me to rethink several important points in my explanation of Roosevelt's actions. Professor Richard Weiss, my old friend and colleague at UCLA, also read the entire manuscript and offered penetrating suggestions for improvement. As important, he generously listened to my ideas as I wrote and raised a number of useful points which I have incorporated into the book. Professor Warren Kimball of Rutgers University, who is preparing a definitive edition of the Churchill-Roosevelt correspondence, eased my way through these extensive materials by providing me with descriptions of the content and location of each exchange. He also read the manuscript for the period 1939–45 and raised a number of valuable questions about interpretation and made useful suggestions for additions. Professor Robert Jervis of the Political Science Department at UCLA and Professor Christopher Thorne of the University of Sussex, England, also helped clarify some of my ideas in conversations about my work. Professor William E. Leuchtenburg of Columbia University called materials in the Robert W. Bingham and James Farley papers to my attention and helped me win fellowships for released time from teaching. Professors Richard W. Leopold of Northwestern University, Ernest R. May of Harvard University and Fritz Stern of Columbia University also generously supported these requests for fellowships.

My thanks to the John Simon Guggenheim Memorial Foundation and to the National Endowment for the Humanities for providing me with fellowships which allowed me to devote two full years to research and writing. The Eleanor Roosevelt Institute of the Franklin D. Roosevelt Library aided me with a generous grant for travel and reproduction of materials during one year. The UCLA Academic Senate supported me with a series of grants for such work during several other years.

I am also indebted to the staff of the Franklin D. Roosevelt Library for helping me work through the Library's rich holdings. To this, I wish to add a special note of thanks to Dr. William R. Emerson, the Library's Director, and to William J. Stewart, the Library's former Associate Director. They helped make my journeys to Hyde Park more valuable and interesting than they may have realized. I also wish to thank the staffs of the Manuscript Divisions of the Columbia University, Harvard University, Hoover Institution, University of California, Berkeley, University of Virginia, and Yale University Libraries and of the Library of Congress, the National Archives, and the British Public Record Office.

A word of appreciation to the excellent people at the Oxford University Press, New York, is also in order. Sheldon Meyer, the Vice President, worked with me on this book from its inception and provided me with valuable encouragement and suggestions throughout the long period of research and writing. Leona Capeless, the Managing Editor, and Annabel Tyrrell, the copy editor on the book, saved me from numerous errors, for which I warmly thank them.

Finally, my wife, Geraldine R. Dallek, helped sustain me in this work with patience, understanding, and a thoughtful critique which has both improved the book and made it more understandable to the general reader.

R.D.

Los Angeles, California
June 1978

CONTENTS

PART FOUR

The Idealist as Realist, 1942–1945

EPILOGUE

Roosevelt as Foreign Policy Leader   529

Franklin D. Roosevelt
and American Foreign Policy, 1932–1945

PROLOGUE

An American Internationalist

ASIDE FROM HIS COUSIN Theodore, Franklin D. Roosevelt was the most cosmopolitan American to enter the White House since John Quincy Adams in 1825. The son of James and Sara Delano Roosevelt, Hudson River Valley aristocrats who habitually lived and traveled abroad, Franklin was introduced to Europe in 1885 at the age of three. His first memories, in fact, were of a lost jumping jack swept away by seawater that entered the family cabin on a return voyage from England in April of that year. Between the ages of seven and fifteen he spent a few months annually in Britain, France, and Germany, where his parents socialized with their European counterparts.

During a typical stay abroad in 1889–90, the family first visited England, where "James had some good shooting with Sir Hugh" Cholmeley and "much riding and hunting" at "Belvoir, one of the most beautiful of the English castles, belonging to the Duke of Rutland." After six weeks, they moved on to France, where Franklin played in the parks and gardens of Versailles and the Paris Tuileries, walked in the Champs-Elysées and the Bois, and accompanied his father to the "dizzying" top of the Eiffel Tower to marvel at "the great city, spread out like a map below." The winter found them in Pau, a health spa in the south of France. There Franklin took bird-watching walks with Cecil Foljambe, an M.P., rode his pony for two hours every morning, listened to his father discuss naval affairs with Lord Clanwilliam, Admiral of the Fleet, and attended a Christmas-day children's party at "Lady Nugent's." In subsequent years, when James Roosevelt took his cures at Bad Nauheim, Franklin bicycled through parts of Holland and Germany, attended the opera at Bayreuth, and climbed the Blauen in the Black Forest.

Even at home in Hyde Park, Franklin was constantly reminded of the world abroad. Each week the *Illustrated London News* brought pictures of Hohenzollerns and Hapsburgs, "of parades and palaces, of international society moving from Paris to London to Vienna, to spa to fox hunt to fancy ball." From the time he was five until he was eleven, European governesses tutored him in German and French, giving him the rudiments of both languages; he still held some command of them during his presidential years.[1]

3

In his formal schooling, which began at Groton in the fall of 1896, the foreign world continued to make itself felt in Franklin's life. Groton, like other leading American boarding schools of the day, resembled the English church or public schools with their classical curriculums of Latin, Greek, French, German, and English, and their central preoccupation with developing "manly, Christian character."

It was in the latter that Groton had a particularly important impact on Franklin's thinking. What he learned from Endicott Peabody, Headmaster and founder of the school, was the Christian gentleman's ideal of service to the less fortunate: the conviction that privileged Americans should take a part in relieving national and international ills. Peabody took considerable pains to assure that his boys kept abreast of what these were. He stocked the library with the leading periodicals of the day, insisted that the school magazine include essays on social problems, and set students to debating current questions: the expansion of the navy, the annexation of Hawaii, British and American responsibility for the integrity of China, Philippine independence, and the Boer War were typical subjects.

No student conformed more fully to Peabody's design than Franklin Roosevelt. He joined the school's Missionary Society, contributed current events articles to the *Grotonian*, and actively participated in school debates on foreign affairs. By the time he left Groton in 1900, Franklin, like other graduates of the school, firmly believed in a useful role for the United States in world affairs.[2]

It would be twelve more years, however, before he gave meaningful expression to this attitude. Though he continued to interest himself in the outside world, touring the Caribbean twice and Europe three times, his concerns from 1900 to 1912 were chiefly personal: social and extracurricular activities at Harvard, marriage, law school at Columbia, and dreams of high political station. He was an ambitious young man who believed himself slated for social distinction.

He came to this belief partly through a well-developed appreciation of his aristocratic background. "His mother," one biographer has written, "could recite pedigrees from a repertoire that seemed to include half the aristocracy of Europe and all that of the Hudson River Valley. At least a dozen lines of Mayflower descent converged in Franklin, and Sara could name every one of them." Franklin himself effortlessly acquired this knowledge from his mother and added to the family's genealogical records through his own research and writing while at Harvard.[3]

His early years also endowed him with a fund of self-confidence. He was the only child of an exceptionally happy marriage, and the household seemed to revolve around him. "There were no brothers or sisters to compete for attention, to wrest toys from him, or to bring the life of school or playground to him outside his parents' ken." His father showered him with attention, acting as "an understanding guide and playmate," affectionately teaching him to sled, skate, toboggan, ride, fish, sail, and farm. Sara also doted on the boy, keeping diaries with almost daily records of his achievements. "Franklin went out before breakfast and shot two bluebirds, one for his collection and one for Martin," a typical entry reads. Everything about Franklin received her loving care: she preserved his childhood clothes, letters, and even examinations, "as though sure they would be of significance to posterity." [4]

Much that he met outside the family home reinforced his feelings of exceptionalism. By the time he was five, he had met many of America's most prominent men, including President Grover Cleveland at the White House. When he began his formal schooling at Groton, he found himself almost exclusively among the sons of social register families, and at Harvard he entered effortlessly into Boston-Cambridge society. During his second year at the university, his cousin Theodore Roosevelt became President of the United States, and two and a half years later he married Eleanor Roosevelt, the President's niece. In 1907, as a matter of course, he began a law career with a prominent Wall Street firm—Carter, Ledyard, and Milburn.

At the same time that Franklin learned to feel himself special, he also learned to dominate and lead. "His father and I always expected a great deal of Franklin, just as my father had always expected a great deal of his sons, and got it," Sara Roosevelt once said. "We thought he ought to take prizes, and we were pleased but not surprised when he did. After all he had many advantages that other boys did not have."

There is evidence that Franklin absorbed this lesson as a child. Once, when his mother chided him for ordering his playmates around, he replied: "Mummie, if I didn't give the orders, nothing would happen!" He was intensely competitive at Groton and Harvard and tried repeatedly to win athletic honors, the object of greatest student esteem. Though a slight physique forced him to settle for what he and his fellows regarded as second rank—the managership of the baseball team at Groton and the editorship of the *Crimson* at Harvard—he worked at these assignments with an "almost desperate energy," revealing a "ferocious drive" for preferment. "Looking back on the Roosevelt career," Rexford Tugwell has written, "I find its most persistent as well as its most astounding feature is this fierce flame burning at its core."

As would become particularly clear after he gained high public station, this drive for preeminence was always closely tied to the idea of service—the responsibility of the well-born to the less fortunate. As he understood by the age of nineteen, this was a noteworthy family tradition. "Some of the famous Dutch families in New York," he wrote in a Harvard history essay, "have today nothing left but their name—they are few in numbers, they lack progressiveness and a true democratic spirit. One reason—perhaps the chief—of the virility of the Roosevelts is this very democratic spirit. They have never felt that because they were born in a good position they could put their hands in their pockets and succeed. They have felt, rather, that . . . there was no excuse for them if they did not do their duty by the community, and it is because this idea was instilled into them from their birth that they have in nearly every case proved good citizens." By the time he was at Harvard, Franklin's background, rearing, and education had led him to feel that he should be a leading American who contributed meaningfully to the national life.[5]

When he was a teenager and a young man, no one encouraged these feelings more than Theodore Roosevelt. As early as 1897, Franklin had begun thinking of him as a special hero. "After supper tonight," he wrote his parents from Groton in the spring of that year, "Cousin Theodore gave us a splendid talk on his adventures when he was on the Police Board. He kept the whole room in an uproar for over an hour, by telling us killing stories about policemen and their doings in New York." In 1898, when T.R. became Governor of New York, Franklin reported himself "wild with delight," and in the following January he accompanied his parents to the inauguration in Albany. In 1900, when Theodore ran for Vice President, Franklin temporarily abandoned his father's Democratic leanings to join the Harvard Republican club and march through the streets of Boston in Theodore's behalf. After T.R. became President in 1901, Franklin's admiration knew no bounds. He visited him a number of times at the White House and listened with rapt attention as the President discoursed on Panama, the Congress, and public service. While Franklin was traveling in Europe in the summer of 1905, he wrote his mother that "Everyone is talking about Cousin Theodore saying that he is the most prominent figure of present day history, and adopting towards our country in general a most respectful and almost loving tone. What a change has come over English opinion in the last few years! Even the French were quite enthusiastic, but the German tone seemed to hide a certain animosity and jealousy as usual."

Sometime during these years, Franklin decided to duplicate Theodore's career. By 1907 at least, he was telling his fellow law clerks at Carter, Ledyard, and Milburn that "he wasn't going to practice law forever, that he intended to run for office at the first opportunity, and that he wanted to be and thought he had a very real chance to be President." The steps he described as leading to this goal paralleled those taken by cousin Ted: a seat in the state Assembly, an appointment as Assistant Secretary of the Navy, the governorship of New York, and the presidency.[6]

There was something almost painfully naïve or surprisingly immature about Franklin's identification with T.R. and his impulse to parallel *every* step of his career. After all, by 1907 he was a well-educated, widely traveled young man of twenty-five who moved in the most sophisticated circles of American society. Yet for all his advantages, he was also the only child of a domineering mother and an older father who had taught him to conform to family and social traditions. Indeed, what seems most striking in his attitude toward T.R. is its lack of originality, or in other words, his readiness to conform to a prefabricated plan. Yet this hardly squares with his later much celebrated quality of flexibility and openness to new economic and social schemes. Clearly, behind the mask of amiability and conformity, which were also hallmarks of his career, there was an impulse to rebel or break out of familiar modes which later found expression in the experimentalism of his New Deal years.

But this would not emerge until later. In 1910, when Democratic leaders in Dutchess County, New York, invited him to run for the state legislature, his eagerness to emulate T.R.'s career made him quick to accept. Though he shortly found himself offered an unpromising nomination for state Senator rather than a relatively safe Assembly seat, he decided to go ahead anyway. His decision led to his first electoral success. Exploiting a state-wide split in Republican ranks with a shrewd campaign in which he identified himself with cousin Ted, Franklin became the second Democrat in fifty-four years to represent Columbia, Dutchess, and Putnam counties in the state Senate. During the two years he served there, he established a solid progressive reputation by opposing Tammany bosses and supporting popular reform proposals for the direct election of U. S. Senators, direct primaries, conservation of natural resources, and aid to upstate farmers.[7]

When he combined his progressivism with early and consistent support of Woodrow Wilson for President, he quickly found himself in a position to achieve his next political goal. Drawing on his credit with the new administration, he asked for an appointment as Assistant Secretary of the Navy. Moreover, he refused to be sidetracked when offered the assistant secretaryship of the Treasury or the collectorship of the port of New York. Hence, an invitation from Secretary of the Navy Josephus Daniels to come to Washington as Assistant Secretary of the Navy evoked the response that it would please him "better than anything in the world. . . . The assistant secretaryship is the one place, above all others, I would love to hold." [8]

FDR saw his entrance into the Navy Department as a chance not only to advance his political career but also to unite his "vocation with [his] avocation." From his earliest years he had been addicted to the sea, spending countless summer hours on his father's and then his own sailing yacht in the Canadian waters off Campobello. His early readings included Admiral Alfred T. Mahan's *The Influence of Sea Power on History* and *The Interest of America in Sea Power, Present and Future.* During his years at Groton he began collecting old prints of sailing ships, and while at Harvard he began a collection of books, pamphlets, articles, and manuscripts on the Navy. When he entered the Navy Department in March 1913, he was a skilled seaman with a substantial knowledge of ships and naval warfare.[9]

Despite his pleasure in joining the Navy Department, Roosevelt saw it primarily as a stepping-stone to his next political goal. The example of cousin Theodore, who within two years after becoming Assistant Secretary had won military glory at San Juan Hill and election to the governorship of New York, remained firmly in his mind. During his first eighteen months in office, Franklin tried to gain administration backing for a New York gubernatorial campaign, and when this failed, he launched an unsuccessful primary fight against Tammany Hall for a U. S. Senate nomination.[10]

At the same time, he responded to international affairs with a militancy reminiscent of T.R.'s. From the outset of his Navy Department service, he made it abundantly clear that he was also a big Navy man. The Navy needed "a fighting force of the highest efficiency," he told a Navy League convention in April 1913. "You can't fight Germany's and England's dreadnoughts with United States gunboats," he declared in the following year. ". . . The policy of our congress should be to buy and build dreadnoughts until our navy is comparable to any other in the world." During a diplomatic crisis with Japan in the spring of 1913, he supported an expansion of American naval power and joined militant admirals and generals in urging ship and troop movements which Wilson rejected as provocative. A year later, when Wilson's nonrecognition policy toward Victoriano Huerta's "unconstitutional" government in Mexico resulted in the American occupation of Vera Cruz, he predicted all-out war. "I do not see how we can avoid it," he said. "Sooner or later . . . the United States must go down there and clean up the Mexican political mess. The best time is right now."

He coupled this militancy with a desire for personal adventure in which, like cousin Ted, he could dramatize himself. Should a war occur, he announced within two months of taking office, he would prefer naval service, but "I suppose that I must . . . follow in the steps of T.R. and form a regiment of rough riders." Speculating later that summer on what he would do if he were in the diplomatic service, he declared: "I would beg for Mexico, as it is the only place just now where there is real action." [11]

Roosevelt's militancy was the product not only of his desire to win a reputation and advance his political career but also of his sincere commitment to ideas he had learned in earlier years and now shared with the diplomatic, military, and political elites he associated with in Washington. Like them, he believed that a major American role in world affairs would serve both the national well-being and the needs of backward peoples around the globe. He also shared their desire for a great Navy to assure that no "enemy" would "supersede us in every outlying part, usurp our commerce and destroy our influence as a nation throughout the world." "Our national defense must extend all over the western hemisphere," Roosevelt said in 1914, "must go out a thousand miles into the sea, must embrace the Philippines and over the seas wherever our commerce may be."

Because he held these views, FDR at once found himself in conflict with administration leaders, including Secretary Daniels, his immediate superior. A small-town North Carolinian reared in poverty and Methodist fundamentalism, Daniels was a pacifist, a prohibitionist, and an agrarian radical. "He was plain; he wore baggy clothes and a parson's broad hat; and he was a little fat. He looked a good deal like [Secretary of State William Jennings] Bryan or like a hundred congressmen who were his contemporaries." Franklin mimicked Daniels before his society friends and described him as " 'the funniest looking hillbilly' he had ever seen." [12]

More important, Roosevelt saw Daniels and other administration pacifists as so unsophisticated and wrongheaded about world affairs that he tried to push them along paths they did not care to go. This was particularly the case after the outbreak of World War I in August 1914. By contrast with his superiors, Roosevelt saw an immediate need to put the Navy Department in a state of alert. When he found Daniels making no such preparations, he took matters into his own hands. "To my astonishment on reaching the Dept.," he wrote Eleanor on August 3, "nobody seemed the least excited about the European crisis—Mr. Daniels feeling chiefly very sad that his faith in human nature and civilization and similar idealistic nonsense was receiving such a rude shock. So I started in alone to get things ready and prepare plans for what *ought* to be done by the Navy end of things. . . . These dear good people like W.J.B. and J.D.," he added, "have as much conception of what a general European wars means as Elliott [FDR's three-year-old son] has of higher mathematics." "I am *running* the real work, although Josephus is here!' he wrote Eleanor three days later. "He is bewildered by it all, very sweet but very sad!"

Roosevelt's view of Daniels and Bryan revealed more about him than it did about them. Both men were more complicated than Roosevelt's view of them suggests. Bryan, after all, had supported the Spanish-American War and Daniels would remain as Secretary of the Navy throughout the period of American involvement in World War I. Both, one suspects, were convenient targets for Roosevelt's annoyance with Wilson and the mass of Americans, who were at odds with his inner wish to join the fighting and allow him to live out his fantasy about literally following in T.R.'s footsteps.

In the fall of 1914, Roosevelt openly began taking issue with the administration's preparedness policies. He informed the press about the

Navy's numerous deficiencies and told Eleanor that even if his statement got him into trouble, he was "perfectly ready to stand by it. The country needs the truth about the Army and the Navy," he explained, "instead of a lot of soft mush about everlasting peace which so many statesmen are handing out to a gullible public." By early 1915 he was predicting that he would "do some awful unneutral thing before I get through," and by June, after Bryan had resigned over Wilson's stiff response to the sinking of the *Lusitania*, he complained that Daniels would not follow the example of the Secretary of State.[13]

Even during the next twenty-two months while Wilson prepared the nation for war, Roosevelt remained a voice for stronger action. In the summer of 1915 he called for a Council of National Defense to supervise industrial mobilization, and by June 1916, with his suggestion still unanswered, he declared himself "the only person in Washington in the Administration who realizes the perfectly wonderful opportunities, nationally and politically, to accomplish something of lasting construction." At the same time, he continued to speak publicly for a stronger Army and Navy than the administration favored, and by the fall of 1916 he began to urge his superiors to take the country into war. Though Wilson moved toward this decision in early 1917, it was still not fast enough for FDR. Shortly before Wilson's request for congressional action, Roosevelt met with prominent administration critics, including T.R., General Leonard Wood, and J. P. Morgan, to discuss ways of pushing the government into a fuller defense of neutral rights and a larger buildup of the Army and the Navy.[14]

Once the United States entered the fighting in April 1917, Roosevelt's differences with Wilson and Daniels became clashes of method and degree rather than of policy and kind. Sharing a common desire for victory with his chiefs, Roosevelt now devoted himself principally to the heavy wartime administrative burdens of the Department.[15]

But he was soon restless in this assignment. A craving for excitement and a keen sense of patriotic duty made him desire a direct part in the fighting. Hence, in June 1918, when a choice arose between traveling to the front for the Department and accepting the gubernatorial nomination in New York, the fruit of a three-year effort at cultivating Tammany Democrats, he chose the former. He did not want to "give up war work for what is . . . very much of a political job in these times," he wrote Wilson. "I cannot accept such a nomination at this time either with honesty or honor to myself." His decision also rested partly on what he saw as good politics: he did not think a Democrat would win New York's governorship in 1918, and he believed that a successful postwar political career required military service of some kind.[16]

But the closest he could come to military service was his trip to Europe in the summer of 1918. Crossing the Atlantic on a newly commissioned destroyer, he joined enthusiastically in submarine alerts that were all false alarms. In France, however, he saw the devastation at the front lines, witnessed heavy fighting, and came under direct shellfire. Attracted more than ever to the idea of a share in this fighting, he returned to the United States in September determined to resign his assistant secretaryship for a Navy commission. But severe influenza and pneumonia contracted on the trip delayed his request, and when he brought it to Wilson in October, the war was coming to an end.[17]

With the conclusion of the war in the following month, Roosevelt once more fixed his attention on the political path ahead. His attitude at this time, historian Frank Freidel has written, "was frankly opportunistic—he wished to advance his political name and reputation as much as possible while he built for a somewhat distant and unforeseeable future."

A possible first step along this road was a trip to Paris, where government chiefs, including Wilson, were to negotiate the peace. He was not very clear on how such a trip would benefit him, except that it would place him near the center of major events and allow him to assure against errors in demobilizing the Navy. Republican control of Congress in the coming year made it almost certain that the direction of the war under Wilson, including the Navy Department, would come under close review. He had no intention of leaving himself vulnerable to any sort of congressional attack.

As things turned out, the most significant part of this journey occurred not in Europe, where he attended to his Navy business and was a spectator at the Paris peace talks, but on his return to the United States. During the crossing, President Wilson chatted with him about the League of Nations and stirred his enthusiasm with the comment that "the United States must go in or it will break the heart of the world, for she is the only nation that all feel is disinterested and all trust." If Wilson's comment was not enough to elicit his support, the President's reception in Boston was. As he paraded through the city, 200,000 Bostonians cheered him wildly. Later that day, when he spoke in behalf of the League, he again received unrestrained acclaim. Even Calvin Coolidge, the Republican Governor of Massachusetts, expressed the conviction that "the people would back the President," and anyone watching the enthusiastic crowds at the stations on Wilson's journey to Washington could not doubt this observation.[18]

Wilson's reception made a strong impression on FDR and persuaded him that an aspiring politician with internationalist commitments could not now make his way with the kind of martial deeds and rhetoric T.R. had used. Indeed, Roosevelt understood that involvement in the fighting had temporarily increased American interest in foreign affairs and made disarmament and peace popular watchwords which no potential candidate for high office could ignore. "This is a time of idealism," he observed, "a time when more ideals are properly demanded of us, and the world looks to us to make good the high purpose with which we came into this war."

Roosevelt also appreciated that unless the government acted on this idealism by entering the League, the country would probably revert to "an old Chinese wall policy of isolation." He considered this morally and realistically unsound. It would not only be wrong for the United States and all mankind, he said, it would also be at odds with international realities. "There will be many crises in international affairs for many years to come," he predicted, and the country will be unable to "escape an important, perhaps even a controlling voice." To prevent this and align himself with current public mood, in March 1919 he began campaigning for American entrance into the League. Instead of viewing it as "a beautiful dream, a Utopia," as he had the year before, he now called it a realistic alternative to continued heavy armament and a potential bulwark against revolution and future war. At bottom, however, one cannot escape the conclusion that Roosevelt's sudden switch from strong military advocate to League of Nations supporter had less to do with a changed perception of international realities than with domestic politics: convinced that Wilson's universalist vision had caught the public imagination, he believed his identification with the League would be a valuable asset in any election campaign.

Yet at the same time that he came out in support of the League, he also continued to call for adequate defense. During 1919 he repeatedly pressed the case for universal military training, saying that it was "the surest guarantee of national safety" as well as a guard against the Bolshevik revolt. By the beginning of 1920, however, he saw pacifist sentiment in the country as so widespread that he declared himself as "not keen for universal military training just now." Instead, he hoped Americans would agree to "have universal training with the military cut out." Such training, he argued, would promote good citizenship and improve the quality of government throughout the United States.[19]

Roosevelt's more pacific approach to foreign affairs was but one expression of his emerging belief that to advance his political career he needed to establish a national reputation as a Wilsonian. Though he appreciated that Wilsonianism was then on the wane, he felt that Americans would ultimately return to their progressive faith and that when they did, he would be in a strong position to command their support. Moreover, by 1919, as some earlier exchanges with his mother indicate, he would have found it difficult to identify himself with the growing conservative mood; by this time he had developed a fundamental, if somewhat hazy, commitment to progressive ideas. Consequently, in 1919–20, he became a vigorous spokesman for Wilsonianism. In addition to arguing for the League, he began denouncing the "conservatism, special privilege, partisanship

[and] destruction" of the Republicans, and celebrating the "liberalism, common sense idealism, constructiveness [and] progress" of the Democrats.

Moreover, during this time he renewed his efforts to win a gubernatorial or senatorial nomination, which, at the very least, he could convert into a forum for dramatizing his Wilsonian ties. Though Governor Al Smith's decision to run again for the State House and a reluctance to identify himself fully with the unpopular Tammany machine blocked Roosevelt from a serious bid for either nomination, a combination of effective preparation and good fortune made him the Democratic Party's vice-presidential nominee. In an appearance at the end of May before the Democratic National Committee in Chicago, he made "a fighting speech" that attacked the Republican old guard and gained him national attention "as a coming leader." In June 1920, on the eve of the Democratic convention, he encouraged rumors that he would make a strong vice-presidential candidate. Further, at the convention he made a highly effective seconding speech for Al Smith's nomination as President. When the convention broke a deadlock between Governor James Cox of Ohio, the candidate of the bosses, and William Gibbs McAdoo, the candidate of the party's rural and progressive forces, by nominating Cox, Roosevelt, a McAdoo backer with a famous name, became a logical choice for the second spot on the ticket. When Tammany boss Charles F. Murphy, who believed it would serve the purposes of his machine, agreed to the idea, Roosevelt gained the nomination on the first ballot.[20]

This placed him in an ideal position to further his long-term political goal. Though vice-presidential candidates usually ran modest, unspectacular campaigns, Roosevelt departed from this tradition to speak and become known all over the nation. Traveling to many of the states, delivering usually seven, and sometimes as many as thirteen, speeches a day, he spoke tirelessly for international cooperation and progressivism. "In our world problems," he declared repeatedly, "we must either shut our eyes . . . build an impregnable wall of costly armaments and live, as the Orient used to live, a hermit nation, dreaming of the past, or we must open our eyes and see that modern civilization has become so complex and the lives of civilized men so interwoven with the lives of other men in other countries as to make it impossible to avoid . . . those honorable and intimate foreign relations which the fearful-hearted shudderingly miscall by that devil's catchword, 'international complications.' "

Despite the country's failure to enter the League, he continued to picture American involvement as the surest means to an effective foreign policy. The League, he said, "is a practical solution of a practical situation. It is no more perfect than our original Constitution . . . was perfect. It is not anti-national, it is anti-war. . . . Through it we may with nearly every other duly constituted government in the whole world throw our moral force and our potential power into the scale of peace. That such an object should be contrary to American policy is unthinkable."

In domestic affairs he promised "organized progress" and "more efficient government": "the bettering of our citizenship," the reduction of illiteracy, the exclusion of physically and morally unfit immigrants, the betterment of working conditions in the cities, the improvement of communications on the farm, "the further protection of child life and of women in industry," the "proper use" of our natural resources, and the handling of government business on at least a level with a well-conducted private industry.

Though James Cox, the Democratic Party's presidential nominee, acted and spoke along similar lines, Harding and Coolidge won by a landslide. In spite of the defeat, Roosevelt ended the 1920 campaign in an upbeat mood. "Franklin D. Roosevelt, Ex. V.P., Canned. (Erroneously reported dead)," he joked in a letter. Having emerged from the election as a much better known national figure and an heir apparent to Wilson, Roosevelt had reason for good humor. He had carried off what Rexford Tugwell, one of his biographers, has called "a political feat of really astonishing cleverness." [21]

During the next eight years, while he waited for the opportune moment to run again, Roosevelt's political problem was how to keep himself at the center of his party and before the public. The onset of poliomyelitis in the summer of 1921, followed by a long period of great personal suffering and the permanent paralysis of his legs, made this highly difficult for him and raised serious doubts about his political future. Yet in spite of his affliction, another of his biographers, James MacGregor Burns, has written, "there was never the slightest chance of Roosevelt's retiring from politics." While Burns in no way makes light of Roosevelt's terrible ordeal, he believes that the illness strengthened rather than altered existent tendencies in his personality and had its chief effect on the timing of his next bid for office. Recent revelations about the near collapse of Roosevelt's marriage in 1918 and continuing strains in his relations with Eleanor lend additional weight to this idea. Despite the polio, retirement to private life had little appeal to FDR; in the 1920s, a public career promised a measure of satisfaction he seemed unlikely to find in the private sphere.[22]

In the seven years between the onset of his illness and a New York gubernatorial campaign, Roosevelt in fact worked continuously to advance his political fortunes. Only a month after his polio attack, he accepted membership on the party's Executive Committee in New York, and in the fall he began writing again to Democratic leaders all over the state and in other parts of the country. In 1922 he took a major part in returning Al Smith to the governorship and acted as honorary campaign chairman for Royal Copeland, the party's U.S. Senate nominee. In 1923–

24 he involved himself fully in the fight for the Democratic presidential nomination, becoming Al Smith's campaign manager. At the convention, moreover, he regained the national spotlight when he dramatized his first major public appearance since his illness with a brilliant nominating endorsement of Smith as the "Happy Warrior." Roosevelt dramatically delivered his speech on crutches, and when he came "to the end and named Al," Will Rogers said, "you would have thought somebody had thrown a wildcat in your face. The galleries went wild and about ten State delegations marched and hollered for an hour." Though John W. Davis of West Virginia became the party's nominee, after Smith and McAdoo had deadlocked the convention for 102 ballots, Roosevelt's appearance at the convention was a personal triumph.

After a disastrous campaign in 1924, in which the Democrats had split into rural and urban factions and Davis suffered overwhelming defeat, Roosevelt had devoted himself to rejuvenating the party. Believing that the Democrats could not outbid the Republicans until they found a set of progressive principles on which they could unite, Roosevelt tried repeatedly from 1925 to 1927 to identify these aims. Though he made little headway toward this end, he managed nevertheless to keep himself at the center of party affairs, and in 1928 he added to his standing by playing a key role in Smith's successful nomination campaign. He was Smith's floor manager at the Democratic convention and made another eloquent nominating speech for him, which once more thrust Roosevelt into the national limelight.[23]

During the twenties, Roosevelt also tried to place himself at the center of party and national affairs by providing leadership on foreign policy. Convinced more than ever that the United States could not turn its back on overseas affairs without injury to itself and the rest of the world, he continued to work for international cooperation. In 1921 he helped launch a Woodrow Wilson Foundation to honor the former President and reward contributions to international harmony. Between 1923 and 1927 he took an active part in setting up the Walter Hines Page School of International Relations at Johns Hopkins University, helped plan the sponsorship of courses on international relations in colleges all over the world, and supported the creation of a Bok Award for the best plan to preserve peace.

More important, he continued to urge American entrance into the League or, barring that, a new, less controversial world body. In 1923 he prepared a plan for submission to the Bok prize committee. He envisaged a new Society of Nations free of the characteristics Americans found objectionable in the League. The United States was not "to become involved in the purely regional affairs . . . of other nations," nor would Americans have to commit themselves to "undertakings calling for or leading up to the use of armed force without our full and free consent, given through our constitutional procedure." Throughout the twenties Roosevelt also continually urged other Wilsonians to accept whatever restrictions American opinion placed on entrance into the League. It was not important how America resumed her proper role in the world, he argued, but that she took part.

While all these activities kept Roosevelt in touch with the Wilsonian internationalists, they did not allow him to reach a mass audience or even a substantial cross-section of the party. To do this, he abandoned his earlier militancy and elitism for a pacifist approach to foreign affairs. Believing that pacifism now dominated public thinking everywhere, he thought it simple political realism to back the international drive for peace. Indeed, the divisions of the immediate postwar years had taught him that the first requirement of an effective role abroad was a stable consensus at home. And in the 1920s this meant advocating a foreign policy aimed at achieving disarmament and peace. "President Harding's Washington Conference of 1921," he told a friend in 1923, "has, without question, removed the greater part of the indefinable something which bred suspicion and competition first in the defense departments, then in Congress, and finally among a large body of people who followed the doings of the government." "The whole trend of the times," he observed in public, "is against wars for colonial expansion. The thought of the world leans the other way. Populations themselves have a say. Subjects of dispute are being worked out more and more by amicable means. No, the millennium has not arrived, but the nations are using greater and greater efforts to prevent war." [24]

To identify himself with and support this trend, Roosevelt wrote an article for *Asia* magazine in 1923 entitled, "Shall We Trust Japan?" His answer was an emphatic yes. Picturing the Japanese as living up to both the letter and the spirit of the Washington treaties on naval disarmament and China, Roosevelt urged Americans to abandon their old suspicions of Japan. If the United States, as so long forecast, fought a war with Tokyo, it would, Roosevelt contended, produce a military deadlock in which both nations would likely bleed to death "through the pocketbook." Drawing on current military thinking expressed in such popular books as Walter Pitkin's *Must We Fight Japan?* (1921) and Hector Bywater's *Sea-Power in the Pacific* (1922), Roosevelt described American and Japanese defenses against each other's fleets as practically invulnerable. If as long as ten years ago naval experts calculated losses for a fleet crossing an ocean during wartime at between a quarter and a third of its fighting strength, "then," Roosevelt asserted, "the principle is even more true today"; for the addition of the submarine and the airplane to sea battles made the defense of capital ships even more difficult than before. In place, therefore, of the old antagonisms, which would profit no one, Roosevelt suggested the development of economic and political cooperation that would benefit the United States and the entire world. [25]

More significantly, in 1928 Roosevelt published an article in *Foreign Affairs* which he hoped Smith and the party would use during the presidential campaign. Unlike the *Asia* essay, the *Foreign Affairs* piece was avowedly partisan and sought to identify him and the Democrats with the effective promotion of world peace. "There have been outstanding periods when American leadership has influenced the thought and action of the civilized world towards international good will and peace," Roosevelt asserted. But the past nine years had not been one of them. "Since the summer of 1919 our country has had to face the charge that in a time when great constructive aid was needed in the task of solving the grave problems facing the whole earth, we have contributed little or nothing save the isolated Naval Conference of 1921." But even in this, Roosevelt complained, Coolidge had failed to supplement the Washington treaty at the 1927 Geneva talks and now wished to revive naval building on "an enormous scale." Roosevelt proposed instead that guarantees of safety for merchant ships in time of war would remove the chief remaining reason for naval expansion and would open the way to "careful preliminary examination and interchange of views—unofficial friendly 'chats around the table'—" for extending and strengthening limitations on naval arms.

Roosevelt also complained that the Republicans had undermined the "principles of peace" by refusing "to have anything to do with either the League of Nations or the World Court." Though he did not wish "to agitate the question" of American membership and though he acknowledged that a majority of American voters opposed entrance "on the conditions under which other nations have joined," he proposed "a far larger share of sympathetic approval and definite official help than we have hitherto accorded." "We should cooperate with the League," he said, "as the first great agency for the maintenance of peace . . . and, without entering into European politics, we should take an active, hearty and official part in all those proceedings which bear on the general good of mankind. So too with the World Court."

Roosevelt found additional grounds for complaint in Republican handling of Allied war debts to the United States. The fact that the United States expected to collect $22 billion on a $10 billion loan to the European governments was by itself, Roosevelt observed, enough to make us "a hated collector." This was chiefly because "in a time of general poverty and retrenchment our Government has seemed greedy." Specifically, at the same time the United States demanded payment on its war loans, it practiced a "discriminatory and exorbitant tariff policy" that made it "doubly hard" for the Europeans to pay.

Finally, Roosevelt saw reason to quarrel with Republican policy in Latin America. Here, however, he freely admitted that shortcomings existed before the Republicans took the reins of government in 1921, and that he himself had partly contributed to the problem. Having been a vigorous proponent of interventions and annexations in Latin America during the Wilson years, and having defended American control of Haiti as recently as 1922, FDR now saw at least two good reasons for altering this approach. On the one hand, informed domestic opinion now seemed strongly against military adventures of any kind, and on the other, interventions, like one that had recently occurred in Nicaragua, seemed destructive to U. S. influence in the Western Hemisphere. Though he did not think that the United States should stand aloof from Latin American affairs, he believed that a new method was in order. "The time has come when we must accept . . . a newer and better standard in international relations," he declared. As before, it might well be that a sister nation would "fall upon evil days" and that a helping hand would be necessary to restore order and stability. But "in that event it is not the right or the duty of the United States to intervene alone. It is rather the duty of the United States to associate with itself other American Republics, to give intelligent joint study to the problem, and, if the conditions warrant, to offer the helping hand or hands in the name of the Americas. Single-handed intervention by us in the affairs of other nations must end; with the cooperation of others we shall have more order in this hemisphere and less dislike."

All in all, he considered this a good time to start a new chapter in American foreign relations: one in which the United States once more pointed the way toward arms reduction, cooperated "whole-heartedly with every agency that . . . works to relieve the common ills of mankind," and renounced "the practice of arbitrary intervention in the home affairs of our neighbors." [26]

Although a desire to set the Democrats off from the Republicans and a hope of enlarging his own reputation moved FDR to prepare this systematic statement on foreign relations in 1928, other political considerations shortly persuaded him to remain silent about world affairs for the next three years. After becoming Governor of New York in January 1929 and deciding to run for the presidency in 1932, Roosevelt believed it best to say nothing about foreign affairs for as long as possible. In the midst of the grave economic crisis besetting the country after October 1929, suggestions that the nation devote attention and energy to world problems seemed certain to offend growing nationalist sentiment. At the same time, a sharp departure from earlier pleas for international cooperation would antagonize the party's small but influential group of Wilsonian internationalists. It seemed most expedient, therefore, to avoid commenting on foreign affairs. In 1931, for instance, Roosevelt refused invitations from the press to discuss President Herbert Hoover's war debt moratorium or Japan's military action in Manchuria.[27]

Once he declared his candidacy in January 1932, though, Roosevelt found it impossible to maintain this posture. Under pressure from isolationist publisher William Randolph Hearst, who attacked him on the front pages of his newspapers as an internationalist, Roosevelt disavowed his earlier support of the League. "The League of Nations today is not the League conceived by Woodrow Wilson," Roosevelt declared in a speech before the New York State Grange on February 2. "Too often through these years its major function has been not the broad overwhelming purpose of world peace, but rather a mere meeting place for the political discussion of strictly European national difficulties. In these," he asserted, "the United States should have no part. . . . The League has not developed through these years along the course contemplated by its founder, nor have the principal members shown a disposition to divert the huge sums spent on armament into the channels of legitimate trade, balanced budgets, and payment of obligations. American participation in the League," he concluded, "would not serve the highest purpose of the prevention of war and a settlement of international difficulties in accordance with fundamental American ideals. Because of these facts, therefore, I do not favor American participation." While Roosevelt had not in fact publicly urged entrance into the League for several years, this statement differed from earlier ones in its failure to urge limited cooperation with the League or even to praise its work.

Similarly, he now reversed himself on the war debts. Instead of reminding his countrymen of how American economic nationalism had crippled Europe's ability to pay, he attacked huge expenditures on armaments as evidence that Europeans could meet their just obligations to the United States.

Though Roosevelt's departure from his earlier internationalism angered many Wilsonians, it served a useful purpose. It appeased Hearst, who, at a strategic moment in the convention, did not block the California and Texas delegations from moving into Roosevelt's camp. "Roosevelt," Frank Freidel has written, "had come in sackcloth and ashes and prostrated himself before Hearst. The humiliation was an essential step toward the ultimate triumph."

Only on tariffs and trade did Roosevelt hold to his old internationalism. In his speech of February 2, he attacked the excessively high Smoot-Hawley tariffs of 1931 as injurious to world trade and the American farmer. He proposed in its place a reciprocal trade program which could start the wheels of American industry turning again and save American farmers from buying in a protected market and selling in a competitive one. The idea, as Roosevelt explained it, was for the United States and other nations to work out a reciprocal exchange of goods which could increase world commerce without compelling nations to put out cash they did not have.[28]

By the time the presidential campaign was over, however, Roosevelt had also backed away from these ideas. Eager not to risk any of the lead he had established over Hoover at the start of the campaign, he made a systematic effort to avoid controversial positions that could antagonize significant groups. Since farmers and manufacturers opposed substituting a reciprocal trade program for tariffs supposedly protecting their goods, Roosevelt shortly abandoned his position of February 2. In public and private he now argued that it was out of the question to reduce tariffs on farm products or to discontinue protection for American industry. At the same time, however, he refused to drop the reciprocal trade idea entirely. Presented with two opposing drafts on tariff policy, Roosevelt told an astonished adviser to "weave the two together." Roosevelt, Hoover complained, was "a chameleon on plaid."

Roosevelt's handling of the tariff was symptomatic of his whole approach to foreign policy during the campaign. Since the internationalism he had favored for years seemed unlikely to capture many votes, and since he had little quarrel with Hoover on foreign affairs, he decided to avoid the subject as much as possible. If compelled to speak, however, he intended to align himself with the current nationalistic mood. Since the Republicans largely ignored the issue, Roosevelt was also content to leave it alone, making no major foreign policy address during the campaign.[29]

Roosevelt's silence on the subject belied his true feelings. Behind the façade of indifference, he remained vitally concerned about international affairs. On the eve of his presidency, two long-standing convictions shaped this concern: a belief in the interdependence of nations, that is the dependence of nations on each other for long-term prosperity and peace, and a conviction that an effective policy abroad required a stable commitment at home. Translated into more specific terms, he believed that American economic well-being would ultimately depend on the return of economic health abroad through the cooperative action of all the major trading powers, including the United States. He also saw an unbreakable link between prosperity and peace; there could not be one without the other. Arms limitation and guarantees against war loomed as large in his mind as the restoration and expansion of international trade. But he was profoundly uncertain about how and even whether the United States could contribute anything to these aims. On the one hand, he saw no easy solutions to the problems of world depression and aggression, and on the other, he doubted whether the grave difficulties in the United States would leave him free to do much of anything overseas. But in the mood of exultation that came with victory, he was determined to try.

PART ONE

The Internationalist as Nationalist,
1932-1934

I

First Things First

IF HE WERE TO MAKE any progress toward international prosperity and peace during his first term, Roosevelt believed that he must begin by working out differences with Britain and France. As he had told an English journalist in the summer of 1932, if Britain and the United States could achieve "a complete identity of political and economic interests," they would ". . . acquire the true leadership of the world." "I am eager to get into personal contact with leading Englishmen, and to find out something at first hand of modern Britain and the new spirit in Europe," he also told the reporter. By October, in fact, he had informed England's Prime Minister Ramsay MacDonald that he hoped to visit Europe during the interregnum, and he used an interview with a Paris newspaper to express similar feelings of friendship for the French.[1]

Yet in spite of these hopes and plans, Roosevelt was under no illusion as to what must come first. Starvation, unemployment, business and financial collapse made foreign relations a secondary concern. "Our international trade relations, though vastly important," he declared in his Inaugural Address, "are in point of time and necessity secondary to the establishment of a sound national economy. I favor as a practical policy," he said, "the putting of first things first. I shall spare no effort to restore world trade by international economic readjustment, but the emergency at home cannot wait on that accomplishment."[2]

Indications that Roosevelt's first priority was domestic affairs appeared immediately following the election. On November 12, four days after his defeat, Hoover invited FDR to discuss war debts, disarmament, and preparations for a world economic conference scheduled for early 1933. With the war debt moratorium coming to an end and the British asking for a fresh review of their obligation, Hoover saw a last chance to reverse the nation's continuing downward slide. Believing that domestic recovery largely depended on swapping debt reductions for a restoration of the international gold standard or currency stabilization, he wished to tie FDR to international negotiations which neither the British nor the Congress would take seriously without Roosevelt's support.[3]

Hoover's request took Roosevelt and Professors Raymond Moley and Rexford Tugwell of Columbia University, his principal advisers, "completely by surprise." Moley, a forty-six-year-old political scientist, and Tugwell, a forty-two-year-old specialist in agricultural economics, could not remember another instance in which an outgoing President had asked the assistance of his successful opponent. More important, they viewed the subject for discussion as economically insignificant and politically dangerous. Advocates of national planning that would eliminate the wastefulness of free competition and rugged individualism, they saw currency stabilization as unlikely to produce significant economic upturn, while debt discussions impressed them as certain to outrage the Congress and jeopardize New Deal reforms. At a time when the federal government faced growing demands to feed the starving, aid the unemployed, and bolster the economy, Americans found it intolerable to give up income that could meet these needs. Moreover, Americans in and out of Congress saw debt reductions as helpful not to the masses but to international bankers demanding payment on private loans.

Roosevelt also believed that a close association with Hoover would jeopardize the first goal of his presidential term: the restoration of hope that America's economic and governmental machinery could work. Seeing Hoover as a prime contributor to the country's mood of gloom, Roosevelt wished to avoid tying the incoming administration to the image of helplessness associated with the old. But because he believed that a need for national unity required him to accept Hoover's invitation, he agreed to it on the condition that their meeting be "wholly informal and personal." For "in the last analysis," he told Hoover, responsibility for government action remained with "those now vested with executive and legislative authority." [4]

Consequently, a November 22 meeting at the White House produced none of the cooperation Hoover wished. Feelings of antagonism from his recent defeat and a profound distrust of Roosevelt's intentions made Hoover "grave, cold and glum." Roosevelt, who reciprocated Hoover's distrust, also seemed strained. When Hoover suggested a joint appeal to Congress for a debt commission that could take coordinated steps on debts, disarmament, and world economic questions, Roosevelt proposed instead that negotiations take place through existing diplomatic channels. As his response made clear to the Congress and the public, the new administration would not follow Hoover's ideas of curing the Depression from abroad. [5]

Hoover felt compelled to reopen the issue with Roosevelt in the following month. With banks collapsing in the western United States and the whole economy taking a further downward turn, Hoover again asked Roosevelt to support international remedies. Arguing that foreign conditions were a principal depressant of prices and employment in the United States, Hoover described an urgent need for an early and successful meeting of the World Economic Conference. He wished Roosevelt to join him in selecting a delegation that would give "coordinate consideration" to debts, world economic problems, and armaments. Two days later, before Roosevelt replied, Hoover proposed this to the Congress and emphasized the need for a restoration of the international gold standard if economic conditions were to improve.

As in November, however, Roosevelt again refused to follow Hoover's lead. Debts, disarmament, and economic arrangements, he told the President, required "selective treatment." The World Economic Conference "should not be submerged in conversations relating to disarmament or debts," and personnel conducting these different conversations should not be identical. Since they held such divergent opinions about the scope of the Conference, Roosevelt concluded, the appointment of delegates and the determination of the agenda should be held in abeyance until after his Inauguration on March 4. On December 18, Roosevelt asked Edmund E. Day and John H. Williams, Hoover's delegates to the preparatory commission for the Conference, to hold off further preliminary talks until late February when his influence on the agenda could be decisive.

Despite Roosevelt's reply, Hoover refused "to admit that cooperation could not be established between the outgoing and incoming administrations." In yet another message, he asked Roosevelt to understand that foreign conditions were increasing economic difficulties in the United States, that debts, disarmament, and world economic questions needed coordination and that all he wanted was a commitment not to common policies but to the establishment of machinery that could expedite solutions to the country's problems. For his troubles, Hoover received one more rebuff, which moved him to release his correspondence with FDR to the press and to comment pointedly: "Governor Roosevelt considers that it is undesirable for him to assent to my suggestions for cooperative action on the foreign problems outlined in my recent message to Congress. I will respect his wishes." [6]

Hoover's statement greatly distressed FDR, who saw it encouraging the mistaken belief that he would pursue a strictly nationalistic course. Though international action remained a secondary priority, Roosevelt certainly did not wish to turn his back on foreign affairs. Quite the contrary, after setting domestic programs in motion, he hoped to deal with economic and political issues abroad. In the meantime, though, he needed to keep international discussions alive by countering Hoover's statement. "It is a pity, not only for this country," he publicly declared, "but for the solution of world problems, that any statement or intimation should be given that I consider it undesirable to assent to cooperative action on foreign problems."

To illustrate his sincerity, Roosevelt at once began communicating with Secretary of State Henry Stimson. Informed that Stimson was above politics and would gladly arrange cooperation between the two administrations, Roosevelt sent him word that he regretted the clash with Hoover and would like to see Stimson at Hyde Park. As tokens of his willingness to cooperate, Roosevelt declared himself ready to see British debt negotiators in the United States before he took office and to have Day and Williams return to the preparatory talks at once if they left final agreement on the Economic Conference agenda until March 4. He also expressed an interest in being "kept in touch with these preliminaries. If at any time you would care to talk things over with me, either by telephone or in person," he wrote Stimson on December 24, "it would make me happy." [7]

Roosevelt revived more hopes for meaningful world talks when he met with Norman Davis on December 26 and 27. An Assistant Secretary of the Treasury and financial adviser to Woodrow Wilson and currently a Hoover delegate to the Geneva Disarmament Conference and the preparatory commission, the fifty-three-year-old Davis was a prominent internationalist whose good will would assure American and foreign opinion that Roosevelt intended more than a nationalistic approach to world affairs. Since Roosevelt strongly shared Davis's internationalist perspective and had consulted him on the *Foreign Affairs* article in 1928 and on European conditions in more recent days, his support was not difficult to obtain. Indeed, by the close of their conversations, Davis reported that he "had a very nice & satisfactory visit with FDR. . . . We are in accord as to what our general foreign policy should be."

On foreign economic questions, however, Roosevelt needed to assure Davis that their differences were smaller than they seemed. In favor of reviving national economies through rapid world action, Davis, like Hoover, regretted Roosevelt's failure to appreciate the need for prompt world talks. By emphasizing, however, that he also saw the World Economic Conference as "of the utmost importance" and was ready to have Conference preparations go ahead at once, Roosevelt disarmed Davis's concern and persuaded him to accept the idea of holding the Conference in the summer of 1933 rather than the spring.[8]

On the evening of the second meeting with Davis, Roosevelt further blunted suggestions of ultra-nationalism by meeting with William Bullitt, another prominent internationalist. A Philadelphia aristocrat who had worked as a European correspondent for the Philadelphia *Public Ledger* and was an assistant to Wilson at Versailles, Bullitt had come to prominence in 1919 when Wilson and British Prime Minister Lloyd George sent him to Russia to negotiate with Lenin. Angered by Wilson's refusal to act on the results of his mission and by the compromise peace agreed to in Paris, Bullitt gave damaging testimony against the Versailles Treaty before the Senate Foreign Relations Committee. During the twenties he took refuge in Europe, where he made the acquaintance of numerous European leaders, wrote a biography of Wilson with Sigmund Freud, and published a novel parodying upper-class Americans. Reintroduced to FDR in October 1932 by Louis B. Wehle, a mutual friend, Bullitt had just returned from Europe where he had made an informal survey of conditions for the President-elect. His report, partly warning that fundamental debt adjustments were imperative to head off European political collapse, encouraged Roosevelt's desire to do something about foreign affairs. Though mounting domestic difficulties had caused Roosevelt to drop his plan for a European trip, Bullitt's report revived this idea. According to Wehle, FDR asked Bullitt to work out an itinerary for such a journey. When pressing domestic matters once more changed his mind, however, he sent Bullitt alone to gather fresh information and ask Prime Minister MacDonald to make a post-inaugural visit to the United States.[9]

Meanwhile, after considerable preliminaries to assure Hoover's approval, Roosevelt arranged a meeting with Stimson at Hyde Park for January 9. In addition to offering further evidence of his interest in cooperating on foreign affairs, the discussion allowed Roosevelt to identify specific policies he wished to carry over into his term. These policies, the conversation showed, included most of what Hoover and Stimson had done. On disarmament, Latin America, and the Far East, Roosevelt largely embraced their ideas. He particularly endorsed their response to Japan's occupation of Manchuria. After learning from Stimson that the League was approaching a judgment on the Sino-Japanese dispute and that the next administration's attitude would materially affect the League's report, Roosevelt endorsed Stimson's nonrecognition of Japanese control. On January 17, one day after Stimson sent word to other countries that his doctrine of nonrecognition would stand, Roosevelt told the press that "America foreign policy must uphold the sanctity of international treaties. That is a cornerstone on which all relations between nations must rest."

Roosevelt had not been so forthcoming with Stimson on economic policy. When the Secretary reminded him of the administration's conviction that recovery depended on currency stabilization, which they could get by reducing foreign debts, Roosevelt put him off by saying that he would not appoint commissioners to negotiate these issues because "such selections would be misinterpreted as cabinet selections. Second, . . . his experience in the campaign made him believe that he could get the necessarily unpopular debt settlement through Congress and through the country better if he did it himself rather than through a commission."

While Roosevelt remained unwilling to support Hoover's internationalist approach to the Depression, he was eager to avoid a repetition of the public dispute he had had with the administration in the previous month. Another such clash seemed certain to intensify economic problems at home and abroad and to add to the difficulties in the way of international talks. Moreover, after hearing from Bullitt about the potential problems which could flow from unsettled debts, Roosevelt had begun thinking about "flexible" schemes for removing them as an irritant from the world scene. For both these reasons, he ended his discussion with Stimson by suggesting that the administration invite a British leader such as former Prime Minister Stanley Baldwin to come see him and Washington officials about the debt.[10]

What Roosevelt had in mind emerged the following day when he met secretly in New York with Paul Claudel, the French Ambassador. Putting the best possible face on everything, Roosevelt expressed confidence that the nations would resolve differences by finding "common ground." Specifically, he predicted a Franco-American accommodation on the debt, suggesting, as in the case of America's Revolutionary War debt to France, that Paris pay the principal but not the interest on its loan.[11]

Though Roosevelt's idea of dealing with one envoy strictly about debts had no appeal to Hoover, he used it as an opening wedge for another proposal to FDR for comprehensive world talks. Armed with a written memo of Hoover's views, Stimson telephoned Roosevelt on January 15 to suggest that the President-elect would want to get assurances from the British on currency stabilization before agreeing to a debt settlement. Such a commitment, he told FDR, "could be a great advantage to us unless our nation proposed to join in the race for national inflation which is now going on among the nations. . . . [Roosevelt] at once said that of course he did not want to join in such a race," and he further agreed to Stimson's proposals that several rather than one British representative come for talks and that he discuss all this with Hoover at the White House on January 20.

What seemed like an important turnabout to Stimson was in fact little more than a gesture on Roosevelt's part. Since it was also agreed that the British would not arrive until after March 1, by which time Roosevelt would have appointed his Secretaries of State and Treasury, it was clear to FDR that he would entirely control the negotiations. Hence, by ostensibly accepting Hoover's suggestions, he was able to avoid another damaging clash with the President and simultaneously assure himself that British-American discussions would be kept in the background until his domestic programs were initiated.[12]

Moley and Tugwell did not see it this way. The meetings with Davis and Stimson, to which they were not invited, followed by the endorsement of Stimson's Manchurian policy and a commitment to discuss the British debt, left his advisers confused about Roosevelt's plans. Having watched him maneuver from one position to another during the presidential campaign, they wondered whether he was about to abandon his domestic priority in favor of policies closer to Hoover's internationalist view.

He was not. But neither was he willing to cast aside that internationalist view and simply follow the Moley-Tugwell lead. In this, he was giving his advisers an initial taste of how he would operate during his presidential years. He would not allow himself to be the captive of one set of advisers or one approach to a problem. He wished to keep his options open and make his own decisions. "Roosevelt had a love affair with power . . . ," the political scientist Richard Neustadt has written. "The White House was for him almost a family seat and like the other Roosevelt he regarded the whole country almost as a family property. Once he became the President of the United States that sense of fitness gave him an extraordinary confidence. Roosevelt, almost alone among our Presidents, had no conception of the office to live up to; he was it. His image of the office was himself-in-office."

The difficulty Moley and Tugwell had with him at this time over his intentions reflected two techniques he used constantly during the White House years to assure his power to decide. Roosevelt "deliberately organized—or disorganized—his system of command to insure that important decisions were passed on to the top," Arthur Schlesinger, Jr., has written. "His favorite technique was to keep grants of authority incomplete, jurisdictions uncertain, charters overlapping. The result of this competitive theory of administration was often confusion and exasperation on the operating level; but no other method could so reliably insure that in a large bureaucracy filled with ambitious men eager for power the decisions, and the power to make them, would remain with the President." A natural complement to this technique was to shield his purposes from his advisers until he was ready to act. "Never let your left hand know what your right is doing," he once told Henry Morgenthau. "Which hand am I, Mr. President?" Morgenthau asked. "My right hand, but I keep my left hand under the table," Roosevelt replied.

On January 17, when Moley and Tugwell confronted FDR with the issue of whether he now intended to accept Hoover's internationalist views, he treated them to some of his famous indirection. Beginning with a discussion of the Manchurian policy, Tugwell pointed out that it could lead to war and that we had "sacrificed much in European policy to win neutrality in our attempt to isolate Japan. We are hated for this," Tugwell said, "and have lost much that we might have gained in forcing the removal of trade restrictions which is where our real interest lies." But these "arguments . . . had no effect." Roosevelt declared his intention to see his policy through, "admitted the possibility of war and said flatly that it might be better to have it now than later." "I have always had the deepest sympathy for the Chinese," he explained, and asked Moley and Tugwell how they could expect him not to go along with Stimson on Japan.

Much of this was overstatement on Roosevelt's part. While he did have a strong feeling for the Chinese, partly based on an old family involvement with the China trade, and while he was indignant at Japan's Manchurian action, he had no intention, as the next five years would make clear, of risking a war in the Far East. Indeed, when he asked Moley and Tugwell how they could expect him not to go along with Stimson on Japan, he was telling them that this was a moral issue on which he had to take a stand. As a longtime advocate of international cooperation against war and now a world leader responsible to millions of people who were asking for disarmament and peace, Roosevelt felt compelled to condemn Japan's armed attack.

When the conversation turned to economic questions, however, Roosevelt tried to assure them that they still shared the same point of view. He explained his willingness to discuss the British debt with Hoover and then with the British themselves as no more than a response to London's payment of a full installment on its obligation and a hope that preliminary talks might advance the work of the forthcoming Economic Conference. To this, he added his agreement in a conversation with Moley on January 19 that only Roosevelt-appointed officials would conduct debt negotiations and that such talks would remain separate from the Economic Conference. When Moley replied that Hoover, Stimson, and Davis would urge another course, Roosevelt "laughingly" told him "not to worry: he felt as strongly on the question as . . . [Moley] did." [13]

His determination to keep international economic reform in the background until domestic legislation could work registered clearly enough at the White House conference on January 20. After general agreement that talks with the British representatives should begin after March 4, an argument ensued over whether debts should be discussed separately or in connection with other international questions. Hoover, Stimson, Davis, and Secretary of the Treasury Ogden Mills all made the now familiar case for tying things together, while Moley represented the opposing point of view. When Roosevelt, who seemed to enjoy the high-powered barrage, finally spoke up, it was to affirm that debts would be considered separately from other matters. But in an attempt to fudge the issue and avoid another public clash with the administration, he also acknowledged that other issues might arise naturally in the course of these talks. But this was too vague for Stimson, who now pressed FDR to make clear whether he would or would not make these discussions inclusive.

In a masterful display of double-talk, Roosevelt presented a formula that satisfied everyone. Suggesting two sets of separate but related discussions, which he called "twins," he managed to persuade both sides that they would have their way. Hoover saw Roosevelt's formula as a means "to state our appearance of separation to the public but a consolidation of them in fact to the British delegations." Stimson believed it an acceptance of the administration's policy, while Moley considered it a firm, unequivocal indication of Roosevelt's determination to separate debts from other issues.

Moley was right, as events that afternoon showed. With Roosevelt about to leave for a holiday in Warm Springs, Georgia, and an aide-mémoire to London expressing his idea on the debt discussions still to be drawn, FDR gave Moley final power to approve the text. This assured not only that debts would be separated from other questions, but also that Roosevelt would avoid another punishing conflict with the administration over what he meant to arrange. Because Moley rather than Roosevelt himself compelled Stimson to write separation into the British note, FDR was allowed to keep his domestic priority without personally emphasizing that international negotiations would play only a secondary role in what he did.[14]

But that was clearly what he intended. Having opened the way to international talks, he now wished to assure that they were kept in proper proportion to his overall goals; he did not want discussions of foreign affairs either to overshadow domestic reform or to reach an impasse. When, for example, Stimson approached him a few days after their White House talk with requests from several more governments for debt reviews, Roosevelt agreed to see each of them if there were no implication that he intended a general round-table discussion. There must be no suggestion, he told Stimson, that they would talk with them all at once. Having been warned before the White House meeting by Vice President-elect John Nance Garner that Congress would not agree to any postponement or reduction of foreign debts, Roosevelt had no desire to stir congressional animosities by allowing rumors that he had agreed to a general conference on debts. On the other hand, when Stimson proposed a formal protest to the French over their failure to pay their December 15 installment, Roosevelt urged "a more informal oral suggestion" which would give less offense. Because he wished to encourage prospects for Franco-American talks, he simultaneously had Bullitt, who was unofficially touring Europe in his behalf, ask that former Premier Edouard Herriot come to America for talks.

Similarly, when British-American relations seemed headed for a deadlock over debts, Roosevelt tried to clear the way to productive talks. In response to a British request that a debt settlement be tied to final reparation payments from Berlin, essentially a proposal for cancellation, Roosevelt asked Sir Ronald Lindsay, the British Ambassador, to visit him in Warm Springs. A veteran diplomat with three years' service in the Washington Embassy, Lindsay had little regard for American leaders. The Republican decision to run Hoover again in 1932 evoked the remark that the party's campaign slogan should be: "Why change toboggans in the middle of a slide." He considered Roosevelt an amiable and impressionable lightweight and warned the Foreign Office that it should not tell Bullitt, FDR's Personal Representative, anything beyond what it might not mind reading later in an American newspaper.

Their conversation on January 29 tended to confirm Lindsay's view of him as superficial. Roosevelt spoke "with obvious desire that eventual agreement" between Britain and the United States be achieved. He assured the Ambassador that world economic revival was central to his thoughts, pointing out that "only by presenting Congress with [the] prospect of curing the world as well as the domestic situation can he hope to ensure its support." He then laid out a timetable for British-American talks, suggesting ten days of discussions in early March, followed by a visit from MacDonald "to finish matters off."

Roosevelt's optimism rested on the belief that he had found a scheme for settling debts which "His Majesty's Government would see the wisdom of accepting." He wanted Congress to forgo the future interest on the British debt and to apply past interest payments to the principle. In this way he could reduce the total debt from $4.2 billion to $1.2 billion, with the new sum to be paid back over a period of fifty years.

As FDR immediately heard from Lindsay, and subsequently from MacDonald, his plan was unacceptable. No settlement, the British told him, was agreeable to them unless it went along with the Lausanne formula of 1932: the scheme already enunciated by the British government for tying reparation and debt reductions together. "The American settlement," MacDonald wrote him on February 10, "must be a European one as well, so that when it is made you and we together will have enabled Europe and America to begin anew a restoration of commercial transactions and trade."

Roosevelt's realization that his plan would not work did not deter him from further efforts to advance British-American talks. In his next meeting with Lindsay on February 20, he acknowledged that the two governments were "in irreconcilable opposition to each other at present over debts," but he urged that they temporarily ignore the issue and concentrate on economic questions instead. This might allow them to find some common ground which they could then describe as "a fairly wide measure of agreement for a programme of world recovery." This, in turn, Roosevelt predicted, would create a better atmosphere in the United States, make possible a visit by a British Minister, and help "Congress towards accepting measures to forestall a crisis over debts in the immediate future."

Though realizing that he was grasping at straws, Roosevelt saw his suggestions as a means of keeping the talks alive. The important thing, he emphasized to Lindsay with particular force, was to avoid any indication that the negotiations had suffered a setback. With the United States in the midst of a banikng crisis that threatened a general financial collapse, Roosevelt feared that any bad news from the international scene would only make domestic conditions worse. Moreover, because he saw the first step toward recovery as the re-creation of faith in governmental power to reverse the downward trend, he wished to encourage a belief in worldwide economic upturn through international talks. Therefore, at the conclusion of his meeting with Lindsay, he gave the press the impression that he would try to promote world revival by broadening the negotiations with the British. "The net result of his conference with Sir Ronald," the *New York Times* reported, "is believed to have been a decision to set up machinery, of which the World Economic Conference will be part, to bring about a readjustment of the economic structure of the world and to do this as quickly as possible." [15]

Roosevelt's announcement the next day of the appointment of Cordell Hull as Secretary of State further encouraged this belief. As a Tennessee Congressman and Senator for twenty-three years, the sixty-two-year-old Hull had established a reputation as a fervent believer in economic internationalism or, more precisely, in world economic improvement through tariff reform. "Gentle" and "frail," with a slight lisp, Hull gave "the appearance of a benign southern gentleman of the old school." But his "air of harmless benevolence" masked a vindictive evangelism which he put at the service of economic internationalism. The protective tariff, he said, was the "king of evils," the breeder of economic wars, and "the largest single underlying cause of the present panic." "We must eliminate these twade baa-yuhs heah, theah and ev'ywheah," the unconverted mimicked him. In December 1932 he had gone on record as calling for recovery through world economic disarmament. He outlined a program in which "a truce on further increases in tariffs and similar trade obstructions" and "a horizontal reduction of 10 per cent in all permanent tariff rates of all countries" were preliminary steps to the gradual reduction of trade barriers through reciprocal agreements. Such a program, he believed, could be set in motion through discussions at a world economic conference on tariffs, monetary rehabilitation, credit policy, and general economic disarmament. Though his long-term political support of FDR and his high standing with party regulars, particularly in the South and in Congress, made Hull an attractive candidate for the senior Cabinet appointment in any case, his internationalism was a highly important consideration in his behalf.

As Undersecretary of State, Roosevelt selected William Phillips, another internationalist. A Boston Brahmin and a friend of Roosevelt's since the Wilson years, Phillips had a long record of diplomatic service in Europe, England, and China. An Assistant Secretary of State during World War I and the Department's Undersecretary from 1922 to 1924, Phillips moved comfortably in elite diplomatic circles where Hull was loath to spend his time. A "distinguished" and "courteous" Foreign Service officer, whose "dress, gentlemanly manners and direct talk" reminded one junior associate of what he "had found admirable in the upper reaches of Boston society," Phillips encouraged the impression that Roosevelt was putting the Department in the hands of the internationalists.

This was no sign, however, that Roosevelt would make international economic reform his first goal. For at the same time that he placed Hull at the head of the State Department, he persuaded Raymond Moley to become an Assistant Secretary of State with responsibility for "the foreign debts, the world economic conference . . . and such additional duties as the President may direct in the general field of foreign and domestic government." In short, the Department under Hull was to espouse both internationalist and nationalist views, and by so doing, lose its ability to direct foreign affairs quickly along an internationalist course. But this was just what Roosevelt wished. While Hull's presence in the new administration's highest foreign affairs post suggested that, in the long run, Roosevelt would not forsake the internationalism of his earlier years, or more immediately, ignore world economic reform, Moley's appointment indicated that Roosevelt intended to deal with domestic problems first.[16]

2

The Diplomacy of Hope

"THIS NATION ASKS FOR ACTION, and action now. . . . I am prepared under my constitutional duty," Roosevelt assured the country in his Inaugural Address, "to recommend the measures that a stricken Nation in the midst of a stricken world may require."

Appreciating that only quick decisive action would break the mood of hopelessness that reached across the nation and around the world, Roosevelt moved at once to fulfill his promise. On March 5, 1933, the day after his Inauguration, he declared a national bank holiday to prevent further financial collapse and called Congress into special session. When it met four days later, he asked and received immediate action on an emergency banking law. On Sunday night, March 12, he gave the first of his Fireside Chats. Speaking to approximately sixty million people over the radio, he explained the banking crisis in language everybody could understand, and urged Americans to put their savings back in banks.

His actions had an electrifying effect. Letters of approval poured into the White House by the thousands, and people immediately redeposited their funds. "In one week," Walter Lippmann wrote, "the nation, which had lost confidence in everything and everybody, has regained confidence in the government and in itself." "He's taken the Ship of State," Raymond Moley said, "and he's turned it right around." [1]

At the same time, Roosevelt began trying to rekindle hope abroad, where discouragement over economic and political affairs was almost as widespread. The first order of business was the Disarmament Conference, which seemed on the verge of collapse. After thirteen months, during which the French demanded security guarantees, the Germans equality of national strength, the British and Americans limitations on offensive arms, and the Japanese naval controls, the delegates were unable to find a common ground. Moreover, the rise of Adolf Hitler to power in Germany on January 30, 1933, and the subsequent transformation of the Weimar Republic into the Third Reich had further blighted prospects for agreement. Indeed, by the end of Roosevelt's first week in office, America's representatives in Geneva were warning that the Conference was "in a precarious state" with "tempers . . . exasperated and discouragement . . . general." Worse, they predicted that a breakdown of the

Conference would aggravate European tensions and jeopardize world economic reform.

In response to this news, Roosevelt moved to prevent a collapse. On March 14 he proposed that the Conference recess for five or six weeks while Norman Davis, who was to become chairman of the American delegation, and other statesmen sought "a further meeting of minds." Three days later he told the press that he saw disarmament as "one of the principal keys to the world situation," and that he intended "to use every possible means to make some kind of a very very definite success of this disarmament conference."

One token of Roosevelt's sincerity was his determination further to reduce the size of America's small 140,000-man Army, a step that also promised to free money for desperately needed domestic relief. This put him into sharp dispute with Army Chief of Staff General Douglas Mac-Arthur. During a discussion at the White House about the Army's budget, MacArthur "spoke recklessly . . . to the general effect that when we lost the next war, and an American boy, lying in the mud with an enemy bayonet through his belly and an enemy foot on his dying throat spat out his last curse, I wanted the name not to be MacArthur but Roosevelt. The President grew livid. 'You must not talk that way to the President!' he roared." MacArthur apologized and offered his resignation, but Roosevelt would not accept it: " 'Don't be foolish, Douglas,' " he said, " 'you and the budget must get together on this.' . . . 'You've saved the Army,' " Secretary of War George Dern told MacArthur after they left the President. MacArthur was not appeased: "I just vomited on the steps of the White House," he recalled.[2]

To save the disarmament talks and simultaneously advance prospects for world economic discussions, Roosevelt renewed his proposal to Prime Minister Ramsay MacDonald that he visit him. Though freely acknowledging that he had no panaceas or set plan for resolving differences, he expressed confidence that a personal meeting would allow them to "work out some practical methods of solution." Such a get-together, he told MacDonald, through Davis, would show that they "were working shoulder to shoulder in good faith on a program which effectively held out some hope of ameliorating general economic conditions." MacDonald's tentative acceptance of this suggestion on March 31 brought forth a reiteration of Roosevelt's feeling that such a meeting was "of the highest importance." After ironing out further details, the White House announced the forthcoming visit on April 5.

In the next three days, Roosevelt extended invitations to ten other countries—France, Italy, Germany, Japan, China, Argentina, Brazil, Chile, Mexico, and Canada—to send their government leaders to Washington to reach "some fundamental understanding" on economic problems and to create "a favorable public opinion" in the world toward the Economic Conference.[3]

To some of Roosevelt's principal advisers—Moley, Tugwell, and Herbert Feis, the State Department's Economic Adviser—there was considerable confusion about what the President hoped to achieve. As far as they knew, he had no practical plan for breaking the Geneva deadlock, no fresh scheme for dealing with debts, nor even a conciliatory response to foreign demands that June 15 payments be postponed. Even more important, though, his initial commitment to nationalistic monetary and economic policies seemed to preclude meaningful international talks.

Considerable tension, for example, seemed certain to arise over currency stabilization. Of the sixty-six nations preparing for the Economic Conference, all but two, Britain and Japan, believed world monetary stability essential to recovery. This was especially true of the French, Germans, Dutch, Belgians, and Swiss, who feared a repetition of the inflation of the early 1920s when their currencies had become almost worthless.

Though Roosevelt initially refused to commit the country to currency inflation, domestic and foreign pressures shortly forced him along this path. With the index of wholesale commodity prices at 59.6 per cent of its 1926 level, and with debts contracted at higher prices threatening to collapse the whole economy, Roosevelt saw an overriding need to raise domestic prices. He initially hoped to do this with his recovery program. But when it became clear in April that his agricultural and industrial measures would not move through Congress fast enough to meet this need, he accepted congressional proposals for currency inflation. At the same time, his desire to regain a share of the foreign markets lost to countries with devalued currencies and a need to halt a speculative drain of $100 million of the country's gold reserves persuaded him to take the country off the international gold standard. Consequently, on April 19, 1933, he halted all gold exports, temporarily removing gold backing for the dollar abroad, and gave his blessings to the Thomas Amendment to the Agricultural Adjustment Act, a congressional grant of Executive power to inflate the dollar.

Though these actions placed the United States at odds with nations seeking currency stabilization and seemed to jeopardize chances for international agreement, Roosevelt was able to put an entirely different face on the matter. At a press conference on the same day, he assured reporters that he hoped "to get the world as a whole back on some form of gold standard" and that in fact dollar devaluation would now make it easier to achieve that end. "It is a constructive move," Roosevelt said. ". . . It puts us on a par with other Nations, and it is hoped eventually that it will aid somewhat to raise prices all over the world." The objective, as Roosevelt saw it, was for the various governments to stimulate their national economies and raise commodity prices through either direct expenditures or subsidies to private industries. When these national programs had had a chance to work and world prices had shown a significant improvement, it would then be appropriate to reestablish the international gold standard on new parities.

For Roosevelt to remain hopeful about the upcoming international talks, he had to rationalize not only his monetary actions but also the emerging contradiction between his domestic and foreign economic policies. The conflict between what he was urging in national affairs and what he was urging in international affairs was clear to his advisers by the second month of his term. On the one hand, he was openly committing himself to a program of freer international trade, and on the other, he was supporting domestic legislation that aimed to revive America's economy strictly from within. In the first six weeks of his term, for example, he declared his intention to ask Congress for a reciprocal trade bill; allowed Cordell Hull to state America's determination to clear away barriers to world trade; and sanctioned proposals to the World Economic Conference for a temporary tariff truce and a horizontal tariff cut by all states.

At the same time, though, he committed himself to a policy of "intranationalism"—the reorganization of American economic institutions without interference from the outside. By mid-April his Agricultural Adjustment Act, a program for raising agricultural prices by reducing surpluses at home and temporarily barring imports from abroad, was well on its way to becoming law. "The strategy of the situation," Moley had concluded on April 17, ". . . is to let Cordell Hull talk one thing re tariffs while the army is marching in another direction."

For Roosevelt, however, this was less of a contradiction than Moley believed. Though accepting a policy of economic self-protection "for the present emergency," FDR did not see it as a viable long-run plan. Ultimately, "it would work against us and our world trade and our industry," he said. Long-term agricultural adjustment impressed him as dependent on new foreign markets gained through reciprocal agreements on trade. It was Roosevelt's hope, therefore, that nationalistic monetary and economic policies might work fast enough to permit him to support stabilization and tariff agreements at the World Economic Conference later in the year. In the meantime, however, he tried to lay the groundwork for such agreements by replacing world despair with new hope that nations would cooperate.[4]

To this end, Roosevelt not only invited heads of government to Washington, he also initiated actions in Latin American and Russian relations which would immediately bolster world hopes and ultimately improve international affairs. In Latin American relations, he had inherited a history of mistrust dating back to the nineteenth century. Though the Hoover administration had reduced these tensions by repudiating Theodore Roosevelt's corollary to the Monroe Doctrine and then carefully following a policy of nonintervention, considerable animosity toward the United States remained. FDR, who wished to give specific meaning to his In-

augural promise that "in the field of world policy, I would dedicate this
Nation to the policy of the good neighbor," seized the occasion of Pan
American Day, April 12, 1933, to apply the concept to the Western
Hemisphere. In an address before the Governing Board of the Pan American Union, he declared his commitment to equality and cooperation
among the American Republics, acknowledging the independence of each
and the need to abolish all artificial barriers hampering the healthy flow
of trade.[5]

At the same time, he had begun investigating the question of United
States recognition of the Soviet Union, which had been withheld since
the Bolshevik revolution of November 1917. Believing that a realistic improvement in world conditions required normalization of Soviet relations
with the United States, Roosevelt was eager to learn how informed Americans would respond to recognition and what he could ask of the Soviets
in exchange. After the experience of the postwar years, in which domestic
divisions had limited America's world role, Roosevelt firmly believed that
an effective policy abroad first required a consensus at home. With this
in mind, he encouraged Senator Claude Swanson of the Foreign Relations Committee to open a national discussion on recognition. As he had
hoped, this quickly told him how businessmen, editors, religious leaders,
veterans, academicians, and government officials felt. By April, for example, he was in possession of a petition from 673,000 Massachusetts voters,
a survey of 329 prominent Americans, a memorandum from the State Department's Far Eastern division, editorials from important periodicals,
and the views expressed at a Washington mass meeting organized by the
American Legion showing him that Americans were generally receptive
to the idea.

Simultaneously, he began gathering information on the U.S.S.R. He
asked his friend Felix Frankfurter of the Harvard Law School to put him in
touch with a Soviet spokesman in the United States, requested information from the White House press corps, and told Henry Morgenthau, Jr.,
his head of the Farm Credit Administration, to see if he could negotiate
the sale of farm surpluses to the Soviets. He also had Colonel Hugh L.
Cooper, a distinguished engineer engaged in building the Dnieper dam,
come talk to him about Russia. Though he was not ready to offer recognition in the spring of 1933, his actions were another expression of his
desire to improve the state of world affairs.[6]

Nothing in world affairs, however, loomed as large for him as the impending Washington talks on the world economy. He appreciated that
world economic recovery and international political stability depended on
getting some measure of agreement in these discussions. But formidable
obstacles stood in the way. "There never was a time when an economic
conference looked less hopeful or was more needed," Tugwell wrote in a
newspaper article shortly before the preliminary conversations in Wash-

ington. "Measures taken by nations individually with the hope of protecting themselves from the impact of the depression," he explained, "have further restricted the exchange of goods and aggravated the distress." Though the nations of the world now appreciated that recovery would be very difficult without common international action, their traditional ways of doing things made this an unlikely event. But even if it were to occur, he foresaw no more than a start toward the revival of world economic life. "Privately," Tugwell wrote in his diary, "we have no hope, or hardly any, that anything will come of it."

America's departure from gold on the eve of the preliminary discussions added to this belief. Roosevelt's action infuriated the British and the French. London viewed it as a blow to Britain's export trade, while Paris saw it as a threat to the gold-backed franc. Moreover, because FDR acted while MacDonald and Herriot were on their way to the United States, London and Paris believed it an attempt to improve America's bargaining position in the talks. "The whole business," one English paper declared, "has been deliberately planned in cold blood as a piece of diplomatic blackmail." [7]

But whatever the appearances, Roosevelt badly wanted to establish fundamental points of monetary and economic agreement with his visitors as initial steps toward a successful world conference. His principal guests reciprocated this wish. Britain's sixty-six-year-old Prime Minister, former Labor Party leader, Ramsay MacDonald, held a "mystic confidence . . . in his providential call to save the world from its present crisis." More to the point, his continued leadership of a national government dominated by Conservatives seemed to require some success in Washington. His French counterpart, Edouard Herriot, who had been forced out of the premiership in December 1932 over his advocacy of paying the war debt to the United States, hoped to vindicate his stance by achieving some agreement with the Americans.

Roosevelt began the talks, on April 21, by disarming British and French fears that the United States might launch a currency war. Bullitt, Feis, Moley, and James P .Warburg, a New York banker brought in by Moley to help on monetary problems, proposed an improved international gold standard and a three-nation stabilization fund. In addition, Roosevelt joined MacDonald and Herriot in calling for "the ultimate reestablishment of equilibrium in the international exchanges," and "the restoration of stable monetary conditions." In Feis's view, Roosevelt led the Anglo-French missions "to infer that the stabilization of the dollar in the near future was a genuine possibility—almost a probability—even though he was not ready yet to determine the precise time when the American government might agree to take action, or what the relative rates for the several currencies would be."

On the intractable debt issue, Roosevelt offered suggestions for both a long-term settlement and an immediate accommodation on the June 15 payment. In the first instance, he suggested the cancellation of all interest, a redetermination of the principal, and a reaffirmation of the debt. On the June 15 installment, Roosevelt told MacDonald that he would probably ask Congress to give him power "to deal with the problem," and he advised Herriot that, if France were to make its December 15 payment, he would "ask Congress for power." But he promised "nothing," since he had no idea of what powers, if any, Congress might grant him. Still, he assured Herriot of his confidence that "a settlement of this whole problem could be reached with the passage of time." With MacDonald and Herriot unable to accept or even discuss Roosevelt's proposals in detail, the three issued optimistic declarations that "progress is being made" and that conversations "can well continue" in London, Paris, and Washington.

On tariff increases and new trade restrictions, Roosevelt gained the support of MacDonald and Herriot for a temporary truce to begin at once and last until the end of the World Economic Conference. Since so much disagreement existed among the Americans themselves as well as between the negotiators about this question, the truce was a satisfying accomplishment which everyone hoped would "have a favorable effect on international commerce and world prices."

Even more satisfying to Roosevelt was Anglo-French willingness to acknowledge the primary importance of coordinating national price-lifting programs. In their final communiqué, MacDonald joined Roosevelt in recognizing "the necessity for an increase in the general level of commodity prices . . . as primary and fundamental" and as partly to be achieved through credit expansion and government spending. Herriot's final joint statement with FDR called for the "sound and permanent solution" of world economic problems through "an international collaboration supplementing the indispensable domestic efforts of each country."

In response to this general "meeting of minds," Roosevelt readily agreed to MacDonald's and Herriot's proposal that the Conference convene in London on June 12. In the belief that a desire to assure the success of the Conference would soften American objections to a British failure to pay, MacDonald wished to have the Conference in session before Britain's June 15 payment fell due. Moreover, MacDonald wanted the Conference to meet before a further decline in the dollar injured British commerce and doomed the Conference by alienating gold-bloc countries. For the French, who a week before had "wondered whether the World Economic Conference could meet at all," the attraction of an early date rested chiefly on the assumption that the sooner the Conference met the sooner the United States would agree to stabilize the dollar.

All in all, the conversations produced feelings of genuine optimism that

Britain, France, and the United States would be able to cooperate effectively in meeting international economic problems. "We have in these talks found a reassurance of unity of purpose and method," Roosevelt and MacDonald announced. "They have given a fresh impetus to the solution of the problems that weigh so heavily upon the . . . men and women of the world." "Our conversations had . . . as their result as complete an understanding as possible between our two countries in regard to our common problems," FDR and Herriot declared. Even as vigorous an exponent of economic nationalism as Raymond Moley came away from these talks believing that there was "good hope of successful understanding at the Economic Conference."

Given this optimism, Roosevelt began attaching ever greater importance to the Conference. In the days immediately following the MacDonald and Herriot visits, he joined Prime Minister Richard Bennett of Canada and Finance Minister Guido Jung of Italy in emphasizing "the vital importance to mankind of the World Economic Conference" and his belief that "if normal life is to be resumed, the . . . Conference must be made a success." In his second Fireside Chat on May 7, moreover, he stated his intention "to restart the flow of exchange of crops and goods between Nations" by seeking a reduction in trade barriers and a stabilization of currencies. "The international conference that lies before us," he declared, "must succeed. The future of the world demands it . . ." [8]

Roosevelt's hopefulness about the Economic Conference was the result not only of the successful Washington talks but also of positive developments in the disarmament negotiations. Believing that disarmament was of transcendent importance and that success at London partly depended on agreement at Geneva, he devoted himself to finding some basis for cooperative action on arms control.

He found it in a security and disarmament plan MacDonald had put before the Geneva Conference on March 16. To prevent a collapse, MacDonald had formulated a fresh scheme for dealing with potential and actual aggression through consultation among the European Powers, and for reducing each nation's armed might by limiting the number of troops and weapons each were to have. Seeing the plan as a major step toward arms control, Roosevelt gave it strong support. More specifically, he assured MacDonald and Herriot that the United States would back the MacDonald plan by relinquishing traditional neutral rights. If the United States, he told the two leaders, found itself in agreement with the Powers when they declared a nation an aggressor, it would refrain from any action that would tend to defeat the collective effort against an aggressor. He emphasized, however, that such a commitment was contingent upon a prior international agreement for substantial reduction of armaments and an effective program of automatic and continuous inspection.

The British-French response to these ideas was generally enthusiastic. MacDonald saw Roosevelt's endorsement of his plan as "a fact of real significance and hope," stating that it could be turned "to good effect at this critical, and probably final, stage of the Disarmament Conference." Herriot "seemed very much pleased" with Roosevelt's ideas, since they represented a considerable step toward assuring French security. Roosevelt added to Herriot's satisfaction by agreeing to oppose German construction of sample weapons that later could be manufactured quickly in large numbers.

By the time his British and French guests had returned home, Roosevelt regarded "Germany as the only possible obstacle to a Disarmament Treaty." Events in Geneva and Germany from the end of April to the middle of May, moreover, strengthened this feeling. At the Conference itself, the Germans demanded the right to limited rearmament with the option to build specimens of sample weapons. Since the British and the French categorically rejected these demands, the Conference reached an impasse. At the same time, reports coming from Berlin indicated that Hitler was intent on rebuilding Germany's military strength and that he would state this aim in a speech to the Reichstag on May 17. Such a declaration seemed likely to end the Geneva talks and to undermine the London ones.

Because Roosevelt feared that Hitler's action might destroy all he had been working for in international affairs for two months, and because he believed that he had sufficient world standing to influence foreign events, in a speech on May 16 he issued an appeal to fifty-four heads of state for "peace by disarmament" and "the end of economic chaos." The London Conference, he asserted, "must establish order in place of the present chaos by a stabilization of currencies, by freeing the flow of world trade, and by international action to raise price levels." Further, he urged the nations to preserve world peace by eliminating offensive weapons, starting the process outlined in the MacDonald Plan, keeping armaments at existing treaty levels while the process went on, and promising not to send an armed force of any nature across a frontier during the disarmament period. Hitler, against whom the whole proposal was obviously aimed, responded with a conciliatory speech in which he skillfully threw the blame for the Geneva deadlock on other countries. He denounced the destructive madness of war and described Germany as ready to disband her entire military establishment if other nations would do the same. Germany, he claimed, wanted not rearmament but equality of rights through disarmament among all states.

In light of Hitler's statement and general world approval for the President's declaration, Roosevelt authorized Norman Davis to reveal his commitment to MacDonald and Herriot to abandon traditional neutral rights in return for adequate disarmament. On May 22 Davis publicly outlined the President's plan to the Geneva delegates, explaining that the United States would consult with other states in response to any threat to the peace and would, in the event of actual aggression, refrain from any action tending to defeat a collective effort to punish a state the United States and other nations saw as an aggressor.[9]

Davis's announcement punctuated a four-week period in which Roosevelt had established himself as a world leader determined to promote international accord. In the eyes of people at home and abroad, he had become the chief sponsor of the World Economic Conference and a central figure in the Geneva talks. More important, though, his actions had created hopes in the United States and around the world that both Conferences could make substantial strides toward prosperity and peace.[10]

By mid-May, however, Roosevelt appreciated that he had helped create extravagant expectations which needed reining in. He knew that debts, tariffs, and currency stabilization continued to be difficult if not insoluble problems in the way of international advance. He understood, for example, that the debts stood suspended between the unbending attitudes of the Congress and the foreign governments. On the one hand, Senator Arthur Robinson of Indiana made it clear to him that the Congress would not look with favor on a request for a debt moratorium for the period of the Conference. In response, Stephen Early, the President's Press Secretary, assured the Senator that there was "no agreement, nor agreement to make an agreement, in relation to debts, cancellation of debts or moratoriums between the President and the Prime Minister of Great Britain . . . [or] between the President and the representative of France." On the other hand, MacDonald expressed the view that a successful Conference depended on a debt settlement. Though he abandoned this position when he realized that a settlement could not be arranged before the Conference met, he insisted instead on a suspension of the June 15 installment. A failure to arrange this, he had written FDR on May 8, "would seriously interrupt the negotiations for a final settlement and jeopardize the Conference." In a reply on May 22, Roosevelt could only suggest that the debts be kept separate from other issues before the Conference, and that if the British could not pay the entire amount due on June 15, perhaps they could pay a part.[11]

Tariffs were another source of unyielding friction. Despite his agreement to the President's tariff truce, MacDonald came under considerable pressure at home to continue building protection for British trade. Since London had been a consistent advocate of freer trade, while the Europeans and the Americans had raised their barriers, the British felt that "a stabilization of the *status quo*" left their trade exposed to damaging attacks, and that at the very least they should be allowed to complete negotiations for preferential treaties. Even with the conclusion of these negotiations, MacDonald told FDR, Britain would still have a less complete system of protection than her competitors.

The French also had strong reservations about a tariff truce. As long as the dollar remained unstabilized and threatened to fall even lower, Paris resisted limitations on its right to restrict American imports. Consequently, the truce that Norman Davis managed to get through the Organizing Committee for the Conference on May 12 included substantial reservations, leaving each government free to interpret how it should be applied.

In his determination to assure America's special interest, Roosevelt did not take a back seat to other leaders. On the day the tariff truce won approval, the President signed the Agricultural Adjustment Act, which authorized an agricultural import tax equal to a domestic processing tax. Since the processing levy was part of an overall plan for reducing farm surpluses and raising agricultural prices, the additional tariff was necessary to assure that foreign producers did not undersell American farm goods. In the last week of May, therefore, when Roosevelt decided to apply a processing tax to cotton, he also agreed to increase the tariff on foreign cotton products. Similarly, the National Industrial Recovery Act, which Roosevelt had sent to the Congress on May 17, carried the prospect of higher tariffs to protect American industrial goods. Finally, despite his talk about a reciprocal trade bill, for which he even initiated the drafting process, he refused to commit himself to such legislation. In the closing days of May, he refused to go beyond the word "probably" in answering whether he would ask for such a measure.[12]

By mid-May currency stabilization also had begun to look like an impossible problem for the Conference to solve. At that time, the dollar began a new downward movement with a simultaneous rise in stock, bond, and commodity prices. Roosevelt confided to Moley that the dollar might fall to lows the experts had not foreseen, and that "he was in no hurry to stabilize until he was sure he was going to get the best bargain there was to be got. New purchasing power was being created in this country, he held. This stimulating movement must not be stopped." The French and the British, who feared economic losses through the export of cheaper American goods to their shores, immediately began demanding provisional stabilization of the dollar. Indeed, they warned that, without a tripartite agreement before June 12, it would be "useless" to convene the Conference. Though Roosevelt agreed to send American financial experts to London for separate discussions beginning about June 10, he refused to make any commitments.[13]

Given all this, it is not surprising that Roosevelt encouraged Moley to published a syndicated newspaper column warning against excessive hopes for the Conference. Explaining in an article on May 16 that a good many of the economic ills of each country were domestic, Moley argued that remedies had to come largely from within the nations themselves. He also contended that international trade problems would be extremely difficult to solve. "Tariffs and other restrictive devices," he wrote, "are deeply rooted in the policies of the various countries and are closely integrated parts of their economic life." The best he could foresee was the initiation of "many bilateral agreements and a more enlightened point of view." It was also possible, he said, to make progress toward removing exchange restrictions, setting up an international monetary standard, and exchanging ideas on how to make domestic programs work. But he did not think the nations should expect more than this. Roosevelt not only approved the article, he also told Moley that it "would be a grand speech for Cordell [Hull] to make at the opening of the Conference." [14]

The President, as Moley at once realized, was not being ironic. He found great appeal in Moley's combined warning against unrealizable goals and suggestions of limited aims on which the nations could build. Also, by mid-May Roosevelt had become convinced that the Conference could succeed only if it met for eight weeks or less, limited itself to statements of general principles, and appointed committees to work out additional details. Roosevelt saw several advantages to this procedure. It would allow the Conference to achieve some measure of agreement and keep hopes for international recovery alive, or, stated another way, it would keep the Conference from moving beyond generalizations into divisive discussions that would tear it apart. Further, Roosevelt's plan of action would leave hard problems like stabilization and tariffs to committees, which could wait for national recovery programs to work before making international accords.

Roosevelt indicated all this in letters to MacDonald in the second half of May and in his instructions to his delegates on the eve of their departure for London. "I feel strongly," he wrote the British Prime Minister on May 16, "that the Conference should come to its conclusion before the summer holidays [in August] and that every effort must be made to reach simple definitive agreements before disbandment. I am convinced that if the Conference is allowed to drag on until Christmas, the chance of reaching agreements will be lessened, not increased," "Do you not agree with me that if we let the Conference drag through this summer," he wrote him again on May 23, "we shall disappoint the hopes which we have aroused in the entire world?" "I wish to urge upon you," he told his delegates on May 30, "that delay in conferences of this nature usually make it more difficult to secure results. . . . I can see no reason why its work cannot be completed by the middle of August." "The Conference," he shortly added, "should confine itself to finding promptly the solution to a few major problems and not diffuse its efforts over too wide a field. It should proceed as rapidly as possible to adopt the general principles of a solution for these problems, appointing immediately such committees as may be necessary to work out the details."

In his instructions to his delegates, Roosevelt even spelled out what these "general principles" or "resolutions" should be. They were to cover the tariff truce, the coordination of monetary and fiscal policies for stimulating national economies and improving prices, the removal of foreign exchange restrictions, the establishment of an adequate and enduring international monetary standard, the gradual abolition of artificial barriers to trade, and the control of production and distribution of certain basic commodities. Moreover, they were to take the form of generalizations on which all nations could reasonably agree. On artificial trade barriers, for example, Roosevelt wished the delegates to state that the tendency toward such barriers must be arrested if world recovery was to be achieved. They were to announce their determination to remove "embargoes, import quotas and various other arbitrary restrictions . . . as quickly as possible," and to reduce tariff barriers by reciprocal bilateral and multilateral agreements.[15]

Since he had worked out just what his representatives would strive for in London, Roosevelt felt free to select delegates who had never been to an international conference and who held widely different views on international economic and financial affairs. In choosing Hull; his former running mate James Cox; Senator Key Pittman, who was Chairman of the Foreign Relations Committee; Republican Senator James Couzens, also of the Foreign Relations Committee; Congressman Samuel McReynolds, Chairman of the House Foreign Affairs Committee; and Ralph Morrison, a financial backer of the Democratic Party from Texas, Roosevelt seems to have been primarily concerned with appeasing congressional sensibilities. But whatever his purpose in selecting them, he clearly wanted the delegates to sponsor general and innocuous resolutions that would hold open possibilities for later, more significant agreements and, more immediately, sustain world hope that recovery could be achieved.[16]

Such was essentially Roosevelt's strategy in dealing with disarmament, debts, and tariffs in late May and early June. By the end of May it was clear to FDR that he could not put across his arms control ideas at that time. His plan for American cooperation with other states in punishing an aggressor partly depended on congressional approval of an arms embargo resolution he had sent to Congress in March. While the House of Representatives had passed the measure in April, giving him power to say when and against whom it should be used, the Senate Foreign Relations Committee balked at this abandonment of traditional neutrality and amended the bill to require impartial use of the embargo. Despite the fact that this denied him the power to join with other states in identifying an aggressor, Roosevelt reluctantly accepted the Senate version. By allowing him to prevent arms shipments which could undermine a collective effort for peace, the resolution took a step in the right direction. Moreover, acceptance of the revised version promised to prevent a congressional fight that could jeopardize domestic legislation and passage of any arms embargo at all. Such a result, Roosevelt feared, would signal a defeat for his policy of international cooperation. When Cordell Hull strenuously objected to the Senate measure, however, Roosevelt agreed to shelve the issue and have Hull announce their intention to fight for the original House proposal at the next congressional session. This then left open the possibility that the United States might yet fulfill the Davis pledge of May 22 to support collective efforts against war.[17]

Similarly, in late May and early June, when it became clear that the Geneva Disarmament Conference could still not reach agreement on disarmament procedures and would adjourn for private talks, Roosevelt was happy to support the Four Power Pact of June 7, an agreement by Britain, France, Germany, and Italy to consult each other about disarmament and peace. The Pact, Roosevelt said, was "a good augury" and gave "renewed courage to all who are striving for the success of the Geneva and London Conferences." In short, Roosevelt backed this general enunciation of good intentions as a way to sustain hopes for disarmament and assure that European political differences would not destroy the London talks.[18]

He had the same goal in mind when he embraced a patchwork solution to Britain's June 15 payment problem. In a letter to the President on June 4, MacDonald had repeated the case for a postponement of the June 15 installment and argued that insistence on even a nominal payment, such as Roosevelt had suggested on May 22, would probably create "a very serious deterioration in mutual confidence and in temper [in Britain], which will have an unfortunate effect upon comprehensive debt negotiations, the International Economic Conference, and, generally, upon international relations." In reply, Roosevelt, expressed his wish that "the momentous Conference" would succeed and explained that "a number of perplexing problems" before the Congress ruled out a debt proposal. This left the issue unresolved, permitting it to be described on the eve of the Conference as "the shadow which hangs over . . . everything." MacDonald illustrated his own preoccupation with the question by publicly discussing it on the first day of the Conference, violating a pre-Conference agreement not to talk debts.

It was with considerable relief, then, that Roosevelt accepted a British offer of June 13 to make a token payment. This allowed him to announce candidly that it was "vitally necessary that during the opening days of the Conference difficult and possibly protracted discussion of the debt be avoided." He was able to say this, he explained, because the British had made a small payment, acknowledged the existence of the debt, and asked for an opportunity to make representations concerning the whole question, which he declared himself willing to receive later in the year.[19]

At this point, tariffs had also become an issue that Roosevelt felt compelled to defuse if the Conference were to succeed. With congressional opposition making tariff legislation seem "not only highly inadvisable, but impossible of achievement," Roosevelt decided to forgo a trade bill in the emergency session. Since this decision would badly sting Hull, who saw the bill as "one of the chief bases . . . for hoping that real results could be achieved at the Conference," and since it would leave foreign governments skeptical of American intentions, Roosevelt made a considerable effort to downgrade the importance of his decision. He told Hull on June 7 that general reciprocal treaties and individual tariff conferences between the United States and other nations could still be negotiated and arranged, and he told a press conference two days later that his decision not to send up a tariff message was "a very unimportant thing." The only difference in not doing it then, he explained, was a matter of two or three months: with a reciprocal trade law, negotiated tariff reductions could go into effect at once; without it, they would have to wait until January for congressional approval, which would be needed ultimately under the tariff bill anyway. When Hull, who accurately saw the difference as Executive rather than congressional control of tariff cuts, seemed about to resign on June 11, the President wired him in London: "I am squarely behind you and nothing said or done here will hamper your efforts. There is no alteration of your policy or mine." Though Hull remained unconvinced, he decided to stay in his post anyway. His decision saved the President from considerable embarrassment.

At the time he was soothing Hull, Roosevelt also pressed his case for a Conference of limited duration and aims. When Hull had reported to him on June 9 that he had repeated and emphasized this idea to MacDonald, Roosevelt wired his approval and suggested the possibility of putting a motion before the Conference that it conclude its work on or before August 12. A report on June 11 that MacDonald had agreed to limit preliminary speeches to ten minutes and to seek a definite conclusion of the Conference by August 12 held out hope that Roosevelt's strategy would work.[20]

But his goal of covering over differences by holding a brief Conference and issuing bland declarations received a sharp jolt in the next several days. Beginning on June 12, the tripartite stabilization discussions he had agreed to hold became the focus of attention in London, and the Conference all but suspended its work while waiting to learn the results. Because the French insisted that the Conference could not proceed without a stabilization agreement and because Roosevelt had encouraged the impression through several pronouncements that he would accept temporary stabilization, Oliver W. Sprague, George L. Harrison, and James Warburg, his negotiators, committed themselves to an agreement. It included provisions for stabilization at about $4 to the pound and for a promise that, in the absence of unforeseen circumstances, Roosevelt would not use his powers under the Thomas Amendment to inflate the dollar. When they forwarded these proposals to Washington, Sprague and

Warburg added warnings that a failure to stabilize "would be most disastrous" for the Conference and would deprive the United States of a chance to bring about lasting economic peace.

Roosevelt, however, now saw compelling reasons to reject their proposals. Since the dollar-sterling rate had reached $4.18 on June 12, well above the $4 level Roosevelt had previously thought it would go, and since rumors of stabilization had increased the dollar's value of $4.02 on June 16, with a simultaneous decline in stock and some commodity prices, Roosevelt wanted no part of temporary stabilization at $4 to the pound. He informed his delegates of this on June 17, explaining that for the present he preferred an informal statement that if the pound went up to $4.25, he would consider unilateral action of some kind. "On the other hand," he added, "if exchange goes the other way, resulting in commodity price declines in this country, we must retain full freedom of action under Thomas' amendment in order to hold up price level at home." Roosevelt also expressed the fear that the agreement was "so worded that London and Paris might later charge us with bad faith if we decline later to go along with their interpertation of it," and he concluded by saying that too much importance is being placed on temporary stabilization and too little on "the bigger ultimate objective of balanced budgets and permanent national currencies."

The exchange left Roosevelt with the feeling that his representatives in London did not seem "to get his drift." It seemed advisable, therefore, for Moley to make a brief trip to London to help get them back on course. With the Congress adjourning and the President about to go off on a cruise in New England waters, he and Moley agreed that, if the reports out of London did not improve in the next few days, Moley would undertake this "nasty chore."

If anything, things in the next two days got worse. On hearing of Roosevelt's reply to the stabilization agreement, Harrison immediately departed for the United States, while Cox, Sprague, and Warburg tried to convince the President to accept the proposal in modified form. Though acknowledging that undue importance was being attached to the "reduction of fluctuations," they argued that a failure to relieve this concern would hinder the larger work of the Conference; it would create the feeling that America had changed its stand on temporary stabilization and had sent a delegation without the authority to present a permanent program.

In fact, with the exception of Hull, the delegation was already viewed as "very weak." Pittman concerned himself only with silver, a special interest of his home state of Nevada, and put other delegates to sleep with his incessant talk about it. He also embarrassed his fellow Americans by drunken sprees in which he shot out London street lights with a six-shooter and chased a technical adviser, whom he suspected of inadequate enthusiasm for silver, down the corridors of Claridge's hotel with a bowie knife. McReynolds treated the whole assignment as simply another congressional junket, while Morrison "made no sense whatsoever on any subject." Warren Robbins, the protocol officer, went about with a monocle, while his wife, who gave out a statement describing her husband as "the mystery man of the conference," appeared "with her hear dyed purple."

Roosevelt was of two minds about the appeal from his monetary experts. For the most part, he found it unpersuasive. As he notified the delegates on June 20, he believed it best to stand on the conclusion he had stated in his June 17 message, and he advised them "to insist on consideration of the larger and more permanent program, working towards a means of exchange among all nations. Remember," he added, "that far too much importance is attached to exchange stability by banker-influenced cabinets." At the same time, he told Moley to go to London, where he was to impress on the delegation and others that the President's primary international objective was to raise the world price level. "If other nations will go along and work in our direction, as they said they would when they were in Washington," he declared, "then we can cooperate. If they won't, then there's nothing to cooperate about." He added that international cooperation in positive, forward measures was a fine idea, but he wanted no part of cooperation to accomplish a negative stability.

But these were not Roosevelt's only thoughts on the matter. As he had been doing since April 19, 1933, he continued to talk about some kind of stabilization effort. In a telegram to Acting Secretary of State William Phillips on June 19, he had reiterated his reluctance to make an agreement with upper and lower limits and his attraction to unilateral steps for keeping the pound from going above $4.25. At the same time, he told Phillips to talk with financier Bernard Baruch and Moley about the advisability of an agreement in which the medium stabilization point for the dollar would be $4.15 rather than $4. "I hesitate to go even that far," he concluded, "but it is worth considering." In his conversation with Moley on the following day, moreover, he discussed the possibility of an "agreement to calm the gold-standard countries and steady the dollar," saying that "if nothing else can be worked out, I'd even consider stabilizing at a middle point of $4.15 with a high and low of $4.25 and $4.05. I'm not crazy about it, but I think I'd go that far."

After Roosevelt told this to Moley, things in London apparently started going as Roosevelt wished. On the evening of the 20th he heard from Warburg that sections (a) and (b) of his resolution on an enduring monetary standard had received unanimous committee approval, which was "precisely what we were working for," while on the 21st Hull signaled him that the delegation would "promptly and wholeheartedly comply" with his instructions of the previous day. Further, on the 22nd he learned from Warburg and Cox that they would remove all doubts about America's position on stabilization by giving a statement to the press and that they had overcome the crisis and gotten past the point where temporary stabilization was necessary to the continuance of the Conference by calming British, French, and Italian fears. Warburg, however, also told the President that violent fluctuations in the dollar would revive the crisis, and he recommended that, without making any declaration whatsoever, Roosevelt authorize "the Federal Reserve banks to take such actions to limit fluctuations as may from time to time be desirable and practicable."

To all this, Roosevelt replied that he was delighted at the way things were going and expressed the belief that the real trouble of the first week lay with the "French and British press trying deliberately to discredit us for certain clear objectives. . . . Most people are saying," he advised, "[that] you were all clever enough to avoid an obvious trap." On June 24 he asked Phillips to talk to Baruch and Secretary of the Treasury William Woodin about steps to prevent the pound from going much higher than $4.25 and to prepare a draft of a further message if they thought it advisable. But he added that the "situation seems quieting down so well that anything further may be unnecessary." Roosevelt now declared publicly that reports from London in the last twenty-four hours "have been altogether satisfactory to the President," while privately he wrote Sumner Welles, his Ambassador in Cuba, that "we seem to have straightened ourselves out in London." [21]

But this was an illusion. Rather than dropping the stabilization issue and giving itself over to the President's resolutions, the Conference now stood still waiting for Moley to infuse it with new life. Moley's exaggerated role as the savior of the Conference was chiefly the product of circumstance. Having suffering serious doubts about a London mission in the three days after he had seen the President on June 16, he asked Roosevelt for permission to come see him on his yacht. When the President agreed, Moley sped to his side by navy plane and destroyer, giving his departure for London on June 21 an importance it was never meant to have. Moley's dramatic actions combined with the inability of the Conference to accomplish anything in its first nine days led American, English, and continental newspapers to describe Moley as carrying new instructions that would revive prospects for success. Even FDR's attempt to minimize the importance of Moley's trip by announcing his function as that of "a messenger or liaison officer" only encouraged the feeling that he was carrying some vital message that could set the Conference on a fresh course.

Circumstances now pushed Moley and the President further along a path neither had intended to travel. When he arrived at the Conference on the 28th, Moley found the delegates agitated anew by a monetary crisis. After Roosevelt's rejection of stabilization in the previous week caused a further devaluation of the dollar to between $4.30 and $4.40 to the pound, the Dutch, French, Swiss, and Belgians began warning that they too would have to go off gold and that this would make the work of the Conference exceedingly difficult if not impossible. When Hull had notified the President of this on the 27th, Roosevelt replied that he did not believe the abandonment of the gold standard by these countries mattered all that much to an "ultimate permanent settlement," nor did he "greatly fear [a] setback to our domestic price level restoration" even if all these nations went off gold. Therefore, he advised the delegation to continue to reject any international agreement to stabilize.

But Hull never got this message. Roosevelt asked Phillips to cable this decision provided Undersecretary of the Treasury Dean Acheson, Baruch, and others expressed no "serious disagreement." Since they did, and since Sprague and Moley sent word that they were already working on a proposal that was in accord with the President's earlier directives, Acheson advised FDR that they were withholding his proposed cable.

That Moley took the lead in discussing an agreement to limit exchange speculation was a more or less natural consequence of what had gone before. Having been told by FDR that he would consider stabilizing at about $4.15 to the pound, having seen a summary of the President's June 24 message to Baruch and Woodin about keeping the pound from going much above $4.25, and having found the Conference immobilized by the new monetary crisis, Moley at once plunged into discussions on foreign exchange. He found the gold countries asking that the President endorse a "wholly innocuous" declaration which "would commit Roosevelt to absolutely nothing except to ask the Federal Reserve to cooperate in limiting fluctuations due to speculation. . . . *It did not*," Moley concluded, "*mean stabilization.*" Indeed, in Moley's judgment, the declaration extended no further than Roosevelt's own pronouncements on ultimate stabilization, reestablishment of an international gold standard, and unilateral action for controlling currency gyrations. More important, however, he and monetary experts in the United States urged Roosevelt to understand that the continuance of the Conference depended on his acceptance of this joint declaration.[22]

However accurately Moley presented the case, this appeal had no influence on FDR. Seeing the declaration from a perspective that differed from that of his advisers, Roosevelt rejected it as an attempt of the gold-bloc countries and the international bankers to commit the United States to the beginnings of permanent stabilization. Having had a chance during his cruise to give further thought to his economic policies and, more specifically, to a variety of contemporary arguments against an international gold standard and for a nationally managed currency, he had concluded that the United States must remain free to pursue domestic price-raising programs for as long as needed, and that any declaration of intent to stabilize the dollar would inhibit this freedom of action. "At this time any fixed formula of stabilization by agreement," he told the delegation in a message on July 1, "must necessarily be artificial and speculative. It would be particularly unwise from political and psychological standpoints to permit limitation of our action to be imposed by any other nation than our own. A sufficient interval should be allowed the United States to permit in addition to the plan [play] of economic forces a demonstration of the value of price lifting efforts which we have well in hand."

To this, Roosevelt added in his famous bombshell message to the Conference on July 3 the contention that "the sound internal economic system of a nation is a greater factor in its well being than the price of its currency in changing terms of the currencies of other nations. . . . Old fetishes of so-called international bankers," he declared, "are being replaced by efforts to plan national currencies with the objective of giving to those currencies a continuing purchasing power which does not greatly vary in terms of the commodities and need of modern civilization." While Roosevelt could still say that "our broad purpose is the permanent stabilization of every nation's currency," he now declared that it would have to wait until the majority of nations had returned to economic health and could "produce balanced budgets" and live within their means.

If Roosevelt had any doubts that the London declaration would be regarded as an initial commitment to permanent stabilization, his advisers and current events relieved them. Moley, for example, had acknowledged in a dispatch on June 30 "that such a temporary project if known might be regarded as the beginnings of permanent stabilization," while Woodin, Baruch, and Acheson had told him that the making of the declaration might strengthen the dollar. The accuracy of their observation seemed to be borne out on June 30 when rumors alone of stabilization increased the value of the dollar and dropped stock and commodity prices.

In publicly rejecting this currency declaration, Roosevelt was saying that for the time being he wanted no part of currency stabilization and that other nations would not be allowed to take advantage of the United States. As one journalist who had spent the afternoon of June 30 in conversation with him recalled, "Roosevelt might be an internationalist, something of an Anglophile through family and friends, a cosmopolitan; but at this stage he was determined that the United States was not to be pushed around." Roosevelt complained that "American investors had trusted the debtor countries as they did their own, and yet they had wound up with worthless or depreciated bonds." He added that "the changing of tariffs could not allow the dumping of products by any cheap producer on American markets. The United States must not reduce the value of the dollar so that foreign governments could trade it at bargain prices in other markets. . . . The time might come when this devaluation would be to American advantage, but it was not beneficial to our country in 1933."

It is difficult to understand Roosevelt's indignation toward the other nations or any of his advisers for urging a limit on currency fluctuations. Much that he had said in the previous two and a half months had encouraged the belief that he would agree to at least an initial step toward stabilization, and it was only during the last days of June that he had firmly decided against any such agreement. His indignation, one suspects, had more to do with his inability to bend others to the idea that the London talks should settle for apparent rather than real agreements, which he wished to forgo until national economic improvement had taken firmer hold. The nub of the problem, therefore, was, first, Roosevelt's miscalculation that national economic programs would be farther along when the Conference met, and second, his mistaken belief that other governments would see the virtue of leaving open the possibility of future agreements by opting for illusory ones for the time being.

There is also reason to think that Roosevelt's rejection of the currency agreement was his way of diminishing Moley's importance. Throughout the spring Moley's prominence in the administration had reached a point where commentators joked that one had to call up Roosevelt to get an appointment with Moley. He had his picture on the cover of *Time* magazine, and when he went to the Conference, where some people expected him to work miracles, skeptical observers gibed, "Moley, Moley, Moley, Lord God Almighty." It was clear to those around him that Moley enjoyed and wished for ever greater notoriety and influence. "This morning," another of Roosevelt's advisers remarked, "he [Moley] acted as if he was running the Government and that Roosevelt was carrying out Moley's suggestions." According to what Joseph P. Kennedy, a Roosevelt financial backer, told Moley in June, FDR was becoming jealous of his adviser's acclaim. Whether or not this was a consideration with the President in rejecting Moley's currency proposal, the fact is that shortly after he returned from London, Roosevelt eased Moley out of power.

The principal architect of this deed, however, was Hull. Offended by the President, whom he referred to with a characteristic lisp as "That man acwoss the stweet who never tells me anything," and infuriated by Moley, who usurped his authority in Washington and eclipsed him in London, Hull bent his considerable political talents to breaking Moley's influence. He sent Roosevelt a list of grievances against Moley, which included charges of bypassing him in negotiations with Heads of State in London and attacking his capacity to function as the President's representative, and reported "an attitude and course of conduct on the part of Professor Moley which has been utterly dumbfounding to me." Hull was less decorous with his London associates: "That piss-ant Moley, here he curled up at mah feet and let me stroke his head like a huntin' dog and then he goes and bites me in the ass!" Forced to choose between Hull, who continued to hold considerable influence with party and congressional barons, and Moley, who held no political power, Roosevelt satisfied the wishes of his Secretary of State.[23]

It was no small bit of irony that the man who in the past had pushed international differences into the background, now felt compelled to confront them with nationalistic declarations that all but ended the Conference. With his almost boundless faith in his ability to bring harmony out of conflict, however, Roosevelt simultaneously tried to keep the Conference alive by pushing it toward another course. "I would regard it as a catastrophe amounting to a world tragedy," he announced in his July 3 message, "if the great Conference of Nations called to bring about a more real and permanent financial stability and a greater prosperity to the masses of all naitons should, in advance of any serious effort to consider these broader problems, allow itself to be diverted by the proposal of a purely artificial and temporary experiment affecting the monetary exchange of a few nations only. Such action, such diversion," he declared, "shows a singular lack of proportion and a failure to remember the larger purposes for which the Economic Conference originally was called together." When told by Hull that his message angered the five gold countries and depressed MacDonald, Roosevelt explained that he had purposely made the language of his message a bit harsh because he felt that "the Conference was getting into stage of polite resolutions about temporary stabilization only and that it was time to be realistic and work towards main objectives."

More specifically, Roosevelt still hoped that he might persuade the member countries to join the United States in domestic price-lifting programs. "If such a united effort should commend itself to other nations," he told Hull on July 4, "the firmest basis would be laid for world-wide recovery, and international cooperation would immediately become possible." Indeed, it seemed to FDR that recovery programs in other nations, like the one operating in the United States, "would remove any necessity . . . for closing our borders to the goods of other nations and for most currency discrepancies and fluctuations."

But the Conference would not follow Roosevelt's lead; instead it exploded in indignation at this message. MacDonald complained to Hull that the President seemed to think that the Conference had been called to do only one thing—raise prices; he told Moley that Roosevelt's message did not sound as though it came from the man he had spent so many hours with in Washington; and he said to Warburg that, "when a man says something with which you disagree, even if he says it unpleasantly, you can argue with him, but if he says nothing in a hurtful way, there is

nothing you can say." The gold-bloc delegates declared continuance of
the Conference a "pure waste of time" and urged immediate adjournment. The message also thoroughly demoralized and confused the American delegation. "Mr. Roosevelt's purposes may be excellent," Walter
Lippmann observed in the New York *Herald Tribune* on July 4, but "he
has completely failed to organize a diplomatic instrument to express
them." Hull now asked the President for explicit guidance in explaining
his tariff and monetary plans.

Despite this response to his message, Roosevelt pressed Hull to keep
the Conference alive. If it adjourned at once, its failure would be blamed
on the United States. "We should first try to see to it that we are not
censored [censured] in any sort of way," he told Hull on July 5. With the
help of Moley, Lippmann, British economist John Maynard Keynes, and
Herbert Bayard Swope, Baruch's associate and Moley's aide at the Conference, Hull staved off immediate adjournment and then kept the Conference going for another three weeks.

By doing so, he fulfilled a second and more fundamental Roosevelt purpose—the preservation of hope that international cooperation would ultimately take place. "You have . . . through your courage and sincerity,"
the President wired him as he prepared to come home, "saved the principle of continued international discussion of perplexing world problems
from a collapse which would have made further deliberations impossible."
The Conference had not failed, he wrote MacDonald at the same time,
because, despite a paucity of formal agreements, "the larger and more
permanent problems will continue to be analyzed and discussed." Others
were not so sure. Toward the end of July, when Robert W. Bingham,
owner of the Louisville *Courier-Journal* and American Ambassador to
London, went to see MacDonald, Prime Minister Richard Bennett of
Canada suggested that he "load him up with flattery, as that was all that
he was willing to listen to." "Even if I had been willing to do so," Bingham noted in his diary, "I had no opportunity, for the Prime Minister
began to flatter himself immediately." [24]

The fact that in spite of his action Roosevelt still had hopes of advancing international understanding can only be understood against the backdrop of other events. The experience of the Hundred Days had given him
extraordinary proof of his ability to handle contentious issues and men. In
a three-month period he had put more major legislation through the
Congress than any other President had during a similar period. Moreover, in June, with production and farm price indexes up from 56 to 101
and from 55 to 83, respectively, much of the press had given him premature credit for ending the Depression. As much to the point, he felt
that he had prevented a European war. After meeting in May with
Hjalmar Schacht, Reichsbank President and Hitler's representative to the
Washington talks, Roosevelt had told Morgenthau that he was "in an

awful jam with Europe," that the European statesmen were "a bunch of bastards," and that he saw "a very strong possibility" of war with Germany. After his May 16 speech, however, he had told Morgenthau that " 'I think I have averted a war. . . . I think that sending that message to Hilter had a good effect.' " [25] In sum, though London produced a result far from what Roosevelt wished, he continued to see the United States as a major force for world prosperity and peace.

3

. . . and Nationalism

B Y THE SUMMER OF 1933 Roosevelt had settled into a routine of White House work which remained his pattern throughout the presidential years. He ate breakfast in bed at 8:30 while he skimmed five or six morning newspapers from New York, Washington, Baltimore, and Chicago and conferred with presidential aides about the day's problems and schedule. Around 10 a.m. his valet pushed him in a small, armless wheelchair to the White House elevator for the descent to the first floor and the Oval Office, where he swung himself into his desk chair. There he remained throughout the day, usually lunching at his desk with aides or visitors. From two to three in the afternoon, the President attended to his mail, dictating the outlines of replies to the handful of correspondence his aides had selected from the thousands of letters and telegrams that arrived at the White House each day. Further conferences followed in the afternoon until about 5 p.m. when, in what he called the "children's hour," he recapitulated the day's events with his staff. Once a week, on Fridays, he met with his Cabinet, and twice a week, on Tuesdays and Fridays, for fifteen to thirty minutes he held off-the-record press conferences with reporters crowded around his desk.

Roosevelt was now backing away from decisive action in foreign affairs. However strong his wish to lead the nations toward cooperative efforts against depression and war, the domestic and foreign conditions he met in the nine months after June 1933 made him increasingly cautious about foreign affairs. In the second half of the year, sagging commodity prices at home and unyielding differences over armaments and trade barriers abroad combined to hold him on a nationalistic course. "I cannot, unfortunately, present to you a picture of complete optimism regarding world affairs," he said at the start of 1934. "In other parts of the world . . . fear of immediate or future aggression . . . prevents any progress in peace or trade agreements." Though American economic policy contributed to this impasse, Roosevelt continued to emphasize United States readiness "to cooperate at any time in practicable measures on a world basis looking to immediate reduction of armaments and the lowering of barriers against commerce." For the moment, expressions

59

of interest in cooperation remained the best contribution he felt free to make to international affairs.

This gap between internationalist hopes and nationalistic actions had also appeared in dealings with Cuba. His difficulties with the Island stemmed from a revolution against the dictatorship of Gerardo Machado. President of Cuba since 1925, Machado was a "'pale, pocked, suspicious butcher" who ruled by "graft" and "bloody vengeance." Killings, imprisonments, and a bankrupt treasury had provoked an uprising in 1929 which had continued for four years. Under the Platt Amendment to the Cuban-American Treaty of 1903, the United States had the right to intervene for the preservation of Cuban independence and the maintenance of life, property, and individual liberty. From 1929 to 1932, despite repeated calls for American action to right Cuban wrongs, Hoover and Stimson refused to intervene or interfere. Since they interpreted the Amendment to mean that the United States had to protect the rights of Americans and foreigners in Cuba, but not of Cubans, and since only the Cubans were suffering under Machado's regime, they disclaimed any justification for intervention. Moreover, since they accepted former Secretary of State Elihu Root's argument that the right to intervene was not synonymous with intermeddling or interference, they also refused to take any actions less drastic than intervention. All this, however, was chiefly a means of expressing what they had learned in Nicaragua—that American intervention, or even interference, would cost more than it was worth.[1]

Roosevelt's entrance into the White House brought a change in Cuban policy. Persuaded that deteriorating conditions in Cuba would ultimately endanger foreign lives, property, and liberty and compel the United States to intervene, the President wished to negotiate a truce in the fighting between Machado and his opponents and open the way to free and fair elections. Such action, the Cubans were told, was not to be construed as intervention but rather as "measures intended to prevent the necessity of intervention."

The architect of this policy was Roosevelt's Ambassador to the island country, Sumner Welles. A descendant of old New York and Boston families, he had been named for his great uncle, Charles Sumner, the Massachusetts Abolitionist Senator. Forty years old in 1933, Wells was an old friend of FDR's and a schooled diplomat, especially in Latin American affairs. He had become Chief of the State Department's Latin American division in 1921 at the age of twenty-eight, and during the 1920s he had served as a diplomatic troubleshooter in Santo Domingo and Honduras. "Tall, slender, blonde and always correctly tailored," Welles was a natural choice for assignment, the most difficult the new administration confronted in Latin America.

During the first three months Welles served in Havana, from May to

August 1933, Roosevelt took almost no interest in Cuban affairs, except to sanction the policies Welles outlined to him. In June, for example, three weeks after receiving a request from Welles for a two-line approval or disapproval of the policy he had formulated, Roosevelt had told him that he had "been altogether too busy to do more than keep in very sketchy touch with all you are doing, but it seems to me that things are going as well as you and I could possibly hope for." Two weeks later, the President sent Welles a public message approving the Cuban political discussions he had been arranging, and privately wrote that, while he had been reading his dispatches, he had dismissed them from his mind "for the very good reason that you seemed to be getting the situation under control."

At the beginning of August, however, a crisis forced Roosevelt to turn his attention to Cuba. On August 4, when a general strike in the Island threatened "utter chaos," Welles proposed the replacement of Machado by a government representing all important political elements. He told the Cuban President that his failure to accept this proposal would cause "absolute anarchy" and compel the United States to honor its obligations under the Treaty of 1903.

Roosevelt at once gave Welles full backing. He approved his plan for dealing with the crisis and told the Cuban Ambassador that Welles had acted with his "fullest authorization and approval," adding "that he had no desire to intervene but that it was our duty to do what we could so that there should be no starvation and chaos among the Cuban people." On the following day Roosevelt rejected a Cuban suggestion that Welles be brought back to Washington for consultation and instead sent Machado a message that he awaited his action and "that time was the essence of the whole problem." Further, when Machado resigned on August 12, Roosevelt extended his warmest congratulations and appreciation to Welles for what he had done.

Though FDR approved and supported Welles's policy of outright interference, he was eager to avoid a military intervention in Cuba or even to allow the impression that he sanctioned uninvited political involvement in its affairs. On June 21, when he had publicly endorsed the talks Welles had been arranging, he emphasized that the request for assistance had originated in Cuba and not in Washington. Further, in the midst of the August crisis, when he had told the Cuban Ambassador that Welles had his fullest backing, he had also told reporters that "we cannot be in the position of saying to Machado, 'You have to get out.' That would be obvious interference with the internal affairs of another nation. . . . I have to be terribly careful not to be in the position of intimating that the Cubans get rid of their President," he said. Finally, though he joined Welles in warning of possible American intervention, he genuinely opposed a military occupation of Cuba. "It would require a case of complete anarchy," he told the press, before we sent troops down there.[2]

Landing troops in Cuba, or just appearing as an interloper, would play havoc with Roosevelt's long-term aim of advancing inter-American cooperation and trade. He was especially eager to revive United States-Latin American commerce, which was now only one-fourth of what it had been four years before. More important, any outright intervention or acknowledged interference would provoke a storm of criticism from pacifists at home and Latins abroad and distract energy and attention from pressing domestic needs.

In the summer and fall of 1933, this was something he could not allow. On July 18 and 19 the farm prices and industrial output he had managed to raise during the Hundred Days began a descent which continued sporadically until late in the year. The *New York Times* Weekly Business Index, which had increased from 60 to 99 during the first three months of his term, dropped to 72 in October, while wholesale commodity prices in general and farm prices in particular showed continuing declines in November and December. In addition to these fresh economic difficulties, Roosevelt confronted extensive problems with his chief recovery agencies, the National Recovery Administration (NRA) and the Agricultural Adjustment Administration (AAA). For three months during the summer of 1933, negotiations with major industries for NRA code agreements consumed much of his time. After that, he struggled with intractable questions about how to use the codes to assure business expansion and increased purchasing power. At the same time, the AAA came under sharp attack for failing to help farmers. In November, when he rejected demands for compulsory production control and price-fixing for basic commodities, strikes and violence erupted across the farm belt.

In the face of all this, Roosevelt found little time for foreign affairs. "This particular autumn is not a particularly propitious time to have any international gathering here in Washington," he told a proponent of such a conference on July 28. "I had hoped to be able to have a talk with you during these two weeks," he wrote Leo S. Rowe, Director General of the Pan American Union, on August 22, "but, as you know, the new [NRA] codes have taken every moment." The need to improve economic conditions at home impressed Roosevelt for the moment as far more important than any issue abroad. He wished, therefore, to quiet Cuban strife, and he shared Welles's feeling, or simply accepted his judgment, that a policy of limited intervention was the best means to this end. These considerations continued to determine his Cuban policy during the next four months.[3]

In the ten days after Machado resigned, Welles had urged Washington to believe that the Cuban problem was under control. On August 14 he had described the new government of President Carlos Manuel de

Céspedes as "a thorough new deal for Cuba," and on the 19th he added that the "Cuban people have a government which commands their confidence." Now headed by a sixty-two-year-old professional diplomat with wide experience in Europe and the Western Hemisphere, the new government in fact inspired greater confidence in Welles than in the Cuban people. On September 5, in what was described as "the bloodless revolt of the sergeants," the rank and file of the Cuban Army overturned the Céspedes government and replaced it with a five-man ruling junta.

Having closely identified himself with the Céspedes government, Welles could neither accept the new government nor resist the impulse to restore the former regime. "The Céspedes government was his government," historian Bryce Wood has written, "and the mutiny was a blow to his newly gained prestige no less than an attack on the position of the traditional ruling groups in Cuba." Welles told Washington that the new junta consisted of "the most extreme radicals of the student organization and three university professors whose theories are frankly communistic." He predicted that a government of enlisted army men and radical students would find it impossible to protect "life, property, and individual liberty," and he called for armed intervention by the United States. Warships in the Havana and Santiago harbors and troops in Havana were his suggestions for dealing with the new regime. Though Roosevelt and Hull agreed to send warships, they did not want to send troops unless there were physical danger to members of the Embassy. "If we have to go in there again," Hull explained on September 6, "we will never be able to come out and we will have on our hands the trouble of thirty years ago." On the same day, the President urged the press "to lay off on this intervention stuff . . . That is absolutely the last thing we have in mind. We don't want to do it."

To underscore this point, Roosevelt met with the Argentinian, Brazilian, Chilean, and Mexican envoys in an unprecedented expression of regard for Latin sensibilities. He was the first President in the nation's history to discuss current United States policy in the Hemisphere with Latin diplomats. Explaining United States actions in Cuba, Roosevelt declared that he "had absolutely no desire to intervene" and was "seeking every means to avoid intervention." He also took pains to persuade the press that the twenty to thirty ships sent to Cuba were, with two exceptions, "little bits of things" which had to cover a seven hundred mile coast line and represented a very limited display of force. He remained convinced that direct military involvement in Cuba would distract from pressing domestic concerns and all but destroy the Good Neighbor idea.[4]

Since Roosevelt and Hull would not agree to any form of direct intervention, Welles now began a more subtle attack on the revolutionists. On September 11, they formed a provisional government under the presidency of Ramón Grau San Martín, a surgeon and University of

Havana anatomy professor. "For the first time in history," one member of the new government declared, "the Cuban people will rule their own destinies." Welles at once recommended against any intimation that we were considering recognition. Instead, he urged a statement that recognition depended on "conclusive evidence" of a representative government and an ability to maintain order. In shifting his attention to the question of recognition, Welles appreciated, as he had stated in a cable on September 10, that "no government here can survive for a protracted period without recognition of the United States."

Though Roosevelt was not willing to accept Welles's intervention proposals, he was ready to follow his lead on recognition. On September 12 he had Hull issue a statement that "our Government is prepared to welcome any Government representing the will of the people of the Republic and capable of maintaining law and order throughout the island." More important, he accepted Welles's estimates of whether the Grau regime fulfilled these conditions. On September 27, after a succession of dispatches in which Welles cited disorder, economic conditions "verging upon complete prostration," and numerous revolutionary outbreaks, Roosevelt told a press conference that "Mr. San Martín is sitting there in the Presidential Palace and he has his local army with him, which consists of about fifteen hundred men and a bunch of students. Apparently they are not collecting any taxes anywhere on the Island and, of course, their government cannot go on there forever without taxes. Something is bound to happen . . . So we are just sitting and waiting." Grau shortly responded that America's non-recognition policy was "a new type of intervention—intervention by inertia."

By the second week of November, however, with the Grau regime still in power after withstanding attempted coups, Welles came under renewed pressure to defend his policy. Latin leaders and American newspapers criticized the failure to recognize Grau as contributing to the latest revolutionary outbreak and renewing the danger of intervention. At the same time, Argentina, Chile, and Mexico quietly urged Latin American recognition of Grau, while Grau himself asked for Welles's recall. Welles returned home to put his case personally before FDR. Their meeting on November 19 gave Welles largely what he wished. Since he apparently convinced the President that Grau was still without majority backing, Roosevelt publicly reaffirmed that the United States would not accord recognition to a Cuban government lacking popular support. He also announced his intention to negotiate a new commercial convention and make changes in the 1903 Treaty once genuine stability returned to the Island, and revealed that Welles and Jefferson Caffery, Assistant Secretary of State for Latin American Affairs, would switch jobs.

Though the President's statement was meant to soften Latin criticism of his Cuban policy, it had the opposite effect. It was seen as an invitation to Grau's enemies to overturn his rule. It suggested that expansion of Cuba's United States sugar market, revival of its badly depressed economy, and repeal of the Platt Amendment depended on a change in government. When William Phillips, the undersecretary of State, pointed out that the President's statement "might not be well received by the present regime," Roosevelt indicated no concern and said that "if the situation grew steadily worse," he would "withdraw the Embassy from Habana and all Americans from the Island." In short, while the President rejected intervention in Cuba, he believed that pressing domestic need and preservation of the Good Neighbor idea required him to interfere in its affairs. Without American pressure to quiet Cuban strife, he saw conflict in the Island forcing eventual intervention, distractions from domestic economic problems, and damage to the fundamental aim of a Good Neighbor policy. Consequently, though political interference violated his commitment to independence and equality for all American states and, in fact, deprived Cuba of the freedom fully to decide its own political fate, it impressed Roosevelt as the best means to both immediate domestic and long-term foreign goals. The Cuban issue now faded into the background until Grau was overturned in 1934.[5]

At the same time that Roosevelt tried to tranquilize Cuban affairs, he wished to defer doing anything about Latin America in general until domestic recovery had taken stronger hold. This view governed his response to the seventh Pan-American Conference scheduled for Montevideo in December 1933. From his Inauguration until October 1933, he gave little attention to preparations for the Conference. Aside from one suggestion about the agenda and a few brief discussions about the delegation, he left the matter entirely to the State Department.

At the end of October, however, he came under strong pressure to decide on a Conference policy. The Chaco border war between Bolivia and Paraguay, the Leticia border dispute between Colombia and Peru, the Cuban difficulties, and the danger of a revolutionary outbreak in Uruguay had persuaded some Latin leaders that the Conference would not accomplish anything and should be postponed. The fact that Mexico might embarrass the United States with objectionable proposals on debts and the Monroe Doctrine led Hull to share their belief. But when he suggested postponement to the President on October 30, Roosevelt opposed the idea unless a majority of Latin American states felt otherwise. He believed that a brief conference on non-controversial subjects would best serve the economic well-being of the United States and the evolution of a Good Neighbor policy.

During the next two weeks, therefore, the State Department and the White House developed a program that reflected this view. Hull, who was to head the delegation, delayed his departure for the Conference from November 5 to 11 to shorten his stay in Montevideo. The Department instructed its delegates to avoid controversies over intervention, the Monroe Doctrine, and debts owed to citizens of the United States. Louis Howe, FDRs secretary and long-time political adviser, warned the delegation against discussions of trade agreements which the "state of flux" in national economic policies temporarily made impossible to achieve. He proposed instead that the "means of communication" or transportation between the two Americas become the major topic of discussion. "We will try up here through our news service," he told Hull, "to magnify everything that is done about transportation in order to build this up as the big achievement of the conference. It looks like the only thing of importance that we can brag about when we come home even if all goes well." The State Department also counseled the American delegation not "to assume a role of leadership in the Conference" or to support anything but "those proposals which would appear to be of common interest and which merit the unanimous approval of the American Republics." In sum, because Roosevelt and his advisers saw little which could give meaning to the Good Neighbor idea without jeopardizing domestic advance, they wished to move the Conference to a rapid and undramatic conclusion before this became abundantly clear. This objective would guide Roosevelt when the Conference met in December 1933.[6]

While Roosevelt felt stymied over Latin American affairs during the summer and fall of 1933, he maintained some hope of pushing forward the disarmament talks. Though appreciating that the odds were heavily against success, he believed the talks too important not to try. At the beginning of July, when Davis, who had returned from Geneva for a "short visit," had told him that he could do nothing useful at the Conference during the next two months, Roosevelt agreed to keep him in the United States. But because he decided this three days after his bombshell message to the London Economic Conference, he worried that "it would be taken as a complete severance of international cooperation." Hence, when the State Department announced that Davis would not return to Geneva until September, Roosevelt publicly explained that this was simply evidence of a summer lull and that the work of the Conference was going forward under the direction of Arthur Henderson, its president.

However positive Roosevelt wished to remain about Conference prospects, though, the news coming to him during the summer left him little hope that anything could be done. In July he heard from Bullitt that the French would not accept "any disarmament agreement whatsoever" and that war in Europe was "inevitable." Later that month, Breckinridge Long, a wealthy Missouri Democrat and campaign contributor he had made Ambassador to Italy, also pictured the French as intransigent and concluded that there was nothing to be done since Paris wanted what Roosevelt could not give—a guarantee that the United States would go to its aid in case of a German attack. In August the President also learned from William E. Dodd, a University of Chicago historian and staunch Jeffersonian Democrat he had appointed Ambassador to Berlin, that war sentiment was sharp. By mid-August, therefore, when he met with Davis again, he described himself as "much discouraged by the prospects for disarmament" and said that only a faith in what Davis called "the logic of the situation" kept his hopes alive. On the following day, when he spoke with Arthur Sweetser, the Information Director for the League of Nations, he declared that we were "nearly through with our crusading and that if the nations did not soon get down to brass tacks they should tell us so and let us go our own way." Roosevelt reiterated that unless some disarmament was soon agreed to, he could see no alternative but a new race in armaments with another eventual European war.

Despite his growing disenchantment, Roosevelt made another effort to save the Geneva talks. In late August he sent Davis back to Europe with a promise of "full backing" and a letter to show MacDonald and Edouard Daladier, the French Premier. In it, he confided his concern for the future peace of Europe should the Conference fail, and his belief that nothing would better promote immediate and permanent economic welfare than disarmament. "I realize, of course, the technical and political problems involved," he said, "but I am satisfied that a sufficient will to solve them will solve them." He also expressed the belief that a meeting between MacDonald, Daladier, Mussolini, and Hitler could get results, and he gave Davis permission, if he thought it advisable, to use his good offices to bring this about. He concluded by pointing out that "controlled disarmament and international supervision form the only answer." In an additional letter to MacDonald, he underscored his "grave concern" for success in Geneva, expressed his apprehension over events in Germany, and begged MacDonald "for the sake of peace, do all you can."

As if in response to his own injunction, he had Davis announce on the day of his departure for Europe that "the President was not only as deeply interested in the [disarmament] question as ever but even more so." He also took time from absorbing domestic problems to write Long that Mussolini had a wonderful chance to force through an agreement in Geneva and to urge Dodd to "do everything possible to pave the way for the possibility that France and England . . . will try to put it up to Germany at the Disarmament Conference. The crux of the matter will be some form of continuous international inspections. . . . Perhaps the German Government," he suggested, "could use as a face saver the claim that they would have equal rights to full knowledge of what the French were doing."

When the negotiations themselves reached an impasse in early October, Roosevelt took a part in trying to unblock them. Since the French demanded a "trial period" during which Germany would not rearm, and after which France would begin to disarm, and since the Germans rejected this as an insult to their national honor, Roosevelt urged Paris to begin limited disarmament at once and urged Berlin to accept this as a face-saving device. After Roosevelt and Davis agreed that this plan provided "a real chance" to break the impasse, Roosevelt spoke to a national audience about a problem "which can be helped by public interest and public discussion"—world peace. "It is only through constant education and the stressing of the ideals of peace," he declared, "that those who still seek imperialism can be brought in line with the majority." FDR's hopes that his message might help advance the Geneva talks were quickly disappointed. On October 14, 1933, in what Davis and Dodd described as a premeditated act uninfluenced by Roosevelt's actions, Berlin announced its decision to withdraw from the Geneva Conference and the League.[7]

On the surface, Roosevelt's hope for disarmament seems naïve. But in fact he was already skeptical about prospects for an agreement when he sent Davis back to Europe in August, and one can only suspect that he had other considerations in mind: it was good domestic politics, assuring his standing with the pacifists and strengthening his case with the Congress and the country for a larger Navy. It was also a means of signaling Germany and Japan that the United States was not indifferent to their actions, and it assured against foreign suggestions that American isolation from Europe had helped kill arms control.

The collapse of the Geneva talks heightened already strong feelings of ambivalence within FDR about foreign affairs. On the one hand, he clung to the belief that the United States should play a major part in checking the world drift toward economic and political tensions, and on the other, he felt largely unable to influence events abroad and saw good reason to focus his efforts on simply improving conditions at home. During the next several months, in fact, he drifted back and forth between these views, combining nationalistic actions with occasional bursts of effort in behalf of international advance.

The response in the United States to the Geneva collapse, for example, moved Roosevelt further to limit American involvement in European affairs. As long as disarmament remained a possibility, he had met little domestic opposition to an American role in advancing the Geneva talks. Once the Conference collapsed, however, opinion leaders began arguing that the United States should shun the coming round of European power politics. "Nationwide editorial reaction to recent events in Geneva," Hull cabled Davis, "combines a wide resentment against the Hitler Government . . . together with a unanimous opinion that we must not allow ourselves to become involved in European political developments."

In response, Roosevelt moved at once to refute suggestions that Davis would participate in discussions between London, Paris, and Rome. On October 16 he instructed Davis to issue a statement that he was "in Geneva solely for disarmament purposes" and that "we are not . . . interested in the political element or any purely European aspect of the picture."

Though he had previously encouraged Davis to aid European talks on disarmament and peace, including the discussions by Britain, France, Germany, and Italy for the Four Power Pact and a possible meeting between the four heads of state, he now greatly restricted his role. On October 19, when Davis suggested a joint Anglo-American proposal to Paris and Berlin, Hull replied that Davis should not support such a project at this time. The United States will want to follow "a distinctly passive role for some time to come," Hull also told him, and he suggested that Davis come home for consultations with the President and the Department.[8]

When he returned in mid-November, Davis found the President firmly convinced that European political problems temporarily ruled out success in the disarmament talks and that attempts to involve the United States in European political conversations should be consistently turned aside. Roosevelt, however, was not about to turn his back on Europe or completely give up on arms control. "Disarmament," one of his Assistant Secretaries observed at the time, "is a bear which one holds by the tail and no one no matter how discouraged may let go." With the Geneva talks stalled, the United States leaving it to Europe to find new means for reviving the negotiations, the League weakened by Germany's withdrawal, and America's advocates of peace and the League declaring themselves "disheartened" and "uncertain" of their "duty," Roosevelt felt compelled to give international peace efforts a fresh boost.

In a speech before the Woodrow Wilson Foundation on December 28, the President warmly praised the League, restated his May proposals for disarming nations and preventing war, and cited 90 per cent of the world's people as favoring peace. Though "political profit, personal prestige [and] national aggrandizement" handicapped the League from its infancy, he declared, it has either directly, or "through its guiding motives indirectly," encouraged the states of the world "to find something better than the old way of composing their differences." By encouraging non-aggression pacts and arms reductions, he asserted, the League has become "a prop in the world peace structure, and it must remain." Though Roosevelt made it clear that the United States would remain outside the League, he nevertheless assured it of America's continuing cooperation, especially in trying to achieve permanent peace. "As you know," he said, "our own country has reduced the immediate steps to this greatest of objectives—reduced those steps to practical and reasonable terms."

Moreover, he stated his conviction that the great majority of people in America and around the world shared this objective, with only some political leaders standing in the way: "We could get a world accord on world peace immediately," Roosevelt said, "if the people of the world could speak for themselves. . . . It is but an extension of the challenge of Woodrow Wilson for us to propose in this newer generation that from now on war by governments shall be changed to peace by peoples." [9]

Roosevelt's speech was aimed more at domestic opinion than at the nations abroad. Despite a highly favorable response to his speech in the American press and among European supporters of the League, Roosevelt still saw no way to support his vision with practical deeds. In fact, during the next month, he and the State Department emphasized in public and private that nothing had happened to change the position they had adopted in October. "In the present European situation I feel very much as if I were groping for a door in a blank wall," he wrote a friend on February 1. "The situation may get better and enable us to give some leadership."

Events shortly proved him wrong. On March 19 the French expressed a desire "to wind up the Disarmament Conference by a correct juridical funeral" and a willingness to discuss "a treaty of limitation on the basis of the status quo for the heavily armed Powers and legalized re-armament for Germany." In response, Roosevelt announced that the United States could not go beyond what it had proposed in May, and that "it would not sign any accord obliging it to use its armed force for the settlement of any dispute whatever." At the same time, Hull expressed the belief that status quo limitation discussions would be "a negation of our disarmament efforts, and . . . an attempt to draw us into a political adjustment in Europe from which we would gain no advantage." In general, the French response created "considerable depression in Washington, where it was regarded as having completed the transfer of world disarmament out of the realm of practical possibility, at least for the immediate future." [10]

The failure of the disarmament talks also weakened Roosevelt's inclinations to ask Senate approval for membership in the World Court or a discriminatory arms embargo. The collapse in Geneva strengthened the hand of a hard-core group of some twenty Senators opposed to even symbolic American involvement abroad. Led by progressive Republicans —William Borah of Idaho, Bronson Cutting of New Mexico, Lynn Frazier and Gerald Nye of North Dakota, Hiram Johnson of California, and Robert La Follette, Jr. of Wisconsin—these Senators were few in number but strong in influence. They were warm supporters of Roosevelt's domestic actions and had the ability to arouse intense emotions in the country over alleged foreign exploitation of the United States. The war debts and involvement in another "unnecessary" war profiting bankers and munitions makers were issues Roosevelt wished to keep firmly under control. In a word, a struggle with his progressive Republican friends for minor foreign policy goals at the likely expense of domestic advance was something he would not do.

Though he had made Senate agreement to participation in the World Court a foreign policy goal in March 1933, he refused to move on the issue during 1933 or 1934. In April 1933, he assured Hiram Johnson that he would not raise the controversial World Court question during the special congressional session. In December he asked Mrs. Roosevelt to tell Esther Lape of the American Foundation, an internationalist group, that "politically speaking . . . it would be unwise to do anything about the World Court." Further, at the beginning of January 1934, after he conferred with Senator Joseph Robinson of the Foreign Relations Committee, Robinson told the press that "the situation in Europe is so complex that this is not the opportune time to take up the World Court protocols."

But it was opposition in the Senate more than European conditions which worried FDR. There had been widespread sentiment in the country for joining the Court since 1923. Both political party platforms, the House of Representatives, a majority of American newspapers, bar associations, chambers of commerce, labor unions, churches, American Legion groups, teachers' associations, state legislatures, and a host of pacifist societies had endorsed the idea. Moreover, in January 1934, Court advocates had sent Roosevelt a poll of the Senate that showed 65 Senators in favor, 16 opposed, and 15 doubtful. Despite all this, Roosevelt was swayed by the fact that the Senate had blocked American admission in the past, and he believed that raising the issue during 1934 would "delay some necessary legislation for the recovery program." If the Court protocols "come before this session of the Senate," Senator Johnson declared on March 24, "the debate will be so bitter and determined as to carry the session into the dog days." A bitter-end isolationist and Anglophobe who had served in the Senate since 1917 and voted against the Versailles Treaty, Johnson feared involvement with the Court as promising the destruction of American sovereignty. Consequently, after the Foreign Relations Committee held hearings in the spring of 1934, Senator Robinson won agreement to shelve the issue until Congress reconvened in January 1935.[11]

Likewise, in the opening months of 1934 Roosevelt decided against a new push for a discriminatory arms embargo. European affairs, bureaucratic politics, and Senate feeling, above all, argued for leaving the issue alone. Since disarmament was a prerequisite to any American commitment to use a discriminatory embargo, there was no urgency about such a law at the beginning of 1934. Further, the State Department split three ways on the question: Norman Davis and Joseph C. Green, the Department's expert on the international arms traffic, urged a fight for the original legislation; Assistant Secretary of State R. Walton Moore, a former Virginia Congressman who replaced Moley in the summer of 1933, argued for an impartial embargo; while the rest of the leadership wanted to leave the issue on the shelf. In the face of this division, to do nothing about the embargo seemed best calculated to preserve departmental peace. Encouraging this view was the belief that opposing Senators had enough votes to defeat a discriminatory embargo. With all this before him, Roosevelt decided on February 16 to let the issue "lie dormant at this session."

The wisdom of this decision registered forcefully in the next twelve days. On February 28, after Roosevelt had asked Pittman to kill the impartial arms embargo resolution, the Foreign Relations Committee sent it to the Senate floor, where it received unanimous approval. Because an impartial embargo would tie the President's hands and partly repudiate the May 1933 pledge on consultation, the administration arranged to have it blocked in the House. While this action left the matter open for the future, it was small comfort to those within and outside of the country who hoped the new administration would expand cooperation in foreign affairs.[12]

At the same time that Roosevelt turned away from political cooperation with Europe, he initiated a monetary policy which put the United States in open conflict with the major European powers. The source of this tension was the President's decision to follow a policy of systematic currency inflation in an effort to raise commodity prices. By October 1933, with those prices sagging badly and farmers threatening a march on Washington, Roosevelt had felt compelled to relieve this distress. When a committee of orthodox advisers proposed stabilization and a return to the gold standard, he asked his Secretary of the Treasury to "tell the committee that commodity prices must go up, especially agricultural prices. I suggest that the committee let you and me have the recommendation of how to obtain that objective and that objective only." "The West is seething with unrest," he had written his mother on October 28, "and must have higher values to pay off their debts."

To achieve this, Roosevelt turned to the theories of Professors George Warren, Irving Fisher, and James Harvey Rogers. They contended that government purchases of gold at rates above the domestic and world markets would force up the price of gold and reduce the value of the dollar. This, in turn, was supposed to push up commodity prices. Ultimately, their idea was to create a commodity dollar, which would have "a constant buying power not for one commodity but for all commodities at wholesale prices, managed in accordance with a price index by manipulation of the gold content."

On October 19 Roosevelt had ordered the Reconstruction Finance Corporation to begin purchasing newly mined gold in the United States, and on the 22nd he explained his new policy in a Fireside Chat. "Our dollar is now altogther too greatly influenced by the accidents of international trade, by the internal policies of other Nations and by political disturbance in other continents," he said. "Therefore the United States must take firmly in its own hands the control of the gold value of our dollar. This is necessary in order to prevent dollar disturbances from swinging us away from our ultimate goal, namely, the continued recovery of our commodity prices. . . . I am authorizing the Reconstruction Finance Corporation," he told his listeners, "to buy gold newy minted in the United States at prices to be determined from time to time after consultation with the Secretary of the Treasury and the President. Whenever necessary to the end in view, we shall also buy in the world market." By November 1 the program had been set in motion at home and abroad.

The foreign reaction was strongly negative. Faced with trade losses and pressure to devalue their own currencies, the gold-bloc countries angrily denounced Roosevelt's actions. After hearing of the program, French officials "nearly jumped out of their skins," while Montagu Norman, Governor of the Bank of England, declared this to be "the most terrible thing that has happened. The whole world will be put into bankruptcy." When Roosevelt and Morgenthau, who had become Acting Secretary of the Treasury in November 1933, heard about Norman's reaction, they pictured "foreign bankers with every one of their hairs standing on end in horror . . . and began to roar with laughter." "A very definite drive," by New York bankers, Republican leaders, and British sources "to have the gold content of the dollar definitely fixed by the United States" gave Roosevelt less amusement. Spreading reports that London would stabilize the pound if Washington stabilized the dollar, they hoped to push Roosevelt into ending his experiment. To counter these rumors, Roosevelt had George Harrison of the Federal Reserve Bank of New York ask Norman whether Britain would take such a course. As Roosevelt anticipated, the British showed little interest. But even if they had, Roosevelt would not have stabilized in November. At that time, as he indicated in a letter to an opponent of gold buying, he wanted no part of a policy that placed "an artificial gold standard among nations above human suffering and the crying needs" of the country.

By January 1934, however, it was clear to FDR that the gold-buying program would not have the price-raising effects he wished. He decided, therefore, to close off the experiment and use the profits from devaluation to create a stabilization fund which could limit alleged British influence over international exchange. On January 15 he asked Congress for power to stabilize the dollar at between 50 and 60 per cent of its former value, and on January 31, the day after Congress passed the Gold Reserve Act of 1934, he returned the United States to the international gold standard with the dollar fixed at 59.06 per cent of its pre-1933 gold value. The end of the managed-currency experiment temporarily eased antagonisms between Europe and the United States.[13]

But conflicts over war debts quickly triggered them again. In October

1933, when the British had initiated yet another round of discussions about their debt, some of Roosevelt's advisers hoped that a settlement could be reached. It was soon clear, however, that it would be almost impossible to achieve an understanding on how much and for how long the British should pay. Roosevelt, in fact, came away from these discussions "horrified" by "the suggestions that were made to us, and . . . [by] the extremely adamant position that was taken in regard even to suggestions of some kind of compromise." A British offer of $460 million in full settlement on a debt of $8 billion moved Roosevelt to say that "our European friends talk such ridiculous sums that no self-respecting Congress and, for that matter, no self-respecting President, could go on with the discussion." With the French defaulting on their December 15 payment, as they had on the previous two, and with the British and the Italians paying only token sums, Roosevelt decided to support legislation introduced by Senator Johnson for punishing defaulting debtor states.[14]

The Johnson bill, as passed by the Senate on January 11, 1934, provided prohibitions against buying bonds from, or making loans to, governments that were in default on obligations to the United States government or its citizens. While Roosevelt wished to punish defaulters on obligations to the United States, he rejected the idea of federal pressure on foreign governments to repay loans from private citizens. Since the administration already faced insoluble problems with intergovernmental debts, he had no reason to think that it could deal more effectively with private ones. The assumption of this task, therefore, impressed him as likely to turn American creditors into critics of the administration for failing to collect their loans and seemed certain to increase tensions with debtor states, especially in Latin America where the governments were largely in default on debts owed to citizens of the United States.[15]

Hence, Roosevelt's price for support of the Johnson bill was its limitation to debts owed strictly to the United States government. In early February, when Johnson agreed to this restriction, Roosevelt signaled Assistant Secretary of State Moore to steer the bill through the Congress. Since it was likely to produce considerable anger abroad, though, he tried to disassociate himself from the measure. His backing "was not stated in the Senate, nor . . . in the hearing before the House Committee," nor before the House itself when it came up for final passage on April 4. By signing the bill on April 13, however, he clearly demonstrated his desire to press debtor nations into equitable settlements with the United States. With Johnson and other progressive Republican Senators like James Couzens, Robert M. LaFollette, Jr., and George Norris warmly backing the law, Roosevelt also strengthened a valuable working relationship he had established with these men. But there were also negative repercussions: the bill never persuaded any of the debtor countries to pay, and it came back to haunt FDR in the first years of World War II when it prevented him from lending Britain money to buy arms in the United States.[16]

If Roosevelt was reluctant to disclose his commitment to a nationalistic policy on debts, he was more direct about his support of American naval expansion. From his first days in office, he backed a naval buildup as contributing to national recovery and making the United States the military equal of Japan. Relying on Navy Department figures, he justified a construction program on the grounds of being likely to employ people from 125 trades and professions in all parts of the country, to use materials from almost every state in the Union, and to make labor, both directly and indirectly, the recipient of 80 per cent of all shipbuilding expenditures. Further, he defended a construction program because it would allow the United States to bring its Navy "almost up to the ship strength of the Japanese navy," to which, he wrote in August 1933, "our navy was and probably is actually inferior. . . . The further fact that the whole scheme of things in Tokio does not make for an assurance of non-aggression in the future," he added, made the building program necessary.

During his first year in office, Japanese actions fanned Roosevelt's suspicions. In March 1933 the Japanese officially withdrew from the League of Nations and disclosed their intention to abandon the naval limitation agreements they had with Britain and the United States. In April, William Phillips informed him that Japanese demands for increased armaments would make a universal disarmament agreement impossible. In May he learned from Ambassador Joseph Grew in Tokyo "that Japan probably has the most complete, well-balanced, coordinated and therefore powerful fighting machine in the world today. . . . The Japanese fighting forces consider the United States as their potential enemy," Grew also said, ". . . because they think the United States is standing in the path of the nation's natural expansion." In June, Carl Vinson, Chairman of the House Committee on Naval Affairs, notified him of a 25 per cent increase in Japan's 1933 naval budget, and in July the State Department told him of a possible Japanese attack on the U.S.S.R. In the fall and winter of 1933, he received news of continuing pressure in Japan for a larger navy and of the inevitability of a Russo-Japanese conflict.

Hence, national economic needs and Japanese militance moved Roosevelt to begin substantial naval expansion. In June 1933 he allocated $238 million in public works funds for the construction of thirty-two ships totaling 120,000 tons. When added to five ships of 17,000 tons already provided for by the Congress, the total amounted to a threefold increase in allocated construction costs and the largest building program since 1916. Further, at the beginning of 1934 he gave his full support to the Vinson-Trammell bill providing for construction and replacement of ships up to the limits of the Washington and London naval treaties of 1922 and 1930.[17]

While Roosevelt was initiating naval expansion, he tried at the same time to assure that it would not weaken him politically and undermine his ability to put across economic reform. Appreciating, as Norman Davis had told him, that the naval program caused "great gloom . . . among a large section of our public," he tried to avoid provoking it. When Navy Department officials spoke publicly, for example, he urged them to use restraint, suggesting that they not overstate the case for a strong Navy, or "hit and assail" the "professional pacifists," since "replies only create a controversy." Moreover, when the White House received more than two hundred letters a day "from every part of the country and from every class of society" opposing the Vincent-Trammell bill as wasteful and contrary to America's professed peace aims, Roosevelt felt compelled to explain that the bill authorized construction of 102 new ships but did not appropriate money for them. Future Congresses, he pointed out, would have to do this, but whether they would depended on upcoming naval talks. "It has been and will be," he assured his countrymen, "the policy of the Administration to favor continued limitation of naval armaments. It is my personal hope that the Naval Conference to be held in 1935 will extend all existing limitations and agree to further reductions." [18]

Similarly, Roosevelt wished to assure that the naval building program did not draw the United States into a crisis with Japan. Consequently, at the same time that he initiated the naval program, he sanctioned a Far Eastern policy of inaction and nonprovocation, which the State Department under Hull and Stanley K. Hornbeck, the chief of the Far Eastern Division, translated into more specific terms. Because he wished to follow a passive policy toward the Japanese in East Asia generally during the thirties, Roosevelt was content to leave the execution, or perhaps more accurately, the nonexecution, of policy to his subordinates. The Far East, as the State Department called it, became one of Hull's special interests. During the next eight years he expended considerable energy lecturing the Japanese about the "principles of good behavior." Hornbeck, the son of a Methodist minister, shared Hull's passion for moral pronouncements. He armed his superior with "an unending flow of policy memoranda" laden with "ponderously complex sentences and fine verbal distinctions." [19]

As interpreted by the State Department, the administration's objective was to avoid all initiatives in the Far East. The experience of the Manchurian crisis, in which the Washington and Kellogg-Briand agreements had proved unworkable and the League members had given American leadership little support, had left the Department wary of cooperative steps against Japan. At the end of March, therefore, when a committee of the League indicated that an anti-Japanese arms embargo depended on American action, Hull declared that he did not intend to have his government "assume the role of mentor to the League or accept a responsibility which initially lies with and belongs to the League." Further, in May, when Alfred Sze, Chinese Minister to the United States, suggested that Washington mediate the Sino-Japanese conflict, Hornbeck strongly advised otherwise. The initiative in such an undertaking, Hornbeck said, properly belongs with the League, or Britain and France, nations whose material interests are more acutely menaced than those of the United States. "The United States," Hornbeck went on, "has not much to lose" from further Japanese aggression in China. "The principles of our Far Eastern policy and our ideals with regard to world peace may be further scratched and dented . . . and our trade prospects may be somewhat further impaired; but from the point of view of material interests there is nothing there that is vital to us." Hornbeck thought it would be better to let the war run its course and give those who had not yet grasped the significance of Japanese actions a fuller chance to see what they meant.

While Roosevelt did not share Hornbeck's inclination to let the war continue, he agreed that the United States should leave it to others to initiate discussions for peace. On May 19 and 22, therefore, after Mussolini told the American Ambassador that Japan's control of China would menace the whole world, Roosevelt suggested that the Italian leader inquire about Japanese interest in mediation by the Great Powers. He also asked, however, that Mussolini describe his inquiry as strictly a personal initiative without any "inspiration whatsoever from the outside." Though nothing came of Mussolini's attempt to implement the President's suggestion, it revealed how concerned Roosevelt was not to increase Japanese feeling against the United States.[20]

The most important expression of this conciliatory policy toward Japan came in response to the Amau Doctrine. In April 1934 Eiji Amau, a spokesman for the Foreign Office, announced Japanese opposition to foreign technical, financial, or military assistance to China, explaining that unification and order in China could occur only through "the voluntary efforts of China herself." The administration's response to this declaration was distinctly passive. Roosevelt himself made no statement, while the State Department sent an aide-mémoire to Tokyo which "was deliberately worded to be as nonprovocative as possible." Cordell Hull then asked the press to avoid stirring up trouble between Japan and the United States and directed the Department's Far Eastern experts to suggest changes in America's China policy which would reduce difficulties with Japan. All in all, the historian Dorothy Borg has pointed out, the administration refused to renew "the Stimsonian effort to champion the movement for world order. . . . Instead the State Department sought to avoid increasing the dangers which already existed in the relations of the United States and Japan and decided not only to refrain from making any move that might provoke the Japanese, but for the most part to remain relatively inactive." [21] In the Far East, as in Europe and Latin America, the domestic and international crosscurrents of the nine months after the London Economic Conference kept Roosevelt on a narrowly self-protective path.

4

Farewell to Internationalism

CONTRARY TO TRADITIONAL BELIEF, the 1930s were not a time of un-relieved isolationism in the United States. During the first two years of his presidency, Roosevelt met not intense isolationism in the country but a general indifference to outside events which left him relatively free to seek expanded American ties abroad. Indeed, in 1933–34, Roosevelt's policies of economic self-protection and political detachment from other nations represented only one side of his foreign policy. At the same time that he charted a separate economic and political course for the United States, he also moved toward greater cooperation abroad.

In the fall of 1933, when domestic and foreign constraints seemed to put international cooperation temporarily out of reach, he channeled his desire for world harmony into improving Soviet-American relations. Strong support for the idea came from American business leaders who hoped that recognition would reopen Russian markets to American manufactured goods. To Roosevelt, there was the additional appeal that recognition might discourage rumored Japanese aggression against the U.S.S.R. But opposition from Catholic and labor leaders and conservative groups like the D.A.R. gave him pause. Though one conservative newspaper publisher belittled the danger of Bolshevism in the United States as "about as great as the menace of sunstroke in Greenland or chilblains in the Sahara," Roosevelt felt compelled to resolve Soviet-American differences and as-sure a consensus before recognizing the Soviet Union.

Because the State Department was unenthusiastic about the idea, Roosevelt turned for help to Henry Morgenthau, his head of the Farm Credit Administration and Acting Secretary of the Treasury beginning in November 1933. Morgenthau first met FDR in 1915 through a shared in-terest in Dutchess County Democratic Party politics. A tall, heavy-set, diffident man, Morgenthau was the child of a wealthy German Jewish family. His father, a man of strong social conscience and a political ac-tivist, had served as Woodrow Wilson's Ambassador to Turkey. Reluctant to involve himself in any of his father's businesses and devoted to the land and the outdoors, the younger Morgenthau became a farmer in Dutchess County and the publisher of the *American Agriculturalist*, one of New York State's two farm papers. There, as a Roosevelt neighbor,

Morgenthau became one of the President's early and consistent political supporters. Sharing "similar backgrounds and habits of mind," they also became close friends. "To Henry," Roosevelt once inscribed a photograph of himself and Morgenthau, "from one of two of a kind." [1]

In early October 1933, Roosevelt asked Morgenthau and Bullitt to approach Boris Skvirsky, Moscow's principal representative in the United States, and explained how they should proceed. Following the President's instructions, Morgenthau invited Skvirsky to his office, where he announced that "in about five minutes Bullitt from the State Department will come here with a piece of paper unsigned and will show it to you."

> His face lit up with a big smile. Bullitt made his entry on the stage as arranged by the President himself, sat down, and said to Skvirsky, 'I have a piece of paper in my hand unsigned. This document can be made into an invitation for your country to send representatives over here to discuss relationship between our two countries. We wish you to telegraph the contents of this piece of paper by your most confidential code, and learn if it is acceptable to your people. If it is . . . the President will sign this piece of paper. . . . If they are not acceptable, will you give me your word of honor that there never will be any publicity . . . and that the whole matter will be kept a secret?' Skvirsky assured Bullitt that that would be the case. He then said, 'Does this mean recognition?' and Bullitt parried . . . , 'What more can you expect than to have your representative sit down with the President of the United States?' [2]

As he was initiating these negotiations, Roosevelt launched a systematic effort to measure public feeling and build a broad consensus for recognition. He saw little potential problem with the press. A State Department survey of 300 newspapers for a thirty-day period revealed little interest in the subject, while direct inquiries from the American Foundation, an internationalist group, to 1139 newspapers showed that 63 per cent favored recognition and only 26.9 per cent opposed.

By contrast, organized religious groups declaring against friendship "with a government avowedly an enemy of God and a persecutor of religion" posed a serious problem. American Catholic leaders, for example, generally opposed recognition, and Hull and Postmaster General James A. Farley shared their view. To meet their objections, Roosevelt revealed that he would ask the Soviets to release religious prisoners and grant religious freedom to Americans in the U.S.S.R. A meeting between FDR and Father Edmund A. Walsh of Georgetown University, the country's leading Catholic opponent of recognition, went far to disarm religious opposition in general and Catholic resistance in particular. Persuading Walsh that he was "a good horse dealer," Roosevelt convinced him to announce that complete confidence could be placed in the President to examine the issue of recognition and to do what was best in light of the evidence. This was a remarkable turnabout, historian Edward M. Bennett has observed, "for a man who had taken a strong public stand against recognition." Walsh himself could only explain it by pointing to Roosevelt's vaunted charm. "In reply . . . to certain observations I had made respecting the difficulty of negotiating with the Soviets," Walsh later recalled, Roosevelt "answered with that disarming assurance so characteristic of his technique in dealing with visitors."

As an additional brake on domestic opposition, Roosevelt indicated that he would seek guarantees against Soviet subversion in America and concessions on repudiated debts and confiscated property. He also assured opponents of recognition that he would negotiate seriously. The agreement to hold talks, he told a press conference, "is a request and acceptance of the thought of sitting together at a table to see whether we can devise means for settling various problems that exist between two great nations, two great peoples. That is as far as it goes. And that is all it is." ³

In the negotiations, which lasted from November 8 to 16, 1933, Roosevelt won the concessions he felt necessary to disarm domestic opponents. This required direct participation on his part. After two days of negotiations between Maxim Litvinov, the Soviet Commissar for Foreign Affairs, and administration leaders, including Hull, Phillips, Bullitt, Moore, Morgenthau, and Robert Kelley, the State Department's chief specialist on Eastern Europe, the discussions reached an impasse. A skilled negotiator with an excellent command of English, Litvinov, of whom it was said he could "come out dry from the water," acted as if he could gain recognition without agreement on religious freedom, propaganda, or debts. Even Hull's prediction that recognition without an accord on religion would overturn the Roosevelt administration at the next election left him unmoved.

Litvinov wanted direct discussions with Roosevelt and a boost to Moscow's international prestige, especially against Japan. Consequently, a single one-hour conversation with the President on November 10 produced a dramatic shift in Litvinov's attitude. In response to FDR's "combination of humor, sincerity, clearness and friendliness," he now agreed to consider the American proposal on propaganda and substantially accept the proposition on religious freedom for Americans in the Soviet Union. "At the end of the conference the President said that he would like to have a man-to-man talk with Mr. Litvinov that evening at 9 o'clock, which would be more informal . . . than any conference which included the Secretary of State and Under Secretary. He wanted, he said, to be able to call Mr. Litvinov names if he felt like it and he certainly hoped that Mr. Litvinov would feel free to call him names too. Litvinov laughed heartily." In a three-hour meeting that evening, they resolved differences over propaganda, subversive activities, and religious practices for Americans in the U.S.S.R., and then settled questions about the legal rights of Americans in the Soviet Union at another two-hour talk on the 12th.

Only the debt problem remained. But with practically all of America's debtors in default, and the British making "ridiculous" propositions,

Roosevelt was unwilling to press the issue very hard. "I want to keep these Russian negotiations on a high plane," he had told Morgenthau on October 23, "and it will be time enough to talk about business after we have come to every other decision." On November 15, therefore, he struck a gentleman's agreement with Litvinov: they committed themselves to a debt settlement at a later date, with the Soviets to pay between $75 million and $150 million on a debt the State Department calculated to be more than $600 million. After a White House party on the following evening, the President and Litvinov simultaneously signed the various agreements at fourteen minutes before one in the morning of November 17, 1933, in the presence of Phillips, Bullitt, Woodin, and Morgenthau. Later that day Roosevelt released the agreements to the press and announced the resumption of normal relations with Russia, emphasizing the guarantees for freedom of religion he had received in exchange.

He emphasized the same point to his Cabinet. Assuming that his remarks would leak to the press and eager to demonstrate that he had disarmed Soviet hostility to religious practice, he painted an exaggerated portrait of how he had embarrassed Litvinov into accepting freedom of worship for Americans in Russia. Roosevelt described himself as telling Litvinov that "every man in his deepest heart knows the existence of God. . . . 'You know, Max,' " the President recounted, " 'your good old father and mother, pious Jewish people, always said their prayers. I know they must have taught you to say prayers. . . .' By this time Max was as red as a beet and I said to him, 'Now you may think you're an atheist. . . . but I tell you, Max, when you come to die . . . you're going to be thinking about what your father and mother taught you.' . . . Max blustered and puffed and said all kinds of things, laughed and was very embarrassed, but I had him. I was sure from the expression of his face and his actions that he knew what I meant and that he knew I was right." As Frances Perkins, the Secretary of Labor, later commented, Roosevelt would only tell the Cabinet what he wanted them to hear.

The public reaction was all Roosevelt could have asked. Most interested Americans, including conservative business leaders, supported his action, believing, like FDR, that recognition would contribute to prosperity and peace by reviving Russian-American trade and inhibiting Japanese aggression against the U.S.S.R. In fact, it did nothing of the kind—neither trade nor international stability received a significant boost from the act of recognition. As historian William E. Leuchtenburg has concluded, it "was an event of monumental unimportance." Roosevelt's caution in handling the issue, then, came less from public resistance or concern with international consequences than from his desire for an unequivocal consensus and his prevailing inclination to move slowly in foreign affairs. The fact that recognition went so smoothly, however, helped revive his hopes for wider cooperation on the world scene.[4]

Events in Montevideo shortly added to this fresh sense of what was possible. In November 1933 Roosevelt had seen little chance for worthwhile accomplishment at the Pan-American Conference to be held in Uruguay in December, and he had instructed his delegation to make the meeting as brief and uncontroversial as possible. Further, to limit expectations, he had issued a pre-Conference statement emphasizing the need to improve inter-American transportation and picturing unsettled economic conditions everywhere as temporarily foreclosing meaningful economic talks.

But Hull, who was to carry the burden of the Conference as delegation chairman and who wished to redeem the failure in London, refused to be so pessimistic. Though initially reluctant to hold the Conference, he took the President's decision to go ahead as a reason to work for significant agreements, especially on inter-American trade. In contrast to the President, he hailed Conference prospects, declaring, "A more substantial step forward in Pan-American unity can and, I believe, will be taken at the Montevideo Conference than at all others within two decades. I am speaking," he explained, "of the possibilities of mutual economic national and international planning." On his way to Uruguay, he drew up a comprehensive economic resolution calling for a tariff truce and bilateral or multilateral negotiations for the elimination of trade barriers. The President responded, however, that domestic economic uncertainties temporarily ruled out a United States commitment to an extended tariff truce or any multilateral commercial agreement. He suggested instead that Hull limit himself to a strong resolution in favor of reduced trade barriers through bilateral discussions. But Hull insisted on a resolution promising long-term liberalization of trade policies. Since, he argued, anything less would imply a highly nationalistic policy with no international plan, Roosevelt acceded to his request. As long as such a commitment would not interfere with immediate actions under the NRA and AAA, the President told him, he was free to pursue his goal.

Despite Roosevelt's concession, Hull faced formidable obstacles to a successful conference. Like the previous Pan-American Conference in Havana in 1928, at which ex-Secretary of State Charles Evans Hughes defended the right of intervention, the Montevideo meeting seemed likely to devote itself to attacks on "Yankee imperialism." When the American delegation arrived in Montevideo, they encountered billboards announcing "Down with Hull' and a hostile press "rawhiding" the United States. "The whole atmosphere and surroundings," Hull later recalled, "were like a blue snow in January."

Hull spared no effort to overcome this animosity. He unceremoniously visited each of the twenty delegations in their hotels, assuring them that the United States sought only fulfillment of the Good Neighbor doctrine at the Conference. He made a particular effort to win over Carlos Saavedra Lamas, Argentina's Foreign Minister and a leading opponent of the United States. It was a difficult task. According to one observer, Saavedra Lamas was an old-school diplomat who conversed "in such formal, rounded periods" that he always appeared "to be reading an oration." At their first meeting, he received Hull "most courteously, but exhibited a noticeable degree of reserve and aloofness with outcroppings of skepticism" as to the Secretary's purposes. To overcome this suspicion, Hull drafted a resolution calling on all the American Republics to adhere to five peace agreements, including one written by Saavedra Lamas. He then suggested that Saavedra Lamas join him in sponsoring his economic and peace proposals, and that Saavedra Lamas himself introduce the peace resolution. In a series of additional conversations, in which Saavedra Lamas became cordial and cooperative, Hull took a major step toward a successful conference.

He assured this success by resolving conflicts over nonintervention and debts. When the Conference considered a convention on the rights and duties of states which contained a provision that "No state has the right to intervene in the internal or external affairs of another," Hull announced American willingness to sign the agreement. Determined, however, to preserve "the right to protect lives and property where government has broken down and anarchy exists," he added the reservation that the United States expected the signatories to work out a codification or definition of the convention's terms. While this work went forward, the Roosevelt administration, Hull announced, would follow the policy of nonintervention it had practiced since taking office. Though some of the "more poisonous individuals and newspapers will attempt to distort" this reservation, Hull told Washington, "sane and reasonable citizens down here" see it as an "absolutely sound and logical position on our part."

Similarly, when José Casauranc, Mexico's Foreign Minister, delivered an emotional appeal for a moratorium on debts owed to "conscienceless corporations in Wall Street," Hull managed to avoid a clash. He persuaded the delegates, who generally shared his concern to avoid a moratorium on inter-American debts, to give the issue to a Conference subcommittee, which referred it to a Pan-American agency for continuing discussion. The result of all this, Hull cabled the President at the close of the Conference, was a better state of feeling toward the United States in Latin America than at any time within a generation. "The American delegation has succeeded in all its plans." [5]

Hull's achievement, following so soon after the successful recognition of the Soviet Union, encouraged Roosevelt to renew his efforts for peace. In his Woodrow Wilson address of December 28, 1933, he tried not only to bolster the League and promote disarmament but also to cite the events in Montevideo as evidence that restraint and cooperation in world affairs could work. "The definite policy of the United States from now on," he announced, "is one opposed to armed intervention. The maintenance of constitutional government in other nations is not a sacred obligation devolving upon the United States alone. . . . If and when the failure of orderly processes affects the other nations of the continent . . . it becomes the joint concern of a whole continent in which we are all neighbors. It is the comprehension of that doctrine," he said, ". . . . that has made the conference now concluding its labors in Montivideo such a splendid success." [6]

On the same day as his Wilson speech, Roosevelt also agreed to revive his request to Congress for authority to negotiate reciprocal trade agreements. Convinced that "a full and permanent domestic recovery" could not be achieved without a restoration of America's badly shrunken world commerce and persuaded that he had new support in the country for such legislation, he sent Congress a reciprocal trade law on March 2, 1934. Only five Republicans voted for the bill, with most of the others denouncing it as "Fascist in its philosophy" and "objective," as "palpably unconstitutional" and "economic dictatorship come to America." But a Henry Wallace pamphlet, America Must Choose, helped to build general backing in the country for the law and to propel it through the Congress by wide margins.

While Hull and the internationalists saw the bill as leading to international tariff reductions and expanded world trade, it also allowed the President to make agreements principally benefiting the United States. On the one hand, he could negotiate reciprocal tariff reductions with one nation and then, as Hull wished, extend them to all other nations that gave most-favored-nation treatment to, or did not discriminate against, the United States. This, the internationalists argued, would lower tariffs and expand world commerce by allowing America's creditors to ship more goods to the United States. On the other hand, the President was free to ignore this multilateral or most-favored-nation approach, which nationalists described as "unilateral economic disarmament," and aim instead at expanded American exports through bilateral agreements, or concessions exchanged with individual nations.

Because immediate economic pressures made Roosevelt uncertain of how he would use these trade powers, he simultaneously encouraged both the internationalist and nationalist interpretations. In March 1934, at the same time he supported Hull's expectations for the reciprocal trade law, he made George N. Peek, a determined nationalist, his Foreign Trade Adviser with responsibility for collecting information on foreign trade and keeping the President informed on developments. While the division of authority suited Roosevelt's purposes, allowing him to delay a decision until his uncanny sense of timing told him to act, it angered Hull. "If Mr. Roosevelt had hit me between the eyes with a sledge hammer," Hull later wrote, "he could not have stunned me more than by this appointment." When the bill became law on June 12, Peek and Hull began a fierce competition to determine how it would be used.[7]

If economic uncertainties in the spring of 1934 made Roosevelt unsure of whether he would use the trade bill as internationalists wished, other conditions were freeing and encouraging him toward fresh internationalist steps. Most important, the near-crisis recession, which had almost totally commanded his attention in late 1933, had now begun to ebb. The *New York Times* Weekly Business Index, which in 1933 had gone from 60 in March to 99 in June and then down to 72 in October, had moved back up to 86 by May 1934. Further, with national income almost a quarter higher and unemployment two million less than in 1933, Roosevelt now felt free to pay more mind to foreign relations. "After months of preoccupation with internal affairs," Clark Eichelberger, the editor of the *League of Nations Chronicle*, observed in May, "the administration in Washington marches forward with its foreign program." Uppermost in Roosevelt's mind was the international arms traffic, an issue of growing public concern.[8]

In 1933 after the Senate Foreign Relations Committee had blocked the administration's arms-embargo law and the Disarmament Conference had collapsed, American demand for regulation of the international arms traffic intensified. The pressure came chiefly from peace groups. Led by women, clergymen, and students disillusioned with the experience of World War I, the American peace movement of the 1930s at its height boasted twelve million adherents and an audience of between forty-five and sixty million people. A declaration in 1931 by 12,000 clergymen against future church approval for any war, a mile-long automobile procession in Washington in 1932 to present President Hoover with a peace petition from several hundred thousand Americans, and a pledge in 1933 by 15,000 students from 65 colleges to either absolute pacifism or military service only in response to an invasion were a few of its activities. The appearance in March 1934 of "Arms and the Men," a widely discussed article in the influential business magazine *Fortune,* and publication the following month of *Merchants of Death,* a Book-of-the-Month Club selection, gave this antiwar sentiment more specific focus. Arguing that munitions-makers instigated wars, these publications urged government controls on the industry. At a time when businessmen stood in low repute, the idea of ruthless arms-makers putting profits above peace had wide appeal. The two axioms attributed to them were: "When there are wars, prolong them; when there is peace, disturb it."

Aided by these writings, Dorothy Detzer, the executive secretary of the Women's International League for Peace and Freedom, led a successful campaign for a Senate investigation of the American munitions industry. During 1932–33 the W.I.L.P.F. and other peace societies had repeatedly called for such an inquiry. In January 1934, after both the

Senate Committee on Banking and Currency and the NRA refused to accept the job, Miss Detzer convinced Senator Gerald P. Nye of North Dakota to do it. A forty-one-year-old veteran of eight years in the Senate, Nye was an isolationist and a progressive with a penchant for crusades against public evils. With four years to go in his term and no munitions industry in North Dakota to oppose him, Nye accepted an assignment shunned by his Senate colleagues. Administration approval, together with a barrage of telegrams, letters, and deputations to Senators, resulted in Senate agreement on April 12 to an investigation.[9]

Roosevelt endorsed the investigation but urged international rather than strictly national action to deal with the problem. In a message to the Senate on May 18, he expressed gratification at the appointment of a committee to pursue the inquiry, urged the Senate to give it generous support, and promised full cooperation from all Executive departments. More importantly, he asked the Senate to understand that it would not be possible "to control such an evil by the isolated action of any one country. . . . This is a field," he said, "in which international action is necessary." He then urged Senate approval of a 1925 Geneva Convention requiring national licensing of international arms merchants and the publication of arms shipments to and from signatory countries. He also expressed the hope that the next meeting of the Geneva Disarmament Conference in May 1934 would agree upon a "much more far-reaching" convention to control the "activities of the manufacturers and merchants of engines of destruction." [10]

At the same time, he fixed his attention on Latin America and Anglo-American naval talks. In June he completed plans for a 10,000-mile summer cruise to the Caribbean and the Pacific with stops in Haiti, Puerto Rico, the Virgin Islands, Colombia, Panama, and Hawaii. The resolution of Cuban problems after the 1933 Pan-American Conference in Montevideo made this Good Neighbor trip, as FDR called it, possible. In January 1934, after more than four months of nonrecognition by Washington, the Grau regime, under pressure from Fulgencio Batista, the country's military chief, had given way to the more conservative rule of Carlos Mendieta, head of the Nationalist Party. Though Roosevelt had refused to promise recognition to a Mendieta government before it took office and unless it fulfilled the conditions of his November declarations, he gave it formal recognition only five days after it gained control. Moreover, during the next six months, Roosevelt gave the new government strong support. In February he started trade negotiations aimed at reducing the tariff on Cuban sugar and expanding Cuban-American trade; in March he approved a $4 million loan to help revive Cuba's economy; in May he signed a treaty abrogating the Platt Amendment, abolishing America's right to intervene in Cuba; and in June, because of "conditions of domestic violence," he limited arms exports to Cuba to those authorized by the Mendieta government.

All this, especially the abolition of the right to intervene, enhanced Roosevelt's standing in Latin America and helped make his Caribbean trip in July a huge success. In Haiti, where Norman Armour, the American Minister, had skillfully resolved long-standing differences over ending America's twenty-year occupation, Roosevelt advanced the withdrawal date from October 1 to August 15, 1934, and initiated negotiations for a mutually beneficial commercial agreement. In Colombia he praised the country's "inestimable service to humanity in the settlement of their Leticia problem" with Peru and announced the start of a new era of nonexploitation by neighbors: "the development of the commerce and resources of the Americas . . . in the spirit of fair play and justice." In Panama he promised to solve all United States-Panamanian problems, and particularly tensions over America's right to intervene under a 1903 treaty, "in the same spirit of justice which we are now displaying." As the first United States President ever to set foot on South American soil and to cross the Panama Canal, Roosevelt gained distinction among Latin Americans as "the world's best neighbor." [11]

During this period Roosevelt was also wrestling with challenges to the international naval-limitation system created by the Washington and London treaties of 1922 and 1930, respectively. The London agreement was to end in December 1936 unless the signatories—Britain, Japan, and the United States—agreed to extend it at a conference in 1935. Moreover, if one of the adherents to the Washington Treaty disavowed its provisions by December 1934, that agreement was also to end in 1936. By early 1934 it seemed almost certain that Japan would repudiate these treaties by asking for parity in tonnage with Britain and the United States. The British, on the other hand, favored continuation of the 5:5:3 treaty ratio, but wanted qualitative—tonnage and gun size—reductions for battleships and heavy cruisers coupled with a quantitative or overall increase in light cruisers, their "handiest ship."

Roosevelt was eager to keep the treaty system intact. To grant Japanese or British demands would unhinge the Pacific security system: parity for Japan or an end to the existing ratios would spark an arms race, while reductions in the size of battleships and heavy cruisers would restrict America's capacity for trans-Pacific cruising. The collapse of the treaty system would also deprive Roosevelt of his public justification for naval building. As long as the system remained, building up to treaty limits carried "an aura of legitimacy" which disarmed some of the intense opposition to arms construction in the United States. Hence, in February 1934, when London approached Washington about a united effort to restrain the Japanese, Roosevelt suggested Anglo-American support for a ten-year continuation of existing ratios with a 20 per cent reduction in each country's overall tonnage. If Japan refused this, Roosevelt suggested that Britain and the United States offer to renew the Washington Treaty for five years. And should the Japanese reject this, Roosevelt proposed a continuation of Anglo-American ratios, with tonnage levels to go up or down according to what the Japanese did.

Though Roosevelt appreciated that the Japanese would probably reject his proposals, he made them anyway as a means of strengthening the domestic and international case for his building program. It was a tactic, historian Stephen Pelz has pointed out, "to neutralize both Congress and the Japanese. By championing disarmament, he silenced his critics in Washington and simultaneously put the responsibility for an arms race on Japan." [12]

By June 1934, when preliminary naval discussions began, London had developed substantial doubts about opposing Tokyo. With the Disarmament Conference unable to check the German threat and with Japan giving fresh signs of aggressiveness in the Amau declaration against foreign assistance to China, Britain's political leaders leaned toward concentrating on Europe and avoiding risks in Asia. Rather than endorse FDR's suggestions for a reduction or standstill in tonnage, London decided to ask for an increase in cruiser strength, which, in turn, would give Tokyo a go-ahead for its own demands. This confronted Roosevelt with a serious dilemma: on the one hand, acceptance of parity for Japan and qualitative alterations proposed by Britain would save the treaty system but compel massive building by the United States to assure its Pacific security; on the other hand, to reject these proposals would dissolve the treaties and burden the United States with responsibility for their destruction. In either case, however, the outcome would be the same—extensive naval building for the United States.

Since an enlarged Navy seemed a near certainty, Roosevelt's principal concern was to throw the onus for expansion on the Japanese. This required British support of his original plans for a 20 per cent reduction. "The difficult situation of modern civilization throughout the world," he wrote MacDonald in June, "demands for the social and economic good of human beings a reduction in armaments and not an increase." He also asked Davis, who represented him in these London talks, to emphasize that his proposals did "not represent a bargaining position but a deep conviction" that naval strength must be brought below, or held at, present levels. If the British and the Japanese insisted on naval expansion, he told Undersecretary of State Phillips, he would make a dramatic public appeal to the King of England and the Emperor of Japan. Though MacDonald rejected Roosevelt's private appeal with the explanation that British naval expansion was "not a question of desire but of realistic need," the President decided to treat these exchanges as preliminary and to withhold any public statement until at least October, when the Japanese would also participate in the talks.[13]

In October, when his latest information indicated that Japan would demand parity and that the British would go along with some increase, the President prepared a public defense of his policy. Written in language that "the man in the street" from "one end of the land to the other" could understand, he explained that the Washington and London treaties "did not involve the sacrifice of any vital interests on the part of their participants; they left the relative security of the great naval powers unimpaired." To abandon these treaties now, he said, would destroy the principle of relative security and result in competitive naval building with unforseen consequences. "Governments impelled by common sense and the good of humanity," he concluded, "ought to seek Treaties reducing armaments; they have no right to seek Treaties increasing armaments."

By the beginning of November, when the Japanese had openly demanded parity and the British appeared ready to grant them an increase, Roosevelt edged toward a public appeal. He told Davis "to inject . . . into the minds" of Britain's leaders the thought that "if Great Britain is even suspected of preferring to play with Japan to playing with us, I shall be compelled, in the interest of American security, to approach public sentiment in Canada, Australia, New Zealand and South Africa in a definite effort to make these Dominions understand clearly that their future security is linked with us in the United States." In addition, he gave the Washington correspondent of the London *Times* a warning against a British compromise with Japan, which the newspaper promptly published. These warnings, combined with pressure on the British government from the dominions and domestic political opponents, forced MacDonald and John Simon, his Foreign Secretary, to disavow intentions of a Japanese deal.

Though differences continued to exist between London and Washington on how to handle Japan, American ideas now largely governed Anglo-American policy. The two governments jointly pressed for a renewal of the existing treaties and a continuation of the talks. Consequently, when Japan denounced the Washington Treaty in December 1934, she alone bore the onus of destroying the naval-limitation system. To underscore this, Roosevelt and Hull publicly restated their faith in limitation and fervently expressed the hope that the two-year period before the Washington Treaty actually lost force would persuade the naval powers to endorse a new plan.[14]

Despite Roosevelt's expression of hope, he had little reason to believe that Japan would reverse course when renewal of the 1930 London Treaty came up for consideration at a 1935 conference. More than ever, therefore, he worried primarily about neutralizing domestic opposition to the naval buildup that would follow the expiration of the treaties. The response in early 1935 to an announcement of American maneuvers in the northern Pacific reminded Roosevelt of the extent of his problem. Warning that the concentration of 177 ships and 447 airplanes near Japan would cause a war, pacifist societies bombarded the government with thousands of protest letters.[15]

Though Roosevelt refused to call off the maneuvers, he was highly sensitive to this public feeling and felt compelled to provide continuing demonstrations of his commitment to naval limitation. When the British tried to downgrade the unpromising 1935 naval conference by suggesting that London Ambassadors rather than special delegations conduct the negotiations, Roosevelt blocked the move. "While it is important that our public . . . not be led to expect too much from such a conference," he wrote Ambassador Bingham in London, "it is equally important for us to do nothing that would make it appear that we are taking this naval conference casually and less seriously than we have taken previous naval conferences and thus run the risk of being blamed for failure." Though he also told his delegates that a renewal of the quantitative limits was beyond reach and that he felt as if he were sending them on "a Cocos Island treasure hunt," he nevertheless instructed them to do all they could to renew the old ratios and to make all their "public statements so simple that the man in the street could easily understand them."

At the same time, he agreed to have the delegation negotiate a qualitative treaty limiting the size of specific types of ships and guns. Though an escape clause requiring conformity by nonsignatories made it a thoroughly innocuous agreement, Roosevelt saw at least two good reasons for accepting this British plan. First, it would preserve and advance Anglo-American cooperation in the Far East, and second, it would encourage the idea that the treaty system had not been entirely abandoned and that American naval building would still be done within treaty limits rather than in response to an open-ended competition with other powers.[16]

The value of Roosevelt's tactics at the naval conference, which began on December 9, 1935 and lasted until late March 1936, emerged in the spring of 1936 when he won approval for what pacifists considered a "tremendous increase" in the naval budget. After the Japanese walked out of the conference in January 1936 and the British announced stepped-up building plans in February, Roosevelt requested the largest peacetime naval appropriation in American history. Despite the fact that the appropriation included funds for only two new battleships and that most of the money would provide replacements for outmoded destroyers and submarines, pacifists sent up a huge outcry. In petitions to the President containing more than a million signatures, such organizations as the National Peace Conference and the People's Mandate to End War pressed Roosevelt to explain his request. Roosevelt answered that these expenditures would be strictly for defense and that his actions in behalf of disarmament illustrated his commitment to peace. Because the President's point was difficult to refute, his proposed naval appropriation stirred little opposition outside of pacifist circles.[17]

The collapse of the naval-limitation system was but one of several indications in the second half of 1934 that international cooperation was in another downward spin. The Senate's continuing refusal to ratify the 1925 Geneva Arms Convention and a cool reception in Geneva for the "more far-reaching" arms-control agreement Roosevelt had suggested in May were two discouraging signs. Unrealized hopes for Soviet-American cooperation were another. After nine months of negotiations on claims and credits, the State Department and Bullitt, who had gone to Moscow as Ambassador, found themselves generally blocked. The easing of Japanese-Soviet tensions, Bullitt told Roosevelt in September, made "the maintenance of really friendly and intimate relations with us . . . [seem] much less important [to Moscow] than it did when Litvinov was in Washington." [18]

All these impediments to international cooperation, however, seemed minor compared to the political news Roosevelt heard from Europe in the summer and fall of 1934. A recess in June of the Geneva disarmament talks after only two weeks, an abortive Nazi coup in Austria and the murder of Austrian Prime Minister Dollfuss in July, the assassinations of King Alexander of Yugoslavia and French Foreign Minister Louis Barthou in Marseilles in October, and a succession of reports from American envoys and travelers abroad suggested that Europe was well on the road to another war. The absence of any means to reverse the trend particularly disturbed FDR. "I too am downhearted about Europe," he wrote Ambassador Dodd in August, "but I watch for any ray of hope or opening to give me an opportunity to lend a helping hand. There is nothing in sight at present." "You and I will continue to preach peace and to live up to our preachings," he told a leading internationalist in September, "but I sometimes think that we are sowing seed in exceedingly rocky ground—at least for the moment." "I cannot with candor tell you that general international relationships outside the borders of the United States are improved," he declared in his 1935 State of the Union address. "On the surface of things many old jealousies are resurrected, old passions aroused, new strivings for armament and power, in more than one land, rear their ugly heads. I hope that calm counsel and constructive leadership will provide the steadying influence and the time necessary for the coming of new and more practical forms of representative government throughout the world wherein privilege and power will occupy a lesser place and world welfare a greater." [19]

While Roosevelt pointed to foreign attitudes that militated against international cooperation, he failed to mention American policies that did little to resolve, or may even have added to, world problems. When implementing the Trade Agreements Act in 1934–35, for example, he saw more reason to apply Foreign Trade Adviser Peek's nationalistic horse-swapping philosophy than Hull's multilateral idea. Though Roosevelt continued to support the rehabilitation of international commerce, he was much taken with a *New York Times* story of July 15, 1934, which described nations that shunned a most-favored-nation approach for special agreements as making significant trade gains at the expense of the United States. He pointedly expressed himself on the issue in November, when he wrote Hull that "in pure theory you and I think alike but every once in a while we have to modify principle to meet a hard and disagreeable fact! Witness the Japanese avalanche of cotton goods into the Philippines during the past six months. I am inclined to think that if you and George Peek, who represents the very hardheaded practical angle of trade, could spend a couple of hours some evening together talking over this problem of the most-favored-nation clause, it would be very helpful in many ways." A few days later, he told a press conference that with self-sufficiency in both agriculture and industry now the policy of other nations, the United States also would have to be economically self-contained. His best hope for foreign trade in these circumstances, he said, was "to get some special agreements with different countries . . . on a barter basis." As an expression of this, he encouraged Peek to make a cotton barter deal with Germany, which Hull dissuaded the President from approving only after a two-month fight.[20]

This reversal signaled the beginning of the end for Peek. In the year after Hull had squelched Peek's bilateral cotton deal, he concluded reciprocal agreements with eight European and American nations which, in his words, "steadily weakened and broke down the Peek program." By July 1935, Peek was ready to resign, but Roosevelt persuaded him to stay on for the time being. By November, however, he could no longer hide his differences with the administration. In an Armistice Day speech before the War Industries Board in New York, he attacked Roosevelt's drift toward internationalism in trade and other policies. He declared that America faced a choice between a general unreciprocated reduction of tariffs, which would throw open American markets to foreign surpluses, and the "preservation of the American market" through real reciprocity or bilateral agreements granting reciprocal advantages. When Roosevelt called this conception of things "rather silly," saying that the government simply did not advocate these internationalist ideas, Peek resigned.

Though Hull and others believed this indicated the triumph of Hull's internationalist principles, Roosevelt thought otherwise. He told Peek that "nobody is asking laissez-faire or unconditional Most-Favored-Nation general reduction of tariffs," and he wrote Raymond Moley that "in actual practice, we are making bilateral treaties insofar as 99% of the articles affected are concerned." Judging from the results of the trade program, Roosevelt saw more clearly than Hull what was going on. In the five years after 1934, Hull's trade agreements did less to revive world trade by increasing imports and reducing America's credit balance than to expand American exports, which increased enough in this period almost to double America's favorable balance of trade. Whatever Roosevelt's or Hull's intentions, the reciprocal trade program chiefly served American rather than world economic interests. Still, as writers on the subject have concluded, it was a less nationalistic program than those pursued by other coutries in the thirties, and it helped set the nations on the road to freer trade.[21]

During the second half of 1934 the administration pursued a silver policy that created severe problems for the Chinese. In June, in response to strong congressional pressure, Roosevelt had signed the Silver Purchase Act, which required the government to buy silver until it constituted one-fourth of the country's monetary reserve or until silver reached $1.29 an ounce on the world market.

Moved by hopes of benefiting America's silver interests and inflating domestic prices, the silver bloc predicted that a rise in silver from its current price of 45 cents "would increase the purchasing power of China and other countries on a silver standard and thus create a potentially vast market for American goods." Other, more objective observers warned against a drain on China's silver reserves which would jeopardize that country's currency system. Silverites, however, rejected this argument out of hand. In March 1935, when Treasury Secretary Morgenthau sent Professor James Harvey Rogers of Yale to China for an evaluation, silver Senators called it " 'the height of assininity' . . . for a professor prejudiced against silver to attempt to learn anything by interviewing Chinese coolies." "My boy," Senator Henry Ashurst of Arizona replied to Morgenthau's invitation to discuss the issue, "I was brought up from my mother's knee on silver and I can't discuss that anymore with you than you can discuss your religion with me." [22]

Within three months after the passage of the American law, Chinese silver exports had increased sevenfold and Nanking began pressing Washington for some kind of relief. Though Roosevelt, Morgenthau, and the State Department worked out a program in December to accommodate the Chinese, angry opposition from silver Senators at once moved the President to abandon the plan. A subsequent suggestion that Nanking send a representative to Washington to discuss financial problems had to be withdrawn when Pittman, the leader of the silver bloc, insisted that there be no discussion of American silver policy. Because this congressional pressure made it politically impossible to modify the silver program, Morgenthau urged FDR to help the Chinese carry out currency reform by giving them a substantial loan. The State Department, however, opposed this as likely to provoke Japanese resentment and create "uncontrollable responsibilities in the Far East." Instead, the Department urged that Roosevelt either alter the silver policy or encourage an internationally organized answer to China's financial crisis.

None of these solutions had much appeal to FDR. He rejected State

Department opposition to silver purchases because he refused to challenge the silver bloc. Not wishing to acknowledge this, however, he defended the assault on China's financial system as likely to have some positive results. "China has been the Mecca of the people whom I have called the 'money changers in the Temple,'" Roosevelt told Morgenthau in December. "They are still in absolute control. It will take many years and possibly several revolutions to eliminate them. . . . I am inclined to believe that the 'money changers' are wrong and that it is better to hasten the crisis in China—to compel the Chinese people more and more to stand on their own feet without complete dependence on Japan and Europe—than it is to compromise with a situation which is economically unsound, and which compromise will mean the continuation of an unsound position for a generation to come."

In February 1935, moreover, when he had received reports of a Japanese proposition to help China fight America's silver policy, the President declared himself "convinced . . . that somehow or other our silver policy is hurting Japan. I have told this to Henry [Morgenthau] and other people, but nobody seems to know why it should hurt Japan, but I maintain that it does." Finally, when the Governor of the New York Federal Reserve Bank told him in July 1935 that American silver purchases were breaking down China's banks and throwing "the business of the people . . . into chaos," Roosevelt replied that "silver is not the problem of the Chinese past, nor the Chinese present, nor the Chinese future. There are forces there which neither you nor I understand but at least I know that they are almost incomprehensible to us Westerners. Do not let so-called figures or facts lead you to believe that any Western civilization's action can ever affect the people of China very deeply." [23]

Although Roosevelt refused to modify the silver-purchase program, he rejected suggestions for either a unilateral or a collective loan to Nanking. Sharing the State Department's concern that unilateral steps would bring the United States into conflict with Japan's Amau Doctrine, Roosevelt vetoed Morgenthau's proposals for American loans or credits to the Chinese. He also believed, however, that international discussions of China's financial plight would raise unwanted questions about American silver policy, and he therefore joined Morgenthau in turning aside State Department proposals for collective action.

In the face of this American policy, by November the Chinese found themselves compelled to abandon the silver standard, sell their bullion, and acquire foreign exchange to support their new currency. To help make this system work, Nanking asked Washington to buy 200 million ounces of silver. Because the Chinese agreed to use the proceeds strictly for currency stabilization, not for military ends, and because the State Department did not think it would offend the Japanese, Morgenthau was able to purchase 175 million ounces of Chinese silver during the next fifteen months. "A way had been found," historian Dorothy Borg concludes, "to repair some of the damage inflicted on China by our silver-purchasing program while keeping our Far Eastern policy intact." [24]

In the midst of these nationalistic actions, Roosevelt saw at least one internationalist gesture he thought would succeed—American entrance into the World Court. Approval of the Court in the United States seemed almost unanimous, and a careful poll of the Senate, where the Democrats now held 69 of the 96 seats, showed more than a two-thirds majority in favor. Further, since the United States could use the Court without formal membership, Roosevelt believed that adherence to its protocols would be seen as a symbolic endorsement of world peace. He saw little risk, therefore, in asking the Senate on January 16, 1935, to approve American admission. [25]

But his request produced an angry response. Led by Father Charles Coughlin, the Detroit radio priest, and the Hearst press, the opposition warned that the Court, like the League, was an instrument of international bankers and "plutocrats." These men, Coughlin asserted, had created the League and the Court "for the purpose of preserving by force of arms . . . [their] plutocratic system against the possible onslaught of communism." American involvement in the Court would only lead to "the pilfering" of Europe's $12 billion war debt to the United States, participation in another war, and the destruction of our American way of life. "Every solid American who loves democracy," Coughlin declared, should stand foursquare with Court opponents "to keep America safe for Americans and not the hunting ground of international plutocrats." Once the Court rendered "advisory opinions in which the United States is interested," Senator Hiram Johnson warned, "the whole fabric we have built up since we were a nation goes crumbling to the ground." "I am a believer in democracy and will have nothing to do with the poisonous European mess," Senator Homer T. Bone of Washington declared. "I believe in being kind to people who have the smallpox, such as Mussolini and Hitler, but not in going inside their houses." "To hell with Europe and the rest of those nations!" Minnesota's Senator Thomas D. Schall announced.

This outcry against the Court struck several resonant cords. It played effectively on American anger over Europe's default on war debts; on fears that Europe would draw the United States, against her better interests, into another war; on the belief, generated by Nye Committee revelations, that involvement in a war would benefit the few at the expense of the many; and on concern that a war would strain America's democratic system beyond endurance. American Liberty League propaganda that New Deal measures had unleashed alien, totalitarian forces in America fueled this last concern. For all these reasons, Americans wished to close themselves off from overseas involvements, and membership in the World Court seemed to be an immediate case in point. [26]

Roosevelt was highly sensitive to these feelings. Having come under increasing attack as a radical who wished to substitute national planning for the traditional competitive system, he was eager to blunt suggestions that he favored bold departures in foreign affairs which might injure the nation's customary habits. In his message to the Senate, for example, he asserted that the World Court, "the movement to make international justice practicable and serviceable," was an "obviously sound and thoroughly American policy." He also offered assurances that such action would "in no way" diminish or jeopardize the sovereignty of the United States, but, on the positive side, would throw America's "weight into the scale in favor of peace." In addition, when Senator Arthur Vandenberg of Michigan offered an amendment reiterating America's traditional non-involvement in the political administration of any foreign state, Roosevelt agreeed to its passage. Further, he reversed himself on an amendment requiring prior Senate approval of Executive action to put an issue before the Court. Initially, he opposed and helped defeat the provision, calling it an unconstitutional limitation on Executive prerogative. But when he saw that 37 Senators supported this limitation on Executive power, he shifted ground to give it his support.[27]

Yet in spite of his efforts to disarm Senate opposition, he could not muster a two-thirds vote. When the Coughlin-Hearst agitation produced an avalanche of telegrams, which messengers carted to the Senate office building in wheelbarrows, and when Hearst lobbyists vigorously pressed the case against the Court, an initial group of ten opposing Senators grew to thirty-six. On January 29, 1935, with only 52 Senators voting in favor, adherence to the Court protocols fell seven votes short of the required two-thirds. The defeat angered FDR, who commented that some Court opponents "are willing to see a city burn down just so long as their own houses remain standing in the ruins." "As to the 36 Gentlemen who voted against the principle of a World Court," he wrote Senator Joseph Robinson, "I am inclined to think that if they ever get to Heaven they will be doing a great deal of apologizing for a very long time—that is if God is against war—and I think He is."

More importantly, the Court defeat impressed Roosevelt and the State Department as something of a turning point in American foreign relations. They believed that the Court fight had awakened a powerful isolationist opposition that would temporarily rob the President of his freedom to act in foreign affairs. Assuming that the country was "substantially behind the Senatorial action," Department leaders predicted that "this defeat will affect our whole foreign policy for some time to come." Roosevelt agreed. "In normal times the radio and other appeals by them [Coughlin, Hearst, and Louisiana Senator Huey Long] would not have been effective," he wrote Henry Stimson. "However, these are not normal times; people are jumpy and very ready to run after strange gods. This is so in every other country as well as our own. I fear common sense dictates no new method for the time being." Therefore, as he put it in another letter, "We shall go through a period of non-cooperation in everything . . . for the next year or two." [28]

Roosevelt and the State Department were correct; an important change had occurred which would bind their hands. In the almost two years between the President's Inauguration and the beginning of 1935, only a small group of Americans had maintained any interest in foreign affairs. Those attentive to external issues had consisted largely of bankers and businessmen concerned with debts, currency, and trade, and idealists principally urging an American contribution to peace. By late 1934 or early 1935, however, the growth of a European war threat made the American people aware of foreign events and evoked an isolationist response, which, as Roosevelt and the State Department understood, now dominated national thinking about world affairs.

PART TWO

The Internationalist as Isolationist, 1935-1938

5

Muddling Through

IN THE THREE MONTHS after the Senate rejected membership in the World Court, events abroad fanned American fears of war. In February 1935, Mussolini responded to a two-month-old border dispute with Ethiopia by sending additional forces to Italian East Africa. In March, Berlin openly repudiated the disarmament clauses of the Versailles Treaty by revealing the existence of a German air force and plans to build a 550,000-man army. In response, France doubled the existing period of service for conscripts, and the League voted to consider economic and financial measures against any state endangering the peace. "These are without doubt the most hair-trigger times the world has gone through in your lifetime or mine," FDR wrote Ambassador Breckinridge Long in Rome. "I do not even exclude June and July 1914." [1]

These developments, coupled with a $1.1 billion defense request by FDR, the largest peacetime budget in American history, stirred American pacifists to fresh actions. "We are rapidly sinking to the level of Hitler and Mussolini in our bowing down before the God of war," Oswald Garrison Villard, the editor of the *Nation*, complained. "That a Christian nation such as we pretend to be . . . is actually planning to spend $1,125,000,000 . . . upon military and naval expenditures . . . when . . . more than 20,000,000 Americans are on the bread line and in receipt of doles, is one of the most humiliating and discouraging happenings of recent years." Arguing that the United States was in no danger of invasion, students, clergymen, and women's groups warned that so large a defense budget signified an intent to make war.

The pacifists took their case to the streets. On April 6, 1935, the eighteenth anniversary of American entrance into World War I, 50,000 veterans paraded through Washington in a march for peace. On April 12, some 175,000 college students across the country staged a one-hour strike against war. In Boston, New York, Washington, D.C., Chicago, and Los Angeles, students by the thousands left their classrooms to demand "schools not battleships" and abolition of the R.O.T.C. The strike, one student leader announced, was "a dress rehearsal of what students intended to do should war be declared." [2]

Most Americans shared the pacifist desire to stay out of war and wished to guard against the conditions that had pushed the country into World War I. As depicted in Walter Millis's national bestseller, *Road to War: America, 1914–1917*, the culprit was traditional neutral rights. Arguing that America's defense of its trade with the Allies made her "a silent partner of the Entente," Millis suggested that a truly impartial America could have avoided war. Published in the spring of 1935, his book encouraged demands for a law that would assure genuine neutrality or bar Americans from supplying a belligerent in another conflict.

Though sentiment in the country and the Congress for abandoning old-style neutrality was widespread by April 1935, no agreement existed on what should take its place. Isolationists, eager to take all possible precautions against involvement in war, urged an impartial law—a bill that would embargo arms, bar loans, and limit trade to all belligerents. On the other side, collective-security advocates and pacifists eager to assure peace through international cooperation urged neutrality legislation that would contain discretionary powers for the President—the freedom to decide when and against whom the law should be invoked, a law, in short, allowing the President to help prevent or end a war by refusing aid to an aggressor.[3]

Roosevelt wished to resolve this argument in favor of the collective-security advocates. But this meant taking the issue away from the Senate Foreign Relations Committee. Realistically fearful that the committee, as in the case of the arms embargo, would favor impartial neutrality, Roosevelt urged Nye's committee investigating the arms traffic to seize control of the problem by preparing a neutrality law. By also asking Nye's committee for "an opportunity to consult the draft of any legislation" before it went to the Senate, Roosevelt implied that mutual cooperation would give the Congress and the country a much-wanted neutrality law and the President discretionary power to punish an aggressor.

Events abroad had convinced Roosevelt that America would eventually need to take a stand against Berlin. The day after Hitler declared his intention to build a half-million-man army, Roosevelt outlined a peace plan in which the United States was assigned a significant part. According to Morgenthau, Roosevelt believed that "England, France, Italy, Belgium, Holland, Poland and possibly Russia should get together and agree on a ten-year disarmament program which would look forward to doing away with all methods of warfare other than what a soldier can carry on his back and in his hand. His thought was that these countries would sign this pact themselves and would then approach Germany and ask her to sign. If she refused, these countries would then establish a two-way blockade around Germany, not permitting anything at all to enter or leave Germany. . . . We would send an Admiral abroad who would assist in seeing that our ships did not run through this block-

ade. . . . 'If this did not succeed,' " the President said, " 'the chances are
we will have a world war.' "

Four days later, Roosevelt described his idea to Undersecretary Phillips,
who "did not respond with any enthusiasm. As a matter of fact," Phillips
observed, "it seemed to me that the President, for once, was completely
off the straight road." Roosevelt surely had his own doubts about the
proposal, but his concern was probably less with identifying a workable
plan than with making it known abroad that he intended to impede aggressors all he could.

During April Roosevelt continued to talk about ways in which the
United States could influence others to keep the peace. He wrote Colonel
Edward M. House, Wilson's longtime adviser, that he considered making
a peace proposal to Europe but had decided against it because "any sug-
gestion on our part would meet with the same kind of chilly, half-
contemptuous reception on the other side as an appeal would have met
in July or August, 1914." He expressed the hope, however, that an Anglo-
French-Italian meeting at Stresa, Italy, on April 11 would give the United
States a chance to take a hand. If the three Powers and the Little
Entente—Czechoslovakia, Roumania, and Yugoslavia—he also told
House, decided to establish "a complete blockade of Germany," and "if
we found it was an effective blockade . . . recognition . . . by us would
obviously follow. . . . A boycott or sanction could not be recognized by
us without Congressional action but a blockade would fall under the
Executive's power after establishment of the fact." The inaction of the
Powers at Stresa, however, quickly ended Roosevelt's hopes for collective
action. But even if the Powers had acted against Berlin, growing sentiment in the United States for strict neutrality would have made any cooperation on Roosevelt's part a substantial political risk.[4]

The movement toward strict neutrality, which culminated in a
Neutrality law on August 31, 1935, had begun to pick up steam in late
March when Representatives and Senators put a number of resolutions
before the Congress. Between March 29 and May 7, Representatives
Frank Kloeb of Ohio and Maury Maverick of Texas, and Senators Nye
and Bennett Clark of Missouri introduced bills to prohibit Americans
from supplying belligerents with loans, credits, arms, or contraband and
from traveling in war zones or on belligerent ships. Moreover, the President's attempt to block impartial neutrality by taking the issue away
from the Foreign Relations Committee failed. On April 1, after hearing
sharp complaints from Foreign Relations Committee members that
neutrality was solely in their province, Nye notified the President that
the Munitions Committee would leave the question to them.

These isolationist pressures persuaded FDR to block congressional
action on neutrality at the 1935 session. Despite his belief that the
European situation made flexible neutrality a good idea, Roosevelt

realized that there was small likelihood of putting such a bill through the Congress, and so he decided to ask Pittman to kill all neutrality laws pending before the Foreign Relations Committee. The fact, moreover, that Senate leaders envisaged an acrimonious neutrality debate that would immobilize an already divided Congress gave Roosevelt another reason to block action at this time.

With fear in the country, however, that worsening Italo-Ethiopian tensions were a prelude to another world war, pressure for a neutrality law continued to grow. In May the radical wing of the American peace movement began shifting its support from international cooperation for peace to narrower guarantees of American neutrality. *Peace Action*, the monthly publication of the National Council for the Prevention of War, came out for impartial neutrality, while the National Peace Conference, an alliance of twenty-eight peace groups, organized a mass antiwar rally at Carnegie Hall in New York, where an enthusiastic audience endorsed appeals by Nye, Clark, and Maverick for strict legislation. In June the Federal Council of Churches declared itself against aid to "all belligerents in any conflict that might arise in the future." At the same time, the Women's International League for Peace and Freedom organized a massive letter-writing campaign, and the National Council for the Prevention of War launched a series of weekly radio broadcasts in behalf of an impartial law.

The message in all these pronouncements was the same. The First World War had been a grotesque disaster; another conflict would be pointless, and worse. American participation in another such struggle would profit no one except bankers, industrialists, and munitions makers. The losers would be the mass of Americans who would pay with their lives, their money, and their democratic institutions. Now was the time to bar American involvement through the enactment of impartial neutrality.[5]

By the second half of June, congressional leaders found it impossible to ignore these demands. Sam McReynolds, Chairman of the House Foreign Affairs Committee, began hearings on the Kloeb and Maverick bills, while Pittman abandoned an agreement with the administration to sit on neutrality by allowing two of the Nye-Clark resolutions to go before the Senate. In response, the administration pressed Pittman to have his Foreign Relations Committee reverse itself: Norman Davis conferred with him on the 27th; Roosevelt saw him on the 29th and again on July 7; and Hull argued the issue with him on July 8. But Pittman, who had refused to lead the Court fight in the Senate and declared himself against involvement in "somebody else's war," resisted this pressure. The most he would concede was temporary recall of the neutrality resolutions for further consideration. When Hull requested this of the Committee on July 10, it agreed on the condition that the State Department and a subcommittee of its members confer on the substance of a law.[6]

Roosevelt was now more eager than ever to block a neutrality debate. For five months beginning in January, while he had tried to hold conservative support, Roosevelt had refused to press Congress for additional reforms. Consequently, only one major law moved through Congress during this time—the work relief bill. "Once more," Walter Lippmann had written in March, "we have come to a period of discouragement after a few months of buoyant hope. Pollyanna is silenced and Cassandra is doing all the talking." By June, however, after the U.S. Chamber of Commerce had denounced the New Deal and FDR had concluded that he could not satisfy conservative critics, he launched a fresh reform effort. Calling House leaders to a White House conference, Roosevelt insisted on passage of "the most far-reaching reform measures" Congress had ever considered. Social security, labor relations, banking, public-utility holding companies, and a wealth tax were the focuses of his program. Though the National Labor Relations Act had already gone through Congress when the neutrality question resurfaced, an "interminable debate" on the matter seemed certain to jeopardize the other major, and a host of minor, laws.

As a device for blocking any action on neutrality, Roosevelt began emphasizing the tactical difficulties in the way of a neutrality bill. "I said to Bill Phillips this morning," he told the press on July 19, ". . . 'I am perfectly willing, if we can get an agreement on neutrality legislation, so long as it does not block the adjournment of Congress. In other words, if you can get it through without waste of time after agreement, that is fine. . . . But no protracted debate on it.' " On the following day, he asked Phillips to tell the Foreign Affairs and Foreign Relations committees "that they must not interfere with his legislative program . . . but . . . if after that was all finished the Senate desired to continue during the rest of the summer and discuss neutrality, he had no possible objection." Appreciating that the legislators would not take kindly to Roosevelt's sarcastic message, Phillips decided to ignore the President's request. "You and I," Roosevelt wrote Congressman Fred Sisson, a proponent of immediate action, "are aware of the legislative situation at this time—after Congress has been in session for nearly seven months. If such legislation can be passed before adjournment, without interminable debate, it would be very satisfactory to you, to me and to the whole country. But can that be done, especially in the Senate?" [7]

By late July Roosevelt appreciated that this tactic would not block the drive for neutrality. By then, a subcommittee of the Foreign Relations Committee was working on a comprehensive law and pressing the administration to state its views. In response, Roosevelt instructed Phillips, Davis, and Moore to support legislation that would allow him to discriminate against an aggressor. Though anticipating significant opposition to this request, Roosevelt hoped that the intense desire for a law would permit him to trade Executive support of neutrality legislation for a flexible bill. As he stated it in a Cabinet meeting on July 26, he would back neutrality legislation in exchange for "freedom of action in applying an embargo." Vice President Garner "thought there was a possibility of such a compromise going through."

The Senate subcommittee quickly dashed Roosevelt's hopes for a compromise; in the first week of August, it rejected the administration's proposal for a flexible law. Instead, it urged the Foreign Relations Committee to recommend an impartial bill which would go into effect automatically at the start of a war. But with the Committee unable to line up decisively behind either flexible or mandatory neutrality, the legislative drive stalled.[8]

The Italo-Ethiopian dispute intervened to change the situation. Though Britain, France, and Italy were to begin fresh conversations about the problem on August 15, Mussolini seemed certain to launch an attack in September after the Ethiopian rainy season ended. To deal with such a war and avoid a battle over comprehensive legislation, Hull suggested that Roosevelt ask Congress for an arms-embargo resolution that would last only until Congress reconvened in January 1936 and would apply only to an Italo-Ethiopian war. The bill, however, was to leave to the President's discretion when and against which country it would be used.

A host of cross-currents made Roosevelt ambivalent about how to proceed. On the one hand, the thought of an Italian attack on Ethiopia outraged him and made him eager for discretionary power to punish the Italians and signal Germany and Japan that America would stand with other democracies against aggression anywhere. On the other hand, he appreciated that the country and the Congress were in no mood for bold steps abroad and that any attempt to push this point would jeopardize parts of the legislative program he was steering through the Congress in the summer of 1935. Indeed, given the domestic constraints on him to affect events abroad, he aimed to counter Fascist advances around the globe by primarily strengthening democracy at home, and encouraging democracies everywhere not to lose faith in their system of majority rule. The five major laws and the bunch of minor bills, many of which would have been seen as major measures in any other session, represented a significant step in this direction.

In addition to this consideration, Roosevelt appreciated that discretionary control over neutrality in an Italo-Ethiopian conflict was of little practical consequence. An arms embargo against Italy alone or against both Italy and Ethiopia would have the same result: since only Mussolini had the wherewithal to buy and ship significant amounts of arms from the United States, an impartial arms ban would work exclusively against Rome. Also, the fact that London and Paris had shown little inclination to block Mussolini's Ethiopian plans and that the British had already tacitly approved German rearmament by signing an Anglo-German naval agreement in June discouraged Roosevelt's hopes of using discretionary neutrality to cooperate with Britain and France against aggression.

These conflicting considerations made Roosevelt's response to Hull's suggested resolution highly erratic. Though he approved the bill and a request to Pittman to sponsor it in the Senate, he also told R. Walton Moore, who carried the message to Pittman, to accept any demand Pittman might voice to make its provisions mandatory and impartial. Hence, when the Senator objected to the President's discretionary powers, Moore at once agreed to modify the bill. Roosevelt then changed his mind and told Moore to discourage action on any kind of neutrality law at the current session.[9]

Additional pressures during the last two weeks of August persuaded Roosevelt to reverse course again. On August 18 the Anglo-French-Italian conversations collapsed, and Mussolini began final preparations for an attack. Believing that the time had come to "make a vigorous effort" to enact the temporary arms embargo they had discussed in the previous week, Hull asked Roosevelt to write Pittman in behalf of such a law. Hull also suggested that FDR mobilize support for the bill by giving his letter to Pittman to the press.

As Hull had judged, significant backing for a discriminatory arms embargo existed in the country. The conservative wing of the pacifist movement, the League of Nations Association and the Carnegie Endowment for International Peace, remained committed to peace through international cooperation, while even the radical peace societies, which had come out for impartial neutrality, continued to express some attraction to the League principle of world cooperation for peace. Secondly, the House of Representatives was sympathetic to flexible neutrality and seemed likely to approve Hull's limited version of this plan. Finally, Hull assumed that most Americans, including a majority of Senators, saw the differences between mandatory and flexible neutrality as secondary to passage of a law that could keep the country out of war. It was against this backdrop that Roosevelt agreed to Hull's request.

Within a few hours after his decision, though, Roosevelt once more reversed himself. When Stephen Early, his Press Secretary, informed Pittman of what the President would ask, the Senator warned that if the President "insists on designating the aggressor in accordance with the wishes of the League of Nations . . . he will be licked as sure as hell." Such a resolution, Pittman explained, "will not be approved by the Foreign Relations Committee and will not be approved by the United States Senate." Indeed, as Pittman pointed out, that very morning his

Committee had unanimously opposed any grant of discretionary power to the President in applying embargoes, and instead had decided by an 11 to 3 vote to back an impartial neutrality law. With ten pieces of domestic legislation still before Congress, Roosevelt at once decided not to test Pittman's judgment.[10]

The events of the next two days vindicated Roosevelt's decision. On August 20 a group of isolationist Senators, led by Bone, Clark, Nye, Long, and Vandenberg, began a filibuster which they vowed to continue until the Senate passed a mandatory neutrality law. Within less than three hours, Pittman presented a compromise bill: it placed a mandatory embargo on "arms, ammunition, or implements of war" to all belligerents, but it gave the President power to define "implements of war" and to say when the embargo should go into effect; it prohibited American vessels from transporting munitions to warring states; it gave the President discretion to withhold protection from Americans traveling on belligerent ships; and it established a Munitions Control Board to regulate arms shipments from the United States. After only twenty-five minutes of discussion on the following day, the Senate approved the bill without a vote of record.

Roosevelt once more warred with himself over what to do. On the morning of August 21, he firmly opposed Pittman's mandatory bill, telling a group of nine congressional supporters that "considerable discretion should be left to the office of the President." By the following day, however, he agreed to accept Pittman's bill if the Congress limited the mandatory arms embargo to six months. His reasons for this turnabout included the fact that Congress was "tremendously excited" over "neutrality to all and shipments to none," and seemed likely to stall on other legislation if it met a challenge to this idea. Assistant Secretary of State Moore, who prepared a defense of presidential discretion, put it aside with the notation that it was "not used or to be used in view of the legislative situation." Further, Roosevelt considered the overall law a compromise; it took "away little Executive authority," he wrote, "except the embargo on certain types of arms and munitions" for a limited period of time. Also, the bill satisfied current needs in international affairs. With the mandatory embargo promising to work exclusively against Italy in a war with Ethiopia, Roosevelt felt free to describe the law as "entirely satisfactory. . . . The question of embargoes as against two belligerents meets the needs of the existing situation," he said. "What more can one ask? And, by the time the situation changes, Congress will be back with us, so we are all right." [11] But Roosevelt was too optimistic about congressional willingness to reverse course. Once he had conceded Executive control over arms exports to belligerents, the Congress was highly resistant to giving it back.

By accepting the law, Roosevelt also hoped to quiet growing fear in the country of excessive presidential control. The rapid expansion of Executive power under the New Deal had moved some Americans to complain that the Constitution was being destroyed. The passage in the spring of 1935 of the Emergency Relief Appropriation Act of nearly $5 billion, the largest single appropriation in the history of the United States or any other nation, had fueled this concern. Giving Roosevelt almost unlimited discretion as to how the money should be spent, the law marked a significant shift of power from Congress to the President. After the enactment of Roosevelt's "Second New Deal," the attack on his leadership from conservatives grew more shrill. In November 1935 columnist Mark Sullivan warned that 1936 might provide "the last presidential election America will have. . . . It is tragic that America fails to see that the New Deal is to America what the early phase of Nazism was to Germany." "The coming election," the Republican National Committee declared in December, "will determine whether we hold to the American system of government or whether we shall sit idly by and allow it to be replaced by a socialist state honeycombed with waste and extravagance and ruled by a dictatorship that mocks at the rights of the States and the liberty of the citizen."

Though Roosevelt realized that he had greatly expanded federal, and particularly Executive, power, he remained thoroughly committed to the national democratic tradition and resented suggestions that he aimed to become a dictator. In the fall of 1935, when Raymond Moley publicly complained that "the furtive character" of the negotiations for a Canadian-American trade treaty did "not fit well with the liberal protestations of an Administration devoted to the masses of the people," Roosevelt replied that "there was nothing 'secret' about the matter in any shape, manner or form." "I suppose . . . ," he told a friend at the same time, "that some of your New York friends and mine will set this down as another communistic decree of a Brain Trust ruled Dictator!"

Despite conservative complaints about the President's growing domestic powers, there was more concern in the country about Executive freedom to lead the nation into another war. By the mid-thirties, Americans generally believed that involvement in World War I had been a mistake, that Wilson's freedom to take unneutral steps had pushed the country into the fighting, and that only strict limitations on presidential discretion could keep this from happening again. As Roosevelt described the problem to Colonel House, "Some of the Congressmen and Senators who are suggesting wild-eyed measures to keep us out of war are now declaring that you and Lansing and Page [the President's pro-British advisers] forced Wilson into the War! I had a talk with them, explained that I was in Washington myself the whole of that period, that none of them were there and that their historical analysis was wholly inaccurate and that history yet to be written would prove my point."

Though mindful of these fears when he accepted temporary restrictions on his control over foreign affairs, Roosevelt believed the loss of presidential discretion a very poor idea. "History," he announced when signing the Neutrality bill, "is filled with unforeseeable situations that call for some flexibility of action. It is conceivable that situations may arise in which the wholly inflexible provisions of Section I of this Act might have exactly the opposite effect from that which was intended. In other words, the inflexible provisions might drag us into war instead of keeping us out." [12]

But Roosevelt did not foresee this happening in the case of the Italo-Ethiopian war. Instead, he saw shifting domestic and foreign conditions allowing him to join indirectly in a growing worldwide movement to punish Italian aggression. On August 27, after having adopted more legislation of permanent importance than in any other session, the Congress adjourned. Shortly thereafter, Roosevelt announced the "substantial completion" of his basic program and the arrival of a "breathing spell" in domestic affairs. "The real news value today," he told a press conference on September 13, "is the foreign situation." He specifically referred to the Italo-Ethiopian crisis, which had assumed worldwide proportions two days before when London unified the League against Rome by calling "for steady and collective resistance to all acts of unprovoked aggression." This was "no variable and unreliable sentiment," Britain's Foreign Secretary Sir Samuel Hoare insisted, "but a principle of international conduct to which they [the British people] and their government hold with firm, enduring, and universal persistence." In a dramatic show of unity, one League delegation after another lined up behind Britain's defense of international law and the rights of small nations.

Though there was more shadow than substance to Hoare's declaration, Roosevelt, like other heads of state and the State Department, took the announcement at face value and began moving toward cooperation with the League. On September 12, he had Hull echo League declarations that nations "contemplating armed hostilities" should resolve their differences by pacific means. On the 25th he approved Hull's proposal that he issue an initial embargo list limited to actual military equipment, but that he reserve the right to extend the list to "certain raw materials the withholding of which would seriously impair the ability of Italy to fight to a successful conclusion."

When the war finally erupted on October 3, 1935, Roosevelt openly displayed his sympathies for Ethiopia to his intimates. Aboard the cruiser U.S.S. *Houston*, while he was on a fishing trip in the Pacific, he "scanned the news dispatches and everything favorable to Ethiopia brought a loud 'Good.'" On the day after the war began, he telegraphed Hull that any evidence of fighting well within Ethiopian borders, regardless of formal declaration, should be taken as reason to invoke the Neutrality law. In effect, this would deprive Italy of American arms. Further, to discourage any kind of American support for Italy, Roosevelt suggested publishing the names of Americans sailing from the United States on Italian ships and the cargo manifests of ships carrying goods, particularly raw materials, to the belligerents.[13]

Hull and most of his advisers urged a more cautious response to the fighting. They preferred to wait on Neutrality proclamations until they knew what the League would do, and they suggested that measures as "drastic" as publishing cargo manifests and the names of Americans traveling on Italian ships be held in reserve as weapons against those who failed to conform to the President's policy. Moreover, they pointed out that since there was no danger to Americans traveling on Italian ships, an attempt to block such travel "might . . . be regarded by Italy as a gratuitous affront in the nature of sanctions." Hull proposed instead that Roosevelt simply issue the arms embargo and a declaration that it was "the plain duty of our citizens to refrain from placing themselves in positions where, were conditions peaceful, they would be entitled to seek the protection of this Government. Accordingly, in these specific circumstances I desire it to be understood that any of our people who voluntarily engage in transactions of any character with either of the belligerents do so at their own risk."

Roosevelt refused to be so circumspect. He insisted that a Neutrality proclamation be issued at once, telling Hull that "they are dropping bombs on Ethiopia and that is war. Why wait for Mussolini to say so." At the same time, he approved the wording in Hull's proposed declaration and agreed to omit publication of names and cargoes for the time being. On the other hand, he instructed Hull to warn Americans against travel on belligerent vessels, stating that the intent of the Neutrality Act was "to prevent aid to either belligerent and American passenger travel on Italian ships gives aid not only financially but also by making access to Italy more easy for Americans seeking commercial advantages." Though acknowledging that no Ethiopian ships or submarines endangered American lives, Roosevelt argued that Italy could not take affront at such a warning because it carried out "the spirit of the law." [14]

By October 10, with the Council and Assembly of the League moving toward sanctions, Roosevelt worked out a formula for expanding American action against Rome. Since the Neutrality law gave him discretion to say what constituted "implements of war," he asked the State Department to identify additional "articles of commerce" that the United States might embargo if the League included them in its sanctions. Further, to assure that embargoed American goods sent to other neutrals would not end up in Italian hands, he suggested "drastic proof of nontransshipment." Finally, he restated his desire to discourage Americans from trading with the belligerents by publishing their names if they did.[15]

In following this course, Roosevelt appreciated that most Americans shared his anti-Italian views. The struggle of Emperor Haile Selassie's primitive army against Mussolini's mechanized forces had generated widespread sympathy for Ethiopia in the United States. For some Americans, the Emperor's mobilization order was enough to make the case: "When this order is received all men and all boys able to carry a spear will go to Addis Ababa. Every married man will bring his wife to cook and wash for him. Every unmarried man will bring any unmarried woman he can find to cook and wash for him. Women with babies, the blind, and those too aged or infirm to carry a spear are excused. Anyone found at home after receiving this order will be hanged." For most Americans, however, it was the sadistic dive-bombing raids of Mussolini's son, Vittorio, which left them shocked and outraged. His widely publicized description of this "magnificent sport" contributed greatly to the anti-Italian mood in the United States: "one group of horsemen gave me the impression of a budding rose unfolding as the bomb fell in their midst and blew them up." Roosevelt also understood that many Americans favored international cooperation as a response to the war. In October "a significant minority" of three thousand pro-Neutrality letters to the State Department praised the administration's "tacit cooperation with the League." A December 1935 *Fortune* poll, moreover, showed 47.9 per cent in favor of economic cooperation with other nations to preserve peace.

Nevertheless, Roosevelt saw serious political dangers in overt cooperation with the League. He realized that the U.S. Senate would see such action as an additional reason for limiting him in foreign affairs. Indeed, if he were to get the sort of flexible Neutrality law he wanted from the next Congress, it was important to encourage the idea that the existing law inhibited the President from an effective contribution to peace. Evidence of direct cooperation with Geneva would blunt this point. Indications of involvement with the League also seemed likely to cut into his domestic political strength. Roosevelt learned in October that Republican Party leaders had mapped plans to use the Italo-Ethiopian conflict to weaken his hold over foreign-born and black voters. Evident ties to the League would allow Republicans to agitate isolationists in general and Italian-Americans in particular in the coming election year. While Roosevelt appreciated that he enjoyed strong support for re-election, he saw that a fight over League cooperation and suggestions of American involvement in a war were likely to undermine his popularity and his ability to lead.

On the other hand, if he went too far in emphasizing his detachment from the conflict, he risked antagonizing black voters, who for the first time since the Civil War were voting Democratic in large numbers. Black leaders in the United States had strong sympathies for Ethiopia, and the conflict was very much on their minds. Betweeen 1933 and 1938,

for example, Haile Selassie was second only to Joe Louis in prominence
on the front pages of the *Chicago Defender*, Chicago's leading black
newspaper. Roosevelt made no direct attempt to align himself with
blacks on the issue, probably because his actions made his sympathies for
Ethiopia transparent; indeed, he feared too much so.[16]

Consequently, Roosevelt made a systematic effort to appear independent of the League and to emphasize his determination to keep out of
war. When the fighting broke out in Ethiopia on October 3, 1935, for
example, he rejected suggestions that he return to Washington. Instead,
he continued his vacation trip aboard the *Houston*, where he could be
"in complete contact with the situation" and simultaneously demonstrate
his confidence that America faced no crisis and would not be drawn into
the conflict. Further, when news came on October 8 and 9 that the
League might invite nonmember states to join in its discussion of sanctions, Roosevelt approved a State Department message to Geneva not to
invite the United States. Because American actions already indicated "our
course and attitude," Hull privately told the League, such a request was
unnecessary. Furthermore, it would also be unwise, because American
public opinion would force the administration to reject it. Despite Hull's
injunctions, the League shortly forced the administration to take a public
stand on sanctions anyway. On October 21, Washington, along with
other nonmembers of the League, received a request for information on
"any action . . . it may be taking" in relation to League sanctions. With
Roosevelt's approval, Hull notified the League that his government was
following an "independent" policy which would keep it free from, and
help prevent a prolongation of, the fighting.[17]

More important than any of these efforts to appear independent of
the League, however, was the administration's decision not to place
strategic raw materials on the embargo list. As first the State Department
and then Roosevelt concluded, "arms, ammunition and implements of
war" had a "commonly recognized definition" which did not include raw
materials. But even if this were in dispute, the "history of the legislation"
showed that the Senate had no desire to include raw materials among
"implements of war." As Roosevelt told one advocate of this idea, "under
ordinary and normal circumstances wheat, cotton and copper ingots
are not implements of war. The letter of the law does not say so and the
trouble is that the spirit of the law, as shown by the debates during its
passage, does not allow me to stretch it that far out—no matter how
worthy the cause." Though internationalists urged a broad interpretation
of the Neutrality law which would allow the administration to join the
League in closing off essential raw materials to Italy, Roosevelt and the
State Department resisted their advice as contrary to the intent of the law
and, more to the point, as too provocative to isolationists in the United
States.

Equally important was the fact that such a step on Roosevelt's part in

October would have placed him miles ahead of the League. After agree-ing on October 11 to recommend four sanctions—an arms embargo, a bar on loans and credits, a boycott of Italian imports, and an embargo on a limited number of raw materials controlled by League states—the League did not actually commit itself to these sanctions until October 31, when it agreed to apply them formally against Rome beginning on November 18. More important, under Anglo-French influence, the League made no move to establish a naval blockade or close the Suez Canal to Italy, which would have cut off supplies to the Italian army in Ethiopia and forced a quick end to the war. "Mussolini," Winston Churchill later wrote, "would never have dared to come to grips with a resolute British Government. . . . If ever there was an opportunity of striking a decisive blow in a generous cause with the minimum of risk, it was here and now." [18]

In these circumstances, Roosevelt would not stretch the Neutrality law to include raw materials on an embargo list. And even if the League had acted more decisively in October, it is doubtful that Roosevelt would have challenged the isolationists by going beyond what he did. For he believed that a moral embargo could work almost as well in aiding the League to deny vital raw materials to Italy's war machine. He tried to indicate this to Geneva in a public statement on October 30, the day before the League Coordination Committee was to reach a final decision on sanctions:

By my statement of October fifth, which was emphasized by the Sec-retary of State on October tenth, we have warned American citizens against transactions of any character with either of the belligerent nations except at their own risk.

This Government is determined not to become involved in the contro-versy and is anxious for the restoration and maintenance of peace.

However, in the course of war, tempting trade opportunities may be offered to our people to supply materials which would prolong the war. I do not believe that the American people will wish for abnormally in-creased profits that temporarily might be secured by greatly extending our trade in such materials; nor would they wish the struggles on the battle-field to be prolonged because of profits accruing to a comparatively small number of Americans.

Accordingly, the American Government is keeping informed as to all shipments consigned for export to both belligerents.[19]

By mid-November, however, it was clear to Roosevelt that his moral embargo was not working very well. Trade records with Italy for 1934–35 showed a significant jump in exports of important raw materials; though a comparison of statistics for October 1934 and October 1935 showed a small overall drop in exports to Italy, shipments of vital petroleum prod-ucts, refined copper, and iron and steel scrap had all more than doubled.

This created a painful dilemma for Roosevelt and Hull. On November 6, the Coordination Committee had voted to extend League sanctions to basic raw materials such as oil if it could obtain simple guarantees of cooperation from nonmember states. Since the United States produced over 50 per cent of the world's oil and could easily replace Italian losses from League states, the burden now fell on Washington to give the League more direct support.

Roosevelt puzzled over how this might be done. He appreciated that his actions to that point had received almost unanimous support and could not be turned against him in a debate over Neutrality revision or in the election campaign of 1936. On the other hand, he now felt that the League was about to begin "a sanctions movement that would seriously cripple Italy," and that unless he took some additional step like publishing a list of American firms making shipments of war materials to Italy, the League program might not achieve its goal. "I know I'm walking a tight rope and I'm thoroughly aware of the gravity of the situation," he told Jim Farley on November 14. "I realize the seriousness of this from an international as well as a domestic point of view."

Roosevelt tried to solve the problem by having Hull on November 15 issue a stronger statement against trade in raw materials with the belligerents. Instead of a general request to Americans to shun such trade opportunities, Hull pointedly announced that essential war materials "such as oil, copper, trucks, tractors, scrap iron, and scrap steel [were] being exported for war purposes" in considerably increased amounts. "This class of trade," Hull declared, "is directly contrary to the policy of this Government . . . as it is also contrary to the general spirit of the recent neutrality act." [20]

Since it was clearly understood that this increased trade in vital materials was exclusively with Italy, Americans and Italians could only interpret Hull's statement as evidence of administration support for League action against Rome. Senator Hiram Johnson now felt compelled to warn the President that his opponents were "hoping and praying that in the present world crisis something will be done which may be distorted into an endeavor on the part of our country to be a part of the League of Nations or of England's policy. It will enable them to make an issue of internationalism next year." Similarly, the publisher of the New York *Post* now informed Roosevelt that criticism of his foreign policy was giving him "grave concern." "I believe that an overwhelming majority of Americans care more about keeping out of war than about any other one thing. If the average citizen suspects, rightfully or wrongfully, that your administration is backing up the League or Great Britain, it would cause a most unfavorable reaction."

The Italian Ambassador also brought pressure to bear on FDR not to line up with the League. In a conversation with Hull on November 22, he objected to American declarations during the previous two months, and especially to Hull's statement of November 15, as "an extension and aggravation, to the principal detriment of Italy, of the meaning of the Neutrality Act of August 31, 1935." He also warned that his government would view any attempt to limit freedom of commerce as not only a violation of the Italian-American Treaty of 1871 but also as a sanction carrying "the positive character of an unfriendly act." Though Roosevelt and Hull parried these comments with assurances that administration policy remained entirely free of the League, they did not make a convincing case. "It may be difficult at the distance of America to appreciate it," Ambassador Long notified Hull from Rome, "but American present policy is so closely in line with League policy that . . . the non-Italian press of Europe . . . comments upon it as being in support of Great Britain and Geneva and as directed [against] Italy. In diplomatic circles the same opinion is held." "As the British understand it," another well-informed American diplomat wrote FDR, your chief goal is "to back up the League and the British position." They believe that "you regard that as almost more important than the fulfillment of our neutrality law or the preservation of peace." [21]

This accord between American and League actions, and the domestic political problems it threatened to pose for FDR, disappeared quickly between November 25 and December 11 when France and Britain crippled League efforts to take a firm stand. Rather than risk losing Mussolini's support against Hitler by pressing the case for an oil embargo, the French postponed a November 29 meeting of the League's Coordination Committee which seemed certain to take such a step. Instead, Sir Samuel Hoare and Pierre Laval, the British and French Foreign Ministers, worked out a proposal for ending the war and the danger of a wider Anglo-French-Italian clash over an oil embargo. In exchange for a seaport on the Red Sea or Indian Ocean, Ethiopia was to give Italy portions of her eastern territories and a "zone of economic expansion and settlement" in the most fertile, southern part of the country. When the press revealed this proposal on December 10, British public opinion denounced it as "a plan that rewarded the condemned aggressor and did not appear in the least bit warranted by the actual military situation." It evoked a similar response in the United States, where, one London newspaper reported, the recently acquired belief that the League could effectively meet "a first-class international dispute" was "utterly shattered." As for Roosevelt himself, he saw the Hoare-Laval scheme to restore peace by dismembering Ethiopia as an "outrageous proceeding" which would sour Americans more than ever on Europe and the League. "Poor old Ethiopia," Roosevelt's Ambassador to Turkey wrote him, "—she is trying to fight her enemies, but can she escape from her 'friends'?" "I feel just the way you do," Roosevelt replied. "What a commentary on world ethics these past weeks have shown." [22]

Though a popular outcry in Britain and other League countries promptly forced Hoare's resignation and an end to the Anglo-French appeasement plan, Roosevelt could no longer be very sanguine about world affairs. The virtual collapse of League unity against Italy and reports from Berlin and London convinced him that the world was about to enter another era of general war. "The international situation is very grave indeed," he told his Cabinet on December 27. ". . . There is an understanding between Germany and Japan which may result in a squeeze play against Russia. Great Britain, concerned as usual for the Empire, and anticipating what a threat this combination would be against the British colonies, especially in Asia, [has] decided to come to some sort of an understanding with Hitler."

Roosevelt gave public expression to these fears in his State of the Union Message on January 3, 1936. "A point has been reached," he declared, "where the people of the Americas must take cognizance of growing illwill, of marked trends toward aggression, of increasing armaments, of shortening tempers—a situation which has in it many of the elements that lead to the tragedy of general war." He blamed these conditions on autocratic rulers in Europe and Asia who had "impatiently reverted to the old belief in the law of the sword, or to the fantastic conception that they, and they alone, are chosen to fulfill a mission and that all others among the billion and a half of human beings in the world must and shall learn from and be subject to them." He also expressed sympathy for the 85 or 90 per cent of the world's peaceful people who "must constantly align themselves on one side or the other in the kaleidoscopic jockeying for position that is characteristic of European and Asiatic relations today. For the peace-loving nations . . . find that their very identity depends on their moving and moving again on the chess board of international politics."

In response to these conditions, Roosevelt urged the continuation of America's "two-fold neutrality"—the policy of denying belligerents American arms, ammunition, or implements of war and of discouraging warring nations from using abnormal amounts of other American products calculated to facilitate their fighting. "I trust," Roosevelt announced, "that these clear objectives, thus unequivocally stated, will be carried forward by cooperation between this Congress and the President." [23]

Roosevelt's statement was a prelude to a fresh congressional discussion of Neutrality. With the arms-embargo section of the 1935 law due to expire on February 29, 1936, it was a foregone conclusion that the Congress would pass a new bill. Roosevelt saw this as an opportunity to win greater presidential discretion, which he believed necessary for both national defense and effective opposition to autocratic aggression. "The crux of the matter," he had written Ambassador Dodd in Berlin on December 2, "lies in the deep question of allowing some discretion to the Chief Executive.

Quite aside from any connection with the League, the President should have some discretion. For example, if some European power were to seek, by force of arms, a raw material source in South America, we should have to take sides and might, without going to war ourselves, assist the South American nation with supplies of one kind or another."

Besides serving the nation's security, Roosevelt believed that presidential power to control exports would help prevent the prolongation of foreign wars. The Ethiopian conflict was an immediate case in point. With American oil flowing to Italy at three times the normal rate in the last three months of 1935 and with the League Coordination Committee postponing an oil embargo until it knew what the American Congress would do about Neutrality, Roosevelt saw a pressing need for controls on oil exports. To be sure, he knew that the British and French governments were reluctant to apply an oil sanction and that they justified their own inaction by focusing on the United States. "It must depend largely upon the decisions to be taken by Congress during the next few weeks," the *Times* of London declared, "what, if any, extension of the economic pressure now applied to Italy by the League powers is practicable and desirable." The United States, Laval had told the Chamber of Deputies on December 28, held the answer to whether France would apply an oil embargo. Despite Anglo-French efforts to blame the United States for not doing what they themselves refused to undertake, Roosevelt could not ignore the fact that American oil was fueling Mussolini's war machine.[24]

To change this and prevent a similar occurrence in a future war, Roosevelt and the State Department drafted a Neutrality bill which Pittman and McReynolds put before the Congress on January 3. Though it contained strong mandatory features—an impartial arms embargo, an automatic ban on loans to belligerents, and an impartial embargo on "materials used for war purposes"—it also included significant discretionary powers for the President: the freedom to limit raw-material exports to "normal" prewar levels, to say what constituted "normal," and to permit short-term loans and commerce with the belligerents only at the trader's own risk. In sum, the bill conceded much to advocates of mandatory Neutrality, but it also gave the President sufficient flexibility to align the United States against an aggressor. The administration "was attempting to beguile the pacifists into giving the President a certain amount of discretion with embargoes on war weapons and material," Arthur Krock wrote in the *New York Times*. "It was trying to allow some legislative room for consultation with foreign nations intent upon putting down treaty-breakers and aggressors, on the entirely sensible ground that this is the only real way to keep the world's peace and ours along with it. The efforts were shrewdly made . . . ," Krock concluded. "But Senators Johnson and Borah can tell a hawk from a handsaw in these matters." [25]

The President's request for discretionary powers evoked intense opposition from several quarters. To deny FDR the power to discriminate between aggressors and victims of aggression, Senators Nye and Clark and Representative Maverick introduced a competing Neutrality bill. This measure also embargoed munitions and war materials and barred loans to belligerents, but it denied the President any say over when and how these things would be done, and it introduced a cash-and-carry formula that would keep Americans from all direct commercial contact with warring states.

Senators Johnson and Borah, together with prominent international lawyers and American exporters, opposed both measures and called instead for a defense of traditional neutral rights. This " 'new neutrality,' " former World Court Justice John Bassett Moore complained, ". . . might be best defined in the terms of the 'new chastity,' which encouraged fornication in the hope that it might reach the stage of legalized prostitution. In other words, the 'new neutrality' appears to be intended to get us into war." The administration's bill, the prominent international lawyer Edwin Borchard declared, allows the President to be as unneutral as he wants. "This is a wild idea," he wrote Borah, ". . . and is calculated to drive us into frequent conflicts." American business groups opposed the trade restrictions in these laws as certain to reduce further America's world trade. The administration bill, they said, would expose "normal" American commerce to attacks by belligerents, while both measures would transfer "legitimate war profits" from Americans to other suppliers. An *impartial* defense of traditional neutral rights, they all agreed, was a better alternative; it would protect American commerce and still keep the country out of war.[26]

The best-organized opponents of Neutrality revision were Italian-Americans. Appreciating that both the administration and the Nye-Clark-Maverick bills would deny Italy essential war materials, groups like the American Friends of Italy, the League for American Neutrality, and the Italian Union of America organized 100 conferences, arranged 75 radio addresses, sponsored 150 articles, sent spokesmen to House and Senate hearings, and flooded the Congress with form mail urging the extension of the 1935 Neutrality law or the exemption of Italy and Ethiopia from the provisions of a new act.[27]

By early February these opponents of new legislation had won the debate. In the House, where some northeastern representatives felt particularly pressured by Italian-American constituents, the Foreign Affairs Committee engaged in table-pounding arguments before reporting out the administration's McReynolds bill. In response to this opposition, though, the Rules Committee blocked the bill from going to the House floor and convinced McReynolds that the House would not pass it. In the Senate, moreover, the Foreign Relations Committee quickly reached an impasse, splitting between administration, Nye-Clark, and traditional-neutral-rights supporters. With Pittman speaking for the administration, Arthur Vandenberg of Michigan for mandatory legislation, and Borah and Johnson against both, the Committee seemed hopelessly deadlocked. After discussing these problems with congressional and State Department leaders and his Cabinet on February 7, Roosevelt decided to follow Pittman's and McReynold's advise that he support a fourteen-month extension of the existing law. Consequently, on February 18, 1936, the Senate joined the House in approving a slightly revised edition of the 1935 law. Reenacting the arms and travel restrictions of the earlier measure, the bill now also forbade loans to belligerents, made the application of an arms embargo to states entering a war in progress mandatory rather than discretionary, and exempted American Republics from the operation of the law if they were at war with a non-American state. "Out of the mountain of discussion and turmoil," William Phillips observed, "has come, in fact, a mouse."

Several compelling reasons decided Roosevelt to accept this compromise. A fight for his bill seemed likely to result in a mandatory measure that would strip him of additional powers. "In view of the violent contrary views and the trend in the Congress to make our original bill mandatory . . . ," Philips wrote, "I am thankful that the legislation will come out in a purely harmless form." Further, a battle for discretionary powers seemed certain to produce "a prolonged, open debate in the Senate [which] would give comfort to Mussolini and have a chilling effect upon the sanctionist group in the League." Moreover, it promised to provoke a filibuster led by Johnson and Borah which would allow the existing law to expire and turn Neutrality into an effective anti-administration issue in the upcoming election campaign. A fight for permanent Neutrality legislation, one commentator wrote, "meant the kind of long and bitter war which those who love peace in an election year were most eager to avoid." [28]

Given all this, Roosevelt gladly accepted the extension law, calling it "a definite step . . . towards enabling this country to maintain its neutrality and avoid being drawn into wars involving other nations." Still, he could not ignore the fact that his request for trade controls had "not been the subject of legislation." Indeed, with a League report of February 12 noting "a very large increase" in American exports to Italy, and concluding that a League oil embargo would be effective if the United States held its shipments to pre-1935 levels, Roosevelt felt compelled to renew his appeal to Americans to conduct their trade with belligerents so "that it cannot be said that they are seizing new opportunities for profits or that by changing their peacetime trade they give aid to the continuation of war."

Paying more attention to American action than to Roosevelt's appeal, the League found grounds for further equivocation. Whereas, according to reports from Europe, the administration's bill would have pushed League states into an oil embargo, the extension of the 1935 law further encouraged them to avoid a decision. On March 2 and 3, for example, when the League returned to the subject of an oil sanction, it again postponed action until it could make a fresh effort to compose Italo-Ethiopian differences. Between March and May 1936, therefore, while Mussolini feigned an interest in peace talks, the Italians destroyed organized Ethiopian resistance and occupied Addis Ababa. Though the Roosevelt administration continued to discourage trade with the belligerents during these months, it was only a symbolic gesture. On June 20, ten days after British Chancellor of the Exchequer Neville Chamberlain had described the continuation of sanctions as "the very midsummer of madness," and two days after Foreign Secretary Anthony Eden had announced the government's intention to recommend a lifting of sanctions, Roosevelt revoked his Neutrality proclamations.[29] It was but one of several indications by the summer of 1936 that Roosevelt had found no effective means to serve the cause of peace.

6

Standing Still

BY THE BEGINNING OF 1936, Roosevelt had felt almost helpless against the worldwide drift toward war. A stream of warnings from abroad filled him with "extreme disquiet" about European and Asiatic affairs. "Nearly all of the political leaders in Europe and even here," Norman Davis wrote from London, "are now thinking of how best to prepare for the war which they think Germany is going to force upon them." "We are back where we were before 1914," Ambassador Bullitt reported from Moscow, "when the familiar and true remark was, 'Peace is at the mercy of an incident.' " "The whole European panorama is fundamentally blacker than at any time in your life . . . or mine," Roosevelt said in response. These "may be the last days of . . . peace before a long chaos." [1]

This deterioration abroad made FDR eager to unify the Americas against any outside threat. Hull had initiated the process in June 1935 when he sounded out other American states on establishing "adequate peace machinery" to deal with future inter-American disputes. Though Roosevelt fully supported Hull's idea, they decided to delay a proposal for a conference on the subject until mediators could settle the Chaco war between Bolivia and Paraguay. In January 1936, nine days after the belligerents had signed peace protocols, Roosevelt had invited the twenty Latin American states "to assemble at an early date . . . to determine how the maintenance of peace among the American Republics may best be safeguarded. . . . With the conclusion of the Chaco War and with the reestablishment of peace throughout the Continent," Roosevelt declared, "there would appear to be offered an opportunity for helpful counsel among our respective Governments which may not soon again be presented." The President's proposal at once received "cordial approval" throughout Latin America, though the formulation of an agenda took until August, when Argentina issued formal invitations for a meeting in Buenos Aires beginning December 1, 1936. [2]

The positive response to Roosevelt's suggestion was partly an expression of confidence in his good intentions. In the year and a half after his Caribbean tour, he and Hull had given further proof of their commitment to the Good Neighbor idea. During 1935 the State Department had concluded reciprocal trade agreements with Brazil, Colombia, Haiti, and Honduras and had begun trade negotiations with nine other Latin states. At the same time, Washington negotiated a new treaty with Panama which abolished American rights under the agreement of 1903 to intervene unilaterally and take unlimited control of Panamanian territory. Under the new treaty of March 2, 1936, Panama was to have joint responsibility for the defense and operation of the Canal and a larger share of its profits.[3]

As important, in 1934–35 the administration resisted considerable pressure from American Catholics to force the Mexican government of President Lázaro Cárdenas to end an anticlerical policy. Dating from the early years of the century, Mexican efforts to restrict the Catholic Church had entered a fresh phase in the fall of 1934 when the government moved to abolish religious education. Viewed as a direct attack on the Church, Catholics in the United States mounted a vigorous opposition campaign. Seizing on a speech by Ambassador Josephus Daniels, in which he praised public or non-parochial education, American Catholics demanded his recall as an expression of opposition to Mexican policy. "What detestable cowardice on the part of the official representative of the mighty nation to the North," declared one American priest, "to jump with both feet upon the weak children of a nation that is being harassed to death in its religious belief and practice by a persecutor that compares favorably with a Nero and a Stalin." Though Roosevelt dismissed these complaints as "fishy" and as "unwarranted by the facts," the pressure on the administration did not subside. In the first half of 1935, William Borah had proposed a Senate investigation of Mexico's religious persecutions, while members of the House introduced fourteen resolutions asking for a response to Mexico's policy. At the same time, the Knights of Columbus led American Catholics in bombarding the administration with thousands of telegrams, letters, and petitions demanding action.[4]

Roosevelt refused to budge. He helped block Senate and House inquiries, specifically allowing Hull to give "every attention to the defeat of the Borah resolution." "It would put our government in the position of claiming the right to say what the laws of another country should be in controlling its internal affairs," Hull told one Senator. The farthest Roosevelt would go in meeting these demands was to discuss his hands-off policy with Catholic and congressional leaders, endorse religious freedom in public statements, and quietly encourage diplomatic conversations between the Vatican and the Mexican government. "I decline to permit this Government," he had written the head of the Knights of Columbus in November 1935, "to undertake a policy of interference in the domestic concerns of foreign governments and thereby jeopardize the maintenance of peaceful relations." [5]

Roosevelt actually had a host of reasons for resisting this pressure. For one, divided opinion among Catholics limited the likely loss of support to the administration from a policy of continued passivity toward Mexico's anticlerical actions. Leaders like Father John J. Burke of the National Catholic Welfare Conference and George Cardinal Mundelein of Chicago sided with the President against interference in Mexican affairs. Secondly, during 1935 the Cárdenas government moderated its religious policies and made the issue less important to Catholics in the United States. Finally, but most important, Roosevelt did not wish to jeopardize a growing reputation for nonintervention in Latin American affairs. This Good Neighbor policy promised not only to encourage inter-American trade but also to promote a common defense against outside threats and to help keep America's millions of pacifists firmly in Roosevelt's camp. This was no small consideration in an election year.[6]

Though the advancement of cooperation in the Western Hemisphere was a high priority with FDR, aiding Europe to keep the peace remained a more pressing concern. In February, Roosevelt asked Samuel R. Fuller, Jr., an old friend and businessman with influential contacts in Germany, to see Hitler and German Finance Minister Hjalmar Schacht on his next trip to Berlin in March 1936. More specifically, he asked him to sound out the Germans on economics, finances, and trade and to propose the idea of meeting Germany's need for raw materials through colonial leases. In March, moreover, after Hitler coupled reoccupation of the Rhineland with a proposal for a twenty-five-year Western nonaggression pact, Roosevelt told Ambassador Dodd to send "immediate word" if events reached a "point where a gesture, an offer or a formal statement by me would, in your judgment, make for peace. . . . But," he cautioned, "the peace must be not only peace with justice but the kind of peace which will endure without threat for more than a week or two." It is difficult to believe that Roosevelt had anything more in mind than a "gesture," or an indication to Hitler that if he pushed too far, the United States could again become a factor on the European scene.[7]

Everything at home and in Europe argued against his doing anything more. American sentiment for strict neutrality, as demonstrated in the recent congressional debate, and the small likelihood that Britain and France would adopt a firm stand against Berlin dictated a "hands off" policy toward Hitler's action in general and a rejection of a French request for a moral condemnation of "any unilateral repudiation of a treaty" in particular. The fact that the Rhineland crisis quickly subsided when London and Paris reinforced each other's inclinations to avoid military or economic sanctions confirmed Roosevelt in his decision to take a detached approach. On March 22, he left Washington for a Bahamas fishing vacation, and on his return in April, when he heard reports of "vast [British] peace proposals . . . to bring about a 'New Deal' in Europe," he acknowledged the need for "some new plan and new leadership," but stated that "perhaps the time is not ripe." With a presidential election only seven months away, he was not about to challenge public sentiment for detachment from Europe's troubles.[8]

More concerned now with organizing his reelection fight than with European affairs, he focused most of his correspondence with his diplomats on arranging their return to the United States for work in the campaign. Initially planning to have Long, Claude Bowers in Madrid, Bullitt, John Cudahy in Warsaw, and two or three ministers return home by May, Roosevelt had expanded the list to include most of his politically appointed envoys. When Ambassador Bingham in London pointed out, however, that the absence of so many American representatives in Europe at such turbulent times might expose him to criticism, Roosevelt asked some of them to stay abroad.[9]

This preoccupation with domestic politics did not spell the end of Roosevelt's interest in European affairs. When an opportunity arose to put some pressure on Germany and simultaneously serve his election campaign, he was ready to act. In April, after Morgenthau explained that differences existed in the Treasury Department and between Treasury and State over whether the 1930 Tariff Act required them to apply countervailing duties or higher tariffs to subsidized German exports, Roosevelt said: "If it is a borderline case I feel so keenly about Germany that I would enforce the countervailing duties." He also saw this as an effective reply to the Republican agricultural program. "The Republicans are most likely going to advocate some form of export debentures for agricultural products so that we can dump our products on the rest of the world," he told Morgenthau. His suggestion was to point out that other countries would respond with higher tariffs, "just the way the Treasury Department evoked countervailing duties against Germany—that is our answer to the Republican agricultural program."

By May 22, after receiving legal advice from the Justice Department and discounting State Department warnings that action against Germany would compel American action against other countries and lead to the collapse of the whole trade-agreement program, Roosevelt told Morgenthau to "try to find an immediate method of carrying out the law. I am convinced that we have to act. It may be possible to make the action apply to Germany only." On June 30 Morgenthau invoked the law exclusively against Berlin. When the Germans quickly stopped subsidizing exports to the United States, Morgenthau considered it "the first check to Germany's career of economic conquests." [10]

At the same time that Roosevelt supported countervailing duties, he also gave quiet backing to a French request for help in devaluating their currency. In the spring of 1936, strikes, street fights between Left and Right, and a flight from the franc plagued France. Worried by conditions he believed "disturbing, not only to France but also to all her neighbors," Roosevelt was eager to help the new Popular Front government of Léon Blum stay in power long enough "to prove . . . itself." Hence, when Blum secretly informed him in June that Poland, Holland, and Belgium were collapsing and that Europe needed a strong France to stand against

Berlin, Roosevelt was ready to help Paris devalue the franc if London would agree. Though he worried that a tripartite currency agreement might expose him to domestic attacks in the midst of the campaign, he went ahead anyway, asking Morgenthau in September after the pact was completed to tell the press that "it supports and sustains the American domestic price level. . . . America's position is fully safeguarded," he said, "while at the same time our action should encourage peace and commerce." Morgenthau was even more enthusiastic: "If this goes through," he said privately, "I think it is the greatest move taken for peace in the world since the World War. . . . It may be the turning point for again resuming rational thinking in Europe."

The French also placed great stock in the agreement. Merle Cochran, the financial expert on the staff of the American Embassy who waited in the French Ministry of Finance while the final details of the agreement were worked out, described Finance Minister Vincent Auriol and his colleagues as "pacing the floor of the magnificent Empire salon, in the Old Louvre Palace . . . glancing at their watches, grinding cigarette stubs into the marvelous carpets, and listening to the rumble of voices from the press representatives outside their door. . . . When you let us know that . . . we were in final agreement," he told Morgenthau, "there was great relief on the French side." "Our common declaration," the Minister himself wrote Morgenthau, ". . . put the definite end to the monetary war and opened the road toward the 'economic peace'—so essential to peace among nations. . . . I do not know how to find words sufficiently expressive to convey to you the thanks of President Léon Blum and his Government." [11]

Roosevelt was also enthusiastic about Morgenthau's tariff and currency actions, but the outbreak of the Spanish Civil War on July 17, 1936, made him more skeptical than ever about helping Europe to keep the peace. From the beginning of the Spanish conflict, leaders everywhere thought it might spark a European war. During the first week of fighting, the Fascist rebels asked aid from Berlin and Rome, while Madrid called on France for support. Convinced that foreign involvement in the Spanish struggle would lead to a wider conflict, British leaders pressed Blum to withhold supplies. Fearing that Stanley Baldwin's Conservative British government might "turn away from a left-wing France to join Germany," Blum agreed to discuss the issue in London. "Are you going to send arms to the Spanish Republic?" British Foreign Secretary Anthony Eden asked him when they met on July 23. "Yes," Blum reported. "It is your affair," Eden countered, "but I ask you one thing. Be prudent." Also pointing to current German movements near the French border, Eden warned that French aid to Madrid might have "grave international consequences." Because he also came under pressure from the French Right and yet could not abandon aid to Madrid without alienating his own supporters in the Popular Front, Blum decided to propose a policy of general non-intervention. In the first days of August, while Paris made this proposal, the French, Germans, and Italians sent war materials to Spain. On August 9, however, after receiving an "almost unanimously favorable" reply to his nonintervention plan and after hearing from London that Britain would not aid France if a war with Germany resulted from intervention in Spain, Blum suspended all war exports to Madrid.[12]

The American response to these developments was predictable. In the words of Richard Traina, the leading student of America's role in the Spanish Civil War, "it was normal, obvious, and unimaginative," reflecting "the major attitudes and policies which preceded it." Though Roosevelt was absent from Washington from July 11 to August 10 and though he apparently gave the State Department no specific instructions, Hull and his advisers notified American representatives in Spain that "in conformity with its well-established policy of non-interference with internal affairs in other countries, either in time of peace or in the event of civil strife, this Government will, of course, scrupulously refrain from any interference whatsoever in the unfortunate Spanish situation."

An inquiry from the Glenn L. Martin Company about the advisability of selling eight war planes to the Spanish government soon illustrated Roosevelt's full conformity with this policy. On August 10, when Phillips asked his instructions on a reply, Roosevelt told him "to intimate that any such sale would not be in line with the policy of the government." As finally drafted and approved by the President, the answer to the Martin Company included a copy of the Department's telegram to its representatives in Spain and a note advising against the sale. Eager to align himself with Britain and France in keeping the conflict from turning into a wider war, Roosevelt was ready to disregard conventional international practice which allowed him to trade and freely send arms to the recognized government of Spain. But his interest at this time in helping that government preserve Spain from Fascist rule was either small or nonexistent. His objective, like that of London, was simply to keep the conflict from becoming a general European war. He also apparently saw some political advantage in this policy, since he decided over Phillips's objection to make administration policy public knowledge. "For once," Hull later wrote, "our position seemed acceptable to both the apparently irreconcilable isolationists and internationalists. Isolationists approved because we were keeping aloof from the conflict. Internationalists approved because we were cooperating with Britain and France." [13]

Specifically, one may see Roosevelt's announcement of his policy as part of a larger campaign to assure his standing with the country's pacifists. The initial response in the United States to the war in Spain was not a grand debate over what the struggle meant and what American policy should be but renewed apprehension that the world was "going on the downfall." With peace sentiment in the country so strong, Roosevelt wished to persuade Americans that he was their best hope against war. On August 8, when he lunched with Mary E. Woolley, the President of Mount Holyoke College and a leading pacifist, he asked her to speak on the radio in behalf of the administration's Good Neighbor idea. When she accepted, the Democratic National Committee was able to announce Miss Woolley's departure from her lifelong allegiance to the Republican Party to support of the President, chiefly because of his record in international affairs. More significantly, in a conversation with Secretary of the Interior Harold L. Ickes on August 10, Roosevelt agreed with his suggestion that it would be "an excellent thing" to state his determination "to leave nothing undone to keep us from becoming embroiled in another European war." A Progressive Republican from Chicago, Ickes urged FDR to use the statement to win an open declaration of support from Senator Nye, who commanded the backing of Progressive Republicans and pacifists alike. "The President seemed very much taken with the idea," Ickes recorded, and thought that a speech scheduled for Chautauqua, New York, on August 14 "might be a good occasion to make such a statement."

Pressure on Roosevelt to act on Ickes's suggestion mounted in the next few days. On August 11, the People's Mandate to Governments To End War, a committee of prominent pacifists seeking twelve million American signatures on a peace petition, asked the President to receive a delegation of its members. Pointing out that they represented "people throughout the country who believe that constructive action by our government to end war is a paramount issue in the coming national election," they reported that Governor Alfred Landon of Kansas, the Republican candidate, has already granted them an interview. In addition, on the 14th Senator Nye led ten Senators and Representatives in "urging every possible effort on the part of the government to prevent shipment of war supplies to Spain. We urge," they wired FDR, "that you make a statement to this effect in your Chautauqua Address." [14]

Though Roosevelt did not speak to this issue at Chautauqua, he made unambiguous appeals to those favoring constructive steps for peace and to those demanding that America, above all, steer clear of war. Reminding the country's pacifists of the administration's efforts for peace, Roosevelt pointed to the practical application of the Good Neighbor idea—the Montevideo agreement on nonintervention, the abrogation of the Platt Amendment, the withdrawal from Haiti, the treaty with Panama, the reciprocal trade agreements, and the upcoming peace meeting in Buenos Aires to "banish wars forever from this vast portion of the earth. . . . Peace, like charity," Roosevelt declared, "begins at home; and that's why we have begun at home, here in North and South and Central America. But peace in the western world is not all we seek. . . . We cooperated to the bitter end" in Geneva and London to reduce armies and navies and to check the international traffic in arms. Yet all this, he acknowledged, had come to "nought." Therefore, he would now "isolate" America from war. "I have seen war," he declared feelingly. "I have seen war on land and sea. I have seen blood running from the wounded. I have seen men coughing out their gassed lungs. I have seen the dead in the mud. I have seen cities destroyed. I have seen two hundred limping, exhausted men come out of line—the survivors of a regiment of one thousand that went forward forty-eight hours before. I have seen children starving. I have seen the agony of mothers and wives. I hate war."

He described himself as spending countless hours "thinking and planning how war may be kept from the United States." There are many causes of war, he said, "ancient hatreds, turbulent frontiers, the 'legacy of old forgotten, far off things,' and . . . newborn fanaticisms." But he saw only one enticement to Americans to fight—war profits. "If war should break out again in another continent, let us not blink the fact that we would find in this country thousands of Americans who, seeking immediate riches—fool's gold—would attempt to break down or evade our neutrality. They would tell you—and, unfortunately, their views would get wide publicity—that if they could produce and ship this and that and the other article to belligerent Nations, the unemployed of America would all find work. . . . It would be hard to resist . . . the clamor of that greed," he warned. But "if we face the choice of profits or peace, this Nation will answer—this Nation must answer—'We choose peace.' . . . We can keep out of war," FDR concluded, "if those who watch and decide . . . possess the courage to say 'no' to those who selfishly or unwisely would let us go to war." [15]

Roosevelt followed up his speech, which received wide acclaim, with additional efforts to secure the peace vote. In response to Ickes's contention that he could persuade Nye to endorse his "re-election on the basis of his peace record and his peace talk," Roosevelt met with the Senator at Hyde Park on August 21. Though Nye would not come out for FDR, neither would he endorse Landon, his party's nominee. On the 23rd Roosevelt also discussed the peace question with representatives of the People's Mandate committee and endorsed their worldwide drive for fifty million signatures against war and their idea that "real peace" depended on majority appeals in all countries for an end to fighting. [16]

Because Roosevelt's speech and private conversations focused more on isolating America from war than on finding new means of preserving peace, he wished to make some gesture toward those in the country asking for fresh efforts against war. Having declared at Chautauqua, "I wish I could keep war from all nations; but that is beyond my power," he now wished to demonstrate that he still had hopes of finding an answer to the problem. Consequently, in the same week he met with the People's

Mandate committee, he invited Arthur Krock of the *New York Times* to spend a night at Hyde Park. In the course of the evening, he outlined a tentative plan for a conference of "the heads of the most important nations in an effort to assure the peace of the world." He also expressed the belief that if he were reelected "over the intense opposition" he was facing, he would be "in the best position any American President has ever been to promote the cause of world peace." One reason that might restrain him "from making a detailed public statement in advance of the election," he also told Krock, was "the certainty that the Republicans will classify it as a campaign device. They will say . . . that it is an attempt to gain re-election on the Wilson issue of 1916, 'he kept us out of war,' and probably deride the plan as a romantic gesture, certain to yield barren results."

A few days later, when Krock informed the President of his intention to publish the story "on the understanding that he would not deny it," FDR sent word through his secretary to "emphasize that . . . Roosevelt had in mind . . . only 'a small committee.'" The story appeared on August 26 while Roosevelt was on a campaign trip in the West with Henry Wallace. In response to inquiries from reporters, he had Wallace announce: "The President has not seen the story and does not know just what was in it, so he can't deny it. But he said that I could tell you that there has been nothing in any shape, manner or form looking toward any meeting of the sort described." Though Roosevelt had no intention of acting on his idea during the election, he had effectively made his point: a fresh mandate for the President promised continued efforts to save the peace.[17]

All this was not simply campaign politics on Roosevelt's part. He had, in fact, been toying with the idea of an approach to other heads of state. In early August he had asked Dodd for his "slant, in the utmost confidence, as to what would happen if Hitler were personally and secretly asked by me to outline the limit of German objectives during, let us say, a ten year period, and to state whether or not he would have any sympathy with a general limitation of armaments' proposal." A few days later, when he saw Mary Woolley, he expressed an interest in holding a "meeting of the Heads of the Seven Great Powers," but also expressed the belief that "it is too 'Idealistic' to be practicable." Still, as Krock pointed out in his *Times* story, "the concept has fascinated him; he returns to it often; and it would not be difficult to convince him that he has made a new discovery in world leadership for what he considers the greatest cause of mankind."

Yet as long as he was in an election campaign, where he might come under attack for pursuing a will-o'-the-wisp or for involving the United States in commitments abroad, he would not follow through on any world peace plan. German replies to Dodd's discreet inquiries also discouraged him from further action. "A hint of the subject mentioned," Dodd had informed him on August 19, "brought a repetition of the present German demand for expansion and colonies." "The Führer . . . will not participate in any world conference if the French-Russian [security] treaty [of 1935] is not renounced by France," he wrote on the 31st. Further inquiries in September and October deepened Dodd's skepticism: if German-Italian control over "all Europe" is agreed to beforehand, he advised, "a peace conference is quite possible; but what sort of peace?" [18]

The only antiwar effort Roosevelt felt free to make during the remainder of his campaign was in response to the Spanish war. By the end of August the war had become his "greatest worry"; he believed the danger of a European outbreak over Spain so great that he decided against going to the West Coast on a campaign trip: "I probably ought not to be four days away from Washington," he confided to reporters on September 15. In the face of this danger, Roosevelt shared Anglo-French convictions that only strict neutrality could confine the war to Spain. "You are absolutely right about . . . what you say of our complete neutrality in regard to Spain's own internal affairs," he wrote Claude Bowers, his Ambassador to Madrid, on September 16. Mounting evidence of Italo-German violations of their nonintervention pledges, or of what Bowers called "an international fascist conspiracy to destroy the democracy of Spain," did not alter British, French, or American thinking; it strengthened it. On October 7, when Russia's representative to the international Nonintervention Committee in London warned that continued fascist violations of neutrality would lead to Moscow's withdrawal, British Foreign Office chiefs angrily asked: "what can Russia hope to gain by throwing over neutrality at this time?" Similarly, French Foreign Minister Yvon Delbos declared that "in spite of the difficulties raised by the Russian démarche, the French Government positively would not abandon its attitude of absolute neutrality and non-intervention."

In Washington, Hull told Fernando de los Ríos, Spain's Ambassador, the same thing. When de los Ríos warned that the destruction of Spanish democracy would bring a similar result elsewhere, and requested American aid, Hull pointed to the Montevideo pledge of noninterference, asked why the French government, "the neighbor and special friend of the Spanish Government," adhered to nonintervention, and stated America's intention to do the same. Clearly, for Roosevelt, as for Baldwin and Blum, the first priority was not saving Spanish democracy but preventing a European war. Since this peace effort required no international commitments of any kind from the United States, and thus carried almost no domestic liabilities, Roosevelt must have found it especially appealing during the closing months of his reelection campaign.[19]

Returns at the polls in November seemed to vindicate Roosevelt's strategy. He carried every state but Maine and Vermont, the largest electoral-vote ratio since 1820. "As Maine goes, so goes Vermont," Jim Farley quipped. The President's popular vote exceeded Landon's by more than eleven million, the biggest popular plurality up to then in American history. There is no evidence, however, that Roosevelt's handling of foreign affairs or the peace issue during the campagin added significantly to his total. At most, it neutralized a potentially explosive issue by assuring that supporters on domestic matters would not desert him over concern about involvement in a future war.

Once the election was over, though, Roosevelt felt freer to make active efforts for peace. On November 4 he made known what he had privately decided in September, that he would lend his prestige to the inter-American peace conference by personally attending the opening session. On November 16, the day before he left for Buenos Aires, he told his Cabinet that if some sort of peace and disarmament understanding came out of the inter-American meeting, "we might later try for something of the same sort in the Pacific Ocean." He raised the possibility of disarming "practically everything in the Pacific except Japan, Australia, New Zealand, and Singapore. This would leave the Philippines, Shanghai, Hong Kong, the Dutch East Indies, British North Borneo, and other important points neutralized." The President also said that he had no intention of disarming Hawaii but would be willing to include American Samoa and the portion of Alaska nearest Japan in such an agreement.[20]

Roosevelt's objectives in going to Buenos Aires were to combine a vacation trip with a demonstration to the "war-weary peoples of the world" of effective cooperation for peace among democratic states. His journey succeeded on both counts. The 12,000-mile sea voyage, which began on November 18, lasted twenty-eight days and gave him ample opportunity to rest and recover from the labors of his election campaign. He slept, reduced weight, sunned himself, fished, and enjoyed the shipboard diversions, including initiation rites for himself and others crossing the Equator for the first time.

His stops in Rio de Janeiro, Buenos Aires, and Montevideo produced tumultuous receptions and strong evidence of excellent relations between the United States and Latin America. In Rio huge throngs gathered at the quay and lined the streets shouting "Viva la democracia! Viva Roosevelt!" The demonstration embarrassed Brazil's President Getulio Vargas. "Perhaps you've heard that I am a dictator," he whispered to Roosevelt as they rode along. "Perhaps you've heard that I am one, too," Roosevelt replied.

In Buenos Aires "approximately two million Argentines, packed in every conceivable point of vantage, greeted the President with wild acclaim and showered him with flowers as he passed. . . . From all reports," one observer recorded, "the reception given the President by the citizens of Buenos Aires exceeded in warmth and spontaneity anything that has ever occurred in Argentina." Despite heavy rains on the final day in Buenos Aires, thousands of people "braved the weather to show President Roosevelt this last evidence of their unbelievably deep admiration for him." Though FDR had no illusion that his reception would have much practical effect on Europe, he hoped that there would be "at least some moral repercussions" in the Old World. "The fine record of our relations is the best answer to those pessimists who scoff at the idea of true friendship between Nations," he declared in Rio. "Let us present a record," he urged, "which our Hemisphere may give to the world as convincing proof that peace lies always at hand when Nations, serene in their sovereign security, meet their current problems with understanding and good-will." [21]

Roosevelt's hopes, however, of a conference that would perfect "the mechanisms of peace" and make "war in our midst impossible" were largely disappointed. Led by Hull, the United States delegation pressed for compulsory consultation among the American Republics when a war threat appeared in the Hemisphere, a permanent Inter-American Consultative Committee, and a common neutrality policy in response to any American war. The United States resolutions met stiff opposition from Argentina's Saavedra Lamas. Committed to strengthening the League of Nations, where he had just presided over the Assembly, and to Argentinian supremacy in Latin America, he saw Hull's proposals as a threat to both goals. A common neutrality policy that embraced an arms embargo, for example, would conflict with League desires to export arms to victims of aggression, while consultation machinery would increase United States influence in the Hemisphere at the expense of Argentina and the League. To torpedo Hull's resolutions, the "dictatorial" Saavedra Lamas began by forbidding the Conference secretariat to publish them, and then summoned the chiefs of the five Central American delegations to his private residence, where he cavalierly insisted that they "immediately reject the proposals favored by the United States." They were, he warned, "nothing more nor less than a means by which the United States hoped to extend its power and influence over the smaller nations of the hemisphere."

To counter Saavedra Lamas, Hull asked Roosevelt "to use the 'steam shovel' " in flattering him. But when this failed, Hull held a series of conferences with him which "became increasingly animated." A last "heated" meeting, at which "some sharp words were exchanged, at least on my side," Hull wrote, broke up in disagreement. "I saw no more of Saavedra Lamas before leaving Buenos Aires. He did not extend the usual courtesy of seeing me off." In another "violent set-to" over the U.S. resolutions, Saavedra Lamas and Brazil's José Carlos de Macedo Soares called each other "pigs" and "liars."

In the face of Saavedra Lamas's opposition, which Bolivia, Chile, and Uruguay supported, Hull felt compelled to accept "watered-down" and "emasculate[d]" resolutions. The Conference agreed to inter-American consultation whenever there was a threat to Hemisphere peace, but rejected the idea of a permanent consultative committee. It made a common neutrality policy a general objective, but declared the Republics free to act in accord with prior treaty obligations and domestic legislation. It agreed to consultation and collaboration when a foreign war threatened peace in the Americas, but made it voluntary rather than obligatory. Only the principle of nonintervention received an unqualified endorsement. Extending the Montevideo commitment, the delegates signed a treaty stating that direct or indirect intervention in the internal or external affairs of any of them was "inadmissible." Despite this achievement, the Conference left Hull dissatisfied. When the time came for a closing address "to emphasize the importance of what we had been able to achieve," he suffered a "diplomatic" cold, which required that Sumner Welles, who was more enthusiastic about Conference results, deliver the speech.[22]

During his Latin American trip, Roosevelt had continued to think about ways of helping Europe avoid war. In the days and weeks after his election, he received numerous reports of European hopes that he would save them from themselves. Bill Bullitt, who was now Ambassador to France, described the "tornado of praise" which greeted his election. "Blum came personally to express his congratulations. That is unheard of. . . . He entered the front door, flung his broad-brimmed black hat to the butler, his coat to the footman, leaped the three steps to the point where I was standing, seized me and kissed me violently! I staggered slightly; but having been kissed by Stalin, I am now immune to any form of osculation. . . ." "The French," Bullitt further reported, "all feel . . . that you will somehow manage to keep Europe from plunging again into war." The Ministers of the small European states told Bullitt the same thing. Though they had no suggestions as to what the President might do, they expressed the hope that he would think of something. "You are . . . beginning to occupy the miracle man position," Bullitt advised. "French Cabinet Ministers and representatives of all the countries of Europe in Paris," Bullitt wrote again in two weeks, "talk as if they had within them the same phonograph record—playing the theme, 'War is inevitable and Europe is doomed to destruction unless President Roosevelt intervenes.' "

But Roosevelt saw no effective way to help. The continuing tensions over Spain, the conclusion on November 26, 1936, of an anti-Comintern pact between Germany and Japan, and reports that no one in the Old World was doing anything constructive for peace left him "most pessimistic about Europe." A world conference now seemed like a poor idea, though he did not give up entirely on a meeting between several chiefs of state. "If five or six heads of the important governments could meet together for a week with complete inaccessibility to press or cables or radio," he wrote Dodd on January 9, 1937, "a definite useful agreement might result or else one or two of them would be murdered by the others! In any case it would be worthwhile from the point of view of civilization!" But "conditions of the moment," he told Ambassador Cudahy in Poland in the following week, ruled out "any move of any kind in Europe." He thought the situation there confusing and described himself as " 'watchfully waiting' . . . I would not dare to say this out loud," he confided to William Phillips, "because sometimes it is better to appear much wiser than one really is." [23]

Only the Spanish Civil War evoked fresh action by FDR. During the last two months of 1936, European tensions over Spain had continued to grow. In November, Germany, Italy, and Portugal blocked a British plan to uncover breaches of nonintervention by posting observers at Spain's frontiers and ports, while Berlin and Rome recognized the Fascists as the government of Spain. In December, Mussolini sharply increased the number of Italians fighting in Spain, leading the British and the French to make urgent representations in Berlin, Rome, Moscow, and Lisbon for an early ban on "volunteers." On December 24, the same day the governments discussed Spain's "armed tourists," and nine days after Roosevelt had returned from Latin America, Robert Cuse, the president of a New Jersey corporation dealing in used aircraft, applied for licenses to export nearly $3 million worth of airplanes and engines to Republican Spain. The State Department, led by R. Walton Moore, who was Acting Secretary in Hull's absence, publicly attacked Cuse's violation of the moral embargo as inimical to American interests. Roosevelt himself joined in, denouncing Cuse's defiance of government policy as "a perfectly legal but thoroughly unpatriotic act."

To head off Cuse and prevent a breach of the Anglo-French neutrality policy or encouragement to European disagreements menacing world peace, Moore and Pittman urged Roosevelt to ask Congress for discretion to embargo arms to countries fighting civil wars. After Roosevelt's record-breaking victory in November, which included top-heavy majorities in both houses of Congress, where the Democrats now held some three-quarters of the seats, Moore believed that the President could retrieve some executive control over neutrality. Pittman agreed, telling FDR that a civil war amendment to the Neutrality law "probably could be passed through both branches of Congress within a very few days." But they were wrong. In early January a "considerable minority" in the Congress jeopardized "early passage" of the amendment by opposing discretionary powers or any kind of additions to the Neutrality law. At the same time, Cuse began speeding up his export preparations, and new applications for $4.5 million worth of arms shipments came into the Department. With the British and the French in the midst of fresh efforts to make the nonintervention agreement effective and reports in the *New York Times* that

London and Paris were concerned that the United States government was "indifferent" to their efforts "to inject some honesty into the nonintervention policy," Roosevelt decided to ask for mandatory legislation applying exclusively to Spain. The Congress responded with near unanimity, approving the proposal on January 6 with only one dissenting vote. According to an opinion survey of January 11, the public largely supported the action: 66 per cent had no special feeling for either side in the Spanish fighting. Moreover, the passage of the Spanish arms embargo generated little debate in the press. Intense feelings over American policy toward the Spanish war did not in fact occur until later. Indeed, in January 1937 American volunteers, who would suffer heavy losses in the Spanish fighting and become martyrs to pro-Loyalist groups in the United States, had not yet even entered the fighting.[24]

All this suggests not that Roosevelt was under great constraints to apply an embargo to Spain but that the state of domestic feeling left him considerable leeway to do what he pleased. Had he chosen to follow conventional diplomatic practice and permitted arms exports to Spain, it is entirely conceivable that the public would have gone along and that the Congress would have been hard pressed to do otherwise. At the very least, it would have compelled advocates of an embargo to argue for a departure from traditional action under international law. But to Roosevelt, the issue was not saving the Spanish Republic or preventing a Fascist takeover in Spain, but aligning himself with what proved to be the egregiously shortsighted Anglo-French policy of preventing a European war. Had he at least won congressional agreement to a discretionary law, he would have been in a position to reverse course. But as things turned out, the mandatory embargo tied him to an inflexible policy for the duration of the war.

Why did he accept the mandatory law? In backing away from a congressional struggle over discretionary powers, Roosevelt was trying not only to assure quick passage of a Spanish arms embargo but also to avoid a congressional debate that could forestall action on judicial reform. His overriding concern in January 1937 was to legitimize New Deal achievements by curbing the Supreme Court. Beginning in the spring of 1935, the Court had struck down several New Deal laws, including the National Industrial Relations Act and the Agricultural Adjustment Act, and in 1937 it seemed ready to overturn other major accomplishments such as Social Security and the National Labor Relations Act. For Roosevelt, Court reform had implications ranging beyond social change in the United States; it was also tied to the question of whether democracy was a more effective system than Fascism or Communism.

This had been one of Roosevelt's preeminent concerns during the 1936 campaign and the Latin American trip. In June he had told the Democratic Nominating Convention that he saw some people in other lands who, having grown too weary to carry on the fight for freedom, had "yielded their democracy. . . . Only our success," he said, "can stir their ancient hope. They begin to know that here in America we are waging a great and successful war . . . for the survival of democracy. We are fighting to save a great and precious form of government for ourselves and for the world." "The election this year," he had written Dodd in August, "has, in a sense, a German parallel. . . . Democracy is verily on trial." After his reelection, he thought the results "may have made the German and Italian populace a little envious of democratic methods." "Democracy is still the hope of the world," he had told the Buenos Aires Conference in December. "If we in our generation can continue its successful application in the Americas, it will spread and supersede other methods by which men are governed." He saw his popularity with the South American crowds shouting "viva la democracia" as stemming from their belief that he had "made democracy function and keep abreast of the time and that as a system of government it is, therefore, to be preferred to Fascism or Communism."

To continue to make democracy work in the United States, Roosevelt believed that he must curb the Court. And to do this, he felt compelled temporarily to put other domestic legislation as well as foreign affairs on the shelf. In his Inaugural Address on January 20, 1937, he entirely ignored foreign policy, which Donald Richberg, who helped draft the speech, described to one journalist as "ticklish stuff to mix into just now." On February 5 Roosevelt astounded the nation, the Congress, and even his closest friends by making the first major action of his second administration a proposal to enlarge the United States Supreme Court.[25]

Despite his eagerness to avoid foreign-policy questions, the May 1 expiration date of the 1936 Neutrality law deprived Roosevelt of this choice. To keep the issue as quiet as possible, though, he left the drafting of a new measure to Pittman and McReynolds and chose a less controversial cash-and-carry method of trading with belligerents than the quota system proposed in 1936. Instead of limiting trade in raw materials to "normal" prewar levels, the new bill required that such exports to belligerents be paid for in cash and carried away on non-U.S. ships. This plan appealed to FDR because it would both satisfy Congress and allow Britain to take advantage of its naval power in a war against Berlin or Rome.[26]

At the same time, despite his preoccupation with Court "packing" and his skepticism about the effectiveness of any peace move, he felt under considerable pressure to continue exploring possible methods of salvaging peace. "There is a tenacious belief in diplomatic circles," Cudahy had written him from Warsaw in January, "that you contemplate some sort of move toward the pacification of Europe and only a few days ago there appeared a story in the Polish press that you were coming over here to preside over an international conference." Simultaneously, word reached the President that Schacht hoped "that the United States would not let slip the opportunity which . . . is now yours, particularly the President's, to take the lead in solving the outstanding questions of Europe, and primarily Germany's problems." In early February Morgenthau advised Roosevelt that Europe was "gradually going bankrupt through preparing for war. . . 'You are the only person who can stop it,' " Morgenthau said. "I feel like throwing either a cup and saucer at you or the coffee pot," Roosevelt replied. ". . . I had Hull, Norman Davis for lunch," he added, "and Davis said, 'The only person who can save the situation is Roosevelt.' "

In response to these pressures, Roosevelt returned to his Pacific-neutralization scheme in February, asking the State Department to comment on his idea. He also gave Morgenthau a go-ahead to ask Neville Chamberlain, Britain's Chancellor of the Exchequer, if he had any suggestions on how to keep the world from going broke over the cost of armaments. At the same time, he came back to the idea of calling a world conference of five or six heads of State. "If I call it," he told Morgenthau, "I will . . . simply outline the situation to them, tell them to adjourn to some other building, tell them that the problem is theirs and that they should try to find a solution and then come back and see me again." He also said that if any country refused to comply with the majority, the rest could threaten it with an economic boycott.

Roosevelt's revival of his conference idea was a momentary enthusiasm or flight of fancy. Ten days later he once more backed away from the scheme, telling Morgenthau on February 26 that it would be "useless" to call a conference, that "the countries would not play ball," and that "they were up against a stone wall." Morgenthau recorded that "the President's attitude is one of complete hopelessness about the European situation." The State Department saw little to warrant greater hope for the Far East. Pointing out that Japan's recent record of broken-treaty pledges and continuing instability in the Pacific made any agreement hazardous, the Department advised against any neutralization treaty at this time.

But Roosevelt was reluctant to drop this plan. On March 1 he sharply complained to Hull that whoever wrote the Department's memo "does not know anything about military and naval facts. The whole tenor of the argument is that this is not the time to do anything; that the proposal is merely idealistic and that an agreement would not be lived up to anyway. In other words, taking it by and large, this argument all the way through is an argument of defeatism." Feeling stymied by his own skepticism about existing peace plans, Roosevelt was venting his frustration with his and the Department's inability to find a proposal that could "fire one's imagination." [27]

A few days later, he and Prime Minister W. L. Mackenzie King of

Canada tried to work out such a scheme. A dominating figure in Canadian politics, where he had been Prime Minister for ten of the previous sixteen years, King was a fervently religious Presbyterian who believed that "a host of unseen witnesses hovered about him and guided his conduct in emergencies." In discussions at the White House on March 5 and 6, they explored the idea of a "Permanent Conference on Economic and Social Problems." Roosevelt was in his best utopian mood and they discussed the possibility of a "continuous" meeting of nations trying to solve the economic and social problems "which are the *fundamental cause of war.*" By investigating and exposing social injustices, the conference was to mobilize world opinion against these wrongs and eliminate national discontent and world strife. Reason or public opinion was to replace force as the best means of guaranteeing collective security. As this method of solving world problems—"peace secured by peaceful means"—proved its effectiveness, Roosevelt and King envisaged a merger of the League and the Permanent Conference into a single world body. On March 19, as a follow-up to this discussion, Roosevelt asked Norman Davis, who was about to leave for an international sugar conference in London, to sound out European leaders on the idea of transforming the League from a political into an economic organization which the United States might join. He also asked Davis to discuss his Pacific neutralization scheme with the British and to search for a means of European cooperation which could halt the slide toward war.

Nothing came of these discussions. British, French, and German leaders in London expressed skepticism about comprehensive world talks, described the difficulties in the way of an initiative by any of them, and argued that Roosevelt was in the best position to make the first move. Moreover, with the exception of Anthony Eden, the British considered a Pacific neutralization proposal to Japan as pointless or premature. The only immediate contribution, in fact, the British believed the United States could make to world peace was through a revision of her Neutrality law. "His Majesty's Government," Chamberlain wrote Morgenthau in March, ". . . have no doubt whatever that the greatest single contribution which the United States could make at the present moment to the preservation of world peace would be the amendment of the existing neutrality legislation. . . . The legislation in its present form constitutes an indirect but potent encouragement to aggression, and it is earnestly hoped that some way may be found of leaving sufficient discretion with the Executive to deal with each case on its merits." [28]

Roosevelt remained fully alert to Chamberlain's point. In January he had told Walton Moore that he strongly favored "permissive legislation." He appreciated, however, especially after he conceded discretionary control over the Spanish arms embargo, that he would probably be unable to win flexible restrictions on arms, loans, and travel, and that the best he could hope for was discretion to embargo raw materials. Though State Department spokesmen, in fact, urged flexible neutrality legislation at congressional hearings in February, the Senate and House bills emerged in largely mandatory form. Aside from granting presidential discretion to withhold raw materials from belligerents and to apply the arms embargo to civil wars, the Pittman bill contained a network of mandatory provisions. The only major difference in the McReynolds bill was in the cash feature of the cash-and-carry provision: instead of requiring that belligerents take immediate title to goods purchased in the United States, thus eliminating the chance that American-owned property would be destroyed in transit, the President was to decide if and when this should be done.[29]

Roosevelt had no intention of asking for more than the congressional bills gave. In the midst of his "bitter" all-consuming Court fight, in which opponents styled him "a remorseless dictator" out to destroy the Constitution and the courts, Roosevelt was in a weak position to ask for greater Executive control over foreign affairs. "I will try to prevent the President's sinister grasp of . . . the war-making power," Hiram Johnson said of the Neutrality bill. ". . . With his reaching into the Supreme Court . . . he will make himself an absolute dictator in fact." Though other Senators were less fearful of Roosevelt's intentions, they also opposed increasing his control over Neutrality. The Neutrality law "is . . . the best that anyone knowing the situation could expect the Senate to pass, and of this I am perfectly satisfied from having being in close contact with Key Pittman from the start," Moore had written Roosevelt on March 4. The President himself was in touch with the Senator who, according to the *New York Times*, convinced him that the Pittman bill went "as far in the direction of discretionary leeway as could be put through the Congress at this time." Only a conference committee impasse over whether the "cash" provision should be mandatory moved FDR to press the case for discretionary power. He asked Senate Majority Leader Joseph T. Robinson to "persuade Key to yield just as far as possible to the House bill," and cautiously added that "you can use my name if you think it advisable." Though Pittman gave in on the "cash" provision, the "permanent" Neutrality law of May 1, 1937, gave Roosevelt far less discretion than he would have liked.[30]

One choice left open to FDR under the law was to invoke embargoes against Germany and Italy for their actions in Spain. This had not become an issue, however, until the middle of March when the defeat and capture of substantial numbers of Italian troops at Guadalajara provided irrefutable proof of Italy's organized military involvement. "Disclosures of the past week have reduced to utter mockery the pretense that the war in Spain is anything other than a foreign war of the Fascist Powers against the Government of Spain," Claude Bowers had written Hull on March 16. After these events, Senator Nye introduced a resolution inquiring whether the Neutrality laws could be applied to nations fighting in a country involved in a civil war. Eager to penalize Franco's foreign supporters and to end America's cooperation with Britain and France, which he saw leading to intervention in Europe's strife, Nye urged an embargo on American munitions to Berlin and Rome.

The loss of American lives in the Spanish struggle now added to this feeling against the Fascists. In February a force of 450 Americans, the Abraham Lincoln Battalion, joined the fighting in the valley of the Jarama, southeast of Madrid. Led by a twenty-eight-year-old Communist and made up mostly of students with no previous military experience other than their training in Spain, the Battalion fought with great gallantry, suffering 120 killed and 175 wounded.

Roosevelt was not ready to act on Nye's proposal. But he believed that an attempt by Mussolini to redeem Italy's military honor by open action against Spain might force his hand. Unwilling to be out of step with London, however, he asked how Britain would react to a move on Mussolini's part. The reply that London would not alter its policy, together with State Department advice that embargoes against Italy and Germany might "seriously endanger the success of the conciliatory efforts being made by Britain and France," discouraged any impulse Roosevelt had to follow Nye's lead. Mussolini's failure to do more than declare that "no Italians could return alive from Spain unless they won a victory" temporarily pushed the idea to the back of Roosevelt's mind.[31]

The bombing of Guernica soon compelled him to confront the question of embargoes again. On April 26, 1937, waves of German planes had bombed and strafed the Basque city for three hours, killing 1,654 people and wounding another 889. "We bombed it, and bombed it and bombed it," declared a fascist staff officer, "and *bueno* why not?" The indiscriminate killing of civilians evoked an angry worldwide response. In the United States prominent Americans from all walks of life and a large portion of the press joined in a denunciation of "the monstrous crime of Guernica," while congressional leaders renewed their appeal for the application of the Neutrality Act to Berlin and Rome. Though the State Department possessed considerable information that indicated direct German and Italian military efforts against the official government of Spain, it took the position that "it would be illogical for the United States to find a state of war between Spain on the one hand and Italy and Germany on the other when the Spanish Government had not taken that position."

Events in May and June made this position increasingly difficult to maintain. On May 31, after Loyalist planes killed 31 German sailors in an attack on the battleship *Deutschland* in Spanish territorial waters, German warships killed nineteen people in a retaliatory attack on the Republican coastal town of Almería. Out of fear that a war with Germany might ensure a Fascist victory in Spain, the Republican Cabinet decided to avoid a confrontation over the bombardment. But there was yet another crisis during the third week of June. After the captain of the German cruiser *Leipzig* claimed that Loyalist submarines staged two unsuccessful attacks on his ship, Berlin and Rome withdrew from the naval-patrol force set up by the Non-Intervention Committee in April. "Italy and Germany *are* at war with the democratically elected government of Spain," one Congressman wrote Roosevelt on June 23. ". . . Their withdrawal from the land and sea control committee removes the last prop from the fiction that they are not." With the Italians now also openly publishing casualty lists and embarkation notices, Roosevelt began to think it "ridiculous" to continue to ignore these facts.[32]

As important, he was under growing pressure from "members of Congress, private individuals and organizations and societies" to extend the arms embargo to Berlin and Rome. Working through organizations like the North American Committee To Aid Spanish Democracy, the American League against War and Fascism, the American Student Union, the League for Industrial Democracy, and the Socialist and Communist parties, supporters of the Republic deluged the President with telegrams, letters, and petitions urging application of the Neutrality law to Franco's foreign backers.

On June 29 Roosevelt responded to these demands by meeting with Norman Thomas, the head of the American Socialist Party, who had just returned from Spain. Thomas gave him a copy of a recently completed Loyalist White Paper describing Italo-German intervention against the Republic and urged him, for reasons of "moral principle" alone, to apply the arms embargo to Germany and Italy. It was grossly unfair, Thomas explained, to deny arms to Loyalist Spain at the same time the nations "doing the real fighting for Fascism" were under no such ban. Roosevelt replied that if German and Italian military efforts were "clearly declared or acknowledged or proved beyond shadow of doubt," the Neutrality law would compel him to act. "After listening to me, rather evasively and then changing the subject," Thomas recalled, "he suddenly said what a great man Cardinal Mundelein [of Chicago] was." Roosevelt, one may conclude, was telling Thomas that he also had to contend with prominent New Deal Catholic supporters who opposed any move to align the United States with the Loyalist regime. Seeing Franco as another George Washington fighting to save Spanish democracy from Communism and anarchism, the American Catholic hierarchy vocally defended his "nationalist" rebellion and opposed any alteration in the administration's neutrality policy.[33]

Though Roosevelt was sensitive to Catholic opinion, he was nevertheless ready in June 1937 to extend the arms embargo to Berlin and Rome. On the same day he saw Thomas, he wrote Hull that, if Mussolini or the Italian government or Hitler or the German government made any official admissions or statements about fighting in Spain, "then . . . we shall have to act under the Neutrality Act. . . . I do not think we can compound a ridiculous situation if after the fight is established, Great Britain and France continue to assert solemnly that they 'have no proof' of Italian or German participation in the Spanish War. Don't you think we should cable Phillips and Dodd to ask for categorical answers?" Roosevelt asked. "According to some of the newspapers," he added, "Mussolini has personally directed participation by the regular Italian armed forces—and Hitler has also made the same kind of statement." Roosevelt asked Hull to check all this and telephone him at Hyde Park.

The response from abroad persuaded Roosevelt not to act. In answer to an inquiry from Hull, Ambassador Bingham in London reported Eden as convinced that a Franco victory would not jeopardize British interests in the Iberian peninsula: Franco's "whole purpose was an Iberian policy . . . with Spaniards in control in Spain and all German and Italian influence eliminated," the Foreign Minister said. Moreover, Eden declared that a state of war between Spain and any foreign nation "cannot be considered" to exist "as long as the Non-Intervention Committee continues to function," and that an extension of the American embargo would "complicate his task." In Bingham's opinion, any application of the Neutrality law to Germany and Italy would likely require that the United States extend it to Russia and France as well. He thought this would endanger Britain's ability to confine the conflict to Spain. Phillips likewise advised that U.S. recognition of a state of war between Italy and Spain "might force other countries to do the very things which . . . they have been united in their efforts to avoid, namely, to spread the conflict beyond the Spanish frontier." When Hull telephoned this information to Roosevelt on July 6, the President "readily agreed" to leave American policy unchanged. When confronted by warnings that an extension of the arms embargo might encourage the wider conflict Britain wished to prevent, Roosevelt felt compelled to drop the idea. He and Hull now agreed that an embargo against Berlin and Rome should occur only in response to a general European war.[34] Despite an upsurge of feeling against German and Italian actions in Spain, he subordinated these feelings to British determination to keep the peace, regardless of what happened in Spain. Like London, he was ready to accept a Franco victory rather than risk a wider war. In July 1937, after repeated discussions about how to save world peace, Roosevelt's actions had brought the nations no closer to blocking aggression and war than they had been eighteen months before. Indeed, in the case of Spain, his policies had even encouraged the aggression he so badly wished to prevent.

7

Gestures

IN THE SPRING AND summer of 1937 Roosevelt felt under continuing pressure to cure the "disease" of war. British, French, German, Italian, and Belgian leaders separately urged him to take the initiative for peace. Such proposals came to him all the time, he told the press in July. Since there was nobody abroad who could provide effective leadership, people were looking "for somebody outside of Europe to come forward with a hat and a rabbit in it. Well," he said, ". . . I haven't got a hat and I haven't got a rabbit in it."

Despite his admission, he felt obliged to respond. As during the first months of 1937, he continued to make suggestions, invite conversations, and entertain proposals that might reverse the downward trend. In April he had returned to his idea of eliminating all but defensive weapons, privately asking Berlin if it would have any interest in this plan. In June he had invited Neville Chamberlain, who had become British Prime Minister in May, to come to Washington for conversations which could "prepare the way for a broader move to establish more healthy conditions in the world." In Chamberlain, Roosevelt saw someone who would spare no effort for peace. Considered the "ablest and most forceful" of Baldwin's Ministers, Chamberlain was known for his conviction that he comprehended "the whole field of Europe and indeed the world. . . . His all-pervading hope was to go down to history as the Great Peacemaker; and for this he was prepared to strive continually in the teeth of facts, and face great risks for himself and his country." Shortly after he wrote Chamberlain, Roosevelt played host to Belgian Prime Minister Paul van Zeeland, who had requested the opportunity to talk with him about international problems. Urging van Zeeland "to draw the world's attention to something quite new," he expressed an interest in the Prime Minister's further efforts to promote "those conditions which alone can lead to the establishment of permanent peace."

As another step in this direction, Roosevelt moved to improve relations with Russia, or align her with the democracies against Germany and Japan. Specifically, in January 1937 he had sent Joseph Davies, a wealthy Wilsonian Democrat, to Moscow with orders "to win the confidence of Stalin." To the distress of the Embassy staff, Davies made a systematic effort to be conciliatory by overlooking arbitrary Soviet actions or by putting a better face on everything the Soviets did. As an extension of this policy, in June 1937 Roosevelt abolished the State Department's anti-Soviet Division of Eastern European Affairs.[1]

The outbreak of fresh fighting in China on July 7 added to Roosevelt's sense of urgency about preserving peace. After troop movements in northern China suggested that the incident of July 7 was a movement toward a full-scale Sino-Japanese clash, he endorsed Hull's idea of issuing a fresh public statement in behalf of peace. On July 16, in a declaration much like one made at the Buenos Aires Conference called the Eight Pillars of Peace, Hull announced American concern with major armed conflicts everywhere. "There can be no serious hostilities in the world," he said, "which will not one way or another affect interests or rights or obligations of this country." Declaring it a "duty" to state the government's position toward international problems of concern to the United States, Hull enunciated American support for the peaceful resolution of all world conflicts. When he sent his statement to all the governments of the world with a request for replies, sixty nations, including Germany, Italy, and Japan, promptly endorsed it. Only Portugal took exception to the Secretary's declaration, complaining about "the habit of entrusting the solution of grave external problems to vague formulae."

Roosevelt himself saw Hull's declaration as only a statement of principle needing practical elaboration. To this end, on July 29 he wrote Mussolini, who in the previous three months had given public indications of welcoming a peace effort on Roosevelt's part. Telling the Duce that his recent statements favoring arms control had gratified him, Roosevelt declared himself "confident that you share with me the desire to turn the course of the world toward stabilizing peace. I have often wished that I might talk with you frankly and in person," Roosevelt added, "because from such a meeting great good might come. But we both realize the great difficulties that stand in the way—international difficulties as well as the distances of the Atlantic Ocean and the Mediterranean Sea." In a letter written the day before to Chamberlain, Roosevelt had been less coy. After receiving word from the Prime Minister earlier in the month that he saw discussions with Berlin as preliminary to any visit to the United States, Roosevelt replied that he appreciated Chamberlain's desire to make initial progress along other lines but declared himself eager nevertheless for suggestions as to additional preparatory steps that might expedite his visit.[2]

By August, pressing questions about American policy in the Far East temporarily replaced Roosevelt's concern with finding a general peace plan. By then, Sino-Japanese tensions had erupted into full-scale fighting, which compelled difficult decisions about American troops in China and the application of the Neutrality law. As a consequence of a long-standing policy to protect American nationals, the United States had some 2300 troops in Peiping, Tientsin, and Shanghai, the areas of most intense current fighting. Fearing that the presence of these forces might inadvertently draw America into the conflict, congressional isolationists and well-organized peace groups began demanding their withdrawal.

Though Roosevelt was distressed that American troops had not been removed from northern China before this latest outbreak and considered making an announcement that Americans remaining in Shanghai did so at their own risk, he agreed with Hull that American forces could not be removed now. In addition, on August 17, after Chinese planes mistakenly killed 1700 civilians in Shanghai, including three Americans, and after the Commander of the Asiatic fleet requested additional troops to protect United States citizens, Roosevelt announced the dispatch of 1200 more marines. When giving this information to the press, however, he explained that the presence of American troops was "an inherited situation" and that he hoped to get them completely out of China as fast as he could. Despite the President's statement, six peace societies launched a campaign for withdrawal from China which, according to the *New York Times*, the administration feared would receive wide public support. When an accidental attack on an American cruiser killed one sailor and wounded seventeen others and a Gallup poll showed 44 per cent of a survey on the East Coast favoring withdrawal, Roosevelt told the press that Americans in China were being strongly urged to leave and that those who refused to go would be staying at their own risk. Moreover, at the end of August, when the Navy asked for more ships to help evacuate Americans, the President refused. According to Admiral William Leahy, the Chief of Naval Operations in Washington, the administration saw such additional forces as likely to arouse both American "peace advocates" and the Japanese.[3]

A more significant problem for Roosevelt was whether to apply the Neutrality Act to the undeclared Sino-Japanese war. Because application of the law would principally hurt China, which needed American arms and loans, and would increase the danger to Americans in China by antagonizing the Chinese, Roosevelt was reluctant to act. At the same time, however, he felt pressured by isolationists clamoring for implementation of the law. On August 17, when asked by reporters about applying the law, he explained that he was operating on a day-to-day basis. Three days later, after twenty-four Congressmen had urged him to invoke the law, "he told Hull that he could not postpone action indefinitely." To counter this pressure, Senator Pittman told a nationwide radio audience on August 23 that, until there was a declaration of war or until neutral nations suffered interference with their commerce, the President should not act.[4]

Events during the next three weeks made it increasingly difficult for Roosevelt to hold his ground. At the end of August, when the Japanese announced a blockade of the China coast and it became known that a government-owned vessel was to carry nineteen bombers to China, several peace groups publicly urged application of the Neutrality law. But with other voices in the peace camp supporting Roosevelt's inaction as the surest way to remain "neutral," and the Chinese privately expressing "bitter resentment" over possible use of the law, Roosevelt took a middle ground. On September 14 he announced that government-owned ships would not be allowed to transport munitions to China or Japan, that other ships flying the American flag would conduct such trade at their own risk, and that the question of applying the Neutrality Act would remain open.[5]

At the same time, Roosevelt turned aside British overtures for joint mediation of the conflict. Reluctant to take a step that would antagonize the Japanese and inflame the isolationists, Roosevelt and Hull declared their preference for "cooperation on parallel but independent lines" to "identical representations." However indirect the language, the British got the message: "We can obviously not rely on American cooperation," British Foreign Office leaders agreed in August, "so we must go ahead under our own steam." [6]

Domestic political problems in the summer of 1937 had made Roosevelt particularly reluctant to risk anything in foreign affairs. The Court fight and a failure to break a series of sit-down strikes had seriously eroded his middle-class support. In August the revelation that Alabama Senator Hugo Black, Roosevelt's choice for a Supreme Court seat, had belonged to the Ku Klux Klan joined with a sharp drop in the economy to bring the President's political fortunes to their lowest point. In this context, Hull and Morgenthau opposed a new Roosevelt idea of offering his services to fifty-five nations as a "clearing-house" for peace. They agreed that the plan had little chance of working and that "the President at this time could not risk another failure." When Morgenthau told this to Roosevelt on September 20, the President agreed and said that he had changed his plans. "I now think that it is a matter of longtime education, and I am not going to do anything which would require a definite response or action on the part of anybody." [7]

Instead, Roosevelt accepted a proposal by Hull and Norman Davis that he counter growing isolationist sentiment in the country by making "a speech on international cooperation . . . in a large city where isolation was entrenched." This idea appealed to FDR as a way to avoid a rejection by a foreign nation of a formal proposal; to express American indignation with German, Italian, and Japanese actions publicly; to begin educating the public to the idea that the United States could not isolate itself entirely from external upheavals, or remain secure in a lawless world; and to propose publicly that neutral nations join together in some nonbelligerent fashion to punish aggression, an idea he had been discussing since the latest outbreak of fighting in China.

On July 8 he had broached this idea with Clark Eichelberger of the

League of Nations Association. Telling Eichelberger that he wished to make "a dramatic statement" that would not be "simply another speech," he expressed a desire to lead the American people to accept "the denial of trade to the aggressor," or "a denial of the economic benefits of the more nearly just international society to the nation that would make war." On September 14 he discussed the same scheme with Harold Ickes. He described a proposal to all nations of the world, except possibly Germany, Italy, and Japan, the "three bandit nations," urging that "if any nation should invade the rights or threaten the liberties of any of the other nations, the peace-loving nations would isolate it." They would cut off all trade with the aggressor and deny it raw materials. He also said that he did not intend to apply his plan to "the present situations in Spain and China . . . because what has happened in those countries has happened." He wished his proposal to be strictly "a warning to the nations that are today running amuck." [8]

The central thrust of a speech on October 5, 1937, in Chicago at the end of a western trip embodied this idea. Beginning with the observation that "the present reign of terror and international lawlessness" had "reached a stage where the very foundations of civilization are seriously threatened," he warned Americans that they would also be attacked. To prevent this, "peace-loving nations must make a concerted effort in opposition to those . . . creating a state of international anarchy and instability from which there is no escape through mere isolation or neutrality." He proposed that this opposition take the form of a "quarantine." "The epidemic of world lawlessness," he declared, "is spreading. When an epidemic of physical disease starts to spread, the community approves and joins in a quarantine of the patients in order to protect the health of the community against the spread of the disease. . . . There must be positive endeavors to preserve peace," he added. "America hates war. America hopes for peace. Therefore, America actively engages in the search for peace." [9]

Though some contemporaries and historians have assumed that Roosevelt had something more specific in mind when he spoke of a "quarantine," the evidence suggests otherwise. His talk with Ickes in September showed that he had no desire to propose any international action toward the current situations in Spain and China and that he wished to do no more for the moment than sound a warning. Moreover, as Dorothy Borg has persuasively argued, discussions held with Cardinal Mundelein, the press, and Norman Davis after the speech suggest that Roosevelt "was not trying through his statements at Chicago to prepare the world for the enforcement of a policy of sanctions against Japan," but rather to give public expression to his long-standing desire to find some new concept for preserving peace. "His plan does not contemplate either military or naval action against the unjust aggressor nation," Cardinal Mundelein recorded after his talk with FDR, "nor does it involve 'sanctions' as generally understood, but rather a policy of isolation, severance of ordinary communications in a united manner by all the governments in the pact." When reporters pressed Roosevelt on the meaning of his speech and whether he had sanctions in mind, he replied: " 'sanctions' is a terrible word to use. They are out of the window." As for the overall thrust of the speech, he said: "The lead is in the last line, 'America actively engages in the search for peace.' I can't tell you what the methods will be. We are looking for some way to peace." When one correspondent pointed out that foreign papers were describing his speech as "an attitude without a program," Roosevelt declared: "It is an attitude and it does not outline a program but it says we are looking for a program." [10]

Roosevelt's search for a "program" drew him to an idea suggested by Sumner Welles on October 6. In July, Welles had become the Undersecretary, replacing Phillips, who had gone to Italy as Ambassador. Selected by Roosevelt despite Hull's preference for Assistant Secretary R. Walton Moore, Welles had easy access to the President, who found him a more congenial adviser than Hull and allowed him to bypass his superior. Welles argued that the solution of the world's specific political, economic, and security problems required preliminary general agreements, and he therefore proposed that Roosevelt ask other nations to join him in working out "fundamental norms" or "standards of international conduct." Believing the proposal a sensible attack on the drift toward world anarchy, Roosevelt raised the possibility of dramatically presenting Welles's peace plan to the Washington diplomatic corps at a White House meeting on Armistice Day. But when Hull, who believed the scheme "illogical and impossible," protested that "a peace conference" would lull the democracies into a feeling of false tranquility at a time when they needed to arm in self-defense and would lead at best to worthless agreements which the Axis states would repudiate at their convenience, Roosevelt shelved the idea.

Roosevelt's only follow-through on the quarantine speech was an agreement to join other signers of the Nine-Power Treaty of 1922, which affirmed China's independence and integrity, in an attempt to settle the Sino-Japanese dispute. On October 6, when the League Assembly denounced Japan's military actions in China and called for a Nine-Power Conference, the administration publicly endorsed this condemnation of Japan and agreed to participate in the talks. In publicly explaining American attendance at the Conference, Roosevelt said it was "an example of one of the possible paths to follow in our search for means toward peace throughout the whole world." [11]

By proposing a "quarantine" of aggressors and accepting a part in the Nine-Power talks, Roosevelt opened himself to considerable foreign pressure for American leadership against Japan. On October 6 the British proposed that the Conference meet in Washington, and on the 12th Eden asked for an "exact interpretation" of the President's "quarantine" idea and whether he was considering a joint boycott against Japan. A week later London told Washington that a policy of "active assistance to China or of economic pressure on Japan" would probably be the only meaningful action for the Conference to take, and that mutual assurances of military support would have to precede such a course. On the eve of the Conference, which was to meet in Brussels on November 3, Eden announced that "in order to get the full cooperation on an equal basis of the United States government in an international conference, I would travel, not only from Geneva to Brussels, but from Melbourne to Alaska, more particularly in the present state of the international situation."

At the same time, the French were also pressing for American commitments of support. On October 22, when Bullitt inquired whether France had agreed to Japanese demands that war supplies not go to China over the Indochina railway, Paris confirmed this and said that it would not resume shipments unless the Brussels conferees, including particularly the United States, offered to help defend Indochina from a Japanese attack.

Roosevelt resisted this Anglo-French pressure. He had rejected the suggestion that the United States arrange to hold the Conference in Washington, proposing instead that Belgium take the lead. He sent word to Eden that the United States would not allow Britain to push her out front at Brussels and "that the attempt which had been made to pin the United States down to a specific statement as to how far it would go, and precisely what the President meant by his Chicago speech, was objectionable and damaging." Since, in Roosevelt's words, "some of the great powers with territorial interests in the Far East were behaving 'like scared rabbits,' " he believed it unreasonable for them to urge that the United States do what they had refused to undertake. Specifically, during the Conference in November he and Hull repeatedly stated that the League's unwillingness to consider sanctions against Japan made it difficult to understand suggestions that the United States lead the way toward strong measures. "The states of the League," Hull told Davis on November 20, "should really be urging us to assume a share in the responsibility for non-application of sanctions rather than attempting, after their refusal to entertain the idea, to put the burden upon us. When the records show that they turned down sanctions at Geneva and when there is not a syllable of law to authorize our Government to participate in sanctions, it is difficult for us . . . to understand why the question of sanctions is a dominant theme of conversations at Brussels." [12]

Domestic opinion more than League inaction, however, deterred Roosevelt from supporting sanctions. Initially, the response to his quarantine speech encouraged him to think that the public might support strong measures against Japan. Though the address evoked some isolationist criticism, it generally received a warm response. Newspapers, peace groups, and White House mail almost uniformly supported his remarks. By condemning aggression and particularly the indiscriminate bombing of civilians, which the Japanese had committed at Nanking on September 21, 1937, the speech provided a release for widespread anger toward Japan. Its appeal, however, chiefly came from Roosevelt's suggestion that he would "quarantine," "isolate," or overcome aggressors by peaceful means. In approving Roosevelt's speech, the Catholic Association for International Peace declared its support for a "concerted effort . . . to uphold the laws and principles of peace"—an effort, the group explained, which "need not, and in our opinion, must not mean war." Among the leading newspapers in the country that endorsed the idea of a quarantine as promising economic and financial steps against Japan, all agreed that "these actions would not lead to war and that the President must not allow them to lead to war." Joining in this endorsement of Roosevelt's quarantine proposal, the American Federation of Labor called for a boycott of Japanese goods, but at the same time declared its opposition to American involvement "in European or Asiatic wars." [13]

With this initial general approval for his speech, Roosevelt was able to envisage a strong American policy at the Brussels meeting. On October 8, when he discussed the Conference with Hull, Welles, and Davis, he had said that if a determined effort at mediation failed, the United States could not "pack up and come home and drop the matter" but would have to "consider taking further steps." Moreover, though his advisers believed it "doubtful" that "public opinion in the United States would support a policy of coercion," he disagreed. If the Japanese rejected all efforts to end the fighting and "persisted in their determination to dismember and conquer China, public opinion of the world and of the United States," he argued, ". . . would most probably demand that something be done."

Roosevelt held this assumption about public opinion for only a few days. When the administration's endorsement of the League's anti-Japanese resolution and its agreement to join the Nine-Power talks demonstrated that the President had no new method for peacefully opposing aggression, enthusiasm for a "quarantine" or more active policy in the Far East began to wane. At the same time, these actions moved isolationists to become more outspoken in their opposition to a "quarantine." As J. Pierrepont Moffat, the Assistant Secretary of State for Western European Affairs recorded at the time, "the press, after two days of jubilation that somebody should have expressed in clear terms what everybody has been feeling, is growing more critical and is beginning to shy away from any risk, however remote, of involvement." Hearst, Moffat noted on October 10, "is alleged to be about to start a campaign against the idea of 'quarantine' or 'positive concerted action.' Those of us who have lived abroad," he added, "were a unit in pointing out that we could not go on to take sanctions, no matter what their form, without risking retaliation."

Since he lacked a program for effective foreign action without the threat of force or risk of war, a program that would have satisfied supporters and appeased some critics of a "quarantine," Roosevelt continued to feel hemmed in by public opinion. On October 12, when he spoke publicly again about international affairs in a Fireside Chat, he felt compelled to answer criticism of his Chicago speech by reminding the nation "that from 1913 to 1921, I personally was fairly close to world events, and in that period, while I learned much of what to do, I also learned much of what *not* to do." In the following week, when he described the response to the quarantine speech to Colonel House, he complained that "as usual, we have been bombarded by Hearst and others who say that an American search for peace means of necessity, war." Though he also expressed surprise that there was not more criticism, and stated a belief that in time the country could be dislodged from its storm-cellar mentality, he did not think that this could be accomplished now.

Some historians have described Roosevelt's failure to follow his quarantine speech with strong action as stemming from excessive sensitivity to isolationist feeling or a failure to realize that there was a strong body of support in the country for his speech. It was not a failure to assess the public mood accurately which restrained FDR but a realistic appreciation that he lacked the means to satisfy the expectations he had aroused through his speech. Because supporting opinion believed a "quarantine" promised effective action against aggressors without the risk of war, something more than conventional political or military steps was expected. Since this was all he had to offer, Roosevelt realistically concluded that public sentiment remained a powerful bar to meaningful pressure on Japan.[14]

A concern not to arouse American public opinion dominated his final preparations for the Brussels Conference. On October 19, when he gave Norman Davis, who was to head the delegation, final instructions, he asked him to tell the British that "there is such a thing as public opinion in the United States," and that we "cannot afford to be made, in popular opinion at home, a tail to the British kite, as has been charged and is now being charged by the Hearst press and others." Any proposal or action coming from Brussels, he added, would ultimately have to reflect "the substantial unanimous opinion of the overwhelming majority of all nations," including, of course, the United States. On the same day he publicly declared that the United States was going to Brussels without prior commitments and that the aim of the Conference was a *peaceable* solution of the Asian conflict.

During the Conference, which lasted from November 3 to November 24, 1937, Roosevelt countered suggestions for sanctions with pronouncements that American public opinion would not support them. On

November 12, after the State Department sent Davis quotes from the *Baltimore Sun, Washington Post,* and *New York Sun* urging concerted action, Roosevelt observed that these newspapers "do not . . . carry any particular weight as expressions of public opinion. . . . It is," he added, "well to remember newspaper opinion and prophesy" about the election of 1936. Further, after Henry Stimson wrote him on November 15 that the United States had paramount interests in China and should provide international leadership to meet the current crisis there, Roosevelt replied that League inaction in October foreclosed "measures of pressure" and that, while there were some nations ready to follow a strong American lead, neither the country nor the Congress would go along. "You and I will agree with him [Stimson] wholly," FDR told Hull, "but we still have not got the answer." With American opinion still divided between those urging strong *peaceful* steps against Japan and those opposing action of any kind as a threat to peace, Roosevelt remained without a program that could win broad public support.[15]

At the same time, major domestic problems continued to make it particularly difficult for Roosevelt to risk a political fight over foreign affairs. By November 1937 the country was in the midst of an economic slump which wiped out most of the gains made since 1935 and defied Roosevelt's powers to improvise a way out. Worse yet, Roosevelt believed the crisis was the result of a business conspiracy which, inspired by fascist gains elsewhere, might lead to unconstitutional steps to turn him out of the White House. On top of this, a special congressional session beginning on November 16 was to consider "must" legislation stalled during the Court fight, and, as things turned out, all the influence he could muster was not enough to win passage of a single bill. Adding a political struggle for bold action in the Far East to these weighty problems was something he would not do, especially since he continued to feel that an effective democratic system at home remained his best answer to fascism abroad. The strongest Far Eastern policies he would follow in these circumstances were another declaration of Hull's "principles of peace" in Brussels and continued resistance to insistent demands that he invoke the Neutrality law.[16]

Though the end of the Brussels Conference temporarily pushed the Far Eastern crisis into the background, the destruction of the American gunboat *Panay* by Japanese planes on December 12, 1937 revived it. On the day after the attack, Roosevelt sent an indignant message to Tokyo. It expressed deep shock at the indiscriminate bombing of an American vessel, asked that the Emperor be informed of the President's response, indicated that Washington would shortly put all the facts about the incident before Japan, and urged that Tokyo prepare a full expression of regret, a proffer of full compensation, and guarantees against a repetition of any similar attack.

Between December 14 and 17, as it became clear that, in Hull's words, "wild, runaway, half-insane men" had deliberately perpetrated the attack, Roosevelt discussed several plans for punishing and restraining Japan. On the 14th he asked Morgenthau to find out what authority he needed to seize all Japanese assets in the United States as security against payment for damages, and if there were no such authority and he did it anyway, what could be done to him in return. When Morgenthau advised that he could use a 1933 amendment to the Trading with the Enemy Act to move against Japanese assets, Roosevelt told his Cabinet on the 17th that he had the right to impose economic sanctions upon Japan, and specifically to embargo cotton, oil, and other items. He also discussed possible naval action. On the 16th he told British Ambassador Sir Ronald Lindsay that he wanted "a systematic exchange of secret information" between American and British naval representatives and plans for a blockade of Japan which would be instituted after "the next grave outrage." On the following day he told the Cabinet that Britain and the United States could block Japan along a line running from the Aleutians to Singapore, and that this would be a comparatively simple task and would bring Japan to her knees within a year. He also referred to naval staff talks with Britain and indicated that he would shortly ask Congress for a larger naval budget than originally planned.

As with his quarantine idea, though, Roosevelt's talk of action against Japan rested on the assumption that it would prevent rather than risk a war. He saw the Trading with the Enemy Act as a way to answer Japan without armed force. "After all," he told the Cabinet, "if Italy and Japan have developed a technique of fighting without declaring war, why can't we develop a similar one? . . . There is such a thing as using economic sanctions without declaring war," he said, "and . . . I want to get that technique. . . . We don't call them economic sanctions, but call them quarantines. We want to develop a technique which will not lead to war. We want to be as smart as Japan and Italy. We want to do it in a modern way." Similarly, he expressed the belief that a naval blockade would be a way to bring Japan to terms without war, and explained that while he wanted the same result as advocates of military action, he "didn't want to go to war to get it." [17]

Behind Roosevelt's concern with finding a new antiwar technique was a realization that the *Panay* episode had raised American peace sentiment to new heights. Though some newspapers, White House letter-writers, and Congressmen saw the attack as grounds for strong action against Japan, the great majority of concerned Americans asked that the incident not lead to war and that the administration prevent a recurrence by withdrawing American ships from the combat zone. Senator Henry Ashurst of Arizona declared that not a single United States Senator would now vote for war with Japan, while Representative Louis Ludlow of Indiana completed a three-year effort to bring a resolution before the House transferring the war-making power from the Congress to the people. As Roosevelt summed up the country's mood in a letter on December 16, "this nation wants peace." [18]

Because he appreciated how strong the peace feeling in the country was and how conventional and risky in fact his ideas for answering Japan were, he immediately backed away from a boycott or a blockade. When Morgenthau saw him a few hours after the Cabinet meeting on the evening of the 17th, he had already "cooled off" and was "not in as great a hurry" for economic steps against Tokyo. Further, instead of giving additional thought and substance to the blockade idea, he decided simply to send an American naval officer to London for technical discussions, which would apply only if both countries found themselves at war with Japan. On December 25, after the Japanese had apologized, offered to pay all damages, and promised to safeguard the rights and interests of American nationals in China in the future, Roosevelt closed the case.[19]

The end of the *Panay* incident allowed Roosevelt to turn his attention back to Europe and to revive plans for bolstering world peace. On December 21, after the Chamberlain government had begun conciliatory talks with Berlin and Bullitt had advised him that Europe was ready for peace negotiations, Roosevelt wrote Mackenzie King of his desire "to chat" with him again about world affairs. "This year has marked little progress toward the goal of peace," Roosevelt observed, "—and now at its close the Far East gives us mutual concern, in addition to the threats of armed banditry in Europe." He asked King if he were planning a visit to Washington in the next month or two and assured him that "the White House door stands ajar." [20]

Shortly thereafter, Roosevelt decided to adopt a revised version of the Welles plan. In a conversation with Welles on January 11, 1938, he agreed to call diplomatic representatives of all governments to the White House, where he would propose discussions of the essential principles of international conduct and the best means to obtain both reductions in armaments and equality of economic opportunity for all peoples. If the nations agreed to this initial suggestion, Roosevelt planned to invite delegates from nine small countries to work with the United States in formulating recommendations. As stated by Welles, the principal aim of the plan was to "lend support and impetus to the effort of Great Britain . . . to reach . . . a practical understanding with Germany." Such a settlement, Welles believed, would also force Japan into peace with China on terms consistent with the Nine-Power Treaty. Before going ahead, however, Roosevelt wished to assure the backing of the British government. On January 11 he informed Chamberlain of the plan, indicated that the state of American public feeling allowed him this only line of action, and asked for the Prime Minister's "cordial approval and wholehearted support." [21]

At the same time, Roosevelt decided to adopt a slightly firmer stance toward Japan. Despite Tokyo's promise of December 24 to safeguard American rights, the Japanese continued to harass and abuse American and British citizens in China. As a response, London considered announcing "the completion of naval preparations," which was "a step prior to mobilization," and on January 8 the British asked Washington to follow such an action with supporting moves. Two days later Roosevelt sent word that he would follow the completion of British naval preparations with steps to ready the American Fleet for a cruise and would set an earlier date for naval maneuvers than mid-March. On January 13 the administration also made known that several American cruisers would visit Singapore in mid-February for the opening of Britain's new naval base. With public excitement about the Far East quieted by settlement of the *Panay* incident, and with the Ludlow Amendment, after strenuous administration efforts, narrowly defeated in the House, Roosevelt felt free to take these modest steps.[22]

The British response discouraged taking any of these moves. Believing it rash in general to count on help from the United States and foolish in particular to think that Roosevelt's proposals for naval action were sufficient to warrant naval preparations, London informed Washington that it would answer Japanese offenses with only a stiff verbal protest. More significantly, Chamberlain asked Roosevelt to delay his peace initiative until Britain's negotiations with Rome and Berlin had a chance to progress. "My fear is," he said, "that if the President's suggestions are put forward at the present time Germany and Italy may . . . take advantage of them both to delay . . . appeasement" and increase their demands. He also explained that Britain was prepared to recognize Italy's Ethiopian conquest if Mussolini showed himself ready to restore friendly relations.

Chamberlain's reply sorely disappointed FDR. Seeing the Welles plan as a means "to appeal for the support of the American people . . . in a new attempt to maintain peace" and as a way to "show the European dictators that the United States was not so indifferent to their plans for world domination as they had been led to believe," Roosevelt took Chamberlain's rebuff as a sign that he placed no great stock in cooperation with the United States. While it is highly doubtful that Roosevelt's proposal would have had any significant impact on the course of European events, Chamberlain's response, as Eden appreciated at the time, added to American suspicions of British intentions and discouraged Roosevelt from trying to arrest the fascist advance toward war. In his direct reply to Chamberlain on January 17, the President objected to the recognition of Italy's conquest, pointing out that a surrender by Britain of the principle of nonrecognition would encourage Japanese aggression in the Far East and have an adverse effect on public opinion in the United States. Speaking more forcefully to the British Ambassador through Welles, Roosevelt said that recognition would reinforce isolationist feeling in the United

States and injure British-American relations. "It would," Welles said for the President, "rouse a feeling of disquiet; would revive and multiply all fear of pulling the chestnuts out of the fire; and it would be represented as a corrupt bargain completed in Europe at the expense of interests in the Far East in which the United States are intimately concerned." [23]

Though Eden, who placed far greater importance on Anglo-American cooperation than Chamberlain did, persuaded the Prime Minister to reverse himself, it did not have the desired effect. On January 21, despite assurances from Chamberlain that he would welcome the President's initiative and that recognition of the Ethiopian conquest would occur only in the context of a general settlement with Italy, Roosevelt deferred action on his peace plan for a week. Offended by the moral compromise involved in recognizing the fruits of Italian aggression and skeptical of the practical effects of Chamberlain's policy, Roosevelt was reluctant to support it directly by initiating peace talks. From Paris, Bullitt added to these doubts in late January when he advised that French political instability and a likely German move against Austria would make a peace overture on Roosevelt's part seem like "an escape from reality. . . . It would be," Bullitt wrote, "as if in the palmiest days of Al Capone you had summoned a national conference of psychoanalysts to Washington to discuss the psychological causes of crime." In February, Hitler's assumption of supreme military command and Eden's resignation in protest against Chamberlain's Italian policy stirred new crises in Europe. By his action, the forty-one-year-old Foreign Secretary provoked a major Parliamentary debate over whether the appeasement policy or constant yielding to pressure could actually preserve peace. Roosevelt now became even more skeptical about appeasement and decided to shelve his plan.[24]

At the same time, Roosevelt remained eager to show aggressors that the United States was not indifferent to their actions. In late January, as a possible prelude to seizing Japanese-owned property in the United States, he asked Hull to begin making clear to the public that Japanese looting of American property in China was in no way "a necessary result of armed conflict." He also asked for more information about "a large number of Italian aircraft and Italian airmen . . . ordered to Japan," and suggested expressing American concern through a direct inquiry in Rome. In February, during an interview with an American peace delegation, he "spent most of his time . . . denouncing international gangsters," and in March, when Hitler annexed Austria, he immediately suggested a strong response.

Yet at the same time that Roosevelt took his distance from Chamberlain's appeasement policy, he did not wish to stand in its way. As he told Claude Bowers at the beginning of March, it was impossible to guess whether Chamberlain would succeed "in establishing reasonable assurance of peace for two or three years" through "concessions" or whether he would fail and be overthrown for giving too much and receiving too little. More specifically, when the British offered a distinctly passive response to the Anschluss in Austria, Roosevelt refused to jeopardize "certain political appeasements in Europe" by objecting strongly to the German action. Instead, he limited Hull to stating American opposition to anything that endangered world peace, removing Austria from the most-favored-nation list, denying her reciprocal trade advantages, and setting up an international committee to facilitate the migration of "political" refugees from Austria and Germany.[25]

Roosevelt followed the same pattern in dealing with British recognition on April 16, 1938, of Italy's Ethiopian conquest. This step, as Roosevelt had made clear to Chamberlain in January, was highly distasteful to him. On the eve of London's action Roosevelt encouraged Representative Byron Scott of California to introduce a resolution asking the administration to name the countries that had violated treaties with the United States. By including Italy in his response, Roosevelt was able to reiterate American unwillingness to alter its nonrecognition stand on the Ethiopian conquest. At the same time that he advanced this idea against State Department resistance, Roosevelt also succumbed to pressure to endorse London's action. When confronted by a request from Chamberlain and Lord Halifax, Eden's successor as Foreign Secretary, for "some public indication of his approval of the agreement itself and of the principles which have inspired it," Roosevelt, under urging from Welles, agreed to announce that the United States saw the conclusion of this agreement "with sympathetic interest because it is proof of the value of peaceful negotiations." "In one breath," Moffat complained, "we praise the British for getting together with the Italians; in the next breath we imply that the Italians are treaty breakers and unworthy to be dealt with on a footing of equality." However contradictory, this was Roosevelt's way of finding a path between rejecting appeasement and not standing in its way. The net effect, though, was to leave him largely immobilized in foreign affairs.[26]

When powerful domestic constraints also came into play in the winter and spring of 1938, they inhibited Roosevelt from doing anything about Neutrality revision, the most significant foreign-policy issue in those months. In January 1938, when Congress reconvened, a variety of American groups, pointing to the ineffectiveness of the Neutrality laws in meeting the wars in China and Spain, had begun a campaign for more flexible legislation. In response, sympathetic Congressmen and Senators introduced bills to repeal the 1937 measure or to allow discriminatory embargoes against aggressors. Though happy to endorse greater discretion for the President, Roosevelt refused to support total repeal or abandonment of the law's principal provisions. In March, moreover, when he gave his "unofficial blessing" to a congressional drive for revision, and the House Foreign Affairs Committee unanimously refused to act, he made no effort to change its mind. In the midst of a seven-month recession that had forced four million Americans back into unemployment and many into near-starvation, Roosevelt was preoccupied with finding a recovery plan.

At the same time, congressional consideration of a Roosevelt proposal for reorganizing Executive agencies was generating wild charges of dictatorial designs. Playing on fears aroused by the Court-packing plan, political opponents pictured Roosevelt's straightforward request as a sinister move to destroy democracy. "You talk about dictatorship," one Congressman announced during the debate. "Why, Mr. Chairman, it is here right now. The advance guard of totalitarianism has enthroned itself in the Government in Washington." Though the Senate narrowly passed the reorganization bill, the House, with 108 Democrats defecting, defeated it by seven votes, marking a new low for Roosevelt's influence over that body. Beset by seemingly insoluble economic problems and by a suspicious and rebellious Congress, Roosevelt was in a weak position to demand more control over foreign affairs.[27]

In early 1938 demands for repeal of the Spanish arms embargo were even more insistent than pressures for general Neutrality reform. Pointing out that nonintervention was a farce and that the embargo was an unneutral aid to Fascist opponents of Spanish democracy, American supporters of the Republic demanded a return to the traditional policy of trading with an established government during a civil war. Further, when indiscriminate bombing of Barcelona, the Republic's new capital, provoked fresh feelings of moral outrage, and when a string of Fascist victories heightened fears of Republican defeat, calls for repeal of the Spanish arms embargo became a constant din.[28]

Though Roosevelt was sympathetic to the Republic, other considerations persuaded him not to help. In February and March, he thought to bolster Loyalist morale by sending Claude Bowers on periodic trips from the Spanish-French border, where the Embassy had moved, to Barcelona; but constant shelling of the roads persuaded him to drop the idea. At the same time, the domestic conditions restraining him from a push for general Neutrality revision also inhibited him from backing repeal of the Spanish arms embargo. In late March, at the height of his concern with the recession and the reorganization fight, he refused to embark on "a violent political fight" with Catholic and isolationist supporters of the embargo, indicating through Hull that the initiative for repeal would have to come from the Congress. He also remained reluctant to challenge continuing British determination to confine the war to Spain. And judging from his remark to Ickes in September that he would not apply a quarantine to Spain and China, "because what has happened in those countries has happened," he simply did not wish to alter policy on Spain.[29]

During April, therefore, when organized pressure in the country for repeal continued to mount and Congressman Byron Scott introduced a repeal measure, Roosevelt discouraged any action. He considered it unwise and pointless. In mid-April, his first concern was to put a recovery program through the Congress, which he described as essential not only to the country's economic well being but also to its political freedom. "Democracy has disappeared in several other great nations," he explained in a Fireside Chat on April 14, "not because the people of those nations dislike democracy, but because they had grown tired of unemployment and insecurity. . . . Not only our future economic soundness but the very soundness of our democratic institutions," he declared, "depends on the determination of the Government to give employment to idle men." In addition, Roosevelt was eager to see a Fair Labor Standards law enacted, to gain congressional support for an antitrust investigation, and to defeat conservative Democrats in various primaries.

The fact that Franco's forces had cut the Republic in half and the Loyalists seemed on the verge of collapse also confirmed his resistance to doing anything for Spain. It was "too late to do any real good," Roosevelt told Senator Borah. Franco was in "complete control of the seas," and arms shipments to Spain would simply fall into Fascist hands, was his answer to queries about the embargo. Though also acknowledging that arms might reach Spain through France, where out of disgust with "the scandal of 'Non-Intervention'" the government had recently opened the frontier, Roosevelt expressed doubts that this situation would continue. In short, at a time when the recovery program, a wages and hours bill, a probe of American monopolies, and a purge of conservative Democrats came first, he was unwilling to expend his dwindling political capital in a fight which, even if successful, seemed unlikely to have a decisive effect.[30]

In spite of Roosevelt's attitude and Loyalist defeats, or because of the latter, several Senators were now ready to repeal the arms embargo. Believing that the embargo worked unfairly against a "friendly recognized government" and that it was time to end "the policy of coming to heel like a well-trained dog every time England whistles," Senator Nye introduced a repeal resolution in the Senate on May 2. With Roosevelt on a Caribbean cruise until May 9, the burden of defining the administration's position fell to Hull. Though the majority of his advisers wanted him to stand above the growing battle by urging that repeal of the embargo apply to both sides, Hull decided to oppose Nye's resolution: it would allow the Congress to usurp Executive authority, reverse a policy that had kept the country "out of a European mess," and take the lead in a European matter from Britain and France, where he thought it belonged. The United States had "enough to do to look out for more immediate interest and affairs than to be watching opportunities to get into a situation fraught with danger," the Secretary told a press conference on May 6. Yet, in spite of his statement, Hull waited to consult with Roosevelt before preparing a declaration of the administration's view.[31]

When Roosevelt returned to the White House on May 9, he found the repeal issue very much alive. That morning, in fact, Nye confided to a reporter that "the resolution was as good as passed, that it would be reported out of committee 4 to 1," and that a roll-call vote, which many Senators feared on so sensitive an issue, could be blocked. But Nye was too sanguine. Even if the resolution were passed by the Senate, which reports of a possible filibuster made doubtful, it seemed certain to be bottled up in the House. In a meeting with Roosevelt on the 9th, House Democratic leaders expressed fears that repeal "would mean the loss of every Catholic vote next fall," and said they "didn't want it done." Roosevelt agreed. Only a month after his sharp rebuff in the lower chamber over reorganization, Roosevelt would not challenge the House on an issue which Spanish and European conditions seemed to put beyond change anyway. Even if the embargo were raised, he told Ickes on the same day, "Spain would not be in a position to buy arms from us," and the French would not allow munitions across the frontier. Though press reports of new controls along the Spanish-French border were less accurate than Roosevelt's statement suggested, it was clear that London intended to continue the nonintervention policy and would persuade Paris to comply, which it did on June 13.

Roosevelt and Hull reflected this understanding in their public response to Nye's resolution. In a letter to Pittman, which Roosevelt reviewed and approved, Hull declared: "We do not know what lies ahead in the Spanish situation. The original danger still exists. In view of the continued danger of international conflict . . . any proposal which . . . contemplates a reversal of our policy of strict non-interference . . . would offer a real possibility of complications. From the standpoint of the best interests of the United States . . . I would not feel justified in recommending affirmative action on the Resolution." Following the administration's lead, on May 13 the Foreign Relations Committee voted 17 to 1 to table Nye's resolution indefinitely.[32]

As soon as Roosevelt had pushed the Spanish arms question into the background, he confronted a crisis over Czechoslovakia. The problem had been building since the end of March when Hitler began implementing plans to destroy the Czech state. Exploiting the discontent of Czechoslovakia's three and a quarter million Germans, Hitler had ordered Konrad Henlein, their leader, to provoke a crisis by making unacceptable demands upon Prague. In April and May, after Henlein had asked for agreements compromising Czechoslovakia's political integrity and military defense, London and Paris encouraged Hitler's design by urging maximum possible concessions and informing Berlin of their eagerness for a settlement. Chamberlain had "yet to find out that Czechoslovakia was a country and not a disease," Prague's Minister to England acidly remarked. In fact, the Prime Minister publicly acknowledged his ignorance of the country and privately told reporters that Czechoslovakia could not continue to exist in its present form. For the sake of peace, Chamberlain said, the Czechs would have to give Hitler the German fringe of their country.

Prague would not accommodate him. On May 20, after receiving reports of German troop concentrations on its border and after negotiations with Henlein had collapsed, the Czech government mobilized part of its Army. When, in a surprising show of determination, the French and the Russians reaffirmed their obligations to the Czechs, and the British told Berlin that they "could not guarantee that they would not be forced by circumstances to become involved also," Hitler was forced to retreat.

Roosevelt was mute throughout the crisis. Though under pressure from two of his Ambassadors and the French Foreign Minister to encourage a negotiated settlement, he refused to intercede. When it became clear on May 21 that France might fight and then on May 22 that Britain also might fight, Hugh Wilson, Roosevelt's new Ambassador to Germany, proposed representations in Berlin and Prague in behalf of "a peaceful solution." At the same time, Foreign Minister Georges Bonnet, a leader of France's appeasement forces, "implored" Bullitt to have Washington pressure the Czech government to make "concessions to the Sudeten Germans which would satisfy Henlein and Hitler." Simultaneously, Bullitt appealed to Roosevelt to stop a war that would bring about "the slaughter of the entire younger generation of France. . . . and Bolshevism from one end of the Continent to the other. . . . an Asiatic despotism established on fields of dead." Bullitt urged the President to ask England, France, Germany, and Italy to send representatives to The Hague, where they "would probably have to recommend" a Czech plebiscite "to determine the will of the different peoples of that country." Should the Czechs reject the suggestion, Bullitt advised, it would free the French from their "desperate moral dilemma." Though predicting that Roosevelt would be accused of "selling out a small nation in order to produce another Hitler triumph," Bullitt urged him to take this brick on his head for the sake of peace. Roosevelt did not reply to any of these proposals. Reluctant to counsel appeasement or to urge anyone else to fight, he remained a detached observer throughout the crisis.[33]

During the next two and a half months, while he principally devoted himself to campaigning against conservative opponents in Democratic primaries, he continued to watch and worry about European affairs. Reports that Hitler still intended to force his will on Prague, even at the risk of a European war, particularly concerned him. Indeed, having acquiesced in Fascist aggression in Spain, Roosevelt now wished the democracies to take a stand. In mid-August, therefore, when he received news of extensive German military preparations and predictions that Hitler would use the Nuremberg Nazi Party Congress in September to bring matters to a head, Roosevelt and Hull agreed to speak out. In well-publicized speeches on August 16 and 18, they tried to deter Hitler by creating doubts about American intentions in case of war. "We in the Americas," the President told a Canadian audience, "are no longer a far away continent, to which the eddies of controversies beyond the seas could bring no interest or no harm. . . . The vast amount of our resources, the vigor of our commerce and the strength of our men have made us vital factors in world peace whether we choose it or not. . . . I give you assurance," he added, "that the people of the United States will not stand idly if domination of Canadian soil is threatened by any other Empire." Though hoping his speech would have "some small effect in Berlin," Roosevelt had strong doubts. An American President could have made the same remarks fifty years ago, he privately remarked. In fact, the speech made no impression on Hitler, who, according to all accounts, remained determined to settle the Czech issue "in his own way and . . . on his own terms." [34]

By the end of August, Roosevelt was ready to explore other ways of backing Britain and France against Berlin. On the 30th, he asked Morgenthau for a plan by which England and France could deposit gold in the United States for use in purchasing war materials. Such a development, he explained, would have a good psychological effect in Berlin and Rome. On the 31st Morgenthau suggested ways to implement this idea, which delighted Roosevelt and moved him to call Hull into the discussion. "I have hatched a chicken," he told the Secretary on the phone. "Do you want to come over and look at it?" When Hull arrived, Roosevelt explained his plan, emphasized the desirability of showing the German government exactly where American sympathies lay, and expressed a desire to tell the German representative of American intentions to apply countervailing duties if Hitler attacked Prague. "It's a hundred-to-one shot that I will do this if you go into Czechoslovakia," and "I hope you won't force my hand," he wished to say. Hull replied that "there was such a thing as doing too much at this time." These moves, added to their recent speeches and a pending trade treaty with Britain, he told Roosevelt, "are apt to get the American people up on their toes over the European situation."

Hull's reservations together with developments on the following day deterred Roosevelt from any action. Diplomatic reports on September 1 suggested that Chamberlain was talking one way to the French, another way to the Germans, and a third way to Joseph P. Kennedy, the American Ambassador in London. Roosevelt told Hull and Morgenthau that Chamberlain was "slippery," that he was not to be trusted under any circumstances, and that he was up to the usual British game of peace at any price. Worse yet, reports in the morning press of British inquiries about American intentions in case of war suggested to Roosevelt that London was trying to make the United States responsible for whether Britain would fight. "If they went in," Roosevelt observed, it would be "on account of the support they would have gotten from us and, if they did not," it.would be "because we held back." In these circumstances, the three of them agreed that the United States should do nothing for the time being, and that Kennedy should delete from an upcoming speech a statement that there was nothing in the Czech situation "worth shedding blood for." "Who would have thought that the English could take into camp a red-headed Irishman?" Roosevelt said. "The young man needs his wrist slapped rather hard." [35]

During the next two and a half weeks, while the Czech crisis deepened, Roosevelt clearly indicated his sympathy for a strong stand against Berlin. Requests from Bonnet on September 8 and 12 that the President consider arbitrating the dispute and asking Hitler not to use force went unanswered. At the same time, Ambassador Lindsay telegraphed London that opinion in Washington favored "a strong stand against German aggression" and that Germany's brutal diplomacy had "aroused" the President, who told a French visitor, "You may count on us for everything except troops and loans." Since he knew full well that he could not fulfill such a promise, Roosevelt was apparently trying to increase French willingness to resist. On September 16, after Chamberlain flew to Berchtesgaden to discuss a Czech surrender of the Sudetenland to Germany, Roosevelt told his Cabinet that Chamberlain was for peace at any price, that England and France would abandon Czechoslovakia to Hitler's aggression, and that after this international outrage, they will "wash the blood from their Judas Iscariot hands." [36]

Appreciating, however, that Czech resistance to Hitler's demands might force Britain and France into a war in spite of themselves, Roosevelt worked on plans for lending them support. On September 19, after testing out his ideas on Ickes and Morgenthau, he invited Ambassador Lindsay to the White House for a secret talk. Urging Lindsay to understand that disclosure of their discussion would threaten him with impeachment, he offered his view of the crisis and outlined a plan for aiding London and Paris against Berlin. He described the Anglo-French pressure on the Czechs as "the most terrible remorseless sacrifice" ever demanded of a state, and said that while he would be the first to cheer if Chamberlain's policy worked, he regarded this as virtually impossible. The Czechs would not acquiesce in the demands on them, and even if they did, he felt certain that other Nazi demands would follow: "Denmark, the [Polish] Corridor or most likely of all a dangerous and forcible economic or physical penetration through Roumania." Though he suggested the possibility of calling a world conference "for the purpose of reorganizing all unsatisfactory frontiers on rational lines," and though he said he would attend if it were held outside of Europe, this idea "was not strongly emphasized."

He was more concerned to persuade London and Paris to fight a defensive rather than an offensive war. A war fought on classical lines of attack, he said, would end in defeat with "terrific casualties." Having received numerous reports of German military superiority, especially in the air, he calculated chances against a successful British-French attack as 6 to 4. He urged that they follow a defensive strategy instead by closing their own frontiers to Germany, standing on a defensive line, and insisting that other states respect their blockade. If Britain and France based this strategy "on loftiest humanitarian grounds . . . the desire to wage hostilities with minimum of suffering and the least possible loss of life and property," he hoped to persuade Americans to recognize the blockade and even to send arms and munitions if the allies avoided an actual declaration of war. He also thought that "somehow or other" the United States might ultimately be drawn into the conflict.[37]

Events during the following week, however, persuaded Roosevelt that war might be averted. On September 21, 1938, Prague surprised him by succumbing to Anglo-French pressure for cession of the Sudetenland. Though Hitler precipitated another crisis two days later by adding humiliating requirements on how the transfer should take place, Roosevelt now felt that the "agreement in principle" between Berlin and Prague made a war over "method and detail" both unnecessary and unjustifiable. Moreover, since the British had given no indication that they would follow his suggestion for a defensive war, and since his latest information confirmed that "neither England nor France is anywhere ready to fight Germany," he decided to make a public appeal for peace.

At 1:13 a.m. on September 26, with the European Powers in various stages of mobilization, Roosevelt asked Prague, Berlin, London, and Paris to continue their negotiations. "The fabric of peace . . . is in immediate danger," he declared. "The consequences of its rupture are incalculable. Should hostilities break out the lives of millions of men, women and children in every country involved will most certainly be lost under circumstances of unspeakable horror. The economic system of every country involved may well be completely wrecked. . . . On behalf of the United States of America and for the sake of humanity everywhere," he announced, "I most earnestly appeal to you not to break off negotiations looking to a peaceful, fair, and constructive settlement of the questions at issue." To avoid "untoward domestic effects," he omitted a tender of good offices and included a statement that "the United States has no political entanglements." [38]

On the 27th, after Hitler showed himself unyielding in a reply to the President and in a speech of unsurpassed invective, Roosevelt made a last-ditch effort for peace. That afternoon he appealed personally to Mussolini to help bring about a negotiated settlement, and approved a request to other Heads of State to make similar appeals to Berlin and Prague. After intensive discussions with his advisers, and after hearing Chamberlain on the radio express disbelief that a quarrel that was so remote from Britain and already settled in principle should have his countrymen digging trenches and trying on gas masks, Roosevelt made an additional appeal to Hitler. Smoking incessantly, shooting questions at Hull, Welles, and Assistant Secretary of State Adolf A. Berle, Jr., who sat nervously near his littered desk, Roosevelt prepared a telegram that again asked Hitler to continue negotiations until a peaceful solution was found. He suggested that the Fuehrer consider widening the scope of the current talks into "a conference of all the nations directly interested in the present controversy." Such a meeting, he explained, could take place at once in some neutral spot in Europe and could deal with both the Czech crisis and "correlated questions." To guard once more against isolationist criticism, Roosevelt also stated his unwillingness to pass upon the merits of the controversy or to assume any obligations in the negotiations. When Hitler reversed course on the following day by inviting Britain, France, and Italy to a Munich conference, and Chamberlain immediately accepted, Roosevelt wired the British Prime Minister: "Good man." [39]

The Munich conference between Chamberlain, Daladier, Hitler, and Mussolini, and excluding the Czechs and the Russians, began at 12:45 p.m. on September 29, 1938. Dominated by Mussolini, who was the only one of the four who could speak the others' languages, the conference proceeded in a disjointed fashion, constantly breaking down into individual arguments or conversations which were made more cumbersome by the difficulties of translation. These exchanges lasted until 2 a.m. the following morning when the participants reached agreement on the details of transferring the Sudetenland to Germany and the destruction of Czechoslovakia's fortifications. In a separate meeting with Hitler later that morning, Chamberlain persuaded the Fuehrer to sign a declaration stating the mutual "desire of our two peoples never to go to war with one another again." "I believe," Chamberlain announced, waving the joint declaration on his return home, "that it is peace for our time."

Though Roosevelt, his advisers, and Americans generally believed that the President had influenced Hitler's action, his appeals were of little consequence. Indications to Hitler that Britain and France would largely concede to his final demands and pressure from Mussolini were far more important in persuading him to make his Czech conquest by negotiation rather than force. To be sure, Roosevelt had also pressed Mussolini to encourage negotiations, but whether this had more than a marginal impact alongside of other considerations is doubtful. In short, Hitler and Mussolini probably viewed Roosevelt's appeals as gestures by a powerless man. [40]

In the fall of 1938, Roosevelt felt himself almost equally powerless to aid Germany's 500,000 persecuted Jews. In the five years after 1933, during which 30 per cent of this group became refugees, the National Origins

Act of 1924 had allowed only a handful to enter the United States. Fearful of adding to the country's swollen unemployment rolls, American officials interpreted the immigration statutes so narrowly that almost three-fourths of the German quota went unfilled. With little counter pressure from American Jews and only occasional broad injunctions from the President to give refugees "the most humane treatment possible under the law," consular officials continued to apply a strict interpretation of the rules. The State Department, Congressman Emanuel Celler had complained in February 1938, had a "heartbeat muffled in protocol." [41]

In March 1938, when the Nazis started expelling Austria's 190,000 Jews after the *Anschluss*, Roosevelt had confronted the refugee crisis. To keep the door open to Austrian immigrants, whose access to the United States would be complicated by the disappearance of their country, Roosevelt combined the German and Austrian quotas. More important, he ensured a full use of the quotas, allowing a little over 27,000 German and Austrian refugees to reach the United States in 1939.

At the same time, Roosevelt invited thirty-two governments to join the United States in setting up a committee to facilate the emigration of refugees from Nazism. With public and congressional opinion apparently opposed to revision of the immigration law, however, he declared that "no country would be expected or asked to receive a greater number of emigrants than is permitted by existing legislation." Furthermore, the conference, which met for nine days in July at Evian-les-Bains, France, proved, in the words of one observer, to be "a façade behind which the civilized governments could hide their inability to act." The British refused to discuss Palestine, or a Zionist solution to the problem, and hopes that Central and South America might become a haven were "drowned in a sea of Latin eloquence." Evian, New Zealand's delegate declared, would become a "modern wailing wall." Though the conference established an Intergovernmental Committee to deal with the refugee crisis on a continuing basis, the new committee quickly found itself powerless to act. With none of the participants willing to offer their homelands as resettlement areas, most committee members saw no point in opening negotiations with Berlin. In early October, for example, an appeal from Roosevelt to Chamberlain for pressure on Hitler in behalf of "orderly emigration" arranged by the committee brought a rebuff. The avenue of appeal, Chamberlain replied, should be through their respective Ambassadors in Berlin. [42]

Events in the following month further tested Roosevelt's ability and willingness to help German and Austrian Jews. During the second week of November, after a Polish Jewish refugee assassinated a German Embassy official in Paris, the Nazis assaulted Jews, looted their property, burned their synagogues, and deprived them of such ordinary civil liberties as attending schools and driving a car. "I myself could scarcely believe that such things could occur in a twentieth-century civilization," Roosevelt told the press. He also announced the recall of Ambassador Hugh Wilson from Berlin and his determination to allow some 15,000 German and Austrian refugees on visitors' permits to remain in the United States for as long as possible. "It would be a cruel and inhuman thing to compel them to leave here" for Germany, the President said.

Roosevelt was unwilling to go beyond these steps. In the months between March and December 1938, sentiment against relaxing immigration laws increased both at home and abroad: mass opinion in the United States against easing restrictions rose from 75 to 83 per cent, while new immigration barriers went up all over Latin America. Opposition in the American Congress to changing the immigration law seemed insurmountable; even a sympathetic spokesman for the Jews like Senator Elbert Thomas of Utah opposed revision. Yet for all this, it is difficult to escape the feeling that a sustained call by FDR for allowing Nazi victims to come to the United States in greater numbers might have mobilized the country's more humane instincts. It was something that surely must have occurred to Roosevelt. But his failure to act upon it suggests that the Jewish dilemma did not command a very high priority in his mind. In the refugee crisis, then, as with other problems in 1937–38, Roosevelt allowed domestic and international constraints to limit him to a series of small gestures.[43]

PART THREE

The Politics of Foreign Policy, 1939-1941

8

Limited Influence

IN THE DAYS AND weeks after Munich, Roosevelt joined the "mass of mankind" in a "universal sense of relief" that peace had been preserved. Overjoyed that they had been spared the "abomination" of another total war, people everywhere showered Chamberlain with expressions of approval: letters, flowers, poems, umbrellas, and fishing rods "rained in on Downing Street"; the Dutch sent tulips; the Belgians struck a medal to the "apostle of peace"; someone requested "a piece of his umbrella to make a relic in a Greek icon"; and city councils across Britain named streets in his honor. "We in the United States," Roosevelt wrote Mackenzie King in Canada, "rejoice with you, and the world at large, that the outbreak of war was averted."

Though Roosevelt also had hopes that Munich might bring "a new order based on justice and law," he invested little faith in the idea. He principally saw Munich as an interlude between threats in which the democracies must rearm. Others shared his belief. Hitler was bent on world domination and would not be satisfied with his Czech gains, Assistant Secretary of State George Messersmith told FDR. Premier Edouard Daladier, Bullitt reported from Paris, anticipated new German demands within six months and intended now, above all, to build French military strength, especially in the air. "Daladier . . . realizes fully that the meeting in Munich was an immense diplomatic defeat for France and England and recognizes that unless France can recover a united national spirit . . . a fatal situation will arise within the next year." "Do not suppose that this is the end," Winston Churchill warned in England. "This is only the beginning of the reckoning. This is only the first sip, the first foretaste of a bitter cup which will be proffered to us year by year unless, by a supreme recovery of moral health and martial vigor, we arise again and take our stand for freedom as in the olden time."

On October 9, 1938, Hitler gave added substance to these fears. He announced increases in Germany's western fortifications to prepare for the possibility that British critics of Munich, such as Churchill and Eden, might come to power. Roosevelt responded two days later with the announcement that he would spend an additional $300 million for national defense.[1]

To deter Hitler, Roosevelt believed that he had to strengthen American, British, and French air power. Reports of Germany's vast air superiority had been troubling him for almost a year. German aviation could fly over France "with impunity," and Paris did not have a single plane that could worry Berlin, a French visitor had told FDR in January 1938. France's air force, Bullitt advised him in early October, included only seventeen modern planes and was but 10 per cent the size of the German air fleet. The Germans "would be able to bomb Paris at will," and the destruction "would pass all imagination." Declaring that possibly "the whole future of freedom in the world" was at stake, Bullitt urged the President to do all in his power to help build France's air arm.

Roosevelt wished to do this and more. On October 14 he told the press that he would probably ask Congress for an additional $500 million in defense funds. On the same day, he asked Assistant Secretary of War Louis Johnson to plan a substantial expansion of America's air force and approved a French mission to the United States to discuss purchases of American planes and the construction of aircraft assembly plants in Canada. During the next two weeks, he discussed expanding annual aircraft production from 2600 to 15,000, assembling 5000 planes a year for France in Canadian factories, where the Neutrality law would not apply in wartime, and having Chamberlain announce that "Great Britain, in the event of war, could rely upon obtaining raw materials from the democracies of the world." [2]

Roosevelt's plans at once ran into a storm of criticism from civilian and military advisers. Though "tickled to death the President is thinking of making this country so strong that nobody can attack us," Morgenthau objected to French plane purchases and reliance on Canadian factories. It would deplete France's foreign exchange and make her dependent on an unreliable source of wartime supply. The French would do better to build planes at home. At the same time, American military chiefs opposed Roosevelt's plans for expanding the air force. "What are we going to do with fifteen thousand planes?" Army Chief of Staff General Malin Craig asked. "Who [are] you going to fight, what [are] you going to do with them, with three thousand miles of ocean?" To Craig and General George C. Marshall, his Deputy Chief of Staff, the need was not simply for combat planes but for a balanced increase in all American forces, ground as well as air.

Roosevelt disagreed. On November 14, in a full-scale discussion of the issue with his civilian and military defense chiefs, he reiterated his desire for a huge air buildup. "A well-rounded ground army of even 400,000 could not be considered a deterrent for any foreign power whereas a heavy striking force of aircraft would." Germany and Italy, he said, had almost 10,000 modern planes and an annual productive capacity of 14,000 more. This was some three times the number held by Britain and France and

5600 above their current annual production. Roosevelt wanted an American air force of 10,000 planes and an ability to produce 20,000 more a year. Basing his estimates on information coming to him from Britain and France, Roosevelt held an exaggerated picture of German air strength. In fact, the British and the French air forces closely approximated those held by Berlin, and Anglo-French plane production also compared favorably with that of Berlin. The real difference was not in material strength but in German willingness and ability to use it. More reluctant to fight a war than Germany, British, French, and American leaders unwittingly expressed this difference by exaggerating Germany's physical capacity to fight.

Roosevelt described the reemergence of German power at Munich as of major consequence to the United States. For the first time since the Holy Alliance of 1818, the country "faced the possibility of an attack on the Atlantic side in both the Northern and Southern Hemispheres. . . . This," he said, "demanded our providing immediately a huge airforce so that we do not need . . . a huge army to follow that airforce. . . . sending a large army abroad was undesirable and politically out of the question. . . . 'I am not sure now that I am proud of what I wrote to Hitler in urging that he sit down around the table and make peace,' " he added. " 'That may have saved many, many lives now, but that may ultimately result in the loss of many times that number of lives later. . . . Had we had this summer 5000 planes and the capacity immediately to produce 10,000 per year . . . Hitler would not have dared to take the stand he did.' " As participants in this conference understood, Roosevelt was less interested in creating a balanced force of planes, crews, maintenance units, and ground troops than in producing airplanes which in American, British, or French hands would intimidate Berlin.

Despite his own wishes, Roosevelt felt compelled to accept a balanced force. At another White House meeting with military chiefs in the second half of December, Roosevelt complained that the services were offering him everything except planes. When his advisers predicted that his 10,000-plane air force would become obsolete before it could be used, he answered that if the Air Corps could not use the planes, the British could. But he could not "influence Hitler with barracks, runways and schools for mechanics." The Chiefs of Staff, however, remained unconvinced and finally persuaded Roosevelt "of the futility of producing planes . . . without producing trained pilots and crews and air bases at an appropriate pace." By the close of the meeting, Roosevelt agreed to use $320 million of the additional $500 million defense appropriation for non-air armament and "non-plane air items." While the remaining $180 million was earmarked for 3000 planes "to impress Germany," Roosevelt agreed in the following month to divide this number almost evenly between combat planes and trainers. Under the weight of the military's argument that aircraft alone would not impress foreign leaders and that sound national defense required a well-integrated, balanced force, Roosevelt substantially altered his plans for a huge air force to back Britain and France.[3]

Conditions beyond FDR's control also blocked a French order for a thousand American planes by July 1939. When the French mission put this proposition before the American government in mid-December, Roosevelt at once approved and put Morgenthau in charge of the negotiations. A firm commitment of $65 million made Morgenthau into an enthusiastic supporter. But American military chiefs opposed the sale of America's most advanced planes as likely to divulge valuable secrets and slow the growth of American air power. These considerations also gave Roosevelt pause. But Morgenthau persuaded him to release the planes: if you want England and France "to be our first line of defense," Morgenthau said, "let's either give them good stuff or tell them to go home, but don't give them some stuff which the minute it goes up in the air it will be shot down."

Production problems compelled a reduction in the French order. It was clear in January 1939 that American manufacturers could not fill the request before the end of the year and that the P-40, the latest American fighter, would not be available until May 1940. As a consequence, the French dropped the P-40 from their shopping list and asked delivery of only 555 planes between May and October 1939. "The President of the United States says that we consider the Maginot Line our first line of defense and for that reason he wants these people to have this thing. . . . I think he's right and the more I hear about airplane manufacturers, the more I think there is something wrong somewhere," Morgenthau complained.

At the same time, the Air Corps continued to put obstacles in the path of the French, refusing to show them the Douglas DB-7 attack bomber, as Roosevelt had ordered. Expressing "astonishment that his order had been incompletely followed," Roosevelt reviewed the issue with Treasury, War, and Navy department officials on January 16. He emphatically rejected a warning from Secretary of War Henry Woodring that release of the Douglas bomber "might put the President in an embarrassing position" and left no doubt that he wished an all-out effort "to expedite the procurement of any types of plane desired by the French Government."

Though the Air Corps now complied with the President's directive, chance intervened to raise yet another obstacle to French plane purchases. On January 23 the French air mission came under public scrutiny when a Douglas bomber crashed in California, killing the test pilot and injuring a French observer. Newspapers at once questioned the presence of a French air force captain on an American test plane, and the Senate Military Affairs Committee began hearings on the French negotiations. Though isolationist Senators attacked the administration for giving away military secrets and involving the United States in European affairs, Roosevelt publicly defended the purchases as good business and told Morgenthau "to go right ahead with the French . . . and let them buy what they want." Since Roosevelt had full authority to encourage these sales, he shortly completed the deal. Production problems, however, slowed deliveries, and at the outbreak of war in September 1939, the French had fewer than 200 of the planes ready for combat. The chief beneficiary of this deal, as Roosevelt foresaw, was the United States. The French orders laid the groundwork for the rapid expansion of America's aircraft industry at a later date.[4]

At the same time that Roosevelt struggled with means of expanding American and French military power to deter Berlin, he was also seeking ways to meet a growing Fascist threat to the Western Hemisphere. By 1938 the German and Italian governments had carried out effective programs of political, military and economic penetration of Latin America: they had organized Fascist and Nazi parties, established propaganda organs, dispatched military missions, underwritten arms sales, gained control of commercial airlines, and expanded trade through barter deals detrimental to the United States. In May 1938 the Integralist Party of Brazil, a group inspired by Nazi and Fascist ideas, staged an unsuccessful coup against the Vargas regime.

In addition to these dangers of internal subversion, the danger of external attack greatly worried Roosevelt and his military advisers. Since Germany supposedly had 2000 planes with a 3300-mile range, or an ability to reach the Americas from the west coast of Africa, Roosevelt declared that "the United States must be prepared to resist attack on the western hemisphere from the North Pole to the South Pole, including all of North America and South America." "As a result of world events in the last few years, and as a result of scientific advancement in waging war," he had told a press conference in November, "the whole orientation of this country in relation to the continent on which we live—in other words from Canada to Tierra del Fuego— . . . has had to be changed . . . Any possible attack," he added, "has been brought infinitely closer than it was five years or 20 years or 50 years ago." [5]

Roosevelt's first line of defense against Fascism in the Hemisphere was the continuation of the Good Neighbor Policy. But during 1938 relations with Mexico threatened to undermine the whole idea. On March 18, after foreign-owned oil companies had defied a ruling of Mexico's Supreme Court in a long-standing labor dispute, President Cárdenas had announced the expropriation of the $400-million oil industry. "This Mexican situation will test our Good Neighbor policy," Ambassador Josephus Daniels advised FDR. "The upholding of that policy, however, is of the highest consideration in a mad world where Pan American solidarity may save democracy. Oil ought not to smear it."

Roosevelt was more sensitive to this injunction than the State Department. Fearful that a passive response to Mexico's action would encourage Colombian and Venezuelan expropriations of American oil holdings and hopeful that vigorous opposition might persuade President Cárdenas to reverse his decision, the Department at once dispatched a strong verbal protest, prodded Morgenthau into suspending monthly silver purchases, and instructed Daniels to return to the United States for consultation. With the cooperation of Roosevelt, however, Daniels and Morgenthau blunted this pressure by the Department. "We are having lots of trouble in Mexico, and you know the President and Daniels have given the Mexicans the impression that they can go right ahead and flaunt everything in our face," Hull complained to Morgenthau in July. "I have to deal with these communists down there, I have to carry out international law." By softening the Department's protest, making ad hoc silver purchases, and leaving no doubt that the United States opposed a right-wing uprising against Cárdenas in May, Daniels, Morgenthau, and Roosevelt prevented an open break with Mexico and a severe setback to the Good Neighbor Policy.[6]

At the same time, Roosevelt warmly encouraged the development of closer military contacts with Latin America and planning for Hemisphere defense. In April 1938 he had "heartily" approved the establishment of a Standing Liaison Committee consisting of the Undersecretary of State, the Army Chief of Staff, and the Chief of Naval Operations. The committee concerned itself principally with strengthening military missions, establishing United States or local control over commercial airlines, and supplying arms to defense establishments in Latin America, and in general helped lay the foundations for later military cooperation with the southern Republics. More significantly, Roosevelt inspired a shift in American military planning from national to Hemisphere defense. In November the Joint Army and Navy Board began considering "various practicable courses of action . . . in the event of . . . violation of the Monroe Doctrine by one or more of the Fascist powers." The five Rainbow Plans of 1939 developed by the Board marked an "epochal advance" over the old idea of preparing strictly for an attack on United States territory by individual nations; they aimed principally to defend the Western Hemisphere against attack from the Old World.[7]

Though recognizing that the United States might have to defend the Hemisphere alone, Roosevelt and Hull were eager to enlist the support of the twenty Latin states. To this end, they sought a formal commitment from the other American Republics "to resist any threat, either direct or indirect, to their peace, safety, or territorial integrity on the part of any non-American country." Using the eighth Pan-American Conference in Lima in December 1938 as the occasion for making this proposal, Hull, as at the Buenos Aires meeting of 1936, ran into opposition from Argentina. Reluctant to sacrifice ties to Europe for exclusive reliance on the United States, Argentina's delegation tried to substitute a "weak," "general" declaration of American solidarity for Hull's strong, binding convention.

For Hull, the ten days at the Conference were "among the most difficult of my career." Meeting "a stone wall of Argentine reluctance to agree to anything that meant anything," he "buttonholed" delegates, engaged in animated, night-long debates, and successfully appealed to Argentina's President Roberto Ortiz over the heads of his delegation and Foreign Minister for a compromise agreement. Settling for a non-binding declaration, which included the provision that "the American Republics will act independently in their individual capacity," Hull won unanimous agreement to defend the principles of American continental solidarity against all foreign threats: should the peace, security, or territorial integrity of any American Republic be threatened, the Conference announced, the American states would share a "common concern" and would "make effective their solidarity."

Though falling short of what Roosevelt and Hull wished, the Declaration of Lima was the first instance in which the American Republics demonstrated a willingness to act as a unit in dealing with the rest of the world. The Declaration, Roosevelt observed, makes "it plain to the world at large that all of the twenty-one American nations are animated by the common desire . . . to assure the security of their independence, their democratic institutions, and their legitimate interests." Morgenthau's Treasury Department reached a more modest conclusion: the Conference "indicated to the totalitarian powers that aggression in Latin America would meet more resistance than it has in the past." [8]

Roosevelt now also considered ways of blocking a Fascist victory in Spain. After Hitler's victory at Munich, Roosevelt was much more reluctant to see Spain's Republic become a Fascist regime. By September 1938, after Loyalist armies had halted Franco's spring offensive and made a successful attack across the Ebro, British and French leaders concluded that neither side could subjugate the other and that a mediated settlement was a reasonable goal. Roosevelt had taken up the idea on October 31, proposing to Assistant Secretary of State Adolf Berle that the Vatican ask him to name a three-man commission to govern Spain for a period of months, or until he could arrange to bring back a Spanish government. "He jokingly suggested that he might appoint someone like me," Berle recorded. "I stipulated for a battleship to bring home our corpses after the inevitable assassination." After another conversation with the President on November 7, Berle inquired in New York "as to whether the Catholic Church would ask the President to try to compose the Spanish Civil War" and went to work on getting the Lima Conference to propose an armistice. "I think that Loyalist Spain would accept";

Berle advised FDR, "there is a possibility that Franco might, but that if he did not, the knowledge that he had declined would liberate political forces which might force peace within a few months. Further, if he did refuse it would clear the way for changing our position in the matter of the Spanish embargo." Though Hull raised the suggestion in Lima, divisions among the Latin Americans killed the idea.

Roosevelt also tried to keep the Republic from succumbing to starvation in the winter of 1938–39, when the whole population of the Republic was living on minimum rations. "In Madrid, over half a million persons existed . . . on a daily issue of two ounces of lentils, beans or rice, and an occasional ration of sugar or salt cod." The problem in Barcelona was "truly appalling," where relief funds were inadequate to feed one-third of 600,000 refugee children one meal a day. By appointing a Committee for Impartial Civilian Relief in Spain, which was to work with the American Red Cross and the American Friends Service Committee, Roosevelt hoped to send wheat held by the Federal Surplus Commodities Corporation. Since the bulk of this aid would go to Republican Spain, or, in the words of two newspaper columnists, "to keep the Loyalists alive and fighting during the winter," Catholic leaders opposed committee efforts to raise funds. "Apparently pressure from radical Catholics has about driven [George] MacDonald [the committee's chairman] crazy, and he, in turn, is about to make the Friends crazy," Norman Davis wrote FDR. Though hoping to gather $500,000 to meet the cost of wheat shipments, the committee was able to raise only $50,000.[9]

Roosevelt's only other means of helping the Republic was through repeal of the Spanish arms embargo. In November he considered recommending that Congress lift the embargo when it reconvened in January, and he asked the State Department and the Attorney General to advise him on whether he could do it on his own. Since he had applied the embargo under the provisions of the general Neutrality law of May 1, 1937, which allowed Executive discretion in applying arms embargoes to civil wars, and since some lawyers believed that the May law cancelled out the mandatory January 1937 resolution, it was conceivable that Roosevelt himself could end the embargo by simply declaring the civil war over and withdrawing his proclamation. Hull, Welles, and State Department lawyers viewed this proposition as "entirely without foundation." Though members of the Attorney General's staff found merit in the contention that the second statute cancelled the first, they acknowledged that the State Department had a "strong argument." Moreover, they pointed out that a presidential announcement declaring the civil war over would elicit complaints that this was patently false. Finally, they predicted that such action by the President would push the Congress into a debate on whether to reenact the January resolution. Though the Attorney General was ready to endorse the idea that the January statute now lacked force, his supporting brief was enough to dissuade Roosevelt from taking this course.[10]

Direct repeal of the congressional restraints on arms shipments abroad impressed Roosevelt as a much more satisfactory way to extend aid to the Republic and deter aggressors. On December 15 he conferred with Senator Pittman about changing the Neutrality laws and tried to persuade him to take the lead. But with Pittman unwilling to do anything until he had talked to other members of the Foreign Relations Committee and with Franco launching an offensive on December 23 which seemed likely to overwhelm the Republic, Roosevelt decided to take the initiative.

In his State of the Union Message on January 4, 1939, he warned of the increasing threat to peace, the need for additional weapons of defense, and the dangers to democracies from indifference to international lawlessness anywhere. Democracies "cannot forever let pass, without effective protest, acts of aggression against sister nations—acts which automatically undermine all of us," he declared. ". . . The mere fact that we rightly decline to intervene with arms to prevent acts of aggression does not mean that we must act as if there were no aggression at all. Words may be futile, but war is not the only means of commanding a decent respect for the opinions of mankind. There are many methods short of war," Roosevelt explained, "but stronger and more effective than mere words, of bringing home to aggressor governments the aggregate sentiments of our own people. At the very least," he recommended, "we can and should avoid any action, or any lack of action, which will encourage, assist or build up an aggressor. We have learned that when we deliberately try to legislate neutrality, our neutrality laws may operate unevenly and unfairly—may actually give aid to an aggressor and deny it to the victim. The instinct of self-preservation should warn us that we ought not to let that happen anymore." [11]

The Congress remained unreceptive to this advice. A week after Roosevelt's speech, Pittman informed him that he would shortly begin hearings on the several Neutrality bills introduced in the Senate, and that any immediate attempt on his or the President's part to push a specific measure would bring a "united attack" from "those holding divergent views." Pittman proposed instead that he take the part of a mediator, airing all the different Neutrality plans in committee hearings and then proposing a compromise bill.

Pittman's Foreign Relations Committee would not go even that far. In January decisive Fascist victories sparked renewed demands in the United States for aid to the Republic. Provoking counteractions, Loyalist and rebel supporters bombarded the Congress and the President with thousands of letters, telegrams, and petitions containing millions of signatures. On January 19, in response to these cross-pressures, the Foreign Relations Committee suspended consideration of Neutrality and Spanish embargo legislation for the time being. "The conflicting avalanche of telegrams from both sides," Pittman told Assistant Secretary of State Moffat, "had convinced individual Senators that they were on too hot a spot to sit with ease and that the sooner they could get off it by avoiding the issue the happier they would be."

Roosevelt saw no way to compel congressional action. His hold over the Congress was weaker than ever. Republican gains in the 1938 congressional elections had strengthened the coalition of Republicans and conservative Democrats which had blocked his demands before November. The likelihood that he would not run again in 1940 had further diminished his ability to overawe opponents or even hold the backing of supporters. Though he still had enough influence to prevent conservatives from dismantling the New Deal, he could not steer any major legislation through the Congress. Specifically, the fear of jeopardizing chances for revision of the general Neutrality law and the belief that American arms would either not reach the Loyalists or get there too late to do any good decided Roosevelt not to press the committee. Nor would he respond to public pressure to repeal the embargo on his own. Such action would rest on dubious legal grounds, seemed certain to antagonize the Congress, and offered no solution to the problem of getting munitions into Loyalist hands.

For what solace it gave to opponents of the embargo, Roosevelt now acknowledged that it "had been a grave mistake. . . . The policy we should have adopted," he told the Cabinet on January 27, "was to forbid the transportation of munitions of war in American bottoms. This could have been done and Loyalist Spain would still have been able to come to us for what she needed to fight for her life against Franco—to fight for her life and for the lives of some of the rest of us as well, as events will very likely prove." [12]

As a last-ditch means of helping the Republic, on January 20 Roosevelt again considered urging a negotiated settlement. But as he quickly recognized, it was too late. "At this moment things look like a victory for one side," he wrote on the 24th. ". . . What a pity it could not have been a negotiated peace." On February 10, when Catalonia fell to Fascist arms, "the world concluded that the Spanish war was over," and Franco refused to entertain any suggestions of a conditional peace. "The Nationalists have won," he announced, "the Republicans must therefore surrender without conditions." In response, London and Paris recognized the Nationalist government on February 27, 1939, and on April 3, after the capture of Madrid and the disappearance of the Loyalist regime, Roosevelt followed suit. [13]

Roosevelt's sense of limits in dealing with the Spanish embargo also extended to general Neutrality reform. During the fall and winter of 1938-39, he found little reason to think that Congress would be receptive to suggestions for either outright repeal of the arms embargo or greater presidential discretion in applying it. In October Pittman had warned that "extreme and foolish pacifist sentiment" might dominate the next Congress and block any expansion of Executive control over Neutrality. His only hope was for a law permitting trade in arms on a cash-and-carry basis. In January, moreover, while Congress showed itself receptive to Roosevelt's suggestions for increased defense spending, it revealed little enthusiasm for his recommendation on Neutrality. "The logical conclusion is another war with American troops sent across the ocean," a Republican spokesman declared. Communists and munitions-makers, "insidious alien influences," were behind Roosevelt's Neutrality plans, one Democratic Congressman said. The Foreign Relations Committee's cautious approach to the issue in the following weeks gave Roosevelt additional reason to think that pressure from him would not do much good.[14]

Events that followed the plane crash involving the French officer further undermined Roosevelt's hopes of directly leading the Congress to revise the Neutrality law. When the furor erupted over this incident, Roosevelt invited members of the Senate Military Affairs Committee to the White House to explain the sale of warplanes to France. Though the group meeting with the President on January 31 included staunch isolationists like Gerald Nye, Bennett Clark of Missouri, and Ernest Lundeen of Minnesota, Roosevelt took them into his confidence and spoke candidly of his fears. Hitler was intent on dominating Europe, he explained, and should he accomplish this, it would imperil the peace and safety of the United States. "That is why the safety of the Rhine frontier does necessarily interest us," Roosevelt said. "Do you mean that our frontier is on the Rhine?" one Senator asked. "No, not that," the President replied. "But practically speaking, if the Rhine frontiers are threatened th rest of the world is, too. Once they have fallen before Hitler, the Germa sphere of action will be unlimited." Despite a pledge of secrecy, one more of the Senators told the press that the President had drawn a "truly alarming" picture of world affairs and said that America's frontier lay on the Rhine.

This breach of confidence outraged Roosevelt, who attacked the description of what he said as a "deliberate lie." "A great many people, some members of the House, some members of the Senate and quite a number of newspaper owners, are deliberately putting before the American people a deliberate misrepresentation of the facts," he declared. "The [country's] foreign policy has not changed and it is not going to change," he assured the public. The President's public remarks greatly angered some Senators, who now described Roosevelt as intent on opposing aggressors and entering a war in spite of the Neutrality laws. The President "seems to have gone perfectly mad because his policy in respect to the world situation is opposed," Senator Johnson complained. He "cares no more for what may happen to us in a war than the man in the moon. He has developed a dictator complex." "I am convinced that we shall be extremely fortunate if Roosevelt does not put us into war," Oswald G. Villard of *The Nation* warned. ". . . FDR now realizes that the New Deal is stopped, that he is not making a dent on the unemployment situation, that the present tremendous spending is doing very little to restore prosperity and that he has lost control of congress." "[I] sincerely hope Nye, Vandenberg, and Borah will not force us into war before I get back to Washington," Roosevelt sarcastically answered these charges. The "Charleston Navy Yard needs three or four days' notice before any actual declaration."

In these circumstances, Roosevelt hesitated to press the case for Neutrality revision. On March 7, after Senator Elbert Thomas of Utah had introduced a Neutrality resolution allowing the President to discriminate between aggressors and victims of aggression, and former Secretary of State Henry Stimson publicly called for collective-security measures, Roosevelt refused to give more than guarded support to Neutrality reform. No, he told reporters, he did not think that the Neutrality legislation of the last three years had contributed to the cause of peace; on the contrary, it had helped push things in "the other direction." In what respects? he was asked. "I cannot go into detail"; he replied, "of course you understand that. I have to answer it generally." [15]

Reports coming from Europe in February and early March eased Roosevelt's sense of urgency about asking a hostile Congress for Neutrality change. During this time, American diplomats and European leaders expressed the belief that British, French, and American rearmament, French resistance to Italian demands in the Mediterranean, and the President's statements, especially his remarks to the Senate Military Affairs Committee, were forcing Hitler to quiet down. "It is unquestionable that your acts have had a cooling effect on Hitler," Bullitt wrote on February 1. The British, Ambassador Kennedy reported from London on the 21st, "believe chances for explosion are small. Halifax reiterated [that] our action . . . and speeding up of British production has been body blow for peace." "The very best thing the United States could do," Winston Churchill sent word through a visitor, "was to keep on beating the drums and talking back to the dictators. The one thing that might make them hesitate in plunging the world into war was the fear that the United States would soon be in it in a big way." These reports heartened FDR, who at the beginning of March wrote that "our policy during the past month . . . has had a definite effect on Germany and only a slightly less effect on Italy." [16]

These convictions were much exaggerated. British, French, and American actions after Munich did little to alter Hitler's plans. On March 15, 1939, German troops completed the destruction of Czechoslovakia by occupying Bohemia and Moravia. Though Hitler called his willingness to use "peaceable" means his "last good deed" for the Czech people and though he described his action as necessary to preserve order in a territory that had belonged to Germany for over a thousand years, trust in Hitler's promises that he intended to bring only German nationals back into the Reich largely collapsed. The annihilation of Czechoslovakia marked the end of British appeasement. On March 17 Chamberlain announced that he would not sacrifice British liberty for peace, and should an attempt be made to dominate the world by force, Britain would use all its power to resist. Less than two weeks later, in a revolutionary break with past policy, Chamberlain committed Britain to the defense of Poland. Though it was a badly needed expression of British determination to halt further Nazi aggression, Chamberlain's guarantee shortsightedly failed to assure Russian support and gave Warsaw the ability to put Britain in a war against Berlin.

In the United States there was also a stiffening of will. Feelings in the State Department and the White House approached "the boiling point." Hitler's actions made the President "madder and madder" and left Sumner Welles "simply gasping for breath." "No one here has any illusions that the German Napoleonic machine will not extend itself almost indefinitely," Adolf Berle concluded. "If Germany invades a country and declares war," Roosevelt told Senator Tom Connally of the Foreign Relations Committee on March 16, "we'll be on the side of Hitler by invoking the [Neutrality] act. If we could get rid of the arms embargo, it wouldn't be so bad." On March 17 the administration publicly condemned "the temporary extinguishment of the liberties of a free and independent people," and announced its determination to continue recognizing the Czech Minister as the representative of his country. On the same day, Roosevelt ordered the immediate execution of a week-old decision to reapply countervailing duties to subsidized German goods, and told the press that European developments of the last few days demonstrated a need for Neutrality reform.[17]

Simultaneously, the State Department pressed Pittman into introducing a revised Neutrality bill, the Peace Act of 1939. Eliminating the mandatory arms embargo and placing all trade on a cash-and-carry basis, the law assured that Britain and France would use control of the Atlantic sea lanes to receive arms and supplies in time of war. On March 21, the day after Pittman introduced his bill, an opinion poll showed that 66 per cent of the public favored selling war materials to England and France if they were fighting Germany and Italy.

Moved by these developments and by suggestions that he support a British effort to separate Mussolini from Hitler, Roosevelt converted a ceremonial visit from Prince Colonna, the new Italian Ambassador to Washington, into a lecture on international affairs. There was no question, he told Colonna, that the overwhelming sympathy of the American people would be with the victims of aggression in a European war, and that with the amendment of the Neutrality law, which was surely coming, the United States would provide the fullest possible aid to these countries. Mussolini, the President also said, had a great opportunity to prevent war and ultimately gain "just concessions" at the conference table. Should he continue to associate himself with Hitler, though, he would eventually become another victim of the Fuehrer's drive for control of Europe.

Roosevelt now also pressed directly for changing the Neutrality law. Convinced that the time was ripe for leadership and that Pittman's bill would victimize the Chinese, who lacked the funds and ships to use cash-and-carry, Roosevelt called for full repeal. "Before the bill gets too far," Roosevelt wrote Hull and Wells on March 28, "it should be called to the attention of Senator Pittman that while the cash-and-carry plan works all right in the Atlantic, it works all wrong in the Pacific. The more I think the problem through, the more I am convinced that the existing Neutrality Act should be repealed in toto without any substitute. I do not mind if you pass this word to Senator Pittman and the leaders." At the same time, Roosevelt asked Welles to draft a brief radio address in which he would point out that the Neutrality legislation had worked to encourage aggression and now needed to be changed. If the United States were to remain at peace, Roosevelt intended to say, it must make it possible for victims of attack to receive American aid. Pittman's reply, however, that repeal was "impossible" and evidence of committee resistance to even Pittman's cash-and-carry plan decided Roosevelt against pressing directly for elimination of the Neutrality law in the spring.[18]

At the same time, conditions continued to deteriorate abroad. On March 23 German forces occupied the Memelland, an area on the northern edge of East Prussia ceded to Lithuania in the Versailles settlement. Simultaneously, Hitler pressed Warsaw to return the Free State of Danzig to Germany and allow the construction of a German extraterritorial road across the Polish Corridor separating East Prussia from the rest of Germany. Polish opposition to these demands and British guarantees to Warsaw produced a threatening speech by Hitler on April 1 and confidential warnings from London and Paris that a German attack might come at any moment. On April 7, moreover, Italian forces occupied Albania and created apprehensions that Mussolini and Hitler would shortly embark on a joint venture. Foreign Minister Bonnet "asked me to inform my Government that 'it was five minutes before twelve,'" Bullitt wrote from Paris. ". . . He could not predict where the first blow would be struck. . . . It was clear, however, that Germany and Italy had decided to rush their attacks and it was now merely a question of where and when general war would begin." "Men are massed on every frontier in Europe, and the British and French fleets are in the Ionian Sea," Berle recorded on April 13. "The chance of getting off without a general war is not great." [19]

In these circumstances, Roosevelt sought ways both to encourage Neutrality revision and inhibit the dictators. In press conferences on April 8 and 11, he reiterated the dangers to the United States from unchecked aggression and the need for the country to come out from behind its "paper guarantees of immunity" and align itself clearly with Britain and France. Commending a *Washington Post* editorial to the reporters, he also endorsed the assertion that Hitler and Mussolini must take account of "the tremendous force of the United States," which "is far from indifferent to their plottings."

Roosevelt used a Pan American Day address on April 14 to make these themes more explicit. He could not accept recent German and Italian claims of imprisonment and encirclement, he said. British guarantees to Poland represented no threat to Berlin. "There is no such thing as encircling or threatening, or imprisoning any peaceful Nation by other peaceful nations." If the dictators wish peace and security, he asserted, they need only give up their dreams of conquest. "Do we really have to assume that nations can find no better methods of realizing their destinies than those which were used by the Huns and Vandals fifteen hundred years ago?" he asked. But should this prove to be the case, he urged others to understand that "we have an interest, wider than that of the mere defense of our sea-ringed continent. We know now that the development of the next generation will so narrow the oceans separating us from the Old World, that our customs and our actions are necessarily involved with hers, whether we like it or not. . . . We, too," he pointedly told the isolationists at home and the dictators abroad, "have a stake in world affairs."

Roosevelt was not content to leave the issue there. To impress his opposition on Berlin and Rome, and possibly dissuade them from further aggression, he sent Hitler and Mussolini extraordinary public messages, which were broadcast to all parts of the world on April 15. People everywhere "are living today in constant fear of a new war . . . ," he declared. "The existence of this fear—and the possibility of such a conflict—are of definite concern to the people of the United States. . . . Any major war, even if it were confined to other continents, must bear heavily on them during its continuance and also for generations to come." Reviewing the recent loss of independence by three nations in Europe and one in Africa and the occupation of a part of China by Japan, Roosevelt cited reports of further plans of aggression against other independent nations and invited the dictators to pledge themselves to peace. "Are you willing to give assurance that your armed forces will not attack or invade the territory or possessions" of thirty-one specific nations for at least ten years? Roosevelt asked. If Hitler and Mussolini would comply, Roosevelt offered to transmit their messages and arrange a conference on disarmament and trade in which the United States would take part. He also proposed that separate political discussions take place at the same time without the United States.

Roosevelt had few illusions about the likelihood of a positive response. He quoted the odds to Morgenthau as one in five. "The two madmen respect force and force alone," Henry Wallace told him. An appeal to Hitler and Mussolini may be put "in the same category as delivering a sermon to a mad dog." Nevertheless, Roosevelt felt that such a move might put the dictators on the spot; it would make clear to people everywhere, and especially to Americans, that the dictators were not intent on limited national gains but on the conquest of Europe.[20]

The response to Roosevelt's appeal confirmed his worst fears. Though it was greeted with widespread popular enthusiasm and hailed in some official circles "as one of the most important events in current history," the Italians and the Germans contemptuously turned it aside. The press in both countries poured rage and scorn on the President's words, while Air Marshal Hermann Goering and Mussolini privately attacked the message as suggesting an incipient brain malady or creeping paralysis. Publicly, Mussolini declared his indifference to "press campaigns . . . or Messiah-like messages," and called the suggestion of a ten-year guarantee "absurd."

Though reluctant to answer a "communication from so contemptible a creature as the present President of the United States," Hitler concluded that the profound impression made in all quarters of the world by Roosevelt's message compelled a reply. In a speech to the Reichstag on April 28, he evaded the President's request for assurances to other nations with a sarcastic harangue which elicited roars of malicious laughter from the assembled delegates: If President Roosevelt believed that all problems could be solved at the conference table, why had the United States rejected membership in the League? If he had inquired about American intentions in Latin America as Mr. Roosevelt had asked about German plans in Europe, he, Hitler, would have been told to mind his own business. Yet, in spite of this, Hitler said he had asked each of the states mentioned by the President whether they felt threatened by Germany and whether they had asked Roosevelt to request guarantees. All replies had been negative. Still, he would gladly give assurances to any of these states if they asked for them, and he would also include the United States and other American countries in this guarantee, should they so wish.

Hitler's speech also shrewdly appealed to American isolationists. He denied charges that he intended to start a war, defended German actions as simply the righting of past wrongs, and described them as indistinguishable from the self-interested deeds of America, Britain, and France. Eager to believe that there woud be no war and that, if one occurred, it would be a traditional European power struggle in which the United States had no interest, the isolationists took considerable satisfaction from Hitler's speech. "Hitler had all the better of the argument . . . ," Hiram Johnson declared. "Roosevelt put his chin out and got a resounding whack. I have reached the conclusion that there will be no war. . . . Roosevelt wants to fight for any little thing. He wants . . . to knock down two dictators in Europe, so that one may be firmly implanted in America." Instead of persuading opponents that a European conflict was imminent, Roosevelt's exchange with Hitler simply strengthened their fears that he wished to overcome problems at home by meddling abroad.[21]

The most effective answer Roosevelt saw to Hitler was not additional words but support for Britain and France through revision of the Neutrality law. By the end of April this seemed less within reach than ever. During the month, Senate Foreign Relations Committee hearings had produced a variety of conflicting opinions leading to an impasse. "We have eighteen members present at this hearing," Pittman told FDR, "and so far, we have eighteen bills." Pittman also acknowledged that his committee was out of hand and that "the isolationists might even win." By the beginning of May he thought the "divisions of opinion among the leading peace societies in the country will tend to prevent any legislation at all." One close observer in the State Department saw "the neutrality situation . . . going from bad to worse," and concluded that Pittman's leadership had broken down.[22]

Though Roosevelt resisted entering the picture directly for fear of creating more opposition in a Congress only too eager to defeat his every wish, he pressed the case behind the scenes. Beginning in mid-April, he met quietly at the White House with "wavering" Senators and Representatives. Emphasizing the likelihood of a conflict and the dangers to the United States from a British defeat, he urged repeal of the arms embargo as the best way to keep the peace and assure the national interest in case of war. Hull shared the burden of this effort, telling numerous legislators that they were "making the mistake of their lives" in thinking that the coming struggle was "another goddam piddling dispute over a boundary line." It would be a worldwide struggle against nations "practicing a philosophy of barbarism." The United States, he added, was encouraging these aggressors and jeopardizing its own safety through retention of the arms embargo. Not to repeal this "wretched little bobtailed, sawed-off domestic statute" was "just plain chuckle-headed."

These arguments had no impact on isolationists. Soundings of congressional sentiment in early May indicated that isolationists remained unalterably opposed to repeal of the arms embargo, that they would put embarrassing public questions to Hull on aiding Britain and France if he appeared before Pittman's committee, and that they would respond to a confrontation on Neutrality with a long filibuster in the Senate. Worse yet, a survey of congressional feeling indicated that a majority did not see a European war as imminent and wished to postpone action on Neutrality legislation until the next session in January 1940. In response to these facts, on May 8 Hull cancelled plans to appear before the Foreign Relations Committee, and on May 16 Pittman stated his intention to do nothing about Neutrality for several weeks.

Roosevelt, however, saw strong arguments for pushing Neutrality reform. Congressional soundings indicated that while a majority in Congress wished to postpone action, it nevertheless also favored repeal of the arms embargo. Public opinion surveys continued to show a majority of Americans favoring revision of the Neutrality law in order to aid Britain and France. A failure to do anything seemed certain to encourage German war moves: according to Bullitt, German Foreign Minister Joachim von Ribbentrop urged the case for war by citing American unwillingness to modify the Neutrality Act and assure supplies for the democracies. British and French leaders predicted that an early revision of the Neutrality law would defeat Ribbentrop's hopes of convincing Hitler to risk an immediate war. Finally, Representative Sol Bloom, the acting Chairman of the House Foreign Affairs Committee, urged the administration to believe that his committee and the House, which was "less rent by faction and divergent opinion" than the Senate, would act promptly on Neutrality reform.[23]

In response, Roosevelt decided to press for revision in the House. In a conference with House leaders on May 19, Roosevelt explained that repeal of the arms embargo would prevent the outbreak of a European war or at least would reduce the likelihood of a victory for the Powers unfriendly to the United States. He made no objection to retaining other sections of the law and approved keeping Americans out of the war zone and placing all trade on a cash-and-carry basis. He further supported his appeal by warning that Germany and Italy had at least an even chance of winning a war and that they would use their victory to penetrate Latin America. "At the end of a very short time," he predicted, "we should find ourselves surrounded by hostile states in this hemisphere. Further, the Japanese, who 'always like to play with the big boys,' would probably go into a hard and fast alliance." Should the United States then get "rough" about this threat, the three Axis states would be tempted "to try another quick war with us." He also assured these Congressmen that he had no intention of sending American troops to Europe and insisted that they put aside their skepticism about achieving Neutrality reform and make the fight for it. He concluded by asking that the House complete approval of a bill before the arrival of Britain's King and Queen for a ceremonial visit on June 12.

To support the President's appeal, Hull met personally with the members of Bloom's committee, and on May 27 he sent a public letter to

Bloom and Pittman recommending Neutrality reform. A letter from Hull seemed best calculated to avoid the congressional antagonism that a direct request from FDR would stir. The letter also shrewdly tried to head off isolationist opposition by emphasizing the administration's desire to stay out of war. Though it noted the impossibility of remaining entirely detached from overseas affairs, the letter principally stressed keeping the country out of war by enacting "measures adapted to the safeguarding of our interests in all situations of which we can conceive." This chiefly entailed repealing the arms embargo and adopting a cash-and-carry policy. Two days after receiving this letter, Bloom introduced a bill that largely conformed to Hull's request. On May 31 Roosevelt asked congressional leaders to take up Neutrality revision even if it delayed adjournment and provoked an isolationist filibuster.[24]

Despite this show of determination, the congressional response remained in doubt. Dozens of Congressmen and Senators declared themselves unsure as to the likely outcome. Some observers likened the legislators to "a flock of sheep in a pen where if one jumped out in a given direction all the rest would immediately follow. . . . The only trouble," Moffat said, "is no one could calculate just which side of the pen the first sheep would jump out." Hull expressed his own uncertainty with "the story of the teacher who was showing off her bright pupils to the members of the school board. She called up Tommy to shine in arithmetic. 'Tommy,' said one of the board members, 'if there are sixteen sheep in a field and one jumps the fence, how many are left?' 'None,' replied Tommy. 'Well,' said the questioner, 'I'm afraid you don't know anything about arithmetic.' 'The trouble is,' said Tommy, 'you don't know anything about sheep.' "

The House demonstrated its unpredictability in the next month. On June 6, despite predictions from Bloom that he could get any kind of a bill the administration wanted through the House, his committee voted to repeal the arms embargo by only 11 to 9. A week later, however, on a straight party vote of 12 to 8, the committee reported a surprisingly flexible measure granting the President discretion to say when, how, and where the law should apply. "No President," Republican members of the committee complained, "has ever had such powers before." Though isolationists from both parties hammered on this point during two days of floor debate, they were unable to win anything like a majority for amendments reducing Executive discretion. On the night of June 29, however, after a hundred Democratic members, who apparently either favored an arms embargo or did not wish to make their opposition to it public, had gone home, the House gave a two-vote margin, 159 to 157, to an amendment embargoing "arms and ammunition" but not "implements of war." The latter, as explained by the author of the measure, Ohio Republican John M. Vorys, meant items, such as airplanes, which also had peacetime uses. On the following day, when the Democratic leadership tried to remove this new version of an arms embargo, they failed by four votes, 180 to 176. The House then passed the Bloom bill by a vote of 200 to 188 with the "obnoxious" Vorys amendment attached.[25]

The administration failed this test of strength in the House because opponents of the unamended Bloom bill were able to combine solid Republican backing with the votes of one-fourth of the Democrats. While isolationist sentiments moved some of the Representatives on both sides of the aisle, antagonism to the President and the New Deal largely accounted for the rest of the votes. In short, isolationism, Republican partisanship, and antipathy toward Roosevelt in his own party joined to sink Neutrality reform in the House. Had Bloom not written so large a measure of presidential discretion into his bill and had Roosevelt fully detached himself from the fight, it is conceivable that the House would have repealed the arms embargo. On the other hand, without administration pressure for repeal, the issue would have gone over to the next session. Would a more vigorous effort by the President and the Secretary of State, as some critics have suggested, have won the fight in the House? Probably not. It would not have converted any of those voting against FDR, and it would probably have lost the administration as many votes as it gained. But even if this tactic had worked in the House, it would not have carried repeal through the Senate. As Hiram Johnson confidently predicted throughout June, there were enough opponents in the Senate to "stop almost any legislation" the administration might ask.[26]

Despite an appreciation of these facts, the response in Europe to the House action persuaded Roosevelt to continue the fight for Neutrality reform. He at once received reports that British and French leaders saw the House vote as weakening the democracies, encouraging the aggressors, and increasing the likelihood of war. Subsequent dispatches from Belgium, Holland, Italy, and Switzerland made the same points. "If we fail to get any Neutrality Bill," Roosevelt asked the Attorney General on July 1, "how far do you think I can go in ignoring the existing act—even though I did sign it?" Though Vice President Garner and Secretary of Interior Ickes urged him to believe that, as President, his constitutional control over foreign affairs freed him from the constraints of the Neutrality, law, Roosevelt did not pursue the question.[27]

Instead, he pushed Neutrality reform in the Senate, where the Foreign Relations Committee had still not acted on Pittman's Peace Act of 1939, which would allow the President to export arms to belligerents on a cash-and-carry basis. To get Pittman's support, Roosevelt agreed to a higher price for domestic silver. During the spring, Pittman had pressed the administration to reduce unemployment in western states by increasing government subsidies to the silver-mining industry. But Roosevelt had resisted, arguing that federal support to silver miners was already too high and that these states could reduce unemployment by other means. When Pittman refused to move on the Neutrality question until the President agreed to his silver policy, however, Roosevelt gave in. "We have got 18 votes—and what are you going to do about it?" Pittman asked FDR. On July 5 the White House persuaded the Senate to approve increased subsidies for domestic silver. At the same time, Roosevelt and Hull pressed other members of the Foreign Relations Committee to help repeal the arms embargo. "Pat, old dear," Roosevelt wrote Senator Harrison of Mississippi, "What is this I hear about your going home ahead of time? Do please don't! I need you here on lots of things, including the next big thing on the calendar—the Neutrality Bill—and I do hope you will help to get it out on Saturday and put it through." [28]

Despite the administration's efforts, opponents of Neutrality reform again gained the upper hand. With the twenty-three-member Foreign Relations Committee split eleven in favor, ten against, and two undecided, Pittman was confident that he could swing one or both of the uncommitted Senators to his side. Both men, Walter George of Georgia and Guy Gillette of Iowa, were Democrats, and both favored Neutrality repeal. But Roosevelt had openly opposed both of them in the 1938 elections. Playing on their antagonism to the President, the isolationists won their support for a motion to shelve the question until the 1940 session. On July 11, with thirty-four Senators already pledged "to keep the neutrality bill before the Senate indefinitely" if it were reported, Pittman's Committee rejected the President's appeal by a vote of 12 to 11.

Convinced that only a prompt demonstration of American willingness to aid the democracies would prevent a war, Roosevelt responded to the committee's decision with private anger and a public request to the Senate to overrule its committee and vote Neutrality change. "I will bet you an old hat," the President told Morgenthau, ". . . that . . . when he [Hitler] wakes up and finds out what has happened, there will be great rejoicing in the Italian and German camps. I think we ought to introduce a bill for statues of [Senators] Austin, Vandenberg, Lodge and Taft . . . to be erected in Berlin and put the swastika on them." Though he also considered publicly venting his anger on congressional isolationists, he decided to follow Hull's advice and send a restrained appeal for legislative action. "It has been abundantly clear to me for some time," he said in a message on July 14, ". . . that the Congress at this session should take certain much needed action. In the light of present world conditions, I see no reason to change that opinion." Appending a lengthy statement from Hull to his letter, Roosevelt endorsed the Secretary's contention that the administration's Neutrality program of May 27 would "to a far greater extent than the present act . . . both aid in making less likely a general war, and . . . reduce as far as possible the risk of this nation being drawn into war if war comes." [29]

On the evening of July 18 Roosevelt made a direct appeal to Senate leaders. At a White House meeting with Hull, Garner, Pittman, Majority Leader Alben W. Barkley, and Republican leaders Charles McNary, Warren Austin, and William Borah, Roosevelt grimly described the likelihood of a war, its possible consequences for the United States, the continuing need for repeal of the arms embargo, and his repeated efforts to preserve peace. "But now I've fired my last shot," he concluded, "I think I ought to have another round in my belt." The opposing Senators were unmoved. "No one can foretell what may happen," Borah declared. "But my feeling and belief is that we are not going to have a war. Germany isn't ready for it." Hull strongly disagreed, predicting a war by summer's end and inviting Borah to read the cables reaching his office. "So far as the reports in your Department are concerned," Borah answered, "I wouldn't be bound by them. I have my own sources of information . . . and on several occasions I've found them more reliable than the State Department." Hull was so angry at Borah's blind refusal to confront the facts that Hull could scarcely proceed further without losing his self-control. Asked by Garner whether Neutrality reform could get through the Senate, all the Senators answered no. "Well, Captain," Garner said to the President, "we may as well face the facts. You haven't got the votes, and that's all there is to it."

Roosevelt believed the impasse would leave Hitler less constrained than ever to make war. The "failure of the Senate to take action now," Roosevelt announced after the White House meeting, "would weaken the leadership of the United States in exercising its potent influence in the cause of preserving peace." In the event of another international crisis, he shortly told a press conference, "I have practically no power to make an American effort to prevent such a war from breaking out." [30]

Though Borah proved to be dead wrong in discounting predictions of an imminent war, Roosevelt and Hull were also well off the mark in thinking that immediate repeal of the arms embargo could affect Hitler's plans. In general, Hitler had little regard for the United States, viewing it as a "mongrel society" which "could not possibly construct a sound economy, create an indigenous culture, or operate a successful political system." More specifically, in the spring and summer of 1939 Hitler considered America "hopelessly weak" and incapable of interfering with his plans. In short, his scheme for a Polish war turned not on whether the United States would revise its Neutrality law but on British-French and German negotiations with Moscow. For all Roosevelt's belief, which was widely shared abroad, that repeal of the arms embargo would be a significant step for peace, the status of the Neutrality law had almost no impact on the course of immediate European events. [31]

The limits on Roosevelt's influence in Europe matched the constraints on his power in the Far East. During 1938, as Japan extended the war in

China, Roosevelt had continued to wrestle with ways of aiding the Chinese and punishing the Japanese. In the spring and summer, after repeated Japanese air raids on crowded Chinese cities, Roosevelt and Hull had imposed a moral embargo on airplane sales to countries bombing civilian populations from the air. In addition, the State Department complained repeatedly to Tokyo about Japanese abuses of American citizens and property in China. But it had no impact. Encouraged by Anglo-French appeasement at Munich and a series of military victories in south and central China, Tokyo had boldly announced its intention in November 1938 of creating a "new order in East Asia" based on the political, economic, and cultural cooperation of Japan, Manchukuo, and China. Declaring itself confident that other Powers would "adapt their attitude to the new conditions prevailing in East Asia," Japan repudiated the Open Door policy and expressed determination to create an East Asian block that would assure her the same degree of economic self-sufficiency enjoyed by Britain and the United States.

In oral and written replies, the State Department took strong exception to the Japanese announcement. Complaining that Japan's action was a unilateral repudiation of binding international agreements, Washington rejected Tokyo's contention that the continued observance of these agreements depended upon American acceptance of a "new order" in the Far East. Washington also argued that the Open Door, or the principle of equality of opportunity, was not beneficial solely to the United States but contributed to economic and political stability in China and among other nations. While declaring itself ready to accept alterations in existing agreements by orderly processes of negotiation, Washington refused to accept the abrogation of any of its rights, or the need for any single Power to declare itself an "agent of destiny" or an architect of a "new order" in areas not under its sovereignty.[32]

At the same time, Roosevelt and Morgenthau helped bolster Chinese resistance to Japan. In the fall of 1938 the Chinese, who, according to Morgenthau, were "busted," had asked for a loan to see them through the next year. "By risking little more than the cost of one battleship," Morgenthau told FDR, "we can give renewed vitality and effectiveness to the Chinese. We can do more than that. By our action we can further the struggle of democracy against aggression everywhere." Roosevelt commissioned Morgenthau to arrange the loan. By mid-November, however, after the Treasury suggested lending the Chinese $25 million against the delivery of tung oil over the next three years, and Chiang Kai-shek had provided assurances of Chinese determination to fight on despite recent defeats, Hull warned that a loan would intensify problems with Japan and even lead to hostilities. Though "very much disturbed" by Hull's warning, Roosevelt felt compelled to take the risk, and on December 14 he announced completion of the deal.[33]

Roosevelt was more cautious about direct opposition to Japan. During the second half of 1938, sentiment in the country mounted for embargoes on war supplies to Tokyo. A June 1938 poll, for example, showed 84 per cent of the public against continued export of military goods to Japan, while private groups like the Committee for Non-Participation in Japanese Aggression pressed the administration to adopt economic sanctions. Though sympathetic to strong action, Roosevelt and Hull saw the consequences as too risky: it could weaken Japan's moderates, produce new aggressions, and precipitate a war in which the United States would be unable to respond effectively to the more serious threat from Berlin.

The administration felt itself under the same constraints during the first half of 1939. Though Japanese forces had occupied China's Hainan Island in February and the Spratly Islands in March, placing themselves within easy striking distance of the Philippines and Singapore and suggesting a determination to dominate the Western Pacific, the administration limited itself to fresh diplomatic protests. Simultaneous Japanese negotiations with Berlin and Rome for a full-scale military and political alliance made Washington more circumspect than ever. A sharp debate in Tokyo between Army proponents and Cabinet, Navy, and business opponents of a treaty persuaded Roosevelt and Hull that any strong American action in the Far East would strengthen Japanese advocates of an Axis agreement. When Congress considered appropriating funds for defensive construction on Guam, for example, Roosevelt helped discourage the idea.[34]

Japanese violations of British rights in China in June demonstrated that London operated under similar constraints. Hoping to eliminate the foreign settlements, which were giving aid and comfort to Chiang, and to persuade opponents of an Axis pact that such an agreement would intimidate rather than arouse the democracies, the Japanese Army stepped up its attacks on British subjects in China. At Tientsin, the Japanese blockaded the British compound and forced its residents to disrobe before they could leave or enter. Convictions that a Far Eastern crisis would encourage a German move against Poland, that Britain lacked enough capital ships to fight effectively in both Asia and Europe, and that the United States would not support Britain inhibited London from making a strong response. Consequently, the British accepted the humiliating Craigie-Arita declaration of July 24, 1939, negotiated in Tokyo by Britain's Ambassador and Japan's Foreign Minister. As a condition of a Tientsin settlement, London recognized Japan's special position in China and acknowledged that Japanese forces had responsibility for law and order in areas they occupied.[35]

The Tientsin violations created the feeling in Washington that without some show of resistance the Japanese would soon drive all Westerners out of China. Though the Japanese, in fact, excluded Americans from their assaults in Tientsin and simultaneously invited the United States to help Japan prevent a European war, Roosevelt and Hull refused. They viewed the suggestion as an attempt to win American acceptance of Japanese actions in China and to drive a wedge between Britain and the United States in their dealings with Japan. While American military and State Department chiefs privately agreed that "we must not get pushed into the front line trench by the British," Roosevelt and Hull felt compelled to object to the Tientsin assaults and to continued "indiscriminate" bombing of Chungking, the current center of the Nationalist government. "Send for the Japanese Ambassador," FDR told Hull on July 7, ". . . and tell him that the President in person asked you to protest to him against a continuation of these [indiscriminate bombing] actions. Further, that the President would like to have an immediate statement from the Japanese Government, without making it a matter of formal notes." Though Roosevelt and Hull also considered moving the Fleet from San Diego to Pearl Harbor and restating American opposition to Japan's "new order" in China, continuing fears of provoking the Japanese into bolder actions deterred them.[36]

In July, because of the Craigie-Arita agreement, Senate inaction on Neutrality reform, and domestic pressure for action against Japan, Roosevelt was moved to suspend a long-standing trade agreement with Tokyo. In the spring and summer of 1939, public opinion polls showed heavy majorities favoring an arms embargo against Japan and a boycott of Japanese goods. The administration came under attack for failing to take these steps. The Congress also pressured Roosevelt by introducing resolutions authorizing restrictions on trade with nations violating the Nine-Power Treaty of 1922. Since economic sanctions might violate a 1911 commercial treaty with Japan and lead to war, Roosevelt and Hull preferred to abrogate the commercial agreement by giving a required six months' notice. Such a step would not only tell the Japanese that they might shortly face a loss of essential supplies from the United States, but would also weaken the conviction generated by inaction on Neutrality that Washington was incapable of meaningful international action and would partly answer the public clamor for opposition to Japan. On July 26, therefore, eight days after Senator Vandenberg introduced a resolution urging abrogation and two days after Japan's victory over Britain in the Craigie-Arita agreement, Roosevelt decided to tell Tokyo that America would abandon the 1911 treaty.

Abrogation of the treaty achieved everything the administration could have wished. It encouraged London to be firmer with Tokyo, raised Chinese morale, and received widespread approval in the United States. More importantly, it created anxiety among some Japanese about pushing the United States too hard. Business and Foreign Office leaders displayed considerable concern over what would follow termination of the treaty, while Cabinet officials showed themselves more determined than ever to resist army pressure for an Axis alliance.[37]

This victory barely compensated for Roosevelt's inability to affect European affairs. By the beginning of August, all signs pointed toward a German-Polish crisis over Danzig in a matter of weeks. Reports from Berlin indicated that "the Germans had everything ready for the end of August and that they could, if they wished, strike almost without further preparation." Roosevelt guessed the date for the explosion as September 10: "I get this by being psychic," he admitted. "If other statesmen are allowed that luxury, I don't see why I shouldn't."

He remained determined, though, to make last-ditch efforts for peace. On August 4 he sent word to Soviet leaders, who were engaged in simultaneous negotiations with Britain-France and Berlin, that a pact with Hitler would simply delay a German attack on Russia until after a French defeat. By contrast, an Anglo-French-Soviet nonaggression agreement would "have a decidedly stabilizing effect in the interest of world peace." Though Soviet Foreign Minister Vyacheslav Molotov said that his government attached "the greatest interest and the utmost importance" to the President's views, on August 22, 1939, Moscow agreed to a Nazi-Soviet nonaggression pact.

The agreement assured that Hitler would attack Poland. On the 22nd, in fact, he called his generals to a conference, where he exuberantly set forth his war plans and described his British and French enemies as "little worms" who were unlikely to intervene. "I shall give a good propaganda reason for starting the war," he declared, "whether plausible or not. The victor will not be asked, later on, whether he told the truth or not. In starting and making war it is not right, but victory, that matters." After this "exultant outburst," Goering "jumped upon the table and offered bloodthirsty thanks while he danced like a savage."[38]

The Nazi-Soviet pact moved Roosevelt to make final peace efforts. On the 23rd he sent a message to Italy's King Victor Emmanuel, asking him to exert his influence in behalf of the American peace proposal of four months before. The next day Roosevelt also sent appeals to Hitler and President Ignacy Mościcki of Poland. Renewing his April proposal and restating American opposition to national gain through war, he suggested an immediate settlement of German-Polish differences through direct negotiation, arbitration, or conciliation, and indicated his willingness to serve as a mediator if both sides agreed to respect the other's independence and territorial integrity.

State Department chiefs vested little hope in these appeals. They all agreed that the message to Victor Emmanuel, who had small influence on Italian policy, was a "weak" move; Ambassador Kennedy described it as "lousy and a complete flop in London." "These messages will have about the same effect as a valentine sent to somebody's mother-in-law out of season," Berle observed, "and they have all that quality of naïveté which is the prerogative alone of the United States. Nevertheless, they ought to be sent. The one certain thing in this business is that no one will be blamed for making any attempt, however desperate, at preserving peace." As anticipated, though, Victor Emmanuel described his government as doing all it could for peace; President Mościcki declared himself ready for negotiation or conciliation; and Hitler offered no response.[39]

Roosevelt made these appeals principally for their domestic effect. Since many Americans believed that the coming war was no more than a traditional European power struggle and since he had no intention of asking Americans to remain neutral in thought, he wished to establish clear responsibility for the fighting. "In the interest of public opinion in the United States, as well as . . . in other parts of the world," he told his Ambassador to Poland, "it is in the highest degree important that history should not record . . . that the first act of aggression of a military character was brought about by Poland. To use the Biblical phrase, a situation should not arise as a result of which it could truthfully be said that Poland 'threw the first stone.'" To "'put the bee on Germany'—which nobody had done in 1914," Roosevelt sent Hitler another message on August 25. Informing him that Poland was ready to solve the conflict by direct negotiation or conciliation, he stated that "countless human lives can yet be saved . . . if you and the Government of the German Reich will agree to the pacific means of settlement accepted by . . . Poland."

The French and the British had other ideas on how the President might save the peace. On August 22, Daladier had suggested a summons to "all the nations of the earth to send delegates immediately to Washington to try to work out a pacific solution of the present situation." But Daladier doubted that Germany would accept, and Roosevelt would only have done his "utmost to prevent a horrible catastrophe for the entire human race, and . . . made the moral issue clear." The British, according to Kennedy, wanted the United States to put pressure on the Poles to make voluntary concessions that would avert a war. Roosevelt and his advisers summarily rejected this suggestion as an attempt to have the United States arrange a new Munich. A message to Warsaw along these lines, Berle sarcastically observed, would have to begin: "In view of the fact that your suicide is required, kindly oblige by etc." [40]

Aside from preparing declarations of American neutrality and industrial mobilization, Roosevelt and the State Department waited on events. "These last two days have given me the feeling of sitting in a house where somebody is dying upstairs," Moffat observed. "There is relatively little to do and yet the suspense continues unabated." "I have a horrible feeling of seeing . . . a civilization dying even before its actual death," Berle lamented. ". . . How delicate a fabric this thing we call modern civilization really is." The "death watch" came to an end at 2:50 a.m. on

September 1, 1939, when Bullitt telephoned Roosevelt from Paris that Germany had invaded Poland. The call left Roosevelt with "a strange feeling of familiarity," reminding him of Navy Department days during the First World War when other tragic messages came to him in the night. It was "like picking up again an interrupted routine." Two days later, despite last-minute rumors of no wider European conflict, Britain and France declared war on Berlin. The sense of America's powerlessness before these events reduced some of the President's advisers to despair. Notifying Roosevelt from London at a little after 4:00 a.m. on September 3 that Chamberlain would make a war speech in two hours, Ambassador Kennedy declared: "It's the end of the world, the end of everything." [41]

9

The Reluctant Neutral

THE OUTBREAK OF fighting in Europe moved Roosevelt to express strong determination to keep the country out of war. In a Cabinet meeting on September 1 he distinguished between preparing for war and preparing to meet war problems. "Pay attention only to the latter," Hull recorded him as saying, "because we were not going to get into war." In a Fireside Chat two days later, he counselled against false talk of sending American armies to European fields. "I give you assurance and reassurance," he declared, that your government will make every effort to prevent a "black-out of peace in the United States." Also telling the country that "this nation will remain a neutral nation," he issued proclamations of neutrality required by international law and the Neutrality Act of 1937.

Though Roosevelt sincerely wished and expected to keep the country out of war, he rejected strict neutrality. "I cannot ask that every American remain neutral in thought . . . ," he announced. "Even a neutral has a right to take account of facts. Even a neutral cannot be asked to close his mind or conscience." Morality and self-interest, Roosevelt believed, compelled American aid to Britain and France: the preservation of American values and national peace depended on the defeat of Berlin. On the eve of the conflict, he asked the Commerce Department for a program that would allow Americans to sell "certain types of war supplies to friendly nations without violating the [Neutrality] Act." Selling airplane motors to motorboat companies in Canada impressed him as one example of how this could be done. He also suggested delaying Neutrality proclamations for five days after the fighting began to allow Britain and France to transport all previously ordered American supplies.[1]

Roosevelt never implemented these ideas for getting around the Neutrality law. Instead, he renewed his campaign for Neutrality reform. Actually, he had never abandoned it. On July 20, two days after Senate leaders dropped the issue, Roosevelt had recommended putting President Nicholas Murray Butler of Columbia University, an advocate of Neutrality change, "on the air." During the next six weeks, he had repeatedly made the case for Neutrality reform in press conferences, and on the eve of the fighting he told Berle that "now is the time to shoot the gun towards getting our neutrality law changed." To this end, Assistant Secretary of

War Louis Johnson had made speeches at the end of August suggesting that the European crisis might not have occurred if Congress had approved the President's Neutrality proposal and that revision was still necessary if the country were to keep out of war.[2]

The outbreak of war was more effective in converting congressional sentiment to Neutrality change. By the second week of September there were strong indications that the Congress would repeal the arms embargo: a number of Congressmen and Senators told Roosevelt this, while surveys of sentiment in both houses indicated that sixty Senators would favor cash-and-carry Neutrality and that "several members of the House . . . may be expected to reverse their position." By September 11, in fact, Roosevelt believed that a Senate filibuster was the only impediment to passage of a revised Neutrality law.[3]

Developments abroad prompted quick action. In the first week of fighting, Hitler's forces destroyed the Polish air force, largely broke Polish ground resistance, and laid siege to Warsaw. According to one report reaching FDR, German Propaganda Minister Joseph Paul Goebbels hoped to destroy Poland in a few days, smash France and England quickly from the air, and conquer the United States ultimately from within. Roosevelt also heard that Daladier expected England and France to hold out for a while, but that without American supplies they could not launch a successful offensive. Bullitt warned that an unrevised Neutrality law would assure the rapid defeat of the Allies and force the United States to fight Hitler in the Americas. Likewise, Kennedy described high government officials in London as "depressed beyond words that it has become necessary for the United States to revert to its old Neutrality Law." They thought it would be "a sheer disaster" if a cash-and-carry bill failed to pass. On September 13, "after a survey of the whole situation," Roosevelt called a special congressional session for September 21 and asked a bipartisan group of legislative leaders to meet with him the day before.[4]

Though surveys of congressional sentiment in the week after Roosevelt called the special session continued to show strong support for Neutrality reform, administration leaders feared that "any evidence of . . . improper action . . . might well lose the battle which at the moment seems won." An effective isolationist drive against Neutrality change created reasonable concern. Led by Senators Borah, Clark, Nye, and Vandenberg, Father Charles Coughlin, and Colonel Charles A. Lindbergh, the isolationists mounted a national radio campaign which generated a spontaneous deluge of pro-embargo mail. In three days alone, a million telegrams, letters, and postcards reached congressional offices, with some Senators receiving 4000 messages a day. A report that the Republican National Committee intended "to disseminate the impression that the President will, if not restrained, get the country into war," also troubled FDR.

The Republicans would ultimately cooperate in drafting a bill that "meets the needs of the Allies and the demands of businessmen," Roosevelt learned, but they would describe the act as a "victory for peace" won by Republicans curtailing presidential demands for "vague and broad" powers.[5]

Public opinion surveys also gave Roosevelt cause for alarm. Polls during the first three weeks of September suggested that any indication of White House readiness to aid the Allies at the risk of war would produce an outpouring of opposition to Neutrality change. While more than 80 per cent of the public favored the Allies in the fighting and while between 50 and 60 per cent of the public consistently supported aid to England and France, the majority of this second group unequivocally wished to keep the United States out of war. An advance copy of a *Fortune* survey that reached the President on September 19, for example, showed only a quarter of the public against "any aid of any kind to either side," but also revealed that 70 per cent of those favoring exports to belligerents wished this trade to be on an impartial cash-and-carry basis or to reach the Allies without risk of war. At the same time, Cornelius Vanderbilt, Jr., a newspaper columnist who had provided Roosevelt with accurate personal surveys in the past, sent him disturbing reports based on 2000 miles of travel through eight southern and midwestern states. He found a fifty-fifty split on Neutrality change, a widespread belief that England, France, and Germany were fighting a "mock war," and a "strong feeling that the President is playing the European war as an end to be elected for a Third Term."[6]

To counter these suspicions and fears, Roosevelt made bipartisanship and determination to keep the country out of war the keynotes of his Neutrality fight. He arranged for prominent Republicans like Alf Landon, Henry Stimson, and Colonel Frank Knox, the publisher of the *Chicago Daily News*, to answer Borah and other isolationist opponents of Neutrality revision; he asked Landon and Knox to attend the White House conference with congressional leaders of both parties; and he told Congress in a speech on September 21 "that regardless of party or section the mantle of peace and of patriotism is wide enough to cover us all. Let no group assume the exclusive label of the 'peace bloc.' We all belong to it." He also announced a request to leaders of both parties to remain in Washington after the extraordinary session in order to continue consultations with him on foreign affairs.

His speech, however, chiefly emphasized the need for Neutrality revision to assure the peace at home. Reiterating his belief that the existing law aided aggressors, he stressed that it also made the United States vulnerable to involvement in war. The embargo provisions, he explained, did not prevent the sale of "uncompleted implements of war" which, when transported to belligerents in American ships, created a "definite danger to our neutrality and peace." It would be far better, he declared, to repeal the embargo and permit the sale of all goods on a cash-and-carry basis. When coupled with provisions to keep American merchant ships and citizens out of war zones and to prevent war credits from going to belligerents, there would be a program offering "far greater safeguards than we now possess, or have ever possessed, to protect American lives and property from danger." It would be a program "better calculated than any other means to keep us out of war." Though Roosevelt preferred full repeal of the Neutrality law and implementation of these measures by Executive proclamation, he appreciated that Congress would insist on writing such restrictions into a revised Neutrality bill. Believing the method by which these measures were carried out to be secondary, he said, "our acts must be guided by one single hard-headed thought—keeping America out of this war." [7]

Though Roosevelt would not say so openly, he chiefly expected a cash-and-carry law to help the Allies defeat Berlin. His determination to aid them was an open secret in official circles. On September 4 Edwin ("Pa") Watson, his secretary, had asked Hull whether an American citizen who enlisted in the armed services of a belligerent without taking an oath of allegiance would lose his citizenship. "P.S." Watson wrote, "I also am authorized to say that it is hoped that the answer will be 'No.'" More significantly, Roosevelt supported Britain and France by trying to detain German merchant ships in United States and Latin American ports, allowing "defensively" armed Allied merchantmen free access to United States harbors, acceding to a British blockade of German-controlled territory, and facilitating the work of Anglo-French purchasing missions in the United States. "I hope you will at all times feel free to write me personally and outside of diplomatic procedure about any problems as they arise," Roosevelt wrote Chamberlain on September 11. "I hope and believe that we shall repeal the embargo within the next month and this is definitely a part of the Administration policy." "I shall at all times welcome it if you will keep me in touch personally with anything you want me to know about," he advised First Lord of the Admiralty Winston Churchill on the same day.[8]

As long as the Neutrality question was before the Congress and the country, however, Roosevelt stressed his determination to keep the country out of war and said nothing about helping the Allies. When Lord Tweedsmuir, the Governor General of Canada, asked the President whether he might "slip down inconspicuously" to Hyde Park at the end of September, Roosevelt and Hull asked him to wait until the conclusion of the Neutrality fight. The visit would become public knowledge, Hull warned, and would be used effectively against repeal of the arms embargo. "I am almost literally walking on eggs," Roosevelt wrote Tweedsmuir, "and, having delivered my message to the Congress, and having good prospects of the bill going through, I am at the moment saying nothing, seeing nothing and hearing nothing."

At the same time, Roosevelt resisted pressure for substantial increases in national defense forces and rapid industrial mobilization. Fearful that these actions would agitate suspicions about his peaceful intentions and make Neutrality change appear as a step toward involvement, Roosevelt temporarily limited expansion of the regular Army and National Guard to less than 50 per cent of what defense chiefs asked and suspended economic and fiscal preparations for war. "Have you noticed that . . . I have been trying to kill all war talk?" he wrote Frank Knox on October 4. "I have treated the report of the War Resources Committee as just an ordinary instance of normal preparedness work and they will go home in two weeks with my blessing." [9]

At the start of the special session, Roosevelt was cautiously hopeful that Congress would revise the Neutrality law. There were indications that the Senate would give a two-to-one vote to a cash-and-carry bill and that 90 per cent of the public favored such a law. Even Borah privately expressed himself in favor of cash-and-carry, but explained that he "must make some sort of fight . . . so as to keep the President from leading us into war." At the same time, though, congressional mail against lifting the embargo was reaching "fantastic proportions," while some twenty isolationist Senators declared their intention to fight "from hell to breakfast" to prevent revision. At the end of September isolationist groups had begun conducting keep-America-out-of-war rallies. Using network radio to carry their message to the nation, isolationists warned that repeal of the embargo would be "the first step in that tramp, tramp of American sons in Europe's war."

Roosevelt and his aides made systematic efforts to counter the isolationists. They encouraged Clark Eichelberger and William Allen White, the prominent Republican editor of the Kansas *Emporia Gazette*, to publicize the case for repeal. Organizing a national Non-Partisan Committee for Peace through Revision of the Neutrality Act, they advertised repeal as the best way to keep America at peace and preserve freedom everywhere. Roosevelt himself privately urged Catholic and labor leaders to state the case for Neutrality revision to their followers, and publicly attacked "orators and commentators" who beat their breasts and proclaimed "against sending the boys of American mothers to fight on the battlefields of Europe." He labeled this "one of the worst fakes in current history . . . a deliberate setting up of an imaginary bogey man." No one in a responsible position in national, state, or local government, he declared, "has ever suggested in any shape, manner or form the remotest possibility" of sending American boys to fight in Europe.[10]

The administration made its greatest effort in the Congress. Its central concerns were to prevent other questions from sidetracking the Neutrality debate, to defeat a possible filibuster, and to answer arguments that might win opposition votes. To meet the first two problems, Vice President Garner advised telling Senate leaders "to keep their mouths shut and to shut off debate." Specifically, he suggested expanding daily sessions from six to twelve hours to break a filibuster and sitting on the war-profits issue until Neutrality was out of the way. No filibuster tested Garner's plan, and Roosevelt successfully discouraged efforts to bring other matters before the special session. He also tried to counter the chief isolationist contention that repeal of the embargo after war had begun was an unneutral act that would draw the United States into the fighting. He emphasized publicly that Neutrality revision had been an administration goal for several months before the war, and privately urged that comparisons with World War I, when Secretary of State Bryan had rejected changes in the arms trade as unneutral, be answered with contentions that "the situations are wholly different."

By mid-October, with success in the Senate apparently assured, the administration turned its attention to the House. On October 13, when Garner told the Cabinet "that nobody knew just how the situation stood in the House," Roosevelt asked Postmaster General Farley to check things out. It produced some discouraging reports: a New Mexico Congressman advised that three administration supporters had changed their minds and others might do likewise; Farley reported a revolt against Neutrality reform led by Irish Catholic Representatives; and Senator Stiles Bridges of New Hampshire, a recent Republican convert to revision, also warned of problems in the House. By contrast, Congressman Pat Boland of Pennsylvania, the Democratic Whip, asserted that Roosevelt had regained twenty-five of the sixty-five votes lost at the regular session and that this was enough to win the Neutrality fight. Likewise, on October 27 Garner reported a margin of twenty to forty votes for the administration's bill. Refusing to take anything for granted, though, Roosevelt asked people in and out of the Congress to continue working on House members and arranged for insertion in the *Congressional Record* of new Gallup polls showing sharp increases in the President's popularity.

Substantial margins in both houses rewarded Roosevelt's efforts. On October 27 the Senate approved Neutrality revision by a vote of 63 to 30, and the House followed suit six days later with a decisive 243 to 181 vote. In the House, where there is some basis for comparison, the administration won the backing of twenty-eight Democrats and nine Republicans who had not voted on the issue in June, and gained the support of twenty-four Democrats and eight Republicans who had previously rejected Neutrality change. Roosevelt's victory was the result of changed conditions abroad and the administration's tactics at home. The onset of the war, which made insulation from the fighting and aid to the Allies compelling issues, were the largest factors in persuading the Congress to revise the Neutrality law. Roosevelt contributed to this outcome by accepting a congressionally determined cash-and-carry policy which quieted fears about getting into war and reassured Southern conservatives, among whom he made his greatest gains, that Neutrality change would not expand presidential power.[11]

At the same time that Roosevelt pushed for Neutrality reform, he also laid plans for the Americas which could assure Hemisphere security and aid the Allies. In line with the Buenos Aires and Lima agreements to consult when events threatened peace in the Hemisphere, Roosevelt had arranged for an inter-American conference at Panama. The conference was to work out common neutrality plans and means of coping with the monetary and commercial problems a European war would bring to the Americas. The administration particularly wished to head off economic instability which could make Latin America vulnerable to Nazi penetration. In addition, Roosevelt was eager to have the conference establish a neutrality zone around the Western Hemisphere which would be closed to belligerent warships. Disturbed by rumors that a fleet of German submarines operating out of a Brazilian island or obscure Caribbean ports would attack Allied shipping and aid assaults against British possessions in the Hemisphere, Roosevelt asked Adolf Berle to find historical precedents for creating such a zone to keep war away from the Americas. When Berle identified several U.S. and Latin American proposals made during the Napoleonic wars and First World War for excluding foreign war vessels from "certain Atlantic waters," Roosevelt proposed this as the centerpiece of the conference.

Moved by considerations of their own safety and feelings of trust engendered by the Good Neighbor policy, the Latin Republics, in a "palpable" display of unity, backed all these proposals. In an eleven-day meeting at Panama beginning on September 23, the American states unanimously agreed to common rules of neutrality and established an Inter-American Neutrality Committee to keep them out of war. The conference also created an Inter-American Financial and Economic Advisory Committee to support monetary stability and relieve the loss of European trade through greater Hemisphere exchange. Most significantly, the conference endorsed Roosevelt's "neutrality zone" in a Declaration of Panama. As "a measure of continental self-protection" and the "inherent right" of neutrals, the twenty-one Republics defined an area ranging from three hundred to one thousand miles off the Atlantic coast south of Canada, which was to be "free from the commission of any hostile act by any non-American belligerent." Though making no commitment to back the declaration with force, the Republics agreed to keep watch over the area by coordinated patrols and to ask the belligerents to respect the zone.[12]

Despite the unparalleled cooperativeness of the Latin states, Roosevelt was unable to give much practical meaning to these agreements. In the fall of 1939, American resistance to new loans or credits to Latin American governments largely undermined plans for greater economic cooperation. Opposition in the Congress, the press, and, most of all, from the Foreign Bondholders Protective Council to financial aid for countries in default on existing debts and expropriated American property forestalled positive replies to Latin requests for such help. Moreover, insurmountable differences between the Treasury and State Departments on how to overcome this opposition and arrange the loans left the administration without an effective plan of aid to Latin America until the second half of 1940.

Similarly, the idea of a war-free zone off the Americas fell short of Roosevelt's expectations. Even before the Panama conference approved the President's plan, American naval chiefs declared effective patrol of so large an area impossible, and the belligerents called it a violation of the freedom of the seas. The British, in particular, declared themselves unable to accept the zone unless the United States assured that German ships would not use it as a sanctuary and deprive the Allies of full use of their superiority at sea. To satisfy this objection and uphold the aim of the declaration, Roosevelt assigned eighty ships to patrol duty in the area and personally worked to assure that effective operations promptly got under way.

Though cooperative patrolling with the Latin states was in effect by the end of 1939, the Republics were unable to prevent belligerent actions in the zone. In December three British cruisers and the German pocket battleship *Graf Spee* fought a spectacular battle off the coast of Uruguay. Toward the end of 1940, after further unsuccessful efforts to bar belligerent warships from the area, Roosevelt abandoned his quest for belligerent recognition of "neutral" waters and accepted Hull's proposal for a "flexible zone" determined by current circumstance. Though the zone did not provide the insulation from war Roosevelt wanted, it allowed American patrol ships to inform the British of German naval movements in the Western Atlantic, and it restrained Hitler. Convinced that Britain and France would not fight him over Poland or would quickly make a compromise peace if they did, Hitler had discounted the importance of the United States in a European war. Once it was clear, however, that London and Paris would make an extended fight, Hitler began taking account of American power, which he was eager to keep out of the war. To avoid provoking the United States, therefore, he gave unspoken recognition to Roosevelt's neutrality zone by keeping German submarine operations in the area to a minimum.[13]

Roosevelt's partiality for the Allies had extended in September and October to refusing to help Berlin arrange a mediated settlement, which would leave it in a more powerful position than before the fighting.

Though he wished the United States to play a major part in arranging a stable peace, he believed this incompatible with the continuation of Hitler's regime. On September 11, after Ambassador Kennedy had suggested that "the President can be the savior of the world" by restoring world peace after Polish defeat, Roosevelt had answered: "The people of the United States would not support any move for peace initiated by this Government that would consolidate or make possible a survival of a regime of force and of aggression." On September 15, however, he met with William R. Davis, an American businessman with extensive German contacts, who was acting as a go-between for Hermann Goering. Learning from Davis that Goering was eager to prevent all-out fighting with Britain and France, and that he or the German Army might force Hitler from power, the President declared himself ready to consider the possibility of mediation if he were officially asked by the interested governments. Roosevelt, however, was less interested in peace talks themselves than in overturning Hitler; he appreciated that the British government could not call for peace talks and survive.

Roosevelt's aversion to mediating a settlement that would assure the continuation of Nazi power registered forcefully in the following month. At the beginning of October, with Kennedy warning that further fighting would mean defeat for Britain and "the complete collapse of everything we hope and live for," Roosevelt complained to Morgenthau that Joe Kennedy "always has been an appeaser and always will be an appeaser. . . . If Germany or Italy made a good peace offer tomorrow . . . Joe would start working on the King and his friend, the Queen, and from there on down, to get everybody to accept it . . . he's just a pain in the neck to me."

During the first two weeks of October, Roosevelt also turned aside suggestions from Berlin and Brussels that he initiate peace talks. On October 7, after Hitler announced that neither the Allies nor Germany had anything to gain from continued fighting and after stories appeared in the press about German interest in American mediation, Roosevelt told his secretary Marvin McIntyre: "If you believe this morning's papers you will expect me to be in Berlin talking peace with Hitler next Monday morning. Fortunately you agree with me about what one reads in the papers." Further, on October 12, when William R. Davis told him that Goering was eager to have the President mediate and that he "could, if he would, force peace on Europe," Roosevelt described himself as able to act only on an official proposal from Berlin, and declared that London would not negotiate now. A few days later, after Goering sent a message urging the President to abandon his fight for Neutrality reform and support the German peace drive and Berle informed him that Davis had misrepresented him to Goering as ready to mediate, Roosevelt "squarely hit the roof." At the same time, a report that King Leopold of Belgium saw the President as "the only person in the world" who could keep the conflict from hardening into "an irrevocable, bitter, real, long and horrible war" moved Roosevelt to reply that an American effort for peace should occur only when it became abundantly clear that it would bring peace.[14]

While Roosevelt refused to embarrass the Allies or to aid Hitler by offering to mediate, he was ready to help prevent the spread of the European war and preserve the independence of small neutral states. But the two aims quickly proved to be incompatible, and Roosevelt gave priority to the first of them. More specifically, when the Soviet Union invaded Poland on September 17, 1939, Roosevelt had agreed not to designate Moscow a belligerent by invoking the Neutrality law. Informed by a diplomatic source that Russia's action did not mean full participation in the European war, he wished to avoid anything that might encourage Moscow to fight Britain and France. In September and October, therefore, when Russia established control over Estonia, Latvia, and Lithuania, the administration interpreted it as directed against Berlin and accepted the nominal independence of these Baltic states as a means of avoiding diplomatic protests.

Despite hopes that Finland would not suffer a similar fate, continuing reluctance to antagonize the Soviet Union and fear of jeopardizing repeal of the arms embargo initially inhibited the administration from pressing Moscow to respect Finnish independence or from raising the question of a Finnish armaments loan. Hull, for instance, told Finnish Minister Hajalmar Procopé that American pressure on Moscow would probably do more harm than good to both Finland and the United States, while Morgenthau explained: "We are not going, with this [neutrality] bill pending on the Hill, to take any risks. The whole picture is *so* important for you and for everybody else, the *whole* picture."

The prospect of wider European fighting through a Soviet attack on Finland and the irresistible attraction of tiny Finland holding its ground against Russian might moved Roosevelt to ask for Soviet restraint. On October 10, while receiving appeals from the Swedish Crown Prince and the President of Finland, Roosevelt, despite Hull's objection that it would create a troublesome precedent, agreed to send a message to Moscow. "The President expresses the earnest hope," FDR cabled President Mikhail Kalinin, "that the Soviet Union will make no demands on Finland which are inconsistent with the maintenance and development of amicable and peaceful relations between the two countries, and the independence of each." Ten days later, in response to reports of an imminent German attack on the Low Countries and a request from the Dutch Minister in Washington, Roosevelt secretly asked assurances that the German government would not violate Dutch and Belgian neutrality.

As Roosevelt anticipated, though, his influence in Berlin and Moscow was "just about zero." German leaders offered unpersuasive replies, while

Kalinin and Molotov rejected "tendentious versions" of Soviet intentions and belittled "American sentimental interest in Finland." More revealing, rumors of a German offensive through the Low Countries continued to plague Europe through the winter, while Moscow maintained its pressure on Helsinki to yield territorial and military concessions. When the Finns refused to comply, the Soviets manufactured a crisis in late November as a prelude to an armed attack. Though having little hope that it would deter Moscow from mopping up Finland, Roosevelt and Hull offered the good offices of the United States to compose the Russian-Finnish dispute. Rejecting the administration's proposal and ignoring its warning against a "further deterioration of international relations," Moscow launched a full-scale assault against Finland on November 30.[15]

The Soviet attack, including aerial bombardment of undefended cities, outraged FDR. He described the United States as "not only horrified but thoroughly angry" at "this dreadful rape of Finland." Under prodding from Sumner Welles, he gave brief thought to breaking relations with Moscow: "People are asking," he wrote on November 30, "why one should have anything to do with the present Soviet leaders because their idea of civilization and human happiness is so totally different from ours." But still reluctant to do anything that would drive Moscow into closer cooperation with Berlin, he used less direct means of opposing the Soviets. He publicly condemned "this new resort to military force," asked the Russians not to bomb civilian populations, and issued a fresh call for a moral embargo on airplane sales to nations guilty of such unprovoked attacks. At the same time, he ordered Morgenthau to end sales of aluminum and molybdenum to the Soviet Union, and countered the Secretary's objection that such sales were perfectly legal with the observation that "you have done worse things before." Though a moral embargo slowed the export of these metals, it did not reduce the flow of other materials to Moscow; in the three months between November 1939 and February 1940, Soviet purchases in the United States more than doubled over the previous year.

Roosevelt also tried to aid the Finns. He refused to proclaim a state of war, which would bar Helsinki from borrowing American funds; he decided to ask Congress to return Finland's current payment of almost $235,000 on her World War I debt; and he arranged a $10 million loan which could help the Finns buy weapons abroad. "We are literally doing everything we can without legislation to help the Finns," Roosevelt declared on December 22. But the Finns could not agree. Asking for $60 million in credits and $20 million in war matériel, Procopé complained that "guarded assistance in the way of surplus supplies" and $10 million "does not help us very much. . . . We need much more money. . . . We need . . . guns and airplanes and shells." [16]

Insurmountable difficulties blocked these demands. Military supplies asked by the Finns were not available. Because it was struggling to equip American forces and preparing to ask the Congress to supply troops that could be called to the colors in an emergency, the administration found little more than forty surplus navy planes it could legally send the Finns. Sharply questioned at a November congressional hearing about America's defense buildup, Chief of Staff General George C. Marshall had retorted that we were not building up but trying to catch up to the level authorized in 1920. Despite these problems, in January 1940, when Procopé declared that American failure to sell arms to his country "would be tantamount to signing a death warrant," Roosevelt proposed selling surplus arms to Sweden for resale to Finland. But this was probably only a gesture on Roosevelt's part. When Marshall identified only a small number of artillery pieces he could legitimately call surplus and when Hull and Secretary of War Harry Woodring, an isolationist from Kansas, warned of the political repercussions that would flow from so unneutral an act, Roosevelt abandoned the idea.

Legal and political bars also restrained him from giving Finland a loan of $60 million. In December, when a friend suggested that he simply waive the payment on the Finnish debt, he had replied: "I may be a benevolent dictator and all powerful Santa Claus and though the spirit has moved me at times, I still operate under the laws which the all-wise Congress passes. . . . Whether we like it or not Congress and God still live!" Further, at the beginning of 1940, when Procopé pressed his $60 million loan request, Roosevelt told Hull that "we cannot make any large loan to Finland under the R.F.C. [Reconstruction Finance Corporation] Act because, frankly, there is not enough security for its re-payment under the existing law." But this was not Roosevelt's real reason for rejecting the request. He believed that pressure for a large armaments loan would revive charges that he intended to involve the country in the war, would undermine his ability to offer guarded assistance to Britain and France, and would weaken his chances for reelection in 1940, if he decided to run again. "Pressure by the Republicans and conservative Democrats continues in relation to the political future!" he observed in a letter of December 13. ". . . The Republicans will raise every particular kind of cain when Congress meets." Hull reinforced this concern by repeatedly telling him that congressional opponents were waiting for the administration to take an unneutral step and "would thereupon start attacking . . . in force."

The state of public feeling also gave Roosevelt pause. Though sympathy for "brave little Finland" abounded in the country, there was also widespread reluctance to do anything that might draw the United States into the Soviet-Finnish war. After an initial outburst of indignation toward the Soviet Union, the public entered "an isolationist period of second thoughts." Letters to the Town Hall Meeting of the Air, a radio program aimed at testing public sentiment, showed little desire for involvement in Finland's behalf. "What worries me, especially," FDR wrote William Allen White in mid-December, "is that public opinion over here is patting itself on the back every morning and thanking God for the Atlantic Ocean (and the Pacific Ocean). We greatly underestimate the serious implications to our own future and . . . . it really is essential to us . . . to warn the American people that they . . . should think of possible ultimate results in Europe and the Far East. Therefore, my sage old friend, my problem is to get the American people to think of conceivable consequences without scaring the American people into thinking that they are going to be dragged into this war." "The country as a whole," he shortly wrote in another letter, "does not yet have any deep sense of world crisis." [17]

In these circumstances, he would take only the most cautious steps in Finland's behalf. Instead of presenting a specific aid program to Congress, on January 10 he sent word to the chairmen of the House Ways and Means Committee and the Appropriations Committee that he would like Congress to help Finland with a bill of its own design. "They both pressed me very hard to indicate to them how much money you would like to see loaned by Congress," Morgenthau reported to the President, "and I said that you had no program." Reports a few days later that House leaders opposed a loan to Finland confirmed Roosevelt in his decision not to advance a specific plan. "There is without doubt in the United States," he told Congress on January 16, "a great desire for some action to assist Finland to finance the purchase of agricultural surpluses and manufactured products, not including implements of war. There is at the same time undoubted opposition to the creation of precedents that might lead to large credits to nations in Europe, either belligerents or neutrals. No one desires a return to such a status. The facts in regard to Finland are just as fully in the possession of every Member of Congress as they are in the Executive Branch of the Government. . . . The matter of credits to that Republic is wholly within the jurisdiction of the Congress. . . . An extension of credit at this time," he assured the legislators, "does not in any way constitute or threaten any so-called 'involvement' in European wars." [18]

The Congress showed little inclination to give Finland much quick help. Senate isolationists at once denounced the President's modest proposal as the first step on the road to war and blocked any swift response. On January 19 Roosevelt complained to the Cabinet that Senators who were delaying aid to Finland were "a bunch of 'Uriah Heeps' . . . who did not realize that what was going on in Europe would inevitably effect this country." His annoyance with opposition to Finnish aid and anger toward Moscow boiled over in a speech before the pro-Soviet American Youth Congress on February 10: The idea that a loan to Finland was "'an attempt to force America into the imperialistic war'. . . . was un-adulterated twaddle based . . . on ninety per cent ignorance." The hope that Russia "would eventually become a peace-loving, popular government . . . which would not interfere with the integrity of its neighbors" was "either shattered or put away in cold storage against some better day. The Soviet Union," he declared, "is run by a dictatorship as absolute as any other dictatorship in the world. It has allied itself with another dictatorship and it has invaded a neighbor so infinitesimally small that it could do no conceivable possible harm to the Soviet Union." The pro-Soviet audience booed and hissed. Meanwhile, after a six-week debate, during which Moscow broke Finnish resistance, the Congress approved a token $20 million credit to Finland for nonmilitary supplies. The sympathy of the United States and other nations, Finland's Foreign Minister remarked, was so great "it nearly suffocated us." [19]

Roosevelt also had difficulties aiding Britain and France. The revised Neutrality law compelled him to designate combat zones, which closed eight Atlantic and Baltic sea routes to ninety-two United States ships earning $52.5 million a year. This, one commentator observed, "aided the German blockade of Britain as effectively as if all our ships had been torpedoed." To prevent this loss of revenue, American shipowners asked permission for the nominal transfer of their vessels to foreign flags not barred from war zones. Roosevelt was not averse to the idea. But complaints in the Congress and the press that this would be "a dirty subterfuge" or "trick" which would violate the spirit of the Neutrality law persuaded him to support only bona fide sales.[20]

Roosevelt also found himself hamstrung by the British and the French. In the two months after revision of the Neutrality law, the Allies placed surprisingly small orders for American supplies. A standstill in the fighting after Poland's defeat and a belief that the war would last three years, or long enough for them to produce most of their own arms, reduced their sense of urgency about buying weapons in the United States. Moreover, with American money markets closed to them by the Johnson Act of 1934 barring loans to defaulters on World War I debts and the Neutrality laws, the Allies tried to protect their gold and dollar reserves by initially limiting imports to raw materials, foodstuffs, machine tools, and aircraft.

Allied purchasing procedures also slowed their acquisition of goods and threatened to create political and economic problems in the United States. "The dear British and French Governments," Roosevelt had complained to Bullitt on November 23, "are failing, as usual, to be definite between themselves and to be definite to me. They shifted back and forth a dozen times . . . on their purchase methods and finally got everyone so disgusted that we had to tell them what to do." Roosevelt asked the Allies to establish a closely coordinated purchasing mission in the United States which would proceed through the Federal Reserve and allow the administration to keep close track of Allied orders and security sales in American stock markets. By these means, Roosevelt hoped to avoid interference with American military needs, excessive price rises, disturbances in the stock markets, and Allied reliance on private banking firms like J. P. Morgan which Americans blamed for involvement in the last war.

Though the British and the French had satisfied the President's complaint in December by establishing a Purchasing Commission and though the Allies greatly increased their orders at the beginning of 1940, especially for planes and engines, Roosevelt now had to overcome resistance in his own administration. Secretary of War Woodring, backed by military chiefs, opposed any foreign purchases that interfered in the least with American needs. They particularly objected to Morgenthau's efforts to sell new American planes, which were in short supply. In a conference with Army and Air Corps officers on January 17, Roosevelt emphasized his desire to speed aircraft deliveries to the Allies and insisted that a percentage of army planes coming off the production lines go to France.

But the "battle of Washington," as Morgenthau called it, did not end there. In March, when Woodring, Assistant Secretary of War Louis Johnson, and Air Corps Chief of Staff General Henry ("Hap") Arnold refused Allied access to secret devices necessary to the planes they had ordered, Roosevelt told Arnold that resistance in the War Department must end, that leaks from Johnson and Arnold to the Republican and isolationist press were to stop, and that uncooperative officers would be sent to Guam. In April, moreover, when Woodring continued to buck the President's wishes, Roosevelt ordered him either to go along or to resign. With safeguards built into the sales contracts to protect American security and Allied investments creating a fourfold expansion of American airplane production, Woodring accepted Roosevelt's lead.[21]

Roosevelt's eagerness for quick aid to the Allies rested on fears that they were too weak to resist a German assault, especially from the air. Throughout the fall of 1939, Bullitt and Kennedy had warned that Britain and France were no match for Berlin. "There is an enormous danger that the German air force will be able to win this war for Germany before the planes can begin to come out of our plants in quantity," Bullitt had reported on October 18. "Although everybody hates Hitler," Kennedy had written from London on November 3, the British "still don't want to be finished economically, financially, politically, and socially, which they are beginning to suspect will be their fate if the war goes on very long." Unless 10,000 planes reached the Allies from the United States during 1940, Bullitt had predicted in December, Britain and France would go down to defeat. Kennedy was even more pessimistic, forecasting that Germany could outlast the Allies economically and militarily and that another year of war would leave all Europe in economic ruin and "ready for communism or some other radical change in social order."

Adolf Berle and Raymond Geist, American Consul General in Berlin, had added to Roosevelt's concern by warning that Russian expansion in concert with Berlin would pose a grave threat to the United States. "If this nightmare proves real (and it seems too damnably logical) . . . ," Berle observed, "you will have two men able to rule from Manchuria to the Rhine, much as Genghis Khan once ruled and nothing to stop the combined Russian-German force at any point, with the possible exception of the Himalayan Mountains north of India." The Western world would then be "besieged on two Americas; and the rest of my life . . . will be spent trying to defend various parts of this world from economic, military and propaganda attempts to establish domination over it." Geist, who had returned to Washington in November, also saw a German-Russian victory as a "distinct possibility." They would then, according to Geist, seek "air bases and outposts pretty much all over the world" and force the United States "to become a militarized nation."

After revision of the Neutrality law in November 1939, Roosevelt had considered voicing these fears publicly. In a draft of a speech attacking isolationist "fallacies," he had argued that anyone thinking "in terms of geography and distance and speed of transportation" would feel compelled to admit that the country's safety depended on a defense of the entire "American Continent, all the way from Alaska and Canada to Cape Horn." "If France and England should be defeated," he said, "the United States will have to watch its step. And make it clear to the dictator victors that they will have another first-class war on their hands if they seek, in any way, to dominate any part of the American Continent." Victory for the dictators, he had also warned, would compel the United States to spend more on military preparedness and would injure our foreign commerce. American trade "would be faced with competition by government-controlled and government-subsidized trade, arising out of every part of a dictator-dominated Europe and a dictator-dominated system of colonies in almost every part of the world." Fearful, however, that such a "theory of self-defense" would be taken as a justification for involvement in the war and would be used against him if he ran again in 1940, Roosevelt never gave the speech.[22]

Russia's attack on Finland had intensified Roosevelt's concern and moved him to think about more specific means of defending the United States from Soviet-German might. While recognizing that Germany itself might be "much concerned over Russia's unexpected policy of action," he leaned toward the idea that "there is a fairly definite agreement between Russia and Germany for the division of European control and with it the extension of that control to Asia Minor, Persia, Africa and the various British, French, Dutch, Belgian, etc. colonies." If there were such a plan, he believed that a Soviet-German victory in the war would place American civilization "in peril." "Our world trade," he had written in December, "would be at the mercy of the combine and our increasingly better relations with our twenty neighbors to the south would end—unless we were willing to go to war in their behalf against a German-Russian dominated Europe." As one step against this danger, Roosevelt laid plans to lease the Dutch West Indies from Holland and fortify them against attack.

Roosevelt gave public expression to this anxiety in his State of the Union message on January 3, 1940. Reassuring the nation that he shared the majority will to stay out of war, he explained that "there is a vast difference between keeping out of war and pretending that war is none of our business. We do not have to go to war with other nations," he asserted, "but at least we can strive with other nations to encourage the kind of peace that will lighten the troubles of the world, and by so doing help our own nation as well. . . . For it becomes clearer and clearer that the future world will be a shabby and dangerous place to live in—yes, even for Americans to live in—if it is ruled by force in the hands of a few. . . . I hope that we shall have fewer American ostriches in our midst," Roosevelt declared. "It is not good for the ultimate health of ostriches to bury their heads in the sand." [23]

Roosevelt was trying not only to dispel isolationist assumptions but also to line up support for peace efforts that would block Soviet-German domination of Europe and assure American security. Within a few days after the Soviet invasion of Finland on November 30, he had told Berle that he "proposed to make peace next spring on the basis of having everybody produce everything they could; take what they needed; put the rest into a pool; and let the countries which needed the balance draw it as needed, through the cartels." Roosevelt did not elaborate on what he meant, probably because he had nothing more in mind than a vague formula for opening peace talks which could delay or possibly avert Anglo-French defeat in the war and the expansion of German-Soviet power. The following week he told the Chicago newspaper publisher Frank Knox that a German victory would produce chaos in Europe, and he raised the possibility of American participation in shaping postwar peace.

More specifically, Roosevelt decided to send a Christmas message to the Pope which would "lay something of a moral foundation for an ultimate peace." As Berle, who was asked to draft the letter, understood the President, the idea was to create some "unity of moral action" that would then allow the resolution of technical or mechanical ills. "The people of this nation," Roosevelt wrote Pius XII, ". . . understand that that which harms one segment of humanity harms all the rest. They know that only by friendly association among . . . the seekers of peace everywhere can the forces of evil be overcome." Though he acknowledged that the moment was not right for a specific peace plan, he confidently predicted that "the time for that will surely come." In the meantime, he declared his intention to send a personal representative to the Vatican so that "our parallel endeavors for peace . . . shall have united expression." [24]

In January 1940, however, Roosevelt decided to seek a peace settlement before a German offensive broke the standstill on the Western front. He appreciated that chances of accomplishing anything were about "one in a thousand," and that to be successful he would need the combined powers of "the Holy Ghost and Jack Dempsey." But indications that both sides might be receptive to meaningful talks and fears of what additional fighting would mean for Europe and especially American security persuaded him to try. "No possibility, however remote and however improbable," he told Welles early in the New Year, "should be overlooked." His "obligations to the American people made it imperative for him to leave no stone unturned."

Consequently, in January and February, Roosevelt initiated three peace moves. He asked James D. Mooney, a General Motors executive with high German contacts, to see if there were interest in Berlin in "a fair and equitable" solution to current world problems. Mooney was to emphasize that the President had no interest in "any scheme of world domination" or in "interposing himself between the belligerents to urge them to peace." Should they ask, however, he was ready to act as a moderator seeking to "reduce and reconcile" their differences. Second, Roosevelt invited forty-six neutral nations to consider exchanging views on the maintenance of postwar peace through arms control and international economic stability. The unstated idea behind this proposal was that "neutrals are parties at interest in a modern war," or, in other words, that an organization of neutrals might propose mediation and peace terms and insist on sitting "at the peace table with equal right." [25]

As the third, and most significant move, Roosevelt asked Welles to go to Rome, Berlin, Paris, and London to learn "the views of the four governments . . . as to the present possibilities of concluding any just and permanent peace." Though he was ready to encourage negotiations with Hitler on such a basis, he expressed "no interest in any temporary or tentative armed truce." Further, though he did not authorize Welles to make any proposals or commitments in the name of the United States government, he empowered him, if he thought it wise, to discuss peace on the "old basis of disarmament and an opening of trade," or to revive the President's peace proposal to Hitler of April 1939. Roosevelt had small hope that any of this would work, but, as he told Breckinridge Long, it might at least delay a German offensive and give the Allies a chance to strengthen their defenses. He also hoped that Welles might discourage Mussolini from entering the war.

Though Roosevelt made two of these initiatives public on February 9, he shielded their real aim. Instead of describing the inquiry to other neutrals as a peace move, the administration explained it as strictly an effort to encourage postwar disarmament and freer trade. Similarly, instead of acknowledging that Welles was to investigate peace possibilities, Roosevelt described his mission as "solely for the purpose of advising the President and the Secretary of State as to present conditions in Europe." Because Chamberlain and Hull warned that avowed peace efforts would aid Berlin by creating disunity and false hopes in Britain and France, Roosevelt felt compelled to disguise his true purpose. An open peace move would also evoke isolationist predictions of American involvement in the war and undermine chances for a third term.

At the beginning of 1940 Roosevelt expressed reservations about running again. The chance to free himself from the exhausting demands of the presidency and write his memoirs in a hilltop "dream house" at Hyde Park probably had some genuine appeal. But a determination to prevent a conservative or anti–New Deal Democrat from succeeding him, the possibility of a German victory, and the prerogatives of office made him reluctant to step aside. In these circumstances, he was careful not to weaken himself politically by challenging widespread public aversion to European interventions of any kind. At the same time, however, Roosevelt appreciated that a successful peace initiative would add greatly to his political strength. Welles sold him on the European trip, Roosevelt told Bullitt, "by saying that it would make a hit with the ladies' peace societies." More important, a Welles mission that led to serious peace talks could make FDR an indispensable candidate for another term. Considerations of American security and domestic politics, then, persuaded Roosevelt to send Welles abroad.[26]

Despite his guarded explanation, Roosevelt's announcement of the Welles mission touched off both Allied speculation that he intended to appease Hitler and isolationist outcries that he would sacrifice American interests "to put the world aright." During the Welles trip, therefore, he felt compelled to quiet Allied fears by stating that peace cannot be lasting if it leads to "oppression, or starvation, or cruelty, or human life dominated by armed camps. It cannot be a sound peace if small nations must live in fear of powerful neighbors. It cannot be a moral peace if freedom from invasion is sold for tribute." In addition, to blunt isolationist charges of dangerous meddling abroad, Hull reiterated the limited nature of the mission, while Welles himself announced from Rome that he had neither received nor conveyed any peace plans and that he was there only to gather information.[27]

Welles, in fact, did little else. Going first to Rome, where he was to discourage Italian involvement in the fighting, he met with Mussolini and Foreign Minister Count Galeazzo Ciano on February 26. Though Mussolini expressed the conviction that successful negotiations for a real and lasting peace were now possible, he gave Welles little substantive reason to think this could be the case. Declaring that a just political peace in Europe would have to precede other constructive steps, he described such a peace as the assurance of Germany's "vital interests" in Central Europe and Italian freedom from British control in the Mediterranean. Though he also expressed a willingness to see Welles again after he had traveled to the other capitals, Mussolini was less than forthcoming during their conversation: "He was ponderous and static, rather than vital," Welles recorded. "He moved with an elephantine motion. Every step appeared an effort. . . . During our long and rapid interchange of views, he kept his eyes shut a considerable part of the time, opening them . . . only when he desired particularly to underline some remark. . . . One could almost sense a leaden oppression."

The reception in Berlin shattered what little hope Roosevelt and Welles had for meaningful peace talks. On the eve of Welles's arrival in Germany, Hitler issued a secret order against any indications of German interest in opening negotiations. Welles was not to be "left in the slightest doubt that Germany is determined to conclude this war victoriously." Foreign Minister Ribbentrop fully met Hitler's request. Receiving Welles "glacially . . . without the semblance of a smile," he treated him to a two-hour harangue, "eyes continuously closed" in the manner of the "delphic Oracle." "Ribbentrop has a completely closed mind. . . . a very stupid mind," Welles observed. "I have rarely seen a man I disliked more." Though Hitler was more pleasant and dignified with Welles, the message was the same: there was no hope for a lasting peace until German arms broke English-French determination to destroy Germany. Worse yet, conversations with the most experienced members of the Berlin diplomatic corps suggested that Hitler had the domestic backing and military strength to accomplish this goal.

French and British officials echoed Hitler's belief that negotiations were not possible. Though the French expressed a willingness to treat with Hitler in return for adequate security guarantees, they did not think these could be arranged. Only additional fighting and Hitler's demise could provide this. The British were even more emphatic. Expressing no faith in talks with Berlin, they uniformly agreed that Europe could not have lasting peace until Nazism was destroyed and Germany learned that "war does not pay." Despite some talk in France that continued fighting would destroy all Europe, neither capital showed much concern for a quick end to the war. Paris "seemed its normal self," with traffic undiminished, food plentiful, and champagne available as an apéritif. A warm spring Sunday brought all London into the parks, and apart from the prevalence of uniforms, there was little to remind one of the war. All in all, Welles returned from Europe at the end of March 1940 convinced that there was not "the slightest chance of any successful negotiation at this time for a durable peace." [28]

On April 9, 1940, Hitler invaded Denmark and Norway, and Roosevelt once more struggled to aid the victims of aggression and educate the public about the dangers to American security. Following Morgenthau's suggestion, Roosevelt promptly froze Danish assets in the United States.

This not only kept some $267 million out of German hands but also helped keep Denmark alive. "You and the Danish Minister and the President and I," Berle told Morgenthau, "are building a Denmark in our heads for the time being. . . . We're just arranging there's going to be a Denmark existing somewhere . . . and just keep on going until the Germans get out of there."

At the same time, Roosevelt urged Americans to consider what this latest round of aggression meant to the United States. It was "a grand thing," he told reporters on April 9, that current events will force "a great many more Americans to think about the potentialities of the war." "Today we can have no illusions," he declared in a Pan American Day address on April 15. "Old dreams of universal empire are again rampant. . . . This is not of mere academic interest. We know that what happens in the Old World directly and powerfully affects the peace and well-being of the new." At a meeting three days later with 275 members of the American Society of Newspaper Editors, he declared it their "duty" to confront the people with questions about what it will mean to the United States if the dictators win in Europe and the Far East. Believing that isolationists would dismiss such representations from him as "alarmist" or as steps toward war and reelection, Roosevelt asked the editors to bring the international situation frankly to the attention of the American public. "You can do it just as well as I can," he told them. To remove any doubts about the need, he gave a detailed description of how the Americas might shortly come under attack. "You are in real danger," he told William Allen White of Kansas, "and do not realize it." [29]

The most immediate danger was to Greenland and Iceland. Germany's occupation of these Danish possessions would present a direct threat to Britain and all of North America. Yet Roosevelt was reluctant to have Britain or Canada take temporary control of either one; it would create a precedent for the Japanese to seize the Dutch East Indies if Germany conquered Holland. Nor did he believe that domestic opinion would support measures to bring Greenland or the more-distant Iceland under American protection. Though he and others in the administration described Greenland as belonging to the American continent, he "stalled" on whether the Monroe Doctrine applied to the area, telling reporters on April 12 that the question was "premature" and "hypothetical." While willing to send "humanitarian" aid to the country's 17,000 inhabitants and to establish a consulate at Godthaab, the capital, he resisted suggestions that the United States take direct responsibility for Greenland's defense. In meetings with Canadian Prime Minister Mackenzie King on April 23 and 24, he left the impression that he wanted the British Navy to defend Greenland against a German attack.

Roosevelt's reluctance to commit himself rested not only on a realistic fear of creating a war scare in the United States, which would cause domestic political problems, but also on the hope that Anglo-French forces would be able to deprive the Germans of their Scandinavian gains. Though giving a good account of themselves in naval engagements off Norway and though confidently declaring that Hitler's actions would prove to be a major strategic blunder, the Allies soon showed themselves unable to throw the Germans back. By the end of April, in fact, it was clear that they had suffered a first-class defeat.[30]

These events gave Roosevelt the "jitters," making him afraid that "the English were going to get licked," and spurring him to new efforts in behalf of the Allies and American defense. During April, while the outcome in Scandinavia remained unclear, Roosevelt had refused to act on Vatican requests for another appeal to Mussolini to keep out of the war. He believed it would encourage concern in the United States that he intended to involve the country in the fighting. By the end of the month, however, when the Allied defeat in Norway increased the likelihood of an Italian move, Roosevelt asked Morgenthau in "strictest, strictest of confidence. . . . to take care of Italy" by preventing it from taking funds out of the United States. The following day he sent Mussolini a secret message. It contained a thinly veiled threat of American intervention, and Roosevelt asked Ambassador Phillips in Rome to present it orally, but not in writing. "A further extension of the area of hostilities," Roosevelt's message said, ". . . would necessarily have far-reaching and unforeseeable consequences, not only in Europe, but also in the Near and Far East, in Africa, and in the three Americas. No man can today predict with assurance, should such a further extension take place, what the ultimate result might be—or foretell what nations, however determined they may be today to remain at peace, might yet eventually find it imperative in their own defense to enter the war." Though replying through his Ambassador in Washington that "Italy definitely does not desire any extension of hostilities," Mussolini also made it clear that the President's threat would not intimidate him.

Despite the Duce's reply, events during the next two weeks persuaded Roosevelt to appeal to him again. With Germany invading the Low Countries on May 10 and overwhelming Holland and parts of Belgium in four days, Roosevelt received several reports that Mussolini would almost certainly enter the war in the near future. Appeals from the Allies to help block this step moved Roosevelt to send Mussolini a fresh expression of his concern. "You whom the great Italian people call their leader have it in your hands to stay the spread of this war to another group of 200,000,000 human souls in the Mediterranean area. . . . As a realist you also will . . . recognize that if this war should extend throughout the world it would pass beyond the control of heads of state. . . . And no man, no matter how omniscient, how powerful, can foretell the result either to himself or his own people." Mussolini, who had told his Foreign

Minister on May 13 that he would declare war within a month, turned aside Roosevelt's appeal with the explanation "that Italy is and intends to remain allied with Germany and that Italy cannot remain absent at a moment in which the fate of Europe is at stake." [31]

Roosevelt now also moved to strengthen American military might. In the first week of May, he had arranged to discuss "basic war plans" with Navy chiefs and asked the War Department for new estimates of Army needs. Though having refused to bring the Army up to full strength in the fall and having reduced its budget request in the winter, he now felt compelled to build up ground as well as air forces. On May 10, the day the war began "in earnest," he had received a War Department report that the United States could field only five divisions totaling 80,000 men and had equipment for less than 500,000 combat troops. By contrast, German forces in the West exceeded two million men organized into 140 divisions. Six days later, with Holland already out of the fighting and German armies having broken through Belgium into northern France, Roosevelt asked the Congress for $1.18 billion in additional defense appropriations, over half of which was for "a larger and thoroughly rounded Army."

Roosevelt remained as convinced as ever, however, of the need for air strength, both to deter an attack on the Americas and to give the Allies a chance to defeat Berlin. His message to the Congress on May 16, in fact, laid greatest emphasis on the danger from air power, warning that planes moving between 200 and 300 miles an hour from any number of Atlantic and Pacific bases largely eliminated the oceans as "adequate defensive barriers." Pointing out, moreover, that one belligerent had more planes and a greater production capacity than all its opponents combined, he proposed that the nation develop "the ability to turn out at least 50,000 planes a year" and commit itself to the creation of a 50,000-plane air force. Still believing that American planes in Allied hands were a prime weapon of self-defense, he asked the Congress not to do anything "which would in any way hamper or delay the delivery of American-made planes" to Britain and France. "That," he said, "from the point of view of our own national defense, would be extremely shortsighted." [32]

Roosevelt's request to the Congress was partly in response to impassioned Allied pleas for quicker and greater help. On May 14 and 15 the French and British had deluged him with requests for planes, old destroyers, anti-aircraft guns, and ammunition. Churchill, who had just become Prime Minister on a program of "blood, toil, tears and sweat," also asked the President to proclaim nonbelligerency, to sell to Britain steel and other materials, to give these supplies after British dollars ran out, to discourage a German parachute descent on Ireland by sending a United States squadron to visit Irish ports, and to keep the Japanese "dog" quiet in the Pacific. While Roosevelt ignored the suggestion of nonbelligerency and denied the request for destroyers as politically inopportune and contrary to American "defense requirements," he replied that the United States was doing all in its power to send the latest types of aircraft and other war matériel, promised to consider sending a squadron to Irish ports, and pointed to the presence of the American Fleet in Hawaii as a deterrent to the Japanese.[33]

Despite Roosevelt's desire to help, the United States now lacked the wherewithal to avert an Allied disaster. Insufficient supplies of planes, guns, and ammunition ruled out substantially expanded shipments to the Allies. In May 1940 the United States had only 160 pursuit planes for 260 pilots, 52 heavy bombers, or 83 fewer aircraft than believed essential for American defense, and a terrible shortage of anti-tank guns and ammunition for anti-aircraft batteries. General Arnold calculated that if 100 pursuit planes were sold to the Allies, that would, at current loss rates, give them only a three-day supply, while delaying American pilot training by six months. Further, since German forces had reached the English Channel by May 20 and trapped the bulk of the Anglo-French troops in Belgium and northwestern France, the swift dispatch of more American matériel would hardly have turned the tide. New German tactics had caught the Allies by surprise, and this had contributed more to Anglo-French defeat than any lack of modern weapons of war.

As their desperation in the third week of May mounted, the Allies made bolder demands on the United States. On May 18 French Premier Paul Reynaud had warned that "the war might end in an absolute defeat of France and England in less than 2 months," and indicated to Bullitt that he would ask the President either to seek a declaration of war against Germany or to announce "that the United States in defense of its vital interests could not permit the defeat of France and England." Though Roosevelt at once informed Bullitt that neither action was possible, Reynaud returned to the subject on May 22. Warning the President that France might feel compelled to make a separate peace, which would leave Britain and ultimately the United States dangerously vulnerable to Nazi might, Reynaud asked FDR to counter a German peace offer by coming into the war with America's Atlantic Fleet and all her air power. At the same time, Churchill predicted an attack on the British Isles before very long, explained that American help must come soon for it to play a part, and warned that a British defeat might bring to power a different government willing to exchange the Fleet for better peace terms.

Though Roosevelt gave no serious consideration to a declaration of war and saw no way to relinquish up-to-date matériel without compromising American security, he felt more compelled than ever to confront the possibility of an early Allied collapse. On May 22, despite an appreciation of the fact that World War I rifles, field pieces, machine guns, and mortars were usable training weapons, the administration declared them "surplus," and Roosevelt ordered aides to clear other legal roadblocks to British acquisition of these stocks. Preparing to defend their home islands in part with pitchforks and museum pikes, the British saw the release of this matériel as welcome indeed. Four days later, after hearing from Bullitt that Allied armies in Flanders would be obliged to surrender in two or three days and that Paris would probably be occupied in ten days, Roosevelt urged Reynaud to assure the safety of the French Fleet. "If the Germans hold out alluring offers to France based on surrender of the Fleet," he advised, "it should be remembered that these offers are of no ultimate value and the condition of France could be no worse, but in fact would be far stronger, if the Fleet were removed as a whole to safe places." [34]

On the same day, in the hope that he might yet prevent an Italian declaration of war, which would almost certainly assure French defeat, Roosevelt sent Mussolini another message. Following Anglo-French suggestions, he told the Duce that if he would state his specific desires in the Mediterranean, he would communicate them to London and Paris. He also promised to seek assurances that the Allies would ultimately honor any agreement and give Italy a full say at the peace table if Mussolini stayed out of the war. But, determined to join the fighting, Mussolini would not even receive Ambassador Phillips. Instead, he sent word through Foreign Minister Ciano that he had no interest in negotiations and that "any attempt to prevent Italy from fulfilling her engagements" was not well regarded. Unwilling to answer Mussolini's rejection by sending the Atlantic Fleet into the Mediterranean, as Bullitt and Reynaud had suggested, Roosevelt decided to send another verbal warning. On May 30 he informed Mussolini that Italian intervention would probably force involvement by the Americas and would certainly cause increased rearmament by the United States and a redoubling of efforts to send matériel to the Allies. Answering that the decision to enter the war had already been made, the Duce declared himself unconcerned about efforts to help the Allies and expressed a desire "not to receive 'any further pressure' as this . . . 'would only stiffen his attitude.' " [35]

With Allied fortunes sinking so rapidly in the last two weeks of May, American defense preparations mounted accordingly. The Congress, which had been so frugal with the military throughout the thirties, suddenly could not do enough. In the two weeks after the President's request for additional appropriations, the Congress voted $1.5 billion more for defense, $320 million above what Roosevelt had asked. On May 21, for example, when naval officers had informally told Senators that they could use $100 million more than requested for air power, the money, with FDR's okay, was added at once. Moreover, on May 31, when Roosevelt told the Congress that "the almost incredible events of the past two weeks . . . necessitate another enlargement of our military program," the legislators took less than four weeks to appropriate an additional $1.7

billion, expand the regular Army from 280,000 to 375,000 men, and grant presidential power to call the National Guard into active service.[36]

At the same time, an hysterical outcry in the country declared the nation unprepared against attack and called for the adjournment of party politics and the adoption of authoritarian controls. Republicans and Democrats now demanded a combined Roosevelt-Willkie ticket, with Wendell Willkie, a leading GOP contender, asked to accept the vice-presidential nomination of both parties. Further, some Americans now demanded industrial mobilization under a war czar or agency which would regulate production and labor at the possible expense of some New Deal gains.

Roosevelt rejected all these suggestions as violations of the very political and constitutional processes the country wished to defend. He privately described the suggestion of a combined ticket as a "silly business," and publicly attacked the idea "that only by abandoning our freedom, our ideals, our way of life, can we build our defenses adequately, can we match the strength of the aggressors. . . . I do not share these fears," he had announced in a Fireside Chat on May 26. ". . . I am not going to set up a War Industries Board and turn a billion dollar or two billion dollar program over to five complete outsiders who don't know anything about running government," he told a group of prominent businessmen. "It would be unconstitutional; the final responsibility is mine and I can't delegate it." Nor would he put one man in charge of national defense. "That had never been done and could not be done under the Constitution and laws," he told Roy Howard of the Scripps-Howard newspaper chain.

Though Roosevelt appointed a seven-member Defense Advisory Commission to answer demands for a tightly controlled preparedness drive, he refused to give it meaningful powers. Instead, he centered industrial mobilization largely in his own hands, where he could assure against a breakdown or cancellation of New Deal achievements. "Government policy [is] in no way to weaken the social gains that have been made in the last few years," he had told the press on May 21. "That is very, very important." "There is nothing in our present emergency to justify making the workers of our nation toil for longer hours than now limited by statute," he declared in his Fireside Chat. ". . . There is nothing in our present emergency to justify a lowering of the standards of employment. . . . There is nothing in our present emergency to justify a breaking down of old age pensions or of unemployment insurance. . . . There is nothing in our present emergency to justify a retreat from any of our social objectives." He also promised to give labor adequate representation in the implementation of his defense program, to oppose the "creation of a new group of war millionaires," and to guard against "the rising spiral of costs of all kinds." [37]

Roosevelt was less scrupulous about constitutional and political processes when combating potential espionage and domestic opponents of his national defense program. In May 1940, when FBI Director J. Edgar Hoover told Henry Morgenthau that a restraining order from Attorney General Robert Jackson had prevented him from using wiretaps against "four Nazi spies . . . in Buffalo," New York, Morgenthau urged Roosevelt to rescind Jackson's order. Despite a Supreme Court ruling that "evidence obtained from the interception of wire and radio communications was inadmissible in court," Roosevelt directed his Attorney General to authorize investigating agents "to secure information by listening devices direct to the conversation or other communications of persons suspected of subversive activities against the Government of the United States, including suspected spies." Roosevelt rationalized this directive by arguing that the Court never intended its ruling "to apply to grave matters involving the defense of the nation," and that after "sabotage, assassinations and 'fifth column' activities are completed," it is too late to do anything.

Roosevelt also asked the Attorney General if there were "any law or Executive Order under which it would be possible for us to open and inspect outgoing . . . or incoming mail to and from certain foreign nations." He expected a mail-opening program to intercept communications relating to " 'fifth column' activities—sabotage, anti-government propaganda, military secrets, etc." Though there was no legal sanction, the FBI, apparently in response to FDR's inquiry, soon began such a program with six agents trained in mail-opening techniques by "an allied country's censorship agency." [38]

At the same time, Roosevelt asked the FBI to investigate hundreds of people who wired their support of Colonel Charles Lindbergh's opposition to his preparedness program. In a national radio address on May 19, Lindbergh, drawing on his fame as a pioneering aviator who had made the first cross-Atlantic solo flight, had belittled the idea that the United States was in danger of attack, and contended that with properly formulated defense policies the country would be virtually impregnable to assault. By contrast with the President, he had also argued that the oceans enhanced America's defensive position, that an air force of 10,000 planes would be ample for defense, and that the United States should not send aid to Britain and France. The speech infuriated FDR, who complained "that it could not have been better put if it had been written by Goebbels himself. What a pity," Roosevelt added, "that this youngster has completely abandoned his belief in our form of government and has accepted Nazi methods because apparently they are efficient."

More importantly, Roosevelt feared that some of Lindbergh's supporters were part of a "fifth column" trying to sow domestic discord. "Today's threat to our national security is not a matter of military weapons alone," FDR had declared on May 26:

> We know of new methods of attack. The Trojan Horse. The Fifth Column that betrays a nation unprepared for treachery. Spies, saboteurs and traitors are the actors in this new strategy. . . . But there is an added

technique for weakening a nation at its very roots. . . . The method is simple. It is first, a dissemination of discord. A group—not too large—a group that may be sectional or racial or political—is encouraged to exploit its prejudices through false slogans and emotional appeals. The aim of those who deliberately egg on these groups is to create confusion of counsel, public indecision, political paralysis and, eventually, a state of panic. Sound national policies come to be viewed with a new and unreasoning skepticism. . . . As a result of these techniques, armament programs may be dangerously delayed. Singleness of national purpose may be undermined. . . . The unity of the state can be so sapped that its strength is destroyed. All this is no idle dream. It has happened time after time, in nation after nation, during the last two years.[39]

Roosevelt had in mind not only Austria, Czechoslovakia, Finland, Norway, and Holland but also Nazi efforts to influence political developments, steal military secrets, and sabotage preparedness in the United States. In September 1939 the State Department had "intercepted" messages from Germany urging people to ask their Congressmen not to repeal the arms embargo. In March 1940 the Nazis had published a White Book containing Polish documents indicating that American diplomats, and Roosevelt by implication, encouraged the Poles to fight Berlin. The objectives, as Roosevelt heard from several sources, were to lend color to isolationist charges that he intended to lead the country into the war, and to undermine his chances for reelection. Believing that only Roosevelt's defeat would assure American neutrality in the war, Berlin subsidized the printing and distribution of large numbers of these books and sent more than $5 million to the United States to promote isolationism and to campaign against FDR in 1940. According to one historian, the extent and effect of these activities "constituted one of the most massive interferences in American domestic affairs in history." Through FBI reports Roosevelt was also aware of the fact that a Nazi espionage ring and Nazi saboteurs were operating in the United States. "The United States cannot plan a warship, design an airplane, develop a new device that we do not know of at once," a Nazi spy boasted. Nazi saboteurs, working in factories, also tried to slow the production of American arms.[40]

There is considerable question, however, about the significance and extent of these activities. Nazi efforts did not prevent repeal of the arms embargo; nor did they affect the outcome of the presidential campaign. Their spies did manage to steal enough information about the Norden bombsight, the most highly prized American military secret of 1940, for German engineers to produce a replica, but technical problems apparently allowed Berlin little or no use of it in the war. As for Nazi saboteurs, their impact on American industrial production was negligible. While some Americans at the time and since believed that Nazi agents conducted extensive operations in the United States, there is good reason to think that these efforts were insubstantial. Although in 1940 FDR could not have known the precise extent or consequences of these Nazi activities, by his own criteria that the country could build adequate defenses and "match the strength of the aggressors" without "abandoning our freedom, our ideals, our way of life," one may doubt whether he used sufficient restraint in sanctioning FBI violations of civil and political rights.[41]

Roosevelt believed, however, that the best means of defending American security was through expanded aid to Britain and France. Though he had begun moving in this direction on May 22 when he ordered the sale of World War I equipment to the Allies, legal and political obstacles initially barred the way. Whereas the cash-and-carry provisions of the Neutrality law allowed private firms to sell arms to belligerents, it was illegal for the United States government to do so. On June 3, after extended discussions, the President's legal advisers agreed that the administration could sell "surplus" military supplies to private parties who could then resell them to the Allies. The decision "delighted" FDR, who ordered Morgenthau to assure speedy delivery by giving the material "an extra push every morning and every night until it is on board ship."

There was strong political opposition to such a policy. On June 3 members of the Senate Foreign Relations Committee strenuously urged Roosevelt not to let other countries have anything that might otherwise serve the national defense. Two days later, the committee overwhelmingly rejected a bill allowing government sales of modern planes and ships to the Allies. What is more, public support for such a policy was erratic. Although opinion polls in April and May consistently showed majorities of between 60 and 70 per cent for greater aid to England and France, more specific suggestions about sending Army and Navy planes or other matériel could not win majority support. A May 29 survey on whether the government should sell all, some, or none of its military planes to the Allies showed 9 per cent in favor of selling all, 38 per cent willing to sell some, and 49 per cent against selling any.[42]

This was an important concern to FDR. With the German victories removing whatever hesitancy he had about running for reelection, Roosevelt was reluctant to push for a controversial policy that might undermine his reviving political strength. Equally important, though, his experience since 1919 had taught him that an effective policy abroad depended on a stable commitment at home. As long as there was uncertainty about public and congressional receptivity to selling some of the Army's and Navy's scarce supplies, Roosevelt hung back from a full commitment to this policy. Contrary, however, to contemporary and subsequent complaints that his reluctance left him behind public opinion, a close assessment of national sentiment at the time suggests that he was abreast and possibly even a little ahead of public feeling and that external events more than anything he might say or do was the necessary catalyst for him to assure a policy of greater aid.

When domestic support for helping the Allies rose sharply in June 1940, Roosevelt promptly took advantage of the change in mood. On June 4, after almost four weeks of uninterrupted reverses, which shook American faith in an Allied victory and weakened inclinations to send help, Britain's successful withdrawal of 300,000 troops from Dunkirk temporarily reversed this trend. The "miracle of deliverance," as Churchill called it, produced an upsurge of hope in the United States that Britain, with American matériel support, might yet defeat Berlin. An opinion poll of June 10 revealed that the 47 per cent in the May 29 survey favoring sales of air force planes to England and France had grown to 80 per cent. Between June 5 and 7, in response to these domestic developments, together with a German drive on Paris and a direct request from Reynaud for fully equipped planes, Roosevelt had approved the sale of 50 old Navy dive bombers and 93 obsolete Army attack bombers for quick delivery to France. Further, on June 7, in answer to an injunction from a friend to step up aid to the Allies and publicly identify himself with this aim, he declared: "I beat you to it! Very many planes are actually on the way to the Allies. . . . I am doing everything possible—though I am not talking very much about it because a certain element of the press, like the Scripps-Howard papers, would undoubtedly pervert it, attack it and confuse the public mind. . . . Very soon," though, he concluded, "there will be the simple statement you speak of." [43]

He announced this policy in the next three days. With public opinion coalescing behind all aid short of war, Churchill indicating that Britain might have to surrender its Fleet, Mussolini entering the war, and Paris about to fall, Roosevelt proclaimed American readiness to give the Allies all possible matériel support. On June 8 he informed the press of the decision to send outmoded arms and planes to the Allies, and observed that nowadays "a plane can get out of date darned fast." On June 10, in an address at the University of Virginia, in Charlottesville, he attacked isolationist ideas, denounced Italy's action, and voiced his determination to help Britain and France. He described the isolationist dream of "a lone island in a world dominated by force" as a "delusion." It would turn into a "nightmare of a people lodged in prison, handcuffed, hungry, and fed through the bars from day to day by the contemptuous, unpitying masters of other continents." Only an Allied victory over "the gods of force and hate," he explained, could prevent such imprisonment.

Italy's involvement in the fighting now made victory more difficult. He had done everything in his power to discourage Mussolini from this step, but, he concluded indignantly, "on this tenth day of June, 1940, the hand that held the dagger has struck it into the back of its neighbor." The United States would respond by pursuing "two obvious and simultaneous courses; we will extend to the opponents of force the material resources of this nation; and, at the same time, we will harness and speed up the use of those resources in order that we ourselves in the Americas may have equipment and training equal to the task of any emergency and every defense. All roads leading to the accomplishment of these objectives must be kept clear of obstructions. We will not slow down or detour. Signs and signals call for speed—full speed ahead." [44]

The combination of Roosevelt's announcement and the rapid deterioration of French resistance now evoked a storm of Anglo-French appeals for all-out help. On June 10, shortly before leaving Paris to escape the onrushing German armies and establish the French government in Tours, Reynaud implored the President to send "new and even larger assistance. . . . I beseech you to declare publicly that the United States will give the Allies aid and material support by all means 'short of an expeditionary force.' I beseech you to do this before it is too late."

On June 11 Churchill expressed gratitude for the President's declaration of the day before and advised that "everything must be done to keep France in the fight. . . . The hope with which you inspired them may give them strength to persevere." He also described an urgent need for thirty or forty old destroyers to prevent Italian submarines from strangling British commerce. On the evening of June 12, after traveling to France for first-hand accounts of the fighting, Churchill notified Roosevelt that, while Reynaud wished to fight on, other French leaders would soon urge an armistice. "This, therefore, is the moment for you to strengthen Reynaud the utmost you can and try to tip the balance in favor of the best and longest possible French resistance. . . . If there is anything that you can say publicly or privately to the French now is the time." On the following morning, he wired Roosevelt that the French had sent for him "again, which means that crisis has arrived. Anything you can say or do to help them now may make a difference." Churchill also expressed his concern about Ireland and renewed his request for an American naval visit to an Irish port. [45]

Roosevelt could give little meaningful response to these messages. He could not promise all aid "short of an expeditionary force." American opinion remained strongly opposed to participation in the war, and Roosevelt himself hoped that British forces, helped by American supplies, might yet resist the Nazi war machine. Destroyers, however, remained one weapon he still could not give. Navy chiefs refused to concede that any were superfluous to the national defense, and the Congress shortly made its opposition clear as well. As for sending naval vessels to Ireland, Roosevelt told Churchill on the 13th that this was ruled out because of squadrons off Portugal and the east coast of South America, patrol efforts providing "a wide safety zone" in the Western Atlantic, and the vital need for the main Fleet at Hawaii.

The only encouragement he felt free to offer was a message to Reynaud explaining that "this Government is doing everything in its power to make available to the Allied Governments the material they so urgently require, and our efforts to do still more are being redoubled." To this, he added his endorsement of French naval resistance from North African and Atlantic bases as the best means to win the ultimate victory. "Naval power in world affairs," he observed, "still carries the lessons of history." Eager, however, to assure that the Allies not use this message as a commitment to future participation in the fighting, Roosevelt asked Reynaud not to publish it.

In a desperate attempt to keep France in the war, Churchill now tried to give just such a meaning to Roosevelt's words. As described by Ambassador Kennedy, Churchill read the President's note to Reynaud as "an absolute commitment . . . to the Allies that if France fights on the United States will be in the war to help them if things go bad at some later date." In the early hours of June 14, Churchill himself wired Roosevelt that in his meeting with French leaders on the 13th he had urged them to put aside discussion of an armistice until they made "a further appeal . . . to you and the United States." Reynaud believed it impossible to fight on without "American intervention up to the extreme limit open to you," and Churchill urged publication of the President's message as the way to provide this. "It may play the decisive part in turning the course of world history. It will I am sure decide the French to deny Hitler a patched-up peace." Reynaud echoed this appeal later that day: "I must tell you . . . that if you cannot give to France in the hours to come the certainty that the United States will come into the war within a very short time, the fate of the world will change. Then you will see France go under like a drowning man and disappear, after having cast a last long look towards the land of liberty from which she awaited salvation."

Roosevelt hastened to restate the limits of his power. "My message to Reynaud," he asked Kennedy to tell Churchill, is "not to be published in any circumstances. It . . . does not commit this Government to the slightest military activities in support of the Allies. . . . There is of course no authority except in Congress to make any commitment of this nature. The French fleet and its disposition for future use was the matter primarily in mind in sending the message." In a direct reply to Churchill, Roosevelt explained that "a certain amount of time must pass" before American supplies would become available "to the full extent desired," and restated his concern that the French not surrender their Fleet. To Reynaud, he sent all the verbal encouragement he could, reiterating his determination to send the fullest possible material aid. He also emphasized, however, that his statements carried "no implication of military commitments," because only the Congress could do that.

Within hours after his reply to Reynaud, Roosevelt received yet two more appeals from Churchill. Though expressing appreciation of the President's difficulties with public opinion and Congress, Churchill warned that events would soon outdistance American public feeling and that France might feel compelled to surrender its Fleet intact. He described the moment as supremely critical: "A declaration that the United States will, if necessary, enter the war might save France. Failing that, in a few days French resistance may have crumbled and we shall be left alone." He also restated the possibility that a shattered Britain might entirely submit to Hitler's will, bringing with it a revolution in sea power and a Nazi-dominated Europe "far more numerous, far stronger, far better armed than the New World." In a follow-up message, he predicted that "if your reply does not contain the assurance asked for, the French will very quickly ask for an armistice, and I much doubt whether it will be possible in that event for us to keep the French fleet out of German hands." Having already answered Reynaud and stated the limits of what he could do, Roosevelt saw no reason for another reply.[46]

On the afternoon of the 17th, however, after learning that Reynaud had resigned and Henri Pétain, his successor, had requested an armistice, Roosevelt vigorously pressed the new French government not to surrender the Fleet. Should it do this, Roosevelt warned, it "will fatally impair the preservation of the French Empire and the eventual restoration of French independence and autonomy. Furthermore, should the French Government . . . permit the French Fleet to be surrendered to Germany, the French Government will permanently lose the friendship and goodwill of the Government of the United States." When the armistice of June 22 left the fate of the Fleet unclear, Roosevelt approved a British decision to prevent German control by either seizing or, if necessary, destroying all French warships in British and North African ports. When the British successfully put the bulk of France's war vessels out of action on July 3, 1940, Roosevelt and most Americans warmly endorsed this act of "self-defense." [47]

Roosevelt's more immediate problem in the face of French collapse was to fulfill the Charlottesville program of increased aid. The French request for an armistice produced a sharp drop in American hopes for an Allied victory and once more weakened public willingness to help "the opponents of force." By late June, only a third of the public believed that Britain would win the war, while the number of Americans favoring increased aid to the Allies had diminished by almost 10 per cent in three weeks. Isolationist leaders like Charles Lindbergh and General Hugh Johnson gave voice to these attitudes in national radio broadcasts which warned that help to Britain might force us into a war we were unprepared to fight. The President's policy was "a sort of reckless shooting craps with destiny," Johnson said. At the same time, Senate isolationists blocked the sale of new torpedo boats to Britain and added a provision to a naval expansion bill which increased the number of legal roadblocks to aiding the Allies.

Since two-thirds of the public continued to favor help to Britain, Roosevelt believed he still had sufficient support to increase material aid. When Morgenthau had asked him on June 17 whether he should continue to give England the same assistance he had been giving England and France, the President replied: "absolutely!" Though still seeing no way to meet repeated British requests for old destroyers, Roosevelt approved the transfer of French munitions contracts to Britain and told his military chiefs to send everything they could spare, and a little more.

On June 19 he also brought Henry Stimson and Frank Knox, two of the country's most pro-Allied Republicans, into his Cabinet as Secretary of War and Secretary of the Navy, respectively. Replacing the two most isolationist members of his Cabinet, Harry Woodring and Charles Edison, the appointments were not only a fresh demonstration to London of Roosevelt's intentions, but also an attempt to create a bipartisan consensus for all aid to Britain short of war and to strengthen his bid for another presidential term. Secretary of War under William Howard Taft and Secretary of State under Hoover, the seventy-two-year-old Stimson favored compulsory military training and the taking of all steps necessary, including repeal of the Neutrality law and U.S. naval convoys, to get supplies to Britain. Knox, who had been the Republican vice-presidential candidate in 1936, favored even stronger action—a million-man army, the strongest air force in the world, and the prompt shipment of large numbers of late-model planes to Britain. Though a vocal minority and influential military chiefs in the United States opposed these steps, by June 1940 Roosevelt believed they were the path along which the country must now advance.[48]

10

Conflict and Compromise

F EW ISSUES GAVE ROOSEVELT more concern in the summer of 1940 than
the threat to Latin America. As Hitler's armies swept across Western
Europe in May and June, Roosevelt received repeated warnings of Nazi
subversion in Brazil, Chile, Uruguay, Colombia, Ecuador, Venezuela,
Panama, and Mexico. Edwin C. Wilson, the United States Minister
in Montevideo, described alleged Nazi plans for an uprising there which
the Uruguayan Parliament made public in June. "It is commonly thought
here," Claude Bowers, now Ambassador to Chile, wrote from Santiago,
"that the Germans, who are numerous, are thoroughly organized with the
view of a coup d'état." By late May, Roosevelt had concluded that continued Nazi victories would lead Berlin to attempt the overthrow of
existing Latin American governments and the transfer of Dutch and
French possessions in the Western Hemisphere to its control. He also saw
Germany's likely acquisition of France's Fleet and West African bases as
a prelude to an attack on Brazil and the rest of South America.[1]

Though Roosevelt had been alive to these dangers for more than two
years, he now saw an urgent need for a strong response. On May 23 he
had approved a request to all the American Republics for secret military
talks between United States and Latin American officers. Shortly thereafter, in response to State Department recommendations for a show of
naval force off Brazil and Uruguay, he sent a heavy cruiser to visit Rio
de Janeiro and Montevideo. At the same time, in answer to Latin request for arms, he signed a congressional resolution authorizing the sale
of coastal guns and ships to other American Republics for cash. Sumner
Welles urged the President to do more. Only three or four heavy cruisers
and a "reasonable" number of destroyers on the east coast of South
America could halt Nazi subversion, and only a systematic program of
credits could allow the Latins to buy defensive arms, he warned. Acquiescence in the creation of American governments subservient to Germany
would render the Monroe Doctrine "nonexistent" and cause the majority
of Latin Republics to "run helter-skelter to Hitler."

Other needs largely compelled Roosevelt to resist this advice. Agreeing
with Admiral Harold Stark, the Chief of Naval Operations, that Ameri-

can naval strength should remain concentrated in the Pacific, he sent only one more cruiser and some destroyers on "shakedown cruises" to South America. Similarly, he agreed to arm the American Republics on financial terms they could meet; but limited supplies and a need to equip United States and British forces first caused him to restrict this aid. The Latin states were to receive only enough equipment to maintain their internal security and blunt external attacks until United States forces could arrive. Further, Brazil and Mexico were to have first call on these supplies, with Ecuador, Colombia, and Venezuela next, and the Central American and Caribbean countries standing third. Nations south of the Brazilian bulge were to have no promise of immediate help.[2]

Roosevelt also found himself unable to meet all of Latin America's economic needs. Wartime reductions in European markets, which normally absorbed over half of Latin America's exports, left the southern Republics with huge surpluses of foodstuffs and economic difficulties comparable to those of the early thirties. Unless the United States provided a market for these goods, the Latin Republics would have to deal with Hitler, who seemed increasingly able to restore their lost European trade. The administration found no ready answer to this problem. Since most Latin surpluses duplicated those in the United States, an administration proposal for a Hemisphere organization to market and control production of staples evoked strong domestic opposition.

Roosevelt's announcement of this plan on June 21 moved financial, agricultural, and business leaders to warn against multibillion-dollar costs, the accumulation of unneeded competitive goods, and the extension of agricultural controls to all the Americas. The reception in Latin America was no better; Latin leaders objected to United States direction of their economies, or "a new version of Yankee imperialism." If these objections were not enough to sink the plan, Hull's opposition to a scheme that might replace his program of reciprocal trade agreements was. In July, Roosevelt turned to more conventional means of helping the Latin economies. Asking the Congress to increase the capital and lending power of the Export-Import Bank by half a billion dollars and to eliminate some of the restrictions on its operation, he proposed that the Bank assist "our neighbors south of the Rio Grande" by principally "financing the handling and orderly marketing of some part of their surpluses." [3]

By contrast with the opposition to economic planning for Latin America, Roosevelt found a strong consensus in the country for denying Berlin control of Dutch, French, or British possessions in the Americas. Congressional leaders urged the administration to purchase Europe's New World bases with gold and credits on defaulted debts. While Roosevelt and the State Department opposed outright acquisition as likely to destroy the Good Neighbor policy and give Japan a pretext for seizing European possessions in the Pacific, they took other steps to prevent the transfer of Hemisphere territory between non-American states. In May, Roosevelt ordered military chiefs to plan the occupation of Hemisphere possessions that Germany might claim as spoils of war. In June the administration won strong congressional backing for a declaration against European changes in control over New World colonies, notified Berlin of its position, and called a Pan-American Conference in Havana to win Hemisphere support.[4]

Though all the Republics promptly agreed to the meeting, several of them were unenthusiastic. With German envoys warning against making any agreements in Havana aimed at Berlin and predicting that Nazi domination of European markets would compel American dependence on Germany's good will, nine Latin American countries, including Argentina, Brazil, and Chile, refused to include their Foreign Ministers in their delegations to the Conference. Moreover, with Argentina leading the way, the Latin Americans resisted a United States proposal for Pan-American trusteeships over Europe's New World possessions threatened with changes in control. The Latins preferred to say nothing about Hemisphere colonies until a specific case arose, and then to turn over the threatened territory temporarily to a single American Republic or to allow it self-determination.

Hull nevertheless aligned the Havana Conference behind the administration's program by emphasizing the need for unified opposition to Nazi plans of subversion and control. As fearful as Washington that any break in Hemisphere solidarity would increase the Nazi threat to their political and economic independence, the Latin Republics declared themselves against direct or indirect efforts to transfer sovereignty over Europe's New World colonies, and agreed that threatened territories would come under inter-American trusteeship until they were ready for independence or could be returned to their original owners.

At the same time, Argentina and Brazil, the countries most exposed to the German threat, tried to preserve some measure of independence from Washington's plans. By insisting that the "no transfer" policy take the form of a convention that required only two-thirds approval, they and other particularly vulnerable Republics were able to withhold support and maintain some aloofness from the United States. More significantly, in 1940–41 President Getulio Vargas of Brazil, without the knowledge of his Foreign Minister, repeatedly portrayed Brazil to the German Ambassador as "the bulwark against the inclusion of South America in Roosevelt's anti-German policy." Similarly, Acting President Ramón Castillo of Argentina relaxed his government's efforts to suppress Nazi activities in his country and made overtures to Berlin for economic support.[5]

As German documents subsequently revealed, Roosevelt and most Americans greatly exaggerated the German threat to the Americas in the summer of 1940. At the time, Hitler had no plans to seize Allied possessions or to launch an attack on the Hemisphere. While there were ongoing efforts to undermine Hemisphere solidarity by holding out promises of economic help and encouraging the establishment of pro-German regimes, Hitler's prime concern was not to push the United States into the war. Henry Stimson, the new Secretary of War, concluded as much when he described "Hitler's so-called fifth-column movements in South America" as principally "attempts to frighten us from sending help where it will be most effective."

But reports from United States and Latin American sources of extensive German subversion, coupled with Britain's occupation of the Dutch West Indies and blockade of the French Antilles to prevent developments favorable to Berlin, convinced Roosevelt that there was a significant threat. Moreover, by the second half of 1940 Hitler's past behavior and growing military capability left Roosevelt little choice but to take all possible precautions against an eventual attack. The fact that Hitler instructed military chiefs in the fall of 1940 to plan the seizure of Atlantic islands as a prelude to a possible assault on the Hemisphere suggests that Roosevelt demonstrated good sense. Indeed, even though Hitler never made detailed plans for an American war, he continued to give general consideration to such action during 1941, and had he won full control of Europe, an attack on the Americas was a possible next step. But whatever the actuality of Hitler's plans or future actions, a rational leader had to view a Nazi drive against the Hemisphere as a possibility against which he must plan.[6]

At the same time that Roosevelt had been working on Hemisphere defense, he had tried to restrain Japan and prevent the outbreak of a Pacific war. Reflecting the mood of the country, the Congress, and the administration in the summer and fall of 1939, he had told Joseph Grew, the American Ambassador to Tokyo, that the United States would not be forced out of China and would support its position in the Far East by reinforcing Manila and Pearl Harbor and holding maneuvers in Haiwaiian waters. More specifically, in September 1939, when Japan renewed its pressure on Britain and France to withdraw from China, Hull had warned Tokyo against actions that would further undermine Japanese-American relations and encourage the introduction of financial and trade policies injurious to Japan. In October, with Roosevelt's explicit approval, Grew had bluntly told an America-Japan Society luncheon in Tokyo that opinion in the United States highly resented Japanese actions in China and favored economic retaliation against further violations of American rights.[7]

In the three months before the Commercial Treaty with Japan expired in January 1940, international and domestic pressure mounted for stronger action against Japan. Steps toward the creation of a puppet regime in Nanking and continuing efforts to drive Anglo-French forces from China suggested that words alone would not alter Tokyo's course. Only economic sanctions, Chiang Kai-shek told FDR, would force Japan into a negotiated settlement "based on reason and justice." Morgenthau, Ickes, Stanley K. Hornbeck, the State Department's senior Far Eastern adviser, congressional leaders, and, according to an opinion poll, 75 per cent of the American public agreed.

Others were not so sure. Fearful that continued resistance to Japanese control in China, especially by the use of sanctions, would lead Tokyo into an attack on their Asian colonies, Britain and France urged Washington to help negotiate a settlement of the China Incident and to renew its trade treaty with Japan. Ambassador Grew also counseled restraint. Seeing "a marked trend" in Japan toward better relations with the United States, he recommended against talk of an embargo and urged negotiations for a new trade treaty. While Hull opposed immediate trade talks, he also opposed the introduction of economic sanctions as likely to "arouse" the Japanese. Instead, he urged the President simply to continue with existing trade practices when the treaty expired.

Roosevelt's own impulse was to deal harshly with Japan. In the summer of 1939 he had spoken of intercepting the Japanese Fleet if it moved south against Indochina or the Dutch East Indies; in September he had answered a Chinese plea for additional credits by telling Morgenthau "to do everything . . . that we can get away with"; in October he had complimented Grew on his blunt speech, saying that "you did it in the right way and at the right time"; and in November he had predicted that Americans would question continued relations with Tokyo "if the Japanese government were to fail to speak as civilized twentieth-century human beings."

In December, however, when he had to make up his mind about economic pressure on Japan, he had adopted a middle ground between advocates of sanctions and conciliation. While accepting Hull's recommendation not to impose sanctions at the expiration of the treaty, he also asked him to tell the Japanese that the withholding of sanctions was "a temporary measure" which would stand as long as there was a reasonable possibility of reaching some accord. Should this possibility disappear, Hull was also to say, the President would restrict trade with Japan. He hoped that such a policy would strengthen Japanese proponents of better relations with the United States and weaken impulses to recoup potential trade losses by seizing Allied colonies to the south.[8]

Though hopes for improved relations rose when a moderate Japanese Cabinet under Admiral Mitsumasa Yonai took power in mid-January, unbridgeable tensions over China kept the two countries apart. Opinion in Japan was practically unanimous on achieving the "new order" in East Asia, which was a euphemism for control of China. During the first three months of 1940, attacks on China's supply line through Indochina and the creation of a collaborationist regime in Nanking made this clear. In response, the administration lent Chiang another $20 million and denounced the puppet government in Nanking as "a further step in a program of one country by armed force to impose its will upon a neighboring country." The United States, Hull declared, would continue to recognize Chiang's regime as the legitimate government of China.

German victories in Scandinavia in April 1940 further sharpened Japanese-American tensions. Hitler's defeat of Denmark followed by Britain's occupation of Iceland aroused concern in Tokyo and Washington about the Dutch East Indies. Anticipating a German attack on Holland and a Dutch request for American occupation of their overseas territory, Japan's Foreign Minister publicly warned against any change in their control. Believing this foretold a Japanese move into the territory, Roosevelt and Hull responded with a statement of American dependence on the islands for rubber and tin and declared against any change in their status quo as inimical to peace throughout the Pacific. Tokyo, in turn, objected to Washington's interpretation of its statement and to the movement of the American Fleet to Hawaii as an unneeded deterrent against Japanese expansion to the south.

In May, Germany's conquest of Holland followed by Britain's occupation of the Dutch West Indies accentuated these concerns. Hull publicly reiterated American support for the status quo in the Dutch East Indies, while he and Roosevelt privately persuaded London to disavow any intention of intervention there. Despite these actions, Tokyo pressed the Dutch to guarantee minimum annual exports from the islands of thirteen raw materials, including principally oil. German victories persuaded the administration to concede these demands and to renew the search for a settlement with Japan. In late May, Roosevelt told Morgenthau that he "would like to do something with Japan, [a] sort of joint treaty to keep peace in the Pacific." Simultaneously, Hull asked his Far Eastern experts "to take a fine-tooth comb and a microscope and go back over our relations with Japan and see if it is humanly possible to find something with which to approach them and prevail upon them not to gallop off on a wild horse." Conversations initiated in Tokyo by the administration on June 10 only highlighted the gulf between the two sides.[9]

In June 1940 Allied losses in Europe touched off a new round of Japanese aggressiveness. Taking advantage of French defeat and British weakness, the Yonai government revived demands for Allied withdrawal from China, pressed France to shut the Indochina border and Britain to close Chinese supply routes through Hong Kong and Burma, and declared "the regions of the South Seas" part of Japan's Greater East Asia Co-Prosperity Sphere. In response, the French asked Washington to oppose their expulsion from China and to send arms to Indochina; the Chinese urged a declaration of American backing for the status quo in Indochina; and the British suggested either halting all exports to Japan or sending a part of the American Fleet to Singapore. The only alternative to these steps, London advised, was to attempt to negotiate a full-scale settlement with Japan which would end the war in China and guarantee the safety of Western possessions in the Pacific.

Roosevelt and Hull refused to alter course. Believing that strong measures would provoke an unwanted Pacific crisis and that appeasement would encourage further Japanese demands, they continued to urge a middle ground. If, Hull told the British, the Western Powers acquiesced in, but did not assent to, Japanese impairment of some of their rights and interests, and if Britain continued to resist Berlin and the United States kept its Fleet in Hawaii, Japan would refrain from any major move. But London thought otherwise. Since it believed that Britain could not hold out against Japanese demands without direct American support, London agreed to close the principal supply route to Nationalist China, the Burma Road, in July and to work for a settlement in China.[10]

Britain's action forced Washington into a hot debate on Far Eastern policy. On July 18, when Morgenthau, Stimson, and Knox questioned the Burma Road decision in a conversation at the British Embassy, Lord Lothian, the Ambassador, protested that Washington's refusal to back strong measures against Japan had forced London's hand. "After all," Lothian said, "you are continuing to ship aviation gasoline to Japan." If, he contended, the United States would stop such shipments and Britain would blow up the oil wells in the Dutch East Indies, Japan would be without fuel for its war machine. Morgenthau, who had been battling to halt the export of strategic materials, put this plan before the President on the following day. Proposing a total embargo on all American oil exports, British acquisition of sufficient supplies from Venezuela and Colombia, Anglo-Dutch destruction of the Dutch East Indies wells, and British air attacks on German synthetic-oil plants, Morgenthau predicted "that this thing might give us peace in three to six months."

Roosevelt was of two minds. On the one hand, he wished to take a stronger stand against Japan. Unhappy over the closing of the Burma Road and aware that Tokyo was about to exert "the utmost efforts" to block inter-American economic cooperation at the Havana Conference and to step up strategic imports from the United States, Roosevelt was "tremendously interested" in Morgenthau's proposal and discussed it with Stimson, Knox, and Welles. At the same time, though, he remained determined to avoid a war in the Pacific. A conflict with Japan would not only reduce Anglo-American power to defeat Berlin, it would also jeopardize the President's political future. Having just been nominated for a third term on a platform of no participation in foreign wars unless attacked, Roosevelt felt constrained to avoid provocative steps. Hence, when Welles argued that this plan would cause Japan to attack Britain, the President ordered more discussions with the British and left the proposal in the air.[11]

But Morgenthau and Stimson would not leave it there. Angered by Welles's "beautiful Chamberlain talk," which suggested that "everything is going to be lovely" and that Japan will come over and "kiss our big toe," Morgenthau asked the President on July 22 to use the Defense Act of July 2, 1940, to forbid the export of petroleum, petroleum products, and scrap metals. In receipt of reports that Japan had significantly increased its orders in the United States for high-grade aviation fuel, Roosevelt directed Welles to limit the export of this gasoline. On the 25th, after hearing from Stimson that Japan was trying to corner the American market on aviation fuel and that delivery of these orders might leave United States forces without adequate supplies for six to nine months, Roosevelt signed a Treasury Department proclamation limiting the export of all oil and scrap metal.

Going much beyond what Roosevelt or the State Department had intended, the Order caused a sharp conflict within the administration. Pointing out that the State Department had not seen the Treasury's proclamation and that it would provoke Japan to move against the Dutch East Indies, Welles won FDR's prompt agreement to modify the Order. On the morning of the 26th, Roosevelt told reporters that he had not introduced an "embargo," as their newspapers were saying, but rather an extension of the government's licensing system to only certain categories of scrap and oil. At a Cabinet meeting later that day, Morgenthau and Welles vigorously argued the question of what the President's Order should include. Roosevelt "raised his hands in the air, refused to participate in it and said that those two men must go off in a corner and settle their issue." Having won a "victory in substance" and appreciating that the President opposed a strong challenge to Tokyo, Morgenthau agreed to restrict the Order to aviation motor fuel and lubricants and high-grade melting scrap. This narrowly drawn embargo fully satisfied FDR: it assured against an oil or scrap shortage in the United States, answered some of the domestic demand for stronger action against Japan, and expressed his own desire for firmer steps without the risk of war.[12]

Though Tokyo objected at once, these restrictions had little to do with the fact that Japan now intensified its drive for an East Asian sphere of control. In the second half of July, in the belief that the Yonai government was not taking enough advantage of German victories, Japanese militants established Prince Fumimaro Konoye at the head of a Cabinet that included avowed expansionists like Yosuke Matsuoka and General Hideki Tojo, the new Foreign Affairs and War ministers. Outlining its policies in formal documents of July 26 and 27, the Konoye government pledged itself to settle the China Incident and solve "the problem of the south" by using stronger measures against the foreign concessions in China, the Netherlands East Indies, and French Indochina. These plans took specific form in August and September when the Japanese intimidated the British into withdrawing troops from Shanghai, the Dutch into discussing Japan's economic demands on the Dutch East Indies, and the French into recognizing Japan's preponderant interest in Indochina.

Roosevelt and Hull felt as constrained as ever in answering these challenges. With the outcome of an air battle over Britain and control of the Atlantic in doubt, they remained firmly opposed to a Pacific war. To ease Japan's need for oil and to control its impulse to seize it in the Dutch East Indies, the State Department interpreted the President's Order of July 26 to include only high-octane aviation fuels. This allowed Japan to buy middle-octane gasolines which were entirely satisfactory for their planes. Though this loophole in the President's proclamation was an open secret in the administration, Roosevelt had no desire to close it. In a conversation with Morgenthau about oil and scrap on August 16, he spoke "in [the] same vein as S. Welles," saying that "we must not push Japan too much at this time as we might push her to take [the] Dutch East Indies." In September and October, moreover, when Japanese negotiators in the islands were pressing Dutch authorities for a sixfold increase in annual oil shipments for five years, the State Department, with Roosevelt's approval, endorsed a settlement satisfying 60 per cent of this demand.[13]

Other developments made Roosevelt less accommodating about scrap metal. In August and September, despite repeated verbal protests by Washington, the Japanese had pressed French Indochina into conceding transit rights for troops, permission to construct airfields, and close economic ties. On September 12, in a telegram that impressed FDR, Grew advised against further efforts to conciliate Japan or attempts to protect American interests merely by expressions of disapproval. Describing Japan as a predatory power temporarily without ethical or moral sense, Grew urged a policy of striving by every means to preserve the status quo in the Pacific. At the same time, increased Japanese purchases of American scrap metal threatened to create shortages in the United States. Roosevelt responded to all this on September 13 by asking Morgenthau to find ways of halting scrap shipments to Japan without denying them to Britain. On the 26th, after Britain had shown itself likely to withstand the German air assault and Japanese forces had marched into Indochina, the administration announced a full embargo on all iron and steel scrap.[14]

These steps were insufficient to deter Japan from the completion of a Tripartite Pact with Berlin and Rome on September 27, 1940. Marked chiefly by an agreement to help each other if attacked by a Power not currently involved in the European or Sino-Japanese fighting, the treaty aimed to prevent the United States from either joining Britain against Berlin or directly opposing Japan's creation of an East Asian sphere. For Tokyo, it was also a way of securing German approval for its drive to the south and help in settling differences with Russia to the north.

In Washington the pact fueled the debate between proponents and opponents of a strong line toward Japan. Believing that Tokyo would back down if confronted by strong action and that the pact was no more than a case of "making a bad face at us," Stimson, Morgenthau, and Ickes renewed their demands for "some straight acting which will show Japan that we mean business and that we are not in the least afraid of her." Specifically, they urged a prompt, comprehensive oil embargo. Complaining that the restrictions on scrap had been too little and too late, they argued that the time to embargo gasoline was before, not after, Japan went into the Dutch East Indies. In addition, with London declaring that it would reopen the Burma Road on October 17 and Churchill asking FDR to send a naval squadron—"the bigger the better"—to Singapore to deter Japan from any strong response, Stimson urged the President to agree and to send a naval force to the Dutch East Indies as well.

Hull, Welles, and American military chiefs believed that an oil embargo or a move into Singapore would provoke an attack that would endanger unprepared American forces and distract the United States from effectively meeting the German threat. In conversations with the President, Hull continued to emphasize the danger to the Dutch islands from reductions in American oil exports to Japan, while General Marshall told Welles and Admiral Stark that this is "as unfavorable a moment as you could choose" for trouble with Japan. Navy chiefs also urged caution. Declaring the Fleet unfit for offensive operations and unlikely to deter Japan, they asked the President to return it from Hawaii to San Diego for proper preparations, even if this were interpreted as retreat before Japanese pressure.

Roosevelt's preference was for active opposition to Japan. During Cabinet discussions about oil in September, he impressed Stimson and Ickes as being agreeable to an embargo, and in a conversation with Knox on October 8 he described himself as considering a total trade embargo against Japan if she responded aggressively to the reopening of the Burma Road. On this occasion, he also discussed the possibility of naval patrols between Hawaii and the Philippines and Samoa and the Dutch East Indies to intercept Japanese commerce. Further, he refused to bring the Fleet back to San Diego, calling it a backward step, and announced in a speech on October 12 that "no combination of dictator countries of Europe and Asia will halt us in the path we see ahead for ourselves and for democracy. No combination of dictator countries of Europe and Asia will stop the help we are giving to . . . those who resist aggression, and who now hold the aggressors far from our shores. . . . The people of the United States . . . reject the doctrine of appeasement."

Yet at the same time, he continued to hold the conviction that meeting problems in the Atlantic and winning reelection required peace in the Pacific. Consequently, he would not risk an oil embargo, telling Morgenthau, who pressed him on this point, to get out of the oil business and leave foreign affairs to him and Hull. Shortly after, he told Hull and Welles that "we were not to shut off oil from Japan . . . and thereby force her into a military expedition against the Dutch East Indies." He also decided against any move into Singapore and abandoned his talk of Pacific patrols. The fact that Tokyo showed no determination to fight over the reopening of the Burma Road also seemed to reduce the need for such steps. Further, the fact that American declarations on the Tripartite Pact led Tokyo to use softer words suggested that the administration's measured response was all it now need do in opposing Japan.[15]

Throughout the summer of 1940, the considerable problems Roosevelt faced in Latin America and the Far East had paled alongside the difficulty of aiding Britain without jeopardizing national security, violating domestic laws, or causing a political crisis. For a month beginning in late June, predictions that Britain would soon have its neck wrung like a chicken's had created considerable reluctance to send supplies which military planners believed would "seriously weaken our present state of defense." Roosevelt, who wanted to send everything American forces could possibly spare, also wished to guard against any significant dilution of national strength in support of a lost cause. On June 24, therefore, he approved the recommendation of his military planners that commitments to sell London war matériel "will be made only if the situation should indicate that Great Britain displayed an ability to withstand German assault, and that the release of such equipment as we could . . . spare would exercise an important effect in enabling Great Britain to resist until the first of the year." On June 28 the Congress went even further by forbidding the sale of Army and Navy supplies unless service chiefs declared it unessential to the national defense.[16]

The issue had taken specific form over insistent British requests for old destroyers. In a message to the President on June 18, Churchill had explained that Germany's conquest of the European coast from Norway to the Channel, the addition of one hundred Italian submarines to Germany's fifty-five in the sea war, and the loss of almost half of Britain's home destroyer force had seriously impaired British ability to hold off an invasion and protect vital trade. The acquisition of some over-age American warships, Churchill advised, was "a matter of life or death." On June 26, King George VI had personally appealed to the President for these destroyers, describing the need as "greater every day if we are to carry on our solitary fight for freedom to a successful conclusion."

During June and July, Roosevelt saw no way to transfer these ships. As he explained to Ickes on July 6, the fact that the United States was recommissioning and using over one hundred of its World War I destroyers in the Atlantic patrol made it difficult to say that the Navy did not need them. Further, the possibility that Germany might defeat Britain and turn American destroyers against the United States also argued against selling them to Britain. British chances for survival, FDR told Farley at that time, were "about one in three." But even if Berlin did not capture these ships, the continuing possibility of German aggression against the Americas made them necessary to Hemisphere defense. Roosevelt also saw insurmountable legal and political barriers to such a sale. The argument that Britain could legally purchase old destroyers because it would strengthen rather than weaken American defense left Roosevelt unpersuaded. He saw recent congressional restrictions on transferring war matériel as "a complete prohibition" against selling destroyers, and even if it were not, he believed that Congress was "in no mood at the present time to allow any form of sale." [17]

A desperate need for these destroyers moved Churchill and American interventionists to press the case further with FDR at the end of July. "I am beginning to feel very hopeful about this war," Churchill cabled Roosevelt on the 31st, "if we can get 'round the next three or four months." But the key to this, Churchill declared, was the prompt dispatch of fifty or sixty old destroyers to reinforce Britain's diminishing warships that were defending trade and shores against attack. "The whole fate of the war," Churchill advised, "may be decided by this minor and easily remediable factor. . . . Mr. President, with great respect I must tell you that in the long history of the world, this is the thing to do now." On August 1 the Century Group, advocates of direct intervention in Britain's behalf, suggested that FDR exchange American destroyers for a guarantee that a successful German invasion of Britain would bring the British Fleet to American waters, or for "immediate naval and air concessions in British possessions in the Western Hemisphere." They also urged Roosevelt to act without congressional authorization, arguing that it was unnecessary and that Wendell Willkie, the Republican presidential nominee and an avowed internationalist, would follow his lead.

Convinced by an effective resistance during three weeks in July that Britain might weather the German air assault and that her "survival . . . might very possibly depend on their getting these destroyers," Roosevelt began exploring means by which this could be done. In a Cabinet meeting on August 2, he endorsed the idea of exchanging the ships for leases on bases in Britain's Western Hemisphere possessions. He also concluded, though, that this measure would depend on a combination of published British assurances about the Fleet and Willkie's willingness and ability to disarm Republican opposition in the Congress. That evening, therefore, he asked William Allen White to arrange for Willkie's support, and four days later, after London agreed to swap bases for destroyers, he asked Churchill to announce his intention to save the Fleet if Britain met defeat.

Neither Churchill nor Willkie, however, felt free to meet the President's requests. On August 7 Churchill replied that he certainly intended to use the Fleet to defend the Empire if Britain were overrun, but that a public discussion now of such an eventuality would create the demoralizing impression that he foresaw a possible collapse. Further, he told Lord Lothian, his Ambassador in Washington, that he would not make an agreement that would give the United States a say over future Fleet movements. Two days later Willkie also frustrated the President's plan by publicly refusing "to enter into advance commitments and understandings" about "specific executive or legislative proposals." Worse yet, informed observers saw the prospects for congressional action as somewhere between poor and nonexistent.[18]

On August 13 the urgency of Britain's need decided Roosevelt to cut through the legal and political constraints against an exchange. With the Battle of Britain reaching an intensity that would allow no additional delays in American aid, Roosevelt and the Cabinet agreed to take the "momentous" step. Persuaded by prominent jurists that the Executive could act without congressional action, Roosevelt cabled Churchill that he thought it possible to furnish Britain immediately with at least fifty destroyers, twenty torpedo boats, and ten modern planes. Since, he told Churchill, such assistance depended on British actions that would enhance the "defense and security of the United States," he asked the Prime Minister to give him unpublished assurances about the British Fleet and to sell or lease to the United States for ninety-nine years naval and air bases in seven of Britain's Western Hemisphere possessions. Though seeing no comparison between the intrinsic value of the "antiquated and inefficient" American ships and the "immense" strategic advantage to the United States of the island bases, the need for the destroyers and the chance to bring America nearer to Britain and the war prompted Churchill to accept.[19]

An exchange of over-age destroyers for highly valuable bases seemed certain to win widespread support and likely to gain the tacit approval of Willkie and Senator Charles McNary, the Republican vice-presidential candidate. Roosevelt still feared that action without Congress would cost him the election. His nomination in July by a contrived draft, which he wished as a defense against criticism of his break with the two-term tradition, and his insistence on Secretary of Agriculture Henry Wallace, a strong New Dealer and anti-Fascist, as a running mate had intensified popular suspicion of his deviousness and impulse toward personal control. Leaks to the press in early August about secret Anglo-American staff conversations also encouraged fears that he wanted to take the country into the war and become a dictator. The announcement on August 18 of a Joint Canadian-American Defense Board directly associated the United States with a belligerent and opened the administration to additional charges of involvement in Britain's war. Roosevelt, therefore, saw an Executive agreement on destroyers as calculated to "raise hell with Congress," fill the air with "cries of 'warmonger' and 'dictator,'" and defeat his bid for another term. Yet despite these fears, he felt compelled to act, saying that Britain's survival was at stake and that any delay "may mean the end of civilization." "I have no right to think of politics in the sense of being a candidate or desiring votes," he told one opposing Senator.[20]

Yet at the same time, Roosevelt did all he could to disarm political opposition. In a press conference on August 16, he emphasized that conversations were under way with Britain for the acquisition of Hemisphere bases, but denied that destroyers had been settled on as a quid pro quo. "The emphasis," he declared, "is on the acquisition of the bases—that is the main point—for the protection of this Hemisphere, and I think that is all there is to say. . . . I am trying . . . to acquire American bases," he added. "Let us make that clear." Roosevelt also consented to Churchill's announcement on the 20th that "without being asked or offered any inducement," Britain was ready to offer the United States ninety-nine-year leases on naval and air bases in the Western Hemisphere as bulwarks against a Nazi attack. Because Roosevelt undoubtedly wished to say nothing about destroyers until he had official legal backing for the deal from the Attorney General and the Chief of Naval Operations, he principally aimed to impress upon Americans what the country would receive. By emphasizing the acquisition of valuable bases, Roosevelt hoped to make the transfer of the destroyers seem of small account and the exchange so beneficial that few would fault him for acting swiftly on his own. When he first justified the deal to an opponent on the 22nd, for example, he declared the trade of fifty destroyers "on their last legs" for bases immensely important to the national defense as "the finest thing for the nation . . . done in your lifetime and mine." [21]

For domestic political reasons of his own, Churchill tried to make a more balanced arrangement with the United States. With the air attack temporarily slackening in the week after August 17, he felt less pressed to conclude the deal and proposed an exchange that would not appear "as a naked trading-away of British possessions." On the 22nd, after receiving formal proposals from Washington for implementing the agreement, Churchill told Roosevelt that he had not contemplated an explicit "contract, bargain, or sale between us." Rather, he suggested that Britain independently offer naval and air facilities and that the United States provide munitions as an entirely separate act; a case of "two friends in danger helping each other as far as we can." In this way, Churchill asserted, the "difficulties, and even risks," which would result from a contrast between what was given and what was received could be avoided. Though Roosevelt explained that it was legally impossible for him simply to give the destroyers, Churchill held his ground, still urging that Britain offer the bases as a gift which the United States would reciprocate independently with a quid pro quo. This would satisfy the American legal requirement without involving Britain in a direct swap.

Roosevelt now responded with a compromise proposed by two aides.

He suggested that Britain offer bases in Newfoundland and Bermuda as gifts, while five other bases in the Caribbean and British Guiana be exchanged for the destroyers. By August 27 a growing Italian threat to Greece renewed Churchill's sense of urgency about the destroyers; they would allow him to reinforce British naval units in the Mediterranean and possibly head off an invasion of Greece. Though he made a final stab at getting the destroyers "not in payment or consideration for, but in recognition of, what we had done for the security of the United States," Churchill now reluctantly agreed to the President's proposal. Subsequently, he also agreed to a public assurance that Britain would neither surrender nor scuttle its Fleet, guarding against any demoralization with the observation that "these hypothetical contingencies seem more likely to concern the German Fleet or what is left of it than our own." Armed with these documents, Roosevelt was able to announce the agreement as "the most important action in the reinforcement of our national defense . . . since the Louisiana Purchase." On his side, Churchill took satisfaction not only from the receipt of the destroyers but also from the fact that the deal brought an end to American neutrality and left the two countries "somewhat mixed up together in some of their affairs for mutual and general advantage. I do not view the process with any misgivings," Churchill said. "I could not stop it if I wished; no one can stop it. Like the Mississippi, it just keeps rolling along." [22]

The response in the United States was widely favorable. If many Americans were not ready to place the exchange on a par with the Louisiana Purchase, they shared the President's conviction that the country had received excellent value for the old destroyers. "You can't attack a deal like that," one Senator declared. "If you jump on the destroyer transfer, you're jumping on the acquisition of defense bases in the Western Hemisphere." "A stockade of steel to the East," one newspaper called it. Yet Roosevelt had been less concerned about the substance of the agreement than the fact that it had been done in secret without congressional sanction. As he anticipated, this moved some critics to complain that he had "committed an act of war" and become "America's first dictator." But the expected outcry from the Congress proved to be no more than a murmur, and the threat to his reelection from the deal never materialized.

If Roosevelt exaggerated the political dangers to himself from the agreement, it was chiefly because he saw the war issue as Willkie's best hope for victory. With the great majority of Americans still opposed to involvement in the fighting, Roosevelt believed that the Republicans might effectively use this sentiment to unite the country against him. The destroyer exchange, with all its implications of an Anglo-American alliance, impressed him as a golden opportunity for the opposition to identify him as a reckless leader playing fast and loose with the peace. By emphasizing the defensive advantages to the United States emanating from the agreement, however, Roosevelt, in conjunction with the pro-British Century Group, was able to defuse the war question more effectively than even he had dared hope.[23]

Roosevelt's cautious approach to selective service in the summer of 1940 had rested on the same concern. In May, in the belief that the United States needed a million-man Army to defend itself and Latin America and that so large a force would require a draft, a group of World War I officers proposed the introduction of universal military training. Since an unprecedented peacetime draft seemed certain to run into heavy congressional opposition and charges that its proponents intended to take the country into the war, Roosevelt would not give it open backing. Privately, however, he encouraged action. In May he told Grenville Clark, a leading advocate of a draft, that he saw no reason why his group should not urge military training. In June, after an anti-New Deal Democratic Senator and a Republican Representative introduced a selective service law in the Congress, he gave Stimson to understand that he sympathized with his advocacy of conscription and approved an Army-Navy recommendation for a "draft act." In July he allowed Stimson and General Marshall to speak in behalf of compulsory training before congressional committees, and worked behind the scenes against inclusion of an anti-conscription plank in the Democratic platform.

In July he also began moving toward public advocacy of compulsory training. With opinion polls in June showing an increase from 50 to 64 per cent in favor of conscription and with Stimson and military chiefs pressing for action, he made guarded public appeals for a draft law. On July 29, moreover, he asked Congress for authority to call the National Guard to active service, and on August 2, in the belief that the draft law would languish in the Congress unless he took the lead, he declared himself "distinctly in favor of a selective training bill." Though fearful that his advocacy of a draft might lead to "political disaster," he believed it was as essential to national defense as the destroyer deal, and so he took the risk.[24]

Roosevelt's appeal caused a substantial outcry and made him reluctant to press the issue further. Isolationists in and out of the Congress denounced conscription as calculated to put American boys in foreign wars and "slit the throat of the last great democracy still living." Hiram Johnson called the bill the "most sinister law" he had encountered during all his years in Congress. "Silver Star Mothers" and "all kinds of mushroom peace societies" helped flood the Senate with mail which ran nine and ten to one against conscription and influenced "timid congressmen." Though polls continued to show increasing public support for the measure, Roosevelt backed away from further public identification with conscription as an issue that Willkie might use to defeat him. In response to the suggestion that he publicly invite his opponent to work out a mutually satisfactory program on compulsory training, Roosevelt complained that inquiries to Willkie had made it "perfectly clear that he has no desire to cooperate and is merely playing politics." "A limited form of selective draft," Roosevelt told one concerned Democrat, ". . . may very easily defeat the Democratic National ticket—Wallace and myself." In Roosevelt's view, the public might simultaneously favor a draft for defense and vote against someone who appeared to want it as a step toward war.[25]

In the second half of August, however, after Willkie had also called for conscription, Roosevelt pressed the case for a draft law. At a press conference on August 23 he made a long, unequivocal appeal for "action now." The President's request, coupled with Willkie's support and widespread feeling that a draft was necessary for national defense, broke a logjam in Congress. Between August 27 and September 14, after narrowly defeating a series of restrictive amendments, the majority gave Roosevelt power to call the National Guard for service in the Americas and passed a selective service law for men between the ages of twenty-one and thirty-five.[26]

This was not the end of Roosevelt's apprehensions about the draft, however. In late September, Willkie was running well behind in the polls. Though an attractive personality whose attacks on New Deal failures to end the Depression and provide for adequate national defense won him substantial public backing, Willkie had not found an issue that could overcome Roosevelt's popularity. Consequently, he decided to break with his bipartisan approach to foreign affairs and attack the President as a warmonger. Advised by Republican Party professionals to scare the people with warnings that Roosevelt's reelection would mean wooden crosses for their sons and brothers and sweethearts, Willkie began depicting American boys as "already almost on the transports." To counter the effects of such attacks on potential draftees and their families, Roosevelt considered postponing the implementation of the draft until after the election. But fears that any delay might hurt the national defense and backfire politically persuaded him to continue as planned.

By the middle of October, with fresh poll results and reports from party leaders indicating that Willkie was cutting into his lead, Roosevelt launched a vigorous effort to demonstrate his commitment to peace. On October 16, 1940, the day sixteen million Americans registered for the draft, he told a national radio audience that "the three-hundred-year-old American custom of the muster" constituted a program "of defensive preparation and of defensive preparation only. . . . It is to . . . the cause of peace," he declared, "that we Americans today devote our . . . national strength." In Philadelphia on the 23rd, he attacked "the fantastic misstatement" that this government "has secretly entered into agreements with foreign nations," and offered a "solemn assurance" that there was no secret treaty, obligation, commitment, or understanding "to involve this nation in any war." At New York's Madison Square Garden on the 28th, he recounted his "affirmative, realistic fight for peace," and on the following day at a lottery drawing to determine initial draftees, he described conscription as a "mustering" of national resources "for one purpose only: the defense of our freedom." [27]

Roosevelt's campaign against the war charge reached a culmination in Boston on October 30. With the latest Gallup poll showing Willkie surging to within four percentage points of the President, with Willkie declaring that FDR's reelection would mean war by April 1941 and party leaders clamoring for a direct response to this warning, Roosevelt decided to offer unqualified assurances of peace. He was unhappy about this. Because he was being compelled to emphasize his peaceful intentions when he preferred to discuss aid to Britain short of war, he complained to aides about pressure from party chiefs for fresh assurances that the country would not fight in foreign wars unless attacked. "How often do they expect me to say that?" he asked. "It's in the Democratic platform and I've repeated it a hundred times." But the fact that these past assurances had not downed suspicions of his intentions drove him not only to repeat them but also to drop the qualifying phrase, "except in case of attack." It had been a signal that he could not give absolute guarantees against war. But in Boston he simply declared, "I have said this before, but I shall say it again and again and again: Your boys are not going to be sent into any foreign wars." Three days later, in Buffalo, he announced: "Your President says this country is not going to war." Convinced by Willkie's surge in the October polls that attacks on him as a warmonger might cause his defeat, he felt compelled to predict that the country would not become involved in fighting of any kind.[28]

While the war issue raised doubts about Roosevelt's intentions and added to Willkie's vote among German-, Italian-, and Irish-Americans, it chiefly benefited FDR. Asked how they would vote if there were no war, voters favored Willkie by 5.5 per cent—48.7 to 43.2. When voters confronted the possibility of involvement in the fighting, however, they preferred Roosevelt to Willkie by a margin of 18 per cent—54.6 to 36.4. Moreover, one post-election analysis of Roosevelt's victory showed that, whereas 11 per cent of FDR's supporters voted for him chiefly because of the critical international situation, only 2 per cent of Willkie's voters backed him principally because he would keep the country out of war. Where Roosevelt was able to offset Willkie's warnings with peace declarations in the closing days of the campaign, the fact of the actual conflict in Europe gave Roosevelt an advantage that Willkie could not overcome. The final count on November 5, 1940, showed the President with 27 million votes to Willkie's 22 million, and a decisive electoral margin of 449 to 82. Willkie had carried only ten states, but he had won five million more votes than Landon in 1936 and he had cut Roosevelt's plurality to the smallest winning margin since Wilson's narrow victory in 1916.

Roosevelt was greatly relieved by the outcome. For weeks he had worried about a defeat which, in spite of Willkie's internationalism, could be interpreted as a victory for anti-British, pro-appeasement forces in the United States. "We seem to have averted a *Putsch*," he remarked privately on election night. "I prayed for your success and . . . I am truly thankful for it," Winston Churchill wrote him. "We are entering upon a sombre phase of what must evidently be a protracted and broadening war. . . . Things are afoot which will be remembered as long as the English language is spoken in any quarter of the globe." [29]

The close of the election contest shifted the country's attention back to the central foreign policy issue of the day—to what extent should the United States help Britain survive. Even in the most hectic days of the campaign, the issue repeatedly forced itself on Roosevelt's attention. In late September, when a combined British-Free French force prepared to seize Dakar in West Africa from Vichy in order to prevent the creation of a German base that could menace British movements in the South Atlantic and threaten Brazil, Churchill asked FDR to send warships to Monrovia or Freetown and to caution Vichy against fighting Britain. While Roosevelt ignored Churchill's proposal on the ships, he warmly endorsed the attack on Dakar and instructed Welles to tell the French Ambassador that, if Vichy declared war on London, it might cost France control over her New World colonies.

In October, after Churchill had asked him to warn the French Ambassador directly against a military pact with Berlin, and after Vichy leaders had met with Hitler, Roosevelt sent a strong personal message to Marshal Pétain. Describing any use of the French Fleet by Germany against Britain as "a flagrant and deliberate breach of faith with the United States Government," he warned that it would "wreck the traditional friendship between the French and American peoples" and would discourage any future American effort to help France retain its overseas possessions. In November, shortly after the election, Roosevelt tried to enhance American influence with the French as much as possible by appointing Admiral William D. Leahy, former Chief of Naval Operations, Ambassador to Vichy. "We are confronting an increasingly serious situation in France," FDR told Leahy, "because of the possibility that one element in the present French Government may persuade Marshal Pétain to enter into agreements with Germany which will facilitate the efforts of the Axis powers against Great Britain. . . . We need in France at this time an Ambassador who can gain the confidence of Marshal Pétain, who at the present moment is the one powerful element in the French Government who is standing firm against selling out to Germany." [30]

More significantly, in the final days of the campaign Roosevelt confronted substantial new orders from London for all types of war matériel. The British wanted American manufacturers to sell them enough equipment in 1941 for ten divisions and to increase airplane deliveries from 14,000 to 26,000. Though accepting such huge orders meant putting the American economy on a full war footing, Roosevelt readily agreed and revealed the British request to the public. Believing this an opportunity to answer Republican charges about insufficient aid to Britain and a chance to tell the nation generally and the "Boston Irish" in particular about the benefits to the United States from these purchases, Roosevelt announced that by accepting these orders "we are following . . . hardheaded self-interest." These purchases were not only fueling the economy in every part of the country, they were also creating a plant capacity for military equipment which could "serve the needs of the United States in any emergency." The speech also reaffirmed the President's determination to give Britain all possible aid short of war.[31]

Roosevelt gave more direct expression to this goal in the days immediately following the election. On November 7 and 8, 1940, he spoke privately and publicly of allocating to Britain half of all newly produced munitions, including the latest model bombers. At the same time, to prevent British shipping losses from jeopardizing the transport of supplies, Roosevelt suggested that the United States build and lease cargo ships to Britain. He also proposed that the Attorney General find ways of overcoming the legal barriers to the sale and lease of these planes and ships. Specifically, the next week, when Stimson could find no way to declare some B-17's (Flying Fortresses) superfluous to the national defense, Roosevelt suggested that General Marshall release them to England so that the Air Force could test them under combat conditions. Further, when the Maritime Commission rejected the idea of building and leasing ships for which the United States would have little long-run need, it was agreed that London should simply purchase the ships from American shipyards.[32]

By the end of November, however, it was clear that none of this would do Britain much good unless the administration could find some way to help London finance its war purchases in the United States. Though it had been obvious for several months that Britain would run out of funds for its multibillion-dollar war orders, London did not signal an urgent need until the British Ambassador, Lord Lothian, put the question in the headlines on November 23: "Well, boys," he told a group of American reporters, "Britain's broke; it's your money we want." He also told them that a British Treasury official would shortly come to the United States to discuss financial aid.

Outwardly, Roosevelt refused to acknowledge this as a pressing problem. On November 8 he told his Cabinet that "England still has sufficient credits and property in this country to finance additional war supplies"; on the 25th he advised Lothian that Britain must liquidate its holdings in the Western Hemisphere before requesting financial help; and on the following day he casually turned aside press inquiries about specific requests from the British Ambassador by saying that "nothing was mentioned . . . not one single thing—ships or sealing wax or anything else." Finally, on December 1, after Morgenthau reported that the British claimed not to have the $2 billion for the arms they had ordered in October, Roosevelt replied that the English "aren't bust." A Treasury Department estimate of British resources suggested to him that "there's lots of money there."

While Roosevelt believed that Britain had more convertible assets available than they would admit, he was far more concerned about their financial plight than his remarks suggested. He appreciated that England would soon need financial help, but he wished to de-emphasize the question until he came up with a workable solution. On December 1, for example, he suggested that the United States government take over the $2 billion order, that the Reconstruction Finance Corporation provide the money for plant expansion, calling it essential to national defense, and that the British ultimately cover the entire cost through payments on finished goods. Since the British had already declared themselves unable to pay, this was Roosevelt's way of deferring the question until he could decide how to proceed. "We have just got to decide what we are going to do for England," he told Stimson that day. ". . . Doing it this way is not doing anything." As the next three weeks made clear, Roosevelt realized that he must now ask Congress to clear away existing legal barriers to all aid short of war, in particular the Johnson act and the Neutrality laws barring loans and requiring cash for all munitions sold to a belligerent.[33]

Roosevelt was loath to fight for direct repeal or revision of these laws. Such efforts seemed certain to agitate the animus toward Britain and increase fears of war, which had produced the legislation in the first place. The election and recent opinion polls suggested that the country remained strongly opposed to involvement in the fighting and painfully divided about risking war to save Britain. In short, Roosevelt understood that a stable consensus for large-scale aid financed by the United States greatly depended on avoiding suggestions that the country was duplicating the experience of World War I. It is conceivable, of course, that Roosevelt could have exploited his fresh mandate from the electorate to win revisions in the Johnson and Neutrality laws. But the memory of 1937, when a much larger mandate proved insufficient to carry Court-packing through the Congress, together with the conviction borne of the experience since 1919 that an effective policy abroad required a solid consensus at home, impelled Roosevelt to seek some other means by which Britain would continue to receive aid despite an inability to pay.[34]

During a two-week absence from Washington for a vacation cruise beginning December 2, Roosevelt received additional inducement from Churchill and his own advisers to solve the problem. In a letter characterized by Churchill as "one of the most important I ever wrote," the Prime Minister described Britain's prospects for 1941. He explained that the danger of a swift, overwhelming blow by invasion had greatly receded, and that, instead, two less spectacular, but equally deadly, threats to Britain's survival had emerged. The first was a "steady and increasing diminution of sea tonnage. . . . The decision for 1941," Churchill declared, "lies upon the seas. Unless we can establish our ability to feed this island, to import . . . munitions of all kinds . . . unless we can move our armies to the various theatres where Hitler and his confederate Mussolini must be met . . . we may fall by the way, and the time needed by the United States to complete her defensive preparations may not be forthcoming."

To meet this difficulty, Churchill suggested that the United States reassert the doctrine of the freedom of the seas and protect its "lawful" trade with ships and planes. This "decisive act of constructive nonbelligerency," Churchill predicted, would not provoke Hitler into fighting the United States and would assure the effective continuation of British resistance. The only alternative Churchill could see to this policy was "the gift, loan, or supply of a large number of American vessels of war," which, in conjunction with a more extensive patrol of the approaches to the Western Hemisphere, could keep the Atlantic route open.

The other difficulty was the problem of finance: the need of dollars to pay for the ships, planes, artillery, tanks, and small arms Britain was asking in ever greater numbers. "The moment approaches when we shall no longer be able to pay cash for shipping and other supplies," Churchill declared. "While we will do our utmost, and shrink from no proper sacrifice to make payments across the exchange, I believe you will agree that it would be wrong in principle and mutually disadvantagous in effect if at the height of this struggle Great Britain were to be divested of saleable assets, so that after the victory was won with our blood, civilisation saved, and the time gained for the United States to be fully armed against all eventualities, we should stand stripped to the bone. Such a course would not be in the moral or economic interests of either of our countries." Churchill also expressed the conviction that the government and people of the United States did not wish to confine their help only to munitions and commodities that could be immediately paid for. Concluding with a reaffirmation of British willingness "to suffer and sacrifice to the utmost for the cause," Churchill expressed confidence that "ways and means" would be found to assure the continuing flow of supplies.

On December 10, the day after Roosevelt received Churchill's message, his principal advisers also underscored the urgency of Britain's financial problem. They advised the President that London apparently had less than $2 billion available to pay for $5 billion in orders, and they recommended to FDR that the British put up $250 million to start production on their latest orders. This would tide the English over until January, they explained, "at which time it is the unanimous feeling of this group that we should present the entire matter to Congress." [35]

Roosevelt's answer was Lend-Lease. While FDR and others had touched on parts of this scheme in the fifteen months since the war began, the overall plan and timing was strictly the product of Roosevelt's fertile political imagination. Conceived on board ship in the two days after the receipt of Churchill's letter, the plan was an attempt to avoid direct loans, or to "get away from the dollar sign." The thing to do, he told Morgenthau at lunch on December 17, was to increase United States arms output and then "say to England, we will give you the guns and ships that you need, provided that when the war is over you will return to us in kind the guns and ships that we have loaned to you."

He elaborated on the idea at a press conference later that day. Emphasizing that he had no desire to repeal the Neutrality or the Johnson acts in order to lend Britain money or to give the English weapons as a gift, he declared himself eager to try "something brand new." The United States could take over British orders, he said, and "enter into some kind of arrangement for their use by the British on the ground that it was the best thing for American defense, with the understanding that when the show was over, we would get repaid sometime in kind, thereby leaving out the dollar mark . . . and substituting for it a gentleman's obligation to repay in kind." Lest the idea appear too great a departure from the norm, Roosevelt invoked the homely analogy of one neighbor lending another his garden hose to put out a fire. "What do I do" in such a crisis? Roosevelt asked. "I don't say to him before that operation, 'Neighbor, my garden hose cost me $15; you have to pay me $15 for it.' . . . I don't want $15—I want my garden hose back after the fire is over." He wished to lend Britain munitions on the same understanding.[36]

Roosevelt now also moved to increase arms production. For weeks before the election Stimson and others in the administration had pressed him to expand defense production by putting the National Defense Advisory Commission (NDAC) under one chief and breaking with the idea that normal, civilian output need not give ground to defense needs. Reluctant to antagonize labor by appointing a defense czar and eager to see more of the millions of unemployed and the idle factories returned to work before pushing going industries into defense production, Roosevelt resisted this advice. By October, however, when increased English orders made it clear that defense production was inadequate to meet British and American needs, Roosevelt asked the automobile industry to shift some of its output to war goods and established a Priorities Board under the NDAC to synchronize military and civilian production. It was not until after the election and discussion of the Lend-Lease plan, though, that Roosevelt committed himself to a major change in defense planning. On December 20 he announced the replacement of the seven-member NDAC by an Office of Production Management made up of Stimson, Knox, Sidney Hillman of the C.I.O., and William S. Knudsen of the old Board. Knudsen was also appointed Director with increased responsibilities and powers.[37]

Nine days later, Roosevelt used a Fireside Chat to justify and encourage support for all aid short of war. Freed from the constraints of the campaign and a reluctance to speak about anything but peace, Roosevelt candidly explained what he felt the United States must do in foreign affairs. Attacking the belief, which continued to hold wide currency in the country, that events abroad, including even Britain's defeat, would not seriously threaten the United States, Roosevelt declared that "never before since Jamestown and Plymouth Rock has our American civilization been in such danger as now." Should Britain go down, the Axis powers, which had avowed their determination to dominate the world, would control Europe, Asia, Africa, Australasia, and the high seas, and "all of us, in all the Americas, would be living at the point of a gun—a gun loaded with explosive bullets economic as well as military. . . . To survive in such a world, we would have to convert ourselves into a militaristic power on the basis of war economy."

The proper response to this danger, Roosevelt asserted, was not, as the isolationists wished, to encourage a "negotiated," or "dictated peace," but rather to continue sending all possible aid to opponents of aggression. Speaking to the some 40 per cent in the country who continued to think it more important to keep out of war than to aid England, Roosevelt said:

> I make the direct statement to the American people that there is a far less chance of the United States getting into war, if we do all we can now to support the nations defending themselves against attack by the Axis than if we acquiesce in their defeat, submit tamely to an Axis victory, and wait our turn to be the object of attack in another war later on.
> If we are to be completely honest with ourselves, we must admit that there is risk in any course we may take. But I deeply believe that the great majority of our people agree that the course that I advocate involves the least risk now and the greatest hope for world peace in the future.
> The people of Europe who are defending themselves do not ask us to do their fighting. They ask us for the implements of war . . . which will enable them to fight for their liberty and for our security. Emphatically we must get those weapons to them in sufficient volume and quickly enough, so that we and our children will be saved the agony and suffering of war which others have had to endure. . . .
> There is no demand for sending an American Expeditionary Force out-

side our own borders. There is no intention by any member of your Government to send such a force. You can, therefore, nail any talk about sending armies to Europe as deliberate untruth.

Our national policy is not directed toward war. Its sole purpose is to keep war away from our country and our people.

Turning to the need for increased defense production, he called for an end to the "notion of 'business as usual.'" The job cannot be done by merely superimposing defense needs on existing productive facilities, he said. It would require an expansion of industrial productivity which "must not be blocked by those who fear the future consequences of surplus plant capacity. The possible consequences of failure of our defense efforts now are much more to be feared. . . . We," he urged, "must be the great arsenal of democracy. For us this is an emergency as serious as war itself. We must apply ourselves to our task with the same resolution, the same sense of urgency, the same spirit of patriotism and sacrifice as we would show were we at war."

Roosevelt's speech was one of the most successful he ever gave. White House messages ran 100 to 1 in favor, while an opinion poll showed that 80 per cent of those who heard or read the talk expressed approval, with only 12 per cent opposed. Though 24 per cent of the public did not know about the Fireside Chat, the 76 per cent who did represented the largest number ever recorded as aware of a Roosevelt speech. The ingredients of Roosevelt's success seem clear: the 61 per cent national approval for the talk was close to the number of people favoring help to Britain even at the risk of war, while the overall 9 per cent disagreement with the speech suggests that Roosevelt's emphasis on assuring peace through expanded aid disarmed the fears of many who felt it more important to stay out of war than help Britain win.[38]

Convinced that he had a broad consensus for expanded American aid, Roosevelt now asked Congress for full authority to provide help. Giving the Treasury responsibility for writing the Lend-Lease bill, he told Morgenthau that he wanted power from Congress to determine how much, where, and when material support should be sent and what would eventually be given in return. He also explained that he wanted the procedure to be entirely aboveboard, with no government agencies or corporations through which indirect help would be sent. "No RFC, no monkey business . . . no corporations . . . ," he said. "We don't want to fool the public, we want to do this thing right out and out."

While Treasury officials were drafting a Lend-Lease bill, Roosevelt used his annual message to Congress on January 6, 1941, to outline his program. Interpreting recent expressions of the public will, and principally the national election, as a mandate for "speedy and complete action" against "obvious danger," he announced a threefold policy of "all-inclusive national defense," "full support of . . . resolute peoples . . .

resisting aggression and . . . keeping war away from our Hemisphere," and opposition to "a peace dictated by aggressors and sponsored by appeasers." Repeating his determination to act as an arsenal for opponents of aggression, he explained that their inability to pay cash for weapons must not force them to surrender. He recommended that the United States continue to send them supplies which they would ultimately repay with "similar materials, or . . . other goods of many kinds." Having identified the country so closely with Britain's cause, which some Americans viewed as less a defense of democracy than of Empire, Roosevelt also felt compelled to voice peace aims that would weaken this belief. Victory over the dictators, he announced at the close of his address, would mean "a world founded upon four essential human freedoms": freedom of speech; freedom of religion; freedom from want; and freedom from fear.[39]

With a further message from Churchill emphasizing the need for prompt American financing of both current and future British orders, Roosevelt quickly put an aid bill before Congress. On January 10, 1941, the day after he had asked Democratic leaders for a law that would limit neither the amount nor the kind of aid he could send, they introduced such a bill. Designated H.R. 1776 and entitled "An Act To Further Promote the Defense of the United States, and for Other Purposes," the bill authorized the President "to sell, transfer title to, exchange, lease, lend, or otherwise dispose of . . . any defense article" to "any country whose defense the President deems vital to the defense of the United States." The Act also left the President free to decide whether repayments should be "in kind or property, or any other direct or indirect benefit" he considered satisfactory.

Though Roosevelt publicly adopted a hands-off attitude toward the legislation, he privately directed administration strategy. He asked the Century Group to lobby for the measure, and he helped draft part of Hull's testimony before the House Foreign Affairs Committee. With suspicion widespread that Britain had greater available assets than it was willing to admit, Roosevelt also ordered a halt to direct British buying for a month, and instructed Morgenthau to reveal the details of Britain's financial exhaustion in open congressional hearings. "So far as I know," Morgenthau told the Foreign Affairs Committee, "this is the first time in history that one government has put at the disposal of another figures of this nature." Explaining that Britain had already paid $1.33 billion for American goods and might be able to pay another $1.4 billion during 1941 for current orders, he demonstrated that British holdings would not provide the dollars for future supplies. At the same time, to discourage suggestions by some administration leaders that Britain put up some $3 billion as collateral against future Lend-Lease orders, Roosevelt wrote Hull that Britain had only about $1 billion in readily available cash in the United States and that an additional $8 billion or 9 billion worth of assets in Canada, South America, Africa, and the Far East were either needed to purchase things in those locales or were of little potential value to the United States.[40]

In the second half of January, Roosevelt moved to prevent intense isolationist opposition from delaying passage of the law and undermining the national consensus supporting it. Though he was confident of safe majorities in both houses, he believed that opponents might use a filibuster to delay enactment beyond February 15. Information that Hitler might invade England before that date and the possibility that a delay would impede the flow of matériel to Britain made Roosevelt more eager than ever for quick action on the bill. Moreover, charges circulated by America First, the most effective isolationist organization, that he wished to use the law to give away the American Navy, convoy supplies, enhance his powers, and make war impressed FDR as likely to weaken the wide support he believed essential to the measure. He was particularly bothered by Senator Burton Wheeler's remark that Land-Lease was "the New Deal's triple A foreign policy; it will plow under every fourth American boy." He responded directly to all these accusations, saying that the President was somewhat fond of the American Navy and didn't expect to get rid of it, that he had never even considered convoying, and that Wheeler's remark was "the most untruthful . . . dastardly, unpatriotic thing that has ever been said." [41]

He also answered these attacks by accepting specific amendments to the bill. On January 26, when Speaker of the House Sam Rayburn contended that the measure could not pass without amendment, Roosevelt promptly agreed to four restrictions: a time limit on Executive authority to enter into Lend-Lease agreements; a requirement for periodic reports to the Congress on actions taken under the law; consultations with Army and Navy chiefs before disposing of defense equipment currently in hand; and a proviso that nothing in the bill sanctioned Executive use of the Navy to transfer Lend-Lease goods. In accepting the last amendment, though, Roosevelt and administration spokesmen made it clear that as Commander in Chief the President could use the Navy to escort convoys.

Churchill also tried to blunt isolationist attacks on Lend-Lease as a "war measure." On February 9, the day after the House approved the bill by a vote of 260 to 165, the Prime Minister discussed Lend-Lease on the radio. Saying that "the Government and people of the United States intend to supply us with all that is necessary for victory," Churchill emphasized that Britain did not expect the United States to send another Expeditionary Force to Europe. "We do not need the gallant armies which are forming throughout the American Union. We do not need them this year, nor next year; nor any year that I can foresee." Churchill then read a quote from Longfellow that was contained in a message from President Roosevelt:

Sail on, O Ship of State!
Sail on, O Union, strong and great!
Humanity with all its fears,
With all the hopes of future years
Is hanging breathless on thy fate!

"What is the answer that I shall give . . . to this great man . . . : Give us the tools and we will finish the job."

Though Roosevelt was justifiably confident that the Senate would echo House approval of the bill, he felt compelled to accept additional amendments to assure the strong votes he wished. None of these, however, vitiated the bill's central purpose. But they allowed him to close out the Lend-Lease fight by March 11 with a Senate vote of 60 to 31 and a House vote of 317 to 71 on the revised Senate version. The strong support allowed Roosevelt to warn the dictators not to doubt "our unanimity. . . . As a united nation . . . our democracy has gone into action," he said in an address to the White House correspondents. ". . . The decisions of our democracy may be slowly arrived at. But when that decision is made, it is proclaimed . . . with the voice of one hundred and thirty millions. It is binding on us all. And the world is no longer left in doubt." [42]

The passage of the Lend-Lease Act opened the way to consideration of the shipping problem Churchill and others had been emphasizing since December 1940. Without forcible intervention to stop the German submarines, Stimson had told the President then, the dispatch of additional supplies to Britain was like pouring water into a leaky bathtub. In January 1941, with the concurrence of Knox, Marshall, and Stark, Stimson had advised that a British victory required American military action to secure the Atlantic lifeline. Roosevelt replied that he "hadn't quite reached that yet." "When a nation convoys ships through a hostile zone," he told reporters in January, ". . . there is apt to be some shooting . . . and shooting comes awfully close to war. . . . That is about the last thing we have in our minds." Yet at the same time, Roosevelt sanctioned Navy planning for escorts, which he feared might become necessary to prevent a British collapse. British losses in the Atlantic during the next two months bore out this concern. Extending the naval war to Greenland and the western Atlantic, Berlin began sinking British merchant shipping at a rate five and one-half times London's annual capacity to build replacements, a critical situation endangering Britain's entire war effort.

In late March, after Congress had appropriated $7 billion to implement Lend-Lease, Roosevelt acted to bolster Britain in the battle of the Atlantic. He agreed to repair British vessels in American shipyards, to transfer ten Coast Guard cutters to the Royal Navy, and to expand Allied shipping capacity by seizing 65 Axis and Danish ships detained in United States ports. He also concluded an agreement with the Danish Minister in Washington placing Greenland under United States control and permitting the construction of bases to defend the Western Hemisphere against attack. At the same time, he took advantage of British victories over Italian forces in East Africa to declare the Red Sea region no longer a combat zone. This allowed unarmed American ships to carry all kinds of supplies to British forces in the Middle East, releasing British merchant vessels for use in the Atlantic.

The principal need, however, was for American sea and air forces to escort convoys moving between America and Britain. On April 3, after two days of discussion with Admiral Stark, the President gave preliminary approval to Navy plans for escorting and assented to the transfer of three battleships, an aircraft carrier, four cruisers, and other units from the Pacific to the Atlantic to implement these plans. But he did not communicate his decision to his Cabinet, and by April 10 he had decided upon a more cautious step. As he explained it to the "War Cabinet"—Stimson, Knox, Morgenthau, Hull, and Harry Hopkins, FDR's chief civilian aide—and reported it to Churchill on the following day, the United States would extend its neutrality or security zone to longitude line 25° west, including all of Greenland and the Azores, and would send air and naval patrols into the area to find German raiders and notify British convoys of their whereabouts. Instead of escorting, with its heightened risks of combat, Roosevelt decided upon a more extensive policy of patrolling.[43]

Roosevelt's reluctance to go beyond patrolling rested principally on the conviction that "public opinion was not yet ready for the United States to convoy ships." Convinced that the consensus for Lend-Lease had been built largely upon the assumption that such aid would prevent rather than bring about American involvement in the war, Roosevelt feared that escorting and subsequent combat would shatter this consensus and leave him with a divided nation on the verge of war. There was persuasive evidence for his conviction: on April 4 Cabinet members reported that the country "wasn't ready to go to the extreme" to get munitions through to Britain; in opinion polls of April 8, the public opposed escorting by 50 to 41 per cent, and opposed going to war by 50 to 40 per cent if German submarines sank American warships that were guarding merchant vessels; at the same time, a majority of editorial writers expressed the hope that "convoying" would not be necessary; and congressional isolationists introduced a joint resolution prohibiting American merchantmen from carrying goods to belligerents and warships from escorting them.[44]

Roosevelt was so wary of public and congressional reaction to extended patrolling that he considered doing it without a "specific announcement." "I may decide to issue necessary . . . orders," he wrote Churchill on April 11, "and let time bring out the existence of the new patrol area." When he met with his advisers on the 15th, he declared that he would make no formal statement on patrolling but would simply give the orders and let the news leak out when the orders went into effect. Though Morgenthau and Stimson advised against this tactic as likely to embarrass the administration and lose it an opportunity to lift British morale, Roosevelt largely followed his own design. On April 24, when the Navy assumed its new patrol duties, Roosevelt allowed Hull and Knox to outline the new policy in public addresses. At a press conference on the following day he confirmed the commitment to extended patrolling, but took pains to distinguish it from escorting and emphasized its continuity with what had been going on for a year and a half.[45]

All these actions, however, could not stem a tide of Nazi victories in the spring of 1941. In October 1940, after British resistance had forced Hitler to abandon plans for an immediate cross-Channel attack, he committed himself to a strategy of cutting British supply lines in the Atlantic and the Mediterranean. While German naval forces mounted their highly successful campaign in the Atlantic in the winter of 1940–41, Hitler's plans for the Mediterranean went all wrong. Despite strong diplomatic pressure, he was unable to persuade Spain or Vichy France to join the war against Britain and give him control of Gibraltar and North Africa. Further, Italian forces attacking Greece and Egypt were badly beaten and driven back into Albania and Libya, while British forces secured control of the eastern Mediterranean by destroying half the Italian fleet at Taranto and occupying Crete. During April 1941, however, Hitler resoundingly reversed this process: German forces pushed the British back to the Libyian-Egyptian border east of Tobruk, overwhelmed Yugoslavia in eleven days, and occupied all Greece after forcing the surrender of the Greek Army and the evacuation of British forces in less than four weeks.[46]

These defeats provoked additional requests from Churchill for help. Fearful that Hitler would now also strike through Spain and Portugal against Gibraltar and North Africa, he asked Roosevelt to help Britain occupy the Azores and Cape Verde Islands ahead of Berlin by sending a naval force to cruise these regions. This would weaken Hitler's ability to pressure Madrid and Lisbon and thus deny Berlin another advantage in the Atlantic war. A few days later, after describing the dangers to Britain and the United States from the deteriorating situation in the Middle East, he also asked the President to apply "the most extreme pressure" on France to oppose German moves into Syria, Morocco, Algeria, or Tunisia. He hoped this opposition would include naval demonstrations at Dakar and Casablanca, as well as verbal representations.

Roosevelt refused Churchill's requests. The Portuguese government had recently objected to a proposed American visit to the Azores or Cape Verde Islands, he told the Prime Minister on May 1, and the best he could promise was the extension of American patrols to the west side of the Islands. Fearful, moreover, that American opinion would view a British move into the Azores before a German attack as a permanent occupation of a Western Hemisphere possession, he asked Churchill to couple any such action with a declaration of intent to restore the Islands to Portugal at the end of the war.

He also rejected Churchill's bleak interpretation of events in the eastern Mediterranean. "If additional withdrawals become necessary," Roosevelt said, "they will all be a part of the plan which at this stage of the war shortens British lines, greatly extends the Axis lines, and compels the enemy to expend great quantities of men and equipment. . . . Both here and in Britain public opinion is growing to realize that even if you have to withdraw further in the Eastern Mediterranean, you will not allow any great debacle or surrender, and that in the last analysis the Naval control of the Indian Ocean and the Atlantic Ocean will in time win the war." As for France and her colonies, he preferred the carrot to the stick. Urging recognition of the fact that Vichy was "in a German cage," he suggested inducing opposition to German occupation of French colonies by promising regular food shipments to unoccupied France and fuel and ammunition to North Africa.

Churchill, who felt "held in such harsh duress by events," pressed the urgency of his case. He responded on May 3 that he might find it impossible to defer a move against the Atlantic islands until Germany attacked Portugal, but that he would promise their return at the end of the war and would welcome a United States guarantee of such a commitment. "We are far from wishing to add to our territory," he assured the President, "but only to preserve our life and perhaps yours." As for the consequences of losing the Middle East, he cautioned Roosevelt that "it would seriously increase the hazards of the Atlantic and Pacific, and could hardly fail to prolong the war, with all the suffering and military dangers that this would entail." Also pointing out that Spain, Vichy, Turkey, and Japan would be influenced by the outcome of this Middle Eastern struggle, he urged Roosevelt to understand that unless the United States took "more advanced positions now, or very soon . . . vast balances may be tilted heavily to our disadvantage." The one decisive counterweight he saw to growing pessimism in Turkey, the Near East, and Spain was an immediate declaration of United States belligerency. With regard to Vichy, he left it to Roosevelt to determine whether threats or favors would get the best from them.

Roosevelt promptly offered what assurances he could. Explaining that he "did not intend to minimize in any degree the gravity of the situation, particularly as regards the Mediterranean," he stated his determination to rush supplies to the Middle East "at the earliest possible moment" and to continue sending them until a decision was reached there. "I know of your determination to win on that front and we shall do everything that we possibly can to help you do it." His previous message, he explained, was meant to indicate that a withdrawal from the Mediterranean would not "mean the defeat of our mutual interests. . . . The outcome of this struggle is going to be decided in the Atlantic and unless Hitler can win there he cannot win anywhere in the world in the end." To this, Roosevelt added the news that American patrols were pushing farther out into the Atlantic, that Pétain had sent fresh assurances of noncollaboration with Berlin, and that he was asking him to resist any German attempt to use French territory as a base for military operations.[47]

Roosevelt's response to this crisis left many of his principal advisers dissatisfied. Led by Stimson, Knox, and Ickes, they urged him to bring the bulk of the Pacific Fleet into the Atlantic, where it could assure effective patrolling, begin escorting, and defend Dakar, the Azores, and the Cape Verde Islands against Nazi control. Patrolling is "a step forward," Roosevelt told his Cabinet in late April. "Well, I hope you will keep on walking, Mr. President. Keep on walking," Stimson replied. They also pressed him to take his case to the public for stronger action. "Without a lead on his part," Stimson said, "it was useless to expect the people would voluntarily take the initiative in letting him know whether or not they would follow him if he did take the lead." By early May, however, all these men thought that the time for words had passed. It would be insufficient for the President "to make another speech and then go into a state of innocuous desuetude again," Ickes observed. "People are beginning to say: 'I am tired of words; I want action.'"

But Roosevelt felt immobilized by international and domestic constraints. While he appreciated that effective patrolling required the transfer of some ships from the Pacific to the Atlantic, he worried that the implementation of Navy plans he had given preliminary approval on April 3 would encourage the Japanese to renew their drive to the south, especially since they had secured their northern flank through the completion of a neutrality pact with Russia on April 13. As important, he did not think that public opinion was ready for actions that were likely to bring the country to the brink of war. In his judgment, the public still did not fully appreciate the threat to American security from Axis power and would object to escorting or the seizure of Dakar and Atlantic islands as pushing the United States into "Britain's war." Moreover, he did not feel that he could persuade the public with another didactic address about foreign dangers, and that it would require some dramatic event to win the country to bolder deeds. Consequently, for ten days in early May, while he waited on events, he took advantage of an intestinal disorder to avoid giving a foreign policy address or discussing the crisis with aides.[48]

By the middle of May, diplomatic developments stirred Roosevelt to fresh action. With Tokyo demonstrating a willingness to continue discussing Japanese-American differences and with Vichy now actively collaborating with Berlin for the use of Middle Eastern and African bases, Roosevelt ordered a quarter of the Pacific Fleet into the Atlantic. Though it was still less than Stimson and Knox believed sufficient to inhibit Berlin, this move allowed Roosevelt to consider a declaration to the Congress that the United States could not respond passively to German control over West African ports and Atlantic islands. It also allowed him to order his Chief of Naval Operations to plan the possible occupation of the Azores by a 25,000-man defense force. "Slowly, and in spite of anything we Americans do or do not do," he candidly wrote an isolationist Congressman on May 19, "it looks a little as if you and some other good people are going to have to answer the old question of whether you want to keep your country unshackled by taking even more definite steps to do so—even firing shots—or, on the other hand, submitting to be shackled for the sake of not losing one American life." [49]

Though Roosevelt had now apparently concluded that the United States would ultimately have to join the fighting, he remained painfully uncertain about how to proceed. On May 17 he told Morgenthau that he was "waiting to be pushed into this situation." Morgenthau took him to mean that "he wanted to be pushed into the war rather than lead us into it." At a Cabinet meeting on the 23rd, when some participants expressed hope that the President would use a speech rescheduled for May 27 to declare the country "ready to do something," he replied: " 'I am not willing to fire the first shot.' So it seems that he is still waiting for the Germans to create an 'incident,' " Ickes concluded. "The President shows evidence of waiting for the accidental shot of some irresponsible captain on either side to be the occasion of his going to war," Stimson observed. But with German forces now driving the British out of Crete and the Bismarck, the most heavily armed ship afloat, on the loose in the Atlantic after destroying the Hood, Britain's largest and fastest capital ship, Roosevelt felt compelled to take some meaningful step. If the Bismarck showed up in the Caribbean, he would consider ordering American submarines to sink her. But his belief that the people might demand his impeachment persuaded him to lay aside the idea.

A dream Roosevelt related to Adolf Berle on May 25 provides additional evidence of his feelings on the issue. "The President was telling us last night of a dream . . . that he was at Hyde Park; that there had been a light bombing of New York; that the Secret Service had provided him with a bombproof cave two hundred feet under the cliff near a little cottage he has up on the hill there; that he and several of his people had gone down into it to stay until a squadron of German planes had passed over Hyde Park." Judging by the German attack, the dream suggests, on the one hand, an expectation of American involvement in the war. On the other hand, the "light" bombing of New York and the absence of an attack on Hyde Park, where "he and several of his people" found shelter, suggest a determination to defend himself and the administration from the political crisis that arbitrary involvement in the war seemed likely to bring.

For the moment, he decided to restrict himself to a forceful speech proclaiming an unlimited national emergency. The Nazis, he warned, were waging a war for world domination, and "unless the advance of Hitlerism is checked now, the Western Hemisphere will be within range of the Nazi weapons of destruction." Recent German successes gave Hitler the power to occupy Spain and Portugal, the "Atlantic fortress of Dakar," and the "island outposts of the New World—the Azores and the Cape Verde Islands." This, he said, would put the Nazis only seven hours' flying distance from Brazil and in a position to dominate South Atlantic shipping lanes. It would jeopardize the island possessions of the United States and "the ultimate safety of the continental United States itself." One requirement of American security, therefore, was to keep Hitler out of the territorial approaches to the Western Hemisphere—Iceland and Greenland in the north, the Azores and Cape Verde Islands in the south. "It would be suicide to wait until they are in our front yard," Roosevelt admonished. ". . . It is stupid to wait until a probable enemy has gained a foothold from which to attack."

To resist the Nazis, Roosevelt also said, the Allies must have "control of the seas." In the Battle of the Atlantic, where the Axis powers were "risking everything they have, conducting desperate attempts to break through to the command of the ocean," the Germans were now sinking merchant ships at a rate more than three times the capacity of British shipyards to replace them and more than twice the combined Anglo-American output. To meet this peril, the United States would have to step up its shipbuilding program and help cut losses on the high seas through expanded patrolling. Further, if Britain, upon which "control of the seas" depended, were to survive, the United States would have to assure delivery of needed supplies. "This can be done; it must be done; and it will be done," Roosevelt declared. Closing with reassertions of the American doctrine of the freedom of the seas, of the solidarity of the twenty-one American Republics and Canada, and of determination to give the democracies material support, he "issued a proclamation that an unlimited national emergency exists and requires the strengthening of our defense to the extreme limit of our national power and authority." [50]

The speech left unclear whether any concrete actions would follow the President's proclamation. The talk "was calculated to scare the daylights out of everyone . . . ," one of its authors observed, "but it did not do much else." It was "more explanatory than dispository," and it left "several main issues to be settled later." Roosevelt eliminated the confusion at a press conference on the following day. Explaining that escorting was outmoded, that he would not ask repeal of the Neutrality law, and that he had no intention of issuing the Executive orders needed to implement the declaration of unlimited emergency, Roosevelt promised no specific follow-up to his speech.[51]

Critics at the time and since have puzzled over Roosevelt's reluctance to take a strong lead during that spring crisis. By May, 68 per cent of the public believed it was more important to help Britain than to keep out of war, while 85 per cent assumed that the United States would eventually enter the conflict. Despite the fact that three-fourths of the population thought escorting would put the country in the war, 55 per cent endorsed such action, with the figure going to 73 per cent when the alternative to escorting was described as Britain's defeat. At the same time, however, 79 per cent of Americans expressed a desire to stay out of the fighting, while approximately 70 per cent felt that the President either had gone too far or was now doing enough to help Britain. Proponents of stronger action argued that clearer guidance by the President would have overcome these contradictory tendencies and mobilized solid majorities behind escorting and, ultimately, stronger measures. An initial 95 per cent favorable response to the May 27 speech was seen as one indication of what presidential leadership could achieve.[52]

But Roosevelt put a different construction on this evidence. He viewed the enthusiasm for his speech as resulting from the fact that he did not go beyond a general discussion of the Nazi threat into controversial details for meeting it. While he believed that the public would strongly line up behind intervention if a major incident demonstrated the need to fight, he did not feel that he could evoke this response simply by what he said or did. A specially prepared poll in late May, for example, showed him that only 51 per cent of the country favored prompt entrance into the war should he and the military chiefs predict that Britain would be defeated unless America intervened in the near future. Subsequent unpublished polls showed him that the use of his name made only a marginal difference in raising or lowering the level of support for stronger war policies. Roosevelt appreciated that he could command a national majority on escorting, on occupation of Atlantic islands, and possibly on direct involvement in the war. But these actions did not promise a broad, stable consensus for fighting which a major provocation abroad could give. In his view, if a substantial minority in the country felt that he, rather than a meaningful threat to the national security, compelled involvement in the conflict, it would be difficult to assure wartime unity in the United States, especially in the face of any temporary defeat. In short, if he were to avoid painful wartime divisions, the nation would have to enter the fighting with a minimum of doubt and dissent, and the way to achieve this was not through educational talks to the public or strong Executive action, but through developments abroad which aroused the country to fight.[53]

News on June 11 of the unprovoked sinking of an American freighter, the *Robin Moor*, by a German sub in the South Atlantic, a nonwar zone, seemed well tailored to the President's desire for an "incident." Hopkins urged him to use this violation of international law and America's freedom of the seas to change the "observation patrol" into a "security patrol," which would give the Navy free reign to assure the safety of American-flag ships traveling outside of danger zones. Though Roosevelt used the incident to reiterate the Nazi threat, telling the Congress that it was meant to intimidate the United States into accepting German conquest of Britain and the high seas, he refused to follow Hopkins's advice or to start escorting; nor did he interpret it as a direct attack on the United States. The destruction of an American freighter was insufficient to push the country into actions that risked war.

While Roosevelt was ready to offer rhetorical defiance to Berlin, announcing that "we are not yielding and we do not propose to yield," he was reluctant to do anything that would either force the war issue with the public or alter Hitler's plan to attack the Soviet Union. Rumors of the plan had been coming in for months, with Churchill writing him on June 15 that "from every source at my disposal . . . it looks as if a vast German onslaught on the Russian frontier is imminent." Since a German move against Russia promised at least temporary relief from the crisis in the Mediterranean and the Atlantic and a potentially powerful ally against Berlin, Churchill and Roosevelt welcomed the attack on June 22 as opening a new phase in the widening struggle to destroy Nazi power. "Any man or state who fights on against Nazidom will have our aid. Any man or state who marches with Hitler is our foe. . . . That is our policy and that is our declaration," Churchill announced in response to the attack. "It follows, therefore, that we shall give whatever help we can to Russia and the Russian people. We shall appeal to all our friends and allies in every part of the world to take the same course and pursue it, as we shall faithfully and steadfastly to the end." [54]

II

The Tortuous Road to War

FROM THE FALL OF 1940 to the summer of 1941, while Roosevelt struggled to aid Britain against Berlin, the Far East continued to force itself on his attention. Though he remained eager to keep things as quiet as possible in the Pacific and to divert the fewest possbile resources from the Atlantic and the Middle East, continuing Japanese pressure on China and Southeast Asia denied him that option.

On October 18, 1940, Chiang Kai-shek sent word that continued resistance to Japan depended on prompt additional help from the United States. He contended that the loss of American and Russian supplies after the closing of the Burma Road in July, rampant inflation, and Communist exploitation of current difficulties in order to weaken Nationalist rule were sapping China's ability and resolve to fight. To meet these difficulties, Chiang asked for 500 planes in the next three months, American volunteers to fly them, and "a single big loan rather than small piecemeal credits" as given in the past. The planes and crews would allow Chiang's Chungking government to oppose Japan's uncontested control of the skies and to defend the recently reopened Burma Road; they would permit raids on naval bases in Japan and Formosa and thus impair Tokyo's ability to fight the United States.

Though Ambassador Nelson T. Johnson strongly endorsed Chiang's request as a way to move beyond "flimsy aid" which demonstrated a "callous and dangerous disregard" for China's plight, Roosevelt and Hull responded skeptically and cautiously. Challenging Chiang's assertions that aid from Russia had ceased and that the Burma Road could be put out of commission, the President and Secretary also pointed out that it was traditional for the United States in peacetime not to enter into alliances or entangling commitments, that "a considerable number" of American planes was already on the way to China, and that additional credits or loans were under discussion in Washington. But Chiang, who feared that current moves toward a Soviet-Japanese agreement and toward Tokyo's recognition of the seven-month-old Japanese puppet regime in Nanking as the government of China would further undermine his power, pressed Washington to make additional commitments. During the first three weeks of November, he asked Roosevelt to ally the United

States with Britain and China, or, at the very least, to declare approval and support for an Anglo-Chinese pact. In addition, he requested an Anglo-American loan of between $200 million and $300 million, the sale of up to 1000 planes a year on credit, with 200 or 300 to be delivered by the end of 1940, and a team of military, economic, and communications experts to organize Sino-American cooperation in the Far East.[1]

Though Roosevelt rejected Chiang's proposal for an alliance, he shared his apprehension that Japanese recognition of the Nanking government would further undermine "free China," and he tried to "do something fast." Asking Welles and Morgenthau to arrange a hundred-million-dollar loan at once, he pressed Morgenthau to go ahead with the credit even if it meant defying Congress. "It is a matter of life and death. . . ," he told the Secretary. "If I don't do it . . . it may mean war in the Far East." On November 30, the same day Tokyo recognized the Nanking regime, Roosevelt announced a contemplated credit to the Chinese government of $100 million, and Hull expressed American determination to continue to recognize "the legally constituted Government at Chungking."

At the same time, Roosevelt encouraged a plan to give the Chinese a limited number of long-range bombers to attack Japan. Since, as Morgenthau told T. V. Soong, Chiang's Personal Representative in Washington, "asking for 500 planes is like asking for 500 stars," Roosevelt saw the idea of giving bombers as a relatively cheap way to bolster Chungking. Originating with the Chinese, who proposed to use foreign pilots and mechanics operating from airfields within 650 miles of Tokyo, the scheme received enthusiastic support from the President, Morgenthau, and Hull. "Wonderful," FDR replied when Morgenthau put the plan before him. "If we could only find some way to have them [the Chinese] drop some bombs on Tokyo," Hull remarked to Morgenthau. When the two of them tried to work out the details of such an operation, however, it drew fire from Stimson and Marshall as "rather half baked" and too costly to the British war effort. Instead, with London's reluctant acquiescence, Stimson and Marshall agreed to divert 100 pursuit planes from British orders to help defend the Burma Road. This help, while less than Chiang had asked or Washington wished to give, promised to keep China fighting and, most importantly, help deter Japan from attacking French, Dutch, or British possessions to the South.[2]

The corollary to tying Japan down in China was checking her directly, either through diplomatic talks or more assertive economic and military means. Though Roosevelt, like all his advisers, wished to assure England the largest possible aid in the Atlantic by keeping peace in the Pacific, he was of two minds about how to do it. At a Cabinet meeting at the end of November he endorsed Hull's description of future policy toward Japan as one of continuing to slow her up as much as possible "by fighting a rear guard diplomatic action, without doing it so stringently as to drive her to get her supplies by making an attack on the Netherlands." Further, in January 1941, when two American priests, Bishop James E. Walsh and Father James M. Drought, returned from a trip to Japan with an unofficial proposal from Prince Konoye for settling Japanese-American differences, FDR, though skeptical of success, encouraged further discussions.

At the same time, however, he was drawn to stronger measures, which advocates of strict diplomacy thought might provoke a war. In late November 1940, he had expressed sympathy with the British idea of sending part of the American Fleet to Singapore, and agreed to prevent Japanese purchases of more steel and iron products than were bought annually before the war. Also, in December, when Francis B. Sayre, the High Commissioner to the Philippines, warned that a war with Japan would divert aid from England, Roosevelt replied that helping Britain partly entailed a defense of Pacific possessions on which she relied for supplies, and implied that the United States must be prepared to take strong action, and even fight in the Pacific, if Britain were to survive. As to which policy he would follow toward Japan, however, he himself could not say. "Our problem being one of defense," he wrote Ambassador Grew in January, "we cannot lay down hard and fast plans. As each new development occurs we must, in the light of the circumstances then existing, decide when and where and how we can most effectively marshal and make use of our resources." [3]

When a fresh crisis arose in the Far East in February 1941 over reports of a Japanese offensive against Southeast Asia, circumstances dictated that Roosevelt not challenge Japan. Though he considered giving a strong response, the battle of the Atlantic and the Lend-Lease debate constrained him. More specifically, the need to answer Hitler's offensive with additional Atlantic patrols and concerns that a war scare would provoke opposition to Lend-Lease decided Roosevelt against moving more ships to the Pacific or sending a naval force to cruise the Philippines as a warning to Japan.

Instead of strong measures, Roosevelt relied on "moral steps" of doubtful consequence. On February 11 he advised Americans in China, the Philippines, and Malaya to leave the Far East, and on the 14th he had "a very serious talk" with Admiral Kichisaburo Nomura, Japan's new Ambassador. Declaring that Japanese movements southward were giving "this country very *serious* concern," he warned that an incident like the destruction of the *Panay* could "cause an overnight uprising . . . of American sentiment against the authors." Though the Ambassador assented to everything the President said, Roosevelt thought the conversation of little importance and made light of it in a discussion with Berle. Describing himself as "really emotional," he recounted his "speech" to

the Ambassador, "interspersing it with [mock] sobs. . . . He hoped
Admiral Nomura would make it plain to his Government that . . .
everybody here was doing their best to keep things quiet . . . should the
dikes ever break (three sobs), civilization would be ended." 4

The British, who took a strong verbal stand against Tokyo, pressed
Roosevelt to go beyond these "moral steps." Describing "the awful
enfeeblement of our war effort" that would result from a conflict with
Japan, Churchill implored the President to inspire the Japanese "with
the fear of a double war." From Churchill's perspective, if this helped
check Japan, all to the good, and if not, it would link the United States
in a military alliance with Britain in the Far East and almost certainly
assure her involvement in the European war. Roosevelt, however, remained convinced that a war scare would jeopardize the "pending" Lend-
Lease bill and that the public would oppose initiatives that risked war in
the Far East. An opinion survey sent to him on February 15, the same
day as Churchill's message, showed 59 per cent favoring American action
to keep Japan out of the Dutch East Indies and Singapore, but only 39
per cent willing to risk war to achieve this end. It was with considerable
relief, then, that London and Washington saw Tokyo back away from
any warlike act in Southeast Asia during the next nine days.5

For four months after this crisis subsided in February 1941, Roosevelt
continued to aim for peace in the Pacific through diplomatic talks,
limited displays of strength, and additional aid to China. Since negotiations with the Japanese held out some possibility of a settlement and
since discussions even if unproductive would at least delay the onset of
a war, Roosevelt encouraged further talks. In a conversation with
Nomura in March, he endorsed the idea that "matters between our two
countries could undoubtedly be worked out without a military clash."
Though the ensuing discussions between Nomura and Hull principally
confirmed American suspicions of Japanese intentions, Roosevelt was
content to let them run on through the spring. They continued to seem
not only the best immediate bar to war, but also the best means to help
Japan's moderates resist, and possibly overcome, advocates of strong
action and firm ties to Berlin.

Roosevelt also tried to restrain Japan by calculated displays of American power and Anglo-American-Dutch unity. While resisting repeated
British proposals to dispatch ships to Singapore, he had naval forces visit
Australia and New Zealand in March and naval officers participate openly
in staff conversations at Singapore with high-ranking British, Dutch, Australian, New Zealand, and Indian officers in April. Similarly, he explored
the possibility of sending Willkie to Japan, where he could indicate "a
hardening of the American attitude in the general conflict," and then on
to China, Singapore, Australia, and the Dutch East Indies, where he could
display "a united front to Japan." 6

The most effective restraint on Japan at that time, Roosevelt felt, remained aid to China. In January he had sent Lauchlin Currie, a high White House aide, to help Chiang Kai-shek with his economic problems and to demonstrate American determination to provide additional assistance. In March, after Currie returned with a list of Chinese needs and after the Lend-Lease bill became law, Roosevelt placed transportation and air force experts at Chiang's disposal and promised to make China eligible for Lend-Lease. In April, after news of the Soviet-Japanese Neutrality Pact threatened to reduce Soviet help to China and further demoralized Chiang, Roosevelt authorized the resignation of American military personnel to become founding members of Colonel Claire Chennault's Flying Tigers, a group of Air Corps volunteers fighting for China; he also gave personal assurances to T. V. Soong of his determination to get Lend-Lease goods through to China. To give substance to his words, he insisted that Chunking receive a loan of $50 million in a lump sum rather than in installments "on evidence of sanity in Chinese finance," advised Chiang of what supplies would go forward at once, and publicly acknowledged China's eligibility for Lend-Lease. In May he also gave Currie a go-ahead to negotiate with American and British military chiefs on planes, or anything else the Chinese requested. At the same time, though, he cautioned Currie against committing him to any of Chiang's requests. These, he explained, "can only be finally worked out in relationship to our military problem and the needs of ourselves and the British." In brief, with the war in the Atlantic and Mediterranean reaching another crisis, help to China would have to remain a secondary concern.[7]

In June and July, despite his undiminished desire to avoid greater involvement in the Pacific, pressures beyond his control pushed Roosevelt toward a confrontation with Japan. Hitler's attack on Russia forced Tokyo into a grand debate on whether to join Germany by invading Soviet Siberia, take advantage of Russian preoccupation in the north to step up expansion and control of raw materials to the south, or redouble its efforts to avoid war and gain its principal ends in China and Southeast Asia through negotiations with the United States. As long as such a debate was in progress, Roosevelt, who was under heavy domestic pressure to relieve American petroleum shortages by embargoing oil to Japan, refused to do anything which might "tip the delicate scales and cause Japan to decide to attack Russia or . . . the Dutch East Indies." "The Japs," he told Ickes on July 1, "are having a real drag-down and knock-out fight among themselves . . . trying to decide which way they are going to jump—attack Russia, attack the South Seas (thus throwing in their lot definitely with Germany), or whether they will sit on the fence and be more friendly with us. No one knows what the decision will be but . . . it is terribly important for the control of the Atlantic for us to help to keep peace in the Pacific. I simply have not got enough Navy to go round—and every little episode in the Pacific means fewer ships in the Atlantic."

Roosevelt did not know that American diplomatic action was discouraging Japan from an accommodation with the United States. On June 21, in response to developments in the talks going on since April, Hull had sent Tokyo a comprehensive statement of America's position on the issues between them. Since Nomura had initially misled his government into thinking that the United States would negotiate on far more generous terms than those outlined in the June 21 proposal, the Japanese interpreted this document as a deliberate stiffening of position in response to Berlin's imminent attack on the Soviet Union. This apparent change in attitude contributed to a high-level Japanese decision of July 2 to proceed with the advance to the south, even if it meant war with Britain and the United States. More specifically, the Japanese now decided to consolidate their hold on Indochina and Siam as a prelude to closing the Burma Road and dominating the Dutch East Indies.[8]

Evidence of this decision provoked a strong response. Believing that negotiation and appeasement had done little to check Japan and would be a highly unpopular answer to its current action, Roosevelt laid plans to answer new Japanese demands for control in Southeast Asia with "various embargoes, both economic and financial." On July 18, after Tokyo had demanded Vichy's acquiescence in the occupation of eight air and two naval bases in southern Indochina, the President worked out a program of sanctions with his Cabinet. Though giving them "quite a lecture" against a total oil embargo, which would be a goad to war in the Pacific, he agreed to answer Japan's action with a freeze on assets, a reduction in oil exports to amounts received in past years, and a limit on gasoline sales to 67 octane or lower. On the 24th, therefore, when Vichy acceded to Tokyo's demands, Welles issued a public condemnation of the action as a prelude to "further and more obvious movements of conquest," and Roosevelt confirmed his decision to freeze Japanese funds and further restrict her trade.

Yet Roosevelt still had no intention of closing off all oil to Japan. While he wanted a comprehensive order that would allow him to do so at any time, he had no inclination to do it at once. The President, Ickes complained, "was still unwilling to draw the noose tight. He thought that it might be better to slip the noose around Japan's neck and give it a jerk now and then. . . . The effect of the freezing order is to require an export license before any goods can be shipped to Japan but the President indicated that we would still continue to ship oil and gasoline." As Roosevelt explained it to a group of civilian defense volunteers on July 24, oil exports to Japan served American and British self-interest by keeping the Japanese out of the Dutch East Indies and thereby preventing a war in the South Pacific which would disrupt essential lines of supply. Roosevelt also tried to forestall a crisis with Japan by proposing that if Tokyo withdrew from Indochina, the Powers would neutralize the area and guarantee equal access to all its resources. Though Roosevelt had little hope of a favorable response to his plan, he saw it as "one more effort to avoid Japanese expansion to [the] South Pacific." [9]

Neither of these efforts at appeasement, however, made an impression on the Japanese. They refused to take the President's neutralization scheme seriously, and they saw no evidence of his intention to permit further oil exports. So as to leave petroleum policy open, the White House announcement of the President's freezing order said nothing about oil. This left the impression both in the United States and Japan that all trade between them, including petroleum exports, had been suspended. Though an announcement of August 1 indicated that applications for petroleum export licenses could be resubmitted if they did not exceed prewar quantities or involve fuels and oils suitable for use in aircraft, the administration's failure to state its policy clearly allowed government agencies to reject these applications and establish a de facto embargo on oil to Japan. Roosevelt, who left on August 3 for a conference with Churchill on board a ship in the Atlantic, did not realize that a full embargo had been introduced until early September, and by then he saw a shift in policy as a show of weakness which Japan would exploit and London and American leaders would deplore.

Roosevelt's acceptance of the full embargo was one expression of his growing belief that only a firm policy would have an impact on Japan. An initial report on the results of the freezing action indicated that it had thrown the Japanese off balance and put them in a quandary about future policy. On the one hand, they asked for further conversations with the United States, even proposing a meeting betweeen Prince Konoye and the President. On the other hand, they made plans for further expansion to the south. Since Roosevelt was aware of these plans because Japanese diplomatic cables could be read through a code-breaking device called "Magic," he viewed their suggestions for talks as insincere. "You will . . . find the President quite ready to talk freely about Japan and about the question of joint action with ourselves if the Japs go for ourselves or the Dutch," Lord Halifax, the British Ambassador to Washington since January, had cabled Churchill in early August. "Opinion has moved so fast during the last few weeks that I don't think you need have any inhibitions about speaking quite freely." Yet, as his actions would shortly demonstrate, Roosevelt remained eager to extend the discussions with Tokyo as a means of deferring a war in the Pacific for as long as he could.[10]

Roosevelt's desire to avoid, or at least hold off, a Pacific conflict rested on his continuing concern that scarce resources be marshaled to fight

Hitler. At the beginning of July, for example, while the crisis with Japan was unfolding, he had debated whether to occupy Iceland. Reports in April of German preparations for an attack had helped decide Roosevelt to take this step, which he believed would also eventually release a British division from ocupation duty and free British shipping from the Iceland to America crossing. Churchill's conviction that "it would have a moral effect even beyond its military importance" may also have played a part. On June 5 Roosevelt ordered a Marine brigade of 4000 men to prepare to sail in fifteen days, and on July 7, after their arrival in Iceland, he informed the Congress that he had sent troops to the island to forestall a German move that could threaten Greenland and the northern portion of North America, all shipping in the North Atlantic, and the steady flow of munitions to Britain. Presented as a strictly defensive move, Roosevelt's actions received strong backing in the Congress and the country. A national opinion poll, for example, showed 61 per cent in favor and only 20 per cent unequivocally opposed.

With the decision to go into Iceland, Roosevelt was at once confronted with the constraints on American power. Though London and Reykjavik wanted Washington to replace Britain's entire 20,000-man force immediately, Roosevelt resisted such a commitment. Forbidden by the Selective Service Act to send draftees outside the Western Hemisphere, which was not normally thought to include Iceland, he was hard pressed to find regular troops for long-term duty in the island. Consequently, he limited the American contingent to 4000 men. It was his wish to announce that they were being sent "to supplement and perhaps eventually replace" British forces, but, under pressure from Iceland's government, he agreed to drop the qualifying "perhaps." Similarly, though plans for the North Atlantic after the occupation of Iceland included a commitment to escort British as well as American and Icelandic ships moving between the United States and Iceland, Roosevelt abruptly reversed this decision at the end of July and approved escorting only for American and Icelandic ships. In the midst of a debate on revising the Selective Service law and a crisis in the Far East, he was reluctant to give congressional opponents ammunition or to assume commitments in the Atlantic that might dilute American naval strength in the Pacific. Though the President's caution left the British somewhat disappointed, Churchill nevertheless took considerable solace from the fact that "at this particularly grim and fateful moment" he could encourage his people by calling America's move into Iceland "one of the most important things that have happened since the war began." [11]

The problem of finding troops for Iceland threw into high relief the question of building a large land force for service anywhere on the globe. In June, Roosevelt had approved War Department recommendations for extending the service of selectees and National Guardsmen for the emergency and for eliminating the provisions of the Selective Service Act limiting induction to no more than 900,000 draftees for service strictly in the Western Hemisphere. Though refusal to extend the term of military service beyond one year threatened to leave the country without an adequate land force, a vigorous opposition to the extension sprang up at once. Effectively playing on sentiments for sending the boys home and keeping out of war, opponents denounced these proposals as violating pledges to limit selectees to a single year of service and as a prelude to sending American troops abroad. When House leaders expressed opposition to breaking "promises" about the conscription law and said they believed that extended duty for selectees was impossible, Roosevelt agreed to confer with congressional chiefs. "In forty years on the Hill," one congressional secretary reported, "he had never seen such fear of a bill." At a White House meeting on July 14 the President won a promise of extended military service in exchange for commitments to ask personally for the legislation and to defer a proposal giving him the power to send draftees outside the Hemisphere.

To satisfy congressional demands that he take full responsibility for an unpopular measure, Roosevelt sent a strongly worded recommendation to Congress on July 21. In what Stimson called a "humdinger" of a message, he warned against the "tragic error" of allowing the "disintegration" of America's comparatively "small" Army. "We . . . cannot afford to speculate with the security of America," he explained, when the danger to the nation "is infinitely greater" than when the draft began. "Time counts," Roosevelt concluded. "Within two months disintegration, which would follow failure to take Congressional action, will commence in the armies of the United States. . . . The responsibility rests solely with the Congress."

With an opinion poll of July 29 showing only 51 per cent of the nation in favor of extending military service beyond a year, the Congress gave a cautious endorsement to the President's appeal. The Senate, with twenty-one members not voting and only forty-five in favor, approved an extension of service for eighteen months rather than for the duration of the emergency as the administration had asked. The situation in the House was even more precarious, where fears of constituent reaction made the vote too close to call. In response, Roosevelt sent another personal appeal to Congressmen in which he stressed the seriousness of the situation if the United States were left with "a weak Army composed mostly of new recruits. The future . . . defense of the Americas," he advised, "may depend on this vote. It is too serious to take a chance." Despite the President's warning, the bill to extend military service to eighteen months passed the House on August 12 by only one vote, 203 to 202.

The congressional action demonstrated how divided and resistant the

Congress and country remained about entering the war. Despite Roosevelt's unequivocal appeals for prompt action, the Congress barely passed a watered-down version of the administration's request. The result undoubtedly confirmed Roosevelt in his belief that proposals to Congress for stronger measures would surely fail. In June, for example, when Grenville Clark, a leading proponent of the draft, had urged Roosevelt to ask for congressional approval for anything necessary to defeat Hitler, the President told an aide that "Grenny Clark could not get elected to Congress in any district—North, South, East or West!" [12]

On no issue did Roosevelt proceed with greater caution than on aid to Russia. Though he had promised to align himself with Churchill on the question, the President's initial declarations were more guarded than the Prime Minister's. Whereas Churchill unhesitatingly pledged to give Russia "whatever help we can," Roosevelt's first statement on the Nazi attack on June 22 came through the State Department and said nothing about helping the U.S.S.R. At a press conference on June 24, while he promised all possible aid to the Soviet Union, he hedged this commitment by pointing out that officially Moscow had not yet asked for anything and that Britain had first call on American arms. Asked if Russia's defense were essential to the defense of the United States, Roosevelt evasively replied: "Oh, ask me a different type of question—such as 'how old is Ann?' "

Roosevelt's reluctance to commit himself rested on at least three considerations: first, that the Russians, according to America's best military opinion, could not hold out against Germany for more than three months; second, that in this "period of respite" limited supplies might best be used to bolster Britain and strengthen America's Atlantic defenses; and third, that opinion in the United States was unsympathetic to providing Russia with all-out support. While only a small segment of the public saw the Soviet-German conflict as a contest between "Satan and Lucifer," in which the United States should take no part, and while almost three-fourths of the country wanted Russia to win, a majority of Americans opposed giving help to Moscow on the same basis as to Britain.[13]

But the conviction that successful Russian resistance would ultimately mean Hitler's defeat overrode these considerations. "Now comes this Russian diversion," Roosevelt wrote Admiral Leahy on June 26. "If it is more than just that it will mean the liberation of Europe from Nazi domination." In line with this feeling, Roosevelt had begun opening avenues of help. On June 24 he had released $39 million of frozen Russian assets and on the 25th announced that, in the absence of any peril to the United States, he would not invoke the Neutrality Act, meaning that American ships could still carry goods to unoccupied Soviet ports. On June 30 Welles took under consideration an official Soviet request for $1.8 billion in supplies and a five-year credit to pay for them. Further, on July 6 Roosevelt asked Prince Konoye for assurances that rumors of a Japanese attack on the Soviet Union were false, and on the 8th, in hopes of heading off potential Catholic opposition, he joined the British in explaining to the Vatican the Anglo-American position on helping Russia.

By this last date, Roosevelt's hesitation about committing himself to prompt, substantial support for the Soviets had largely disappeared. Under the influence of a better Soviet military performance than either London or Washington had anticipated, predictions by Joseph E. Davies, former Ambassador to the Soviet Union, that the Red Army "would amaze and surprise the world," and indications that Japan would strike south and defer an attack on Russia, Roosevelt moved "to supply urgently to the Soviet Union" the war material requested on June 30. On July 10, in his first interview with a Soviet representative since the outbreak of war in 1939, he told Ambassador Constantine Oumansky that he wanted this help to reach Russia before October 1. "If the Russians could hold the Germans until October 1," he explained, "that would be of great value in defeating Hitler since after that date no effective military operations with Russia could be carried on and the consequent tying up of a number of German troops and machines for that period of time would be of great practical value in assuring the ultimate defeat of Hitler."

Roosevelt's desire to aid Russia promptly did not easily translate into action. A paucity of supplies and shipping, uncertainty about financing, division of administrative responsibility, and an outright reluctance to pile goods on what many saw as a sinking ship limited Soviet supplies in July to $6.5 million. Roosevelt made direct efforts to cut through these barriers. On July 21 he made General James H. Burns, an official in the Lend-Lease office, responsible for Soviet aid, and asked for a report in forty-eight hours on what matériel could go to the Soviet Union at once. When a list of articles totaling $22 million came in on July 23, Roosevelt asked General Edwin ("Pa") Watson, his appointments secretary, to "get the thing through" by the night of the 25th.

Roosevelt now also decided to send Harry Hopkins to Moscow. A social worker, FDR's head of the Federal Emergency Relief Administration, chief of the Works Progress Administration, and Secretary of Commerce, the unconventional, tough-talking Hopkins, who frequented racetracks, disdained religion, and showed little patience with conservatives and moralists, had become Roosevelt's chief aide. In 1940 he had moved into the White House, where, despite declining physical powers due to stomach cancer and the aftermath of an operation to cure it, Hopkins became the President's alter ego. "He had almost an extrasensory perception of Roosevelt's moods," James MacGregor Burns writes, "he knew how to give advice in the form of flattery and flattery in the form of advice; he sensed when to press his boss and when to desist, when to talk and when to listen, when to submit and when to argue. Above all, he had a marked ability to plunge directly into the heart of a muddle or mix-up, and then to act. 'Lord Root of the Matter,' Churchill dubbed him."

On July 26, after Hopkins, who was in Britain seeing Churchill, suggested that he fly to Moscow to show Stalin that "we mean business on a long-term supply job," Roosevelt agreed and sent him a message for Stalin:

> Mr. Hopkins is in Moscow at my request for discussions with you personally and with such other officials as you may designate on the vitally important question of how we can most expeditiously and effectively make available the assistance which the United States can render to your country in its magnificent resistance to the treacherous aggression by Hitlerite Germany. I have already informed your Ambassador, Mr. Oumansky, that all possible aid will be given by the United States Government in obtaining munitions, armaments and other supplies needed to meet your most urgent requirements and which can be made available for actual use in the coming two months in your country. . . .
> I ask you to treat Mr. Hopkins with the identical confidence you would feel if you were talking directly to me. He will communicate directly to me the views that you express to him and will tell me what you consider are the most pressing individual problems on which we could be of aid.

Despite these actions, Roosevelt was nowhere near solving the problem of supplying Russia. Requests for some $1.75 billion in equipment, including all the arms and planes the Soviets had asked for, remained untouched. The intense competition of American and British forces for these scarce materials created considerable antipathy in the War Department to meeting Soviet needs. "Oumansky . . . said that he was absolutely getting the run-around and not getting anywhere," Morgenthau reported to FDR on August 1. At a cabinet meeting later that day, Roosevelt talked for forty-five minutes on the need to get supplies to Russia. Directing "most of his fire at Stimson," he declared himself "sick and tired of hearing that they are going to get this and they are going to get that. . . . He said he didn't want to hear what was on order; he said he wanted to hear what was on the water." In addition to 200 fighters, which had already been committed to the Russians, the President wanted to send them "token" shipments of four-engine bombers and Garand rifles.

As Stimson and Morgenthau explained to the President, however, the tie-up was partly the result of administrative confusion. Stimson complained that he had never seen a list of what the Russians needed, aside from planes, and that Soviet insistence on sending requisitioned fighters from England via Vladivostok instead of Archangel had contributed to the delay. When Morgenthau also pointed out that Hopkins's absence left no one to get things done, Roosevelt announced that he was putting Wayne Coy, one of the best administrators in Washington, in charge of Russian orders. "Please get out the list and please, with my full authority, use a heavy hand—act as a burr under the saddle and get things moving!" FDR directed Coy on the eve of the President's departure for an Atlantic conference. If Germany can be held until October 1, "Russia is safe until spring. Step on it!" [14]

Roosevelt's decision to meet Churchill dated from at least as far back as the end of 1940 when he had expressed a desire to discuss aid to Britain directly with the Prime Minister. When Hopkins went to London in January 1941, Roosevelt instructed him to say that he hoped to meet Churchill "some day to talk over the problem of the defeat of Germany." Churchill was entirely receptive, and they tentatively agreed to meet in March or April at Bermuda or Newfoundland. Though the Lend-Lease debate in Congress and the spring fighting in the Balkans and the Middle East destroyed that plan, Roosevelt continued to think about a conference. Aside from a chance to cement personal ties, he chiefly saw a meeting with Churchill as a way to dramatize and clarify for American and world opinion the vital principles at stake in the war. As Roosevelt told reporters after he returned from the Conference off the Newfoundland coast, the talks met a need for an exchange of "views relating to what is happening to the world under the Nazi regime, as applied to other Nations. The more that is discussed and looked into," he said, "the more terrible the thought becomes of having the world as a whole dominated by the kind of influences which have been at work in the occupied or affiliated Nations. It's a thing that needs to be brought home to all of the democracies, more and more." [15]

By July, Roosevelt had a sense of urgency about making this point. The increasing likelihood of a partnership with the Soviet "dictatorship" in the war against Hitler and rumors of postwar economic and territorial deals between Britain, Russia, and the smaller Allies heightened Roosevelt's desire to enunciate the humanitarian principles Hitler's opponents would follow after the war. In the three weeks after Berlin had attacked Moscow, Roosevelt had tried to preserve the sharp contrast between Nazism and the democracies by picturing the "Russian dictatorship" as less of a menace than Hitler's and by privately urging Churchill to announce "that no postwar peace commitments as to territories, populations or economies have been given." On July 11, the same day he drafted this message to Churchill, he sent Hopkins back to London to arrange a meeting with the Prime Minister which was to exclude any discussion of postwar economic or territorial deals or of American involvement in the war.

This Atlantic Conference began on August 9, 1941, in Placentia Bay off of Argentia, Newfoundland. Roosevelt was delighted to be meeting the extraordinary Churchill, whose careers as a soldier, journalist, and government leader dating from the turn of the century had already made him famous before he became Prime Minister. Now, almost fifteen months after he had become the head of Britain's government, his qualities as an inspirational leader made him a match for FDR as a world-renowned figure. Churchill reciprocated Roosevelt's pleasure at the chance for a meeting. "You'd have thought he was being carried up into the heavens to meet God," Hopkins said of Churchill's state of mind on the way to the Conference. The two leaders held their first meeting aboard the President's ship the *Augusta*, a heavy cruiser, where their military and civilian staffs exchanged introductions. In addition to his military chiefs, Roosevelt's aides included Undersecretary of State Sumner Welles, Harry Hopkins, and W. Averell Harriman, a liberal industrialist, who was serving as a Lend-Lease expediter. Welles's presence and Hull's absence was another demonstration of Roosevelt's preference for his Undersecretary over his Secretary of State.[16]

The only item Roosevelt had proposed for the agenda of the talks was a joint declaration of war aims. It was his principal reason for calling the conference. As he explained to Churchill, he wished the meeting to conclude with a short statement that they "had held conversations at sea; that they had been accompanied by members of their respective staffs; that the latter had discussed the working-out of aid to the democracies under the Lend-Lease Act; and that these naval and military conversations had in no way been concerned with future commitments other than as authorised by Act of Congress. The statement would proceed to say that the Prime Minister and the President had discussed certain principles relating to the civilisation of the world and had agreed on a statement of them." This announcement would guard Roosevelt from inevitable charges that he had made secret commitments and would focus attention on the declaration of war aims, which he hoped would educate Americans to what was at stake in the struggle and would make them more willing to fight. The President attached a great deal of "importance to the Joint Declaration, which he believes will affect the whole movement of United States opinion," Churchill cabled his Cabinet from the Conference. ". . . I fear the President will be very much upset if no Joint Statement can be issued," Churchill added, "and grave and vital issues might be affected."

Roosevelt took considerable pains to assure that the declaration served his purpose. On the first day of the Conference, he expressed his desire for "a joint declaration laying down certain broad principles which should guide our policies along the same road." Though Welles had prepared a statement, Roosevelt preferred to have a first draft from Churchill's pen. The Welles document seemed likely to provoke a fight over colonialism and trade discrimination. By the second morning of the Conference, Churchill had produced a five-point declaration which renounced any intention of Anglo-American aggrandizement, announced opposition to territorial changes without the freely expressed consent of the peoples concerned, endorsed the rights of all peoples to determine their form of government and enjoy freedom of speech and thought, advocated "a fair and equitable distribution of essential produce," and called for an "effective international organization" assuring the security of all states, freedom of the seas, and general disarmament.

After several discussions over the next two days between Roosevelt, Churchill, Welles, and Sir Alexander Cadogan, Permanent Undersecretary for Foreign Affairs, the President won a declaration to his liking. Beginning with a preamble that expressed their desire "to make known certain common principles . . . on which they base their hopes for a better future for the world," the Atlantic Charter, as their handiwork came to be called, enunciated eight propositions: eschewal of any Anglo-American "aggrandizement"; opposition to imposed or undemocratic territorial changes; sovereign rights and self-government for all peoples, including those "forcibly deprived of them"; access on equal terms, but "with due respect for their existing obligations," to the trade and raw materials of the world for "all States, great or small, victor or vanquished"; international economic collaboration to secure "improved labor standards, economic advancement and social security"; a postwar peace assuring safety to all nations and freedom from fear and want for all men; freedom of the seas; and, "pending the establishment of a wider and permanent system of general security," the disarmament of aggressor nations and the reduction "for peace-loving peoples [of] the crushing burden of armaments."

The fourth and eighth statements on international trade and postwar peace-keeping provoked considerable debate. Whereas Churchill wanted an innocuous declaration on trade and raw materials, which would not contradict the Ottawa Agreements granting special trading privileges to British Commonwealth countries, Welles and Roosevelt favored an unqualified endorsement of international economic opportunity, or the elimination of "all those artificial restrictions and controls . . . which had created such tragic havoc to world economy during the past generation." Though Welles objected to any qualifications on the postwar "restoration of free and liberal trade policies," Roosevelt, to assure his larger purpose, acceded to Churchill's request that article four include the phrase, "with due respect for their existing obligations."

On article eight, where, for fear of isolationist "suspicions," Roosevelt eliminated Churchill's mention of an "effective international organization," he also accepted a compromise. Though declaring himself opposed to a new Assembly of the League of Nations for the time being, or at least until an Anglo-American international police force had had a chance to function, he agreed to appease the "extreme internationalists" by promising the ultimate "establishment of a wider and permanent system of general security." Roosevelt, in fact, was happy to accept Churchill's amendment here, since it made clear that "a transition period" would follow the war and that a permanent international body "would only be set up after that experimental period had passed." This, as Roosevelt and Churchill fully agreed, was simple "realism." [17]

Roosevelt made every effort to get the Charter and all it implied before the public. He insisted that everything about the Conference, including the fact that it was taking place, be kept secret until he could couple its announcement on August 14 with the release of the Charter. Moreover, on August 16, at his first press conference after returning from Placentia Bay, he emphasized the "very remarkable religious service on the quarter-deck of the *Prince of Wales* last Sunday morning." He described the intermingling of British and American servicemen, the service conducted by two chaplains, one English and one American, the ship's altar decked with British and American flags, and the singing of three hymns "that everybody took part in. . . . It was one of the great historic services." It was not only an experience that, as Churchill wrote, "none who took part in it will forget," it was also "a deeply moving expression of the unity of faith of our two peoples" which, as with the Charter, contrasted Anglo-American values with those of Hitler.

Roosevelt came back to this theme in another news conference three days later. Drawing a parallel with Lincoln's experience during the Civil War when the "country hadn't yet waked up to the fact that they had a war to win," Roosevelt declared that "a lot of people" had not waked up to the current danger. "A great many people," he emphasized. He then advanced the point by quoting from a letter Supreme Court Justice Felix Frankfurter had just sent him: "We live by symbols and we can't too often recall them," Frankfurter declared. "And you two in that ocean . . . in the setting of that Sunday service, gave meaning to the conflict between civilization and arrogant, brute challenge; and gave promise more powerful and binding than any formal treaty could, that civilization has brains and resources that tyranny will not be able to overcome. . . . The deed and the spirit and the invigoration breathed there in the hearts of men will endure and will kindle actions toward the goal of ridding the world of this horror."

The public response to the Conference and the Charter disappointed Roosevelt. Instead of sparking an upsurge of public willingness to take up arms, the Conference, as historian Theodore A. Wilson has shown, principally served to harden already familiar battle lines: interventionists voiced enthusiastic approval, while isolationists warned of secret commitments to war and complained that the Charter included nothing about freedom of religion or speech. Roosevelt effectively blunted these criticisms in statements to the Congress and the press, and the Conference received general approval in the United States. As an inducement to belligerency, though, the meeting was "a propaganda bust." An opinion survey conducted immediately after the Conference showed that 74 per cent of the country still opposed involvement in the war, only a one per cent drop from a pre-Conference poll. Subsequent surveys confirmed this finding. "The meeting and the announcement," one commentator observed at the time, "have not caught the public imagination." [18]

There seems little question that Roosevelt now wished to take the United States into the war. After British reverses in the spring of 1941, he had apparently concluded that Nazi defeat required the use of American air and naval power. This was certainly the case by the time of the Atlantic Conference. Churchill gained the impression there that Roosevelt "was obviously determined that they should come in." Though FDR ruled out any talk of American involvement in the war, Churchill could not resist the topic. He raised it on the first evening of the Conference in a review of the war situation before the President and his advisers, and in a subsequent meeting he told Roosevelt's "circle that I would rather have an American declaration of war now and no supplies for six months than double the supplies and no declaration." According to Churchill's account to his War Cabinet, the President responded to his appeals by explaining that "he was skating on pretty thin ice in his relations with Congress, which, however, he did not regard as truly representative of the country." A request to the Congress for a declaration of war, he complained, would produce a three-month debate. Instead, he "said that he would wage war, but not declare it, and that he would become more and more provocative. . . . Everything was to be done to force an 'incident.' . . . The President . . . made it clear that he would look for an 'incident' which would justify him in opening hostilities." [19]

Roosevelt gave meaning to these statements at the Atlantic Conference by promising to occupy the Azores and escort British convoys in the Atlantic. Fearful that Hitler would follow a Russian collapse with steps against Spain and Portugal, the British pressed for preventive occupation of the Canary Islands and the Azores. Since London lacked sufficient strength to mount both operations, Churchill asked that the United States defend the Azores and approve a British move into the Canaries scheduled for September 15. Roosevelt agreed and promised to send occupation forces into the Azores as soon as London arranged for Portugal's President Antonio de Oliveira Salazar, to invite them. In September, however, continued Russian resistance and a shortage of British and American forces persuaded Churchill and FDR to postpone these operations indefinitely.[20]

Roosevelt's commitment to escorting, however, went forward as planned. In a discussion with his military advisers at Argentia before Churchill arrived, the President had stated his intention to protect convoys in most of the Atlantic, drawing a line on a map running from east of the Azores to east of Iceland. Reversing decisions of late July, he now committed himself to escort British shipping between Iceland and America and to tell the country about this policy in September. "The American Navy would have their convoy system in full operation between their country and Iceland by September 1st," Churchill advised his Cabinet. ". . . The President's orders to these escorts were to attack any U-boat which showed itself, even if it were 200 or 300 miles away from the convoy. . . . Everything was to be done to force an 'incident.' This would put the enemy in the dilemma that either he could attack the convoys, in which case his U-boats would be attacked by American Naval forces, or, if he refrained from attack, this would be tantamount to giving us victory in the Battle of the Atlantic." Churchill wished to "provoke Hitler by taunting him with this difficult choice" in six or eight weeks' time. By committing himself to this action, Roosevelt apparently wished to release British destroyers for escort duty on other routes, particularly the treacherous run to Murmansk and Archangel, to bolster British morale by giving the Atlantic Conference some concrete meaning, and to open the way to an "incident" that might trigger fighting with Berlin.[21]

When Roosevelt returned from Argentia, he struggled with the question of when and how to reveal his naval policy to the public. Though he had told the Congress in July that "all necessary steps" were being taken "to insure the safety of communications in the approaches between Iceland and the United States," and though he had subsequently told the press that his orders were "to keep the communications open against attack, or the threat of attack," he resisted making any "frank statement" on escorting of American and Icelandic ships. Since his naval policy, especially after the commitment to protect British ships, was partly aimed at provoking an "incident" that could lead to war, Roosevelt wanted it to have public support. But during July and August he saw the country as still unreceptive to such an announcement. And in a matter of this kind he believed timing of the utmost importance. "From what extremes do the pendulums swing for us as individuals," he wrote one recent convert to stronger action. "Governments, such as ours, cannot swing so far or so quickly. They can only move in keeping with the thought and will of the great majority of our people." [22]

Though he still did not see a clear consensus for his naval actions by September 1, the imminent extension of protection to British shipping and pressure from Churchill edged him toward an announcement. On August 29, Hopkins had received "one of the gloomiest messages" the

Prime Minister ever sent to the White House. Describing his Cabinet as deflated by Roosevelt's public assurances that the Atlantic Conference had brought the United States "no closer to war," Churchill declared himself unable to say what would happen if England found itself fighting alone when 1942 came. He also pointed out that Hitler's current naval policy gave little prospect of an "incident" and asked Hopkins if he could express any hope for the future. "I told the President," Hopkins recorded in a memo, that the British "believed that ultimately we will get into the war on some basis or other and if they ever reach the conclusion that this was not to be the case, that would be a very critical moment in the war and the British appeasers might have some influence on Churchill."

In a radio address on Labor Day, 1941, Roosevelt responded with an announcement that "unless we step up the total of our production and more greatly safeguard it on its journeys to the battlefields," America's enemies would find encouragement to push their attack against democracy. "I know," he added, "that I speak the conscience and determination of the American people when I say that we shall do everything in our power to crush Hitler and his Nazi forces." Though he also attacked the "very dangerous assumption" that Hitler's slower progress than in the year before meant that he had been "blocked and halted," he remained silent about changed naval policy.[23]

Roosevelt found the basis for an announcement of his policy in an exchange of fire between a German submarine and the American destroyer *Greer* in the North Atlantic. On September 4, after a British plane informed the *Greer* of the presence of a U-boat ten miles ahead, the destroyer and the plane stalked the submarine. Before returning to its base, the plane unsuccessfully attacked the U-boat with four depth charges. Some two hours later, with the *Greer* still in pursuit, the submarine fired a torpedo. The *Greer* answered with eight depth charges, and the submarine fired one or two more torpedoes. When the *Greer* relocated the U-boat two and a half hours later, it dropped eleven more depth charges without effect, and an hour later ended its chase. There was "no positive evidence that [the] submarine knew [the] nationality of [the] ship at which it was firing," the Navy reported to FDR on September 9.

Two days later Roosevelt used the *Greer* incident to announce his policy of escorting and "shoot on sight" in the Atlantic. Telling a national radio audience that a German submarine "fired first upon this American destroyer without warning, and with deliberate design to sink her" in American defensive waters, he described her identity as an American ship as "unmistakable" and denounced the attack as "piracy— piracy legally and morally." Recalling other attacks that Nazi raiders had made on United States and Latin American ships, he called them "acts of international lawlessness" which manifested a "Nazi design to abolish the freedom of the seas."

> To be ultimately successful in world mastery, Hitler knows that he must get control of the seas. He must first destroy the bridge of ships which we are building across the Atlantic and over which we shall continue to roll the implements of war to help destroy him. . . .
>
> It is time for all Americans, Americans of all the Americas, to stop being deluded by the romantic notion that the Americas can go on living happily and peacefully in a Nazi-dominated world. . . .
>
> This attack on the *Greer* was no localized military operation in the North Atlantic. This was no mere episode in a struggle between two Nations. This was one determined step toward creating a permanent world system based on force, on terror, and on murder.

Turning to the policy he would now apply, Roosevelt declared:

> We have sought no shooting war with Hitler. We do not seek it now. . . . But when you see a rattlesnake poised to strike, you do not wait until he has struck before you crush him.
>
> These Nazi submarines and raiders are the rattlesnakes of the Atlantic. . . .
>
> In the waters which we deem necessary for our defense, American naval vessels and American planes will no longer wait until Axis submarines lurking under the water, or Axis raiders on the surface of the sea, strike their deadly blow—first.
>
> Upon our naval and air patrol . . . falls the duty of maintaining the American policy of freedom of the seas—now. That means, very simply, very clearly, that our patrolling vessels and planes will protect all merchant ships—not only American ships but ships of any flag—engaged in commerce in our defensive waters. . . .
>
> . . . Let this warning be clear. From now on, if German or Italian vessels of war enter the waters, the protection of which is necessary for American defense, they do so at their own peril.

Roosevelt concluded with the frank acknowledgement that he had "no illusions about the gravity of this step. I have not taken it hurriedly or lightly," he said. "It is the result of months and months of constant thought and anxiety and prayer. In the protection of your Nation and mine it cannot be avoided." [24]

Roosevelt's announcement of an undeclared war in the Atlantic won solid majority support. Sixty-two per cent of a national poll approved of the "shoot on sight" policy, and though a congressional inquiry led by Senate isolationists shortly revealed the distortions in the President's account of the *Greer* episode, neither a congressional nor a national majority demanded a change in policy. As the writer Joseph Lash recently concluded, this was because a majority in the country and the Congress shared the President's belief that "a Hitler victory would constitute mortal danger for American interests and the American way of life and that the United States had a vital stake in supporting the nations fighting Hitler. The majority also shared the Administration's conviction that Hitler must be defeated."

Yet the public and the Congress also clung to hopes of staying out of war and did not wish to take responsibility for anything that forced the issue. Indeed, much of the country and its representatives continued to hope that aid to Hitler's opponents short of war would ultimately bring Nazi defeat. As Lord Halifax reported Roosevelt's description of public opinion: "his [Roosevelt's] perpetual problem was to steer a course between . . . (1) the wish of 70% of Americans to keep out of war; (2) the wish of 70% of Americans to do everything to break Hitler, even if it means war. He said that if he asked for a declaration of war he wouldn't get it, and opinion would swing against him. He therefore intended to go on doing whatever he best could to help us, and declarations of war were out of fashion." In light of the national unwillingness to face up fully to the international dangers confronting the country, it is difficult to fault Roosevelt for building a consensus by devious means. Had he directly presented his view to the public of what it must do in response to the world crisis, it would have won him few converts and undermined his popularity and ability to lead by confronting ambivalent Americans with a choice they did not care to make. Further, if he had advised the public of the fact that the U-boat had fired in defense and that Hitler did not then seem intent on attacking America's Atlantic traffic, as Churchill had reported, he would have risked having to wait for the collapse of Russia and Britain's near demise before gaining broad national support for a resort to arms. As he suggested in his radio speech, that would have been a failure of his responsibility as Commander in Chief.[25]

Yet for all the need to mislead the country in its own interest, the President's deviousness also injured the national well-being over the long run. His action in the *Greer* incident created a precedent for manipulation of public opinion which would be repeated by later Presidents in less justifiable circumstances. "The fact that Roosevelt and Truman were substantially right in their assessment of the national interest," Senator William Fulbright asserted in 1971, "in no way diminishes the blamefulness of the precedents they set. FDR's deviousness in a good cause made it easier for LBJ to practice the same kind of deviousness in a bad cause."

Roosevelt's use of the FBI also formed an important precedent for arbitrary action by subsequent Presidents. In his determination to combat the Nazi threat, Roosevelt sanctioned FBI actions and the establishment of an agency for "special operations" which undermined the democratic institutions he wished so much to preserve. He not only allowed FBI investigations of political opponents and unlawful wiretappings and mail-openings, he also used the Bureau to gather information on "the attitude of Congressional groups toward the President's international relations or foreign policy." To be sure, in September 1941, when J. Edgar Hoover performed this task, some members of Congress were helping circulate anti-British propaganda, and, in general, congressional support for the President's foreign policy was less than the administration wished; but this hardly warranted FBI scrutiny of congressional attitudes toward foreign affairs.

Further, in July 1941 the President had appointed William J. Donovan Coordinator of Information (COI) to collect information and plan "covert offensive operations." Though FDR's announcement of Donovan's appointment indicated that his assignment was to collect and coordinate data for the President bearing on national security, he said nothing about Donovan's responsibility for "special operations" in cooperation with the British, especially the British Security Coordination, an intelligence group operating in the United States with FDR's specific sanction. "Special operations" was a euphemism for waging undeclared war against the Nazis abroad. As with naval policy in the Atlantic, it was in the country's best interest, but it created another precedent for secretly involving the nation in later, more questionable, wars.[26]

Once Roosevelt committed the country to an undeclared war in the Atlantic, the elimination of Neutrality Act restrictions on arming merchant ships and sending them into combat zones became logical next steps. Roosevelt had considered asking for Neutrality revision in July, but with Selective Service extension under discussion and Senators George and Connally warning that revision could be had only at the cost of a prolonged debate and an isolationist filibuster, Roosevelt temporarily dropped the idea.

Events in September, however, forced him to confront the question again. Unarmed and unescorted cargo ships traveling to Iceland, Berle reported to FDR on the 15th, had "not much better than an even chance" of survival. Two requisitioned Danish ships making the journey had been sunk with the loss of most of their Danish crews. At the same time, Churchill asked for the use of twelve United States liners and twenty cargo ships manned by American crews for four months beginning in October. He needed them to transport additional British troops to the Middle East, where they would help "hold Turkey and sustain Russia, and by so doing bar further advance eastward by Hitler." Roosevelt at once replied "that we can provide transports for 20,000 men. These ships will be United States Navy transports manned by Navy crews. Our Neutrality Act permits public ships of the Navy to go to any port."

"After long conferences with congressional leaders," however, Roosevelt decided to suspend this offer and directly ask the Congress for Neutrality reform. "I have determined to send a message to Congress in the immediate future recommending sweeping amendments to our Neutrality Act," he informed Churchill on October 7. "I am convinced that the Act is seriously crippling our means of helping you. I want not only to arm all of our ships but I want to get the authority from Congress to send American flagships directly into British ports. . . . I have reached the conclusion that it would be disastrous to this legislation if one of our transports proceeding to or from Britain, and in British waters . . . were to be sunk, when manned by U.S. Navy officers and men. Such an event might jeopardize our lend-lease and other aid." Two days later, the President asked the Congress, as "a matter of immediate necessity and extreme urgency," to provide for the safety of American crews and "the almost priceless goods" aboard their ships by rescinding the prohibition against arming them.[27]

Though a great majority of the press endorsed full repeal of the law and though the public seemed increasingly receptive to having American ships with American crews carry war materials to Britain, the President directly asked the Congress only for power to arm merchant ships. He also proposed that the Congress "give earnest and early attention" to allowing Americans to enter combat zones and deliver Lend-Lease goods to friendly ports, but he refrained from recommending this outright. His strategy was first to put arming of merchant ships through the House with a strong vote and then to broaden the measure in the Senate to include repeal of restrictions on entering combat zones. A Gallup poll showing 72 per cent of the public in favor of arming merchant ships, and the loss of eleven American seamen in a German submarine attack on the destroyer *Kearny* on October 16, brought added pressure and helped carry Neutrality revision through the House by an almost two-to-one vote on the following day.

In line with the agreed strategy, Senate leaders then put through the more comprehensive changes. But this was only after the President had publicly announced that he had come into possession of secret Nazi documents revealing plans to divide all of South and part of Central America into five vassal states and to abolish all existing religions, and after a German submarine had killed 115 American sailors in a torpedo attack on the destroyer *Reuben James*. Though Roosevelt made no effort to demonstrate the validity of the Nazi documents, his speech, which was the most "histrionic" he ever gave, added to American fears about Nazi plans. Yet despite all this and the fact that pollsters now reported 61 per cent of the public in favor of sending Lend-Lease goods to Britain in American ships, Neutrality revision passed the Senate by a vote of only 50 to 37, the smallest Senate majority on a major foreign policy question since the beginning of the war. Senator Hiram Johnson exalted in the "nearness" of isolationist success, "particularly," he wrote his son, "when you recall that the Administration, and every department of government, the bundles to Britain crew and all the Anglophiles, were pulling and hauling, and doing everything they could."

The result in the House was no more encouraging for advocates of

American involvement in the war. Opponents denounced revision as a British device for getting America to do her fighting. In a joke that made the rounds in Washington, a German, a Greek, and an Englishman were in a faltering aircraft. When the pilot announced that the wings were icing badly and that he was losing altitude, the German got up, threw out his hand in salute, said "Heil Hitler," and jumped out. A little later, the pilot again turned and said, "I am still unable to maintain altitude. The load is too heavy." The Britisher got up and said, "There'll always be an England," and threw the Greek out!

Opponents also complained that the country was being driven into an unprepared for war. "We are determined our sons shall not leave this country," the United Mothers of America wired the President, "and there will not be enough concentration camps . . . to hold the mothers and fathers." Only after Roosevelt predicted that failure to take favorable action on the Senate amendments would bring "rejoicing to the Axis Nations" and weaken America in the struggle against aggression did the House pass revision on November 13, 1941, by a scant 18 votes, 212 to 194.[28]

The close votes on neutrality revision reinforced Roosevelt's conviction that winning a declaration of war from the Congress would require a substantial provocation from abroad. However strong his impulse to create incidents with the Germans in the Atlantic, as he had over the *Greer*, or to take advantage of episodes like the *Kearny* and the *Reuben James*, he had now concluded that it would take some more dramatic event than any single clash in the Atlantic to draw the United States into the war.

At the same time that Roosevelt struggled to expand America's role in the Atlantic war, he intensified his efforts to aid Russia. At the Atlantic Conference he had received detailed reports from Hopkins on his trip to Moscow. Returning from Russia in time to accompany Churchill to Argentia, Hopkins provided the President and the Prime Minister with strong confirmation of their decision to send aid. In extended interviews of "unparalleled" frankness, Stalin had impressed Hopkins with his determination to fight a long war. "Give us anti-aircraft guns and the aluminum and we can fight for three or four years," he declared. He asserted that Hitler had underestimated the strength of the Soviet Army and the difficulties of crossing the Russian terrain: "Germany has already found that 'moving mechanized forces through Russia was very different than moving them over the boulevards of Belgium and France.'" Predicting that heavy rains would throw the Germans on the defensive by October 1, Stalin "expressed great confidence that the line during the winter months would be in front of Moscow, Kiev and Leningrad—probably not more than 100 kilometres away from where it is now."

Stalin also provided Hopkins with previously undisclosed information about the quality and quantity of Soviet military equipment and asked for large supplies of light anti-aircraft guns, aluminum for planes, 50-calibre machine guns, and 30-calibre rifles. Hopkins, who wished to be sure of continued Soviet resistance before making large, long-term commitments, proposed an Anglo-American-Soviet conference for October, when "we would know whether or not there was to be a front and approximately the location of the front during the coming winter months." He told Stalin that the United States and Britain would be unwilling to send heavy munitions to Russia until the three governments had explored the relative strategic interests of each front and the Soviet Union had provided full information about its existing and future capacity to produce supplies. Stalin endorsed the idea of a conference, promised to make all required information available, and concluded by urging American participation in the war. He would "welcome . . . American troops on any part of the Russian front under the complete command of the American Army." Such a request for aid in August 1941 probably offered a truer measure of Stalin's estimate of Soviet capacity to resist Hitler than his confident predictions of a long war.[29]

Roosevelt, Churchill, and Hopkins, however, chose to take Stalin's expressions of confidence at face value. It was Roosevelt's hope that if he could keep the vast Russian armies fighting, he might not have to land American troops on the Continent, as in World War I, and the United States could limit its contribution to matériel and sea and air forces. At Argentia, therefore, he had agreed to follow through on Hopkins's proposal for a conference, and consequently Russia was invited to become, in Churchill's words, "a welcome guest at [a] hungry table." On August 15 Roosevelt and Churchill sent a cable to Stalin suggesting a meeting in Moscow between him and their "high representatives" to decide on "the future allocation of our joint resources." On the 30th Roosevelt formally told Stimson that aid to Russia was of "paramount importance for the safety and security of America," and instructed him to draw up recommendations at once on how to distribute American munitions among the United States, Britain, and Russia during the next nine months. Much to Stimson's and Marshall's distress, he also began discussing reductions in American land forces as a way to free equipment for Russian use. Oumansky, the Russian Ambassador, "will take everything we own if we submit to his criticisms," Marshall complained. He is "nothing but a crook" and "a slick, clever little beast," Stimson said.

Stimson and Marshall nevertheless appreciated the enormous value of continued Russian resistance and did all they could to help Moscow. In a joint estimate of overall production needs dated September 11, Marshall and Stark acknowledged that "the best opportunity for a successful land offensive against Germany" rested on "*the maintenance of an active front in Russia.*" Only she possessed "adequate manpower, situated in favorable proximity to the center of German military power. . . . The effective arming of Russian forces [therefore] . . . would be one of the most important moves that could be made by the associated Powers." On the following day, Stimson recommended a 50 per cent reduction in equipment for American forces in training during the next nine months and a reallocation of Lend-Lease matériel for Britain to allow large deliveries of guns, tanks, and planes to the Soviet Union during that period until June 30, 1942.[30]

Recent Russian military reverses gave a sense of urgency to these recommendations. In late August and September, German forces had overwhelmed Soviet defenders in the Ukraine and threatened Leningrad in the north. In a message to Churchill on September 3, Stalin had complained that the arrival of between thirty and thirty-four fresh German infantry divisions with huge numbers of tanks and planes had upset the relatively stable Ukrainian and Leningrad fronts. The only way out of that "more than unfavorable situation," Stalin asserted, was for Britain to open a second front in the Balkans or France, which would divert thirty to forty German divisions from the Eastern front, and "simultaneously to supply the Soviet Union with 30,000 tons of aluminum by the beginning of October and a minimum monthly delivery of 400 airplanes and 500 tanks (of small or medium size). Without these two kinds of aid," he warned, "the Soviet Union will be either defeated or weakened to the extent that it will lose for a long time the ability to help its Allies by active operations at the front against Hitlerism."

Churchill at once replied that there was no possibility of British action in the west, other than air attacks, which could draw German forces from the east before the beginning of winter. But he promised that Britain would fill one half of Russia's monthly need for aircraft and tanks and expressed the hope that the United States would provide the other half. "We could not exclude the impression that they [the Russians] might be thinking of separate terms," Churchill cabled FDR. ". . . Hope you will not object to our references to possible American aid." [31]

Roosevelt did not object in the least. Through Hopkins, he informed Churchill of his directive to Stimson for a plan of supply allocations, suggested that British and American officials hold preliminary talks in London starting on September 15, and proposed that the Moscow Conference begin by September 25 rather than October 1. Hopkins added that the President was "convinced that substantial and comprehensive commitments should be made to Russia" at the Conference.

The problem was where to find the resources. American and British service chiefs were understandably reluctant to relinquish supplies essential for actual and potential combat. "We endured the unpleasant process of exposing our own vital security and projects to failure for the sake of our new ally," Churchill later wrote. ". . . The Service departments felt it was like flaying off pieces of their skin." The British, led by Lord Beaverbrook, their Minister of Supply, tried to control the division of American matériel between themselves and the Russians. "Your function," Churchill advised Beaverbrook, "will be not only to aid in the forming of the plans to aid Russia, but to make sure we are not bled white in the process." At the pre-Conference meeting in London, Beaverbrook pressed to have all aid channeled through his hands. But Averell Harriman, FDR's chief representative, would have none of it. He objected that that "would relieve the Americans of the necessity of going to Moscow. 'Oh, no, no, no,' the horrified Beaverbrook replied. 'We must go together.' "

Roosevelt and Hopkins made the strongest possible effort to meet British and Russian needs. When Harriman reported that American plans to supply 611 medium tanks to Britain and 795 to Russia "stunned" the British, Roosevelt directed the War Department to double production. Advised at a White House conference on September 17 that tank output would reach 1400 by May 1942, "the President paused, placed a cigarette in his famous long holder, lit it, and then calmly issued this short directive: "Double it!' " "I am going to develop a program which I hope will . . . get our full tank capacity up to a minimum of 2500 a month and a maximum of 3000 a month," he cabled Churchill. While this "cheering" news "encouraged everyone" in London, there was no "disguising" the fact that these "necessary and worthwhile offers" to Russia made "grievous inroads" into what America needed to expand its forces and Britain required to intensify its war effort. The "all-important thing now," Hopkins informed Churchill, was for the United States to expand "very substantially" its total output of all weapons, or fulfill what Washington planners now described as their Victory Program, the overall production of American goods needed to defeat the Axis.[32]

Harriman gave expression to this plan in Moscow. The objective, he told one of his fellow delegates, was to "give and give and give, with no expectation of any return, with no thought of a *quid pro quo*." During four days of discussion in the Kremlin at the end of September 1941, Harriman and Beaverbrook worked out a one-billion-dollar schedule of aid to the Soviet Union which left Stalin openly enthusiastic and "completely satisfied that Great Britain and America meant business." At a final negotiating session, when Beaverbrook asked whether the proffered help pleased Stalin, he "smiled and nodded. At this point, Litvinov [former Commissar for Foreign Affairs and translator in these talks] . . . bounding from his chair, cried, 'Now we shall win the war!' " The demonstration of Anglo-American determination to destroy Hitler gave the Russian war effort a badly needed boost.

If Stalin was so pleased with the promised aid, why, as Ambassador Bullitt had urged FDR at the time, was there no attempt to compel Soviet renunciation of territorial gains made since 1939? Chiefly because Roosevelt saw a substantial quid pro quo in some 280 Russian divisions fighting a like number of German troops, he was unwilling to raise questions that might weaken the Soviet resolve to fight. He and Churchill feared that suspicions about Anglo-American aims might drive Stalin into another deal with Hitler. Roosevelt also believed that a Soviet commitment to self-determination would be no more than a paper promise which Stalin could break at any time.

Also, because they were uncertain of their ability to deliver promised supplies, Roosevelt and his aides hesitated to make demands of any kind. "At times I get terribly discouraged about getting the matériel fast enough," Hopkins told Churchill on September 29. ". . . There is still an amazing number of people here who do not want to help Russia and who don't seem to be able to pound into their thick heads the strategic importance of that front." "It is of the utmost importance that prompt action confirm the confidence the Russians now have in the sincerity of our aid," Harriman wrote a few days later. "I am also delighted with the outcome of the Moscow Conference," Roosevelt cabled Churchill on October 8. "The important thing now is to get the goods to them." In short, at a time when neither American nor British troops were engaged in mass battles, it seemed farfetched to use uncertain commitments of matériel support as reasons to ask for more than continued Soviet resistance.[33]

In the fall of 1941, Soviet inability to pay for supplies threatened to defeat the administration's goal. Though existing dollar balances and credits on future deliveries of gold and raw materials financed initial Soviet purchases, it was clear by September that a continued flow of war matériel to Russia must be done under Lend-Lease. The difficulty, as FDR had explained to Ambassador Oumansky on September 11, was "the unpopularity of Russia among large groups in this country who exercise great political power in Congress." In particular, the President had reference to an opinion poll of August 5 which showed only 38 per cent of the country in favor of Lend-Lease for Russia, and to a conference of August 18 in which congressional leaders told him that a further request for almost $6 billion in Lend-Lease funds would run into problems if it included Russia as a recipient. More especially, the President had in mind strong Catholic opposition expressed in a papal encyclical of Pius XI forbidding collaboration with Communism in any form.

In September the President had made a concerted effort to disarm Catholic opposition. He asked Pope Pius XII to declare that help to Russia was distinct from support of Communism. He believed it ultimately possible, he told the Pope, to persuade the Russian government to accept freedom of religion, but not the Nazis, whom he described as a far greater threat to religion and humanity. All American church leaders should recognize these facts clearly, FDR urged, and not "by their present attitude . . . directly assist Germany in her . . . objectives." At the same time, Roosevelt told Oumansky that "if Moscow could get some information back to this country regarding the freedom of religion . . . it might have a very fine educational effect before the next lend-lease bill comes up in Congress." Roosevelt also asked Harriman to press Stalin for official assurances that constitutional guarantees of religious freedom in the Soviet Union meant what they said.[34]

While waiting for the Pope and Stalin to respond, Roosevelt tried to convert American Catholics to aid for Russia by other means. He encouraged leading Catholics in his administration to speak out on the issue, and he told a press conference on September 30 that Article 124 of the Russian Constitution guaranteed freedom of conscience: "Freedom equally to use propaganda against religion," he said, "which is essentially what is the rule in this country, only we don't put it quite the same way." Religious leaders of all faiths immediately took strong exception to the President's comments, declaring it utterly misleading to suggest that Soviet and American citizens shared similar religious freedoms. The President should invite Stalin to the White House, Congressman Hamilton Fish proposed, "so that he might be baptized in the swimming pool" before all the members of Congress. Afterward, all those present could "join the Stalin Sunday School." In response, Roosevelt explained that he did not see religious freedom operating in the Soviet Union, but he was making efforts to bring it about. Under pressure form Harriman, the Soviets released a statement on October 4 contending that the President correctly interpreted the existence of religious freedom under their Constitution. But this only intensified antagonism to the President's remarks by confirming the belief that Moscow would give no more than lip service to freedom of worship.

Despite this, the President continued his crusade to convince religious opponents of aid to the Soviet regime that the aid was justified. In October he helped publicize a petition of one thousand leading Protestants who supported help to Russia. He also made a vigorous effort to depict the Nazis as more dangerous opponents of organized religion than the Soviets were. In a speech on October 27, he described Germany as intent on replacing the "churches of our civilization" with an international Nazi church, the Bible with the words of *Mein Kampf*, and the "cross of Christ" with "the swastika and the naked sword."[35]

Many supporters of Russian aid thought the President's actions unnecessary. They believed the country would support aid to Moscow without false claims of Russian sympathy for free worship. "Most editorial commentators," a survey of newspaper opinion showed him, were "quite ready on the simple basis of expediency to give aid to the Red Army." They saw any further justification of the policy as "needless and even injurious. . . . 'Let's not pretend that there is anything sweet-smelling about the commies,'" a Scripps-Howard editorial declared, "'Give them guns, tanks, planes—but keep on saying: Don't call me brother.'" In a more rational and eloquent expression of this attitude, diplomat George Kennan wrote at the time: "To welcome Russia as an associate in the defense of democracy would invite misunderstanding of our own position and would lend to the German war effort a gratuitous and sorely needed aura of morality." Such a course, Kennan believed, would identify the United States and Britain with Soviet violations of territorial integrity, the destruction of religion throughout Eastern Europe, and Russia's undemocratic treatment of its own people. All of which, Kennan concluded, "would not preclude the extension of material aid wherever called for by our own self-interest. It would, however, preclude anything which might identify us politically or ideologically with the Russian war effort."

Roosevelt knew full well that there was no freedom of religion in the Soviet Union. Nor was he blind to the fact that he could extend Lend-Lease help to Russia without demonstrating her devotion to religious freedom. But his concern to associate the Soviets with this democratic principle extended beyond the question of aid to the problem of American involvement in the war. Convinced that only a stark contrast between freedom and totalitarianism would provide the emotional wherewithal for Americans to fight, Roosevelt wished to identify the Russians, regardless of Soviet realities, with Anglo-American ideals as fully as he could. The effort to depict the Soviet Union as reformed, or reforming, on the issue of religious freedom was chiefly an expression of this concern.[36]

As matters developed in the fall of 1941, Roosevelt was able to bring the Russians under Lend-Lease without a significant political fight. On September 18, when the President's request for almost $6 billion in additional Lend-Lease funds went to the Congress, the administration had taken pains to emphasize that gold and raw material sales to the United States would finance Russian aid for the time being. Further, to avoid an acrimonious debate in Congress on the appropriation bill, Roosevelt disingenuously assured congressional leaders that he had no immediate intention of bringing Russia under Lend-Lease. He emphasized, however, that Russian exclusion from Lend-Lease help would impair her morale, and would inhibit him from action he might ultimately need to take in the national interest. Congressional hopes that continued Russian resistance might preclude an American need to fight prompted Congress to leave the President free to give Russia Lend-Lease help when he saw fit.

This was at once. By late September, Russian finances were "in a hell of a mess. . . . We made this large size commitment," Hopkins told Morgenthau on the 23rd, "and now, by god, we can't deliver on it. . . . It's just god damned discouraging." In a Cabinet meeting a few days later, Hopkins complained that Russia could have bought $50 million worth of goods that afternoon if she had had the funds. Although

Roosevelt arranged these purchases with additional credits against future gold deliveries, he refused to make long-term commitments until the Lend-Lease appropriation had cleared "the Hill." When this happened on October 24, he promptly earmarked part of the money for Russia. In response to a report from Harriman that Moscow would find it impossible to pay for additional supplies, the President notified Stalin on October 30 that a Lend-Lease credit needing no repayment until five years after the war would provide up to a billion dollars in matériel.

This still did not assure the arrival of promised American supplies. A shortage of merchant shipping now played havoc with efforts to meet scheduled deliveries. Forty-one ships were to carry goods to Russia in October and November, but with only twelve available by November 21, some seventeen shiploads of cargo lay inadequately cared for in American ports. Whereas ninety-eight ships were needed to meet Russian supply shipments in December, "insurmountable physical limitations" held the available number to forty-nine. By December 6, however, herculean efforts by Roosevelt and his aides made the fulfillment of aid schedules possible by the end of the month. But Pearl Harbor at once disrupted all these plans, and Russia received only about a quarter of the aid the United States had pledged to send by the end of the year.[37]

The Pearl Harbor attack on December 7, 1941, ended the long struggle to check Japan without going to war. In August at Argentia, after the British had also answered Japan's move into southern Indochina with sanctions, Churchill had pressed Roosevelt to confront Tokyo with an ultimatum. Under pressure from the Dutch and the Australians to win a commitment from the President to follow a Japanese attack on the Netherlands East Indies or Malaya with a request to Congress for a declaration of war, Churchill proposed parallel warnings to Tokyo by America, Britain, and Holland. These were to say that any further encroachment in the Southwest Pacific would compel countermeasures that might lead to war. The American note was also to indicate that Japanese aggression against British or Dutch possessions would move the President to ask Congress for authority to aid them. Churchill asserted that only some such declaration could restrain Japan and that without it there would almost certainly be a war which would destroy all of Britain's merchant shipping in the Indian Ocean and the Pacific and cut the lifelines between the Dominions and the British Isles. "The blow to the British Government," Churchill declared, "might be almost decisive."

Since Churchill wished to assure that America would not leave Britain to fight Japan alone, he also saw such a warning as a way to bring the United States into the war. As he shortly indicated to one American representative in London, his preference was for the United States to enter the conflict in the Atlantic without Japanese involvement. But as a second choice, he favored American and Japanese belligerency over noninvolvement by both. The "unthinkable" possibility was Japanese involvement without America. An ultimatum to Japan such as he proposed to Roosevelt at Argentia, therefore, would rule out the last possibility and enhance the likelihood that the United States would join the fighting.

Roosevelt would not make the commitments Churchill asked. He refused to give "an assurance that [he] would go to Congress for authority to give armed support" if Japan attacked British or Dutch possessions, and only after considerable pressure from Churchill did he agree to send Tokyo a warning. Though he promised to maintain the economic measures against Japan "in full force . . . he seemed to think that this was the most that he could do. He did not offer to give any further warning to Japan," Churchill reported to his War Cabinet. But after further discussion, "he finally agreed" to warn the Japanese Ambassador that in response to further military expansion "various steps would have to be taken by the United States notwithstanding the President's realization that the taking of such further measures might result in war between the United States and Japan." Since the British were subsequently to associate themselves with the President's statement, Churchill took FDR's agreement to issue this "severe warning" as "a very great advance towards the gripping of Japanese aggression by united forces."

While Roosevelt shared Churchill's concern that Britain not fight Japan alone, he saw the warning to Tokyo as chiefly another means to deter Japan from going to war. The President's "chief objective in the Pacific for the time being," Welles had told Cadogan on the first day of the Atlantic Conference, was "the avoidance of war with Japan." Two days later Roosevelt himself told Churchill "that he felt very strongly that every effort should be made to prevent the outbreak of war with Japan." His idea, as he also told Churchill, was to seize on possibilities, slim as they were, for continued negotiations which could give them at least thirty more days to strengthen Pacific defenses.[38]

When he returned to Washington in mid-August, therefore, and learned that Nomura had urgently requested a resumption of informal conversations, Roosevelt "readily agreed" to Hull's suggestion that he tone down the "hard language" Churchill expected him to use and to indicate American willingness to resume exploratory talks on certain conditions. Instead of a warning that further Japanese aggression would evoke steps by the United States which "may result in conflict between the two countries," the President instead declared that he would respond to additional Japanese action with any and all measures "necessary . . . toward insuring the safety and security of the United States." Though FDR's warning was much weaker than promised and though he felt compelled to defend his revised language as "no less vigorous than and . . . substantially similar to the statement we had discussed," Churchill had little ground for complaint. Having pressed Roosevelt for a warning as a way to restrain Japan from war, he could hardly quarrel with the American emphasis on another round of talks which might produce the same result. In a conversation with Nomura on August 17, Roosevelt stressed his interest in improved relations. In presenting the cautious warning against further Japanese aggression, the President further reduced its importance by asking that his prepared remarks not "be considered as oral statements," but as "only reference material" which he gave to Nomura on the condition that they were only for his "information." Furthermore, Roosevelt explained that if Japan were ready "to suspend its expansionist activities" and furnish a clearer statement than previously of its "attitudes and plans," the United States would consider a "resumption of the informal exploratory discussions," and he would be receptive to a possible meeting with Prince Konoye in Juneau, Alaska, in mid-October. Though FDR's wish to see him immediately after returning from Argentia indicated to Nomura the "graveness" with which Roosevelt viewed Japanese-American relations, the Ambassador left their meeting with "no room for doubt . . . that the President hopes that matters will take a turn for the better." [39]

Yet Roosevelt actually had little hope that a meaningful rapprochement was possible. While he talked with Nomura, a large Japanese force on the Siberian border seemed poised to attack the Soviet Union, and Japanese newspapers discussed the possibility of an attack on American oil tankers headed for Vladivostok. The progress of the Nazi-Soviet conflict rather than "regard for the United States," FDR told Halifax on August 18, was the principal influence on current Japanese policy. For FDR, the realistic objective in these talks was not a fundamental shift in Japanese-American relations, which seemed almost certainly beyond reach, but time—the extension of peace in the Pacific while America, Britain, and Russia increased their military strength. If matters could be strung out long enough, or until Hitler could be destroyed, the change in international circumstance might even force Japan to shift policy without a war.

Consequently, on August 28, when Prime Minister Konoye responded with an "urgent" plea for a meeting as soon as possible, Roosevelt "complimented the tone and spirit" of the reply and declared himself "keenly interested in having three or four days" with him. According to Hull, Roosevelt "relished a meeting with Konoye, and . . . was excited at the prospect." Vice President Henry Wallace left a Cabinet meeting on the following day with the impression that Roosevelt was ready to adopt an "appeasing or partially appeasing stand" toward Japan.

Yet Roosevelt would take only limited risks in these negotiations. While describing himself as looking forward to his meeting with the Prince, he also "cynically" asked Nomura "whether [an] invasion of Thailand can be expected during these conversations just as an invasion of French Indochina occurred during Secretary Hull's conversations with your Excellency." Fearful that a meeting with Konoye would produce only vague commitments which could be bent in almost any direction later, Roosevelt now followed the State Department's advice that he and Nomura resolve fundamental differences before a meeting. In another conversation with Nomura on September 3, therefore, the President asked for assurances of Japan's detachment from the Tripartite Pact, its readiness to withdraw troops from China, and its adherence to principles of nondiscrimination in economic relations.[40]

High-level Japanese conferences between September 3 and 6 demonstrated that Japanese-American differences were irreconcilable. Convinced that they must act before American economic sanctions and weather conditions hindered their ability to fight, Japan's military leaders now insisted that Konoye be given only until mid-October to settle matters with the United States. If there were no agreement by that date, Japan was to prepare itself for war against America, England, and Holland. The conditions for a settlement agreed to by an Imperial Conference on September 6 set Japan firmly on the road to war. At a minimum, America and Britain were not to interfere with Japan's efforts to conclude the China Incident, were to do nothing that threatened Japan in the Far East, including the establishment of additional military bases or the strengthening of existing forces, and were to cooperate with Japan's efforts to secure adequate supplies of raw materials and assure her economic well-being. In return, Japan would promise not to use Indochina as a military base against other countries, except China, would agree to follow a Far Eastern settlement by withdrawal from Indochina, and would guarantee the neutrality of the Philippines. As for China, it was shortly decided that troops would remain for "a necessary period" in Inner Mongolia and north China to defend against Communism, while other army units would be withdrawn at the close of the China Incident. Manchukuo was not to be returned to China.

The statement to the American government of these conditions in documents of September 22 and 25 simply confirmed Roosevelt's determination not to hold a summit meeting without prior guarantees. Even if FDR believed that he could extend these discussions by a personal meeting with Konoye, he appreciated that sentiment in the United States and China made it nearly impossible without preliminary assurances against trading Chinese interests for peace. Newspaper, public, and official opinion was uniformly opposed to any appeasement of Japan. In September, for example, Roosevelt had learned that 67 per cent of the public was ready to risk war with Japan to keep her from becoming more powerful. Moreover, because Japanese aggression and German aggression were firmly linked in American minds, Roosevelt feared that any appeasement of Japan would produce a cynical outcry in the United States which would weaken public resolve to oppose Berlin. At the same time, his principal advisers counseled against anything that further weakened Chinese resistance, pointing out that the combination of ineffective aid and the current negotiations left the Chinese feeling neglected and resentful. They "feel the same way the Czechs did when Chamberlain and Hitler were deciding upon their fate," Lauchlin Currie advised FDR.[41]

In these circumstances, Roosevelt simply tried to string out the negotiations for as long as he could. At the end of September, in response to Hull's outline of what they should say next to Japan, Roosevelt "wholly" agreed that Hull should "recite the more liberal original attitude of the Japanese when they first sought the meeting, point out their much narrowed position now, earnestly ask if they cannot go back to their original attitude, start discussions again on agreement in principle, and reemphasize my hope for a meeting." "Very little was going on as regards these talks," Roosevelt told the British Chargé d'Affaires on October 1, adding that nevertheless he was "gaining useful time."

Encouraged by Stimson, Roosevelt hoped that the expansion of American air power in the Philippines would now restrain Japan. The stationing of new B-17 Flying Fortresses in the Islands, Stimson believed, gave America the ability to "completely damage" Japanese supply lines to the Southwest Pacific, endowing the United States with "a vital power of defense there." "The President had a good deal to say," Halifax informed Churchill on October 11, "about the great effect that their planting some heavy bombers at the Philippines was expected to have upon the Japs." [42]

As events five days later suggested, however, the bombers in no way intimidated Japan. Though Konoye sincerely wished to continue the negotiations and pressed General Hideki Tojo, the War Minister, to satisfy the American demand for troop withdrawals from China, the latter would not agree. Give in to America now, he warned, and there would be no end to their demands. Instead, Tojo suggested that Konoye resign and allow a new Cabinet to examine the situation afresh. When Konoye acceded to this request on October 16, the Emperor appointed Tojo in his place.

These developments seemed to suggest the advent of a military dictatorship and a final turn toward war. "The Jap situation is definitely worse," FDR had cabled Churchill on the 15th, "and I think they are headed North." Konoye's resignation on the following day served to confirm this fear: "Hostilities between Japan and Russia are a strong possibility," Admiral Stark warned his commanders in Hawaii and the Philippines after a meeting at the White House. An attack on Britain and the United States was also considered a distinct possibility. The commanders were to "take due precautions," and they were to avoid "provocative actions against Japan." The "delicate question" now, Stimson recorded after this meeting, was "the diplomatic fencing" to assure "that Japan was put into the wrong and made the first bad move—overt move." If Japan were now intent on war, Roosevelt wished to relieve American opinion of any doubts about who was at fault.[43]

Tojo's rise to the premiership moved the British and Chinese to put fresh pressure on the United States to oppose Japan. With the "Japanese menace" now "sharper" than ever, Churchill renewed his plea for "stronger . . . action." This, he told Roosevelt, would either deter Japan or produce a Japanese-American war which Britain would join "within the hour." In either case, it would serve Churchill's aim of assuring that the United States would take the lead in the Far East and not leave Britain to face Japan alone. Fearful that Tojo's accession to power would spark an offensive to cut the Burma Road and deal Chungking a decisive blow, Chiang asked FDR to tell Tokyo that America could not "remain indifferent" to such a step. He also urged Roosevelt and Churchill to counter such an attack with air power from Singapore and the Philippines.

Churchill seized on Chiang's message to restate the case for directly confronting Tokyo:

> What we need now is a deterrent of the most general and formidable character. . . . When we talked about this at Placentia you spoke of gaining time, and this policy has been brilliantly successful so far. But our joint embargo is steadily forcing the Japanese to decisions for peace or war. . . .
>
> The Chinese have appealed to us, as I believe they have to you, to warn the Japanese against an attack in Yunnan. I hope you might think fit to remind them that such an attack . . . would be in open disregard of the clearly indicated attitude of the United States Government. We should of course be ready to make a similar communication.
>
> No independent action by ourselves will deter Japan, because we are so much tied up elsewhere. But of course we will stand with you and do our utmost to back you in whatever course you choose. I think myself that Japan is more likely to drift into war than to plunge in.[44]

Roosevelt, however, still wished to play for time. Though he initially considered answering Chiang's message with a warning to Japan that "a move to close the Burma Road would be inimical" to good relations with the United States, his military advisers quickly changed his mind. In a review of the Far Eastern situation on November 5, Marshall and Stark urged against an "ultimatum" to Tokyo or any offensive operations to prevent Japan from severing the Burma Road. The Japanese, they advised, would be unable to complete preparations for such an offensive in less than two months, and the Chinese, given the favorable terrain, would have a good chance of defeating such an attack. More importantly, by the middle of December "United States air and submarine strength in the Philippines will have become a positive threat to any Japanese operations south of Formosa," and by February or March, American air strength "might well be a deciding factor in deterring Japan in operations

. . . south and west of the Philippines. . . . In any case, an unlimited offensive war should not be undertaken against Japan, since such a war would greatly weaken the combined effort in the Atlantic against Germany, the most dangerous enemy." Only if Japan struck directly at "the territory or mandated territory of the United States, the British Commonwealth, or the Netherlands East Indies," or if Japanese forces moved into Thailand west or south of Bangkok, Portuguese Timor, New Caledonia, or the Loyalty Islands should the United States respond with military force.

In a cable to Churchill on November 7, FDR gave an indication of this cautious policy. Expressing "doubt whether preparations for a Japanese land campaign" had advanced to a point where they would move in the "immediate future," the President advised that in the meantime the United States would increase and expedite Lend-Lease aid and expand the American volunteer air force in China. "We feel that measures such as the foregoing . . . together with continuing efforts to strengthen our defenses in the Philippine Islands, paralleled by similar efforts by you in the Singapore area, will tend to increase Japan's hesitation, whereas in Japan's present mood new, formalized verbal warning or remonstrances might have, with at least even chance, an opposite effect." [45]

At the same time, Roosevelt tried "to think of something" that would give the military the time it asked. In a talk with Stimson on November 6, he had said that "he might propose a truce in which there would be no movement or armament for six months, and then if the Japanese and Chinese had not settled their arrangement in that meanwhile, we could go on on the same basis." Stimson, however, discouraged this idea as tying "our hands just at a time when it was vitally important that we should go on completing our reenforcement of the Philippines" and as a blow to the Chinese who would feel deserted by any such arrangement. At a Cabinet meeting on the following day, the President expressed the belief that they had to "strain every nerve to satisfy and keep on good relations" with the Japanese negotiators. Don't let the talks "deteriorate and break up if you can possibly help it," he told Hull. "Let us make no move of ill will. Let us do nothing to precipitate a crisis."

The President also stressed the great danger of an outbreak in the Pacific. He polled Cabinet members on whether they thought "the people would back us up" if the administration answered a Japanese attack on British or Dutch possessions with military action. When all agreed they would, it was decided that high government officials should emphasize the critical situation in public speeches during the next few days. Roosevelt's concern sprang from a knowledge through "Magic" intercepts of Tokyo's latest coded messages to Nomura. On November 4, the Foreign Minister had informed Nomura that the government had decided to make a "last effort" at an accommodation with the United States, and on the 5th that if nothing happened quickly, "the talks will certainly be ruptured," and relations would be "on the brink of chaos." "Because of various circumstances," Nomura was told, "it is absolutely necessary that all arrangements for the signing of this agreement be completed by the 25th of this month. . . . Please understand this thoroughly and tackle the problem of saving the Japanese-U.S. relations from falling into a chaotic condition." "This to us," Hull later recorded, "could mean only one thing. Japan had already set in motion the wheels of her war machine, and she had decided not to stop short of war with the United States if by November 25 we had not agreed to her demands."

Japan's final proposals offered little hope of forestalling the threatened war. Divided into parts "A" and "B," with the "B" section to be presented only if negotiations stalled on "A," Nomura put the first set of proposals before FDR on November 10. Though addressing their central differences on relations with the Axis, trade, and China, Tokyo's review of these issues offered no way around the impasse. Japan would not withdraw from the Tripartite Pact. If we went into an agreement with Japan while she maintained an obligation to Germany to go to war with us, Hull told Nomura, "it would cause so much turmoil in the country that I might well be lynched." On China, a "Magic" intercept indicated that Tokyo would only try to dispel suspicions by shifting regions of occupation. "We will call it evacuation; but . . . in the last analysis this would be out of the question." [46]

By November 14, Tokyo had given up on these initial proposals and ordered Nomura and Saburo Kurusu, a professional diplomat flown to the United States to help in the negotiations, to present plan "B." But reluctant to take an "irretrievable" step, Kurusu proposed a temporary arrangement that would buy more time for the discussion of fundamental differences. On November 18, he suggested a modus vivendi to Hull in which the United States would ease its economic pressure on Japan in return for a Japanese withdrawal from Indochina. Tokyo at once rejected this suggestion, however, and ordered its diplomats to seek a temporary agreement conforming to proposal "B." Consequently, on November 20 the envoys presented a five-point program to Hull which they described as "an amplification" of their previous suggestion. Under its terms, Japan and the United States were to make no armed advances in Southeast Asia and the southern Pacific, with the exception of French Indochina, where Japan could still move against China; Japan was to withdraw troops from southern Indochina and transfer them to northern Indochina at once and pull out completely after the establishment of an equitable Pacific peace; both governments were to cooperate in the acquisition of goods from the Dutch East Indies; both sides were to restore trade to pre-freeze conditions; and the United States was not to interfere with efforts to restore Sino-Japanese peace.

Encouraged by Japan's suggestion of a temporary accommodation, Roosevelt and Hull worked on truce proposals of their own. On or shortly after November 17, the President had proposed to Hull that they seek a six-month agreement with Japan by which the United States resumed economic relations and initiated Sino-Japanese talks. In return, Japan was to send no more troops to Indochina, the Manchurian border, "or any place South (Dutch, Brit., or Siam)," and would agree not to invoke the Tripartite Pact even if the United States entered the European war.

At the same time, the State Department drafted its own version of a modus vivendi. As described by Roosevelt in a message to Churchill on the 24th, it was "an alternative proposal" to the unsatisfactory one made by Japan on the 20th and would contain mutual pledges of peaceful intent and a reciprocal agreement against armed advances in Northeast and Southeast Asia and the North and South Pacific. Japan was also to commit itself to withdraw troops from southern Indochina and to limit troops in northern Indochina to 25,000. The United States in return was to resume some trade with Japan, including the export of petroleum for strictly civilian needs. Lastly, the modus vivendi was to operate for three months while the two parties determined whether prospects for a peaceful settlement covering the entire Pacific warranted its extension.[47]

Roosevelt had little hope that these proposals would come to anything. A dispatch from Tokyo on November 22 had indicated that the Japanese were ready to extend the deadline for successful talks from the 25th to the 29th, but not beyond this date. "After that," the cable advised, "things are automatically going to happen." Another message on the 24th declared that Japan would "require the realization" of the five points in proposal "B," and that the cessation of aid to Chiang as well as the receipt of supplies from the Dutch East Indies and petroleum from the United States were "essential" conditions. The acceptance or rejection of the modus vivendi, FDR told Churchill on the 24th, "is really a matter of internal Japanese politics. I am not very hopeful and we must all be prepared for real trouble, possibly soon." On the following day, in a discussion with Hull, Knox, Marshall, Stark, and Stimson about the Far East, the President focused on the likelihood of a Japanese surprise attack. "The question was how we should maneuver them into the position of firing the first shot without allowing too much danger to ourselves." The chief concern was how to justify an American declaration of war to Congress and the public if Tokyo struck only at British and/or Dutch possessions. Roosevelt later told Churchill and Stalin that if "it had not been for the Japanese attack, he would have had great difficulty in getting the American people into the war."

Chinese and British opposition, combined with Japanese troop movements on the 26th, killed the administration's truce plan. On November 25 news of the American modus vivendi had evoked "hysterical" protests from Chiang Kai-shek. Opposed to any relaxation of economic pressure on Japan while she maintained forces in China, Chiang sent direct and indirect warnings that Washington's modus vivendi risked the collapse of Chinese morale and resistance. Churchill supported this warning in a cable to Roosevelt in the early hours of the 26th: "What about Chiang Kai-shek?" he asked. "Is he not having a very thin diet? Our anxiety is about China. If they collapse, our joint dangers would enormously increase." On the morning of the 26th Roosevelt also received word from Stimson that five Japanese divisions on ships out of Shanghai had been sighted south of Formosa. The President "fairly blew up" over this news and said "that that changed the whole situation because it was evidence of bad faith on the part of the Japanese that while they were negotiating for an entire truce—an entire withdrawal—they should be sending this expedition down there to Indochina." Given the near certainty that the modus vivendi would be rejected and that its presentation might bring disintegration in China and complaints in the United States against sacrificing China to help Britain against Berlin, Roosevelt and Hull decided "to kick the whole thing over." [48]

Though they now agreed to give Japan a ten-point outline of a "proposed basis for agreement," which had been drafted simultaneously with the modus vivendi, neither had serious hopes that it would lead anywhere. Both agreed that negotiations with Japan were for "all practical purposes" at an end, and that hostile action by Japan was "possible at any moment." At a War Cabinet meeting on November 28, it was everyone's opinion that the Japanese troopships moving south posed a "terrific" threat to "Britain at Singapore, the Netherlands, and ourselves in the Philippines," and that the next move was for the President to address a secret warning to the Japanese Emperor and a public message to the Congress alerting it to the danger. With intercepted messages from Tokyo indicating that nothing would happen for at least a few days, the President left it to his advisers to draft these messages while he took a belated Thanksgiving holiday in Warm Springs.[49]

When Roosevelt returned to the capital on December 1, he met with Lord Halifax to discuss a coordinated response to Japan. On November 29 the British Foreign Office had instructed Halifax to "ask for an urgent expression" of American views on a plan to counter a Japanese attack on Thailand and the increased danger to Singapore with a rapid move into the Kra Isthmus. "You will realise," the Foreign Office advised Halifax, "how important it is to ensure ourselves of American support in the event of hostilities." A Churchill message to FDR on the following day had expressed the same concern: "It seems to me that one important method remains unused in averting war between Japan and our two countries, namely a plain declaration . . . that any further act of aggression by Japan will lead immediately to the gravest consequences. . . . I beg you to consider whether, at the moment which you judge right which may be very near, you should not say that 'any further Japanese aggression would compel you to place the gravest issues before Congress.' " Roosevelt told Halifax that he wished to precede a parallel warning with a query to Tokyo on where and for what purpose her troop transports were bound.

He also made strong commitments to action. He assured Halifax that in case of a direct attack on British or Dutch possessions, "we should obviously be all together." But he wished to know what Britain would do if Japan reinforced Indochina or attacked Thailand. "I think that whatever action . . . His Majesty's Government are prepared to take," Halifax reported to London, "he [FDR] would be disposed to support." Roosevelt spoke of using air forces in the Philippines and a "long distance naval blockade, 'which of course means shooting.' " On the "immediate question" of a possible British move into the Kra Isthmus, Halifax's report continued, Roosevelt "said that we could certainly count on their support, though it might take a short time, a few days, to get things into political shape here." In further conversations on December 3 and 4, the President assured Halifax that "support" meant "armed support," and agreed that the United States, Britain, and Holland should issue independent warnings to Japan against an attack on Thailand, Malaya, or the Dutch East Indies. He wished the American warning to come first, however, as a way to convince American opinion that he was acting in the country's defense and not simply following a British lead.

Roosevelt also wished to postpone the warning until Tokyo had answered his inquiry and he had decided whether to approach the Emperor about a truce. Kurusu had sent him word, he told Halifax, that this was the only means left of preventing a break. While he did not attach much importance to this suggestion, believing it a means to stall the United States until Japan had its troops in position, he was reluctant to ignore any chance for a settlement and believed a message to the Emperor would strengthen his case with the public if there were a war. On December 6, therefore, after Japan had replied evasively that troop movements in Indochina were a response to Chinese actions on the frontier, and after the Japanese force had entered the Gulf of Siam, where it could strike at Thailand or Malaya, Roosevelt sent a message to the Emperor. Describing the concentration of Japanese troops in Indochina as creating a "deep and far reaching emergency" which threatened the Philippines, East Indies, Malaya, and Thailand, and peaceful relations with the United States, Roosevelt asked for a withdrawal of Japanese forces as the only sure way to have peace in the South Pacific and dispel "the dark clouds." "This son of man has just sent his final message to the Son of God" he told some White House guests shortly after making this last try for peace.[50]

The President needed no reply from the Emperor to know that his appeal would fail. The same evening his message went to Tokyo he received thirteen parts of a fourteen-part Japanese reply to the ten-point American proposal of November 26. "This means war," he told Hopkins. "Since war was undoubtedly going to come at the convenience of the Japanese," Hopkins answered, "it was too bad that we could not strike the first blow and prevent any sort of surprise." "No, we can't do that," the President said. "We are a democracy and a peaceful people." Raising his voice, he added: "But we have a good record." As the military courier who delivered the intercept to the President understood him, the United States would stand on that record and not make the first overt move. "We would have to wait until it came." As Stimson explained it later to a congressional investigating committee, despite the risk involved "in letting the Japanese fire the first shot, we realized that in order to have the full support of the American people it was desirable to make sure that the Japanese be the ones to do this so that there should remain no doubt in anyone's mind as to who were the aggressors."

Even at this late date, Roosevelt had strong reason to fear that American opinion would be divided and unenthusiastic about full-scale involvement in the war. To be sure, a public opinion survey that reached him on December 5 had shown 69 per cent of the country willing to risk war with Japan to prevent her from becoming more powerful; but only 51 per cent of this group believed the United States would go to war with Japan in the near future. At the same time, a summary of editorial opinion indicated that most of the press saw "American involvement in a Pacific war as an imminent probability." But these papers had "by no means relinquished hope that war may be avoided." Indeed, a majority of the press held "to the hope that the Axis can be defeated without full-scale American participation at the actual fighting fronts."

An oppressive fear as to the economic consequences of fuller American involvement fueled this wish. A detailed report to the President in November on the current public mood had concluded that, unlike the people of many warring countries, Americans believed "that the sun will never shine as brightly after the storm as it did before." Despite expectations of military victory, between 60 and 70 per cent of the public foresaw themselves working harder for less money, paying higher prices, and suffering higher unemployment after a war.

There was also disturbing evidence of resistance to full-scale involvement in a report from Professor Paul Douglas of the University of Chicago on public sentiment in downstate Illinois. In a one-month speaking tour of twenty-two cities and towns, Douglas had found "no evidence" that public opinion was ahead of the President "or that any large section demands more violent action. . . . There is a tremendous fear of another A.E.F. [American Expeditionary Force] with its heavy losses," Douglas wrote. "I think the people are in favor of (a) economic aid (b) material aid and probably even (c) use of an airforce but they are opposed at present to an A.E.F." This more or less echoed a national survey of mid-November in which 47 per cent favored and 44 per cent opposed sending a large American Army to Europe, even if it were required for German defeat. Though there was stronger sentiment in the country for directly confronting Japan, the cumulative evidence suggested that the nation would be less than united in a war sparked by Japanese aggression against Thailand, or British or Dutch possessions.[51]

The Japanese solved the President's dilemma on December 7, 1941. At approximately 7:55 a.m., Hawaii time, 190 carrier-based Japanese dive bombers, torpedo planes, and fighters struck at the American fleet and military installations in and around Pearl Harbor, Honolulu, Hawaii. Followed by a second wave of 170 planes, the attack lasted almost two hours. Catching the American defenders by surprise, the Japanese planes killed 2403 Americans and wounded an additional 1178 men. Though no American aircraft carriers were in the Harbor, the bulk of the American battle fleet, seven battleships, along with most of the Navy and Army aircraft on the Island of Oahu were destroyed or put out of commission. However successful in immediate military terms, the Pearl Harbor attack principally served to unite the American people for a war against Japan as nothing else could have.

Though the surprise attack profoundly distressed FDR, it also relieved him. As told by Hopkins, the President said it took the question of peace and war "entirely out of his hands, because the Japanese had made the decision for him." He had always believed that the Japanese would try to avoid fighting the United States while they moved against the other Powers in the Pacific. This would have left him "with the very difficult problem of protecting our interests. . . . Hence his great relief at the method that Japan used. In spite of the disaster at Pearl Harbor . . . it completely solidified the American people and made the war upon Japan inevitable." "In spite of his anxiety," Eleanor Roosevelt later said of her husband, that day "Franklin was in a way more serene than he had appeared in a long time."

When Frances Perkins, the Secretary of Labor, saw Roosevelt at a Cabinet meeting on the evening of the 7th, she found him "having actual physical difficulty in getting out the words that put him on record as knowing that the Navy was caught unawares. . . . It was obvious to me that Roosevelt was having a dreadful time just accepting the idea." But she also saw evidence in him of relief that "the long tension of wondering what they would do and when they would do it, and would we have to go to the defense of Singapore without an apparent attack upon ourselves . . . all these conflicts which had so harassed him for so many weeks or months, were ended." She thought that this "wave of relief," which he was reluctant to acknowledge, was reflected in an evasive look on his face, a "facial expression of tenseness and calmness."

Churchill was even more relieved. "This certainly simplifies things," he told the President via transatlantic telephone. "To have the United States at our side," he later wrote, "was to me the greatest joy. . . . Now at this very moment I knew the United States was in the war, up to the neck and in to the death. So we had won after all! . . . Hitler's fate was sealed. Mussolini's fate was sealed. As for the Japanese, they would be ground to powder. . . . No doubt it would take a long time. . . . But there was no more doubt about the end. . . . Being saturated and satiated with emotion and sensation, I went to bed and slept the sleep of the saved and thankful." [52]

Even after Japan's attack, Roosevelt remained intensely concerned with assuring public unity. When Cabinet members led by Hull pressed him to present a long war message to Congress reviewing the whole history of "Japan's lawless conduct," he resisted. Because he believed it essential to have the message read by as many people as possible, he insisted on making it brief and confining it to "the treachery of the present attack." Further, when Churchill inquired whether he wanted him to wait to ask Parliament for a war declaration until the President had acted, Roosevelt answered: "I think it best on account of psychology here that Britain's declaration of war be withheld until after my speech." On December 8 Roosevelt put his war message before the Congress. "Yesterday, December 7, 1941—a day which will live in infamy—the United States of America was suddenly and deliberately attacked by naval and air forces of the Empire of Japan." Describing in some 500 words the diplomatic background to and the consequences of Japan's surprise offensive throughout the Pacific, the President asked for a Declaration of War, which the Congress promptly gave with only one dissenting vote.

Despite strong pressure from Stimson, Roosevelt refused to include Germany and Italy in his request. The President, Halifax advised Churchill on December 9, still felt that he had to persuade part of the American public to fight Germany as well as Japan. "I seem to be conscious of a still lingering distinction in some quarters of the public between war with Japan and war with Germany," FDR told Halifax. Hopeful, because of intercepts of Japanese messages, that Hitler would take the initiative and relieve him of a step that seemed likely to generate debate in the United States, Roosevelt waited to see what Germany would do. On December 11, Hitler and Mussolini obliged him by declaring war on the United States, an act, in their view, of anticipating the inevitable. [53]

In the years after Pearl Harbor, critics of Roosevelt's leadership argued that the President had provoked the Japanese attack as a "backdoor" to the European war. They even suggested that FDR expected the Pearl Harbor assault but allowed American forces to be surprised in order to assure unity at home. This argument, as Roberta Wohlstetter has shown, is without merit. The surprise at Pearl Harbor, she effectively demonstrates, resulted from a national failure to anticipate. The country's political and military leaders simply discounted or underestimated the likelihood of a Japanese attack on Hawaii. Yet the authors of the assertion that FDR allowed American forces to be surprised did not enunciate it simply to discredit FDR. Voiced by a group of writers who believed the United States would have done better to stay out of the war, the refusal to see the Pearl Harbor attack as a surprise was essential to a vindication of old isolationist beliefs. Having consistently argued that American security was not at stake in the war, or that the United States was invulnerable to attack, diehard isolationists tried to answer a devastating refutation of this theme by placing the blame for Pearl Harbor on FDR. Only by explaining away America's vulnerability to attack as the product of something Roosevelt and others around him contrived could isolationists keep their faith alive.

The isolationist tenet that described involvement in the war as certain to damage the nation's democratic institutions was a more realistic concern. By setting precedents for arbitrary use of Executive power, Roosevelt and subsequent Presidents gave meaning to isolationist warnings that the defense of democracy abroad would compromise it at home. It is an irony of history that in his determination to save democracy from Nazism, Roosevelt contributed to the rise of some undemocratic practices in the United States. But it is an even greater irony that the isolationist failure to appreciate the threat posed by Nazi might helped force Roosevelt into the machinations which later Presidents used to rationalize abuses of power on more questionable grounds.[54]

PART FOUR

The Idealist as Realist, 1942-1945

12

The Struggle for Unity

Though the response of the nation and the Congress to the Pearl Harbor attack was one of overwhelming unity, Roosevelt refused to take this support for granted. One of his chief concerns at the start of the war was to build a commitment to the fighting which initial defeats and the burdens of a long struggle would not weaken. "We are now in this war. We are all in it—all the way," he told a national radio audience two days after Pearl Harbor. "Every single man, woman, and child is a partner in the most tremendous undertaking of our American history." Describing the nation as "fighting for its existence and its future life," he tried to rally the country around a long-range positive goal, a vision "far above and beyond the ugly field of battle." "When we resort to force," he declared, "we are determined that this force shall be directed toward ultimate good as well as against immediate evil. We Americans are not destroyers—we are builders. We are now in the midst of a war, not for conquest, not for vengeance, but for a world in which this Nation, and all that this Nation represents, will be safe for our children."

At every opportunity in these opening weeks of the struggle, Roosevelt emphasized the themes of unity and ultimate goals. Pledges of cooperation from the Republican and Democratic National Chairmen evoked the announcement that there could be no partisan domestic politics in wartime, but "only a determined intent of a united people to carry on the struggle for human liberty." The 150th anniversary of the ratification of the Bill of Rights became the occasion for a public declaration of national determination to defeat Nazi "barbarism" and preserve "the great upsurge of human liberty" embodied in the Bill of Rights. A conference of industrial and labor leaders to prevent future conflicts disruptive to production became a forum for declaring that labor and management were "like the old Kipling saying about 'Judy O'Grady an' the Colonel's Lady.' They are both the same under the skin." He was confident, he added, that they all appreciated "the spiritual side of this war emergency": the fact that "our type of civilization," "our freedoms," were at stake.[1]

Roosevelt also saw a need to tie the country closely to its allies. On December 9, when Churchill proposed a meeting in Washington to "review the whole war plan," Roosevelt warmly endorsed the suggestion and invited the Prime Minister to stay at the White House. At the same time, however, he feared the domestic reaction to such a meeting: "I had a slight feeling," Halifax cabled Churchill, that the President ". . . was not quite sure if your coming here might not be rather too strong medicine . . . for some of his public opinion." One of the British Chiefs of Staff also voiced doubts about dropping the "cautious approach to America that had seemed politic when her intervention was in doubt." "Oh!" Churchill replied, with a wicked leer in his eye, "that is the way we talked to her while we were wooing her; now that she is in the harem, we talk to her quite differently!" [2]

Though Churchill's purpose in coming to Washington was to discuss military plans, Roosevelt viewed the meeting in broader terms. He wished this Arcadia Conference, as it was called, not only to coordinate Allied strategy but also to enunciate political goals. Indeed, his first concern was to draw up a statement that could inspire unity at home and abroad. The inspiration for this idea actually came from Hull, who immediately after Pearl Harbor saw a pressing need for an expression of unity and common principle that would bolster morale and forestall postwar conflicts. On December 19 he gave the President a Declaration in which the anti-Axis nations affirmed the principles of the Atlantic Charter, described themselves as defending life, liberty, and independence, and pledged full wartime cooperation and determination not to cease hostilities except by common agreement. After the State Department assured him that a pledge to conclude the fighting in conjunction with the Allies was not an unconstitutional assumption of congressional power, Roosevelt put this Declaration before Churchill shortly after their talks began on December 22.[3]

Discussions of the Declaration at once raised threats to the domestic and international unity it was supposed to promote. After learning of the "declaration of common purpose" on Christmas eve, the British War Cabinet urged Churchill to include "social security" as a postwar Allied goal. But fearful that it would strike congressional conservatives as a call for a global New Deal, Roosevelt rejected the suggestion. The British also proposed that all the Allies sign the statement as a demonstration that the war was "being waged for freedom of small nations as well as great." Roosevelt agreed, believing it "a distinct advantage to have as long a list of small countries as possible in this Declaration." In January, at a White House dinner party twelve days after they had released the statement, someone mentioned King Zog of Albania. " 'Zog!' cried Roosevelt. . . . He leaned over the table and pointed a finger at Churchill: 'Winston, we forgot Zog! . . . Albania is a belligerent on our side,' said the President. . . . 'I believe there's an Albanian Minister or representative here—we must get him to sign our little document.' "

Roosevelt also pressured the Russians to appease domestic and international feelings by including "religious freedom" in the document. "I am anxious that the most careful thought be given to the language in this Declaration, which will supplement the Atlantic statement," he told Hull, "particularly in reference to the real purposes for which we fight." On December 27, he had pressed Litvinov, who had just become Ambassador to Washington, to urge his government to accept "religious freedom" in the Declaration. But Litvinov, who, according to Churchill, lived in "evident fear and trembling" of Stalin, resisted the suggestion. The President, Churchill whimsically recorded later, "had a long talk with him [Litvinov] alone about his soul and the dangers of hellfire. The accounts which Mr. Roosevelt gave us on several occasions of what he said to the Russian were impressive. Indeed, on one occasion I promised Mr. Roosevelt to recommend him for the position of Archbishop of Canterbury if he should lose the next Presidential election." As Roosevelt told the story to Berle, he overcame Russian objections by pointing out that religious freedom "meant freedom to have a religion or not to, as one saw fit." [4]

For the sake of domestic and foreign opinion, Roosevelt also pressed Churchill to include India among the signatories. By late December, Japanese military advances, including the destruction of Britain's two largest ships in the Far East, the *Prince of Wales* and the *Repulse*, and the fall of Hong Kong, posed a substantial threat to India. With Indian political leaders adding to this danger by demanding commitments to independence in return for support of the Allied war effort, American opinion became increasingly vocal in behalf of Indian independence. Though Churchill and the Cabinet consented to have India sign the Declaration, they refused to make additional concessions to Indian or American opinion. The President "first discussed the Indian problem with me, on the usual American lines, during my visit to Washington in December, 1941," Churchill recalled in his war memoirs. "I reacted so strongly and at such length that he never raised it verbally again." [5]

Roosevelt also tried to preserve domestic unity by not asking the Senate to approve a treaty of alliance with America's allies. He believed a demoralizing debate in the Senate a distinct possibility. Only eight days after Pearl Harbor, a House committee refused to extend the draft to include men under the age of twenty-one, and Stimson believed it "a stiff proposition . . . to make that House committee reverse itself. The scare of these wretches is getting over," Stimson recorded in his diary, "and they are beginning to slip back into their old attitude of laissez-faire." Though the Declaration agreed upon by Roosevelt and Churchill had all the ingredients of a military alliance, FDR shunned the title. Instead of a "Joint Declaration of Allied Unity," or "by the Associated Powers," Roosevelt proposed the words "United Nations," which Churchill considered "a great improvement." "This is much better than 'Alliance,' which places him in constitutional difficulties, or 'Associated Powers,' which is flat," Churchill told his Cabinet. Out of a regard for American "susceptibilities," Eden advised Churchill, "we propose . . . to speak of the U.S. not as an 'Ally' but as 'co-belligerent.' " "The expression 'co-belligerent' is awful," Churchill replied, but he had no alternative suggestion.

As published in its final form on January 1, 1942, the "Declaration by United Nations" read:

A JOINT DECLARATION BY THE UNITED STATES OF AMERICA, THE UNITED KINGDOM OF GREAT BRITAIN AND NORTHERN IRELAND, THE UNION OF SOVIET SOCIALIST REPUBLICS, CHINA, AUSTRALIA, BELGIUM, CANADA, COSTA RICA, CUBA, CZECHOSLOVAKIA, DOMINICAN REPUBLIC, EL SALVADOR, GREECE, GUATEMALA, HAITI, HONDURAS, INDIA, LUXEMBOURG, NETHERLANDS, NEW ZEALAND, NICARAGUA, NORWAY, PANAMA, POLAND, SOUTH AFRICA, YUGOSLAVIA

The governments signatory hereto.

Having subscribed to a common program of purposes and principles embodied in the Joint Declaration of the President of the United States of America and the Prime Minister of the United Kingdom of Great Britain and Northern Ireland dated August 14, 1941, known as the Atlantic Charter,

Being convinced that complete victory over their enemies is essential to defend life, liberty, independence and religious freedom, and to preserve human rights and justice in their own lands as well as in other lands, and that they are now engaged in a common struggle against savage and brutal forces seeking to subjugate the world,

Declare:

(1) Each Government pledges itself to employ its full resources, military or economic, against those members of the Tripartite Pact and its adherents with which such government is at war.

(2) Each Government pledges itself to cooperate with the Governments signatory hereto and not to make a separate armistice or peace with the enemies.

The foregoing declaration may be adhered to by other nations which are, or which may be, rendering material assistance and contributions in the struggle for victory over Hitlerism.[6]

The same concern with unity dominated Roosevelt's discussions of strategy, command, and supply at the Washington meetings. Churchill came to these talks in some apprehension that he would find himself at odds with the President and his Chiefs over fundamental strategy: that the Americans, losing sight of the fact that Germany's defeat would assure victory over Japan, but not the other way around, would now wish to make Japan the prime enemy in the war. But in their first discussion at the Conference, Roosevelt set Churchill's fears to rest. "The discussion," the Prime Minister advised his War Cabinet, "was not *whether* but *how*" to apply the Atlantic-first strategy. On this as well, Churchill found the President singularly forthcoming. He agreed with the Prime Minister that "it was vital to forestall the Germans in Northwest Africa and the Atlantic islands," where they thought Hitler might strike if he were held in Russia. They agreed, therefore, to make plans for an American invasion of North Africa which would begin at Casablanca and eventually meet up with British forces driving west from Libya. The American assault, however, was to depend on British success in Libya and the availability of adequate shipping.

In reaching these decisions with Churchill, Roosevelt relied on his own judgment or asked no advice from his military chiefs. A long-standing interest in naval affairs and geography, or what he called geopolitics, and his eight years as Assistant Secretary of the Navy endowed him with the confidence to be his own decision maker on major military questions or grand strategy. When it came to "Keynesianism or medical economics or the ever-normal granary," Joseph Lash has written, "the New Dealers tutored him; in the field of military strategy and world politics, he taught his advisers." The President's "grasp of the principle of geopolitics," Sumner Welles believed, was "almost instinctive."

A North African invasion appealed to FDR for three reasons. First, it had the virtue of denying to German control an area that could provide a significant peripheral base for future operations against Axis-held territory. Secondly, with only French forces in the area and the possibility that Vichy would agree not to resist, it offered the best opportunity for an initial success against Berlin. Finally, and perhaps most important to FDR, it provided a chance for quick action which would boost American and Allied morale, while simultaneously confronting the Germans with the discouraging fact of American might. "The President," General Marshall recorded after the first formal meeting of the Conference, "considered it very important to morale, to give the country a feeling that they are in the war, to give the Germans the reverse effect, to have American troops somewhere in active fighting across the Atlantic." At the very least, as Roosevelt made clear in ensuing meetings with military chiefs, he put considerable value on prompt action by American bombers operating from England and a public announcement of American troops in the British Isles as means of bolstering Allied hopes.[7]

Developments before the end of the Conference, however, denied Roosevelt the chance for a quick victory in North Africa. George Marshall, the Army Chief of Staff and principal military adviser to the President since September 1939, found little attraction in a North African campaign. A reserved and aloof personality, who resisted the President's charm by refusing to laugh at his jokes, Marshall won Roosevelt's respect by his transparent integrity and his ability to argue a case with precise logic. In the matter of the North African invasion, code-named GYM-NAST, Marshall laid a host of logistical problems before FDR. In addition, he pointed to the possibility of French resistance, which made this "a very dangerous operation." An initial reverse, he also told the President, would have "a very detrimental effect on the morale of the American people." "We can take no chances on the possibility of our first major expedition being a failure," Roosevelt acknowledged, ". . . if the risk looks great, we must think twice before we go ahead." By the last week of the Conference, a British failure to defeat the Germans in Libya and the need to use available shipping to reinforce hard-pressed Allied forces in the Western Pacific ruled out an African assault before May.

Roosevelt now considered other ways to unify the war effort. On Christmas eve, when it had appeared that the Philippines would fall before American reinforcements could reach the besieged defenders, the President offered to turn these forces over to the British to "be utilized in whatever manner might best serve the joint cause in the Far East." When Stimson, who "thought it . . . very improper to discuss such matters while the fighting was going on" in the Philippines, declared himself ready to resign over the issue, Roosevelt at once reversed himself. If this agreement "had gotten into the hands of an unfriendly press," Stimson observed, it would have created considerable trouble for the President. In his eagerness to foster Anglo-American unity, he had, Stimson noted, "pretty nearly burned his fingers." [8]

Stimson's response to Roosevelt's action was but one expression of a general hostility among American military planners toward the British. The President's impulse to follow Churchill's military plans distressed a number of American Army chiefs, who saw British strategy as wasteful of resources and calculated to serve their imperial interests. "The Limeys have his [FDR's] ear, while we have the hind tit," General Joseph W. Stilwell of the War Plans Division complained. "Events are crowding us into ill-advised and ill-considered projects. . . . The Limeys want us in, committed. They don't care what becomes of us afterward, because they will have shifted the load from their shoulders to ours. So they insist that speed is essential, and [Roosevelt] has acquired this same itch . . . and is continually pressing for action, against the considered opinion of all his advisers." To prevent "the ineffectual bleeding away of Army strength in pursuit of British sponsored projects," Lieutenant General Lesley Mc-Nair asked Stilwell to provide "65 reasons why we should not do GYM-NAST." [9]

Mindful of potential tensions between American and British military chiefs, Roosevelt had made unity of command a primary goal of the Washington talks. "There will have to be a Supreme Council," he had told Canadian Prime Minister Mackenzie King on the eve of the conference, "and I am determined it shall have its headquarters in Washington." Anticipating British opposition over what he considered an essential of an effective war effort, he added: "There will possibly be quite a time over this." Indeed, a proposal by Marshall that American, British, Dutch, and Australian forces (ABDA) in the Southwest Pacific operate under one chief evoked strong British resistance. Churchill contended that Allied forces were too dispersed in the Pacific to be effectively controlled by one man and that individual commanders would do better to report directly to Washington. But with Marshall insisting that unity of command in the Far East was imperative if the Allies were ever "to apply the maximum of power where it was most needed," and with Roosevelt proposing that the command go to Britain's General Archibald Wavell, Churchill accepted the idea as "a war-winner." In turn, however, he had to override the opposition of his Chiefs of Staff, who saw this as an American attempt to fasten looming defeat in the Pacific on a British commander.

The logical follow-up to Wavell's appointment as Supreme Commander of ABDA forces was the creation of a "joint body," the Combined Chiefs of Staff. This proposal also "kicked up a hell of a row." Roosevelt had to persuade the British to concentrate the machinery in Washington rather than divide it between London and Washington and to omit the Dutch, Australians, and New Zealanders from a fixed part in the work. Though the British Chiefs were unhappy with the arrangement, Churchill persuaded them to try it for a month. The Prime Minister "is just now possessed with one idea to the exclusion of all others," his personal physician, Sir Charles Wilson, said of this concession. "He feels he must bring the President into the War with his heart set on victory. If that can be done, nothing else matters." [10]

By the time Churchill left Washington on January 14, he and the President had gone far toward establishing the bonds of unity both believed supremely important. Living together in the White House "as a big family, in the greatest intimacy and informality," they had established a regard and admiration for each other which lasted through the most difficult days of the war. "I formed a very strong affection, which grew with our years of comradeship, for this formidable politician . . . whose heart seemed to respond to many of the impulses that stirred my own," Churchill later wrote. After they had set up combined production and distribution boards, Roosevelt told Churchill that he did not "much mind what appeared on paper." FDR was confident that they "would be able to compose any difficulties which might arise." "Trust me to the bitter end," Roosevelt told the Prime Minister at the end of their talks. Roosevelt also "made it perfectly clear" to Hopkins that he was very pleased with the meetings.[11]

Still, the meetings did not end in perfect harmony. During their talks

Roosevelt had difficulty getting Churchill to appreciate that American support partly depended on Britain's identification with idealistic post-war aims. Because Churchill was skeptical of the assertion, especially when raised in connection with India, Roosevelt asked him to read *Two-Way Passage*, a recent book by Louis Adamic, which addressed the issue. He also arranged for Churchill and Adamic to meet at a small White House dinner party. Describing the strong divisions in the country before Pearl Harbor, Adamic's book outlined a postwar aid plan for Europe which could give "strength and coherence" to America's "unifying impulses." The book, FDR told Adamic's wife during dinner, "opens vistas. . . . It appeals to the imagination."

"You know, my friend over there," FDR also said, "doesn't understand how most of our people feel about Britain and her role in the life of other peoples. Our popular idea of that role may not be entirely objective—may not be one hundred per cent true from the British point of view, but there it is; and I've been trying to tell him that he ought to consider it. It's in the American tradition, this distrust, this dislike and even hatred of Britain—the Revolution, you know, and 1812; and India and the Boer War, and all that. There are many kinds of Americans of course, but as a people, as a country, we're opposed to imperialism—we can't stomach it." These feelings "make for all kinds of difficulties," the President added. "Those feelings were certainly evident in the mail I received during the weeks just before Pearl Harbor," Adamic responded, "and I don't doubt that they will be extremely important again after we and Britain are both out of military danger, or even sooner." "Yes indeed," Roosevelt replied. "I can't tell you how grateful we are that you came tonight," Mrs. Roosevelt told Adamic after dinner. "The President has been having considerable trouble in getting the Prime Minister to grasp what kind of a country we are." [12]

In the month after Churchill's visit ended in mid-January, Roosevelt came back to this point in connection with an economic pact. In early February, after negotiations for a mutual aid agreement had reached an impasse over British concern not to abolish Imperial preference, or special trading rights among members of the British Empire, for Lend-Lease, Roosevelt advised Churchill that further delay in signing the agreement would weaken their "unity of purpose" and "be harmful to your interests and ours." When the British suggested an exchange of qualifying notes or reservations about Imperial preference, Roosevelt complained that "attaching notes to this interim agreement would seem . . . to give an impression to our enemies that we were overly cautious." More important, he wished to avoid anything that suggested reservations about economic democracy after the war. "I believe the peoples not only of our two countries but the peoples of all the world," he told Churchill, "will be heartened to know that we are going to try together and with them for the organization of a democratic postwar world. . . . Can we not, therefore, avoid the exchange of notes which . . . seems to dilute our statement of purpose with cautious reservations . . . ? I feel very strongly that this would demonstrate to the world the unity of the American and British people. . . . There are very important considerations here which make an early understanding desirable." Accepting Roosevelt's personal assurances that endorsement of the agreement in no way signified a commitment to abolish Imperial preference, Churchill completed the agreement at once.[13]

Differences between them over India were not so easily resolved. In the second half of February, after the Japanese captured Singapore and made rapid advances across Burma toward India, an outcry went up in the United States for a change in Britain's imperial policy. "We should demand that India be given a status of autonomy," members of the Senate Foreign Relations Committee announced. "The only way to get the people of India to fight was to get them to fight for India." One report coming to FDR described "bitter anti-British expressions . . . everywhere," and warned that one Senator was about to ask a halt in Lend-Lease aid to Britain until it granted India independence. After visiting New Delhi and Calcutta in February, Chiang Kai-shek also publicly called for a transfer of political power. "The danger is extreme," he privately advised FDR. "If the British Government does not fundamentally change their policy toward India, it would be like presenting India to the enemy and inviting them to quickly occupy India."

At the end of February, in hopes of bolstering Indian resistance and quieting American antagonism, Roosevelt reluctantly approached Churchill. Hesitant, after Churchill had expressed strong opposition in December to American interference in the Indian problem, to send him a direct message, FDR broached the issue through Harriman, asking his Special Representative in London to get the Prime Minister's slant on what he "thinks about new relationships between Britain and India." Churchill promptly responded that the great bulk of India's fighting forces were Moslems antagonistic to proponents of independence. "There is ample manpower in India willing to fight," Churchill asserted. "The problem is training and equipment." Britain was nevertheless considering a declaration of Dominion status after the war with the right to secede if desired, Churchill advised. But they were concerned not "to throw India into chaos on the eve of invasion."

Japan's capture of Rangoon on March 10, 1942, created a greater sense of urgency in the United States about the problem of India. Consequently, Roosevelt directly approached Churchill with "a new thought" which might be of assistance to him. Invoking the experience of the American states under the Articles of Confederation between 1783 and 1789, he suggested the creation of a temporary Dominion government in India which would set up a body to work for five or six years on the creation of a more permanent government for the whole country. He thought this might cause the Indians "to forget hard feelings, to become more loyal to the British Empire, and to stress the danger of Japanese domination." He also hoped that such a step could be taken without "criticism in India that it is being made grudgingly or by compulsion. For the love of Heaven don't bring me into this," Roosevelt said to soften resentment over his intrusion, "though I do want to be of help. It is, strictly speaking, none of my business, except insofar as it is part and parcel of the successful fight that you and I are making." [14]

Churchill gave no direct reply to the President's message and later dismissed it as illustrative of "the difficulties of comparing situations in various centuries and scenes where almost every material fact is totally different." "The President might have known that India was one subject on which Winston would never move a yard," one of the Prime Minister's closest associates later told Hopkins. Hopkins himself believed that no suggestions from Roosevelt to Churchill "in the entire war were so wrathfully received as those relating to the solution of the India problem." But concluding that "publicity and the general American outlook" made it impossible "to stand on a purely negative attitude," Churchill decided to send a special mission to India in March to "still febrile agitation" and "prove our honesty of purpose."

Headed by Sir Stafford Cripps, a left-wing Labourite and champion of Indian nationalism, the mission was highly approved of in the United States. In less than three weeks, though, it foundered on differences over who would control the country's wartime defense and over the freedom of individual states and provinces not to join an Indian Union. When Roosevelt's Personal Representative in New Delhi, former Assistant Secretary of War Louis Johnson, advised him that London wanted the negotiations to fail and that the Indian rejection of Cripps's offer "is a masterpiece and will appeal to free men everywhere," the President directly asked Churchill to make one last effort to prevent a breakdown of talks. Though American opinion was now as critical of the Indians as of the British for the failure of negotiations, Roosevelt urged Churchill to believe that Britain would ultimately bear the chief burden for the deadlock. "If the present negotiations are allowed to collapse because of the issues as presented to the American people," Roosevelt cabled the Prime Minister on April 11, "and India should subsequently be successfully invaded by Japan with attendant serious military or naval defeats for our side, the prejudicial reaction on American public opinion can hardly be over-estimated." Urging him to make one more effort to solve the problem along the lines described in his message of March 10, Roosevelt predicted that any subsequent failure would then "clearly be placed upon the Indian people and not upon the British Government." [15]

Roosevelt was not using American opinion as a stalking-horse for some higher moral purpose or principally to save the Allied cause from a self-inflicted defeat in India. His largest concern was with the impact of reverses in India on American feeling toward Britain. Roosevelt's first priority was a stable, smoothly working Anglo-American alliance. His fundamental concern was not India's independence or even the prevention of a temporary defeat in Asia if that meant jeopardizing Anglo-American cooperation. His desire to extend the Indian negotiations rested chiefly on a wish to forestall developments that might undermine effective unity with Britain.

The President's handling of similar British difficulties with Burma illustrates the point. During the first four months of 1942, when the Japanese systematically overran Burma, British unwillingness to satisfy nationalist demands had weakened Burmese resistance. But unlike Indian pressure for independence, Burmese demands stirred little interest in the United States. Roosevelt, therefore, saw no need to press the case for Burma's independence with Churchill. On the contrary, he wholeheartedly supported British resistance to it. In January, when Churchill had asked his help in transporting Burma's Prime Minister U Saw from Lisbon to the Middle East, where the British could arrest him for communicating with the Japanese after unsuccessful talks in London, Roosevelt was happy to comply. In April, moreover, at the height of the difficulties over India, and perhaps as a means of easing the tension generated by them, Roosevelt sent Churchill information about other Burmese leaders who were negotiating with the Japanese. "I have never liked Burma or the Burmese!" he added. "And you people must have had a terrible time with them for the last fifty years. Thank the Lord you have HE-SAW, WE-SAW, YOU-SAW under lock and key. I wish you could put the whole bunch of them into a frying pan with a wall around it and let them stew in their own juice." [16]

While Churchill welcomed Roosevelt's support on Burma, he firmly turned aside his suggestion of April 11 on India. Explaining that Cripps's departure from India made it too late to do anything, Churchill also declared that he could not take responsibility for the defense of India if he had to throw everything again "into the melting pot at this critical juncture. . . . Anything like a serious difference between you and me," he ended, "would break my heart and surely deeply injure both our countries at the height of this terrible struggle." To Hopkins he said that he would rather resign than give ground on the issue, and in his memoirs he was scathing about the President's proposal. "I was thankful that events had already made such an act of madness impossible. . . . The President's mind was back in the American War of Independence, and he thought of the Indian problem in terms of the thirteen colonies fighting George III." Since Roosevelt's chief objective was to preserve an effective working relationship with the British, he now resisted suggestions that he press the issue further with Churchill.[17]

At the same time that Roosevelt was working for unity with Britain, he was also struggling for harmony with China. Although he was unwilling on strategic grounds to make China a major war theater, he was eager to keep the Japanese fighting there and equally eager to avoid the blow to Allied morale from a Chinese collapse. Roosevelt therefore did all he could to give Chiang a sense of central participation in the war. In December, in response to Chiang's request for a full-scale military alliance, Roosevelt had arranged military conferences in Chungking and Singapore which were to provide campaign plans for consideration at the Arcadia talks in Washington. The principal result of the meeting in Chungking, however, was open hostility between Chiang and Britain's General Wavell. Outraged by British confiscation of Lend-Lease supplies in Burma and Wavell's rejection of all but one Chinese division for Burma's defense, Chiang communicated his displeasure to Washington and threatened to turn his back on the British.

The dispute made Roosevelt all the more eager to bolster Chiang's morale. At the Arcadia Conference he persuaded the British to make Chiang the Supreme Commander of the United Powers in China, Thailand, and Indochina, to establish a joint planning staff in Chungking, and to create links between Chiang and other Allied headquarters in India and the Southwest Pacific. "Such arrangements," FDR told Chiang, "would enable your counsel and influence to be given effect in the formulation of the general strategy for the conduct of the war in all theaters." To give Chiang's "seat of operations a recognition and dignity which we have not thus far afforded" them, it was also decided to send "one of our most important [military] figures to China." "The finger of destiny," as Stimson put it, pointed at "Vinegar Joe" Stilwell, one of the Army's best corps commanders. He was appointed Commander of United States Army Forces in China, Burma, and India, and he was also to be Chief of Staff to Chiang.

Roosevelt's insistence on a strong positive approach to the Chinese bothered Churchill. He later complained that in Washington he had "found the extraordinary significance of China in American minds, even at the top, strangely out of proportion." The Americans "accorded China almost an equal fighting power with the British Empire," and compared the Chinese Army favorably with that of Russia. "I told the President," Churchill recalled, "how much I felt American opinion overestimated the contribution which China could make to the general war. He differed strongly," citing China's huge population and postwar potential. But Churchill discounted this talk of the future alongside of current problems, and declared himself unwilling "to adopt . . . a wholly unreal standard of values." "If I can epitomise in one word the lesson I learned in the United States," he informed Wavell after returning from Washington, "it was 'China.' " [18]

Roosevelt appreciated better than Churchill the extraordinary grip China held on American opinion. She was the favorite ally. Untainted by Communism or imperialism, a victim rather than a practitioner of power politics, China above all was seen as America's natural democratic ally. When Roosevelt praised America's allies in his annual message to the Congress on January 6, 1942, his tribute to the "brave people of China . . . who for four and a half years have withstood bombs and starvation and have whipped the invaders time and again," received the loudest and most spontaneous applause. Between 80 and 86 per cent of those questioned in polls in 1942 expressed the belief that China could be depended upon to cooperate with the United States during and after the war. In May 1942, when asked whether Stalin, Chiang, or Churchill had the most support from their people, 23 per cent of a survey chose Chiang, 24 per cent picked Churchill, and 30 per cent selected Stalin. Almost two years later, when pollsters asked Americans which countries they would like to have the greatest say in an international organization, 63 per cent included China along with Britain, Russia, and the United States.

Roosevelt had a far better appreciation of China's limitations than Churchill's recollections suggest. In treating China as a great power, he was acting less out of personal conviction than from a desire to encourage the Chinese and satisfy widespread feeling in the United States that China be accorded a major role in world affairs. In designating Chiang as Supreme Commander of the United Powers in China, Thailand, and Indochina, he appreciated that Chiang was not "getting much of a command." With few Allied troops to lead in China and no operations planned against Japanese control in Thailand or Indochina, Chiang was left to command the same forces and area he had controlled before becoming Supreme Commander. Even more telling, the Chinese were given no place on the Combined Chiefs of Staff. It was a case of all shadow and no substance.[19]

Roosevelt had given some indication of his approach to China in a discussion with Stilwell in February before he left on his mission. Stilwell was not impressed with the President, whom he described as "cordial and pleasant—and frothy." Roosevelt "rambled on about his idea of the war . . . 'a 28,000 mile front. . . . ' " He did not want Chiang to think that Hitler was the one enemy. "The real strategy," FDR said, "is to fight them *all*." "Just a lot of wind," Stilwell believed. "After I had enough, I broke in and asked him if he had a message for Chiang Kai-shek. He very obviously had not and talked for five minutes hunting around for something world-shaking to say. Finally, he had it—'Tell him we are in this thing for keeps, and we intend to keep at it until China gets back *all* her lost territory.' Then he went on to say he thought it best for Madame Chiang not to come here, as invited by some organization or other. It would be too much like a lecture tour of women's clubs."

Behind Roosevelt's pleasant banter were the outlines of his China policy. Determined to pursue a Europe-first strategy which precluded immediate large-scale help to China, he tried to encourage Chiang with assurances of China's central place in the Allied coalition and a promise of ultimate gain—the return of lost territories. In addition, fearful that a visit by Madame Chiang would stir domestic pressures for greater help to China, he asked that she be discouraged from coming. In short, having decided that China would not bulk large in the immediate war effort, he wished to keep her going and forestall demands for greater help by feeding illusions about her status and emphasizing long-term gains.[20]

Roosevelt, however, could not foster these illusions without some measure of substantive support. In the winter of 1941–42, this principally took the form of a $500 million loan. At the end of December, Chiang had requested the money as a means to strengthen China's economy, especially against an accelerating inflation. Though practically everyone having anything to do with the request, including the President, was skeptical of its economic value, they supported the demand. Clarence Gauss, the American Ambassador to China, believed that only $10 million was enough to hold the line against inflation, and expected a larger credit to end up in the hands of "the retrogressive, self-seeking, and . . . fickle elements" associated with Chiang; but he acknowledged that there might be psychological benefits from giving the help. Likewise, Roosevelt and Morgenthau appreciated that there would likely be no return on the loan and that the money might be squandered. As a bar against the latter, they asked Chiang to let them pay part of the money directly to China's soldiers in the form of a special currency FDR wished to call the D-E-M-O. As Morgenthau described it to his staff, "I was trying to think of some way so that while the boys fight they get their money, and if they don't fight, no money."

When Chiang rejected the scheme and "urgently" asked the loan without security or other prearranged terms, the President gave in. "Nothing but blackmail," Litvinov told Morgenthau. "Yes," the Secretary agreed. Though members of Congress also had their doubts about the economic consequences of such a loan, a resolution supporting it swept through both houses without debate. It was considered a political and military loan aimed at bolstering Chiang's government and keeping China in the war. It "testified," Roosevelt wrote Chiang in a calculated overstatement, "to the wholehearted respect and admiration which the government and people of this country have for China."

Similarly, for the sake of continued Chinese resistance, Roosevelt pushed the development of a dangerous and costly air supply route to

China. By the beginning of February 1942, the impending loss of Rangoon and the closing of the Burma Road made Roosevelt extremely anxious to find new ways of getting goods to Chiang. "Miraculously enough that new life line is conveniently at hand," T. V. Soong advised FDR. It was an air route of only 700 miles from northeast India to Kunming "over comparatively level stretches." Though Soong was referring to the treacherous crossing of the Himalayas, which threatened great loss of life and would not accommodate the delivery of heavy supplies, the pressure to do something for China persuaded Roosevelt and his advisers to accept Soong's idea. Nine days later, the President sent Chiang "definite assurances" that supplies would continue to come to China via India by air.[21]

By the end of January, Allied defeats in the Pacific had opened rifts in both Britain and the United States which intensified Roosevelt's concern with unity. During the first two months of fighting, the Japanese had captured Guam and Wake Island, destroyed American air power in the Philippines and seized Manila, brought Singapore under siege by overrunning the Malay Peninsula, endangered Australia by entering Borneo, the Celebes, New Guinea, and the Solomon Islands, and launched their offensive against Rangoon which threatened to close the Burma Road. On his return to Britain from Washington in January, Churchill found "an embarrassed, unhappy, baffled public opinion . . . swelling and mounting about me on every side." Deciding to meet the issue head-on, he asked for a vote of confidence from the House of Commons. After three days of debate, he won a resounding mandate, 464 to 1. "Congratulations on yesterday's vote," Roosevelt cabled him in relief. "We also had one vote in opposition" on the war declaration against Japan.[22]

These reverses in the Far East also gave Roosevelt difficulties with American public opinion. By early February, the unrelieved bad news from the Pacific had weakened the upsurge of enthusiasm produced by Pearl Harbor and had brought on a national mood of apathy or seeming indifference to the fighting. Asked at a press conference on February 10 to comment on the "complacency" in the country, the President acknowledged its existence, but also described the public as becoming more and more realistic "every day . . . in regard to the existing situation." This public demoralization, however, greatly worried him, particularly the rising call for a Pacific-first strategy which urged an all-out effort against Japan at the expense of Britain and Russia. A February poll, for example, showed 62 per cent of the public in favor of concentrating all or most of the country's war effort against Japan, with only 25 per cent preferring to focus principally on the defeat of Hitler. This mentality, Roosevelt complained in another press conference, was encouraged by distortions, such as the contention that "the British want to fight to the last American," or the argument that helping Russia now would allow her to "turn on us later."

The loss of Singapore on February 15, 1942, "the greatest disaster to British arms" in history, Churchill called it, added to this feeling in the United States. The fall of Singapore "gives the well-known back-seat drivers a field day," Roosevelt cabled Churchill, "but no matter how serious our setbacks have been, and I do not for a moment underrate them, we must constantly look forward to the next moves that need to be made to hit the enemy." Thanking the President for his "warm-hearted telegram," Churchill confided: "I do not like these days of personal stress and I have found it difficult to keep my eye on the ball. . . . Democracy has to prove that it can provide a granite foundation for war against tyranny."

Because he temporarily lacked the means to improve morale by hitting the enemy, Roosevelt resorted to reassuring words. Using Washington's Birthday as an "appropriate occasion for us to talk with each other about things as they are today and things as we know they shall be in the future," FDR gave one of his most effective Fireside Chats. Describing the "fearful men" of Washington's day who called his cause hopeless and urged a negotiated peace, Roosevelt depicted "Washington's conduct in those hard times" as a "model for all Americans ever since—a model of moral stamina." To meet the arguments of those who wished to fight principally in the Pacific, or only for narrowly conceived American interests, he asked the nation to understand that they were fighting "a new kind of war," which involved "every continent, every island, every sea, every air lane in the world." He warned against "the old familiar Axis policy of 'divide and conquer,' " or the separation of the United States, Britain, China, and Russia from each other. Axis propagandists, he added, "are now trying to destroy our confidence in our own allies. They say that the British are finished—that the Russians and the Chinese are about to quit. Patriotic and sensible Americans will reject these absurdities."

To rekindle some of the hope that had been lost in the series of recent defeats, Roosevelt confidently promised future victories. "We have most certainly suffered losses," he acknowledged, ". . . and we shall suffer more of them before the turn of the tide. . . . We Americans have been compelled to yield ground but we will regain it. . . . We are daily increasing our strength. Soon, we and not our enemies will have the offensive; we, not they, will win the final battles; and we, not they, will make the final peace." Concluding with reminders of how much the British and the Russians and the Chinese had endured without yielding, he called their resistance "the conquering spirit which prevails throughout the United Nations in this war." [23]

Though Roosevelt's speech calmed "jangled editorial nerves" and produced a dramatic upsurge in public hope, additional defeats in the Pacific in March created fresh dissension at home. Between February 27 and March 9, the Japanese destroyed Allied naval forces in the Java Sea and conquered the Dutch East Indies, placing Australia and India in "dire danger." Forty-seven per cent of the public now felt that unless "we worked a lot harder" the United States would not be able to beat Japan; yet only 56 per cent of the public favored sending as much of the Army and Navy abroad as possible to defeat the Axis. The administration's direction of the Pacific war and mobilization of national resources now also came under a barrage of press criticism. More than ever, the country wished to make its principal effort against Japan.

Roosevelt tried to answer some of these complaints and counter some of this divisiveness through press releases. On March 12 he announced through a letter to the Economic Club of New York that "the supreme achievement of enemy propaganda would be to create disunity. Those who cry for divided efforts in an indivisible war," he declared, ". . . those who encourage divided counsels in this crisis, [and] . . . viciously or stupidly lend themselves to the repetition of distortion and untruth, are serving as obliging messengers of Axis propaganda." In a press conference on the 17th, he used a quotation from the Roman historian Livy to attack "typewriter strategists," whose criticisms, as in ancient times, interfered "with the successful prosecution of a war."

He also ridiculed suggestions that strikes were reducing the country's war output. Telling reporters about an economist who believed that the Allies had lost the Philippines, the Indies, and Singapore because of strikes, Roosevelt said: "The dear fellow wrote to me . . . honestly believing it. And I wrote him back: . . . do you realize that if it hadn't been for the common cold in America today, we would be in Berlin?" If not for "that scourge of Satan, called the common cold, we could understandably have had enough planes and guns and tanks to overrun Europe, Africa and the whole of Asia. Take good care of yourself," he ended. "Don't go on strike and for God's sake don't catch a common cold."

Though some supporters urged the President to take his case directly to the people once more by going on the air again, he resisted the suggestion. "The one thing I dread," he told one proponent of the idea, "is that my talks should be so frequent as to lose their effectiveness." "From now on, for the duration of the war," he wrote another, "there are going to be periods of hysteria, misinformation, volcanic eruptions, etc., and if I start the practice of going on the air to answer each one, the value will soon disappear. . . . For the sake of not becoming a platitude to the public, I ought not to appear oftener than once every five or six weeks." Besides, he also said, the real trouble was not with the people or their leaders, but with "a gang" of "mostly" pre-Pearl Harbor isolationists, who encouraged disunity and even wanted a negotiated peace. This "gang" consisted of newspaper publishers, columnists, radio commentators, political opportunists, racial and religious fanatics "like the K.K.K.

crowd," and "extreme nationalists like some of the wild Irish." He thought the journalist Elmer Davis had best described their motives when he said: "Some people want the United States to win so long as England loses. Some people want the United States to win so long as Russia loses. And some people want the United States to win so long as Roosevelt loses." [24]

To blunt these critics and strengthen morale at home and among America's allies, Roosevelt saw the need for both symbolic and substantive blows against the enemy. Toward the first end, he ordered General Douglas MacArthur to leave the Philippines for Australia, where he was to assume command of American forces in the Southwest Pacific. Chief of Staff of the United States Army from 1929 to 1935 and Commander of all U.S. forces in the Far East since being recalled to active duty in November 1941, MacArthur, whose strong defense of the Philippines had greatly slowed the Japanese conquest of the Islands and given Americans their only taste of effective military action in the war, impressed FDR as the best bet for rallying ABDA forces for the defense of Australia. Reaching his destination in mid-March after a dangerous journey, MacArthur bolstered Allied spirits with the declaration that he had broken through enemy lines to organize the American offensive against Japan, including the relief of the Philippines. "I came through," he said in a memorable pronouncement, "and I shall return."

More substantively, Roosevelt helped develop a bold plan for sixteen Army B-25's to bomb Tokyo and other cities from an aircraft carrier 500 miles off Japan. After striking their targets, the planes were to head for airfields in eastern China. On April 18, despite less than a month's training and the decision, forced by fear of detection, to launch the planes in rough seas almost 700 miles from the coast, the aircraft, led by Lieutenant Colonel James H. Doolittle, all managed to bomb Japan and escape without being shot down. Though none of the planes found their way to the Chinese airfields and had to be crash-landed or abandoned when they ran out of fuel, only five of the eighty crew members involved in the raid lost their lives. The news elated Roosevelt and the nation. To guard the secret of how the bombers had reached Japan, the President announced that "they came from our new secret base at Shangri-La (the mythical Asian paradise in James Hilton's popular novel of the mid-1930s, Lost Horizon)." [25]

Roosevelt's decision in February 1942 to intern all the Japanese on the West Coast of the United States had been another way to relieve feelings of powerlessness toward Japan and quiet a potentially divisive issue. A government report on Pearl Harbor describing widespread espionage by resident Japanese before the attack, together with false reports of espionage and potential sabotage and long-standing racial antagonism, had joined together at the end of January to produce an outcry from the

Pacific Coast for the prompt removal of the Japanese to the interior. Though it was clear to FDR that any action against aliens and citizens alike would stand on shaky constitutional ground and that a failure to take similar action against all Germans and Italians would encourage charges of racial discrimination, he nevertheless gave the War Department carte blanche to do what it thought necessary, asking only that it be as reasonable as possible. As a consequence, some 110,000 Japanese were "relocated" in "concentration camps," as Roosevelt called them, where most of them lived in mass discomfort and psychic distress through most of the war. Though represented at the time as a "military necessity," the action, in fact, had no sound military justification, and, in the view of the American Civil Liberties Union, was "the worst single wholesale violation of civil rights of American citizens in our history."

For Roosevelt, however, these considerations were secondary alongside of War Department assertions of "military necessity" and public demands for action. "I do not think he [FDR] was much concerned with the gravity or implications of this step," his Attorney General, Francis Biddle, later wrote. "He was never theoretical about things. What must be done to defend the country must be done. . . . The military might be wrong. But they were fighting the war. Public opinion was on their side, so that there was no question of any substantial opposition, which might tend toward the disunity that at all costs he must avoid."

As James MacGregor Burns has pointed out, "Roosevelt was not a strong civil libertarian," and "the wartime White House was not dependably a source of strong and sustained support for civil liberties in specific situations." Indeed, in the midst of the war, Roosevelt had little patience with traditional rights that in any way jeopardized the war effort. "That delightful god . . . 'The Freedom of the Press'" he told Churchill in March of 1942, was one of the "additional burdens" by which they were "both menaced" in time of war. To meet some of the difficulty, Roosevelt pressed Biddle for judicial action against critics of his war policies. When the Attorney General described himself as reluctant to do anything unless there were clear evidence of sedition, the President pressed him all the harder. Roosevelt "was not much interested in the theory of sedition, or in the constitutional right to criticize the government in wartime," Biddle recalled. "He wanted this antiwar talk stopped."

His diminished concern for individual rights extended to other situations as well. "Have you pretty well cleaned out the alien waiters in the principal Washington hotels?" he inquired of J. Edgar Hoover in April 1942. "Altogether too much conversation in the dining rooms!" In June, when he received reports that private transatlantic telephone calls to Sweden, Switzerland, Vichy, Spain, and Portugal might be the source of Nazi information on American ship movements, he insisted on ending diplomatic as well as private telephone communications to those countries and instructed that only government messages by specific officials be permitted "—and then these would be monitored." In sum, he felt that arbitrariness in wartime was an unpleasant but necessary reality. "I am perfectly willing to mislead and tell untruths," he had told Morgenthau in May 1942, "if it will help win the war."

Roosevelt's hypocrisy in these matters is striking. At a time when he was contrasting Nazi "barbarism" with "the great upsurge of human liberty" embodied in the American Bill of Rights and the American conception of individual freedom, he was breaking constitutional guarantees by interning American-born Japanese, urging limitations on freedom of the press and sanctioning invasions of individual privacy. He was not acting out of some general desire to destroy American freedoms or, as some have charged, to make himself the country's "first dictator." On the other hand, he was aware that his actions violated the Constitution and constituted racial bias against the Japanese. But he undoubtedly justified these actions to himself by seeing them as expedient. Military necessity suggested that these things be done, and he faced no opposition that might have made him think more carefully about these measures. "There was practically no discussion of the plan [to evacuate the Japanese] and I interjected nothing," Harold Ickes recorded after the Cabinet considered the issue. "However, I feel it is both stupid and cruel." Roosevelt's action in interning the Japanese was of a piece with his policies toward the Spanish Civil War and Jewish refugees from Nazi persecution. Each of these issues required him to take a stand on grounds of principle against prevailing political, military and/or foreign opinion. But this he would not do. In these matters, there is considerable truth in Clare Booth Luce's observation that "every great leader had his typical gesture—Hitler the upraised arm, Churchill the V sign. Roosevelt? She wet her index finger and held it up." [26]

Roosevelt appreciated that the best way to silence wartime critics was with effective military action. By the beginning of March, Japanese victories had forced a fresh discussion in Washington of where and how this could be done. The immediate catalyst for this was a "gloomy" telegram from Churchill to FDR on March 7 lamenting the grave deterioration of affairs since December 7, asking for the reinforcement of Australia and New Zealand by additional American troops, and declaring that further British reverses in North Africa and an unrelieved want of ships were continuing bars to GYMNAST. In a discussion at the White House on the following day, Roosevelt's military advisers rejected the Prime Minister's "appeal for further dispersion on the already over-extended world front." Disturbed by the erosion of a Europe-first strategy through growing ad hoc commitments in the Pacific, Stimson and Army planners urged a prompt buildup in Britain which, by threatening to attack the Germans in France, would relieve the Russian front and stimulate sagging British morale.

The proposal strongly appealed to FDR. In two long cables to Churchill on March 7 and 9, he outlined this emerging strategy. Acknowledging that "the Pacific situation is now very grave" and that the command arrangements they had made in January were "largely . . . obsolescent," he agreed to send two additional Army divisions to Australia and New Zealand, and suggested that operational responsibility for the Pacific be entirely in American hands. Further, a "middle area" extending from Singapore and India to the Middle East was to come under direct British control, with all operational matters there decided by them. Thirdly, there was to be joint Anglo-American responsibility for the Atlantic region, where they should formulate "definite plans for [the] establishment of a new front on the European continent. . . . I am becoming more and more interested in the establishment of this new front this summer, certainly for air and raids," he told Churchill. ". . . And even though losses will doubtless be great, such losses will be compensated by at least equal German losses and by compelling [the] Germans to divert large forces of all kinds from Russian fronts." "This may be a critical period," he also told Churchill, "but remember always it is not as bad as some you have so well survived before." [27]

This plan also allowed Roosevelt to resist Russian demands for recognition of their 1941 frontiers. In December, when Britain's Foreign Secretary Anthony Eden had gone to Moscow to discuss ways of strengthening Anglo-Russian ties, Stalin had asked for formal acceptance of the Soviet Union's June 1941 boundaries. In substance, Britain was to recognize the Soviet annexation of the Baltic states, the territories gained from Finland and Roumania, and the eastern parts of Poland seized in 1939. At the time, Eden held Stalin off with the explanation that Britain had promised the United States not to make territorial arrangements before the end of the war, though he also promised to reopen the issue with Washington. When Churchill and Roosevelt discussed the subject at the Arcadia Conference, they agreed that their acceptance of Stalin's demands "would be contrary to all the principles for which we are fighting" and that frontier questions must be left for settlement at a peace conference. For Roosevelt, the discussion of Stalin's postwar territorial aims would not only violate accepted American standards of international morality as expressed in the Atlantic Charter but would also jeopardize domestic and Allied unity.

In February, Churchill found himself under growing pressure to accommodate the Soviet demands. His War Cabinet believed that both wartime and postwar cooperation with the Soviet Union required some kind of commitment to its future security. If Soviet territorial demands were not to be accepted, it seemed wise to promise Anglo-American support of postwar Soviet bases in, or control over the foreign and defense policies of, strategically adjacent states. When Halifax consulted Roosevelt and Welles about this idea, however, they rejected it as contrary to the Atlantic Charter and as likely to have a "disastrous" impact on American opinion. Instead, the President declared his intention to deal directly with Stalin, with whom he was confident he could reach agreement.

Unconvinced that the President could budge Stalin and disturbed by hints that the Soviets might reach an accommodation with Hitler if they lacked confidence in Anglo-American intentions, Churchill pressed Roosevelt to endorse his acceptance of Stalin's demands. "The increasing gravity of the war," he cabled the President on March 7, "has led me to feel that the principles of the Atlantic Charter ought not to be construed so as to deny Russia the frontiers she occupied when Germany attacked her. . . . I hope . . . that you will be able to give us a free hand to sign the treaty which Stalin desires as soon as possible. Everything portends an immense renewal of the German invasion of Russia in the spring and there is very little we can do to help the only country that is heavily engaged with the German armies."

Though sensitive to Churchill's concern, Roosevelt was confident that Russia would not "quit the war" over the boundary issue and believed that he could solve difficulties with Stalin through a combination of personal assurances and a European offensive. As he told Morgenthau on March 11, the Russians did not trust the English because after promising them two divisions and help in the Caucasus, they had failed to deliver. "Every promise the English have made to the Russians, they have fallen down on. . . . The only reason we stand so well with the Russians is that up to date we have kept our promises." He also said that "nothing would be worse than to have the Russians collapse. . . . I would rather lose New Zealand, Australia or anything else than have the Russians collapse."

Roosevelt now asked Litvinov to tell Stalin that territorial arrangements before the end of the war would have an explosive effect on American public opinion and that it was in Russia's interest for American sentiment to favor close cooperation with the U.S.S.R. He also declared himself in full sympathy with postwar "measures of legitimate security" for the Soviet Union, including guarantees against another German attack. In a letter to Churchill on March 18, Roosevelt promised shortly to send a more definite plan for a joint attack in Europe, and expressed the belief that he could "personally handle Stalin better than either your Foreign Office or my State Department. Stalin hates the guts of all your top people. He thinks he likes me better, and I hope he will continue to do so."

Stalin, however, promptly deflated this idea by dismissing the President's message with a curt acknowledgment and by continuing to press the British for a formal agreement on postwar frontiers. When the British informed Roosevelt of their intention to go ahead, he reiterated his opposition and urged that the agreement include a Soviet pledge to allow people in annexed territories to emigrate freely with their property. The Russians also rejected this proposal.[28]

Roosevelt now sought to overcome public demoralization in the United States and Britain and head off an Anglo-Soviet agreement on frontiers by pressing plans for a European attack. On April 1, Stimson and Marshall put a plan before him which largely met these aims. As developed by Army planners under the direction of General Dwight D. Eisenhower, the proposal called for a buildup of some 48 divisions and 5800 planes for an assault on Western Europe about April 1, 1943. In the meantime, to meet the need for earlier action, they proposed the introduction of air and coastal raids on Europe beginning in the summer of 1942. It was also agreed that if conditions on the Russian front threatened a collapse, or if Germany greatly reduced its strength in Western Europe in the immediate future, an emergency invasion would be launched in the fall of 1942.

Roosevelt at once gave the plan his complete support and put it before Churchill. "I have come to certain conclusions which are so vital," he cabled the Prime Minister the same day, "that I want you to know the whole picture and to ask your approval. . . . Harry and Marshall will leave for London in a few days to present . . . the salient points. It is a plan which I hope Russia will greet with enthusiasm and, on word from you . . . I propose to ask Stalin to send two special representatives to see me at once. I think it will work out in full accord with trends of public opinion here and in Britain. And, finally, I would like to be able to label it the plan of the United Nations." In a follow-up message Roosevelt gave Hopkins for Churchill on April 3, he explained that "what Harry and Geo. Marshall will tell you all about has my heart and *mind* in it. Your people and mine demand the establishment of a front to draw off pressure on the Russians, and these people are wise enough to see that the Russians are today killing more Germans and destroying more equipment than you and I put together. Even if full success is not attained, the *big* objective will be." After arriving in London, Hopkins also impressed on Eden "the President's belief that our main proposal here should take the heat off Russia's diplomatic demands upon England."

In discussions with Churchill and his military chiefs between April 8 and 14, Hopkins and Marshall received agreement "in principle" to the American plan for a major European offensive in 1943 and an emergency landing, if necessary, in 1942. Yet Churchill and his advisers, as Hopkins and Marshall appreciated, had serious reservations. They emphasized their concern first to strengthen Britain's position in Egypt and the Indian Ocean to prevent a linkup of German and Japanese forces "somewhere east of Suez and west of Singapore." They also had grave doubts about the feasibility of any cross-Channel assault in 1942, explaining that insufficient troops, fighter planes, and landing craft would make this a "sacrificial" operation which would dangerously weaken the security of the British Isles. Lastly, Churchill himself did not think a cross-Channel strike against Cherbourg or Brest, fortified German positions, nearly as attractive or helpful as simultaneous attacks on French North Africa and northern Norway: the first was "possible and sound," and the second meant direct, combined action with Russia and a possible new avenue for Russian supplies. But eager not to weaken American determination to give Germany priority over Japan, Churchill encouraged the buildup of forces in the British Isles and voiced no preference for North African or Norwegian operations over a cross-Channel assault in 1942. Under closer study, he believed the latter would fall of its own weight.[29]

British agreement in principle to a European attack allowed Roosevelt to take up the matter with the Russians. On April 11, after hearing from Hopkins that British support for their plan was in the offing, the President had informed Stalin that he had a "very important military proposal" for relieving his "critical western front," and he asked the opportunity to discuss it with Soviet Foreign Minister Molotov and a trusted Soviet General. On the 20th, six days after Roosevelt had told Litvinov the details of his plan, Stalin assented to "a meeting between V. M. Molotov and you for an exchange of views on the organization of a second front in Europe in the near future." Since Stalin also indicated that Molotov would go to London, where he was to reach a final agreement on Soviet frontiers, Roosevelt suggested to Churchill that Molotov come to the United States first. Churchill answered, however, that he did not feel free to suggest a change in the order of Molotov's visits and would feel compelled to reach agreement with him on a treaty. He promised to ask him, though, to go to Washington before anything was finally signed.

Molotov's trips to London and Washington took on additional meaning in early May when Roosevelt had to alert Stalin to the possibility of reduced supply shipments. By late April, increasingly effective German attacks on convoys to Murmansk and Archangel had decided the British to reduce the number and size of convoys on this principal supply route and to suggest a new understanding with the Russians on the amount of matériel they would receive. "In view of the impending assault on their armies" and "the very disquieting impression" it would leave in Russia, Roosevelt asked Churchill not to raise the issue with Stalin and to push ahead with planned convoys. But when Churchill responded that this was "beyond our power to fulfill" and begged the President "not to press us beyond our judgment," Roosevelt promised to ask the Russians to reduce their requirements to "absolute essentials" on the grounds that they needed all possible munitions and shipping for the buildup in Britain. "We are having grave difficulties with the northern convoy route and have informed Litvinov of the complications," he told Stalin on May 4. "You may be sure, however, that no effort will be omitted to get as many ships off as possible." [30]

Stalin was ready to give ground on convoys and postwar boundaries for the sake of an early second front. By May 1942, in spite of successful winter counterattacks and a spring offensive to disrupt German campaign plans, Soviet ability to deal with fresh German assaults against Leningrad in the north and vital production centers in the south seemed at best uncertain. In his first meeting with Churchill and Eden in London on May 21, Molotov candidly declared their talks about a second front more important than those concerning the treaty. Indeed, when the British stubbornly resisted additional Soviet territorial demands and, in conjunction with U.S. Ambassador John Winant, emphasized the negative impact an agreement on frontiers would have in the United States, Molotov agreed to substitute a twenty-year mutual security pact that omitted any reference to borders. "I am certain that this treaty will be of great importance in promoting friendly relations . . . between our two countries and the United States," Stalin cabled Churchill. The Prime Minister characterized this reaction as "almost purring." "We have done very good work . . . with Molotov," he informed Roosevelt, "and . . . we have completely transformed the treaty proposals. They are now . . . free from the objections we both entertained, and are entirely compatible with our Atlantic Charter."

Soviet flexibility on the treaty was not reciprocated with any assurance on a second front. When Molotov inquired whether the Allies would draw German forces from Russia in 1942 by an assault on Western Europe, Churchill was quick to discourage the hope. Explaining that they lacked sufficient landing craft to make an effective invasion, he asserted that an unsound operation which ended in disaster would be of no value to either Russia or the Allies. When Molotov responded by raising the possibility of a Soviet collapse, Churchill assured him that "our fortunes were bound up with the resistance of the Soviet Army," and that Britain and the United States intended to share fully "in conquering the evil foe." Churchill now also put his reservations about a 1942 attack before the President. At FDR's request, he sent a report on his discussion of a second front with Molotov, and asked Lord Louis Mountbatten, Churchill's Chief of Combined or Commando Operations, who was on his way to the United States, to "explain the difficulties of 1942" to the President. In a cable advising Roosevelt of Mountbatten's mission, Churchill also described his interest in a Norwegian operation and concluded: "We must never let GYMNAST pass from our minds." [31]

Roosevelt confronted these political and military problems directly with Molotov between May 29 and June 1. The difficulties of communicating with the Soviet Foreign Minister were as great, or greater, than any Roosevelt had yet met in his public career. The "enormous language" problem made him "unusually uncomfortable" and cramped his style. Also, he had "never before encountered anyone like Molotov." The Foreign Minister arrived in Washington with a chunk of black bread, a roll of sausage, and a pistol which he kept close at hand during the night. In England, Soviet police officers had thoroughly searched his room, meticulously examining cupboards, furniture, walls, floors, and mattresses for "infernal machines." Two Russian chambermaids, who kept constant watch over the room, rearranged the bedding so as to allow its occupant to arise at a moment's notice. As a signatory of the Nazi-Soviet pact and the 1941 neutrality agreement with Japan, Molotov had some reason to think that his Anglo-American hosts might wish him harm.

Roosevelt pursued three goals in these conversations. For one, he tried to encourage Soviet inclinations to leave frontier questions alone by offering assurances that their security needs could be met in other ways. On the first evening of their talks, when Molotov asked his views on the new Anglo-Soviet treaty, Roosevelt expressed pleasure over its omission of border questions, which he believed inappropriate to deal with then. That evening, and in a subsequent conversation on June 1, Roosevelt emphasized his desire for a postwar settlement that would disarm aggressor nations and leave the United States, Russia, Britain, and possibly China responsible for international security. Instead of "another League of Nations with 100 different signatories," the four "policemen," with a combined population of over one billion people, were to secure the peace. He also stated his belief that an end to colonial possessions would serve world peace by preventing postwar struggles for independence and that international trusteeships should be set up for former colonies until they were ready for self-government.

In putting these ideas before Molotov, Roosevelt was offering a sincere expression of postwar hopes. His desire for arms reduction and an effective replacement for the League of Nations were two long-standing aims. But his objective in stating them now was less to advance them than to diminish Soviet interest in territorial changes which would offend American opinion and weaken the Allied coalition. Indeed, as subsequent developments would show more clearly, Roosevelt was less concerned with the details of these postwar arrangements than with their impact on attitudes at home and abroad.

Roosevelt also tried to use the talks with Molotov to strengthen American and British commitments to a 1942 cross-Channel assault. On the evening of the 29th, when Molotov had raised the question of a second front, Roosevelt explained that he was thinking of a diversionary operation in 1942 consisting of ten divisions that would make a temporary landing on the Continent. When Molotov objected that a force of at least thirty-five divisions was necessary to relieve the Russian front, Roosevelt pointed out that he "had to reckon with" military chiefs, who leaned toward "a sure thing in 1943 to a risky adventure in 1942," and that Churchill probably shared their point of view. On the following morning, in a meeting with Molotov, Hopkins, Marshall, and Admiral Ernest J. King, the new Chief of Naval Operations, Roosevelt reported what Molotov had told him the night before: in London, the British had been polite but noncommittal on the question of a second front in Western Europe; German power in Russia made "the situation precarious"; and it was necessary to the Soviets that the Allies land sufficient troops on the Continent to draw off forty German divisions. The United States, FDR said, had an obligation to help the Soviets to the best of its ability, "even if the extent of this aid was for the moment doubtful." This, he added, raised the question of "what we can do even if the prospects for permanent success might not be especially rosy."

At Roosevelt's request, Molotov expanded on his remarks. He warned that Hitler might so strengthen his forces in Russia that "the Red Army might not be able to hold out." This would make Russia a "secondary" front, and Hitler, with Soviet raw materials at his disposal, would be able to fight a "tougher and longer" war. If Britain and the United States, however, were to open a new front that reduced German forces in Russia, "the ratio of strength would be so altered that the Soviets could either beat Hitler this year or insure . . . his ultimate defeat." Molotov then posed the question directly: "could we undertake such offensive action as would draw off 40 German divisions?" Instead of answering the question himself, Roosevelt asked Marshall "whether developments were clear enough so that we could say to Mr. Stalin that we are preparing a second front. 'Yes,' replied the General. The President then authorized Mr. Molotov to inform Mr. Stalin that we expect the formation of a second front this year." Troubled, however, by so strong a commitment, Marshall tried to qualify the President's statement by adding a description of the difficulties in the way of "a successful continental operation." Appreciating that a shortage of landing craft would make this a "sacrificial" assault, which his Army chiefs would ultimately feel compelled to resist, FDR used this conversation with Molotov to ask for Marshall's commitment to such an attack.

On the following day Roosevelt tried again to pin down his military chiefs on the question of a second front and to involve them in pressing the case with the British, who would have to provide the majority of the troops for a 1942 assault. In a conference with Marshall and King, he discussed the final statement he would make to Molotov. "He thought the matter was a little vague and the dangerous situation on the Russian front required that he, the President, make a more specific answer to Molotov in regard to a second front." He then read a cable he proposed to send Churchill, in which he described Molotov's anxiety about the coming months as "sincere and . . . not put forward for the purpose of forcing our hand." He described himself, therefore, as "more anxious than ever" for a cross-Channel attack beginning in August 1942 and for

Molotov to "carry back some real results of his mission and give a favorable report to Stalin." When Marshall objected to proposing an operation by August, warning that the British would strongly resist, Roosevelt agreed to ask only that action begin "in 1942." Roosevelt, however, would not make the date more flexible than that. At the end of the meetings, Molotov proposed a public statement saying that "full understanding was reached with regard to the urgent tasks of creating a second front in Europe in 1942." When Marshall urged that Roosevelt remove all references to a date, the President refused.

At his last meeting with Molotov on June 1, Roosevelt used his agreement to a second front to reduce supply commitments to Russia. To speed the opening of the new front, he told Molotov, he needed to reduce Lend-Lease goods for Russia from 4.1 to 2.5 millions tons in the coming year. Explaining that he intended to eliminate only nonmilitary items and that this would release shipping for the buildup in England, he declared that "the Soviets could not eat their cake and have it too." Molotov sarcastically replied that "the second front would be stronger if the first front still stood," and asked what would happen if the Soviets accepted these reductions "and then no second front eventuated." Molotov asked the President for specific reassurance on this point. Roosevelt answered that Anglo-American discussions of the operation were already in train and that "we expected to establish a second front." [32]

Appreciating, however, that the issue was less certain than his remarks indicated, Roosevelt followed Molotov's visit with fresh efforts to pin down the British and American military chiefs. "We are disturbed here about the Russian front and that anxiety is heightened by what appears to be a lack of clear understanding between us as to the precise military move that shall be made in the event the Russians get pushed around badly . . . ," Hopkins wrote Churchill on June 6. "I am sure there are certain matters of high policy which you must come to grips with the President on," Hopkins added, "and he is hopeful that you can make a quick trip and I fancy will be cabling you about it at once."

Roosevelt expressed his concern directly to Lord Mountbatten three days later. Stressing the great need to get American soldiers into battle as soon as possible, he wished to remind Churchill of their agreement to a "sacrifice landing" in France that summer if things went badly for the Russians. He expressed concern at the possibility of sending a million soldiers to England, where they would be immobilized if a Russian collapse made an assault on France impossible. When Mountbatten replied that the Allies could not land enough troops to compel German additions to the twenty-five divisions already in France, Roosevelt raised the possibility of sending American troops to the Middle East. He also asked Mountbatten to tell Churchill how much he had been struck by his recent injunction: "Do not lose sight of GYMNAST." In short, Roosevelt wished to help the Russians and bolster domestic morale by getting American forces into combat quickly, and if this were not possible in Western Europe, he was ready to open a battlefront in North Africa or the Middle East.

Churchill was also eager to discuss strategy with Roosevelt, especially after Molotov and Mountbatten reported their conversations with him. Determined to head off a "sacrifice landing" on the Continent in 1942, Churchill persuaded his War Cabinet that there should be no substantial landing in France unless they intended to remain and that there should be no such landing that year unless another failure against Russia demoralized the Germans. At the same time, he handed Molotov an aide-mémoire declaring that preparations were going forward for a cross-Channel assault in August or September, but said that limiting factors, especially a want of special landing craft, made it impossible for them to *promise* such an attack. "The Americans, with the best possible intentions," Eden told Molotov, "could not do much in 1942." Though a fierce battle was raging in the Libyan desert, where retreating British forces were once more trying to hold a line at Tobruk, Churchill returned to Washington on June 18 to settle "the grave strategic issues which were upon us." [33]

Roosevelt at once seized upon Churchill's visit to press his military advisers for a decision on relieving the Russian front. On June 17, the day before Churchill arrived, he had told Stimson, Knox, Marshall, King, and Arnold that his chief concern was to do something in 1942 that would help the Russians. "If the Russians held until December, he would give odds that we would win the war," while if they "folded up," he thought the Allies would have less than an even chance. He wished his advisers, therefore, to choose between three alternatives: a cross-Channel assault, which he preferred but now had doubts could be mounted that year; an invasion of North Africa by early September; or the dispatch of American forces to the Egyptian-Libyan border to support hard-pressed British forces. Though Stimson and Marshall at once offered "robust opposition" to an African or Middle East operation as "untimely, ineffectual" departures from a cross-Channel buildup, Roosevelt insisted they be considered as possible alternatives.

As Roosevelt had wished, Churchill's arrival in the United States forced consideration of American action in 1942. During initial talks on June 19 and 20 at Hyde Park, Churchill urged the case for GYMNAST, the invasion of North Africa. After giving assurances that he remained committed to a cross-Channel attack in 1943, Churchill then dwelt on the shortcomings of such an operation in 1942. An attack "that was certain to lead to disaster" would offer no help to the Russians, would expose French supporters to Nazi vengeance, and would gravely delay the main operation in 1943. "No responsible British military authority," Churchill emphasized, "has so far been able to make a plan for September 1942 which had any chance for success. . . . Have the American Staffs a plan? If so, what is it?" If there were none, Churchill wished to know what they were going to do. "Can we," he echoed Roosevelt's concern, "afford to stand idle in the Atlantic theatre during the whole of 1942? Ought we not to be preparing within the general structure of BOLERO [the buildup for a cross-Channel assault] some other operation by which we may . . . directly or indirectly . . . take some of the weight off Russia? It is in this setting and on this background that the operation GYMNAST should be studied."

Anticipating Churchill's argument, Stimson and the Chiefs of Staff attacked GYMNAST as a diversion that would weaken BOLERO and lengthen the war. On June 19, in a letter signed by Stimson and endorsed by the Chiefs, they told Roosevelt that the buildup in Britain was "the surest road" to the "shaking" of Hitler's 1942 Russian campaign and ultimate German defeat. The movement of American forces into Britain, they contended, had already produced "unmistakable signs of uneasiness in Germany as well as increasing unrest in the subject populations." Further, if Russia collapsed, the concentration of forces in Britain would help ward off a possible German attack, while GYMNAST would leave Britain vulnerable to such an assault. Finally, Germany could gain success in Russia over a prolonged period only by using increased forces, and that would make it easier for the Allies to attack France. "Thus German success against Russia, whether fast or slow, would seem to make requisite not a diversion from BOLERO but an increase in BOLERO as quickly as possible."

These arguments, however, did not answer Roosevelt's main concerns. The Stimson letter said nothing about bringing American troops into action in 1942, nor did it offer a realistic proposal for weakening German pressure on Russia. On the contrary, it seemed to accept the possibility of either prompt or long-term Russian defeat. Consequently, on June 20 Roosevelt asked Marshall and King to prepare a response to a general Russian retreat in July and a threatened loss of Leningrad, Moscow, and the Caucasus in August. Specifically, under these circumstances, he wished to know where American ground forces prior to September 15 could "plan and execute an attack" which would compel the withdrawal of German forces from the Russian front.

Discussions at the White House on the following day largely gave Roosevelt what he wished. Churchill and Marshall vigorously disputed the benefits and drawbacks of a European versus a North African assault in 1942, but they finally agreed to push preparations for a 1943 invasion of Europe as energetically as possible and to accept the "essential" need to prepare for offensive action in 1942. It was also agreed that a European front in 1942 would "yield greater political and strategic gains than operations in any other theatre," but that it should not be attempted if further close examination showed success to be "improbable." GYM-NAST was then to be considered as the possible alternative.

The outcome must have pleased FDR. By threatening to opt for GYM-NAST, he had forced his military chiefs to advocate a 1942 European attack. The difficulties involved in such an operation, Marshall now told him, were not "insurmountable." At a minimum, a cross-Channel attack would bring on a major air battle over Western Europe, which would be the greatest single aid they could then give Russia. Equally important to Roosevelt, if closer examination disputed Marshall's conclusions, there was now ample ground to push him and his fellow planners into a North African attack.

It remained clear, however, that the President's military advisers would resist any North African or Middle East operation as an impediment to the main business of a full-scale European attack. But in the midst of the talks on the 21st news arrived that Tobruk had fallen with 25,000 troops taken prisoners, and discussion then focused on the Middle East. The garrison's surrender to a force perhaps one half its size surprised and dismayed Churchill. "Defeat is one thing; disgrace is another," he later wrote. When Roosevelt without a hint of recrimination asked what the United States could do to help, Churchill asked for the prompt dispatch of as many new-model Sherman tanks as possible to the remaining British forces. Filling the request meant that American armored divisions would be left with obsolete equipment. "It is a terrible thing to take the weapons out of a soldier's hands," Marshall declared. But appreciating the urgency of the British need, he agreed to send 300 tanks and 100 large self-propelled guns. To make it easier for his advisers to accept the decision, Marshall told them that in return for the weapons the British had promised to maintain their commitment to a 1943 European attack.

Roosevelt's willingness to go beyond this help provoked the open resistance of his military advisers. At a late night discussion on the 21st, when the President suggested that the United States might consider putting a large force into the "denuded" Middle East between Alexandria and Tehran, Marshall complained "that that was such an overthrow of everything they had been planning for, he refused to discuss it at that time of night in any way" and walked out of the room. In another meeting on the 22nd, Stimson and Churchill engaged in a fresh debate on the virtues of GYMNAST. When the President again raised the possibility of sending a large force to the Middle East, Churchill, much to Stimson's relief, replied that he had no idea of asking that. Stimson nevertheless felt compelled to reiterate his support for BOLERO. As he later recorded, he had asserted that "we could only be ready next spring by making every effort to go ahead, but that if we were delayed by diversions I foresaw that BOLERO would not be made in '43 and that the whole war effort might be endangered."

Though Stimson and Marshall thought the President's attitude toward

BOLERO was "irresponsible" and that he spoke "with the frivolity and lack of responsibility of a child," Roosevelt's suggestion of a Middle East front expressed his deep concern not to lose Egypt, the Suez Canal, Syria, the Persian Gulf, and vital oil supplies. It also expressed his unrelieved concern to bring American troops into action against Germany in 1942. Though the conference ended on the 25th with the strategy decisions of the 21st intact, Roosevelt appreciated that the issue of precisely when and where the United States would act was still unresolved.[34]

In the two weeks after he returned to England, political and military developments moved Churchill to press for a commitment to GYMNAST. The defeat at Tobruk provoked a renewed attack on his leadership in the House of Commons. Though he overcame a Vote of Censure by a margin of 475 to 25, the challenge made him less receptive than ever to the military and political risks involved in an early cross-Channel attack. "My Diary for 1942," Churchill's physician later observed, "has the same backcloth to every scene: Winston's conviction that his life as Prime Minister could be saved only by a victory in the field." Consequently, on July 8, after British Chiefs reiterated their opposition to invading France in 1942, Churchill reported this conclusion to FDR. Not only would such an operation probably end in disaster, he advised, but it would also "decisively injure the prospects of well-organised large-scale action in 1943." Instead, he urged GYMNAST as by far the best chance for effective relief to Russia in 1942. "Here," he declared, "is the true second front of 1942. . . . Here is the safest and most fruitful stroke that can be delivered this autumn."

The British decision brought matters to a head between Roosevelt and his Chiefs. After learning of the British recommendation, Marshall and King sent Roosevelt a counterblast against GYMNAST as an indecisive operation that would undermine possibilities for a European invasion in 1943. They also recommended that if the British refused to "go through with full BOLERO plans," the United States should turn to the Pacific, where it would go all out against Japan. "My object," Marshall stated bluntly in an additional note, "is again to force the British into acceptance of a concentrated effort against Germany, and if this proves impossible to turn immediately to the Pacific."

Though Marshall meant the Pacific-first strategy as a bluff to deter the British and the President from GYMNAST, Roosevelt emphatically turned it aside. "My first impression," he told Marshall, "is that it is exactly what Germany hoped the United States would do following Pearl Harbor." Knowing that Marshall had no well-developed program for implementing this shift in strategy, he asked for a full, immediate exposition of the Pacific alternative, including a statement of its effects on the defense of Russia and the Middle East. When the Chiefs responded that they had no immediate plan to submit, nor any hopes of improving current strategic conditions with a Pacific campaign, Roosevelt informed Marshall that he would not accept their Pacific proposal, and wished him, King, and Hopkins to go to England immediately to work out a final agreement on plans for 1942. Marshall and his colleagues now concluded that "apparently our political system would require major operations this year in Africa."

The following day, July 15, Roosevelt thrashed matters out with Stimson and the Chiefs. In a series of meetings at the White House during the day, the President made it clear that there would be no shift to the Pacific and no threat or ultimatum to the British. The Marshall-King proposal, he said, was "a little like 'taking up your dishes and going away.'" He also called it "something of a red herring, the purpose of which he thoroughly understood," but he thought the Chiefs might wish to alter the record so that they would not appear later as wishing to abandon the British. At the same time, though, he vigorously supported the continued buildup in Britain for a European attack in 1943 and expressed displeasure with the quick British decision to abandon a cross-Channel assault in 1942.

In a detailed statement of his wishes for the London conference, Roosevelt instructed Hopkins, Marshall, and King to reach agreement with the British on "definite plans" for 1942 and "tentative" ones for 1943. "It is of the highest importance," he told them, "that U.S. ground troops be brought into action against the enemy in 1942." If at all possible, he wished this to be in France. But if SLEDGEHAMMER, the code name of the attack, were finally ruled out, he wanted a commitment to operations that would save the Middle East: either the dispatch of aid and ground forces to the Persian Gulf, Syria, and Egypt, or an attack through Morocco and Algiers which would "drive in against the backdoor of Rommel's armies." In any case, he wanted no all-out effort in the Pacific which would enhance German chances of completely dominating Europe and Africa. Japanese defeat, he reminded them, would not overcome Germany, but German defeat would mean victory over Japan. "The immediate objective," he reiterated at the close, was "U.S. ground forces fighting against Germans in 1942." [35]

A week of negotiations in London and a series of transatlantic cables finally brought the unity of strategic purpose Roosevelt wanted for 1942. It was not easily achieved. On July 18, after Marshall and King decided to begin their visit with staff talks in London rather than with Churchill in the country, where he had invited them, the Prime Minister threw a fit. Visitors should see him first, he angrily told Hopkins. The British Chiefs of Staff were under his command. Producing a book of Army regulations to prove his point, he tore out each page as he read it and threw it on the floor. "The Prime Minister threw the British Constitution at me," Hopkins reported to FDR. Talks between the British and American Chiefs on SLEDGEHAMMER led Marshall to acknowledge its shortcomings. But in hopes of heading off a North African operation which would delay the 1943 European attack, Marshall declared the talks deadlocked and insisted on referring the issue to the President. Roosevelt at once urged fulfillment of his original request for other ground operations in 1942, and stated a preference for a North African attack. Though Marshall now agreed to prepare for an invasion of North Africa, he insisted that a final decision be deferred until September 15 while they continued to watch developments in France and Russia. The British Chiefs were willing to accommodate Marshall, but Roosevelt would not. In response to news of this decision from Hopkins, he instructed that a landing be planned for no later than October 30 and that orders should now be "full speed ahead." "I cannot help feeling that the past week represented a turning-point in the whole war," he cabled Churchill on July 27, "and that now we are on our way shoulder to shoulder." [36]

This upsurge of unity with Britain paralleled growing difficulties with the Soviet Union. In the middle of July, after the Germans had sunk twenty-three out of thirty-four merchant ships in a convoy bound for Archangel and the Admiralty had advised Churchill that the Germans could completely destroy any convoy bound for north Russia, the Prime Minister again proposed the suspension of these convoys, at least until the end of perpetual daylight. With Allied shipping losses in the North Atlantic reaching 400,000 tons in one week, a rate two-and-one-half times greater than Allied building capacity, Roosevelt reluctantly agreed.

Stalin was outraged. With a German summer offensive now driving Russian forces east and south of the Don and threatening the industrial and mineral-rich areas of the south, Stalin described the British explanation for suspending the northern convoys as "wholly unconvincing," and declared that "in wartime no important undertaking could be effected without risk or losses. You know, of course, that the Soviet Union is suffering far greater losses," he added, and concluded with an expression of disbelief that Britain would "deny" the Soviet Union war materials when matters were so "grave" at the front.

Also anticipating the outcome of the London talks on a second front, Stalin objected to delaying a cross-Channel assault beyond 1942. The matter, he complained, "is not being treated with the seriousness it deserves. Taking fully into account the present position on the Soviet-German front, I must state in the most emphatic manner that the Soviet Government cannot acquiesce in the postponement of a second front in Europe until 1943." Though Churchill, who had taken pains to discourage expectations of an early second front, felt aggrieved at these complaints from an ally who had been willing to see Britain destroyed until it also was attacked by Berlin, he decided not to argue the case with

Stalin. Instead, he told Roosevelt that he would inform Stalin of their intention to take other action in 1942, of their hope to resume convoys in September, and of their desire, if the battle in Egypt went well, to send air units to Russia's southern front.

Roosevelt, who now considered a Russian collapse a distinct possibility, endorsed and encouraged Churchill's positive approach. "Your reply to Stalin must be handled with great care," he answered the Prime Minister. "We have always got to bear in mind the personality of our ally and the very difficult and dangerous situation that confronts him. No one can be expected to approach the war from a world point of view whose country has been invaded. I think we should try to put ourselves in his place." He also urged Churchill to give Stalin unqualified assurance that they had determined upon a course of action in 1942, to consider running a northern convoy if there were "any possibility of success," and to offer unconditional air support to Stalin's southern front as an effective means of boosting Russian morale.[37]

Churchill now decided to go even beyond Roosevelt's suggestions and to ask Stalin for an invitation to come to Russia, where he could tell him personally of the plans for offensive action in 1942 and demonstrate his concern for Russian fortunes. When Stalin gratefully agreed, Churchill traveled to Moscow, feeling as if he were "carrying a large lump of ice to the North Pole." On August 12, in his first meeting with the "profound Russian statesman and warrior," Churchill began by explaining why there would be no cross-Channel attack in 1942. This produced two hours of "bleak and sombre" conversation, with Stalin becoming very glum and restless. When Churchill moved on to the bombing of Germany, however, Stalin expressed general satisfaction at the effect of these raids. This eased the tension and created a sense of shared purpose. "Between the two of them," Harriman reported to the President, "they soon had destroyed most of the important industrial cities of Germany." Churchill now brought TORCH, as the North African attack was renamed, "into action." It marked a turning point in the conversation: with Churchill drawing a picture of a crocodile to illustrate how after North Africa they would strike at both the soft underbelly and the hard snout of Hitler's Europe, Stalin "in a flash" grasped the full strategic advantages of the assault. His interest now "at high pitch," Stalin exclaimed: "May God prosper this undertaking." Delighted with the outcome of the talk, Churchill told Harriman that it was the most important conference of his long life.

When they met again on the next night, however, Stalin was surly and rude. He attacked the Allies for failing to open a second front and deliver promised supplies. He accused the British Army of being afraid to fight the Germans, while the Russians were sacrificing 10,000 men a day. He complained that the British and American governments regarded the

Russian front as of only secondary importance. Undoubtedly, Stalin's change in mood had something to do with reports received that day of serious deterioration on his southern front. But to judge from a conversation Churchill had earlier in the day with Molotov, Stalin may have been trying to assure an Allied commitment to the African attack. The Russians wanted something done to relieve the pressure on their armies, Molotov told Churchill. While it was clear that there would be no second front in Europe in 1942, Molotov wondered whether they could in fact count on the African campaign. Since Stalin appreciated that his hectoring would not produce a European invasion that year, it must have been directed at assuring other kinds of aid, particularly the North African attack, which he had found so appealing on the previous night.

Stalin's words had the desired effect. Churchill became extremely defensive. "The democracies would show very soon by their deeds that they were neither sluggish nor cowardly," Churchill declared. "They were just as ready as the Russians to shed blood. . . . It grieved him that the Russians did not think the Western Allies were doing their utmost in the common cause." Churchill spoke so rapidly in response to Stalin that his translator could not keep pace with the flow of words. But Churchill, who wished to assure that Stalin did not miss a single point, pressed his aide to get it all across. " 'Did you tell him this?' the Prime Minister demanded, punching Dunlop's [the translator's] arm. 'Did you tell him that?' Stalin at last intervened, smiling broadly. 'Your words are of no importance,' he said to Churchill. 'What is important is your spirit.' "

The atmosphere improved considerably over the next two days, with Stalin even inviting Churchill to his private apartments during a final seven-hour talk. The Prime Minister departed with a strong sense of need to back the Russians materially and spiritually. When Stalin concluded the talks by saying that there were only differences of method between them, Churchill replied that "we would try to remove even those differences by deeds." In post-conference cables to Roosevelt, Churchill suggested that "any consoling or heartening message" to Stalin would be helpful, and that having gotten the Russians to swallow the "bitter pill" of no European attack, "everything for us now turns on hastening TORCH and defeating Rommel." "The fact that the Soviet Union is bearing the brunt of the fighting and losses during the year 1942 is well understood by the United States," Roosevelt now cabled Stalin, "and I may state that we greatly admire the magnificent resistance which your country has exhibited. We are coming as quickly and as strongly to your assistance as we possibly can and I hope that you will believe me when I tell you this." [38]

But words were no substitute for swift material support, and this remained as difficult as ever to provide. At the end of August, Churchill and Roosevelt made further plans for Anglo-American air units to defend the Caucasus, and in early September they dispatched another large convoy to Archangel. By late September, however, Churchill concluded that the fighting in Egypt would inhibit the use of air power on the Russian front until December at earliest, and that the need for warships in operation TORCH would force another suspension of northern convoys until the end of the year. With German forces now in the foothills of the Caucasus and on the outskirts of Stalingrad, Churchill cabled Roosevelt on September 22: "This is a formidable moment in Anglo-American-Soviet relations and you and I must be united in any statement made about convoys." Believing that a message to Stalin simply telling him about the convoys would be "a great danger," he suggested saying that they were "trying to find means of sending supplies on a reduced scale by the northern route" and that they wished to discuss a Norwegian invasion "this winter."

Roosevelt was even more apprehensive than Churchill and wished to find more immediate and specific means of support. He suggested not telling Stalin about plans to suspend the next convoy until its scheduled departure date in early October, when they could also send him word about a trans-Caucasian air force. "I can see nothing to be gained by notifying Stalin sooner than is necessary, and indeed much to be lost." After further consideration, partly influenced by a request from Ambassador William H. Standley to return from Moscow with "a very important message," Roosevelt urged a "firm commitment to put an air force in the Caucasus," regardless of events in Egypt. He offered to replace all the planes transferred from the Middle East to Russia. He also advised against delaying the next convoy. Instead, he wished to divide it into groups of two or three ships which would travel with fewer escorts and rely on evasion and dispersion to get through. He believed it "better that we take this risk than endanger our whole relations with Russia at this time."

Though Churchill refused to send the entire convoy in small groups or to see any shift in air power before success in Egypt, he agreed to have ten ships sail the northern route individually, to give Stalin the details of the air force they planned to put on the Russian front early in the New Year, and to promise immediate increases in aircraft deliveries, which Russia desperately needed for the battle at Stalingrad. Trusting that this would be "sufficient to bridge the gap before TORCH opens," he cabled Stalin on October 9 to this effect. Roosevelt echoed these commitments in a cable of his own to Stalin, and added a description of how he was trying to increase supply shipments across the Pacific and through the Persian Gulf.

During the next two weeks, when Stalin offered no comment on these proposed actions, except for a cryptic "thank you," Churchill described himself as baffled and perplexed. "I wonder whether anything has occurred inside the Soviet animal to make it impossible for Stalin to give an effective reply," he told FDR. But Roosevelt, who had by then learned that Standley's important message from Stalin was a request for additional supplies, particularly aircraft, and that Stalin was "behind in answering because [of] front affairs," expressed himself as "not unduly disturbed about our . . . lack of responses from Moscow. I have decided that they do not use speech for the same purposes that we do," he answered Churchill. "I feel very sure that the Russians are going to hold this winter and that we should proceed vigorously with our plans both to supply them and to set up an air force to fight with them. I want to be able to say to Mr. Stalin that we have carried out our obligations one hundred per cent." [39]

At the same time that Roosevelt struggled to sustain the British in the Middle East, prepare the North African attack, and help the Russians survive into the winter, he confronted unrelenting pressure in the Pacific and Asia. In May and June, American naval victories over the Japanese in the Coral Sea and at the Battle of Midway had provided some measure of relief to hard-pressed American forces. But continuing Japanese expansion in the South and Southwest Pacific provoked a series of battles in the Solomon Islands and New Guinea which created fresh demands on American military resources. Despite the consensus in Washington that the Pacific should remain a secondary theater, insistent warnings of disaster from Admiral King and General MacArthur compelled the movement of ever greater amounts of arms and men to the area. In October, when the battle for Guadalcanal in the Solomons reached a critical stage, Roosevelt ordered that "every possible weapon" be sent there, even at the expense of other areas. By the close of 1942, contrary to fundamental plans, nine of the seventeen divisions and nineteen of the sixty-six air groups that had been sent overseas were in the Pacific.[40]

There were also incessant tensions with and demands from the Chinese. In the spring of 1942, when the Japanese overwhelmed British and Chinese forces in Burma, difficulties had mounted with Chiang Kai-shek. Stilwell, who had been sent to Burma to command two Chinese armies, found himself increasingly at odds with Chiang and his generals. Despite commitments to allow Stilwell a free hand, Chiang repeatedly countermanded his orders for an offensive strategy, and, according to General Claire Chennault, head of the American Volunteer Air Group in China, would have ended Stilwell's performance with a firing squad, had he been a Chinese general. Stilwell reciprocated the Generalissimo's displeasure by privately calling him "Peanut" and complaining that Chiang had fooled him completely and "made it impossible for me to do anything." High on Stilwell's list of reasons for defeat in Burma were "stupid, gutless command" and "interference by CKS." In contrast to Chinese reports of spectacular victories over the Japanese in Burma, which American newspapers reported uncritically, Stilwell told the unvarnished truth. "I claim we got a hell of a beating," he told reporters in New Delhi at the end of May. "We got run out of Burma and it is as humiliating as hell." [41]

Tensions with Chiang over China's place in the overall Allied war effort had become particularly acute. In April, after Marshall decided to divert air forces assigned to Stilwell to help the British defend India, Chiang complained to FDR that "in the all-important matters of joint-staff conferences and war supplies, China is treated not as an equal like Britain and Russia, but as a ward. . . . Gandhi told me when I visited India: 'They will never voluntarily treat us Indians as equals; why, they do not even admit your country to their staff talks.' " In May, moreover, with new Japanese attacks in southern China threatening a collapse of morale and "an undeclared peace involving virtual cessation of hostilities," Chiang warned the President that without visible evidence of help from the Allies, "Chinese confidence in their Allies will be completely shaken," and total collapse might follow. Asking the President to send Harry Hopkins to China "so that I could . . . consult you intimately through him," Chiang described China's war of resistance as at its "most crucial stage."

Though Roosevelt pressed Air Corps Chief of Staff Hap Arnold to keep supplies moving over the Hump, the route from northeast India to southwest China over the Himalayas, and agreed to restore diverted air forces to Stilwell's command and to ask the British to try to recapture the Burma Road, his principal support for China remained soothing words. "The news in Burma tonight is not good," he had reported in a Fireside Chat on April 28. "The Japanese may cut the Burma Road; but I want to say to the gallant people of China that no matter what advances the Japanese may make, ways will be found to deliver airplanes and munitions of war to the armies of Generalissimo Chiang Kai-shek. . . . And in the future," he added, "still unconquerable China will play its proper role in maintaining peace and prosperity, not only in eastern Asia but in the whole world." Shortly after, in a message turning aside Chiang's request for an equal part in Anglo-American staff talks and munitions control, Roosevelt assured him that as a member of the Pacific War Council in Washington no question concerning his "illustrious country" would be acted upon without the "full" collaboration of "your distinguished representative." The Pacific War Council, FDR wrote Ambassador Winant in London in June, "serves primarily to disseminate information as to the progress of operations in the Pacific—and, secondly, to give me a chance to keep everybody happy by telling stories and doing most of the talking!" [42]

Chiang was not appeased. Little interested in the overall war picture, he wished the United States to fight Japan and supply his armies for any possible postwar challenge to his domestic rule. His chief concerns were to draw all possible American forces into China and to expand deliveries over the Hump. After thanking Roosevelt at the beginning of June for the restoration of air forces that had been diverted to India, he pressed him to use new DC-4 transport planes on the Himalaya route and to reverse the policy of keeping China off the Munitions Control Board. When Roosevelt rejected the latter request, and the fall of Tobruk decided American Chiefs to send bombers and transports slated for China to the Middle East, the Generalissimo and Madame Chiang made a huge fuss. "Is the U.S. interested in maintaining the China Theater?" they wished Stilwell to ask Washington. "The Generalissimo wants a yes or no answer whether the Allies consider this theater necessary and will support it." On June 29, Chiang presented a formal ultimatum containing three demands: unless the United States sent three divisions to India by September to help reopen the Burma Road, began operating 500 combat planes in China in August, and simultaneously began delivering 5000 tons of supplies a month over the Hump, there would be a "liquidation" of the China theater.

Roosevelt's response, in Stilwell's words, "was quiet and dignified and promised nothing." Asking Chiang to look at the larger picture, Roosevelt pointed out that losing the Middle East would sever Allied lines to India and China and "jeopardize the whole of the Far East." He also asked Chiang to see this shift of air power as a temporary diversion, and to rest assured that the United States was "doing absolutely all in our power to help China win this war." As another gesture of support, he advised Chiang that Lauchlin Currie would come to China as his Personal Representative. "It will be the next best thing to our having personal talks," Roosevelt wrote.

While Currie headed for China to discuss Chiang's three demands, the Generalissimo pressured Roosevelt to shift control over Lend-Lease supplies in China from Stilwell to himself. It was the beginning of an open war between Stilwell and the Chiangs. Pressed by the Generalissimo and Madame to ask Washington uncritically for everything they wanted, Stilwell resisted. "I'm to be a Chinese, a stooge that plugs the U.S. for anything and everything they want," Stilwell noted in his diary. " 'We're going to see that you are made a full general!' " Madame told him. "The hell they are," Stilwell recorded defiantly. At the beginning of July, when Stilwell quarrelled with Chiang over the use of two transport planes, the Generalissimo complained to FDR that existing arrangements compelled him as Supreme Commander to "beg" his "own" Chief of Staff for Lend-Lease supplies already in China. He wished Roosevelt to make Stilwell subordinate to him in all matters and to end his independent control over Lend-Lease. But in a reply drafted by Marshall, Roosevelt bluntly refused. In all defense aid matters, anyone serving in Stilwell's capacity was to remain responsible only to the United States government. Unwilling to confront the Generalissimo with so direct a denial, the Chinese Embassy in Washington revised the President's message and prevented the actual text from reaching Chiang for several weeks.[43]

The issue of Chiang's three demands, however, and what could be expected of the Chinese in return, still remained. Stilwell favored substantial American help for a Burma campaign, but urged commitments from Chiang to military reforms and combat as conditions of increased aid. "The probabilities are that the Chiang Kai-shek regime is playing the USA for a sucker," he told Currie in a memo of August 1, "that it will stall and promise but not do anything; that it is looking for an Allied victory without making any further effort on its part to secure it; and that it expects to have piled up at the end of the war a supply of munitions that will allow it to perpetuate itself indefinitely." Like Stilwell, the War Department also wished to put strings on help to Chiang, but, in light of more urgent commitments, proposed at that time to give far less than Chiang asked. There were to be no American divisions; the Tenth American Air Force of 265 planes was to be built up to full capacity for use in the theater as soon as possible after October 31; and 100 transports carrying 5000 tons a month over the Hump was promised for 1943. To Stilwell, the whole thing amounted "to doing *nothing* more than at present." "Peanut and I are on a raft, with one sandwich between us, and the rescue ship is heading away from the scene," he wrote his wife.

Roosevelt endorsed the War Department's program of limited help. But by contrast with his military advisers, he did not wish to attach meaningful strings to the aid. As with the Russians, he was reluctant to put demands on an ally suffering under enemy invasion, especially when the United States was offering so little direct help. "I am only grieved that our Allies should have to bear the brunt of the fighting in the next few months," he had written Chiang in July. Moreover, pushing Chiang into effective military action concerned him less than simply keeping China in the war. In the summer and fall of 1942, he received repeated warnings that China might collapse. "China's morale is low," the Combined Chiefs of Staff advised in late August. "The Chinese suffer naturally from the weariness of five years of war, but they also feel bitter disappointment that the Pacific war brought them no relief. . . . In this atmosphere, it may be difficult for Chiang . . . to maintain the morale necessary for a continuance of active national resistance." Though Chiang partly manufactured these rumors of a collapse to strengthen his case for aid, even the most skeptical observers were ready to concede the possibility. Fearing such a development would be a serious blow to Allied morale and ultimate strategic plans for defeating Japan, Roosevelt refused to demand anything that might add to the burdens of his faltering ally.

Instead, he tried to soften differences and encourage hopes for the future. This principally meant dumping Stilwell, who, Currie advised FDR, was in open, irreconcilable conflict with Chiang. "I cannot help feeling that the whole situation depends largely on the problem of personalities rather than on strategic plans," Roosevelt told Currie in September with unwarranted optimism. Consequently, at the same time he removed the conditions on aid to Chiang, he raised the question of replacing Stilwell: "What is the situation with regard to Stilwell in China?" he asked Marshall. "Apparently the matter is so involved between him and the Generalissimo that I suppose Stilwell would be more effective in some other field." When Marshall insisted, however, that they needed "a troop leader rather than a negotiator or supply man who would only serve to promote harmony in Chungking," Roosevelt let matters stand. The immediate consequence was a temporary upsurge of cooperation in Chungking, where, Marshall told FDR in early November, the situation had improved. Things "were looking up," Stilwell now wrote his wife, "and the right people are beginning to listen." [44]

Throughout these difficult days of 1942 during which Roosevelt struggled to overcome tensions dividing the Allies, domestic problems plagued him as well. Despite the Atlantic Charter of 1941, the United Nations Declaration at the start of 1942, and repeated statements by the President and other government leaders about the war as a contest between freedom and tyranny, democracy and brute force, the country lacked a clear idea of its war aims. A confidential Gallup poll in September had shown that 40 per cent of the country did not know "what this war is all about." Pronouncements like the Atlantic Charter were too vague to capture the public imagination. In January 1942, for example, a poll had revealed that only 23 per cent of those questioned knew about the Atlantic Charter, and only a third of these respondents could accurately identify one of its eight points. A German peace offensive seemed likely to profit from the uncertain sense of ultimate purpose about the war in the United States; a September opinion survey indicated that a third of the nation would favor peace discussions with the German Army if it overturned Hitler and offered to stop the war. Another poll in October revealed that 60 per cent of those interviewed wanted the President to inform the people more often about the war, and that 30 per cent of this group wished him to discuss war aims, or "what we are fighting for." [45]

Though mindful of the problem and happy to have members of his administration speak in general, idealistic terms about the peace, Roosevelt would not be more specific about postwar goals. A commitment on his part to any specific peace plan seemed certain to generate greater domestic and international tensions than it would relieve. In the spring of 1942, for example, enunciations of strongly contrasting visions of the postwar world had revealed how difficult it might be to gain a consensus on the issue. Henry Wallace's "The Price of Free World Victory," a speech announcing "the century of the common man," or a "people's peace," and Herbert Hoover's and Hugh Gibson's *The Problems of Lasting Peace*, a book urging postwar reliance on the military power of the victorious nations, simultaneously generated widespread enthusiasm and strong differences. While liberals celebrated Wallace's speech as the Gettysburg Address of World War II, conservatives attacked it as "globaloney." A world such as Wallace described, Adolf Berle told an English visitor, "would need gods to run it. I don't know how it is with you, but here in Washington there's quite a bottle-neck in archangels." A report of the New York Council on Foreign Relations, summarizing the views of national opinion leaders, underscored the existence of sharp divisions on how to organize the peace. All these opinion leaders agreed, however, that it was too early to make detailed postwar plans, and a national poll also showed that a majority of Americans wished to postpone peace planning until they had won the war.

In these circumstances, Roosevelt took refuge in generalizations about saving freedom and independence through victory in the war, and avoided discussing specifics which could bring on a divisive, demoralizing debate. In May, when Clark Eichelberger of the League of Nations Association informed the White House of his efforts to win the people to the cause of international organization, Roosevelt wrote his secretary Marvin McIntyre: "Tell him . . . for heaven's sake not to do anything specific at this time." At the end of the month, after telling Molotov his ideas on policing the postwar world, Roosevelt impressed upon him "the importance of making no public announcement about this matter until we defeat Germany." "The President was opposed to any formal Anglo-American discussion on postwar questions," the British Foreign Office heard in August. "The impression that an Anglo-American peace was in contemplation would be dangerous." "The President," Harry Hopkins told the Counsellor of the British Embassy at the same time "was determined not to go to the Senate with any treaty before the end of the war." [46]

As important, Roosevelt believed that any serious effort at postwar planning would injure relations with Russia and Britain. American antagonism to spheres of influence and imperialism was bound to clash with Russian border plans and British attachments to world empire. Specifically, British-Indian problems in the summer of 1942 raised the possibility that advocacy of anti-imperialism in general or Indian nationalism in particular would provoke mass antagonism to Britain in the United States and hurt the war effort. During August, for example, when Richard Law, the Undersecretary of the British Foreign Office, visited the United States, he found little interest in India among the general public but intense concern among "thoughtful Americans everywhere." He feared that

Indian violence would provoke a "public storm" in the United States which would endanger the war effort by raising intense demands for a Pacific-first policy. "There are ghosts which haunt the American scene—" he told the Foreign Office, "ghosts of [Lord] North and the Hessian troops . . . [and] of ancient tyrannies from which so many of the American people have fled in the past hundred and fifty years." "I did not think the Indian situation was so very much on the American people's mind," Henry Wallace told another Englishman in October, "but . . . when it was called to their attention the great bulk of the people were against the British, believing that the situation in India was a little bit like that of the American colonies in 1765."

Roosevelt opposed anything that would agitate the Indian question. In the summer, when Gandhi and Chiang had appealed to him to intercede with Churchill in behalf of Indian independence, he urged them to submerge current differences for the sake of the "common cause against a common enemy." In the fall, moreover, when Wendell Willkie, who was in Chungking on a round-the-world trip, called for firm commitments to end colonial rule, Roosevelt complained of his insensitivity to the British. As Henry Wallace recorded in his diary, FDR had asked Gardner Cowles, one of Willkie's traveling companions, "to see that Willkie did not say anything that would antagonize the Allied nations. The President feels that Willkie had his chance and has muffed it." When Willkie on his return pressed the case against imperialism in a national radio address, Roosevelt told a friend: "He had a good thought, but was just a bit too immature to carry it through. He could only see the little things—and he has not yet forgotten that he ran for President two years ago." [47]

To Roosevelt, the cardinal sin in those most difficult days of the war was "selfish politics," or anything that contributed to national disunity. Though appreciating that the country saw the need to fight, he also worried that its sheltered experience discouraged belief in any serious threat to the national existence and made it difficult for people to feel that they had a direct, urgent stake in the war. By contrast with the Russians, Chinese, and British, Americans had little sense of impending danger. As a consequence, Roosevelt feared that the country might fall into familiar habits of debate and dissipate energies needed for the fighting. He had tried to make this point at a press conference in March by praising a new book by Marquis Childs, *This Is Your War*. Its virtue, he indicated to reporters, was its emphasis on the country's pampered past and inexperience in war, and on the need for Americans to devote themselves unstintingly to the struggle.

This concern for unity led Roosevelt to shun all controversy. His principal domestic goal during 1942 had been to adjourn politics and submerge all differences. In the spring, when an accelerating inflation threatened to disrupt the economy and generate domestic strife, he had considered doctoring the statistics "so as to make it appear that the cost of living was not really rising so much as it really is." But appreciating that he could not sidestep the problem, he pushed the Congress into unified action in the fall by calling congressional temporizing a peril to the war effort and by threatening to use his war powers to act on his own. In August, when racial tensions erupted in Detroit, he called it a "temporary problem" caused by a wartime influx of population and "an effort on the part of a great many people to create trouble." In October, though he privately complained about the farmers of the Middle West, who were showing no "ingenuity" or "imagination" in finding manpower to run their farms, he publicly described "evidences" that the people were trying to meet the problem "as well as possible."

Party politics was particularly out of bounds. With but two exceptions—support for his old progressive ally, Senator George Norris of Nebraska, and limited forays into New York's political wars—he had refused any direct participation in the 1942 state and congressional elections. In September, in the midst of the campaign, he departed Washington for a two-week tour of inspection. Traveling almost 9000 miles to see defense plants, army camps, and naval training stations around the country, he made the trip without publicity or partisan effort. Aside from eleven governors, with whom he discussed no politics, he saw "nobody running for Congress or the Senate, or for local or state office." With the arresting example of Wilson's partisanship and defeat in the 1918 elections before him, Roosevelt decided to stand aloof from the current political fights. "We are in the last week of a campaign which I wish to heavens was over," he wrote Winant in London. "When the time comes next Tuesday, I hope the country will forget politics for two years. That, however, is an almost impossible miracle."

The result of Roosevelt's failure to campaign was general apathy, low voter turnout, and big Republican gains. In its best showing since the 1920s, the GOP gained seventy-seven seats in the House of Representatives, seven short of a majority, and captured several governorships, including New York and California. According to one analysis, the President had drawn the wrong lesson from Wilson's experience—in 1942 the Democrats lost twice as many congressional seats as in 1918. Yet there was some solace for FDR: his own high political standing, which he would need in the coming military and political discussions at home and abroad, remained intact. Moreover, after eleven months of almost uninterrupted military defeats, the four Allies still stood, tied to one another in a common struggle to overcome the Axis.[48]

13

Balancing Needs

I N THE SUMMER AND fall of 1942, Roosevelt impatiently awaited the assault on North Africa. Eager for a victory over German arms that would open the way to a European campaign and answer domestic and Russian demands for action, he pressed all concerned "to start the attack at the earliest possible moment. Time is of the essence," he told Churchill at the end of August, "and we are speeding up preparations vigorously." When facing a choice in the following month between a full-scale convoy to Russia and TORCH as scheduled, he refused to delay the attack for "a single day. We are going to put everything in that operation," he cabled Churchill, "and I have great hopes for it."

There were also substantial fears. The Germans might learn of the attack prematurely; Axis submarines might inflict heavy losses on convoys carrying men and matériel from Britain and the United States; high swells and surf on the African Atlantic coast might jeopardize the Moroccan landings; the Germans might move through Spain into Spanish Morocco, close the Strait of Gibraltar, and trap ships and troops invading Algeria inside the Mediterranean; French forces might offer effective resistance.

The hours before the invasion on November 8 were particularly difficult for FDR. His tension was so apparent that he told uninformed companions that he was awaiting an important message. When a call came in from the War Department, his "hand shook as he took the telephone. . . . 'Thank God. Thank God,'" he exclaimed after hearing the full message. "We have landed in North Africa. Casualties are below expectations," he told those present. "We are striking back." Despite initial French resistance, Allied invaders gained control of Algiers, Oran, and Casablanca within three days. "I am happy today," he wrote Josephus Daniels on November 10 "in the fact that for three months I have been taking it on the chin in regard to the Second Front and that this is now over." The attack was "moving according to plan." [1]

Political difficulties at once cast a shadow over this military success. The entrance of American forces into French possessions drew Roosevelt into an unwanted involvement in French politics. Though he had maintained relations with Marshal Pétain's Vichy regime since its inception in June 1940 and refused to recognize General Charles de Gaulle's Free French movement in London, his policy was one of strict expediency. He had no intention of recognizing "any one person or group as the Government of France," he told Robert Murphy, his diplomatic representative in North Africa, "until a liberated French population could freely choose their own government. ' . . . I will not help anyone impose a Government on the French people.' " He had hoped recognition of Vichy would allow him to discourage the French from placing the remainder of their Fleet or African possessions in German hands.[2]

The decision to invade North Africa strengthened Roosevelt's Vichy policy. His "best information" indicated that Vichy military and political authorities in North Africa would resist an invasion by the British and Free French, but not by the United States. "An American expedition led . . . by American officers will meet little resistance from the French Army in Africa," he had told Churchill in September. "On the other hand, a British-commanded attack in any phase or with de Gaullist cooperation would meet with determined resistance." Since French political leaders seemed likely to respond in the same way, and were "essential to friendly relations," he also proposed that American political representatives be responsible for civil cooperation. British troops, who were to follow an inadequate number of American invaders into Algiers, were to be described to the French as striking "axis-held Tripoli from the rear." [3]

Roosevelt wished to deny the Free French any part in the attack. British experience with them in assaults on Dakar and Syria suggested that their involvement might reveal the operation to the Germans and cause a French civil war. De Gaulle, who had early inklings of the invasion, showed himself distinctly irritated at his exclusion. During their visit to London in July when Marshall and King had turned aside de Gaulle's personal request for information about their plans, he had abruptly departed after declaring that he would not take up any more of their time. "Regardless of how irritated and irritating he may become," Roosevelt declared, de Gaulle must not receive any information. He even rejected Churchill's suggestion that de Gaulle be told of the operation a day in advance: "I am very apprehensive in regard to the adverse effect that any introduction of de Gaulle into the invasion situation would have on our promising efforts to attach a large part of the French African forces to our expedition," he answered Churchill. He advised telling de Gaulle nothing until after a successful landing.[4]

Roosevelt's hopes for French cooperation were disappointed. Despite a message to Pétain, a personal appeal in French beamed to North Africa by the BBC, and elaborate arrangements with Frenchmen sympathetic to an American invasion, he could not prevent resistance, especially in Morocco, where French naval and land units put up a stiff fight. In addition, General Henri Giraud, whose escape from Nazi imprisonment and loose ties to Vichy made him an attractive choice to lead French forces in Africa, did not reach Algiers until after the invasion began, and then was unable to command the obedience of his fellow officers. These circumstances forced General Dwight D. Eisenhower, the commanding general of the Allied invading force, into an agreement with Admiral Jean Darlan, the Commander-in-Chief of all Vichy forces, who happened to be in Algiers on the day of the attack visiting a gravely ill son. In response to superior Allied force, Pétain's approval, and the German occupation of all France, Darlan agreed to full cooperation with the Allies. In return, French North Africa was to be under his political control.[5]

The Darlan deal, as it was called, provoked bitter objections in Britain and the United States and threatened widespread demoralization. Opponents denounced the arrangement as "a sordid nullification of the principles for which the United Nations were supposed to be fighting." They called it "a base and squalid" agreement with the enemy, and warned that "if we will make a deal with a Darlan in French territory, then presumably we will make one with a Goering in Germany or with a Matsuoka in Japan." "We are fighting for international decency," the British Foreign Office told its Washington Embassy, "and Darlan is the antithesis of this." "We must not overlook the serious political injury which may be done to our cause," Churchill advised FDR, "not only in France but throughout Europe, by the feeling that we are ready to make terms with local Quislings. . . . A permanent arrangement with Darlan or the formation of a Darlan Government in French North Africa would not be understood by the great masses of ordinary people, whose simple loyalties are our strength." North Africa, Morgenthau told FDR, was "something that affects my soul."

Eisenhower was not insensitive to these feelings. But any arrangements with someone so indelibly identified with collaboration, he told the Combined Chiefs of Staff, rested solely on military considerations. He believed Darlan was the only man in North Africa who could effectively control military and political leaders. "All concerned profess themselves to be ready to go along with us provided Darlan tells them to do so, but they are absolutely not . . . willing to follow anyone else." Not only had Darlan been able to halt the fighting in Morocco, Eisenhower explained, but he was also the key to an early conquest of Tunisia, cooperation with the Allies in French West Africa, and possible denial of the French Fleet at Toulon to the Nazis. "I realize that there may be feeling at home that we have been sold a bill of goods," he added, "but I assure you that these agreements have been arrived at only after incessant examination of the important factors and with the determination to get on with military objectives against the Axis and to advance the interests of the Allies in winning the war." [6]

Like Eisenhower, Roosevelt saw the arrangement with Darlan as a temporary expedient for advancing the war. On November 17, he announced his acceptance of Eisenhower's political arrangement in Africa for the time being, but also declared himself fully sympathetic with the feeling that no permanent arrangement should be made with Darlan. "We are opposed to Frenchmen who support Hitler and the Axis," he said. "No one in our Army has any authority to discuss the future government of France or the French Empire. The future French Government will be established not by any individual in metropolitan France or overseas, but by the French people themselves after they have been set free by the victory of the United Nations. The present temporary arrangement in North and West Africa is only a temporary expedient, justified solely by the stress of battle." He also described this temporary arrangement as having saved American, British, and French lives, and speeded up current and future operations. Lastly, he emphasized that he had asked for the release of all anti-Nazi political prisoners and the abrogation of all Nazi-inspired laws in North Africa.

Privately, he sent Eisenhower assurance of his "complete support." But he also asked him to understand that "we do not trust Darlan," and that it was "impossible to keep a collaborator of Hitler and one whom we believe to be a fascist in civil power any longer than is absolutely necessary." Darlan's movements were to "be watched and his communications supervised." Roosevelt confidentially told reporters that an old Balkan proverb sanctioned by the Orthodox Church nicely summed up the arrangement: "My children, you are permitted in time of great danger to walk with the Devil until you have crossed the bridge."

Roosevelt's explanations did not overcome objections to the arrangement. Americans, British, and Free French continued to criticize the Darlan deal. This greatly bothered FDR. "He showed more resentment and more impatience with his critics throughout this period than at any other time I know about," Samuel Rosenman, his long-time aide and speechwriter, later wrote. "At times he refused to talk about the deals in North Africa at all; at times he bitterly read aloud what some columnist had written about them, and expressed his resentment." When two of de Gaulle's representatives in a meeting at the White House insistently protested the arrangement with Darlan, Roosevelt lost his temper: "Of course I'm dealing with Darlan," he shouted, "since Darlan's giving me Algiers! Tomorrow I'd deal with Laval, if Laval were to offer me Paris!" He had little patience with those he believed too shortsighted to see the immediate military advantages in his North African policy, or to appreciate his own long-term commitment to total Nazi defeat.[7]

The imperfect results of this policy may partly explain Roosevelt's testiness toward his critics. Though the arrangement with Darlan brought a quick halt to French resistance, saved lives, and put Dakar under Allied control, it had no effect on the fate of the Fleet at Toulon, which was scuttled, and small impact on the fight for Tunisia, where the Germans quickly sent substantial forces and the French were unable to provide significant help. In addition, it left pro-Nazi Frenchmen in positions of power, which they used to continue victimizing Allied sympathizers and to impede the repeal of Vichy civil restrictions. Moreover, Darlan, who privately complained that he was "only a lemon which the Americans will drop after they have squeezed it dry," publicly challenged Roosevelt's description of their arrangement. He described himself as having assumed "the rights and responsibilities of a government," and established a High Commissariat and an Imperial Council which would "represent France in the world." Because of these developments, Churchill told Roosevelt on December 9, "not only have our enemies been thus encouraged, but our friends have been correspondingly confused and cast down." "What is going on in North Africa," the New York *Herald Tribune* commented, "is an elaborate maneuver to preserve the men, the jobs, the reactionary institutions and anti-democratic philosophy of . . . Vichy. . . . And the United States . . . is now witlessly involved in this enterprise."

Roosevelt took additional steps to meet the problem. He pressed Darlan into announcing his relaxation of discriminatory Vichy laws, especially against the Jews, his intention to retire to private life after helping free France from Axis rule, and his hope that "the French people themselves and no one else" would select the future leaders of France. On December 16 Roosevelt gave Darlan's statement to the press, with the observation that the people of North Africa "have definitely allied themselves on the side of liberalism against all for which the Axis stands in Government." He also tried to dilute some of the effects of the Darlan deal by inviting de Gaulle to visit him in Washington at the end of December. But when Darlan was assassinated in Algiers by a young French monarchist on December 24, he suggested that de Gaulle postpone the meeting until there was a new arrangement in North Africa. Darlan's death, in Churchill's words, "relieved the embarrassment at working with him," and allowed the less controversial Giraud to take his place. It did not, however, remove all fears that the Allies would ultimately associate themselves with collaborators, or even enemy leaders, for the sake of an early peace, and Roosevelt felt compelled to find some formulation that would answer this concern.[8]

A more pressing consideration with Roosevelt during November and December was to formulate future Allied military moves. By November 11, with a British victory at El Alamein driving German forces back into Libya from Egypt, and with Anglo-American troops in control of Morocco and Algeria and looking forward to an early conquest of Tunisia, Roosevelt had told Churchill that it was time to explore "the additional steps that should be taken when and if the south shore of the Mediterranean is cleared and under our control." To Roosevelt's thinking, this included possible forward movements against Sardinia, Sicily, Italy, and Greece and other Balkan areas, including a possible attack, with Turkish support, through the Black Sea against Germany's flank. In discussing these Mediterranean operations, Roosevelt was acknowledging that the invasion of North Africa had all but ruled out a major cross-Channel assault in 1943, and that follow-up attacks across the Mediterranean provided the only way to assure significant Anglo-American operations against Axis land forces in the coming year.

Churchill was in full agreement. "Our enterprises have prospered beyond our hopes," he cabled the President on November 13, "and we must not neglect the good gifts of fortune. . . . Everything you say . . . is in absolute harmony with our views." Five days later, he sent the President a detailed statement of strategic plans he had put before his Chiefs of Staff. The paramount task, he argued, was, "first, to conquer the African shores of the Mediterranean and set up there the Naval and Air installations which are necessary to open an effective passage through it for military traffic: and secondly, using the bases of the African shore, to strike at the soft underbelly of the Axis in effective strength and in the shortest time." He suggested Sardinia or Sicily as the prime objective.

At the same time, he wished to assure American military chiefs that further action in the Mediterranean would not endlessly delay a cross-channel invasion of France. In September, despite repeated earlier warnings by American Chiefs about the "inescapable costs of TORCH," Churchill expressed astonishment that American military planners did not think a major land assault on northwest Europe possible in 1943. American Chiefs were equally astonished at Churchill's belated appreciation of this fact. "Either the original TORCH decision was made without a clear realization of all its possible adverse consequences," Eisenhower cabled Marshall, ". . . or that these considerations were ignored in the anxiety to influence the TORCH decision." Whatever the case, Churchill now vigorously espoused the need for a continued buildup in Britain as "vital to all our plans." Every argument previously used for the cross-Channel attack, he told FDR in September, "counts even more in 1943 and 1944 than it did in 1942 and 1943." In November, moreover, when he learned that American planners expected to have only 427,000 men in the British Isles by April 1943, instead of 1,100,000, he asked the President for assurance that this did not signal the abandonment of ROUNDUP, the cross-Channel assault, and a turn toward the Pacific. He suggested another summit meeting to sort this out.[9]

Roosevelt at once reassured Churchill that there was no intention to abandon ROUNDUP. On the contrary, he intended to "build up as rapidly as present active operations permit a growing striking force in the U.K." for quick use in response to a German collapse, or as the nucleus of "a very large force" for later use. Like Churchill, though, he saw the need for more immediate action in the Mediterranean. Hoping they could secure the North African coast in the next six weeks, he suggested a conference of American, British, and Russian military chiefs in Cairo or Moscow to decide their next steps. Churchill, who declared himself delighted at having the misunderstanding over ROUNDUP "cleared away," urged that instead of a conference between Chiefs, there be a meeting of the Big Three in Iceland. Any meeting with the Soviets, Churchill predicted, would consist of pressure for "a strong front in 1943 by the heavy invasion of the continent." Only "principals," the President and the Prime Minister, he asserted, could effectively meet this argument after they had worked out "a joint and agreed view." In short, Churchill hoped to reconcile Stalin to the choice of Mediterranean operations over a cross-Channel assault in 1943 through a face-to-face meeting in which he and the President would take a common stand.

Roosevelt saw the point. He agreed that "the only satisfactory way of coming to the vital strategic conclusions the military situation requires, is for you and me to meet personally with Stalin." But he opposed Anglo-American discussions beforehand. He did "not want to give Stalin the impression that we are settling everything between ourselves before we meet him. I think that you and I understand each other so well that prior conferences between us are unnecessary." He also wished the meeting to be in Africa south of Algiers or at Khartoum rather than aboard ship in Iceland. "I prefer a comfortable oasis to the raft at Tilsit," he concluded with allusion to a meeting between Napoleon and Alexander I of Russia in 1807. On the same day, December 2, 1942, he cabled Stalin urging a meeting between the three of them in mid-January as the only way to reach "the vital strategic decisions which should be made soon by all of us together."

Churchill was ready to meet the President "anywhere." It was the only way to make "a good plan for 1943. . . . which was on the scale or up to the level of events." But still uncertain of American agreement to follow-up action in the Mediterranean, he continued to press for prior Anglo-American talks. "We still think that Marshall, King, and Arnold should come here in advance," he answered the President on December 3, "so that at least we have some definite plans as a basis for discussion when we all meet in January. . . . Otherwise Stalin will greet us with the question, 'Have you then no plan for the second front in Europe you promised me for 1943?' " [10]

But Stalin would not come. In the midst of a decisive Soviet offensive at Stalingrad, he described things as "now so hot that it is impossible for me to absent myself for even a single day." Though that was un-doubtedly a central consideration in his decision, Stalin apparently also feared a conference as likely to compromise his ability to demand a second front in Europe in 1943. In messages to Churchill on November

28 and December 6, he asked for fresh assurances of a cross-Channel attack in the coming year. Moreover, when Roosevelt answered his rejection with a suggestion for a delayed meeting about March 1, Stalin explained that "Front affairs" required his continuous presence in the Soviet Union and expressed the hope that Britain and the United States would fulfill their commitment to a second front in the spring. "I suspect," Churchill told FDR on December 10, "that he [Stalin] thought he would have put across him by us both 'no second front in one nine four three' and that he thought he might just as well get that by post as verbally. We," Churchill concluded in some exasperation, "have got to go into the whole of this matter again." Stalin's refusal also annoyed FDR. He had sent a second invitation, he told Churchill, "for the sake of the record," which would "put the responsibility for declining up to our friend." Like Churchill, Roosevelt did not relish the thought of further acrimonious exchanges over a second front.[11]

Despite Stalin's decision, Roosevelt saw several reasons to hold the meeting anyway. It would allow him to escape "the political atmosphere of Washington," see his commanders and troops in Africa, and go on a precedent-making trip. He would become the first President to fly and the first to leave the country in wartime. But above all, Hopkins believed, there was the excitement of a secret trip to places he had never been. He and Hopkins would assume the code names Don Quixote and Sancho Panza, FDR informed Churchill. "How ever did you think of such an impenetrable disguise?" the Prime Minister teased. To make it harder for the enemy, Churchill suggested "Admiral Q and Mr. P. (NB) We must mind our P's and Q's." Churchill traveled to the conference in a blue R.A.F. uniform under the alias Air Commodore Frankland. "Any fool can see that is an air commodore disguised as the Prime Minister," one of his Chiefs remarked. The exhausting five-day trip by train and plane via Miami, Trinidad, Belem, Brazil, across the Atlantic to Bathurst, British Gambia, and on to Casablanca, where they had agreed to meet in the suburb of Anfa, exhilarated the President who treated the journey "as a first-class holiday." [12]

He probably also saw a conference as a way to relieve himself of some responsibility for fastening further Mediterranean actions on his Chiefs of Staff. The evidence for this is more implicit than explicit, but it seems persuasive nevertheless. On November 25, when he had discussed operations after North Africa with the Chiefs, he found Marshall full of reservations about the Mediterranean and Balkan attacks suggested to Churchill on November 11. Marshall saw diplomatic and supply problems blocking action in Turkey, and he cautioned against attacks on Sicily, Sardinia, and Crete without "a careful determination" of whether the results of such operations justified the cost in large air and ground forces. In short, Marshall feared further operations in the Mediterranean as a drain on Allied resources which would jeopardize a full-scale cross-Channel assault in 1944. While both he and the President agreed that a major attack on Western Europe was already beyond reach for 1943, they differed on whether further ground action in 1943 should be in the Mediterranean or across the Channel, and whether further immediate fighting in the Mediterranean would hold back a cross-Channel attack in 1944.

The issue received its fullest airing between them in a discussion on January 7, 1943. In preparation for the Conference, which was to begin on January 14, FDR asked the Chiefs for their current views of future plans. Marshall responded that while the British were agreed on further operations in the Mediterranean, which they hoped would force the collapse of Italy and a diversion of German forces in response, American Chiefs differed among themselves as to what to do. They were more favorable toward operations in the north than in the Mediterranean, "but the question was still an open one." Marshall himself favored an attack on the Brest Peninsula of France as soon as possible after July. He acknowledged that this would be costly in troops but he pointed to the cruel fact that they could be replaced. By contrast, he predicted that operations in the Mediterranean would cause a heavy loss of shipping which "might completely destroy any opportunity for successful operations against the enemy in the near future." Marshall also warned that further Allied action in the Mediterranean threatened a German move into Spain, where they could cut Allied lines of communication. The Americans, one British military leader observed, "regarded the Mediterranean as a kind of dark hole, into which one entered at one's peril. If large forces were committed . . . the door would suddenly and firmly be shut behind one." There was, Marshall summed up, "a very decided difference of opinion between the American and British point of view" with no compromise in sight.

The President gave indirect expression to his preference for the British plan. He questioned the practicality of a landing on the Brest Peninsula, and drew Marshall into acknowledging that the British shared this view. He also pointed out that the conclusion of North African operations would free 500,000 men for combat elsewhere. Further, he asked Marshall to consider going to Moscow after the Casablanca meeting, explaining that it would be principally to boost Russian morale. He "thought that Mr. Stalin probably felt out of the picture as far as Britain and the United States were concerned and also that he had a feeling of loneliness." One may take this to mean that FDR saw no cross-Channel operation emerging from the meeting, and he hoped to ease inevitable tensions by sending Marshall to give Stalin the news. As with Churchill's earlier visit, it would be a symbolic demonstration of concern for Soviet wishes that still could not be met in full.

Finally, though Roosevelt predicted that the British would come to the

Conference with a firm plan, obviously for Mediterranean operations, he did not instruct his Chiefs to prepare a unified counterproposal for a cross-Channel assault. Instead, he suggested that they agree to build up a large force in Britain which could attack the Brest Peninsula or fight in the Mediterranean, and that they wait a month or two before making the choice. With the Russians completing the defeat of trapped German forces at Stalingrad, Roosevelt did not wish to foreclose the possibility of moving swiftly into Europe to exploit weakened German defenses in the West. At the same time, though, he leaned strongly toward the Mediterranean operations which the British were expected to make a compelling case for at the Conference.[13]

He was not disappointed. The British came to the Conference with an elaborate staff prepared to present "every quantitative calculation that might be called for." Churchill counseled his Chiefs "not to hurry or try to force agreement, but to take plenty of time; there was to be full discussion and no impatience—'the dripping of water on a stone.' " More important, the logic of the British case was irresistible. The close of North African operations would free a large number of veteran troops to attack Sicily without major demands on scarce Allied shipping. Their movement to Britain for a cross-Channel assault would aggravate the "situation in the Atlantic," where U-boats continued to take a heavy toll of Allied transports. Further, the capture of Sicily promised to "effect an economy of tonnage" by improving air coverage for shipping in the Mediterranean and releasing some 225 vessels for operation elsewhere. The fact that an attack on Sicily might force Italy out of the war and Germany into assuming her commitments also made this an attractive operation. In addition, there were telling arguments against an early cross-Channel assault: the experience in North Africa suggested that they would need twice the force and far more landing craft than originally thought necessary; and the British, who would supply the majority of troops and ships, refused to make this the major operation for 1943. Finally, Roosevelt favored a Mediterranean attack. "I am satisfied the President is strongly in favor of the Mediterranean being given prime place," Churchill advised his War Cabinet on January 18. "Although nothing definite has been settled between us . . . I feel sure that we are in solid agreement on the essentials." [14]

Since the American Chiefs agreed among themselves early in the Conference to accept the Mediterranean strategy, they aimed discussions with the British largely at securing commitments for a 1944 cross-Channel attack and continuing forward movement against Japan. They pressed the British to say what part an attack on Sicily would play in the overall strategic plan. Was "it to be a part of an integrated plan to win the war or simply taking advantage of an opportunity?" Marshall warned against "interminable" operations in the Mediterranean, saying "every diversion or side issue from the main plot acts as a 'suction pump.'" It was time, the American Chiefs insisted, to commit themselves to the cross-Channel assault as the main line of attack and to make step-by-step plans for its advance. Though the British committed themselves to a continuing buildup in Britain for a major cross-Channel attack in 1944 and agreed to the creation of a combined command and planning staff for the operation, the Americans left Casablanca unconvinced that they had seen the last of British demands for peripheral attacks which would defer head-on operations against German strength in France.

There were even greater differences over how to proceed in the Pacific. Having gained the initiative against Japan in November with a naval victory at Guadalcanal, the American Chiefs pressed the case for a continuing offensive in the South-Southwest Pacific against the Solomons, New Britain, and New Guinea, and a further one in the Central Pacific against the Gilbert, Marshall, and Caroline Islands. The British vigorously opposed such extended operations as likely to force a shift in focus from Germany to Japan. They urged a static, defensive war in the Pacific until they had defeated Berlin. But by arguing that this might permit Japan to regain the initiative and bring on a disaster that would compel a diversion of resources to hold the line, the Americans pushed the British into a compromise: offensive operations in the Pacific and Far East were to continue as long as they did not endanger Anglo-American capacity to exploit a favorable opportunity for German defeat in 1943. At the same time, Churchill tried to ease American concern about the Pacific by offering to sign a treaty promising that all of Britain's resources would be turned against Japan after Hitler's collapse. But Roosevelt, who fully supported continued advance in the Pacific, declared this "entirely unnecessary." Instead, he wished to win such a commitment from Russia, and urged that efforts be made to that end.

As stated in a final memorandum of January 23, the priority of operations for 1943 closely reflected Roosevelt's and Churchill's wishes. Anglo-American forces were, first, to secure sea communications in the Atlantic by overcoming the U-boat menace; second, to do everything short of "prohibitive cost" to send assistance to Russia—"a paying investment," Roosevelt called it; third, to continue operations in the Mediterranean, aiming principally at the capture of Sicily; fourth, to conduct "operations in and from the United Kingdom," led by a bomber offensive against Germany and the continuing buildup for the cross-Channel attack; and fifth, to carry out operations in the Pacific and Far East which would throw back Japanese forces and support China.[15]

Though military planning dominated the Casablanca talks, politics also entered the discussions. Attention focused on how to use a growing concern with postwar aims to bolster morale and sustain ties between the Allies. The victories in early November at El Alamein, Guadalcanal, and in North Africa, and the Russian defense of Stalingrad encouraged the belief that the war had reached a turning point. Fearful that these gains might slow the war effort, Churchill and Roosevelt tried to discourage the impulse to believe that the end was in sight. "This is not the end," Churchill declared in a famous speech. "It is not even the beginning of the end. But it is, perhaps, the end of the beginning." Shortly after, Roosevelt acknowledged in a speech that "the turning point in this war has at last been reached. But," he cautioned, "this is not time for exultation. There is no time now for anything but fighting and working to win."

Despite these injunctions, in the winter of 1942–43 Americans began focusing on postwar plans. A December poll had indicated that earlier public reluctance to discuss peace aims had largely disappeared. Roosevelt himself reflected this feeling by entering into private and public discussions of postwar goals. In November he had talked with Clark Eichelberger about postwar peacekeeping, and wrote Jan Christian Smuts, the Prime Minister of South Africa, of his desire to talk with him "about drawing plans now for the victorious peace which will surely come." In December he spent several hours one weekend discussing postwar affairs with Canada's Mackenzie King. Moreover, in his Annual Message to the Congress on January 7, 1943, he tried to "get on the right side" of the postwar-security issue. "Victory in this war is the first and greatest goal before us," FDR declared. "Victory in the peace is next." To assure this peace, he asserted, the United States would have to play a continuing part in world affairs, and the aggressor nations—Germany, Italy, and Japan—would have to be disarmed and compelled to abandon the philosophy that had brought so much suffering to the world.[16]

Roosevelt's most striking attempt to deal with this issue in January was his announcement of Allied insistence on unconditional surrender. As early as May 1942, Roosevelt had privately endorsed the idea that the war should end with an unconditional surrender rather than a negotiated armistice. Eager to prevent a repetition of the post-1918 experience, when the Nazis used the World War I armistice as evidence that political arrangements rather than battlefield reverses had caused German defeat, Roosevelt wanted a full acknowledgment of German and Japanese surrender. He had made this clear in a conversation with Mackenzie King on December 5. By this time, moreover, the Darlan deal, with its demoralizing implications that the Western Allies might negotiate with Berlin, and the certainty that the failure to open a second front in 1943 would heighten Soviet suspicions of Allied intentions made announcement of an unconditional-surrender doctrine a particularly appealing idea.

Roosevelt, in fact, had partly wanted the Casablanca meeting with Churchill as a forum for announcing their commitment to this aim. In his meeting with the Joint Chiefs of Staff on January 7, he said that "he was going to speak to Mr. Churchill about the advisability of informing Mr. Stalin that the United Nations were to continue on until they reach Berlin, and that their only terms would be unconditional surrender." In addition to this statement and his subsequent actions at the Conference, there is some indirect evidence of Roosevelt's intentions. When Churchill had suggested bringing Eden with him to Casablanca, Roosevelt objected on the ground that in that event he would have to bring Hull. The Secretary, he told Harriman, was "forceful, stubborn, difficult to handle. He had some rigid ideas and . . . would be a nuisance at the conference." More specifically, though Roosevelt did not say it, Hull was opposed to the unconditional-surrender idea, and was closely identified with the Darlan deal. His presence in Casablanca would impede and call into question the sincerity of an unconditional-surrender announcement. At the very least, it would give such a declaration the appearance of a contrived attempt to counter the effects of the association with Darlan.[17]

The precise course leading to the President's announcement of the doctrine at Casablanca is difficult to trace. It is clear that by the fifth day of the Conference Roosevelt and Churchill had discussed the subject. In a meeting between them and the Combined Chiefs of Staff on January 18, the Prime Minister suggested that at the close of the Conference they "release a statement to the effect that the United Nations had resolved to pursue the war to the bitter end, neither party relaxing in its efforts until the unconditional surrender of Germany and Japan had been achieved." On the following day Churchill asked the War Cabinet's judgment on the publication of such a statement, and explained the omission of Italy as aimed at encouraging "a break-up there." While the Cabinet did not oppose the idea, it advised against excluding Italy as likely to create misgivings in Turkey and the Balkans and unlikely to help in discouraging Italian resistance. By the time Churchill received this message on the 21st, he and the President had drafted a press communiqué which included a statement of their intention to demand the unconditional surrender of Germany and Japan. Churchill then amended the statement in his own hand to include Italy.

The record beyond this point is unclear. Though Churchill, who did not want to apply the doctrine to Italy, recalled no further conversation with FDR about the issue, the final press release contained no mention of unconditional surrender. Instead, Roosevelt announced the doctrine orally at a press conference on the 24th, where he said: "I think we have all had it in our hearts and heads before, but I don't think that it has ever been put down on paper by the Prime Minister and myself, and that is the determination that peace can come to the world only by the total elimination of German and Japanese war power. . . . The elimination of German, Japanese and Italian war power," he added, "means the unconditional surrender by Germany, Italy, and Japan." The President also said that this meeting "is called the 'unconditional surrender' meeting."

Roosevelt and Churchill subsequently claimed that the announcement was a spontaneous act on the President's part. Roosevelt asserted that the announcement came at a press conference for which he and Churchill "had had no time to prepare," and was the result of a thought that "popped" into his mind. Churchill recorded that he heard the President's announcement "with some feeling of surprise," and Hull was told that "the Prime Minister was dumbfounded." Roosevelt's spontaneity and Churchill's surprise are difficult to credit. Roosevelt had with him at the press conference the statement on unconditional surrender contained in the draft press release and notes precisely foretelling what he would say to the reporters. Moreover, it is difficult to believe that the final press communiqué, which Churchill later described as "a carefully and formally worded document" both he and the President "considered and approved," would have omitted the unconditional-surrender section without their discussion. It seems logical that such a discussion was also the source of a decision to have FDR present the doctrine as his spontaneous creation.

It allowed Roosevelt and Churchill to avoid an open split on an important issue. Once his War Cabinet had pressed him to include Italy in the announcement, Churchill, according to his own recollection, was reluctant to issue any statement at all on unconditional surrender. "I would not myself have used these words," he wrote Robert Sherwood in 1948. Judging also from a statement in his war memoirs, his endorsement of the President's announcement was certainly grudging. Despite his surprise, Churchill wrote, "I of course supported him and concurred in what he had said. Any divergence between us, even by omission, would on such an occasion and at such a time have been damaging or even dangerous to our war effort." Another statement of Churchill's at the January 24 press conference also suggests that he had his differences with Roosevelt at Casablanca. "One thing I should like to say, and that is— I think I can say it with full confidence—nothing that may occur in this war will ever come between me and the President. He and I are in this as friends and partners, and we work together. We know that our easy, free conversation is one of the sinews of war—of the Allied Powers. It makes things easy that would otherwise be difficult, and solutions can be reached when an agreement has stopped."

Roosevelt's oral statement of the doctrine, then, may be seen as a compromise between FDR's strong support of the announcement and Churchill's opposition. An oral declaration would carry less weight than a written one, and would allow Churchill to keep a certain distance from the whole idea. The fact that both of them later described the announcement as Roosevelt's invention which Churchill supported, in spite of his surprise, may be seen as an extension of this compromise. Finally, Churchill was probably faithful to this story after the war out of a sense of honor. In the postwar years, when the unconditional-surrender doctrine came under strong attack as a mistake that extended the war, Churchill undoubtedly believed it dishonorable to throw the whole responsibility on the President by telling the full details of what had occurred at Casablanca. "I certainly take my share of the responsibility," he said in his war memoirs. By so doing, he also honored Roosevelt's belief that some exchanges between heads of state should never see the light of day.

Churchill need not have been so ready to accept his share of "responsibility" for extending the war through the enunciation of the unconditional-surrender doctrine. As Paul Kecskemeti, a social scientist who has examined the impact of the doctrine on wartime German behavior, has concluded, the call for unconditional surrender did not prolong the war by rallying the German people behind the Nazi regime and inducing them to fight to the last. "The length of the war was determined largely by other factors, including the Allies' objective of total victory and Hitler's . . . refusal to admit the possibility of any kind of surrender." German actions in the last stages of the war "also indicated that unconditional surrender to the Western Allies was not unthinkable for them." On the contrary, Kecskemeti shows that both anti-Nazi dissidents and Nazi loyalists were willing to accept unconditional surrender as an end to the war.[18]

Roosevelt's difficulties with the unconditional-surrender idea at Casablanca were mild compared with the problems of French politics. His idea was to avoid any commitment to one French faction or another during the war by making temporary arrangements with local authorities as they liberated French territory. After the war, the French were to settle their own differences by democratic means. "In regard to de Gaulle," he had told Churchill at the start of the North African campaign, "I have hitherto enjoyed a quiet satisfaction leaving him in your hands—apparently I have now acquired a similar problem in brother Giraud. . . . The principal thought to be driven home to all three of these prima donnas [de Gaulle, Giraud, and Darlan] is that the situation is today solely in the military field."

Darlan's assassination did not greatly ease the problem. Segments of British and American opinion continued to complain loudly of arrangements with Vichy officials, and de Gaulle, with British support, continued to press for recognition as the only legitimate representative of France. In a cable of January 1, Roosevelt had reminded Churchill of his determination to avoid any such commitment. "Why doesn't de Gaulle go to war?" he asked sarcastically. "Why doesn't he start North by West half West from Brazenville? It would take him a long time to get to the Oasis of Somewhere." Telling his Chiefs on January 7 that the British Foreign Office was trying to organize a French government under de Gaulle, Roosevelt "indicated that the United States has the whip hand" and that he would tell Churchill that de Gaulle is a military officer who could not be given political authority because the French people have had no opportunity to confer it on him.[19]

One of Roosevelt's objectives at Casablanca was to find a way out of this "French quagmire." One solution, which Robert Murphy and Harold Macmillan, Murphy's British counterpart in North Africa, worked out, was to offer de Gaulle joint political control with Giraud in the area. Churchill, who saw de Gaulle as an indispensable symbol of French resistance, urged Roosevelt to accept the arrangement. Convinced that Giraud was "a rather simple-minded soldier" lacking in any administrative ability, and that such a settlement would largely silence British and American critics and still leave a decision on political power for the future, Roosevelt agreed.

But de Gaulle resisted. When Churchill invited him to come to Casablanca to confer with Giraud, he refused. He was reluctant to meet under Allied auspices, where he might come under pressure to compromise with Vichyites, and he was insulted that the invitation did not also come from FDR. Assurances from Churchill that he would be free of Allied pressure and injunctions not to miss an opportunity to advance his own and the Allied cause still failed to persuade him. Roosevelt, who believed that Churchill would eventually succeed, took a certain amount of pleasure in these British difficulties with their handpicked man. "Here was our great hero, the winning horse that we had bred and trained in our stable; and when the great day came it refused to run at all," Macmillan later wrote. "I have got the bridegroom, where is the bride?" Roosevelt cabled Eden in London. "The temperamental lady de Gaulle. . . . is showing no intention of getting into bed with Giraud," he wired Hull. After Roosevelt added his name to the invitation and Churchill threatened to abandon him, de Gaulle reluctantly agreed to come.[20]

But he was no easier to deal with in Casablanca than he had been in London. Arriving at the Conference on the 22nd, he met in succession with Giraud, Churchill, and Roosevelt. He upbraided Giraud for agreeing "to meet in a barbed-wire encampment among foreign powers." He complained to Churchill of being surrounded by American bayonets on French territory, and answered his description of the Anglo-American proposal for governing the French Empire as "adequate at the quite respectable level of an American sergeant." He dismissed the plan as a violation of French sovereignty which he would not support. He arrived "cold and austere" for his first meeting with the President, who complained afterward that he "found the General rigid and unresponsive to his urgent desire to get on with the war." De Gaulle saw the President as charming but imperious. "Behind his patrician mask of courtesy," he later wrote, "Roosevelt regarded me without benevolence." He "meant the peace to be an American peace, convinced that he must be the one to dictate its structure, that the states which had been overrun should be subject to his judgment, and that France in particular should recognize him as its savior and its arbiter." De Gaulle again rejected the Anglo-American plan, which Roosevelt also put before him. But "we took care not to meet head on," de Gaulle later recorded, "realizing that the clash would lead to nothing and that, for the sake of the future, we each had much to gain by getting along together."

Roosevelt was never as dictatorial and unbending about the postwar peace as de Gaulle believed. But he was correct in thinking that Roosevelt envisaged a role for France well short of de Gaulle's ideas. In his discussion with Molotov eight months before, Roosevelt had included France as one of the nations that should be disarmed after the war. When Molotov specifically asked about the re-establishment of France as a Great Power, he "replied that might perhaps be possible within 10 or 20 years." Further, he reproached Robert Murphy at Casablanca for having given Giraud a guarantee about the return of every part of the empire to France. He also discussed with Murphy and Eisenhower his plan to encourage extensive reductions in the French Empire, and in front of Churchill and the French Resident General, Auguste Noguès, at a dinner with the Sultan of Morocco he pointedly sympathized with colonial aspirations for independence and discussed the possibility of postwar economic cooperation between the United States and Morocco.[21]

During the last day and a half of the Conference, furious efforts by Churchill, Roosevelt, and their aides to impose an agreement on de Gaulle failed. In a meeting later described by de Gaulle as "the most ungracious" he had had with Churchill during the war, the Prime Minister showered him "with bitter reproaches." When Roosevelt heard that de Gaulle proposed to Giraud that he, de Gaulle, would be Clemenceau and Giraud, Foch (French military chief of staff in World War I), the President exclaimed, "Yesterday he wanted to be Joan of Arc—and now he wants to be the somewhat more worldly Clemenceau." At a final meeting between the President, Churchill and de Gaulle on the 24th, despite an "urgent plea" by Roosevelt expressed "in pretty powerful terms," de Gaulle would not agree to a communiqué with Giraud drawn up by Murphy and Macmillan.

When Roosevelt, however, coupled further pressure by him and Churchill with the argument that even a show of unity would serve the needs of Allied morale, de Gaulle promised that he and Giraud would put out a communiqué of their own making. "In human affairs," he [FDR] said, "the public must be offered a drama. The news of your meeting with General Giraud in the midst of a conference in which Churchill and I were taking part, if this news were to be accompanied by a joint declaration of the French leaders—even if it concerned only a theoretical agreement—would produce the dramatic effect we need." With that same end in view, de Gaulle also agreed to shake hands with Giraud before press photographers. For all their differences, de Gaulle shared Roosevelt's belief in the need for at least a show of unity against the common enemy.[22]

Despite these last-minute concessions by de Gaulle, which temporarily quieted public complaints in Britain and the United States about French policy, Casablanca principally served to intensify Roosevelt's antagonism toward him. In Roosevelt's view, de Gaulle was objectionable on three counts: he would not temporarily abandon political antagonisms for the sake of the war effort; he wished to establish himself as France's political chief by undemocratic means; and he would vigorously oppose the President's conception of a secondary role for France after the war. As one token of this antagonism, on his last day at the Conference, Roosevelt, without Churchill's knowledge, signed two documents, the Anfa agreement, binding the United States and Britain to aid Giraud in preserving all French military, economic, financial, and moral interests, and to give him "every facility" to unite all French opponents of Germany under one authority. When Churchill learned of these agreements in February, he insisted on amending them to include de Gaulle.

On his return to the United States, Roosevelt left little doubt among intimates about his feelings. During his first week back in Washington, he asked Hull to convey his "annoyance" to Eden "at the continued propaganda emanating from de Gaulle headquarters in London." He labeled the Free French attitude "a continuing irritant," and asked that steps be taken "to allay the irritation." At the same time, Roosevelt also began telling the apocryphal story that de Gaulle compared himself to Joan of Arc and Clemenceau, and that he had urged him to choose one or the other, since he could not be like both of them. At a meeting with the American Society of Newspaper Editors, he further vented his annoyance by describing how he had tricked de Gaulle into shaking hands with Giraud. "If you run into a copy of the picture," he said with obvious amusement, "look at the expression on de Gaulle's face!" He had no intention, he also said, of satisfying de Gaulle's desire to be recognized as the "spirit" or "soul" of France. Decisions about French rule, he firmly declared, must wait until the people of France can have their say. Clearly, after Casablanca, Roosevelt saw the French political problem as still very much alive.[23]

At the same time that Roosevelt and Churchill wrestled with French problems, they also struggled to avoid recriminations with Stalin over their military decisions at Casablanca. In a carefully prepared message to him of January 25, they had expressed their hope that a combination of Anglo-American and Russian attacks in the first nine months of 1943 might bring Germany to her knees. They also described themselves as primarily concerned to divert German forces from the Russian front and to send the maximum flow of supplies to Russia over every available route. They described their means to the first two ends as large-scale amphibious operations in the Mediterranean, a continuing buildup in the United Kingdom in preparation for the earliest practicable return to the Continent, and a stepped-up bomber offensive against Germany.

Churchill had little hope that this would satisfy Stalin. "Nothing in the world will be accepted by Stalin as an alternative to our placing 50 or 60 divisions in France by the spring of this year," he cabled the War Cabinet. "I think he will be disappointed and furious with the joint message. Therefore I thought it wise that the President and I should both stand together. After all our backs are broad." Stalin's initial response, however, was restrained. Receiving the message from American Ambassador William H. Standley and the British Chargé, he read it without comment or change of facial expression. In his reply to Roosevelt and Churchill three days later, he simply asked for concrete information on the plans and timing of a second front, which he assumed was part of their design for German defeat in 1943. He also cautioned that the Soviet winter offensive, which was about to complete the victory at Stalingrad, could not continue beyond the middle of February.[24]

Greatly bothered at how little they would be doing in the spring compared with the Russians, Churchill now wished to promise more than they could deliver. "I think it is an awful thing," he wired Hopkins, "that in April, May and June, not a single American or British soldier will be killing a single German or Italian soldier while the Russians are chasing 185 divisions around." Hence, he wanted to tell Stalin that after overcoming the 250,000 Axis troops in Tunisia, they intended in July, or possibly sooner, "to attack Italy across the central Mediterranean with the object of promoting an Italian collapse, and establishing contact with Yugoslavia." He also wished to report themselves as "aiming at August for a heavy operation across the Channel." If weather delayed the operation, they would prepare it for September with stronger forces. But Roosevelt persuaded Churchill to be more restrained. Instead of describing their Mediterranean plan as an offensive against Italy, their message spoke more candidly of seizing Sicily, with the object of clearing the Mediterranean and promoting an Italian collapse. It also described them as "pushing preparations to the limit of our resources for a cross-Channel operation in August," and making "the timing of this attack . . . dependent upon the condition of German defensive possibilities." [25]

Though toned down, this message also exaggerated the likelihood of a cross-Channel assault, but, even so, it did not satisfy Stalin. In an answer on February 16, he complained that the slowdown in their Tunisian operations had allowed the Germans to shift twenty-seven more divisions from the West to Russia, and that the delay in opening a second front until the second half of the year would give the enemy a chance to re-cover. Roosevelt candidly answered at once that heavy rains had delayed their offensive in North Africa and that they were doing everything pos-sible to resume aggressive action. He also reminded Stalin of the Allied shipping shortage, and promised to project the American war effort on to the continent of Europe as soon as adequate transportation would allow.

Churchill now was even more explicit about their limitations. After a bout of pneumonia, which kept him from replying until March 11, he explained in rich detail how enemy strength, bad weather, and difficulties of supply over bad roads and single-track railways had slowed the Tunisian offensive. In an equally candid statement, which he asked Stalin to keep strictly between themselves, he provided a full description of Anglo-American resources "for an attack upon Europe across the Mediterranean or the Channel." Britain had thirty-eight divisions of some 40,000 men each spread over 6300 miles between Gibraltar and Calcutta; all had ac-tive and definite assignments for 1943. There were an additional nineteen divisions in the United Kingdom, sixteen of which were preparing to cross the Channel. "You must remember," Churchill pointed out, "that our total population is forty-six millions, and that the first charge upon it is the Royal Navy and Mercantile Marine, without which we could not live. Thereafter came our very large Air Force, about twelve hundred thousand strong, and the needs of munitions, agriculture, and airraid defence. Thus the entire manhood and womanhood of the country is and has been for some time fully absorbed." In addition, he underscored the fact that a severe shipping shortage had allowed the United States to send only eight out of a planned twenty-seven divisions to Britain and North Africa, and would permit only three more to come in the next several months.

As for crossing the Channel, he made clear that this was an open ques-tion. If the enemy weakened sufficiently, they would seize the opportunity and strike before August. If he did not weaken, an attack with insuffi-cient forces would merely lead to a bloody repulse and a great Nazi tri-umph. "The Channel situation," he concluded, "can only be judged nearer the time, and in making this declaration of our intentions there for your own personal information I must not be understood to limit our freedom of decision."

With a German counteroffensive, however, momentarily driving back Soviet forces on the southern front, Stalin renewed his demands for Allied action. He complained that the slowdown in North Africa had allowed Germany to move thirty-six more divisions from the West to Russia, where they were easing the German position. Further, he emphasized that an attack on Sicily could not replace a second front in France, which Russia would need in the spring or early summer to prevent a further

German reinforcement of operations against the U.S.S.R. While he also acknowledged the difficulties Roosevelt and Churchill had described in the way of a cross-Channel attack, he gave "a most emphatic warning, in the interest of our common cause, of the grave danger with which further delay in opening a second front in France is fraught." [26]

Roosevelt was not surprised at Stalin's response, and neither he nor Churchill thought it useful to reply. This may partly have stemmed from a growing feeling among British and American officials that "when we are on sound ground, nothing is gained with the Russians by letting them kick us around." More important, they now had to tell Stalin that a German naval concentration at Narvik, Norway, would force cancellation of the March convoy to Russia, and that they would have to suspend all northern convoys during the attack on Sicily. Churchill wished to say nothing about the March convoy until the offensive in Tunisia had begun, while Roosevelt suggested telling him only that it had been postponed. FDR also wished to delay saying anything about the overall suspension for at least three or four weeks while they waited to see if a dispersal of German forces would allow them to run another convoy.

At the end of March, they told Stalin about the convoys. Information from Churchill during the month about successful air raids on Germany and strong advances in Tunisia had evoked congratulations from Stalin, who now denounced "those scoundrels . . . who allege that Britain is not fighting but merely looking on." In a message of March 30, therefore, Churchill explained that the concentration of a powerful German battle fleet made it impossible to send forward the next convoy, and that between early May and early September the Mediterranean offensive would also rule out northern convoys. He promised, however, to do everything possible to increase the flow of goods over other routes. Though this at once brought forth a protest against "a catastrophic diminution of supplies," Churchill and Roosevelt thought the response "very natural" and "not too bad." An end to the German counterattack in southern Russia and continued bombing of Germany and advances in Tunisia also helped ease the tension. "We are delighted," Stalin cabled Churchill on April 12, "that you are not giving respite to Hitler." [27]

During these winter and spring days of 1943, difficulties with China more than matched those with France and Russia. By December 1942, an uncommon note of harmony had crept into relations between American, British, and Chinese planners, when all seemed agreed on a Burma offensive, code-named ANAKIM, in the spring. Aimed at opening supply routes into China, where air bases for attacks on Japanese shipping and home islands were to be developed, the attack was to consist of a Chinese drive into northern Burma from Ledo, India, and Yunnan, China, and a British offensive in the west against Akyab and toward the Chindwin River. On December 8, Roosevelt had approved a Joint Chiefs recommendation that Stilwell receive an additional 63,000 tons of material and 6000 men for the offensive.

During the following month, however, British and Chinese reluctance killed the plan. Though the British had agreed to prepare for an attack, they were unwilling to follow through. Convinced that logistical and medical problems made a spring offensive in north Burma too risky, and fearful that Chinese invaders might later be difficult to expel, British commanders in India urged a halt to the operation until the dry season in the fall. They explained that only three instead of seven divisions would be available in the spring and that they would be unable to control the Bay of Bengal for an attack on Rangoon.[28]

Chiang at once seized on these British limitations to threaten a withdrawal from the campaign. He complained to FDR that the British were not fulfilling their commitments, and that unless they did, Chinese troops would not move. While Roosevelt tried to persuade Chiang that opening a land route across northern Burma need not depend on British action in the south, he also promised to take up "with the highest allied authorities . . . the matter of opening the Burma Road without any avoidable delay." In a follow-up message to Churchill, he stressed the importance of Chinese action in Burma as a prelude to "our air offensive from China against Jap sea lanes (if not Japan itself)." The problem, he told Churchill, was to "do something to ensure that the Chinese put their full weight into the operations" scheduled for March. "Can you suggest any assurance which we can give Chiang Kai-shek which will have this effect?" he asked.

Because neither the British nor the Chinese wanted the attack, Roosevelt could not bridge the gap between his Allies. On January 8, without waiting to hear the results of the President's consultation with the British, Chiang withdrew from the operation. Without "a landing force to take the Japanese in the rear in South Burma," he declared, "the enemy will be in a position to concentrate rapidly against our armies in the North." This would risk a defeat which "would be a disaster for China so grave that the results cannot now be predicted." An answer from Churchill two days later underscored British opposition to an attack. There had been no promises to send the Eastern Fleet into the Bay of Bengal or to use seven divisions to recapture Burma in the spring, he said. But he saw these limitations as less inhibiting than the fact that men could not be maintained "in these mountainous and rain sodden jungles." "We got the horse almost to the water," Stilwell cabled Washington, "but he is not going to drink."

Instead of the Burma attack, Chiang urged an offensive by General Chennault's Air Task Force. Such action, he told FDR in his message of January 8, would not impinge upon United Nations' air efforts elsewhere, and would bring a return "out of all proportion to the investment."

Though Chiang also promised to continue preparing his land armies for a Burma campaign, which he would launch "whenever our Allies are ready," his intent was to have American air forces fight Japan while he preserved his land armies for any postwar challenge to his rule. As Stilwell advised Washington at the time, "the Americans are expected to go on carrying the load in the air, bringing in supplies, and building up a force that will make China safe for the Kuomintawo." [29]

The idea for the air offensive belonged to Chennault. An advocate of the unmatched importance of air power, he believed that a small air force under his command would be sufficient to defeat Japan. With a 147-plane air force of 105 fighters, 30 medium bombers, and 12 heavy bombers, all kept up to strength, he had written the President in October 1942, he could "accomplish the downfall of Japan." His plan was to force the Japanese air force into a decisive battle in China, where he would destroy it at a rate of between ten and twenty to one. When Japanese air power had been destroyed, he would strike at Japan itself and burn up its two main industrial centers. This would leave Japan incapable of supplying its newly conquered empire and would lead to its collapse.

However farfetched, Chennault's appeal had compelling elements which Roosevelt found hard to resist. Judging from the performance of his small air force against Japanese planes and ships during 1942, he seemed able to injure Japanese air and sea power at small cost to American arms. Moreover, in late 1942, when large question marks remained about Allied ability to mount an effective spring offensive in Burma, Chennault offered a way to initiate quick action against Japanese forces in China. On December 30, therefore, after learning that Chiang might not go ahead with the Burma campaign in March, Roosevelt had suggested to Marshall that Chennault become an independent commander in China with a task force of 100 planes. But when Marshall argued that Chennault's force should remain under Stilwell for use in the Burma attack, which he called an essential prerequisite for expanded air operations in China, Roosevelt did not press the point.[30]

The question of how to proceed against Japan in Burma and China received a full hearing at Casablanca. Marshall and King pressed the case for a strong Burma offensive beginning in November. They contended that a combined assault by the British in the south and the Chinese in the north might divert Japanese forces in the South Pacific to Burma. This, they also said, might prevent a disaster in the Pacific which would put an end to Europe-first. A Burma attack could also reopen a land route into China for a buildup of air forces against Japan. The British, however, remained skeptical of the resources for, and outcomes of, such a campaign. They saw no way to provide the shipping for an amphibious assault in the south, still doubted Allied ability to overcome supply and medical problems in the north, and feared that such a campaign would turn into a full-scale operation and divert supplies from other theaters. Though Marshall and King blunted these objections by promising to supply landing craft from American resources in the Pacific and to reevaluate the feasibility of a Burma campaign in July, Roosevelt gave a Burma attack second priority behind air operations from China.

At meetings with the Combined Chiefs during the Conference, Roosevelt stressed the political advantages in expanding Chennault's air power in China. A periodic bombing raid on Japan, he pointed out, "would have a tremendous morale effect on the Chinese people." In response to expressions of concern about being able to supply this air force without control of the Burma Road, he urged the use of additional transport planes. Though operations in Burma were "desirable," he told the Combined Chiefs, they "would not have the direct effect upon the Chinese which was necessary to sustain and increase their war effort. Similarly, an island-to-island advance across the Pacific would take too long to reduce . . . Japanese power. Some other method of striking at Japan must be found." He saw this in an attack on Japanese shipping which would cripple its ability to supply garrisons stretching from Burma to New Guinea. Though the job was primarily one for submarines, he also thought that aircraft operating from China could do their share, and make an occasional raid on Japan as well. In messages to Chiang at the end of the Conference, Roosevelt emphasized his determination to reinforce Chennault at once "in order that you may strike not only at vital shipping routes but at Japan herself." At the same time, he and Churchill sent the Combined Chiefs a note underscoring the urgency of getting reinforcements to Chennault and of making them "fully operative." [31]

At the end of the Conference, Roosevelt and Churchill sent a high-level mission to Chiang to report their decisions and enlist his support. Led on the American side by Generals Arnold and Brehon B. Somervell, Chief of Army Service Forces, the mission had a spokesman for air operations in Arnold, and one for reopening the Burma Road in Somervell. In New Delhi, where they went first, they found the British "plan" for driving the Japanese out of western Burma nothing more than "several pages of well-written paragraphs telling why the mission could not be accomplished." Though the British showed themselves receptive to suggested improvements in their plans, Arnold could not shake the feeling that India was a place for British officers "who had more or less outlived their usefulness in other theaters."

Things in Chungking were worse. Chiang confronted his visitors with unreasonable demands he insisted on putting before the President as conditions for continuing in the war. Chennault, under Chiang's command, was to head an independent air force in China; monthly deliveries over the Hump were to increase from 3000 to 10,000 tons; and China was to have an air force of 500 planes by November. Though Arnold pointed to insurmountable difficulties in the way of such demands, "the Generalissimo and Chennault glossed over these things with a wave of their hands. They could not, or would not, be bothered with logistics." Though he omitted the threat to quit the war and, after much hectoring by Arnold and Stilwell, included a promise to participate in the November campaign in Burma, Chiang gave Arnold a letter for the President containing his three demands.

Along with Chiang's letter to Washington, Arnold also carried a memo from Stilwell describing the state of the Chinese Army. It amounted to a "God awful" tale of corruption and inefficiency which "no one dares to tell the Peanut. . . . Anything that is done in China," Stilwell predicted, "will be done in spite of, and not because of, the Peanut and his military clique." He also sent a letter to Marshall commenting on Arnold's discussions with Chiang. The Generalissimo, he reported, "has been very irritable and hard to handle, upping his demands no matter what is given him, and this attitude will continue until he is talked to in sterner tones. For everything we do *for* him we should exact a commitment *from* him." The letter, which Marshall passed along to the President, also discussed the progress of Chinese training in preparation for the Burma attack, and ignored Chiang's demands for expanded air action.[32]

Roosevelt responded to all this by largely giving Chiang what he asked. In a message to the Generalissimo on March 8, he committed himself to the organization of a separate 500-plane air force in China under Chennault, to be built up as fast as facilities in China would allow, and the ultimate delivery of 10,000 tons a month over the Hump. In line with the views of his Chiefs, however, he also cautioned Chiang that the air freight route alone would "never be able to transport the combat essentials for your armies, your air force, and Chennault's air force. . . . Accordingly, we must keep constantly in mind our first essential, namely, that the land route of supply to China through Burma must be opened at the earliest possible moment."

Roosevelt's decision to accommodate Chiang rested partly on military considerations. With the British and the Chinese, who were to do the fighting in Burma, so grudging in their support of an attack, he had substantial doubts about American ability to compel a campaign. It seemed best, therefore, to let Chennault, who was intensely eager to fight, show what he could do. While Roosevelt did not expect a Japanese collapse from Chennault's air attack, he believed that Staff planners in Washington gave too little weight to the attrition which China-based air power could visit upon Japan's air and sea forces. Besides, he could not resist the feeling that some unorthodox boldness might pay the same kind of dividends it had in North Africa. "Just between ourselves," he told Marshall in a memo explaining his decision, "if I had not considered the European and African fields of action in their broadest geographic sense, you and I know we would not be in North Africa today—in fact, we would not have landed either in Africa or in Europe!"

Marshall did not accept Roosevelt's decision passively. While he promised to impress upon Stilwell the need to assist Chennault fully, he warned the President that "as soon as our air effort hurts the Japs, they will move in on us . . . on the ground." Without a well-trained, well-supplied Chinese Army, which Stilwell was trying to provide, there would be no way to defend the American airdromes or the terminals for the air transport route. Only "with a land supply route through Burma, and dependable forces to secure our air bases in China," Marshall asserted, could the United States take effective air action against Japan. This meant recapturing Burma with well-prepared Chinese troops. Chinese leaders, Marshall added, had "a let the other fellow do it" approach to the war. They wished to substitute an American air effort for the creation and use of an effective Chinese Army which would make that air effort count. To reverse this attitude and "the present low combat worth of the Chinese Army . . . must be the primary objective of any representative dispatched to this theater to represent American interests."

To this memo Marshall attached a message from Stilwell complaining of American actions that were adding to his problems with the Chinese. "The continued publication of Chungking propaganda in the United States is an increasing handicap to my work. Utterly false impression has been created in United States public opinion. Army is generally in desperate condition, underfed, unpaid, untrained, neglected, and rotten with corruption. We can pull them out of this cesspool," Stilwell declared, "but continued concessions have made the Generalissimo believe he has only to insist and we will yield." [33]

In meeting Chiang's demands, Roosevelt was mindful of Marshall's and Stilwell's concerns. He appreciated that the Chiang regime was corrupt and ruthless, that the Chinese Army badly needed reform, and that Stilwell was correct in describing Chiang as very irritable, hard to handle, and always upping his demands. If Stilwell's reports had not been enough to convince him, his experience with Madame Chiang was. Arriving in the United States in November, ostensibly for medical treatment, she moved into the White House in February, where she lobbied vigorously for China aid and showed herself to be more of an imperial potentate than First Lady of a democratic regime.

In a meeting with Hopkins she showed no interest in the war against Germany, or even in the Pacific, confining herself "entirely to what we are doing in China proper." In addresses to the two houses of Congress, which "enraptured" her audiences, she stressed the same theme. Her advocacy of helping China fight Japan was so effective that the Combined Chiefs thought it might unhinge the Europe-first strategy in the United States. At a press conference with the President, in which he said that aid to China would go forward "just as fast as the Lord will let us," she embarrassed him with the observation that "The Lord helps those who help themselves." To resist her pressure for greater help, he made a point of keeping her at a distance, and soon confided to Morgenthau that he was "just crazy to get her out of the country." Her personal behavior, moreover, "did not suggest a leader who was guiding her country toward a democratic future." At a time when John L. Lewis was threatening a coal miners' strike, Roosevelt asked Madame during a dinner how China would deal with such a labor leader in wartime. When she expressively drew a finger across her throat, the President laughed and called out to Eleanor, "Did you see that?" Later, in private, he asked his wife, who had described Madame as "small and delicate," "Well, how about your gentle and sweet character?" Madame's determination, he told Eleanor, was "as hard as steel." [34]

Despite his appreciation of the shortcomings in Chiang's regime and Army, Roosevelt would not make aid to China conditional on internal reforms and commitments to fight. He did not think it possible to impose American habits on the Chinese, and he refused to do anything that might undermine Chiang, for whom he had genuine regard. Stilwell, he told Marshall,

> has exactly the wrong approach in dealing with Generalissimo Chiang who, after all, cannot be expected, as a Chinese, to use the same methods that we do. . . . When he [Stilwell] speaks of talking to him in sterner tones, he goes about it just the wrong way.
>
> All of us must remember that the Generalissimo came up the hard way to become the undisputed leader of four hundred million people—an enormously difficult job to attain any kind of unity from a diverse group of all kinds of leaders—military men, educators, scientists, public health people, engineers, all of them struggling for power and mastery, local or national, and to create in a very short time throughout China what it took us a couple of centuries to attain.
>
> Besides that the Generalissimo finds it necessary to maintain his position of supremacy. You and I would do the same thing under the circumstances. He is the Chief Executive as well as the Commander-in-Chief, and one cannot speak sternly to a man like that or exact commitments from him the way we might do from the Sultan of Morocco.

A more important consideration for Roosevelt in refusing to extract concessions from Chiang was the fear that it might precipitate a political collapse, force China out of the war, and destroy plans for Japan's defeat. At the beginning of 1943, reports from China had indicated that Chiang's hold on some Kuomintang provinces had noticeably weakened, and that a rampant inflation made Chiang's political future and a continuing war effort doubtful. In these circumstances, Roosevelt opposed anything that might add to Chiang's burdens and lose China as a base of attack in the war. He had no intention, he announced in February, of spending the time "it would take to bring Japan to final defeat merely by inching our way forward from island to island across the vast expansion of the Pacific." "If we took one island, in the advance from the south, once a month . . . ," he told reporters, "I figured out it would take about fifty years before we got to Japan." The way to defeat Japan, he added, was to use China as a base of operations. Since pressuring Chiang to fight in Burma might be a spur to his and China's collapse, Roosevelt would not take this risk. It seemed better to let Chennault take air action, which, even if only temporarily effective, might buy time until the United States could make the necessary effort in Burma and China to defeat Japan.[35]

Roosevelt also worried that a China collapse would play havoc with postwar plans. He looked forward to having China help the United States preserve peace in the Pacific after the war. Though she was now occupied and weak, he believed that her large population would eventually make her a Great Power, and he wished to win her good will by treating her as if that day had already arrived. In the fall of 1942 he had sanctioned the negotiation of a treaty relinquishing extraterritorial rights in China, which, in Chiang's words, placed "an independent China on an equal footing with Great Britain and the United States." In March 1943, moreover, when Anthony Eden came to Washington to initiate discussions on postwar arrangements, he found the President insistent on the idea that China be treated as a major force in world affairs. "The President spoke of the need to associate China with other Powers in the solution of world problems," Eden cabled Churchill after one conversation. "I was not enthusiastic but the President maintained that China was at least a potential world Power and anarchy in China would be so grave a misfortune that Chiang Kai-shek must be given the fullest support." In further discussions, the President urged the inclusion of China as one member of a Four-Power executive committee which "would make all the more important decisions and wield police powers" in a postwar peacekeeping body. He also raised the possibility of having China act as a postwar trustee with the United States and Russia for Korea and French Indochina.

Churchill and Eden were distinctly unenthusiastic about the President's ideas. In October 1942 Churchill had told Eden that he could not "regard the Chungking Government as representing a great world Power. Certainly there would be a faggot vote on the side of the United States in any attempt to liquidate the British overseas Empire." While Eden was in Washington, Churchill spoke on the radio in Britain about postwar plans without mentioning China. When a member of the Foreign Office suggested that Eden rectify this notable omission in a speech in the United States, Churchill objected: "It is quite untrue to say that China is a world power equal to Britain, the U.S., or Russia, and I am reluctant to subscribe to statements." Eden held a similar view: When FDR told him "that China might become a very useful power in the Far East to help police Japan and that he wanted to strengthen China in every possible way," Eden "expressed a good deal of doubt . . . that . . . China could stabilize herself." He thought she might "have to go through a revolution after the war." Eden also said that he "did not much like the idea of the Chinese running up and down the Pacific." [36]

As with everyone else who had received realistic accounts of conditions in China, Roosevelt appreciated that China was not then a world power and might not become one for a long time after the war. His caution about China's postwar role was reflected in a letter of December 1942 from Owen Lattimore, an American expert on Asia, to Chiang. Closely worked on by the President, the letter was a response to Chiang's ideas on postwar peace, which he had asked Lattimore during a discussion in Chungking to put before FDR. Lattimore's letter emphasized that the President did "not wish to embarrass you [Chiang] by seeming to commit either you or himself in advance." Where the next sentence read, "this is the way his [the President's] mind is running," FDR had substituted, "I told the President that broadly speaking the following is the way my mind is running." Further, while the letter discussed the trusteeship idea and the possibility that China, America, Britain, and Russia would become "the four 'big policemen' of the world," Roosevelt cut out specific references to where China would play this part. He left in, however, the observation that "south of Korea the question of actual bases from which China and America might protect the peace of the western Pacific is one of those details which may be left for later consideration." The fact that the letter came from Lattimore rather than the President was alone evidence that FDR wished to avoid specific commitments to China's postwar role.

Despite his appreciation of China's weakness and caution about her ability to act as an international force after the war, Roosevelt saw the picture of a great-power China as a highly useful fiction. For one, he hoped to use China as a counterweight to Russia. He wanted China to be one of the four policemen in a postwar world organization, he told Eden, because "in any serious conflict of policy with Russia, [China] would undoubtedly line up on our side." He expected the same principle to apply to any occupation or trusteeship involving the three of them. For the sake of harmony in the North Pacific, he told Chiang in the Lattimore letter, Russia would have to be included in postwar arrangements, certainly for Korea, and possibly for Japan. If he could include China as one of the three trustees for these areas, it would give the United States an even greater political advantage over Russia than it would enjoy through China's great-power status in a world body. The United States, Eden told the War Cabinet after his visit, "probably regarded China as a possible counterpoise against Russia in the Far East." [37]

Another consideration for Roosevelt was popular insistence in the United States on a major part for China in world affairs. Madame Chiang's visit aroused the greatest outpouring of admiration and welcome received by anyone in the United States since Lindbergh flew the Atlantic. Conveying a sense of similarity and shared purpose with Americans, Madame, in the words of one British observer, consolidated "the American obsession for China . . . to an extent that it requires a definite mental effort on the part of persons in this country [Britain] to understand." Her visit moved Roosevelt to declare that for well over a century the people of China "have been, in thought and in objective, closer to us Americans than almost any other peoples in the world—the same great ideals. China," he added, "in the last—less than half a century has become one of the great democracies of the world." Roosevelt's rhetoric hardly squared with his first-hand reports of Chinese conditions, or his own observation about the differences between Chinese and American methods. But it was partly through this false picture of China that Roosevelt hoped to draw the United States into full-scale involvement in world affairs. "We have strong impressions," Eden reported at the close of his visit, "that it is through their feeling for China that the President is seeking to lead his people to accept international responsibilities." Since Americans seemed to find considerable attraction in the idea of working with a reliable "democratic" China, Roosevelt wanted her in the highest councils of power to act as a magnet drawing in the United States to do its part.[38]

Military developments in March and April confirmed Roosevelt in his decision to make the Chiang-Chennault proposal for air action America's principal military effort in China in 1943. The shipping shortage in March, which had persuaded Roosevelt and Churchill to cancel convoys to Russia temporarily, also convinced FDR to abandon the amphibious or southern part of the Burma attack in November and primarily "keep China going by air." In response to fresh pressure from Chiang for greater aid to Chennault, he promised to add to Chennault's forces as soon as ground facilities in China were ready for them, and to supply more transports to increase deliveries over the Hump. More specifically, he promised to give Chennault approximately 40 per cent of each 4000 tons coming to China each month. "I am fully convinced," he assured Chiang, "that from a strategic point of view one of the most important things we can do this year is to strike the enemy by air from China."

But this was not enough to satisfy Chiang. Frightened that a Japanese offensive launched in March might lead to the loss of Chungking, he now asked the President to call Chennault back to Washington to present the case for an air offensive. Roosevelt was ready to comply, but when Marshall pointed out that this would be an irreparable blow to Stilwell's authority, he agreed to have Chennault and Stilwell return at the same time. In another message to the President on April 29, the day before FDR began discussions with his two commanders, Chiang made clear what he wished: all resources—"the entire air transport tonnage" coming to China during the next three months—was to supply an early air offensive. "In the event the enemy attempts to interrupt the air offensive by a ground advance on the air bases," Chiang asserted, "the advance can be halted by the existing Chinese forces." [39]

A three-day argument, with Marshall, King, Arnold, and Stilwell on one side, and Admiral William D. Leahy, personal Chief of Staff to the President and Chairman of the Joint Chiefs since July 1942, Hopkins, and Chennault on the other, did not change Roosevelt's mind. Though Chennault's opponents had a powerful case, arguing that without an effective Chinese ground force, China could not be maintained as a base for bombing Japan, Roosevelt felt compelled to meet Chiang's wish for immediate action in the air. As he made clear to Marshall on May 2, he was completely against any delay in Chennault's program. While he wished to continue supplying Chinese land forces under Stilwell, and promised to "handle Chiang Kai-shek on that," he declared that "politically he must support Chiang . . . and that in the state of Chinese morale the air program was therefore of great importance." He also declared himself in favor of a modified Burma attack, ANAKIM, or strictly north Burma campaign; but he gave Marshall the impression that "nothing for ANAKIM should delay Chennault's air operations." It was evident to the Joint Chiefs from this discussion with the President that Chiang's situation "was critical and that there was a possibility of the collapse of his whole government," which "would affect seriously our prospects of success in the war against Japan." [40]

Before Roosevelt told Chiang of this decision, however, he wished to consult with Churchill and the British Chiefs, who were coming to Washington on May 11, 1943, for another full-scale discussion of military plans. The Washington or Trident Conference, as Churchill dubbed it, had been largely his idea. For a month beginning at the end of March, reports from North Africa and Washington had made him apprehensive about American willingness to mount more than air strikes against Italy after operation HUSKY, the invasion of Sicily, and about their inclination to help China at the expense of Europe-first.

During April, Roosevelt had done little to relieve Churchill of these concerns. On April 5, after Eden had brought him word that the President was ready to follow a successful invasion of Sicily with prompt action against Italy, to drop ANAKIM, the Burma attack, keep China going by air, and "continue as now" in the Southwest Pacific, Churchill cabled that "we are thinking along the same lines. . . . Now that

ANAKIM has receded," he said, ". . . Mediterranean operations gain more prominence." His hope was to exploit a success in Sicily with the invasion of Italy, or an attack in the eastern Mediterranean, and he asked that Hopkins and Marshall come to London to discuss these plans. But Roosevelt, who wished to modify, not abandon, ANAKIM, and had no desire to make commitments to post-Sicily operations until they had cleaned up the "Tunisian business" and were confident that HUSKY would take place, rejected the proposal for immediate talks.

Though Churchill was "much disappointed," he waited until the end of April to press the issue again. With the victory in Tunisia all but clinched, he cabled Roosevelt that it was "most necessary" for them to settle HUSKY, its subsequent exploitation, and the future of ANAKIM. There were "also a number of other burning questions" which he wished to "bring up to date." "I am conscious of serious divergences beneath the surface," he told Hopkins in a follow-up message, "which, if not adjusted, will lead to grave difficulties and feeble action in the summer and autumn. These difficulties we must forestall." "As recent telegrams from America show," General Alan Brooke, Britain's Chief of the Imperial General Staff, observed at the same time, ". . . we are just about where we were before Casablanca. Their hearts are really in the Pacific and we are trying to run two wars at once." [41]

The American Chiefs were as conscious of these "divergences" as the British. In a memorandum of May 8 for the President, they urged him to intimate at the upcoming Trident Conference in Washington that the United States would focus more on the Pacific if the British insisted on an unsound course of action in Europe. The continued bombing of Germany and a cross-Channel assault in 1944, they said, should "constitute the basic strategy" which "must not be delayed or otherwise prejudiced by other undertakings in Europe." While the American Chiefs recognized "certain advantages in prompt post-HUSKY operations in the western Mediterranean," they were irrevocably opposed to action east of Sicily and wished to ensure that anything done in the Mediterranean after HUSKY would not impede the transfer of forces to the United Kingdom for the invasion of France in 1944. In Asia, they warned against British depreciation of efforts against Japan in support of China: "ANAKIM should be undertaken and pressed to successful conclusion." If British opposition made this impossible, the United States should support China through expanded and intensified operations in the Pacific.

To deal with these differences, Churchill counselled his Chiefs not to commit themselves to any particular plan. "If we show ourselves unduly keen on any one plan others will be pressed as superior alternatives owing to the natural contrariness of allies." Hence, at the first meeting of the Conference on May 12 with the Combined Chiefs, he offered ideas for discussion rather than "fixed plans," and announced himself confident that the "questions of emphasis and priority" outstanding between the two Staffs would be "solved by mutual agreement." He then put forward the idea of following HUSKY with efforts to get Italy out of the war. It "would cause a chill of loneliness over the German people, and might be the beginning of their doom. But even if not immediately fatal to Germany, the effects . . . would be very great." The principal benefits he foresaw were: bases in Turkey for bombing Roumanian oil fields and clearing the Aegean, German reinforcement of the Balkans with divisions from the Russian front, and the elimination of the Italian fleet, which would free British naval units to fight Japan. Even more important, though, the campaign against Italy offered the best means of using the considerable forces concentrated in the Mediterranean during the seven or eight months before a cross-Channel attack. These forces "could not possibly stand idle, and he could not contemplate so long a period of apparent inaction. It would have a serious effect on relations with Russia, who was bearing such a disproportionate weight."

Churchill also took pains to assure the Americans that these operations were all a prelude to crossing the Channel as soon as possible. For Churchill and his Chiefs, further action in the Mediterranean was not essentially the product of a peripheral strategy or postwar political calculation, but of the conviction that it would make for a successful cross-Channel assault. As the British explained during the Conference, an Italian collapse would compel a German troop reduction in France, and "create a situation which will make the difference between success or failure of a re-entry into North West Europe in 1944!" Remembering the unsuccessful invasion of Turkey at Gallipoli in World War I, Churchill and his Chiefs were eager to assure against another major unsuccessful amphibious operation in World War II. The fact that additional steps in the Mediterranean might ultimately check Soviet expansion in the Balkans was another consideration in British minds. The fact, however, that Churchill made British willingness to cross the Channel contingent upon "a plan offering reasonable prospects of success," and that any additional large-scale attack in the Mediterranean might compel greater commitments than intended still left the American Chiefs skeptical of British determination to invade the Channel coast of France in 1944.

As for helping China, Churchill also took a flexible approach. In private, he had made clear to his Chiefs that ANAKIM was "physically impossible for 1943," and that he preferred not to fight in Burma at all. It would, he told General Brooke, be like "munching a porcupine quill by quill!" "Going into swampy jungles to fight the Japanese," he confided to his Chiefs on the way to the Conference, "is like going into the water to fight a shark." He favored demolishing the shark with axes after hauling him onto dry land. At the Conference, however, he was less blunt. "The difficulties of fighting in Burma," he said, "were apparent." The jungle prevented the use of modern weapons; the monsoon strictly limited the campaigning season; and sea power could play no part. He also pointed out that even if ANAKIM succeeded, they could not reopen the Burma Road until 1945, and then its maximum capacity would be only 20,000 tons a month. "Nevertheless," he asserted, "he had not gone back on the status of ANAKIM." He raised the possibility, though, of bypassing Burma for an operation against the tip of Sumatra and the waist of Malaya. He concluded with a reaffirmation of determination to carry the struggle home to Japan.[42]

Roosevelt's response to Churchill at this first session of the Conference demonstrated that he was more in harmony with his own Chiefs than at Casablanca and that British plans would have to conform more to American aims than in the past. Roosevelt left no doubt that he shared Churchill's desire to keep the large Allied forces that were concentrated in the Mediterranean engaged with the enemy. Leaving United Nations' forces idle meant "losing ground," he said, and he extolled the virtues of breaking German lines of communication through the Balkans and of seizing Sardinia. At the same time, however, he voiced concern about the drain on Allied resources from an occupation of Italy, and he urged a thorough investigation of the comparative costs of occupying "Italy proper," seizing only the country's "heel" and "toe," or striking her only by air from Sicily. Like his Chiefs, Roosevelt did not want further Mediterranean action to stand in the way of a cross-Channel attack. An invasion of northwest Europe had been talked about for two years, he said, but there was still no concrete plan. "Therefore he wished to emphasize that SLEDGEHAMMER [the limited cross-Channel assault] or ROUNDUP [the full-scale attack] should be decided upon definitely as an operation for the spring of 1944." He wished, he explained, to take the weight off Russia by meeting German forces head-on. "It was for that reason that he questioned the occupation of Italy, feeling that this might result in releasing German troops now in that country. . . . The most effective way of forcing Germany to fight was by carrying out a cross-Channel operation." [43]

Roosevelt's insistence on giving an invasion of France first priority carried the point. The fact that "the President intended to decide himself on the ultimate issues," Churchill later said of the Trident talks, ". . . exercised throughout . . . a dominating influence on the course of Staff discussions." In addition to six meetings with Roosevelt and Churchill during the two-week Conference, the Combined Chiefs presented them "each day with the questions on which they desired decisions as a result of their ceaseless labours." It was a tribute to the President's authority, Churchill advised his War Cabinet toward the close of the talks, that a satisfactory agreement on strategy emerged from the "most serious" differences between the Staffs. On May 19, after a week of argument over whether cross-Channel action first required the elimination of Italy, the Combined Chiefs agreed that twenty-nine divisions should be concentrated in the United Kingdom for an invasion of the Continent by May 1, 1944. In return for this commitment to the size and timing of a cross-Channel attack, the Americans agreed to instruct Eisenhower "to mount such operations in exploitation of HUSKY as are best calculated to eliminate Italy from the war and to contain the maximum number of German forces." A final decision on any operation, however, was to rest with the Combined Chiefs, and only those forces already in the Mediterranean, less seven divisions which were to go to Britain for the invasion of France, were to be available for such action.

Though Churchill agreed to this resolution on the 21st, by the 24th he had developed serious reservations about having no commitment to invade Italy. This, he later wrote, had been his main purpose for crossing the Atlantic, and he could not let the matter rest. Fearing that Eisenhower might select Sardinia as "the sole remaining objective for the mighty forces which were gathered in the Mediterranean," he pressed the Combined Chiefs and the President to commit themselves to invade Italy. But when they resisted, he asked to have Marshall accompany him to North Africa for talks with Eisenhower. This would allow him to continue the argument with his "chief antagonist at the conference." It would also assure that if Eisenhower agreed to an invasion of Italy, other American Chiefs would not be able to attack Eisenhower's decision as the consequence of uncontested pressure by Churchill.[44]

At the same time that Roosevelt gained his objectives for Europe, he also put across his China plans. Appreciating that the British would favor an air campaign in China over a Burma attack, he waited until the Conference to settle the Stilwell-Chennault debate. At the first meeting with the Combined Chiefs on May 12, he had emphasized the need for China as a base against Japan, the critical danger of a Chinese collapse, and the necessity of giving quick help by air. Like Churchill, he played down the importance of a Burma campaign, saying that the results of ANAKIM would not be felt until the spring of 1944 and that full use of the Burma Road would not be possible until 1945. While he also acknowledged Stilwell's point about the unreliability of Chinese armies without American-inspired reforms, he declared it "important to give the Generalissimo . . . what he wants at this time." He asked the Chiefs of Staff to "bear in mind the political fact that China was in danger of collapse."

Over the next six days, with British support and additional Chinese pressure, Roosevelt worked out a compromise with Marshall and Stilwell for the buildup of Chennault's air force. On the 14th, Churchill and his

Far Eastern commanders endorsed "a passionate development of air transport into China, and the buildup of air forces in China, as the objective for 1943." After ascertaining that Stilwell needed 2000 tons a month of supplies in the next five months for the Chinese Army, and that Chennault estimated his needs at 4700 tons a month for four months, Roosevelt concluded that "the immediate objective for the air route should . . . be 7,000 tons a month." On the 18th, after T. V. Soong, China's Foreign Minister, had warned the Combined Chiefs on the previous day that a failure to satisfy Chiang's demands for help might force China out of the war, Roosevelt gave Soong explicit commitments to an air buildup. With Marshall's agreement, he promised that, except for 500 tons each month, all supplies going over the Hump in May and June would be for air forces, and that beginning on July 1, Chennault would receive the first 4700 tons a month flown into China, with the next 2000 tons a month going to other purposes, including ground forces. This decision was reflected in the final report of the Conference: the first priority in CBI (the China-Burma-India theater) was "the building up and increasing of the air route to China to a capacity of 10,000 tons a month by early fall, and the development of air facilities in Assam [India] with a view to: (a) Intensifying air operations against the Japanese in Burma; (b) Maintaining increased American air forces in China; and (c) Maintaining the flow of airborne supplies to China."

Difficulties over Burma were harder to resolve. In the meeting on the 14th, the British had left no doubt that they wanted to scrap the whole ANAKIM plan. Stilwell's assertion that this would leave the Chinese feeling deserted and suspicious of the British moved Churchill to declare that he would not "undertake something foolish in order to placate the Chinese." He would not make war by "carrying out costly operations to no purpose." Bearing out Stilwell, Soong pressed the case for a Burma offensive in his presentation to the Combined Chiefs on the 17th. He emphasized that Chiang regarded the capture of Burma in 1943 as "a U.S./British commitment." Though Chiang wished to give first priority to an air buildup, by which the Americans would fight the Japanese, he also wanted his allies to make a full-scale effort in Burma to reopen the Road and supply his armies for a likely postwar clash with his domestic foes.

Churchill and Soong clashed openly about a Burma campaign at a Pacific Council meeting on May 20. Churchill's description of the difficulties involved in such an effort brought a strong response from Soong. The difficulty in Burma, Soong suggested, was with Britain's commanders, who were breaking commitments made at Casablanca and in Chungking to a Burma attack. "The situation of China is indeed desperate," Soong said with considerable feeling, ". . . she requires help by land as well as by air." The recovery of the Burma Road was a psychological as well as a material necessity, and the results of the failure to help China "in time could not be predicted." Churchill responded that the leadership in Burma "left little to be desired," that there were no commitments, and that "it would be a very foolish thing to consider pushing troops into Burma at the present time." Churchill's uncompromising language expressed his underlying belief that "the President and his circle. . . . feared unduly the imminence of a Chinese collapse if support were not forthcoming." It also demonstrated his conviction that Russia, and not China, was "the real answer to bringing about the *coup de grace* of Japan." He was not convinced, he said during the Conference, that China was an essential base.[45]

In response to pressures he met in the United States, however, he also tried to encourage the Chinese. Roosevelt made it clear to him that a Chinese collapse, which they could in any way blame on the United Nations, would have profound repercussions in the United States. His visit to Washington, Churchill told the War Cabinet on his return, showed him that American public opinion "was much more concerned about the war against Japan—it was almost true to say that the American public would be more disturbed if China fell out of the war than if Russia did so. Though this was not the view of Roosevelt and the leaders of his Administration," he assured his colleagues, "they could not fail to be influenced to some extent by public opinion."

Hence, in an address to the American Congress on May 19, Churchill spoke sympathetically of "tortured China." At the Pacific Council meeting on the following day, he promised Soong "that the British Empire would do everything humanly possible to support China," and he announced that British air squadrons would be added to the American and Chinese air forces fighting in China. He also urged Soong not to "send a report home that will be too discouraging to his people. We must all try to maintain the morale of all our allies," he said. Further, under direct prodding from the President, he agreed to meet Madame Chiang in Washington. But she refused the invitation "with some hauteur," and insisted that Churchill "make the pilgrimage to New York," where she was then staying. "To preserve unity in the Grand Alliance," Churchill offered to go halfway, if she would do the same. But Madame considered the offer "facetious." Churchill later wrote with evident sarcasm, "I never had the pleasure and advantage of meeting this lady until the Cairo Conference."

These American pressures also moved Churchill to accept a limited Burma campaign. Despite his aversion to these "unprofitable operations," he did not dispute the President's assertion at the meeting on the 14th that opening land communications through Burma should be their objective after the air buildup in China. Though there is no explicit record of additional discussion on Burma between him and the President during the next four days, Roosevelt had told Soong on the 18th that the United States was firmly committed to ANAKIM in the winter and "that he has advised the British that he expects them to carry out their part of this commitment." Moreover, Churchill agreed that the final report of the Conference should include a commitment to a north Burma campaign "at the end of the 1943 monsoon . . . as an essential step towards the opening of the Burma Road." He also subscribed to "the continuance of administrative preparations in India for the eventual launching of an overseas operation about the size of ANAKIM," and gave his consent to a message telling Chiang that "no limits, except those imposed by time and circumstances, will be placed on the above operations, which have for their object the relief of the siege of China." [46]

Accommodating Chiang was less difficult than satisfying Stalin. The plan for no second front until the spring of 1944 meant he would exert renewed pressure for an earlier attack. Suspended convoys and differences over Poland now threatened to make relations with Moscow particularly tense. Since the beginning of 1943, when Soviet military fortunes had improved, Moscow had increased pressure on the Polish Government in exile in London to accept the Polish-Soviet frontier of 1941 and the loss of eastern territories this entailed. But convinced that the Soviets intended to control Poland and that any agreement to Russian demands would discredit them with their underground movement at home, the London Poles resisted this pressure.

These demands raised inevitable questions in Roosevelt's mind about postwar Soviet intentions. In the first three months of 1943, William Bullitt encouraged these concerns in written and oral communications. On January 29 he had sent the President a long letter about Soviet relations which they subsequently discussed over lunch sometime during the next three months. Bullitt told FDR that America's national interest compelled an "attempt to draw Stalin into cooperation with the United States and Great Britain. . . . We ought to try to accomplish this feat, however improbable success may seem." Bullitt was deeply suspicious of Stalin's intentions, predicting that he probably aimed to dominate Europe and that he would take advantage of American preoccupation with Japan after Germany's collapse to put this across. To prevent this, Bullitt urged the President to meet Stalin in June in Washington, D.C., or Alaska. He suggested that Roosevelt use the talks to indicate to Stalin that unless Russia promised to fight Japan after Germany collapsed, to refrain from annexing any European country, and to dissolve the Comintern, the United States would shift from a Europe-first to a Pacific-first strategy and deny Russia additional wartime and postwar aid. Bullitt also suggested that the President consider invading Europe through the Balkans to assure that Stalin kept these promises.

Bullitt's thinking had an impact on FDR. In his conversations with Eden in March, he asked the Foreign Minister's view of Bullitt's warning that Stalin aimed to overrun and communize the Continent. Eden believed it impossible to give a definite opinion, but expressed the belief that, even if this were the case, nothing would be lost by trying to work with Stalin and assuming that he meant to honor his treaty with Britain. When Eden also said that Russia intended to absorb the Baltic states after the war, the President replied that American and English opinion would resist this development. He assumed, however, that the Russians would have control of these countries at the end of the war and that "none of us can force them to get out." He hoped, therefore, that the Russians would go through the motions of holding a plebiscite, and expressed his desire to use Anglo-American agreement to Soviet control of the Baltic states "as a bargaining instrument in getting other concessions from Russia."

As for Poland, Roosevelt was more sanguine than Eden about solving her difficulties with the U.S.S.R. Though Eden described the Poles as having very large ambitions after the war, hoping to emerge with her prewar boundaries intact and "as the most powerful state in that part of the world," Roosevelt expressed his determination to make arrangements for Poland and other small states which would help assure the postwar peace. He did not intend to bargain with Poland at the peace table, he said, but rather to give her control of East Prussia in exchange for territorial concessions to Russia in the East along the Curzon line.[47]

Roosevelt's hopes of arranging Polish affairs received a rude jolt in the following month. In mid-April the Germans announced the discovery of a mass grave in the Katyn Forest near Smolensk containing the remains of some 10,000 Polish soldiers. They accused the Russians of having executed them in the spring of 1940. In response, the London Poles asked the International Red Cross to conduct an inquiry. By contrast, British and American leaders initially blamed the atrocity on the Germans, calling their charges against the Russians "propagandist lies." Mindful of terrible German crimes against the Poles, including the destruction of Polish Jews in the Warsaw Ghetto at the moment of this announcement, Churchill told General Wladyslaw Sikorski, the head of the exile government, that the German statement was an obvious attempt to sow discord among the Allies. Later evidence, however, suggested to Churchill and others in the West that the Soviets were, indeed, responsible for this crime. Hence, in what now seems to have been an apparent attempt to cover up their guilt, the Soviets rejected Sikorski's request for a Red Cross inquiry and broke relations with the London Poles.

Churchill and Roosevelt tried to heal the breach. Promising to oppose any investigation in territory under German control as certain to be a "fraud," and warning that an open break would "do the greatest possible harm in the United States where the Poles are numerous and influential," Churchill asked Stalin to reverse himself. In a separate cable, Roosevelt added the suggestion that the diplomatic break be labled simply "a suspension of conversations," and explained that, while several million Polish-Americans were bitterly anti-Nazi, "the situation would not be helped by the knowledge of a complete diplomatic break between yourself and Sikorski."

Though Stalin replied that the issue was already settled, Churchill took further steps to change Stalin's mind. After persuading the Poles to issue a communiqué that shifted "the argument from the dead to the living and from the past to the future," he sent Stalin another message explaining that the London Poles had dropped their request to the Red Cross and now wished "to work loyally with you." He also urged against setting up a left-wing Polish government in Russia, saying that neither he nor Roosevelt would recognize it, and proposed a restoration of relations with Sikorski after a convenient interval. Ending with an expression of devotion to ever closer cooperation between Russia, America, and Britain, he asked: "What other hope can there be than this for the tortured world?" But Stalin, who was now determined to use renewed relations as a concession for Polish agreement to Soviet demands on frontiers, would concede nothing more than the possibility that better relations might follow the reconstitution of the Polish government.[48]

Though Churchill urged Roosevelt to send Stalin another message on this issue, FDR's thoughts were already fixed on how to cope with the tensions that would follow another deferral of a cross-Channel attack, and how to assure against the postwar dangers Bullitt had described. Certain, as he made clear at the opening of the Trident talks, that there could be no second front in France in 1943, he looked ahead to gaining Stalin's acceptance in the least acrimonious way. As before Casablanca, his idea was to do it face to face. Bullitt's warnings and recommendations had also strengthened his desire for a meeting. Consequently on May 5, he sent Joseph Davies, former Ambassador to Moscow and uncritical friend of the Soviet Union, to Russia to invite Stalin to meet on one side or other of the Bering Strait in the summer. A summer meeting, Roosevelt explained, would allow them to prepare for a possible German crackup in the winter, while the suggested locale would save them both from difficult flights and a meeting on or near British territory, where they would have to include Churchill. The meeting, he emphasized, was to be "an informal and completely simple visit" without staffs or "the red tape of diplomatic conversations." He would bring only Harry Hopkins, an interpreter, and a stenographer, and they would try to "get what we call 'a meeting of minds.'" There were to be no official agreements or declarations. In this setting, he would later tell Churchill, he hoped to avoid "collisions" over an immediate second front, and induce Stalin to speak more frankly about fighting Japan and about relations with China, the Balkan states, Finland, and Poland. He wished "to explore his thinking as fully as possible concerning Russia's postwar hopes and ambitions." [49]

Blunting difficulties over a second front, however, remained his principal concern. When he and Churchill were faced with telling Stalin of the Trident decisions at the close of the talks, they agonized over how it should be done. Animated by both a profound sense of obligation to the Russians for having endured unparalleled losses, while tearing "a large part of the guts out of the German army," and a desire to forestall impediments to wartime and postwar cooperation, they tried to sidestep the second-front issue. Instead of sending Stalin "an explanatory telegram," they agreed to send him a "version" of the Combined Chiefs' final report through "normal official channels." On the last night of the Conference they struggled unsuccessfully until two in the morning trying to prepare this communiqué. Finally, much to Roosevelt's relief, Churchill proposed completing the message himself during his return flight on the following day. During his journey, however, when he found himself stymied again, Churchill turned the task over to Marshall, who was with him, and the latter completed a draft in two hours which elicited Churchill's admiration.

Accepted by Roosevelt with only slight changes, the message described an overall strategy that gave first priority to securing overseas lines of communication and providing Russia with every practicable means of support. Translated into specific operations, this help was to include intensified air operations in Europe and the elimination of Italy from the war. Almost buried in the next-to-last paragraph was the information that "the concentration of forces and landing equipment in the British Isles should proceed at a rate to permit a full-scale invasion of the Continent . . . in the spring of 1944." [50]

Stalin would not accept the postponement of a second front until 1944 without a fight. On June 3, the day after Roosevelt sent Stalin the Trident communiqué, Davies indicated as much in a report on his Moscow visit. Stalin, Davies related, refused to consider either the success in North Africa or the air offensive against Germany a satisfactory substitute for a cross-Channel attack. He also gave Davies the impression that a failure to deliver on the second front in the summer would have far-reaching effects on Soviet attitudes toward the prosecution of the war and participation in the peace. Stalin expressed himself directly on the issue in a letter to FDR. The outcome of a massive German offensive in Russia that summer, he told the President, would greatly depend on the "speed and vigour" with which Anglo-American operations in Europe were launched. While he agreed to meet the President in July or August, he begged him to understand that he would not make a specific date until "these important circumstances" had been clarified. In short, he would not commit himself to a meeting until he was confident that it would not be used to blunt his pressure for a prompt cross-Channel attack.

The news of the Trident decisions evoked an angry response. The postponement of a second front contradicted promises earlier in the year for a second front in August or September, Stalin complained in a cable on June 11, and it created exceptional difficulties for the Soviet Union. It "leaves the Soviet Army, which is fighting not only for its country, but also for its Allies, to do the job alone, almost single-handed, against an enemy that is still very strong and formidable." It would produce a "dishearteningly negative impression" in the Soviet Union, where the people and the Army, "which has sacrificed so much," had anticipated substantial support from the Anglo-American armies. The Soviet government, he concluded menacingly, could not align itself with this decision, which had been made "without its participation and without any attempt at a joint discussion of this highly important matter and which may gravely affect the subsequent course of the war." [51]

Though Churchill expected the "castigation" they received from "Uncle Joe" and promised Roosevelt that he would prepare an "entirely good-tempered" reply, he was incensed at "these repeated scoldings" which "have never been actuated by anything but cold-blooded self-interest and total disdain of our lives and fortunes." He was particularly annoyed at Stalin's complaint about being excluded from their deliberations. In view of their efforts to bring about a tripartite conference, he thought Stalin's objection was "the limit." But it also made him anxious to know more about the President's exchange with Stalin through Davies, which Roosevelt had described to him in only general terms. Assuming, however, that FDR had proposed a meeting between the three of them, Churchill now urged that it be at Scapa Flow in Britain and that the moment had arrived "to make such a suggestion to U.J." Hence, in a message sent to Stalin with Roosevelt's approval on June 19, Churchill not only defended their strategic decisions as the best way to give Russia "substantial relief and satisfaction," but also urged the great need of a meeting between the three of them, which he would attend "at any risk" and in "any place."

Churchill now found himself compelled to make the case for a tripartite meeting to FDR as well. On the evening of June 24, Harriman told him of the President's desire to meet Stalin without him. It would create the opportunity for an "intimate understanding" which would be "impossible" in three-party talks, Roosevelt explained through Harriman. It would also have great appeal to the American people, who would be less favorable to a conference on British soil in which Churchill seemed to be the broker between Stalin and the President. But Churchill was not sold on the idea. He at once urged against anything but a full-scale conference at which the three of them would plan future strategy and lay the foundations for postwar peace. It "would be one of the milestones of history," he cabled FDR. Enemy propaganda, moreover, would make much of a meeting without Britain. "It would be serious and vexatious and many would be bewildered and alarmed thereby. . . . Nevertheless," he concluded, "whatever you decide, I shall sustain to the best of my ability here." [52]

An "offensive" reply from Stalin to the message of June 19, however, at once pushed Churchill's hopes for a tripartite meeting into the background. Reviewing earlier Anglo-American expressions of intent to invade Europe, Stalin declared his bewilderment at the fact that, despite greatly improved conditions since February, when an attack was promised for August or September, Britain and America had now decided to postpone the assault. Complaining again of their failure to invite Soviet representatives to the Washington talks, he stated that "the Soviet Government cannot become reconciled to this disregard of vital Soviet interests. . . . The point here," he concluded, "is not just the disappointment of the Soviet Government, but the preservation of its confidence in its Allies, a confidence which is being subjected to severe stress. . . . It is a question of saving millions of lives in the occupied areas of Western Europe and Russia and of reducing the enormous sacrifices of the Soviet armies, compared with which the sacrifices of the Anglo-American armies are insignificant."

In a spirited reply, Churchill declared that he had at all times been sincere with Stalin, reminded him that Britain had been left alone to fight the Nazis until June 1941, that he had instantly begun helping Russia after the Nazi attack, and that he had done "everything in human power to help you. Therefore the reproaches which you now cast upon your Western Allies leave me unmoved." Reviewing once again the shipping difficulties which stood in the way of a sufficient buildup to make a cross-Channel attack possible, he asserted that only the course of events had modified their decisions, and that their Mediterranean operations had delayed Hitler's summer offensive in Russia and might even save her entirely from any heavy summer attack. Churchill, however, as Sir A. Clark Kerr, his Ambassador in Moscow, pointed out, failed to persuade Stalin with these arguments—not because the case against opening a second front was weak, but because they had allowed him to believe they would.

Churchill, who feared that this exchange might mark the end of his correspondence with Stalin, now urged Roosevelt to meet Stalin alone "if you can get him to come." He thought it curious, he told FDR, that Stalin had recalled his Ambassadors from Washington and London, and that there was no German offensive on the Russian front, which he did not believe "necessarily due only to our Mediterranean activities." Yet he refused to believe that they would see a Russian about-face; "the deeds done between the German and Russian masses" and Russia's interest in the future world seemed to rule this out. Nevertheless, he felt the important thing now was for the President to establish contact with "Uncle J."

Having used Churchill to create some greater rapport with Stalin, first by suggesting his exclusion from a meeting, and second, by leaving the burden of the argument with Stalin to him, Roosevelt now tried to balance accounts between his allies. He tried to relieve Churchill's resentment over his possible exclusion from a meeting by falsely reporting that it was Stalin's suggestion and by arguing that it would be only a "preliminary" or "preparatory talk on . . . a lower level." He proposed that they and their staffs follow this with a conference in Quebec in late August and a full-dress meeting with the Russians in the fall. "I have the idea," he asked Churchill to believe, "that your conception is the right one from the short point of view, but mine is the right one from the long point of view. I wish," he said about the difficulties between them, "there were no distances." [53] But there were, and the military and political decisions they confronted in the second half of 1943 further tested their ability to cooperate not only with each other but also with France, China, and above all, the U.S.S.R.

14

Alliance Politics

THE ONLY THING WORSE than having allies, Churchill once said, is not having them. When it came to de Gaulle, Roosevelt was not so sure. His continuing drive for political power after Casablanca seemed to jeopardize wartime and postwar goals: it created instability and the danger of civil strife in North Africa; it raised the possibility of a postwar dictatorship in France; and it threatened to bar the United States from a say in Dakar and Indochina, which Roosevelt believed essential to postwar security in the Americas and Asia. During the Trident Conference, Roosevelt and Hull had told Churchill that continued British backing of de Gaulle would cause serious friction with the United States. But Churchill, who appreciated that de Gaulle had wider French support than FDR believed and considered de Gaulle an indispensable symbol of French resistance and a potential ally against postwar Soviet expansion in Europe, asked Roosevelt to suspend judgment until de Gaulle and Giraud completed pending negotiations in North Africa.

The de Gaulle-Giraud discussions in Algiers beginning on May 31, 1943, increased Roosevelt's antagonism to de Gaulle. Though de Gaulle agreed to the establishment of a French Committee of National Liberation under his and Giraud's shared control, he also demanded power over all French forces and the removal of Pierre Boisson, the Vichyite Governor General of West Africa. Roosevelt at once advised Eisenhower and Churchill that he would not "remain quiescent" in the face of such developments. He might send troops and naval vessels to prevent de Gaulle's control of Dakar, he declared, and he would not allow him to endanger Anglo-American forces in the Mediterranean by controlling the French Army in North Africa.

Roosevelt now unequivocally urged Churchill to abandon de Gaulle. Declaring himself "fed up" with him and "absolutely convinced that he has been and is injuring our war effort . . . that he is a very dangerous threat to us . . . and that he would double-cross both of us at the first opportunity," Roosevelt suggested a "break" in relations. To meet "emotional" criticism to such a move, he proposed identical action by Britain and the United States in this "miserable mess" and the creation of a committee of Frenchmen eager to put the war above politics.

Churchill resisted the President's plan. He shared Roosevelt's feeling that no confidence could be placed in de Gaulle's friendship for the Allies and endorsed his decision to prevent de Gaulle's "potentially hostile control" of the French Army. But he remained opposed to the idea of breaking with de Gaulle or the Committee of National Liberation, "on which many hopes are founded amongst the United Nations as well as in France." Instead, he urged that the onus of a break be put on de Gaulle, who would probably resign from the Committee rather than accept the President's conditions for "trustworthy" control of the French Army and the safety of Anglo-American forces. De Gaulle, however, avoided a showdown over the issue by agreeing to have Giraud command French forces in North and West Africa while he controlled all forces in the rest of the Empire.[1]

The argument now shifted to the National Committee, which was asking recognition as the director of France's war effort and protector of all French interests. Since recognition would give the Gaullists claims to a say in both wartime and postwar arrangements, Roosevelt was opposed. While Churchill was much more sympathetic, he wished to defer the decision until he knew more clearly how the Committee was going to behave. He worried, however, that the Soviets would undermine postwar Anglo-French unity in Europe by promptly recognizing the Committee. Consequently, he asked Stalin to withhold recognition until they "had reasonable proof that its character and action will be satisfactory to the interests of the Allied cause." Though Stalin grudgingly agreed, Churchill appreciated that he could not hold off either Stalin or the French Committee indefinitely.

In July, therefore, when Eisenhower and Murphy recommended recognition, Churchill was ready to act. He was "under considerable pressure" from his Foreign Office, Cabinet colleagues, and "force of circumstances," he told FDR. Since he already had had numerous dealings with the Committee on a de facto basis and preferred to deal with it rather than de Gaulle "strutting about as [a] combination of Joan of Arc and Clemenceau," he wished to grant "a measure of recognition" in conjunction with the United States, or to have Britain act alone. But Roosevelt sent a "chilling" response. He advised waiting for more satisfactory evidence of the Committee's genuine unity and single-minded determination to fight the Axis, and suggested that, instead of recognition, which would be distorted to mean that they had recognized the Committee as the government of France, they acknowledge the " 'acceptance' of the Committee's local, civil authority in various colonies on a temporary basis." Convinced that the President's formula would not end the agitation for recognition in their respective countries, Churchill proposed a statement of recognition that would include the requirement that the Committee afford them "whatever military and economic facilities and securities in the territories under its administration" they needed for the war effort. This, he contended, would give "us complete power to override or break with them in the event of bad faith or misconduct." Since this was also unacceptable to FDR, they agreed to leave "this tiresome business" until they met again at Quebec in August.[2]

Their discussion of the subject at the Quebec meeting only served to underscore existing differences. With the fighting moving from North Africa to Sicily and toward Italy, the issue now was less de Gaulle's ability to cause immediate military problems than the possibility that he would create long-run political ones. Roosevelt wanted "a sheet anchor out against the machinations of de Gaulle," and "he did not want to give de Gaulle a white horse on which he could ride into France and make himself the master of a government there." Since he believed recognition of the National Committee tantamount to endorsing de Gaulle's drive for postwar control and since he considered this destructive to his postwar plans for arms control in Europe and decolonization in Africa and Asia, FDR wished to maintain the status quo, or "let the whole thing rock along."

In this, Roosevelt had an unyielding advocate in Hull. Strongly antagonistic to the Gaullists for their attacks on him, Hull, in Eden's words, had "an obsession against [the] Free French which nothing can cure." Eden himself, who made no bones about his desire to rebuild France "so far as I could," was equally stubborn in his determination to recognize the National Committee. When their discussion of the subject became "quite heated," Hull remarked that Eden reminded him of a politician in his own country. "Are you . . . not a politician too?" Eden asked. "I retired from politics, and now I'm a statesman," Hull declared. "If you are a statesman, what am I?" Eden asked. "A statesman," Hull retorted, "is a retired politician like myself." "A statesman," Eden said, "is a politician with whom one happens to agree." By that standard, Eden added, he was unable to apply the title to Hull that day. "Hull laughed and matters became a little easier, but the Committee still stuck in the American throat."

When neither Roosevelt nor Churchill could find a formula on which both sides could fully agree, they decided to issue separate statements on relations with the Committee. While both welcomed its establishment as a vehicle for fighting the war, which both also described as the "paramount" concern, they diverged sharply on the measure of recognition each would accord. The American declaration explicitly ruled out recognition "of a government of France or of the French Empire," and limited its acceptance of the Committee to the administration of "those French overseas territories which acknowledge its authority," and to functions "within specific limitations during the war." By contrast, the British said nothing about the Committee as a government of France or the Empire, and specifically acknowledged it "as the body qualified to ensure the conduct of the French effort in the war within the framework of inter-allied cooperation." Other differences in wording suggested that the British were more confident of the Committee's determination to cooperate in the fighting and more receptive to having it become a full-blown ally. In short, the American statement was decidedly more restrained in its acceptance of de Gaulle.[3]

Despite the tension it generated, France was a secondary problem at Quebec, where operations in the Mediterranean after Sicily was the issue of first concern. At the end of May, Churchill's discussions with Marshall, Eisenhower, and the military chiefs in Algiers had ended in no clear-cut decision on post-HUSKY action. The invasion of Sicily on July 10 helped focus the issue. By July 20, rapid Allied progress along with growing signs of Italian reluctance to fight decided American and British Chiefs to follow the capture of Sicily with an invasion of the mainland. American and British Chiefs, however, had different conceptions of what this meant. Where Stimson and Marshall saw an advance into Italy as a limited operation that would get no farther than Rome and do nothing to impede the progress of cross-Channel preparations, Churchill and his Staff viewed it as a first step toward the conquest of all Italy and as a prelude to seizing additional opportunities in the Mediterranean and southern Europe. All this, Churchill believed, would help assure the success of a cross-Channel attack, or prevent a disaster marked by a Channel full of Allied corpses. It also opened the possibility of checking Soviet power in the Balkans.

Though Roosevelt had firmly committed himself during Trident to a cross-Channel attack in May 1944, he was ready to take advantage of other strategic opportunities, even if it meant some reduction or delay in cross-Channel operations. At the end of June, for example, when a possible Allied occupation of the Azores and a defense of Portugal raised the likelihood of reduced forces for post-HUSKY and cross-Channel attacks, Roosevelt had believed it necessary to "accept this interference." Further, in mid-July, when Churchill used a message from General Smuts to make the case for capturing Rome, knocking Italy out of the war, and creating new bases for advances "northward as well as eastward to the Balkans and Black Sea and westward toward France," Roosevelt declared his liking for Smuts's idea and hope that "something of that kind can be undertaken."

Political developments in Italy at the end of July increased the attractions of a significant effort against the Italian mainland and subsequent attacks on the Balkans. On July 25, a bloodless coup led by King Victor Emmanuel III forced Mussolini's resignation and raised hopes for an early Italian capitulation. In response, the Combined Chiefs approved the addition of four British aircraft carriers to Mediterranean forces and authorized Eisenhower to invade Italy near Naples at the earliest possible moment. The American Chiefs, however, remained determined to prevent additional forces from going to the Mediterranean and to assure that scheduled withdrawals for the cross-Channel attack would not be changed. Though a renewed warning from Marshall on July 25 against Churchill's continuing desire for peripheral attacks in Europe evoked a sympathetic response from FDR, he continued to find merit in Churchill's ideas. If any peace overtures come from Rome, he cabled Churchill the following day, "we must be certain of the use of all Italian territory and transportation against the Germans in the north and against the whole Balkan peninsula, as well as use of airfields of all kinds." In another message to Churchill on July 30, Roosevelt declared himself in agreement with his belief that they should also exploit an Italian collapse by considering action north of Rome, seizing Corfu and the Dodecanese islands, and sending "agents, commandos and supplies by sea across the Adriatic into Greece, Albania, and Yugoslavia." 4

Roosevelt's attraction to these Mediterranean operations rested on military and political considerations. On the one hand, he was strongly committed to crossing the Channel: it promised the quickest road to victory in Europe and a friendly Soviet response which might be converted into a full-scale accommodation. On the other hand, he did not wish to miss a military and political opportunity in southern Europe which might quicken the pace of German collapse and shield the Balkans from Soviet power. Since, contrary to the conventional view of FDR's wartime attitude toward Moscow, he was uncertain about postwar relations with Russia, he wished to assure against the possibility that Stalin aimed at extensive European control.

During the second week of August, when Stalin reneged on his promise to meet, Roosevelt's interest in Mediterranean operations increased. On July 15, as he began making plans with Churchill for their Quebec conference, he had asked Stalin to name a date for their meeting, which he still considered "of great importance to you and me." He still had hopes that Stalin would meet him, he had told Halifax on July 7, and if they met, "he thought he might get something out of him on his real thought about one day joining in on Japan." On August 8, however, Stalin responded that his presence at the front had delayed his reply and that his need "to subordinate all else to the interests of the front" would prevent him from making good his promise through Davies for a meeting in the summer or autumn. Unwilling to take Stalin's explanation at face value, Roosevelt concluded that he was giving "us . . . [the] runaround." On the following afternoon Roosevelt told Marshall that he wished to send seven more divisions from the United States to the Mediterranean, and said "in a humorous vein" that "he wanted assistance in carrying out his conception rather than difficulties placed in the way of it." These troops were to replace the veteran forces going to Britain in the fall for the cross-Channel attack, now code-named OVERLORD.

When Roosevelt made this suggestion, he emphasized his commitment to OVERLORD and obscured his real purpose by avowing his opposition to an attack in the Balkans. His intention, he explained, was to obtain control north of Rome and create a serious threat to southern France by seizing Sardinia and Corsica. But Marshall was not misled. On the following day he successfully countered the President's proposal by pointing out to him and the Joint Chiefs that Eisenhower already had enough troops to fulfill these tasks and that an additional seven divisions from the United States would simply invite an invasion of the Balkans. This, Marshall added, would "have a disastrous effect on the main effort from England."

Though Roosevelt at once backed away from his plan and reaffirmed his opposition to invading the Balkans, his earlier messages to Churchill and future flirtations with such operations suggest that Bullitt's ideas about preventing Soviet expansion by entering Europe through the Balkans had not left his mind. It is certainly striking that his proposal for strengthening Mediterranean forces came on the same day he received Stalin's rejection. It is also striking that in a discussion with the Joint Chiefs on August 10 he showed himself much preoccupied with the Balkans, which he said the British wanted to shield from Russian influence by getting there first. Though he also declared himself at odds with the belief that the Russians wished to take over the area, he said that "in any event, he thought it unwise to plan military strategy based on a gamble as to political results." In short, since his Chiefs were so uniformly opposed to action in southeastern Europe, he could not see going ahead on political grounds alone. Even Bullitt had firmly opposed that.[5]

The likelihood of an Italian collapse raised questions not only about future strategy but also about terms of surrender. The problem Roosevelt confronted after Mussolini's collapse was to find a practical middle ground between liberal demands for a prompt replacement of fascism by democratic rule and Churchill's determination to sustain a constitutional monarchy, even if it meant relying on some of Mussolini's collaborators. "We should come as close as possible to unconditional surrender," FDR had told Churchill on July 26, but he opposed any rigid application of the idea. Though he publicly announced that "we will have no truck with Fascism in any way, in any shape or manner," and promised that "we will permit no vestige of fascism to remain," he openly rebuked his Office of War Information for attacking Victor Emmanuel, Mussolini's accomplice, as that "moronic little king," and took pains to explain at a press conference that the political transformation of Italy could not occur overnight.

There are two essential conditions a victorious army wants to meet in a conquered country, he told reporters on July 30. "The first is the end of armed opposition. The second is . . . to avoid anarchy. . . . I don't care with whom we deal in Italy," he added, "so long as it isn't a definite member of the Fascist Government, as long as they get them to lay down their arms and so long as we don't have anarchy." But that was only a first step. In the long run, the objective would be to assure self-determination or democratic rule. This was his answer, he told Churchill, to those "contentious people here who are getting ready to make a row if we seem to recognize the House of Savoy or Badoglio," Mussolini's former Chief of Staff who replaced the Duce as Prime Minister.[6]

Where Churchill warmly endorsed Roosevelt's willingness to deal with Victor Emmanuel and General Pietro Badoglio, he resisted the President's suggestion that they make a pronouncement on self-determination. The issue between them of Italy's ultimate form of government expressed itself more fully through a debate over the contents of armistice terms and the means by which they would put them into effect. Roosevelt favored a proposal limited to military matters, which Eisenhower would present in response to an Italian overture. Churchill, by contrast, wanted to negotiate an armistice through diplomatic channels: it was to include political and economic as well as military conditions and was to recognize the authority of the existing Italian government, excluding Fascists, to implement the agreement. "I am not in the least afraid . . . of seeming to recognize the House of Savoy or Badoglio," Churchill cabled FDR, "provided they are the ones who can make the Italians do what we need for our war purposes. Those purposes would certainly be hindered by chaos, bolshevisation or civil war. . . . It may well be that after the armistice terms have been accepted, both the King and Badoglio will sink under the odium of surrender and that the Crown Prince and a new Prime Minister may be chosen."

But unwilling to tie himself to any regime or its heir, Roosevelt opposed Churchill's armistice plan. On July 30, he insisted that Eisenhower be ready with a precise statement of military terms if he were "suddenly approached" by the Italian government. While Churchill accepted this procedure as a way to deal with an "immediate emergency," he pressed Roosevelt to accept the more detailed British document as the ultimate "instrument of surrender." But Roosevelt seriously doubted the "advisibility of using it at all." He believed the surrender terms given to Eisenhower were all that was necessary. "Why tie his hands by an instrument that may be oversufficient or insufficient?" he asked Churchill. "Why not let him act to meet situations as they arise? You and I," he concluded, "can discuss this matter at Quadrant [the conference in Quebec]."[7]

At the Conference, Churchill persuaded FDR to adopt his more comprehensive armistice plan. By the time the President and Churchill met at Quebec on August 17, the Badoglio government had made serious overtures to the Allies for an end to the fighting and had been told to present a document offering unconditional surrender. On the 18th, Roosevelt and Churchill instructed Eisenhower to put the limited armistice agreement before Badoglio's representative in Lisbon, where the surrender discussions were in progress. On August 23, however, Churchill and Eden "apparently" persuaded Roosevelt to substitute their "long document" for the President's military terms, and Eden notified the British Ambassador in Lisbon to do just that. Three days later, Roosevelt sent Eisenhower the same instruction.

Churchill apparently converted the President to his view by arguing that without a measure of recognition Badoglio's government would collapse, Italian forces would not resist Germany, and Italy would turn "Red." In a report Churchill described to Roosevelt as having "substantial" worth, one of Badoglio's envoys declared that "20 years of Fascism has obliterated the middle class. There is nothing between the King and the patriots who have rallied round him and rampant Bolshevism." On August 19, after two days at the Conference, Roosevelt had joined Churchill in telling Stalin that the Badoglio government would probably not last very long. Either the Germans would overthrow it and set up "a Quisling Government of Fascist elements," or "Badoglio may collapse and the whole of Italy pass into disorder."

Circumstances now intervened to prolong the argument over extending recognition to Badoglio's government. Because Eisenhower feared that the more comprehensive terms might delay Italy's surrender, he received permission to limit the initial capitulation to the brief military agreement. This was signed on September 3, 1943, the day British forces invaded the southern tip of Italy across from Sicily, and made public on the 8th, the day before the main attack on Italy began at Salerno. In response to strong German resistance in Italy in the two weeks after the attack, Roosevelt suggested withholding the "long-term Armistice provisions" or recognition of Badoglio's government until it declared war on Germany, when it could become a "cobelligerent." Such recognition, however, was in no way to prejudice the "untrammelled right" of the Italian people to decide their future form of government. But with Churchill and Stalin wishing to support the King and Badoglio as strongly as possible against a new Mussolini government set up by Hitler, Roosevelt agreed to implement the comprehensive surrender terms and accept Badoglio's rule.

Once this was done, though, Roosevelt pressed the case for an Italian declaration of war and a statement of intent to accept a popularly elected government after German defeat. On October 13, when Badoglio complied with these demands, Roosevelt and Churchill recognized Italy's cobelligerency, and endorsed the "absolute" right of the Italians to decide "by constitutional means . . . the democratic form of government they will eventually have." This signaled the start of an Anglo-American competition to decide whether the King and Badoglio or a more liberal, anti-Fascist regime would lead Italy into the postwar era. With regard to the Italian government, FDR told his Joint Chiefs in the following month, "the British are definitely monarchists." Though he declared himself eager "to get the King out," he would not go against a request from Eisenhower "to get to Rome before there is any 'bust-up.'" Consequently, the issue remained unsettled for another six months.[8]

Between August and October, while Roosevelt and Churchill debated Italian politics, they also continued their discussion of future strategy. During his conference with the Joint Chiefs on August 10, FDR had backed away from stepped-up efforts in the Mediterranean and reaffirmed his commitment to a cross-Channel attack as the primary goal for 1944. During the Quebec talks, moreover, he remained a steadfast supporter of the cross-Channel operation, aiding his Chiefs to extract a fresh, but still qualified, commitment from the British to an invasion of northwest France in May 1944. Though the British avowed their determination to carry out OVERLORD, they emphasized the need to reduce German strength in France and the Low Countries through prior Mediterranean operations. Marshall called this support by "indirection," and said that unless an overriding priority were given to OVERLORD, it would never take place, or would become a "subsidiary operation."

By the close of the Quebec talks on August 24, the British had agreed to affirm cross-Channel operations in 1944 as "the primary U.S.-British ground and air effort against the Axis in Europe," and to use "available resources" to ensure the success of OVERLORD before sending more of them to the Mediterranean. Churchill cautioned, however, that he would defer the cross-Channel attack if there were more than twelve mobile German divisions in northern France, or if the Allies had not gained definite superiority over German fighter forces at the time of the assault. Though the British also agreed to limit Mediterranean operations to those forces allotted at the Trident Conference, they overrode Marshall's objections to including the qualification that "these may be varied by decision of the Combined Chiefs of Staff."

Roosevelt's reaffirmation of OVERLORD at Quebec demonstrated his determination to put military above political considerations and his hopes for a postwar accommodation with the U.S.S.R. His comments at Quebec and after, though, also suggest his continued interest in European operations that might act as a bar to postwar Soviet control. In meetings at Quebec with the Combined Chiefs, he expressed his desire for the "stepped up" movement of American troops to England and asked about plans for an emergency landing in Europe, indicating "that he desired United Nations troops to be ready to get to Berlin as soon as did the Russians." He also inquired about plans for action in the Balkans if the Germans withdrew to "the line of the Danube." He declared himself "most anxious to have the Balkans [sic] divisions which we have trained, particularly the Greeks and Yugoslavs, operate in their own countries." Later in these talks he "reiterated his desire to use the Yugoslav and Greek divisions in the Balkans if the opportunity arose." If getting Anglo-American forces into the Balkans ahead of the Russians were beyond reach, he apparently wished native troops to do the job. Judging also from his comment to Churchill, Eden, and Mackenzie King during the Conference that he needed China "as a buffer state between Russia and America," he wanted some means of checking the Russians in Europe as well.[9]

Roosevelt's and Churchill's suspicions of the Soviets reached something of a climax on the last day of the Conference. On August 24 they received a cable from Stalin which attacked them for failing to keep him fully informed about the Italian negotiations. Though they had in fact tried to do this, a long cable sent from Quebec on August 19 had reached him garbled and incomplete. When he still had not received the complete text on the 22nd, his suspicions were aroused that they were intentionally excluding the U.S.S.R. He declared the time "ripe" to set up a tripartite military-political commission to conduct all surrender negotiations and to stop treating the Soviet Union "as a passive third observer. I have to tell you," he stated, "that it is impossible to tolerate such a situation any longer. I propose to establish this Commission and to assign Sicily at the beginning as the place of residence." Roosevelt "was very much offended at the tone of this message," and told his dinner companions on the 24th that he and the Prime Minister were "both mad" about Uncle Joe's cable. Churchill "arrived with a scowl and never really got out of his ill humor all evening—up to three A.M." Churchill "foresaw 'bloody consequences in the future. . . . Stalin is an unnatural man,' " he said. " 'There will be grave troubles.' "[10]

Though subsequent exchanges during the next three weeks were much friendlier, Churchill and Roosevelt remained uneasy about Soviet intentions. Churchill, who had told Harriman at the end of June that Stalin saw a second front in Western Europe as a way to keep Anglo-American forces out of the Balkans, returned to the idea of a Balkan campaign during further talks in Washington in September. On the 9th, the day after Italy had surrendered and Anglo-American forces had begun their invasion of the Italian mainland, Churchill asked for a fresh strategy review to evaluate the prospects opened by Italy's collapse. In a meeting that afternoon with the President and Combined Chiefs, he urged that after capturing Naples and Rome, they should construct a strong fortified line across the narrow part of the Italian peninsula and "divert a portion of our troops for action . . . to the West or to the East. We are both of us acutely conscious of the great importance of the Balkan situation," he told FDR, and suggested the possibility of later sparing "some of our own forces assigned to the Mediterranean theater to emphasize a movement North and North-Eastward from the Dalmatian ports." He was also eager for operations against the Dodecanese Islands in the Aegean.

Though Marshall and his planners viewed any shift of forces to the east, particularly to the Dalmatian coast, as "a dangerous diversionary idea," Roosevelt was receptive to the suggestion. He said that "operations in the Balkans would be largely a matter of opportunity" which he wished them to "be prepared to take advantage of." Though Churchill and Roosevelt found considerable appeal in exploiting possible German weakness in the Balkans, they were also thinking of long-run political consequences. The fact that they were both "acutely conscious of the great importance of the Balkan situation" suggests that they had more than a strategic opportunity in mind.[11]

Roosevelt and Churchill also expressed their anxiety about postwar relations with Russia through an atomic-energy agreement concluded at Quebec. Joint efforts to build an atomic bomb had begun in the fall of 1941 when British and American scientists had advised them that this would be the fastest way to get the job done. In the second half of 1942, however, when the work shifted from basic research to development and manufacture, the President's advisers recommended "restricted interchange" of information on atomic energy. Arguing that work on the bomb was now almost exclusively American and that sharing the military secrets would in no way advance the British war effort, the criterion for providing information, they convinced Roosevelt to reveal only that which the British or Canadians could "take advantage of . . . in this war." The decision promised to give the United States exclusive postwar military and commercial control of atomic power.

Churchill did not accept the President's decision passively. In February 1943 he had pressed Roosevelt through Hopkins to resume full collaboration on atomic development. Complete wartime cooperation, he told Hopkins, "had always been taken for granted. . . . When the President and I talked of this matter at Hyde Park in June 1942, my whole understanding was that everything was on the basis of fully sharing the results as equal partners." Though Churchill emphasized speed of development as the reason for full collaboration, he and his advisers wanted the information for postwar purposes. Wartime development of the bomb had little to do with their request. As historian Martin J. Sherwin has shown, Churchill and his advisers were determined not "to face the future without this weapon and rely entirely on America, should

Russia or some other Power develop it." Whatever reasons Churchill cited "for his determination to acquire an independent atomic arsenal after the war," Sherwin points out, "it was Great Britain's postwar position with respect to the Soviet Union that invariably led the list." At a meeting in July 1943 with Stimson and Vannevar Bush, the Chairman of the President's Military Policy Committee on Atomic Energy, Churchill said that Britain was "vitally interested" in having all information on atomic energy because it would be "necessary for Britain's independence in the future as well as for success during the war; that it would never do to have Germany or Russia win the race for something which might be used for international blackmail; and that Russia might be in a position to accomplish this result unless we worked together."

During the Trident Conference in May 1943, Churchill had persuaded the President to resume full collaboration on atomic energy. Though there is no record of their conversation, it is clear from post-conference documents that Roosevelt agreed to a renewed exchange of information, and "that the enterprise should be considered a joint one, to which both countries would contribute their best endeavours." Roosevelt also probably knew that the British would not be able to use this information during the war but desired to develop the bomb promptly after the war as a defense against "some other country [than the United States] which might have it far developed at that time."

But even if this were not entirely clear to Roosevelt at the Trident talks in May, it became so during the following month, and this in no way inhibited him from implementing his agreement with Churchill. On the contrary, he not only asked Bush in July to "renew, in an inclusive manner, the full exchange of information with the British Government" on atomic energy, he also made a formal agreement on the subject with Churchill at Quebec in August. In a document signed on the 19th, they pledged never to "use this agency against each other," nor "against third parties without each other's consent." Further, they promised not to "communicate any information" about atomic development "to third parties except by mutual consent," agreed, in view of America's principal role in production, to give the President power to determine what postwar commercial advantages Britain might receive, and to establish a Combined Policy Committee "to ensure full and effective collaboration . . . in bringing the project to fruition." While Roosevelt made this agreement partly to help safeguard wartime harmony with Britain, he was also mindful of the fact that it might help check postwar Soviet power. If Russia emerged from the war within easy reach of the bomb and set out upon extended European control, Britain could effectively counter her plans.[12]

At the same time, however, Roosevelt continued to hope and work for a friendly accommodation with the U.S.S.R. On the day before he and Churchill signed the atomic energy agreement at Quebec, they sent Stalin a joint appeal for a personal meeting in Alaska, where they could "survey the whole scene in common" at this "crucial point in the war." If it were impossible to arrange this "much needed meeting," they declared themselves ready to accept the suggestion in Stalin's message of August 8 for a meeting of "responsible representatives." On August 24, after receiving their full message on Italy, Stalin again turned aside their proposal for personal talks, but agreed to a Foreign Ministers' conference. In response to this "distinctly more civil response," Roosevelt and Churchill at once agreed to "secondary" or Foreign Office talks and to the creation of a tripartite peace commission.

Roosevelt was still eager to see Stalin in person. On September 2, in a discussion with Harriman, who had agreed to become Ambassador to Moscow, he described his desire to negotiate postwar matters with Stalin personally. Convinced that the Russians intended to annex the Baltic states and would have the power to do it, Roosevelt wished to dissuade Stalin from unilateral action. He planned to tell him that the arbitrary seizure of territory would jeopardize Russia's place among the Great Powers at the council table as well as weaken American support of her security claims and postwar reconstruction. He hoped to convince Stalin to give a color of decency to Baltic annexations by holding plebiscites and to guarantee the right of migration to anyone choosing not to live under Soviet rule. Consequently, on September 4, in a cable to Stalin outlining his ideas for the Foreign Ministers' talks, he again urged a meeting of the three heads of governments, suggesting a conference in North Africa sometime in the month after November 15.

Stalin now agreed. With a final report from Quebec indicating that the Allies had a large-scale buildup under way in the United Kingdom for the promised cross-Channel attack, with Italy quitting the war and an invasion of the Italian mainland in motion, Stalin was ready to confront Roosevelt and Churchill face to face. On September 8 he cabled his willingness to meet in November or December in Iran, and proposed that the Foreign Ministers confer at the beginning of October in Moscow. Both responded with unguarded enthusiasm. Though FDR preferred to meet in Egypt, he declared himself "delighted" at Stalin's agreement to personal talks, and "cheerfully" endorsed his plan for their Foreign Ministers. "I really feel that the three of us are making real headway," he replied. Similarly, Churchill was "pleased and relieved" at the prospect of a conference. "On this meeting . . . ," he told Stalin, "may depend not only the best and shortest method of finishing the war, but also those good arrangements for the future of the world which will enable the British and American and Russian nations to render a lasting service to humanity." [13]

For Roosevelt, the Foreign Ministers' meeting in Moscow provided a chance to resolve domestic rather than diplomatic problems. If the

Russians raised the question of Finland or the Baltic states in these talks, FDR had told Churchill and Eden at Quebec, he wished his representatives to plead ignorance and remain silent. Since the President himself intended to discuss frontier questions with Stalin, Hopkins had told Eden at that same time, he very much doubted if Roosevelt would allow someone else to speak for him. In September and October, Roosevelt told his diplomatic advisers that he planned to speak frankly to Stalin about Russian territorial expansion, but it was a delicate topic which he would have to handle himself. "I am sure we are going to find a meeting of minds for the important decisions which must finally be made by us," he cabled Stalin on October 5. "And so this preliminary conference will explore the ground, and if difficulties develop . . . I would still have every hope that they can be reconciled when you and Mr. Churchill and I meet." [14]

Roosevelt viewed the Moscow conference as principally a chance to blunt Republican efforts to make postwar peacekeeping an issue in the 1944 campaign and to end a feud between Hull and Welles which might jeopardize postwar goals. During the first half of 1943, Roosevelt had opposed detailed public discussion of how the Allies would organize the peace. Fearful that close attention to the issue would provoke isolationist attacks disruptive to the war effort, Roosevelt and Hull discouraged attempts to put the Senate on record as favoring postwar participation in a world organization. Specifically, while Roosevelt readily expressed general support of a future peacekeeping role for the United States, he opposed pressure from four internationalist Senators to have the upper chamber consider a detailed resolution on American participation in a new world body.

By the summer of 1943, however, Republican leadership on the postwar issue persuaded Roosevelt to act. In April, Wendell Willkie had published *One World*, an account of his travels through the Middle East, Russia, and China and a plea for American cooperation to preserve postwar peace. The book was an instant bestseller; in only three months it became the third non-fiction book in American history to sell more than a million copies. In July the Republicans announced their intention to draft a statement on postwar foreign policy at a Mackinac Island conference in September. Unless the Democrats did something, Representative J. William Fulbright had told FDR at the end of June, they would lose the foreign policy issue in the next campaign. Roosevelt registered his agreement by asking Hull to consider pushing a Fulbright resolution favoring the creation of international peacekeeping machinery supported by the United States. At Quebec, moreover, Roosevelt told Churchill, Eden, and Mackenzie King that he would need to make a pronouncement on postwar peacekeeping before it was done by other presidential aspirants in the 1944 campaign. [15]

The vehicle for this pronouncement was to be a Four-Power Declaration. On August 10, Hull, Welles, and other State Department advisers put a four-power pact before the President which committed the Allies to united action for peace. After learning that the agreement substituted a worldwide peace organization for postwar regional councils proposed by the British and that it would not need Senate approval if it were issued as a declaration, Roosevelt promised to take it up with Churchill and Eden at Quebec. The agreement pledged continued cooperation for the organization and maintenance of postwar peace and security, but sidestepped the question of a permanent peacekeeping body by simply promising the establishment "at the earliest practicable date of a general international organization." Also, by promising to create a technical commission which would advise on the forces needed to meet an emergency threat to the peace, the pact avoided sensitive questions in the United States about a permanent international police force. Lastly, the agreement gave recognition to Bullitt's suggestion about gaining a Soviet pledge against annexations: it included a promise not to "employ military forces within the territory of other states except for the purposes envisaged in this declaration and after joint consultation and agreement."

At Quebec, after Roosevelt explained the domestic political pressure on him for a statement on postwar organization and characterized the arrangements under the Four-Power Declaration as "interim" ones which "in no way prejudice final decisions as to world order," Churchill endorsed an American approach to the Russians about the pact. After Quebec, when they made firm commitments to a Foreign Ministers' Conference, Churchill and Roosevelt further agreed to put the Four-Power Declaration at the top of the agenda. But the Russians objected. They wished the Conference to give first attention to "measures for shortening the war against Germany," or to a cross-Channel attack, and they opposed the Four-Power Declaration as inappropriate at a Conference between only three of them. The Soviets, Roosevelt concluded, wanted no association with China, which Japan might interpret as provocative. Churchill assumed that "they do not want to be mixed up in all this rot about China as a great Power, any more than I do."

But Roosevelt saw China's inclusion as essential to his postwar plans. Her exclusion would weaken the value of the Declaration in the United States and increase the difficulties of assuring her a central place in the postwar peacekeeping body. Either some way should be found to "absolve" Russia from involvement in Pacific questions until Japan's defeat, he and Hull agreed, or provision should be made for China's later adherence to the Declaration. But whatever the case, Roosevelt was determined to preserve "the four-power concept . . . even at the cost of getting no agreement at this time." "Two three-power arrangements," he and Hull also agreed, "will not be nearly as good as one four-power arrangement." [16]

Roosevelt also wished to use the Moscow conference to end Welles's service as Undersecretary. In August, before the Quebec meeting, Hull had asked Roosevelt to choose between him and Welles. Long-standing antagonism toward the Undersecretary for usurping his authority and for making embarrassing comments to the press about their conflict, as well as apprehensions about the consequences to the Department and the administration from rumors about alleged homosexual activities on Welles's part, made Hull determined to act. Appreciating that Welles had become a political liability and, more important, that he could not afford to sacrifice Senate cooperation, which Hull's departure seemed certain to entail, Roosevelt agreed to remove Welles. To avoid embarrassment to Welles and the administration, Roosevelt and Hull agreed to couple his resignation with a mission to Moscow and Chungking in behalf of the Four-Power Declaration. At the beginning of September, therefore, when the Foreign Ministers' Conference was being arranged, Roosevelt proposed to make Welles his chief delegate. But when Welles resisted the assignment and newspaper stories about his resignation moved Hull to describe him as "disqualified for that job," Roosevelt decided to send Hull.

Welles's resignation on September 25 distressed FDR. There was a sense of personal loss. After ten years of loyal service, his old friend and closest aide in the State Department was departing under a cloud. When William Bullitt, a Welles rival and the alleged author of rumors about Welles's personal indiscretions, appeared at Roosevelt's office after Welles resigned, the President told Bullitt: "William Bullitt, stand where you are. Saint Peter is at the gate. Along comes Sumner Welles, who admits to human error. Saint Peter grants him entrance. Then comes William Bullitt. Saint Peter says: 'William Bullitt, you have betrayed a fellow human being. You-can-go-down-there.'" The President told Bullitt that he never wished to see him again.

There was also the fact that Welles was the most eloquent spokesman in the government for the Wilsonian or universalist vision of a postwar peace. Though Roosevelt had his reservations about Welles's postwar plans, as he had about the peace initiatives Welles had urged upon him during the years 1937–40, Roosevelt valued him as a reflection of the idealism in the country about world affairs. Probably also troubling FDR was the fact that Welles was partly a victim of the President's system of administration. Having encouraged the rivalry between Hull and Welles as a way to divide the State Department against itself and keep control of foreign affairs in his own hands, Roosevelt had created the tension that had moved Hull to push for Welles's removal.[17]

The Moscow conference encouraged Roosevelt's hopes for a postwar accommodation with the U.S.S.R. Soviet responsiveness to Hull's explanations of why the American government needed a Four-Power

Declaration on postwar arrangements greatly pleased FDR. Public opinion in the democracies, Hull told Stalin and Molotov, wanted a clear idea now about postwar peace plans. If his government waited until the end of the fighting to formulate a postwar program, it would be impossible to unite diverse groups in the United States behind a suitable plan. "If an official in my country should announce that he were opposed to formulating the fundamental policies for a postwar world until after the war is over," Hull said, "he would be thrown out of power overnight." As for China, he told Molotov that dumping her from the four-power agreement would create "the most terrific repercussions, both political and military, in the Pacific area, and that this might call for all sorts of readjustments by my Government." Public opinion in the United States would be "hopelessly torn and rent" by the news that they had thrown China "out of the war picture." As a consequence, both the United States and Britain, Hull predicted, would have to give more attention to the Pacific. The implication of how this might affect the Anglo-American war effort in Europe could hardly have escaped Molotov.

Hull's pressure, coupled with firm indications that there would be a second front in Europe in 1944, won a strong response from the Russians. Not only did they agree to Hull's Four-Power Declaration, they also proposed the creation of a tripartite commission to plan the establishment of a world organization. Though concerned with satisfying public pressure for postwar planning, Hull and Roosevelt had no desire to pass much beyond a general declaration of intent in the fall of 1943. Hull told Molotov he was fearful that the creation of the proposed special commission would "stir up agitation" in the United States about a future would organization. Instead, he suggested finding an informal means of discussing this subject behind the scenes.[18]

Even more gratifying to Roosevelt than Soviet willingness to help with his domestic problems on postwar planning were Russian expressions of determination to join the war against Japan. During the second week of the Conference, Harriman reported indications that after Germany's collapse, Moscow would give some help in the Pacific, where they would want the fighting to end "as soon as possible." On October 30, the last day of the Conference, Stalin specifically promised to help beat Japan after German defeat. The news encouraged Roosevelt to assert that the spirit of the Conference "was amazingly good" and had created a "psychology of . . . excellent feeling." The "Moscow accomplishments," he told reporters, "refuted predictions of cynics who thought [the] talks would be clouded with suspicion and would accomplish little." The fact that Russian involvement against Japan would ease American dependence on China as a base and reduce the likelihood of Soviet expansion in Europe while the Allies fought in the Far East after Germany collapsed was enough to make FDR feel that the Conference had been a great success.

At the same time, though, as Harriman informed Roosevelt, "certain real difficulties" remained. "Certain of the doubts which some people have had regarding Soviet intentions," he observed in a post-Conference report, "are now laid to rest. . . . Their acceptance of China is a clear indication that they are genuinely satisfied with the way things went and are ready to make important concessions to further the new intimacy. On the other hand, it cannot be assumed that this policy is already so set that we can take liberties with them." Much depended, Harriman believed, "on their satisfaction in the future with our military operations."

But satisfaction on this score, Harriman predicted, would not alter Soviet determination to control East European affairs. Though they never discussed territorial questions at the Conference, Harriman inferred that they still intended to demand their 1941 frontiers. Further, though they gave "no indication during the conference that they were interested in the extension of the Soviet system," Harriman took "this with some reservation, particularly if it proves to be the only way they can get the kind of relationships they demand from their western border states." The fact that Molotov had opposed the provision in the Four-Power Declaration against using armed forces in other states without prior consultation and agreement suggested Soviet determination to "take unilateral action" in Eastern Europe. Arguing that this commitment might interfere with existing defense agreements between one of the four Powers and another state, Molotov persuaded Hull to drop the requirement for prior agreement. Harriman hoped, however, that growing Soviet confidence in British and American determination to create a system of overall world security would temper the rigid Soviet attitude toward their Western neighbors.[19]

Though Roosevelt hoped to assess Soviet attitudes for himself when he met Stalin, it was not easy to arrange the meeting. While both agreed on the end of November as the time, they could not decide on a place. Stalin was insistent on Tehran, where his lines of communication and security would be under strict Soviet control. Roosevelt pressed for a meeting in Cairo, an eastern Mediterranean port, or a site near Baghdad. Unlike Tehran, they were all within a ten-day round trip of the United States. With the Congress in session, he explained to Stalin, he had a constitutional obligation physically to receive and act on all legislation within that period of time. The two now entered into a contest of wills: Stalin would not risk the loss of secure communications beyond Tehran, and Roosevelt, who would be traveling ten times as far as Stalin, insisted that his constitutional obligation take precedence. "I cannot go to Tehran," he cabled Stalin on October 21, and he offered "one last practical suggestion," a meeting in Basra at the head of the Persian Gulf in southern Iraq. He ended with an appeal on historical and personal grounds: A meeting was "of the greatest possible importance . . . to a peaceful world for generations to come. It would be regarded as a tragedy by future generations if you and I and Mr. Churchill failed today because of a few hundred miles. . . . Please do not fail me in this crisis."

But Roosevelt, who felt the need for an early meeting more intensely than Stalin did, gave in. Whereas FDR saw pressing international and domestic reasons for a conference as soon possible, Stalin was content to wait until his Allies opened the second front. During the next three weeks, therefore, Stalin declared himself ready to defer a meeting until the spring and hinted that he might not be able to leave the U.S.S.R. now anyway. Roosevelt at once agreed to go to Tehran. The "present excellent feelings" produced by the Moscow talks, coupled with the expectation that a conference "will have far-reaching effect on the good opinion within our three nations and will assist in the further disturbance of Nazi morale," he cabled Stalin on November 8, demanded that they get together. If the Congress passed a bill requiring his veto, he would fly to Tunis to meet it and then return to the conference. In that way, he could meet with Stalin in Tehran for as long as the latter felt able to be away. Stalin's concurrence evoked an expression of relief: "I have heard that U.J. will come to Teheran," FDR informed Churchill on the 11th. "I received a telegram from him five days ago which made me think he would not come even to that place. . . . I wired him at once that I had arranged the Constitutional matter here, and therefore that I could go to Teheran. . . . Even then I was in doubt as to whether he would go through with his former offer." [20]

Arrangements with Churchill were also a problem. By late October, existing plans for the 1944 campaign greatly troubled him, and he wished them to have a full meeting of the Combined Chiefs of Staff before the conference with Stalin. "Our present plans for 1944," he had told Roosevelt on the 23rd, "seem open to very grave defects." Where they in-intended to put twenty-seven divisions into OVERLORD and maintain twenty-two more on the Italian front, he believed that Hitler could concentrate at least forty to fifty divisions "against either of these forces while holding the other. . . . It is arguable," he said, "that neither the forces building up in Italy nor those available for a May OVERLORD are strong enough for the tasks set them." He feared that they might give Hitler a chance for "a startling comeback" unless they gathered "the greatest possible forces for both operations, particularly OVER-LORD. . . . This is much the greatest thing we have ever attempted," he concluded, "and I am not satisfied that we have yet taken the measures necessary to give it the best chance of success." In short, he wished to review the OVERLORD decision before they confronted Stalin's pressure for renewed assurances about a second front in the spring.

But Roosevelt would not agree. Full-scale military talks before they saw Stalin, he told Churchill, would probably have unfavorable results in Russia. During the last week of October, therefore, when he thought they might not be able to fix a meeting with Stalin, he had asked Churchill to meet in North Africa anyway and to invite Molotov with a Russian military mission to join them. But Churchill would not hear of it. "I deprecate the idea of inviting a Russian military representative to sit in at the meetings of our joint staffs," he replied. He "would simply bay for an earlier second front and block all other discussions. . . . The year 1944 is loaded with danger. Great differences may develop between us and we may take the wrong turning. Or, again, we may make compromises and fall between two stools. The only hope is the intimacy which has been established between us. . . . If that were broken, I should despair of the immediate future."

Though Churchill pressed Roosevelt for agreement on this point and though FDR assured him that they and their Staffs "will have many meetings before the Russians or Chinese meet with us," he nevertheless asked Stalin to send Molotov and a military representative to Cairo on November 22 when the Anglo-American Staffs would begin pre-Tehran talks. When Churchill heard of this from his Ambassador in Moscow, he called Roosevelt's attention to this "most unfortunate misunderstanding," and asked him to postpone the arrival of the Russians until November 25. But Roosevelt urged Churchill to see "that it would be a terrible mistake if U.J. thought we had ganged up on him on military action." Moreover, he asked Churchill to understand that it would hurt nothing to let Molotov and the Russian military man in on some of their planning talks. It would be a way to encourage Soviet confidence in the sincerity of their intentions without giving them much information: "They will not feel that they are being given the 'run around,'" Roosevelt explained. "They will have no staff and no planners. Let us take them in on the high spots. . . . I think it essential that this schedule be carried out. I can assure you that there will be no difficulties." [21]

Roosevelt also arranged for Chiang to come to Cairo. Advised in the spring of 1943 that a meeting with Chiang would bolster Chinese morale and help check China's rampant inflation, Roosevelt had invited Chiang to meet him sometime in the fall. During the summer and fall, continuing difficulties between Stilwell and Chiang, an inability to get promised supplies to Chennault, and a failure to mount the projected air offensive intensified Roosevelt's desire to give Chiang symbolic support. "I am still pretty thoroughly disgusted with the India-China matter," FDR advised Marshall on October 15. ". . . Everything seems to go wrong. But the worst thing is that we are falling down on our promises every single time. We have not fulfilled one of them."

In October, therefore, while he tried to arrange a meeting with Stalin in the Middle East, Roosevelt also laid plans to have Chiang confer with him and Churchill in Egypt beforehand. Though Churchill was also unhappy about having the Chinese in Cario before he and the President could talk, Roosevelt specifically arranged for Chiang to arrive at the same time he and Churchill did and made a point of telling his Joint Chiefs that he wished their meeting with Chiang "to be separate from and precede any meeting with the British." Though Roosevelt hoped that substantive agreements would emerge from his talks with Chiang, he principally expected the meeting to advance China's symbolic standing as one of the Big Four. An immediate consequence of this arrangement, however, was Stalin's decision to keep Molotov away from Cairo. Concerned not to provoke Japan, he cabled Roosevelt and Churchill that the representatives of any other country "must be absolutely excluded" from their meeting in Tehran. Churchill did not object in the least.[22]

At Cairo, beginning on November 22, Roosevelt made China the first order of business. Much to Churchill's annoyance, he held long conferences with Chiang, and Chinese affairs, which Churchill described as "lengthy, complicated and minor . . . , occupied first instead of last place at Cairo." "To the President, China means four hundred million people who are going to count in the world of tomorrow," Churchill's physician noted in his diary, "but Winston thinks only of the colour of their skin; it is when he talks of India or China that you remember he is a Victorian."

Churchill and Roosevelt found themselves particularly at odds over military plans for Burma. With Chiang showing interest "for the first time" in using his ground forces to reopen the Burma Road, the American Chiefs urged acceptance of his plan for a north Burma assault combined with simultaneous operations in the Bay of Bengal. Roosevelt strongly supported his Chiefs, and despite Churchill's opposition, he promised Chiang "a considerable amphibious operation across the Bay of Bengal within the next few months." In response, Churchill put himself on record as specifically refusing Chiang's request for amphibious operations which would parallel land action. Roosevelt also promised to arm and equip ninety Chinese divisions at an indefinite time in the future.[23]

In supporting his Chiefs and making these promises, Roosevelt was less interested in immediate military operations than in long-term military and political goals. At Cairo, Roosevelt had few, if any, illusions about Chiang's capacity and willingness to fight. He had been directly informed of the questionable combat potential of Chiang's troops and of the Generalissimo's tendency to conserve his strength for any postwar challenge to his rule. Furthermore, Chiang's performance in Cairo inspired little confidence in his intentions. He not only insisted on simultaneous amphibious operations as a condition of a Burma attack, he also demanded an uninterrupted flow of 10,000 tons of supplies a month over the Hump. American and British Chiefs rejected this as an impossible request. Despite this, the Chinese continued to demand supplies in these amounts until Marshall angrily replied that the Chinese could have more matériel only by fighting to open the Burma Road. There were no additional planes to increase the air lift over the Hump, and he warned against any misunderstanding about this. "You are talking about your 'rights' in this matter," Marshall told the Chinese. "I thought these were *American* planes, and *American* personnel, and *American* material. I don't understand what you mean by saying we can or can't do thus and so." Chiang also kept changing his mind about the proposed operations, confirming and withdrawing his approval in a bewildering succession of orders. The first experience of dealing with Chiang, Lord Mountbatten observed, drove Roosevelt, Churchill, and the Combined Chiefs "absolutely mad." [24]

There is other evidence that Roosevelt supported Chiang's Burma plan more to boost morale and create closer Sino-American ties than to assure its execution. For one, Roosevelt was mindful of the fact that his promise of amphibious operations rested on British willingness to cooperate. As he made clear in conversations with his Joint Chiefs on the way to Cairo, the implementation of any military operation greatly depended on who provided the bulk of the forces. Since any attack across the Bay of Bengal depended on the Royal Navy, Roosevelt knew that Churchill's opposition made it impossible for him to give a meaningful promise to Chiang. Secondly, in a conference with Stilwell at Cairo, when the General tried to persuade him to send American troops into Burma and to arrange American control of Chinese forces, Roosevelt turned aside these proposals with unresponsive banter. He would send a brigade of Marines to Chungking, he answered Stilwell's request for troops, because they "are well known. They've been all over China. . . . The Army has only been in Tientsin." This "remarkable irrelevancy" masked Roosevelt's unwillingness to use American troops in an unpromising operation or to offend Chiang with demands for Stilwell's full command of his forces. The President heard him with "little attention," Stilwell complained. ". . . FDR *is not interested.*"

Finally, after the Tehran Conference and further Anglo-American talks in Cairo, Roosevelt agreed to give up the Bay of Bengal attack and see Burma operations postponed until the following November. This was a victory for Churchill, who argued that European operations set at Tehran left insufficient landing craft for the Bay of Bengal, that Stalin's confirmation of his pledge to enter the war against Japan eliminated the need for Chinese bases, and that continued deliveries over the Hump would be enough to keep China in the war and preserve the option of using her bases should Stalin fail to fulfill his pledge. "We're in an impasse," FDR told Stilwell on December 6. "I've been stubborn as a mule for four days but we can't get anywhere, and it won't do for a conference to end that way. The British just won't do the operation, and I can't get them to agree to it." In a cable to Chiang explaining the need to call off the Bay of Bengal attack, Roosevelt suggested either coupling the north Burma operations with modified naval action, or delaying the whole attack until November 1944 and expanding Hump deliveries in the meantime.[25]

Problems that threatened to arise with Chiang over the reversal on Bay of Bengal operations did not greatly concern FDR. His acceptance of the attack in the first place and long-term political commitments to China had largely satisfied Chiang. "The President will refuse me nothing," Chiang told Mountbatten during the Cairo talks. "Anything I ask, he will do." "The Generalissimo wishes me to tell you again how much he appreciates what you have done and are doing for China," Madame Chiang wrote Roosevelt at the end of the conference. "When we said goodbye to you this afternoon, he could not find words adequately expressive to convey his emotions and feelings, nor to thank you sufficiently for your friendship. . . . On my own behalf . . . my heart overflows with affection and gratitude for what you have done."

Roosevelt's efforts to assure China's national aspirations and postwar status as a Great Power particularly pleased the Chiangs. In Cairo, Roosevelt suggested a public declaration "that Japan shall be stripped of all the islands in the Pacific which she had seized or occupied since the beginning of the first World War in 1914, and that all the territories Japan has stolen from the Chinese, such as Manchuria, Formosa, and the Pescadores, shall be restored to the Republic of China." To meet Chiang's concern that Russia would try "to communize China" and annex part of her territory, Roosevelt promised to seek Stalin's approval of this Cairo declaration and to discuss Russian territorial aims in the Far East. Chiang, according to FDR, agreed that Russia would receive all of Sakhalin and the Kurile Islands after the war, and that Dairen would become a free port under international control to satisfy Russian aspirations for an ice-free port in Siberia. Chiang's price for the latter was Soviet cooperation with China and the nonimpairment of Chinese sovereignty. Roosevelt also favored giving the Ryukyu Islands and Hong Kong back to China. He told Chiang that he had already urged the British to return Hong Kong on the condition that China made it a free port. Last, Roosevelt declared his support of China's participation in a postwar world body as one of the four Great Powers.[26]

Roosevelt's desire to satisfy China's territorial aims and assure her postwar security and international influence did not rest on a sentimental concern for the Chinese. His central goal was to safeguard America's wartime and postwar interests in the Pacific and around the world. More than ever, he appreciated that China was an ineffective military power.

But he still wished to include her among the Big Four. In the short run, it would boost Chinese morale and encourage American acceptance of a major role abroad. His first concern, he told Stalin at Tehran, was to assure that China did not fall out of the war. Though he did not think that Japan would offer China "terms she could accept," he feared an internal collapse which would close off the possibility of Chinese bases for bombing Japan and demoralize American hopes for the postwar world. From a longer perspective, he looked forward to having China's political support against other Pacific Powers, namely, Britain, Russia, and ultimately a resurgent Japan. During and immediately after the war, he counted on China's backing in potential political disputes with Britain and Russia over Pacific affairs. "Now, look here, Winston," he answered Churchill's objections at Tehran to postwar plans for Indochina, "you are outvoted three to one." In the even longer run, in twenty-five to fifty years, when he expected China to realize its potential as a Great Power, he looked forward to having her help "in holding Japan in check." Roosevelt had all this in mind at the Cairo talks when he expressed the belief that "this meeting would . . . not only bear fruit today and in the immediate future, but for decades to come." [27]

Roosevelt also wanted a stable, cooperative China to help him establish a postwar system of international trusteeships for colonies and mandates detached from their ruling countries by the war. Under this plan, three or four of the United Nations were to share responsibility for subject peoples until they were ready for self-rule. He also favored a system of international inspection and publicity for areas remaining under colonial control, which he envisaged as "powerful means of inducing colonial powers to develop their colonies for the good of the dependent peoples themselves and of the world." At the same time, he hoped the trusteeship system would allow the United States to establish long-term naval and air bases at strategic points in the Pacific and elsewhere without confronting traditional American antipathy for power politics. Since the annexation of Pacific islands, or even exclusive American responsibility through mandates granted by a world body, seemed likely to provoke domestic opposition, a system of collective rule for the benefit of emerging nations would effectively de-emphasize American military control. In Roosevelt's judgment, this could provide a means of both aiding exploited peoples and creating a workable Pacific security system for at least twenty years.

Anticipating considerable difficulties with the British over these plans, Roosevelt tried to enlist Chinese support. "We will have more trouble with Great Britain after the war than we are having with Germany now," FDR had said in the summer of 1942 to Charles W. Taussig, his chief adviser on Caribbean affairs. In the fall, the appointment of Oliver Stanley as Minister of State for Colonies, a man Welles characterized as the " 'most narrow, bigoted, reactionary Tory' that he had ever met in his official career," and Churchill's comments on the Empire to Taussig did not ease the President's concern. "Nations live on their traditions or die," Churchill pointedly told Taussig. ". . . As long as I am here, we will hold to them and the Empire. We will not let the Hottentots by popular vote throw the white people into the sea." In March 1943, when Secretary Knox asked Roosevelt whether it would be out of order to seek British support for postwar American control of Japan's mandated islands as naval bases, FDR advised against any action. "I am anxious to clean up the problem of all the islands in the Pacific," he said, "and the British would probably be delighted to confine the discussions to the Japanese Mandated Islands." At Cairo in November, after further exchanges with military and State Department advisers on where and how to establish these postwar bases in the Pacific, he invited China's participation in a Pacific trusteeship system. The fate of this and other issues, however, was left for consideration at Tehran.[28]

Roosevelt's first concern at his meeting with Stalin was to settle military operations in Europe. In the almost three months since Quebec, he had remained largely committed to the idea of crossing the Channel in the spring of 1944. In early October 1943, when Churchill pressed a case for seizing Rhodes and the other Dodecanese Islands as promising to lead to control of the Aegean, the likely accession of Turkey to their cause, and possibly "measureless" consequences in the Balkans, Roosevelt blocked the action as certain to divert forces from Italy and delay the invasion of France. Moreover, on November 15, in a meeting with the Joint Chiefs on the way to Cairo, Roosevelt endorsed their recommendation to the Combined Chiefs that operations in the "Balkan-Eastern Mediterranean region" be limited to supplying guerrillas, minor commando action, and strategic air raids which would in no way interfere with the agreed strategy for German defeat or "the successful accomplishment of our commitments elsewhere." "Amen," Roosevelt said after reading this paper, adding that they should send it to the British and "definitely stand on it" during the Cairo talks.

At the same time, however, he did not wish to foreclose the possibility of invading the Balkans. Reports from Moscow had given him some reason to think that fresh German pressure on the Russian front would move Stalin at Tehran to demand more intensive Mediterranean operations in the winter, even at the expense of OVERLORD. In regard to the Eastern Mediterranean-Balkan area, Roosevelt told the Joint Chiefs in another discussion on the 19th, "we must be concerned with the Soviet attitude. . . . The Soviets are now only 60 miles from the Polish border and 40 miles from Bessarabia." They "might say, 'If someone would now come up from the Adriatic to the Danube, we could readily defeat Germany forthwith.'" Further, at a meeting in Cairo with Churchill and the Combined Chiefs on the 24th, he predicted that Stalin would insist on the retention of OVERLORD "in all its integrity" while also demanding that they "keep the Mediterranean ablaze" between now and OVERLORD. More specifically, if the Russians reached the Roumanian border in a few weeks, he expected them to suggest "an operation at the top of the Adriatic with a view to assisting Tito [the Yugoslav Partisan leader]." There were twenty-one German divisions in the Balkans and the Dodecanese, he told his Joint Chiefs a few hours before seeing Stalin in Tehran. "What should we say if the Soviets inform us that they will be in Rumania soon, and inquire what can the United States and Britain do to help them?" More favorably disposed to operations from the Adriatic than from the Dodecanese, he suggested commando raids into Yugoslavia or an invasion of the Adriatic coast by a small force thrusting northward through Trieste and Fiume.[29]

At his first meeting with Stalin in Tehran on the afternoon of November 28, Roosevelt probed his views on military matters. He asked first about conditions on the Russian front. After hearing that the Germans were exercising strong pressure with new divisions brought from the West, he expressed his desire to divert thirty or forty German divisions from the Eastern fighting, declaring that this was one of the things he wished to discuss with him. He was also eager for a reaffirmation of Stalin's pledge to fight Japan. But believing this a delicate question, he approached it obliquely. He instructed his Joint Chiefs not to discuss it with the Russians unless they raised it, and then to be extremely cautious. Though making no overt reference to the matter in his initial discussion with Stalin, Roosevelt broached it by describing the plans for a Burma offensive made with Chiang at Cairo. But Stalin, who was not yet ready to state his military plans, ignored the hint. He saved an expression of his views for the first full-scale session of the Conference later in the afternoon.

Roosevelt and Churchill opened the meeting with comments on the historic importance of the Conference. "A lot of blah-flum," General Brooke called it. "Thrifty of gush," Stalin endorsed their sentiments as "appropriate to the occasion," and declared: "Now let us get down to business." In response, Roosevelt surveyed the fighting fronts from the "American point of view." He began with "a subject that affects the United States more than either Great Britain or the U.S.S.R. . . . the Pacific." After describing American strategy against Japan, he turned to the "more important" European theater. For the past year and a half, he said, he and the Prime Minister had discussed means of relieving the Russian front. It was not until Quebec, however, that they had been able to solve their problems of sea transport and set a firm date for crossing the Channel—no later than May 1944. The question they needed to settle now, he added, was the best way to use their forces in the Mediterranan to aid Soviet armies in the East. They could step up operations in

Italy, or initiate attacks in the Adriatic, the Aegean, or Turkey. Since these actions might delay OVERLORD by one to three months, they wished to have Stalin's views. He ended, however, with an expression of belief that nothing should delay the cross-Channel attack.

Stalin now made his wishes clear. Though the fighting on his western front had made it impossible for him to join the war against Japan, he would be ready to do this after Germany's defeat. As for the European fighting, he emphatically declared himself in favor of attacking Germany through northern and southern France. Italy was not a suitable place from which to strike directly at Germany, and while Turkey and the Balkans would be better in this respect, it seemed best to attack the heart of Germany from northern France, supported by a diversionary assault in the south.

But still fearing a repetition of the World War I bloodletting in France, Churchill was reluctant to agree. Though calling Mediterranean operations no more than a stepping-stone for the main cross-Channel attack, he emphasized his concern that Anglo-American forces not remain idle for six months between the possible capture of Rome in January 1944 and the start of OVERLORD in June. He thought it better to mount an operation across the Adriatic or in the Aegean with Turkish help. Turkey's entrance into the war might "start a landslide among the satellite States" in the Balkans, and he wished to know whether any of these operations would appeal to the Soviet Union, considering that they might entail a two- or three-month delay in OVERLORD.

Before Stalin could answer, Roosevelt interjected his plan for a Balkans attack. He suggested "a possible operation at the head of the Adriatic to make a junction with the Partisans under Tito and then to operate northeast into Rumania in conjunction with the Soviet advance from the region of Odessa." Further, when Stalin took exception to this dispersion of Allied forces and urged instead an invasion of southern France to assist the main cross-Channel attack, the President pointed out that eight or nine French divisions would be available to do this job. "Who's promoting that Adriatic business that the President continually returns to?" Hopkins asked in a note he slipped to Admiral King. "As far as I know it is his own idea," King replied. "The Russians did not appear to grasp the military advantages to be gained in that part of the world," General Brooke told the War Cabinet on returning from Tehran, "though their apparent lack of interest might have sprung from other motives." Roosevelt's attraction to the Balkans attack may also have rested on political considerations.[30]

But the wishes of the Joint Chiefs, together with the likely domestic opposition to postwar American involvement in European political questions and a desire to accommodate Stalin, constrained Roosevelt from pursuing the plan. Toward the close of this first session, after Churchill and Stalin had debated the virtues of continued operations in the Mediterranean versus all-out attention to OVERLORD and ANVIL, the invasion of southern France, Roosevelt declared himself opposed to a delay in OVERLORD, "which might be necessary if any operations in the Eastern Mediterranean were undertaken." He suggested, therefore, that the Staffs promptly work out a plan for striking at southern France. On the following day, at a second plenary session of the Conference, when Churchill and Stalin resumed the debate on military operations, Roosevelt reiterated his support for keeping OVERLORD on schedule, or at least avoiding anything in the Mediterranean that would push cross-Channel operations past the first part of May. After Stalin bluntly asked whether the British really believed in OVERLORD or were "only saying so to reassure the Russians," Churchill gave in. On November 30, the British agreed to mount OVERLORD during May in conjunction with an attack on the south of France.[31]

This decision allowed Roosevelt not only to satisfy his Joint Chiefs but also to limit America's postwar involvement in Europe to what he believed American opinion would permit. Though appreciating that public and congressional opinion was currently sympathetic to an expanded American role abroad, he was not confident that this mood would outlive the war. He was less impressed with opinion polls showing 80 per cent in favor of American participation in a union of nations than with those indicating a threefold greater concern with postwar problems at home than with those abroad. More specifically, he did not think that American opinion would readily accept substantial, long-term involvement in European affairs. It would take "a terrible crisis such as at present," he told Stalin at Tehran, before the American Congress would agree to send troops back to Europe. He also said "that if the Japanese had not attacked the United States he doubted very much if it would have been possible to send any American forces to Europe."

In light of this, he wished to limit America's postwar occupation of Europe to northwest Germany, Norway, and Denmark, where there would be greater political stability and less likelihood of long-term, acrimonious involvement. He did not want the United States, he told the Joint Chiefs, to "get roped into accepting any European sphere of influence," which he believed any peacekeeping responsibility for France, Italy, or the Balkans would compel. He expected America's occupation force to be about one million troops, who would remain in Europe for at least a year, possibly two. Were there a future threat to the European peace, he also told Stalin, the United States would send planes and ships, while Britain and Russia would have to supply the land armies.[32]

Roosevelt's candor was calculated to encourage Stalin to see the President as a trustworthy ally. Indeed, now giving full rein to his hope for a long-term accommodation with the U.S.S.R., Roosevelt made an all-out effort at Tehran to encourage Soviet-American harmony. As a way of exhibiting his "trust," his "complete confidence in them," Roosevelt later told Frances Perkins, he stayed at the Soviet Embassy in Tehran. He also "osentatiously" took Stalin's side in some of his disputes with Churchill. At a dinner meeting on November 29, Stalin took every chance to tease Churchill, "making known in a friendly fashion his displeasure at the British attitude on . . . OVERLORD." "Just because Russians are simple people," he had told the Prime Minister, "it was a mistake to believe that they were blind and could not see what was before their eyes." After suggesting that Churchill "nursed a secret affection for Germany and desire to see a soft peace," Stalin proposed the liquidation of between 50,000 and 100,000 German officers. While Churchill vigorously objected to "cold-blooded executions of soldiers" for political purposes, Roosevelt jokingly proposed that the number be put at 49,000 or more.

On the last morning of the Conference, when Roosevelt found Stalin stiff and unsmiling, he used Churchill to cut through the Marshal's reserve. "I hope you won't be sore at me for what I am going to do," he told Churchill on their way into the Conference room. As soon as they had sat down, he began teasing Churchill "about his Britishness, about John Bull, about his cigars, about his habits. . . . Winston got red and scowled, and the more he did so, the more Stalin smiled. Finally, Stalin broke into a deep, heavy guffaw, and for the first time in three days I saw light," FDR later told Frances Perkins. "I kept it up until Stalin was laughing with me, and it was then that I called him 'Uncle Joe.' He would have thought me fresh the day before, but that day he laughed and came over and shook my hand. From that time on our relations were personal. . . . The ice was broken and we talked like men and brothers." [33]

More significantly, Roosevelt tried to make political arrangements with Stalin that would both satisfy idealistic hopes in the United States and create a realistic structure for preserving the peace. In a private conversation with Stalin on the second day of the Conference, Roosevelt had raised the question of a postwar peacekeeping body based on the United Nations. He described a three-part, "worldwide" organization consisting of a thirty-five to forty-member body which would meet periodically in different places to work out recommendations, an Executive Committee of ten nations, including the Big Four, which would deal with all nonmilitary questions, and a third group, "the Four Policemen," which "would have the power to deal immediately with any threat to the peace" or any sudden emergency requiring action. Stalin, like Churchill, did not like the idea of a worldwide organization. He predicted that small nations would object to the global power of the Four Policemen. A European state, for example, would resent Chinese control over its affairs. He preferred regional committees limited to the nations directly concerned with the area. Roosevelt, however, indicated that American public opinion, particularly the Congress, would object to any regional arrangement as creating spheres of control and would insist on a worldwide approach to keeping the peace. Though he did not push the issue, telling Stalin on the last day of the talks that it was "premature" to decide anything now about the world body, Stalin was apparently sufficiently convinced to declare himself ready to accept the President's idea of a world organization as "worldwide and not regional."

But Stalin did not think that a world organization, in whatever form, would be enough to check future German and Japanese aggression. He emphasized the need for "strong physical points" or strategically located bases near Germany and Japan. Since this neatly complied with FDR's ideas about converting mandated islands and former colonies into trusteeships, Roosevelt warmly endorsed Stalin's plan. Stalin's strong expression of opposition to restoration of France's colonial empire particularly gratified him. "The entire French ruling class was rotten to the core," Stalin said, "and . . . was now actively helping our enemies." He therefore felt that "it would be not only unjust but dangerous to leave in French hands any important strategic points after the war." Roosevelt agreed and urged that Indochina, New Caledonia, which represented a threat to Australia and New Zealand, and Dakar, which, "in unsure hands," posed a direct threat to the Americas, should all be brought under trusteeship. Mindful of the need to couple the realistic with the idealistic, he insisted that these strategic points come under United Nations control. By this means, considerations of power politics, which would offend American opinion, would be submerged under a "new" system of collective rule.

Roosevelt envisaged satisfying specific Soviets interests by the same means. He suggested the possibility of bringing the approaches to the Baltic Sea under "some form of trusteeship with perhaps an international state in the vicinity of the Kiel Canal to insure free navigation in both directions." In a later discussion, when Churchill assured Stalin that "we all hoped to see Russian fleets, both naval and merchant, on all seas of the world," Roosevelt repeated his idea about the approaches to the Baltic Sea. He proposed turning the former Hanseatic cities of Bremen, Hamburg, and Lubeck into some form of a free zone, with guaranteed free passage for world commerce through the Kiel Canal. After declaring this "a good idea," Stalin asked what could be done for Russia in the Far East. Roosevelt suggested the possibility of also making Dairen into a free port, and indicated that the Chinese would not object if there were an international guarantee. "It was important," Churchill said in closing this discussion, "that the nations who would govern the world after the war . . . should be satisfied and have no territorial or other ambitions. If that question could be settled . . . he felt then that the world might indeed remain at peace. He said that hungry nations and ambitious nations are dangerous, and he would like to see the leading nations of the world in the position of rich, happy men. The President and Marshal Stalin agreed."

On all other major political issues discussed at Tehran, Roosevelt also tried to assure Stalin of American willingness to share responsibility for postwar peace and Soviet security needs. The Baltic Republics were a case in point. He "fully realized" the historic ties between Lithuania, Latvia, and Estonia, Roosevelt told Stalin, and "jokingly" assured him that when Soviet forces reoccupied these countries, "he did not intend to go to war with the Soviet Union on this point." But, he explained, "the question of referendum and the right of self-determination" would form a "big issue" with public opinion in the United States. World opinion as well would ultimately want some expression of the will of the people. Stalin objected that no one had raised the question of public opinion when the last Czar ruled the Baltic states, and he did not understand why it was being raised now. To which Roosevelt replied, "The public neither knew nor understood." "They should be informed and some propaganda work should be done," Stalin answered. He added that there would be ample opportunity for popular expression, but he could not agree to any form of international control. It would be helpful to him "personally," the President concluded, if there were some public declaration about the future elections to which Stalin had referred.[34]

Poland threatened to be even more of a problem for FDR. As Russian forces advanced toward the Polish frontier, the Poles become extremely anxious about the future of their country. They asked London and Washington to guarantee Polish independence and territorial integrity by sending troops into Poland and getting Stalin to resume relations with the Government in Exile. The London Poles also declared themselves opposed to any discussion of territorial questions without guarantees of independence and security. They rejected the idea of receiving East Prussian territory in compensation for the cession of eastern Poland to the U.S.S.R., and they called any attempt by Soviet authorities to arrange a "popular vote" on the issue a meaningless expression of the public will.

Roosevelt had little sympathy with the Polish demands. In early November, when an English visitor to Hyde Park had mentioned the growing Polish alarm over the Soviet advance toward their borders, Roosevelt said, "I know it. I am sick and tired of these people. The Polish Ambassador came to see me a while ago about this question," he added, mimicking the Envoy. ". . . I said, do you think they will just stop to please you, or us for that matter? Do you expect us and Great Britain to declare war on Joe Stalin if they cross your previous frontier? Even if we wanted to, Russia can still field an army twice our combined strength, and we would just have no say in the matter at all. What is more . . . I'm not sure that a fair plebiscite if there ever was such a thing would not show that those eastern provinces would not prefer to go back to Russia. Yes I really think those 1941 frontiers are as just as any."

At Tehran, he and Churchill approved Soviet intentions to redraw Poland's boundaries. On the first evening of the Conference, after the President had retired, Churchill initiated a discussion of the Polish question with Stalin. Explaining that he "had no attachment to any specific frontier between Poland and the Soviet Union," he declared Soviet security in the west a governing factor, and himself in favor of moving Polish boundaries to the west, as Stalin had suggested during dinner. In a conversation with Stalin on the last day of the meeting, Roosevelt endorsed this view, saying that he would like to see Poland's eastern border moved to the west and the western border shifted to the Oder River.

At the same time, however, a fundamental sense of justice and domestic politics moved Churchill and Roosevelt to speak for Polish interests. In his conversation with Stalin on the first night, Churchill emphasized that Britain had gone to war with Germany over Poland and was committed to the reestablishment of a strong, independent Poland as "a necessary instrument in the European orchestra." He came back to this point in a final tripartite discussion on December 1. While reiterating his desire for Soviet security against another German attack in the west and for a readjustment of Polish boundaries to meet this need, he also reminded Stalin that the British people had gone to war because of Poland, and that this remained an unforgettable fact for them. Roosevelt also made it clear that he would not ignore Polish interests. In a private talk with Stalin on December 1, Roosevelt explained that his need for the Polish vote in the 1944 presidential election would inhibit him from participating "in any decision here in Tehran or even next winter" on Poland's boundaries. Further, in their tripartite talk later that day, Roosevelt urged the reestablishment of relations between Moscow and the London Poles, supported equal compensation in the west for what Poland ceded in the east, and asked Stalin whether "a voluntary transfer of peoples from the mixed areas was possible," meaning that no Poles should be held in Soviet-acquired territory against their wills.

Though Stalin saw a transfer of peoples as "entirely possible," he offered little hope that he would resume relations with the London Poles. He said they "were closely connected with the Germans and their agents in Poland were killing partisans." Only if he were convinced that the Government in Exile would not again join the Nazis in "slanderous propaganda" and would support the partisans and sever all connections with German agents in Poland, could he envision renewed relations with the London Poles. Neither Churchill nor Roosevelt objected to what one historian has called "this outrageous slander." But convinced that the surest road to renewed relations and the revival of an independent Poland was through a Soviet-Polish accommodation on frontiers, Churchill pressed Stalin to state his intentions on this issue. He wished, he told Stalin, to present the Soviet viewpoint unofficially to the Poles, whom he would wash his hands of if they refused a reasonable settlement. After a detailed discussion over maps of Poland, Churchill declared himself satisfied that the picture they drew would give the Poles "a fine place to live," and he stated his intention to tell the Poles that a failure to accept it "would be foolish." Partly in deference to Roosevelt, "nothing definitely was settled," but it was clear to all, including FDR, who gave his silent acquiescence, that they had reached a general agreement on the outlines of the new Polish state.[35]

Roosevelt felt less constrained about Germany. As he had told his Joint Chiefs on the way to Cairo, he wanted Germany divided into three permanent states: "a sort of southern state" including everything south of the Main River; a northwestern state taking in everything to the north and the west, including Hamburg, Hanover, and the whole area up to and including Berlin; and a northeastern state consisting of "Prussia, Pomerania, and south." At Tehran, however, when he found Stalin insistent on a more drastic division, Roosevelt proposed the creation of five self-governing sectors, including a Prussia "as small and weak as possible," and two regions—one consisting of the Kiel Canal and Hamburg, and the other, the Ruhr and the Saar—under international control.

Churchill disagreed. Fearful of leaving Russia as the only powerful state on the Continent, he suggested the isolation of Prussia from the rest of Germany and the detachment of Bavaria, Baden, Württemberg, the Palatinate, and Saxony for inclusion in a confederation of Danubian states. But Stalin objected that this would open the way to German control of a large state which could threaten the peace. Though Churchill now directly confronted the possibility of Soviet dominance and asked Stalin whether he "contemplated a Europe composed of little states, disjointed, separated and weak," Roosevelt "said he agreed with the Marshal. . . . Germany had been less dangerous to civilization when in 107 provinces," he added. Though the details of Germany's dismemberment were left to a European Advisory Commission established during the Moscow talks, it was clear that FDR wished to do all he could to relieve Stalin's fears of a resurgent German state.[36]

Roosevelt left Tehran convinced that he had significantly advanced the cause of world peace at home and abroad. The general harmony achieved at the Conference allowed him to encourage American acceptance of a major postwar role in world affairs. Believing that anything short of a portrait of full cooperation for a Wilsonian peace would revive American impulses to withdraw from foreign affairs, FDR took pains to emphasize the high ideals of the agreement attained at Tehran. Using a Christmas Eve Fireside Chat to discuss the Middle Eastern conferences with the nation, he assured Americans that they could "look forward into the future with real, substantial confidence that . . . 'peace on earth, good will toward men' can be and will be realized and insured. . . . At Cairo and Tehran we devoted ourselves . . . to plans for the kind of world which alone can justify all the sacrifices of this war." He, Churchill, and Chiang had discussed "certain long-range principles which we believe can assure peace in the Far East for many generations to come": the restoration of annexed territories to rightful owners and the right to self-government without molestation.

With Stalin, they had discussed international relationships in general terms, and he foresaw no insoluble differences. "I got along fine with Marshal Stalin," Roosevelt reported. ". . . I believe he is truly representative of the heart and soul of Russia; and I believe that we are going to get along very well with him and the Russian people—very well indeed." Moreover, he looked forward to cooperation between the Big Four and "all the freedom-loving peoples" of the world. "The rights of every Nation, large or small," he declared, "must be respected and guarded as jealously as the rights of every individual within our own Republic. The doctrine that the strong shall dominate the weak is the doctrine of our enemies—and we reject it." The President's idealistic or Wilsonian rhetoric coupled with plans for postwar peacekeeping by global rather than regional means, a system of trusteeships, and outward adherence to national self-determination were the means by which domestic opinion was to be put firmly behind a continuing American part in overseas affairs.

Actually, Roosevelt believed that he had gone far toward working out a realistic accommodation with Stalin for world peace. By subscribing to Soviet control of the Baltic states, their views of altered Polish boundaries, the need for permanent restraints on German and Japanese power through strategic bases and territorial divisions, and the predominant role of the Big Four in a new world league, Roosevelt thought he had disarmed some of Stalin's suspicions about postwar Anglo-American intentions and advanced the cause of long-term cooperation between the Allies. What were "your personal impressions of Marshal Stalin?" a reporter asked at the President's first press conference after Tehran. "We had many excellent talks," Roosevelt replied, which would "make for excellent relations in the future." "What type would you call him?" another reporter asked. "Is he dour?" "I would call him something like me," Roosevelt added, ". . . a realist." The President "was very much taken with Stalin," Harold Ickes recorded after a Cabinet meeting. ". . . He likes Stalin because he is open and frank." [37]

Churchill did not share the President's enthusiasm. He doubted Stalin's interest in postwar cooperation. "There might be a more bloody war," he had confided to Eden, Clark Kerr, his Ambassador in Moscow, and Lord Moran, his physician, after two days in Tehran. "I shall not be there. I shall be asleep. I want to sleep for billions of years." A "black depression . . . had settled on him," Moran reported. After the others had left, Churchill told Moran, "I believe man might destroy man and wipe out civilization. . . . Stupendous issues are unfolding before our eyes, and we are only specks of dust, that have settled in the night on the map of the world." After Tehran, despite physical exhaustion, Churchill conferred with General Harold Alexander in Italy. "He may be our last hope," Churchill cryptically told his physician, who had urged against the journey. "We've got to do something with these bloody Russians."

For all Roosevelt's expressions of optimism, he also had continuing doubts about Soviet intentions. On December 5, during follow-up talks in Cairo on Far Eastern operations, he expressed some skepticism about Soviet determination to fight Japan. He was "a little dubious about putting all our eggs in one basket," was his answer to Churchill's contention that the promised Russian involvement in the Far East reduced the importance of a Burma campaign. "Suppose Marshal Stalin was unable to be as good as his word; we might find that we had forfeited Chinese support without obtaining commensurate help from the Russians," FDR said. It was a "ticklish" business keeping "the Russians cozy with us," FDR subsequently told his Cabinet. It was "nip and tuck" on whether he could hold them to their promise to fight Japan. He was also doubtful about Stalin's acceptance of his plan for a postwar league. In a conversation with Senator Tom Connally after returning from Tehran, Roosevelt described Stalin as favoring Churchill's regional plan. "I'll have to work on both of them," he said.

He also saw public and congressional opinion in the United States as a potential problem. He believed the country was too optimistic about an early end to the fighting and too ready to resume partisan conflicts which could weaken the war effort and jeopardize the peacemaking. "It really would be a good thing for us if a few German bombs could be dropped over here," he told Harold Ickes on his return from the Middle East. "It is impossible to get along with the present Congress . . . ," he complained to his Budget Director. "No out-and-out Republican Congress could possibly be worse than this one." "I see a tendency in some of our people here to assume a quick ending of the war . . . ," he told the country. "And . . . I think I discern an effort to resume or even encourage an outbreak of partisan thinking and talking. I hope I am wrong. For, surely, our . . . foremost tasks are all concerned with winning the war and winning a just peace that will last for generations."

He particularly feared that American insistence on idealistic postwar goals would make realistic agreements with the U.S.S.R. impossible. In the first three months of 1944, congressional critics and journalists complained of administration silence about postwar plans, and concluded that the President had probably made secret deals with Churchill and Stalin at Tehran for European spheres of control. Roosevelt bristled under this criticism. In a conversation in mid-March with Edward R. Stettinius, Jr., his new Undersecretary of State, he said that whereas Woodrow Wilson saw the United States making the world safe for democracy, the issue was not whether America could make the world safe for democracy, but whether democracy could make the world safe from another war.[38]

15

1944: Victories and Doubts

B Y THE END OF 1943, Roosevelt believed that he would need a fourth term to conclude the war and design the peace. He was not entirely happy with the idea. "God knows I don't want to," he told one adviser early in 1944, "but I may find it necessary." "I just hate to run again for election," he told Admiral Leahy in the spring, and expressed the hope that progress in the war would make it unnecessary for him to be a candidate.

He found considerable appeal in the idea of retiring to Hyde Park. In the winter of 1944 he was sixty-two years old, tired, and in poor health. A number of physical ailments and illnesses—the flu, bronchitis, occasional inability to concentrate, and a blackout once while signing a letter—prompted him to have a full examination at the Bethesda, Maryland, Naval Hospital. The findings shocked his doctors: hypertension, hypertensive heart disease, or an enlarged heart, and evidence of cardiac failure. There is no evidence that the physicians ever gave FDR the results of their examination. He apparently conveyed the impression that he did not want to know or that the findings would not influence him. Believing it a poor idea to change leaders during the war, or for him to abandon the peacemaking he had begun at Tehran, he had resigned himself to staying in office, whatever the personal sacrifice, and wished no challenge to that decision.

During 1944, however, the issue of his health did not impress him as quite that dramatic. Under the care of his doctors, who prescribed more rest, fewer cigarettes, reduced weight, and various medications, including digitalis, which he took without asking their name or purpose, he recovered rapidly from the flu and regained much of his strength. Moreover, though he found he could not concentrate as he formerly had—a result of a generalized arteriosclerosis—and thus was occasionally depressed about his health, Roosevelt unquestioningly accepted the advice of his physicians that he could serve another term if he reduced his work load.[1]

Roosevelt had begun making campaign plans as soon as he returned from Tehran in December 1943. Opinion surveys suggested a focus on the postwar domestic economy. Polls taken during 1943 had indicated continuing mass ignorance about international affairs and fears of re-newed domestic ills after the war. In a September 1943 survey, for ex-ample, only 11 per cent of the public saw international cooperation for a lasting peace as the chief postwar worry, while 80 per cent expected it to be domestic economic problems. Almost half the country, this same survey demonstrated, feared that postwar foreign aid would lower America's standard of living, and if this were the case, two out of every three Americans opposed giving it. In light of this evidence, one aide told Hopkins, the President's State of the Union Address "should give primary emphasis to domestic affairs."

Roosevelt considered this sound advice. But he wished to combine it with the idea that continuing sacrifices to win the war would have to precede a renewed focus on internal economic concerns. He acted on this plan at the end of December when he privately told a reporter that he wished the press would drop the term "New Deal," for which there was now no need. Would he care to elaborate on this statement? an-other reporter asked at his next press conference. "Oh, I supposed some-body would ask that," the President declared with feigned distress. It was all very simple, he went on. Back in 1933 "an awfully sick patient called the United States of America" was treated for "a grave internal disorder" by "Dr. New Deal." After a number of years, the patient was cured. But two years ago on December 7 the patient was in "a pretty bad smashup" in which he broke a number of bones. To get the patient back on his feet, "Old Dr. New Deal" had to call in his partner, "Dr. Win-the-War." The patient was making a good recovery, but he was not entirely well yet, "and he won't be until he wins the war." Once that happened, however, there would have to be a new program of economic expansion to prevent a return to the conditions of 1933.

The President's remarks baffled some of the press. Did he mean to say that social reform had been temporarily shelved until the end of the war, or that the patient had been cured and the New Deal was dead? Roosevelt answered the question in his State of the Union Message on January 11. In what James MacGregor Burns, a biographer, has called the "most radical speech of his life," FDR combined a call for unstint-ing war measures with a promise of a postwar economic bill of rights. Beginning with an attack on "selfish pressure groups who seek to feather their nests while young Americans are dying," he asked Congress for a program of economic restraints, including a national service law which would prevent strikes and make every able-bodied adult in the country available for service until the end of the war.

The end of the fighting, he said, would also mean a new domestic emphasis on economic security. Addressing himself to the widespread fear of postwar economic dislocation registered in polls, Roosevelt of-fered a fourth-term declaration that promised "the establishment of an

American standard of living higher than ever before known. We cannot be content," he declared, "no matter how high that general standard of living may be, if some fraction of our people—whether it be one-third or one-fifth or one-tenth—is ill-fed, ill-clothed, ill-housed, and insecure." The country must have "a second Bill of Rights under which a new basis of security and prosperity can be established for all—regardless of station or race or creed. . . . And after this war is won," he concluded, "we must be prepared to move forward, in the implementation of these rights, to new goals of human happiness and well-being."

In putting forward a wartime stabilization program and calling for a postwar return to economic reform, Roosevelt was challenging Congress to do its worst. Eager to refurbish his image as a reformer in this election year, he skillfully maneuvered the Congress into giving him a fresh claim to that role. During the first three months of 1944 he purposely pushed confrontations with the Congress on issues he saw as not only central to the national well-being but calculated to polish his image as a progressive. On legislation guaranteeing servicemen the right to vote and setting taxes that would provide needed revenue and hold the line on inflation, Roosevelt invited defeat. Attacked as a means of lining up servicemen to back a fourth term and as an intrusion into states' rights, the voting bill had little chance to pass. "Why, God damn him," one Senator exploded over Roosevelt's charge that the Congress was letting the soldiers down. "The rest of us have boys who go into the Army and Navy as privates and ordinary seamen and dig latrines and swab decks and his scamps go in as . . . [officers] and spend their time getting medals in Hollywood. Letting the soldiers down! Why, that son of a bitch."

His tax bill ran into a buzzsaw of special interests. It emerged from the Congress with only one-tenth of the increased revenues FDR had asked. In a stinging veto message on February 22, Roosevelt declared the law "not a tax bill but a tax relief bill providing relief not for the needy but for the greedy." When Senator Alben Barkley of Kentucky, a consistent supporter, resigned as Majority Leader over the issue and the Congress overrode the President's veto, he appeared unperturbed. "Members of Congress were just naturally unsettled at this time before election and . . . there was no reasonable hope of statesman-like action," he told Harold Smith, his Budget Director. But he was "losing no sleep over the matter." Indeed, Roosevelt welcomed this fresh chance to test his campaign skills as a diversion from the harsh problems of war.[2]

But he could not escape these for long. In January 1944 he wrestled anew with the question of how to save Europe's Jews. The problem had taken on an urgency few had foreseen at the start of the war. In 1939 the problem had revolved around finding new homes for displaced persons, refugees from Nazi-dominated countries. Roosevelt's "basic solution" was "the development of a suitable area to which refugees would be admitted in almost unlimited numbers." Believing public enthusiasm for such a scheme essential, he wished to put the problem "on a broad religious basis, thereby making it possible to gain the kind of world-wide support that a mere Jewish relief set-up would not evoke." To this end, he took steps to gain Vatican backing and announced his plan in a speech before the Intergovernmental Committee on Refugees, which met in Washington in October 1943 at Roosevelt's behest. Predicting that the refugee problem would grow to huge proportions involving between ten and twenty million people, Roosevelt urged the delegates to devise a large-scale, long-term scheme for massive resettlement in one of the earth's many vacant spaces—a plan that would capture worldwide support and permanently end the plight of homeless peoples.

But Roosevelt got nowhere with this idea. Arguing that their victory in the war would eliminate the problem, the British and the French blocked action by the Intergovernmental Committee. And because of reluctance to do anything that might increase the threat to the Catholic Church in Nazi Germany, the Vatican turned aside Roosevelt's efforts to put the refugee problem "on a broad religious basis." Roosevelt could not even muster much enthusiasm among Jews. Convinced that British opposition made Palestine an unrealistic choice as a haven for mass relocation, FDR tried to sell the idea of an alternate haven or "supplemental Jewish homeland." But Zionists found small appeal in the scheme. And even if they had, it would have meant little; Roosevelt could find no "suitable area" for large-scale resettlement. Governing authorities in Latin America and Africa, the focal points of most resettlement plans, offered either outright resistance or proposals that lacked practical merit. In Bolivia, for example, talk of accepting Jewish refugees provoked attempts to prohibit "Jews, Mongols and Negroes" from entering the country. Suggestions that Angola might make an ideal locale for resettling Europe's Jews moved Lisbon to discourage Washington from an official approach. In the Dominican Republic, where the government declared itself ready to accept 100,000 settlers on a 26,000-acre tract of improved land, a variety of domestic and international difficulties eventually limited the settlement to 500 refugees.[3]

In pressing the case for resettlement in other nations, Roosevelt labored under the handicap of American unwillingness to do the same. Though the United States gave sanctuary to 90,000 immigrants in 1939 —6000 more than all of Latin America and twice the number accepted by Britain and her colonies—it was clear that Americans would resist opening their country to the kind of mass influx Roosevelt described in his plan. Indeed, in 1939–41, when international conditions and American neutrality had not foreclosed the possibility of mass migration to the United States, the Congress showed little interest in relaxing immigration restrictions. The United States, moreover, would not give entry to the full quota of Europeans allowed under the law. Convinced that the admission of immigrants gave foreign agents easy access to the country, the administration transferred the Immigration and Naturalization Service from the Labor Department to the Justice Department in 1940 and barred anyone even faintly under suspicion. As a result, the flow of European immigrants to America in 1939–41 fell some 15,000 a year below what the quotas would allow.

Roosevelt himself was not willing to press the case for greater immigration to the United States. At a time when he desperately needed congressional backing for a greater American role in foreign affairs, he refused to clash with the Congress by asking for a change in immigration laws. Also convinced that national security dictated a rigorous application of those laws, Roosevelt refused to challenge the State Department's narrow interpretation of who could come to the country. To Breckinridge Long, the Assistant Secretary of State responsible for immigration control, he declared himself in full accord with the policy of excluding anybody about whom there was any suspicion.

In 1942 information that the Nazis had become committed to the total destruction of the Jews produced no dramatic shift in policy. To be sure, on October 7 the administration announced its intention to try Nazi war criminals guilty of murdering innocent persons, and on December 17 it specifically denounced the policy of Jewish extermination, but Roosevelt showed little inclination to mount an immediate rescue effort. In a discussion with Vice President Henry Wallace and House Speaker Sam Rayburn in November 1942, Roosevelt raised the possibility of loosening immigration restrictions. But when Rayburn indicated that this would meet with "great opposition . . . the President said that all he wanted to do was to make it clear that the responsibility was that of Congress." In December, moreover, when he discussed the plight of the Jews with Morgenthau, he showed more interest in plans for postwar resettlement than in immediate action.[4]

Roosevelt's approach to the Jewish refugee problem remained the same through 1943. Though the administration took a leading part in a Bermuda Conference on refugees, engaged in negotiations for the rescue of some 100,000 European Jews, and encouraged Arab-Jewish talks on Palestine, little came of these efforts. More concerned with blunting pressure for action in Britain and America than with initiating steps to save potential victims, the Bermuda meeting, in the words of a British delegate, was "a façade for inaction. We said the results of the conference were confidential," Richard Law of the Foreign Office later acknowledged, "but in fact there were no results that I can recall." In a post-conference discussion of follow-up action, Roosevelt agreed with Hull that there should be no promise of unlimited relief, that North

Africa should be used as a temporary depot for only limited numbers of Jews, that they not ask the Congress to relax immigration bars, and that they not bring in any more refugees as temporary visitors.

Likewise, Roosevelt made no serious effort to overcome State Department and British resistance to rescuing Jews offered for ransom in Roumania, Bulgaria, and France. The fact that the transactions were planned with funds to be frozen in Switzerland until after the war made no difference. He saw other reasons for not pressing the issue: removing large numbers of refugees from enemy territory threatened to divert scarce shipping from military tasks and to agitate Arab opposition in the Near East, where the victims would have to be sent. Though Roosevelt had made inquiries in 1942–43 about Arab receptivity to a settlement with the Jews, by the summer of 1943 he agreed with Churchill that the Palestine issue should be left until after the war. After Tehran, Roosevelt "triumphantly" told his Cabinet that the subject of Palestine "had not even been mentioned."

Finally, the administration also turned aside requests from rescue advocates for bombing crematoria, gas chambers, and rail lines leading to the death camps. Such an operation, the War Department replied, would divert air support from other "essential" tasks, would be of "doubtful efficacy," and "might provoke more vindictive action by the Germans." "What 'more vindictive action' than Auschwitz was possible," the historian Henry L. Feingold writes, "remained the secret of the War Department." Bombing the camps and their railway lines, Feingold believes, would have expanded international awareness of the mass murder of Jews, disrupted the physical means of getting people to the camps, and weakened inclinations of Eastern European officials to cooperate with the Nazis in the extermination program.[5]

Roosevelt was not indifferent to the plight of the Jews. On the contrary, Nazi crimes profoundly disturbed him, and he looked forward to the day when Nazi leaders would face the consequences of their actions. Yet at the same time, he saw no effective way to rescue great numbers of Jews from Hitler's Europe while the war continued. Nazi determination to kill as many Jews as possible placed even the most ardent rescue advocates under an insurmountable constraint. The congressional restrictionists, the British, the Arabs, the Latin Americans, the Vatican, the neutrals, the exiled governments, and even the Jews themselves, divided between Zionists and non-Zionists, threw up additional direct and indirect obstacles to effective mass rescue which Roosevelt saw no way to overcome. Yet if mass rescue was out of reach, there were opportunities which Roosevelt would not take to save many thousands of lives; he saw these opportunities as destructive to the war effort. Unwilling to compromise his unconditional-surrender policy toward Germany and jeopardize Soviet confidence in his determination to fight the war to a decisive end, he rejected appeals for rescuing Jews through negotiations with Berlin. And unwilling to risk divisions at home and abroad which he thought might prolong the war, he refused to press the case for greater Jewish immigration to the United States or other parts of the world. In short, the best means he saw for saving the Jews was through the quickest possible end to the fighting—a policy of "rescue through victory." [6]

At the beginning of 1944, however, Roosevelt agreed to a more active rescue policy. On January 16, Morgenthau gave him a report prepared in the Treasury Department "on the Acquiescence of this Government in the Murder of the Jews." It described "gross procrastination" by the State Department in issuing visas and transferring funds for the rescue of European Jews, and it charged Breckinridge Long and others in the Department with willfully blocking rescue efforts. It also demonstrated that the Department had purposely kept information on the Final Solution from reaching the United States, where, as a later poll would show, the great majority of Americans remained ignorant of what Hitler was doing to the Jews. Coinciding with growing expressions of concern in the country about the fate of the Jews, the report moved Roosevelt to agree to the creation of a War Refugee Board. Made up of the Secretaries of State, Treasury, and War, the Board replaced the State Department as the principal agency concerned with the immediate rescue and relief of the Jews and other minorities singled out for extermination. At "stake," as Morgenthau put it, "was the Jewish population of Nazi-controlled Europe. The threat was their total obliteration. The hope was to get a few of them out."

During the remaining sixteen months of the European fighting, the Board gave "an entirely new tone" to the administration's rescue efforts. It facilitated the removal of Jews from France, Bulgaria, Poland, Slovakia, and Hungary to safety in North Africa, Italy, and the United States. To avoid violations of immigration quotas, Roosevelt set up "Emergency Rescue Shelters" in America, where these refugees were to have temporary havens. The President's action received wide approval in the United States and influenced other countries to do the same. The success of these actions suggests that Roosevelt had exaggerated the negative impact on the war effort which he believed would have resulted from a greater effort to rescue Jews earlier in the fighting. If a War Refugee Board had been set up in 1942 or even earlier, it might have saved many more thousands of lives. Yet an effort of that kind would still have had only a limited impact: Nazi determination to carry out the slaughter consigned such rescue efforts to comparatively small results. Even when the Nazis knew "they had lost the war," Feingold writes, "the cattle cars rolled to Auschwitz as if they had a momentum of their own." To deter Berlin from the slaughter required a "miracle" that no one in Washington could perform. [7]

In the weeks and months after he returned from the Middle East, Roosevelt tried to hold strictly to the agreements reached at Tehran. Believing that the success of OVERLORD would depend partly on German inability to shift forces from the East, Roosevelt opposed anything that would shake Soviet determination to launch a simultaneous offensive in the spring of 1944. At the end of December, however, a stalemate on the Italian front at Cassino, some ninety miles south of Rome, had raised this possibility. The Allied intention of tying down German troops in Italy "succeeded almost beyond expectation." By the end of October, Hitler had concentrated twenty-five divisions in Italy, where German forces took advantage of rugged terrain to establish a series of defensive lines across the peninsula south of Cassino. To break the stalemate, Churchill urged an amphibious assault at Anzio, some sixty miles behind the German lines, which would compel a three-week delay in the transfer of fifty-six LSTs (landing-ship tanks) from the Mediterranean to England for OVERLORD. Convinced that a vigorous effort in Italy during the first half of 1944 was essential to the invasion of France, he warned Roosevelt against allowing the Italian battle to "stagnate and fester." Since he also gave assurances that the Anzio attack would not delay OVERLORD, Roosevelt agreed. FDR added the qualification, however, that he would insist on "Stalin's approval" for "any use of forces or equipment elsewhere that might delay or hazard the success of OVERLORD or ANVIL." "I thank God for this fine decision," Churchill replied, "which engages us once again in wholehearted unity upon a great enterprise." [8]

When the Anzio assault at the end of January failed to break the deadlock in Italy, the problem of holding Churchill to the Tehran agreements intensified. "I had hoped that we were hurling a wildcat onto the shore," Churchill said of the Allied effort at Anzio, "but all we had got was a stranded whale." For eight days after an unopposed landing at Anzio, Allied forces unwittingly failed to take advantage of German weakness in the hills surrounding the beachhead. By the time they pushed forward on January 30, 1944, Hitler had reinforced the area with parts of fourteen divisions totaling 125,000 men. The Anzio fighting now duplicated the stalemate below Cassino. Despite repeated attacks on what the Germans had dubbed their Gustav line, Allied forces could not capture Cassino and break into the Liri Valley. Similarly, a decision to bomb the 1400-year-old Abbey of Saint Benedict atop Monte Cassino, which Allied commanders believed was serving the Germans as an observation post, also backfired. The destruction of the Abbey on February 15 allowed the Germans to construct effective defenses in the rubble and keep Allied troops at bay.

Now convinced that Hitler intended to give no ground in southern Italy and that this afforded the Allies a chance to bleed his divisions, Churchill and his Chiefs urged the cancellation of ANVIL for the sake of "two really good major campaigns—one in Italy and one in OVERLORD." Roosevelt opposed the idea as likely to antagonize the Russians. In early January, when Churchill had first raised the possibility of modifying ANVIL and expanding and delaying OVERLORD until June 2, Roosevelt reminded him of their promise to "Uncle J." to do OVERLORD in May while also making the "strongest practicable landing in the south of France. . . . I think the psychology of bringing this thing up at this time," he cabled, "would be very bad." In February, therefore, he countered British suggestions for cancelling ANVIL with the warning that "the Russians would not be happy." The commitment could not be abandoned without consulting the Russians, he told the Joint Chiefs, and he did not wish to raise the matter with them now, because "we have given up promises [to them] in the past and had better not do it again." When the British, however, continued to press the point, Roosevelt agreed to a compromise which deferred a decision on ANVIL until the spring. Acknowledging that the Italian campaign had first priority in the Mediterranean, the agreement stipulated that the fate of ANVIL would depend on the fighting in Italy during the next month. Meanwhile, preparations were to continue for an attack on southern France.

By the end of March, when a continuing stalemate in Italy moved Allied planners to propose a delay in ANVIL until July, FDR insisted that Stalin be fully informed as soon as there was a firm decision on this change in plans. In the meantime, though, he wished to leave no doubt in Stalin's mind that OVERLORD remained on the books. On April 10 the Chiefs of the Anglo-American military mission in Moscow informed the Chief of the Soviet General Staff that OVERLORD would occur two or three days before or after May 31, 1944. On the 18th Roosevelt and Churchill directly informed Stalin that "the general crossing of the sea" would occur at full strength about May 31 and would follow a maximum-strength offensive in Italy beginning in mid-May. Since they were also eager to receive confirmation of Soviet plans, they expressed their "trust that your armies and ours, operating in unison in accordance with our Tehran agreement, will crush the Hitlerites." Stalin replied at once that the Red Army would support the Anglo-American attack with a simultaneous campaign. In May, almost a month after the Combined Chiefs had decided to leave a final decision on ANVIL until they could assess the next offensive in Italy, Roosevelt and Churchill informed Stalin that the demands of OVERLORD and the Italian fighting had forced them to postpone an attack on southern France until "later." Stalin expressed no dismay. The important thing, he answered, was the success of OVERLORD.[9]

In the six months before OVERLORD, Roosevelt believed that coordinated Soviet military action also depended on holding Polish difficulties in check. It was a formidable task. On January 5, as Soviet forces crossed the Polish border, the Polish Government in Exile had issued a declaration calling for "the earliest reestablishment of Polish sovereign administration in the liberated territories of the Republic of Poland," and describing itself "as the only and legal steward and spokesman of the Polish Nation." This declaration, Stalin cabled Churchill, suggested that the London Poles could not be brought to reason. "These people," he said, "are incorrigible." Stalin gave public voice to this attitude in a Soviet counter declaration of January 11 disputing Polish territorial claims and attacking the Government in Exile as "incapable of establishing friendly relations with the Soviet Union."

A more conciliatory Polish declaration of January 15 received a similar response. It asked Anglo-American intervention to arrange Polish-Soviet discussion of "all outstanding questions." Washington asked Moscow to accept the Polish offer as a way to advance "the cause of general international cooperation," and, as Hull told Harriman privately, as a means of assuring "important elements" in the United States that the Soviet Union intended to defend its interests through an international security system rather than by unilateral action. Before the American initiative reached the Soviet government, however, Moscow had refused the Polish overture as an attempt to skirt the main question between them—the acceptance of the Curzon Line.

Churchill now tried to break the impasse. In a meeting with representatives of the London Poles on January 20, he pressed them "to accept the Curzon Line as a basis for discussion," explaining that they would be compensated with German territory up to the Oder. The need for Soviet security from another devastating German attack and "the enormous sacrifices and achievements of the Russian armies" to liberate Poland, he told them, entitled the Russians to ask revision of Poland's frontiers. If the Poles would agree to these conditions, Churchill promised to challenge Moscow's demand for changes in their government. While the Poles discussed these proposals with their colleagues, Churchill reported his conversation to Stalin: he expressed optimism about the Polish response, transmitted several questions raised by the Poles about future relations with Russia, and questioned Stalin's right to interfere in Polish affairs. "The creation in Warsaw of another Polish government different from the one we have recognized up to the present, together with disturbances in Poland," he warned, "would raise issues in Great Britain and the United States detrimental to that close accord between the Three Great Powers upon which the future of the world depends." While Stalin readily subscribed to Churchill's position on frontiers, he strongly objected to his ideas about the Polish government. "No good can be expected" unless its composition were "thoroughly improved," he declared. Indeed, he predicted that the resolution of border questions and the rebirth of "a strong, free and independent" Poland would follow such a change.[10]

Roosevelt now felt compelled to enter the argument. On February 7 he asked Stalin not to allow the Polish issue to undermine future international cooperation: "While public opinion is forming in support of the principle of international collaboration, it is especially incumbent upon us to avoid any action which might appear to counteract the achievement of our long-range objective." His solution to the Polish problem was to win a "clear-cut acceptance" from the Polish Prime Minister for the desired territorial changes, and then leave it to him to alter the makeup of his government "without any evidence of pressure or dictation from a foreign country." He put the same proposal before Churchill on the following day. Expressing a concern that Stalin may have interpreted Churchill's attitude toward the London Poles as evidence of a desire to establish a hostile government along the Soviet frontier, Roosevelt urged a clarifying message. He suggested some reference to the possibility that, after frontier problems were solved, the Polish government, "of its own accord," would accept the resignations of its well-known anti-Soviet members. He had taken this initiative, the President explained, because of the "potential dangers . . . to the essential unity . . . so successfully established at Moscow and Tehran."

Neither Roosevelt's proposal nor additional efforts at conciliation by Churchill swayed Stalin. The Polish government, he answered the President on February 16, had made no constructive move on the border question. Nor would it. It was principally made up of "hostile to the Soviet Union pro-fascist imperialist elements," who could not establish friendly relations with Soviet Russia. "The basic improvement of the Polish government appears to be an urgent task." As a result of further conversations with the Poles, Churchill advised Stalin on the 21st that the Government in Exile was ready to accept the Curzon Line as a basis for talks, and offered assurances that by the time they resumed diplomatic relations with the Soviet Union, their government would include only members determined to cooperate with Moscow. Though it did not actually say so, Churchill told FDR, this message to Stalin contained the essentials of the settlement outlined at Tehran.

Stalin was still unconvinced. He told Harriman that the London Poles were fooling Churchill, and he cabled Roosevelt that "the solution of the question regarding Polish-Soviet relations has not ripened yet." "Now that I have read the detailed record of your conversations with the leaders of the Polish émigré Government," he answered Churchill, "I am more convinced than ever that men of their type are incapable of establishing normal relations with the U.S.S.R." Although Churchill offered a well-reasoned response to this message, Stalin turned it aside with the complaint that distorted leaks to the British press of his messages violated the confidentiality of their correspondence and inhibited him from giving a reply.

Churchill now threatened to publicize their differences. "I shall have very soon to make a statement to the House of Commons about the Polish position," he cabled Stalin on March 21. "This will involve my saying that attempts to make an arrangement between the Soviet and Polish Governments have broken down; that we continue to recognize the Polish Government . . . ; that we now consider all questions of territorial change must await the armistice . . . ; and that in the meantime we can recognise no forcible transferences of territory." Churchill concluded with an expression of "hope that the breakdown which has occurred between us about Poland will not have any effect upon our cooperation in other spheres where the maintenance of our common action is of the greatest consequence."

But Stalin refused to encourage that hope. In one of the sharpest messages he ever sent Churchill, he complained of the "threats" by the Prime Minister, and accused him of breaking the Tehran agreement on the Curzon Line and of attributing false intentions to the Soviet Union toward Poland. "You are free to make any statement you like in the House of Commons—that is your business. But should you make a statement of this nature I shall consider that you have committed an unjust and unfriendly act. . . . I have been, and still am, for cooperation. But I fear that the method of intimidation and defamation, if continued, will not benefit our cooperation." [11]

Roosevelt tried to avoid jeopardizing joint military efforts by placating Stalin. In March, while he pointedly refrained from any message to him about the controversy, he signaled his willingness to see the creation of a Soviet-inspired Polish regime. On the 24th he acceded to a Soviet request for passports to Russia for two conspicuously pro-Soviet Polish-Americans invited to discuss participation in a new Polish government. Concerned, however, that this might provoke a hostile reaction from a majority of Polish-Americans, he asked Stalin to provide transportation and cautioned that if their trip became "the subject of public comment," he would feel compelled to make it clear that they were traveling as "private citizens" without official sanction for "their views or activities." At the same time, he resisted Churchill's suggestion that Polish Prime Minister Stanislaus Mikolajczyk come to the United States to show Stalin that the London Poles had friends. He also encouraged him temporarily to push political questions about Poland into the background: "It seems to me," he commented on a proposed British response to Stalin's accusations, "the essential consideration in the Polish-Russian controversy . . . is to get the Polish military power, including the underground, into effective action against the Nazis." [12]

Though a British decision not to pursue the argument with Stalin temporarily quieted the Polish question, it resurfaced in May. The growing concern of Polish-Americans over the intentions of Soviet forces advancing in Poland moved Roosevelt to invite Mikolajczyk to visit the United States in early June. The visit, which he had repeatedly put off for six months, was a "sop" to the seven million Americans of Polish extraction whom he considered was the only ethnic group in America likely to vote as a bloc. He remained as concerned as ever, however, about weakening the Soviet resolve to launch their promised offensive.

On June 6, 1944, 156,000 Allied troops established five beachheads along the Normandy Coast of France. Code-named Omaha, Utah, Gold, Juno, and Sword, the beachheads became the sites of an Allied buildup that grew to almost a million men by the end of June. In a month of hard fighting against German forces totaling 65 divisions of approximately 850,000 men, the Allies seized Cherbourg on the north coast of the Cotentin Peninsula and extended their control over a seventy-mile-wide front. Allied forces, however, had not been able to make a significant breakthrough at any point and nowhere was the front more than twenty miles from the beaches. To many in the Allied camp at the beginning of July, "the prospect of trench warfare appeared distressingly real."

On June 7, the day after the invasion of France had begun, Stalin advised the President that the Soviet summer campaign would begin in mid-June and turn into a general attack between late June and the end of July. This was "a little later than we hoped for," FDR cabled Churchill on the 9th, "but it may be for the best in the long run." Still, as he told the visiting Poles, he "had no idea what this offensive was or where it would be." He also said that he "must win Russia's confidence," and that "the Russians trusted him" more than they did Churchill. But he added that they did not "even trust him completely."

Consequently, he wished to assure that Mikolajczyk's visit did not arouse Soviet suspicions. He had instructed Harriman, while he was on leave in Washington in May, to assure Stalin that he was firm in his resolve to fulfill the understandings reached at Moscow and Tehran, and "that no minor difficulties would affect this determination to work out agreements on all questions." The Mikolajczyk visit, Harriman was also to say, would not result in any public agitation of the Polish issue in the United States, and would give the President a chance to urge confidence in Soviet desire for Polish independence, acceptance of the Curzon Line with some adjustments, and the removal from the Polish Government in Exile of four members objectionable to Moscow.

Mikolajczyk's visit, FDR cabled Stalin on June 17, "was not connected with any attempt on my part to inject myself into the merits of the differences which exist between" the Polish and Soviet governments. "I can assure you that no specific plan or proposal in any way affecting

Polish-Soviet relations was drawn up." His personal impression of Mikolajczyk was that he craved Soviet-Polish military cooperation and was ready to go to Moscow if "you would welcome such a step. . . . In making this observation," Roosevelt added, "I am in no way attempting to press upon you my personal views in a matter which is of special concern to you and your country." But Stalin had no complaints. He was, in fact, "greatly pleased" with the President's attitude and "highly appreciated" his efforts.[13]

At the same time that Roosevelt worked to avoid tension with Stalin over Poland, he also tried to prevent Anglo-Soviet differences over the Balkans. In the spring of 1944, when Soviet forces had entered Roumania and a Communist-inspired political crisis erupted among the Greeks, Churchill asked his War Cabinet: "Are we going to acquiesce in the Communisation of the Balkans and perhaps of Italy?" To meet this problem, the British proposed to Moscow that Russia take principal responsibility for Roumanian affairs and that Britain do the same for Greece until the war ended. In May, after the Russians accepted the idea on the condition that the United States also agree, Churchill asked FDR's approval: "There have recently been disquieting signs of a possible divergence of policy between ourselves and the Russians in regard to the Balkan countries and in particular towards Greece. We therefore suggested . . . that the Soviet Government would take the lead in Roumanian affairs, while we would take the lead in Greek affairs. . . . I hope you may feel able to give this proposal your blessing. We do not of course wish to carve up the Balkans into spheres of influence and in agreeing to the arrangement we should make it clear that it applied only to war conditions. . . . The arrangement now proposed would be a useful device for preventing any divergence of policy between ourselves and them in the Balkans."

But Roosevelt feared contrary results. The consequence of such an agreement, he cabled Churchill in June, would be the extension of the control of the responsible party "to other than military fields. . . . In our opinion, this would certainly result in the persistence of differences between you and the Soviets and in the division of the Balkan region into spheres of influence. . . . Efforts should preferably be made to establish consultative machinery to dispel misunderstandings and restrain the tendency toward the development of exclusive spheres." Roosevelt's objection was not to spheres of influence per se; he was ready to accept Soviet control of the Baltic states and, at least in the short run, expected Britain to dominate Western Europe and the United States to police the South Atlantic and the Pacific. His objections were to the Anglo-Soviet agreement itself: the arrangement to share control between traditional competitors for influence in the Balkans seemed certain to inflame rather than inhibit tensions between America's allies; secondly, done without reference to plebiscites or trusteeships, the agreement promised to agitate American demands for self-determination in the Balkans.

Expediency, however, persuaded Roosevelt to give the plan a brief try. When Churchill argued that a consultative committee would paralyze rather than facilitate action in the unstable Balkans, where events would continually outrun current plans, Roosevelt agreed to try his scheme on two conditions: that the three powers review the situation after three months, as Churchill suggested, and that it was made clear, as Roosevelt insisted, "that we are not establishing any postwar spheres of influence." [14]

At the end of June, Anglo-American differences over Mediterranean operations renewed Roosevelt's concern about an Anglo-Soviet confrontation in the Balkans. After a campaign that began on May 11 had broken the stalemates at Cassino and Anzio, the Allies had captured Rome on June 4. This again raised the question of whether the Allies should continue to make an all-out effort in Italy or combine operations there with an attack on the south of France. The British, led by Churchill, strongly opposed doing ANVIL. Though granting that OVERLORD should receive "supreme priority" and that this entailed getting thirty-plus American divisions from the United States to France as quickly as possible, the British disputed the need for a major port in the south of France; they argued that various small ports on the French Atlantic coast could provide what they would gain from the capture of Marseilles. Further, they did not think that ANVIL would provide significant help to OVERLORD: the Germans could effectively resist an advance up the Rhone valley without withdrawing a single division from northwest France. Instead, the British urged continued forward movement in Italy, with the aim of striking eastward across the Adriatic and through the Ljubljana Gap into southern Hungary. This would not only give them a major victory in Italy, Churchill asserted, it would also raise the possibility of political upheavals in the Balkans and the submission of Hitler's satellites—Bulgaria, Roumania, and Hungary. "Let us resolve not to wreck one great campaign for the sake of winning the other," Churchill concluded. "Both can be won."

Roosevelt saw strong military reasons for resisting these plans. Their main effort, he reminded Churchill, must be directed against the heart of Germany through the grand strategy agreed upon at Tehran—OVERLORD, ANVIL, and a Soviet drive from the East. This, Roosevelt emphasized, remained the surest and quickest way to end the war. Besides, he asserted, the difficulties of an advance through the Ljubljana Gap "would seem to far exceed those pictured by you in the Rhone Valley. . . . The Rhone corridor has its limitations, but is better than Ljubljana, and is certainly far better than the terrain over which we have been fighting in Italy." Moreover, he predicted that the movement of additional American divisions from the United States to France would be difficult without Marseilles.

He also had strong political doubts about the British plan. It would violate their agreement with Stalin for an attack on southern France and challenge his belief that other Mediterranean operations were of secondary importance to the European campaign. More to the point, it seemed certain to arouse Stalin's suspicions that his allies were intent on checking Soviet influence in the Balkans, and would jeopardize the military and political understandings Roosevelt was so eager to sustain. "I cannot agree to the employment of United States troops against Istria and into the Balkans," he told Churchill. It would not only cause difficulties with Stalin but would also risk problems with the French and in the United States. He could not see the French agreeing to keep their forces out of France for the sake of secondary operations in Italy or the Balkans, and he predicted that he would "never survive even a slight setback in OVERLORD if it were known that fairly large forces had been diverted to the Balkans."

Though Churchill assured him that "no one involved in these discussions has ever thought of moving armies into the Balkans," and repeated the case against a campaign in the Rhone valley, including the loss of "all" the "dazzling possibilities" in the Italian campaign, Roosevelt held fast to his view: "the right course of action is to launch ANVIL at the earliest possible date." Despite further attempts to turn aside the attack on southern France, the British finally agreed to an invasion, which began August 15.

By then, Allied forces were on the verge of breaking enemy resistance in Normandy, driving German forces across the Seine River, and capturing Paris, which they did on August 25. The attack on the south of France by three American and seven French divisions fully met the expectations of its advocates by capturing Toulon and Marseilles in two weeks and linking up with OVERLORD forces in less than a month. But Churchill still disputed the wisdom of the move. The army in Italy, he complained in his memoirs, lost a chance to strike "a most formidable blow at the Germans," while the forces coming up the Rhone drew no German troops from northern to southern France. There were also political consequences: speculating at the time that Stalin wished American and British forces to fight in France, while eastern, central, and southern Europe fell "naturally into his control," Churchill later observed that the forces in Italy lost the possibility of getting to Vienna before the Russians, "with all that might have followed therefrom. . . . Except in Greece," he concluded, "our military power to influence the liberation of southeastern Europe was gone." [15]

These military and political differences with the British remained minor compared to difficulties with the French. Events during the last two months of 1943 had more than ever convinced Roosevelt that de Gaulle and his Committee would openly defy the principle of self-determination and provoke civil strife in France. In November, de Gaulle had forced Giraud out of the National Committee and limited him to nominal control over the Army. At the same time, he responded to Lebanese demands for independence by suspending their constitution, dismissing their Parliament, and imprisoning their ministers. Churchill himself saw these "lamentable outrages" as "a foretaste of what de Gaulle's leadership of France means. It is certainly entirely contrary to the Atlantic Charter. . . . ," he told FDR. "Everywhere people will say: 'What kind of a France is this which, while itself subjugated by the enemy, seeks to subjugate others?' " "The general attitude of the Committee and especially de Gaulle," Roosevelt told Hull, "is shown in the Lebanon affair. De Gaulle is now claiming the right to speak for all of France and is talking openly about how he intends to set up his government in France as soon as the Allies get in there." In December the arrest of three prominent Vichyites, who had aided the Allied attack in North Africa, further persuaded Churchill and Roosevelt that de Gaulle's Committee intended to impose itself upon France without regard for the popular will or the risk of civil war.[16]

During the first half of 1944, arguments that de Gaulle spoke for most of France and that recognition of his Committee as the provisional government would serve the cross-Channel attack left FDR unmoved. He refused to believe that "there are only two major groups in France today—the Vichy gang, and the other characterized by unreasoning admiration for de Gaulle." The great majority of the people, he believed, "do not know what it is all about," and had "not made up their minds as to whether they want de Gaulle and his Committee as their rulers." This put him under "a moral duty" not to recognize the Committee as the provisional government of France, and "to see to it that the people of France have nothing foisted on them by outside powers. . . . Self-determination is not a word of expediency," he told Marshall, who had recommended recognizing de Gaulle. "It carries with it a very deep principle in human affairs."

Nor did he believe that the OVERLORD attack depended on accepting de Gaulle as the provisional ruler of France. "I am in complete agreement with you that the French National Spirit should be working with us in OVERLORD to prevent unnecessary loss of American and British lives," he cabled Churchill ten days before the attack. But "at the present time I am unable to see how an Allied establishment of the Committee as a Government of France would save the lives of any of our men." After all, he told Churchill in a follow-up message, "we do not know definitely what the state of that French spirit is and we will not know until we get to France." Also, "as a matter of practical fact," they would not be calling on "French military strength" to help OVERLORD until well after D-Day or the invasion of southern France.

As for the argument that they needed de Gaulle's full cooperation to assure easy control of occupied France, Roosevelt dismissed it as an effort to "stampede us into according full recognition to the Comité." Specifically, de Gaulle's refusal to endorse Allied military francs as a legitimate currency unless they agreed to issue them in the name of his provisional government impressed Roosevelt as an empty threat. If for any reason the supplemental currency were not acceptable to the French public, FDR assured Churchill, the Allied authorities could use "yellow seal dollars and British Military Authority Notes. . . . I would certainly not importune de Gaulle to make any supporting statement whatever regarding the currency," he advised Churchill. "Provided it is clear that he acts entirely on his own responsibility . . . he can sign any statement on currency in whatever capacity he likes, even that of the King of Siam." [17]

Though Roosevelt insisted that it was "utter nonsense" to describe his behavior toward de Gaulle as animated by personal dislike, it is difficult to discount this as a contributing factor. "I am perfectly willing to have de Gaulle made President, or Emperor, or King or anything else," he told Marshall, "so long as the action comes in an untrammeled and unforced way from the French people themselves." Yet other FDR comments on de Gaulle belie these words. "The only thing I am interested in," he told Stettinius in May, "is not having de Gaulle and the National Committee named as the government of France." He expected no cooperation from de Gaulle, he advised Churchill in June. "It seems clear that prima donnas do not change their spots." He "would not now permit that 'jackenape' to seize the government," he told Stimson ten days after the Allies had landed in France.

"Arrogant" and even "vicious" in his defense of what he considered legitimate French rights, de Gaulle provoked other Americans as well. Hull, Stimson recorded in June, "hated de Gaulle so fiercely that he was almost incoherent on the subject." De Gaulle's refusal to broadcast his support of the invasion as it began, to endorse the supplemental currency, or to send more than a handful of French liaison officers with the invading forces put Marshall in "a white fury." If the American public learned what de Gaulle had been doing to hamper the invasion, Marshall declared, it would demand a break with the French National Committee.[18]

Roosevelt's desire to assure popular control in France and his personal antagonism only partly explain his opposition to de Gaulle. There were also postwar considerations. Civil strife in France, which FDR believed a likely consequence of de Gaulle's assumption of power, would create not only instability in Europe but also American reluctance to take a meaningful part in European affairs. As important, de Gaulle's control of France would undermine Roosevelt's plans to abolish the French colonial empire and place some of its strategically located colonies under United Nations control. More specifically, it would play havoc with FDR's plans for Dakar in West Africa and French Indochina.

High on Roosevelt's list for assuring postwar security was the conversion of Dakar from a French colony to a United Nations trust territory under American military control. "Dakar is of such vital importance to the protection of the South Atlantic and South America," FDR had advised Eisenhower in June 1943, "that I should be compelled to send American troops there if any problematical changes were sought by de Gaulle." Instead, Roosevelt sent Rear Admiral William A. Glassford as his Personal Representative to protect American interests. The specific objective of his mission was the transformation of Dakar into "one of the prime United Nations strategic strongholds" under the administration of the United States. By November 1943, however, the crystallization of de Gaulle's power convinced Glassford that the French would never give up their colonies without a fight, and that it was time to induce the French to join the United States in making Dakar into a military base under shared control.

But Roosevelt was not ready to concede the French this role. At Tehran in December 1943, he left Eden with the impression "that the United States might take over Dakar." But he told Taussig in February 1944 that "he was having so much trouble with de Gaulle and the French Committee that he did not think the time was right to start any conversation on Dakar." Indeed, as long as he saw a chance for the emergence of a more pliable French regime than de Gaulle's, he would not abandon his hopes for a shift in control over Dakar.[19]

The same was true of French Indochina. Roosevelt was "more outspoken . . . on that subject than on any other colonial matter," Churchill said in May 1944. During 1943 and the first half of 1944, FDR had repeatedly stated his intention to free Indochina from France and bring it under United Nations rule until it was ready for self-government. " 'We' would have great trouble over this with the French," he told a group of diplomats in December 1943, but added that "nevertheless it would have to be done. At recent meetings it has been decided that peace must be kept by force. There was no other way and world policemen would be necessary who would need certain places from which to exercise their function without bringing up questions of changes in sovereignty. He mentioned Dakar which in the hands of a country too weak to defend it or of a hostile country constituted an immediate threat to the whole of the Western Hemisphere." The implication was clear that Indochina, like Dakar, should become a strategic base which the United Nations, and the United States in particular, would use to keep the peace.

Fearing that "any such deprivation" would jeopardize "friendly collaboration with France in postwar Europe," the British Foreign Office urged continued French control over Indochina, on the condition that "she agrees to the establishment of international bases at strategic points (under U.S. control or otherwise)."

As with Dakar, in the first half of 1944 Roosevelt was in no mood to concede the restoration of Indochina to French rule. "No French help in [liberating] Indochina," Roosevelt told the State Department in February 1944. He wanted the country to become a United Nations trust territory. "Before we could bring the French officially into the Indo-China area," Churchill answered a Foreign Office proposal in May, "we should have to settle with President Roosevelt. . . . Do you really want to go and stir all this up at such a time as this?" he asked Eden.[20]

At the same time that Roosevelt had strong reasons for withholding full recognition from de Gaulle's National Committee, he also believed that de Gaulle would fail to survive the rigors of France's political process. Growing evidence in the first week after the invasion of de Gaulle's popularity in France did not convince him that he would emerge as the popular choice to head a new regime. "De Gaulle will crumble," he told Stimson on June 14, and his supporters "will be confounded by the process of events." Though Stimson asserted that this was contrary to everything he had heard, Roosevelt predicted "that other parties will spring up as the liberation goes on and that de Gaulle will become a very little figure." He also made this clear to de Gaulle, who visited the United States in July. As de Gaulle recorded it, the President "was anything but convinced of the rebirth and renewal of our regime. With bitterness he [Roosevelt] described what his feelings were when before the war he watched the spectacle of our political impotence unfold before his eyes. 'Even I, the President of the United States,' he told me, 'would sometimes find myself incapable of remembering the name of the current head of the French government. For the moment, you are there. . . . But will you still be there at the tragedy's end?' "

Roosevelt's decision to invite de Gaulle to America rested on considerations of military expediency. Fearful that his continued refusal to accord de Gaulle a fuller measure of recognition might deprive Anglo-American forces of help from the Resistance and jeopardize the use of French divisions in the ANVIL assault, Roosevelt agreed to have him visit the United States. When de Gaulle comes, Roosevelt told Ambassador Winant on June 13, "I will try . . . to direct his attention toward our war effort for the liberation of France." "We should make full use of any organization or influence that de Gaulle may possess and that will be of advantage to our military effort," he informed Marshall on the following day. But he still wished to be sure that "we do not by force of our arms impose him upon the French people as the Government of France."

He skillfully implemented this policy. Refusing to invite de Gaulle for fear it would accord him status as a head of government or state, Roosevelt insisted that de Gaulle ask to come. When de Gaulle resisted this suggestion, however, as a slight to French dignity, Roosevelt agreed to leave the terms of the invitation undefined. In Washington, where he held three lengthy conversations with de Gaulle during four days, Roosevelt avoided all references to immediate issues, talking instead about long-run political goals. He sketched his plans in "light touches . . . and so skillfully," de Gaulle related in his memoirs, "that it was difficult to contradict this artist, this seducer, in any categorical way." Nevertheless, Roosevelt made it clear to de Gaulle that France was not to share in the postwar responsibilities assigned to the Big Four, that she was to lose her overseas empire, and that some French territory would have to serve as United Nations bases under American military control. Though de Gaulle argued against the President's conception of France's postwar role, he appreciated that he had no impact on FDR. "To regain her place," he told Roosevelt at the close of their talks, "France must count only on herself. 'It is true,' " the President replied, " 'that to serve France no one can replace the French people.' "

The only concession Roosevelt was in fact ready to grant was recognition of de Gaulle's Committee as the "temporary *de facto* authority for civil administration in France." But this was to be on the condition that complete authority remain with Eisenhower to carry out effective military operations, and that the French people retain the opportunity to choose their own government. On this basis, Roosevelt announced on July 11, the United States government recognized the French Committee of National Liberation as the dominant political authority in France.

Though Roosevelt "felt that he had made considerable progress with de Gaulle" and "that we were not going to have much more difficulty with him so long as 'amour propre' was satisfied," others were less certain. At a dinner for de Gaulle hosted by Hull, the General and the Secretary "sat stiffly in informal silence, the American drooping a little, the Frenchman solemnly and forbiddingly erect, all the six feet six of him, balancing a chip like an epaulette on each martial shoulder." After dinner, de Gaulle sat in isolated dignity, unsmiling, and without interest in anyone's remarks. Urged by Bill Bullitt to break the ice, Congressman Solomon Bloom offered de Gaulle a trick cigar. When he put out his hand, the cigar disappeared up Bloom's sleeve. " 'Now you see it, General, now you don't. . . .' " Bloom teased. "Puzzled, suspecting that he was being laughed at, the General turned to his aide. 'What does the American statesman wish?' he inquired. The other did not seem to know, and no one dared to laugh. It was not a successful evening," Attorney General Biddle recalled. Though outwardly far more cordial and responsive in Roosevelt's presence, de Gaulle left Washington little more convinced of the President's good will toward him and his committee than before he arrived. Nevertheless, the visit temporarily eased problems with de Gaulle.[21]

In the summer of 1944 the Polish issue also took a momentary turn for the better. In late July, with the question of who would administer Polish territory pushed to the forefront by Soviet advances across the Curzon Line, Churchill asked Stalin to see Prime Minister Mikolajczyk if he requested a meeting. Stalin at once replied that, out of a desire not to interfere in Polish affairs, Soviet forces would leave the administration of captured Polish territory to the Polish Committee of National Liberation, a coalition of groups dominated by Polish Communists which set up a temporary capital in Lublin. Though dismissing the "so-called underground organisations" of the London Poles as "ephemeral," Stalin tried to soften his announcement by saying that he did not consider the Committee a Polish government, and that he would see Mikolajczyk. He suggested, however, that Mikolajczyk approach the National Committee, which was "favourably disposed towards him." Persuading Mikolajczyk to go to Moscow, Churchill cabled Stalin that he hoped for a fusion of all Poles in behalf of a strong and independent Poland. "It would be a great pity and even a disaster if the Western democracies find themselves recognizing one body of Poles and you recognizing another," he also told him. "It would lead to constant friction and might even hamper the great business which we have to do the wide world over." Roosevelt also sent Stalin an expression of hope that this whole matter could be worked out to the best advantage of our common effort.

Stalin now sent a reply which Churchill described as "the best ever received from U.J.," and led Roosevelt to think that a settlement of the Polish controversy was in the offing. Stalin declared the creation of the Committee a good start toward the unification of Poles friendly to Britain, the U.S.S.R., and the United States and the eclipse of those Polish elements incapable of harmony with democratic forces. He also acknowledged the importance of the Polish question to the Allied cause, and he declared himself ready to assist all Poles and "to mediate in attainment of an agreement between them." Cordial conversations with Mikolajczyk between August 3 and 9, moreover, added to the belief in a settlement of Polish-Soviet differences.[22]

These hopes were short-lived. On August 1, with Russian forces some six miles from Warsaw, with Moscow radio appealing for an insurrection to speed the moment of liberation, and with the London Poles eager to demonstrate their power, the Polish underground had launched an uprising in Warsaw. Though Stalin promised in his final talk with Mikolajczyk on August 9 to aid the insurgents, it was soon clear that the Russians would not help. When a German counterthrust halted the Soviet advance toward Warsaw, Churchill and the Poles asked Stalin to airlift supplies to the hard-pressed Polish fighters. But Stalin was content to let the Germans destroy his principal adversary for control of Poland. On August 16 he answered an appeal from Churchill for help to the Poles by denouncing the Warsaw action as "a reckless and fearful gamble," which had been launched without Soviet knowledge. Consequently, the Soviets would assume neither direct nor indirect responsibility for "the Warsaw adventure." In addition, the Russians rejected an American request to land planes on Soviet airfields after dropping supplies over Warsaw.

On August 20, at Churchill's suggestion, Roosevelt drafted a joint appeal to Stalin. "We are thinking of world opinion if the anti-Nazis in Warsaw are in effect abandoned. We believe that all three of us should do the utmost to save as many of the patriots there as possible. We hope that you will drop immediate supplies and munitions to the patriot Poles in Warsaw, or will you agree to help our planes in doing it very quickly?" But Stalin was adamant. In a reply of August 22, he attacked the underground as "a group of criminals" who staged the uprising in order to seize power, and were sacrificing the inhabitants of Warsaw to gain this end. He also denounced the uprising as harmful to Soviet efforts to take Warsaw, where he claimed the insurrection had caused the concentration of greater German forces.[23]

Churchill and Roosevelt now disagreed on a response. FDR did not see anything useful that could be done. Churchill, by contrast, wished to ask Stalin whether he would object to having American planes land on Soviet fields without indicating their mission along the way. This would allow the Soviets to dissociate themselves from supply drops to the Poles. Should Stalin fail to reply to this message, Churchill advised FDR, they should assume that the Russians would neither maltreat nor detain the planes, and send them anyway. While the President had no objection if Churchill sent such a message, he believed his association with it would hurt current efforts to gain Soviet commitments to later American use of Pacific bases against Japan. With American planes involved, however, Churchill saw little point in acting on his own. On September 4, therefore, as the Poles seemed to reach the limits of their resistance, Churchill appealed to FDR again: warning of the far-reaching effects on Polish-Soviet and Allied-Soviet relations from Stalin's refusal of airfields and a Polish collapse, Churchill asked that American planes supply Warsaw and simply land at Soviet fields without formal consent. Still believing that it would injure "our long-range general war prospects" in the Pacific, FDR again rejected Churchill's request: "I am informed by my Office of Military Intelligence that the fighting Poles have departed from Warsaw and that the Germans are now in full control. . . . There now appears to be nothing we can do to assist them."

Roosevelt either was misinformed or was simply putting off Churchill. The revolt lasted another month. And when the British made yet another appeal to Moscow to help the Warsaw uprising, the Soviets consented. In an apparently cynical effort to refute accusations that they wished to see Poland's non-Communists underground destroyed, they resumed their offensive against Warsaw, airlifted food and arms to the Poles, and agreed to have American planes land on Soviet fields after dropping supplies. The Soviet offensive and a 104-plane airlift on September 18, however, were insufficient to save the Poles. The Soviet attack petered out in the Warsaw suburbs, and American and Russian supplies lasted only until the end of the month, when Moscow refused to agree to another American air drop. On October 4, 1944, the rebellion ended with some 250,000 people, or one-fourth the population of Warsaw, counted as casualties. For the Russians, however, who had lost a million people in the 900-day siege of Leningrad, one-third of the city's population, it was difficult to see the Warsaw debacle as an unusually tragic event of war, especially when they believed that many of the 250,000 Poles wished to create an anti-Soviet regime.[24]

In the summer of 1944 the Polish issue had merged with other developments to challenge Roosevelt's hopes for extended cooperation with the U.S.S.R. In July, with their campaigns in Europe "moving so fast and so successfully," Roosevelt urged Stalin to agree to another Big Three meeting in the first half of September. But Stalin insisted that the fighting on his front made it impossible for him to withdraw from the personal direction of Soviet affairs for the foreseeable future. Advised by Hopkins that Stalin "obviously" meant to wait on a meeting until Germany had collapsed, Roosevelt sent him another appeal, emphasizing that they would soon need to make "further strategic decisions" and that it would help him domestically. Stalin, however, simply repeated his earlier reply. In August, at the same time that Harriman warned that Soviet actions toward Poland were based "on ruthless political considerations" and gave evidence of Soviet hope to "force . . . their decisions without question upon us and all countries," the Russians demonstrated little interest in advanced planning for help against Japan. Discussions on American use of Siberian airfields had become "bogged down in a mass of Soviet indifference and red tape." Though Roosevelt appealed directly to Stalin to expedite the joint preparation of plans, he received only an evasive reply, and Soviet authorities continued to ignore American inquiries about air bases in the Far East.

Harriman summed up these doubts about Soviet behavior in a message of September 10. Communicating through Hopkins, Harriman asked for a chance to report to the President as soon as possible. With the end of the war in sight, "our relations with the Soviets have taken a startling turn evident during the last two months. They have held up our requests with complete indifference to our interests and have shown an unwillingness even to discuss pressing problems." He pointed specifically to unanswered requests to continue air-shuttle operations between Britain and Russia by American bombers and American photo reconnaissance of German targets from Russian fields, to transport trucks through the Soviet Union to American air forces in China, to allow American officers to appraise the results of bombing attacks on the Ploesti oil fields in Roumania, or to act on the "major future planning" promised by Stalin.

He also complained of Soviet "indifference to world opinion regarding their unbending policy toward Poland," and of Soviet inclination to "become a world bully wherever their interests are involved." To alter this trend, the United States would have to make clear what it expected of Moscow "as the price of our good will." There was a need for "a firm but friendly *quid pro quo* attitude." The President was eager to discuss all these problems and the general state of Soviet-American relations, Hopkins replied, but it would have to wait until the meetings that were then in progress at the Dumbarton Oaks estate in Georgetown were completed. These conversations between Britain, Russia, and the United States about a postwar world security organization were at a "critical stage," and Roosevelt feared that Harriman's departure from Moscow at that time would encourage public speculation about Soviet-American differences over postwar plans.[25]

The talks at Dumbarton Oaks were raising further doubts in Washington about Soviet interest in long-term cooperation with her Allies. On August 28, a week after the Conference began, the Soviets had announced their desire to have all sixteen Soviet Republics included among the initial members of the organization. "My God," Roosevelt said to Stettinius on hearing the news, "explain to Gromyko [the Ambassador to the United States and chief delegate at the talks] that we could never accept this proposal." It "might ruin the chance of getting an international organization approved by the United States Senate and accepted publicly in the country." Roosevelt, Hull, and Stettinius considered the proposal so "explosive" that they agreed to keep it secret and persuaded Gromyko to make no further reference to "the X-matter" during the formal talks. At the same time, the President sent Stalin a cable, warning that "to raise this question at any stage before the final establishment and entry into its functions of the international organization would very definitely imperil the whole project, certainly as far as the United States is concerned and undoubtedly other important countries as well." Roosevelt, however, saw no objection to raising the matter after the organization had been formed.

Stalin's answer was not very reassuring. "I attach exceptional importance to the statement of the Soviet delegation on this question," he replied, and explained that recent changes in the Soviet Constitution granted autonomy in foreign affairs to all the Soviet Republics, some of which surpassed in "population" and "political importance" other initiators of the proposed world body. He hoped "to have an opportunity to explain to you the political importance of the question" raised by his delegation. Undoubtedly also a consideration, Stalin wished to balance the control Britain and the United States would have over British Commonwealth and Latin American votes in the world body.[26]

The Americans also found themselves in fundamental disagreement with the Russians over voting rights for six permanent members of an executive council. The Russians insisted that permanent states have an all-inclusive veto. The Americans and the British objected to giving council members the right to vote in disputes involving themselves, saying that this could destroy the effectiveness of the council and would risk rejection of the whole organization. But the Russians countered that the Anglo-American position would violate the principle of Great-Power unity. When it became apparent in early September that the Conference was at an impasse over voting procedure, Stettinius arranged for the President to see Gromyko. At a conference in the President's bedroom on the morning of September 8, Roosevelt cordially told Gromyko that the Soviet idea ran counter to American custom and would create great difficulties for him in the United States Senate. He described the problem to Stalin in a cable on the same day: parties to a dispute in the United States have never voted in their own case, and American public opinion would neither understand nor support a plan of international organization which violated this principle. Smaller nations would also object to the Soviet idea as "an attempt on the part of the great powers to set themselves up above the law. Finally, I would have real trouble with the Senate." He asked Stalin to accept the American position.

But Stalin would not give ground. In a reply on the 14th, he declared the principle of Four-Power unanimity imperative in dealing with future aggression, and said "that among these powers there is no room for mutual suspicions." He also implied that "certain absurd prejudices" against the U.S.S.R. made an absolute veto necessary for Soviet self-defense. He hoped the President would accept the Soviet viewpoint, and that they would find a harmonious solution to the problem. This impasse and "other recent developments" raised "most serious doubts" in Hull's mind about long-range Soviet policy. To Roosevelt, it was another expression of a larger pattern of difficulties which put relations with the Soviets and international cooperation generally in question. To preserve an appearance of harmony and avoid further immediate tensions over the issue, Roosevelt agreed to close the Dumbarton Oaks meeting with a detailed statement of progress and an explanation that there were still outstanding questions which would be settled at a later meeting. On this basis, the talks ended on September 28.[27]

On September 11, in the midst of these difficulties with the Soviets, Roosevelt had met Churchill in Quebec for their eighth wartime conference. The Prime Minister had been pressing for another round of talks since March. But Roosevelt, who wished to avoid a confrontation with Churchill over preserving Tehran plans and to include Stalin in their next meeting, resisted Churchill's urgings. On a vacation in April during which Leahy and the President drove past road markers in South Carolina recalling visits of Lafayette, Washington, and Monroe, Leahy had suggested the need for a future marker saying that in 1944 Roosevelt had also come this way to escape the British. In August, however, with Tehran plans being fully met and Stalin rejecting FDR's invitation to meet soon, Roosevelt had agreed to confer with Churchill in Quebec beginning on September 11.

Though Roosevelt expected the Conference to focus on military matters, it principally concerned itself with postwar problems. An unbroken run of military successes in the seven weeks before the Conference assembled had largely driven German forces out of France and Belgium to the Siegfried Line or West Wall along the German border and had persuaded Allied planners that Germany would collapse before the end of the year and that operational strategy in Europe could be left to the field commanders. "Everything we had touched had turned to gold," Churchill declared at the opening session in Quebec. He predicted that "future historians would give a great account of the period since Teheran." With American military chiefs unenthusiastic about discussing Pacific strategy, which they wished to set without consulting the British, the Conference became the first in a series during the next eleven months devoted chiefly to postwar questions.[28]

Churchill was particularly eager to discuss ways of checking postwar Soviet power in Europe. By September 1944, the "dangerous spread of Russian influence" in the Balkans, where they might "never get out," greatly worried him. At the beginning of September he saw evidence of this in armistice negotiations that brought Roumania and Bulgaria under Soviet control. He also believed that the Russians would encourage civil wars in Yugoslavia and Greece in order to set up puppet Communist regimes.

To head off "chaos," "street-fighting," and the creation of "a tyrannical Communist government" in Greece, Churchill asked that American planes transport British paratroops to Athens when the Germans left. Further, he urged plans to follow the collapse of German resistance in Italy with a move across the Adriatic onto the Istrian peninsula, where Anglo-American forces could occupy Trieste and Fiume and position themselves to beat the Russians into Vienna. He also wanted the President to join him in telling Stalin of "certain anxieties which are in our minds about political developments in Europe. With the defeat of the enemy's armies," his proposed message read, "political problems will arise in all parts of Europe. It is essential that we should work to-

gether to solve these. We mention in particular the situation in Yugoslavia and Greece, in both of which countries there has been, and in
the former of which there still is, the danger of civil war. There is also
the position in Poland, which causes us much anxiety. . . . It would be
gravely embarrassing to the smooth-working of our affairs if events should
so fall out that we were left recognizing Monsieur Mikolajczyk . . .
while you supported some other authority in Poland." [29]

Roosevelt was not indifferent to Churchill's fears. "Our main concern," he told Archduke Otto of Austria during the Conference, "is now
how to keep the Communist[s] out of Hungary and Austria." He emphasized his desire for a Hungarian surrender "only to the Americans and
British. If this were done, Hungary could be saved from communism.
. . . It is evident," the Archduke stated in a record of their conversation, "that the relationship between R. and the Russians is strained.
. . . There was a general interest in keeping the Russians away as far
as possible. R. seems to have been particularly disgusted by Russia's
handling of the Bulgarian question. . . . From all of R.'s remarks it is
quite evident that he is afraid of the Communists and wants to do everything to contain Russia's power—naturally *short of war.*"

Though Roosevelt's remarks undoubtedly were meant in part to satisfy the Archduke, who he thought might be helpful in arranging Hungary's surrender, his answers to Churchill's proposals demonstrate his
genuine concern to limit Soviet control in Europe. Before they met in
Quebec, he approved Churchill's plan for putting British forces in
Greece. He was also "completely openminded" about the possibility of
using their forces in Italy to strike at Istria, Trieste, and ultimately
Vienna. At the Conference, Roosevelt and the Joint Chiefs endorsed
British plans for amphibious operations against the Istrian peninsula,
and agreed to instruct General Henry Wilson, the Allied Commander in
the Mediterranean, to follow a sudden German collapse with the im-
mediate seizure of Austria by four divisions and a small tactical air force.
Churchill and the British Chiefs left no doubt that they viewed such
action as having both a military and political value, "in view of the
Russian advances in the Balkans." Further, at Hyde Park on September
18, in additional talks between FDR and Churchill after Quebec, the
President "provisionally" agreed to the Prime Minister's message to
Stalin "on the political dangers of divergencies between Russia and the
Western Allies in respect of Poland, Greece and Yugoslavia." [30]

Roosevelt also believed that checking excessive Soviet power in
Europe and assuring Anglo-American security around the world required a strong Britain. Specifically, he wished to aid what the British
described as the "recovery of U.K. civilian economy and the progressive
restoration of U.K. export trade." The British believed that this required a change in American Lend-Lease policy. Since the start of the

program in 1941, American aid had aimed to supply material that Britain's full-scale war production could not provide. In the period between German and Japanese defeat, however, the British wished the United States to continue Lend-Lease help while Britain converted some of its industrial output to civilian production for use at home and export abroad. Such a course would afford Britain the opportunity both to fight Japan and to begin restoring her badly depleted home economy. This matter, Churchill told FDR at the start of the Quebec talks, was "of extreme and vital importance . . . for reasons which are only too painfully apparent."

Roosevelt's acceptance of this proposal evoked strong feelings in Churchill. On the third day of the Conference, when the President delayed initialing the memorandum on Lend-Lease by telling stories, Churchill burst out: "What do you want me to do? Get on my hind legs and beg like Fala*?" "Churchill was quite emotional about this agreement," Morgenthau recorded, "and at one time he had tears in his eyes. When the thing was finally signed, he told the President how grateful he was, thanked him most effusively, and said that this was something they were doing for both countries." Roosevelt agreed. In the week after the Conference, he told one adviser of his belief in "the necessity for maintaining the British Empire strong," and "went very far" in expressing his desire for postwar collaboration.[31]

The Conference also backed full cooperation in the development of atomic energy for military and commercial purposes between the two nations after the war. As important, it was specifically agreed that the Russians were not to share in the control and use of atomic power. Embodied in an aide-mémoire of a conversation between Roosevelt and Churchill at Hyde Park on September 19, these agreements evolved out of developments dating from the end of 1943. In September of that year, Niels Bohr, a prominent nuclear physicist, had escaped from Nazi-occupied Denmark to England, where he quickly became an advocate of postwar international control of atomic energy. After coming to the United States at the beginning of 1944 as a consultant on atomic power, he renewed his acquaintance with Supreme Court Justice Felix Frankfurter, before whom he put the case for international control. In late February 1944, Frankfurter related Bohr's argument to the President: It might be disastrous, Frankfurter told FDR, if Russia should learn on her own about "X." Would it not be better for Britain and the United States to explore the possibility of an international agreement with Russia to meet the problems raised by "X"? Bohr, Frankfurter also reported, believed the Soviets would have little difficulty gaining the information to build their own bomb. The issue, as the historian Martin Sherwin has argued, involved the whole question of postwar cooperation

* FDR's pet Scotch terrier.

with the U.S.S.R. A decision to exclude the Russians from the military and diplomatic advantages of the bomb, "with the implied coercion that was its corollary," was bound to affect prospects for postwar harmony.

Roosevelt's response to Frankfurter was ambiguous. He neither accepted nor rejected Bohr's proposal. He gave it informal encouragement by having Frankfurter tell Bohr to advise "our friends in London that the President was most eager to explore the proper safeguards in relation to X." Yet at the same time, he made no effort to discuss the issue with Stimson, his science advisers, or Churchill. Yet again, in the summer of 1944, after Churchill had rebuffed Bohr's proposals in a face-to-face talk, Roosevelt agreed to grant him an interview. More importantly, in his meeting with Bohr on August 26, FDR "agreed that contact with the Soviet Union had to be tried along the lines he [Bohr] suggested," and he promised to take up the matter with Churchill when he saw him in Quebec.

In encouraging Bohr to think that he shared his views, Roosevelt was playing a double game. He had known for almost a year that the Russians were aware of American work on a bomb and were receiving secret information on its development from agents in the United States. Moreover, the agreements he reached with Churchill in Quebec were entirely contrary to what he had told Bohr: "Enquiries should be made regarding the activities of Professor Bohr and steps should be taken to ensure that he is responsible for no leakage of information, particularly to the Russians," a third proviso of the Roosevelt-Churchill agreement states. Roosevelt had every intention of fulfilling his commitment to Churchill. "The President was very much in favor of complete interchange with the British on this subject [atomic energy] after the war in all phases," Vannevar Bush recorded after a conversation with FDR on September 22, "and apparently on a basis where it would be used jointly or not at all." "The President evidently thought," Bush shortly wrote a co-worker on the atomic project, "he could join with Churchill in bringing about a US-UK postwar agreement on this subject by which it would be held closely and presumably to control the peace of the world."

Why, then, had Roosevelt given a sympathetic hearing to Bohr's views? Because while he joined Churchill in seeking to shore up British power and guard against Soviet domination of the Balkans and possibly all Europe, he at the same time wished to continue promoting Soviet-Western accord. Aware through Bohr himself that the Soviets had invited him to live and work in Russia, Roosevelt undoubtedly assumed that his conversation with Bohr would become known to them. The talk, therefore, was his way of telling Moscow that he was ready to entertain a Soviet role in ultimate control of atomic power, or that postwar cooperation on other matters could be a prelude to shared control of the bomb. Though there is no direct evidence that this motivated his response to Bohr, it is clear from his reluctance to force matters with Stalin over Poland and his postwar plans for Germany in September 1944 that he remained genuinely eager for postwar cooperation with the U.S.S.R.[32]

Postwar plans for Germany formed the most controversial subject of discussion at Quebec. After Tehran, the European Advisory Commission, the State Department, and the Civil Affairs Section of Eisenhower's headquarters gave extensive attention to the occupation and postwar treatment of Germany. In the second half of August 1944, after the results of these efforts had come to Morgenthau's attention, a sharp controversy erupted in Washington. Strongly put off by the preference of these agencies for "a soft policy" which would allow the Germans to pay reparations and "wage a third war" in ten years, Morgenthau told Roosevelt that nobody "has been studying how to treat Germany roughly along the lines you wanted." The President left no doubt in Morgenthau's mind that he shared his view: "We have got to be tough with Germany," FDR said, "and I mean the German people not just the Nazis. We either have to castrate the German people or you have got to treat them in such manner so they can't just go on reproducing people who want to continue the way they have in the past."

With this encouragement from the President, Morgenthau prepared his own "analysis of the German problem." Its central tenet was the elimination of all industry from Germany and the conversion of her people "to an agricultural population of small land-owners." Coupled with the idea of dividing Germany into several small states, Morgenthau's plan promised to make her incapable of waging future wars. These ideas greatly appealed to FDR. Confronted by a debate between Morgenthau and Stimson over a "Handbook of Military Government" for Germany which advocated the gradual rehabilitation of peacetime industry and a highly centralized administrative system, Roosevelt sided with Morgenthau. "This so-called 'Handbook' is pretty bad," FDR told Stimson on August 26.

It gives me the impression that Germany is to be restored just as much as the Netherlands or Belgium, and the people of Germany brought back as quickly as possible to their pre-war estate.

It is of the utmost importance that every person in Germany should realize that this time Germany is a defeated nation. I do not want them to starve to death, but, as an example, if they need food to keep body and soul together beyond what they have, they should be fed three times a day with soup from Army soup kitchens. . . . The fact that they are a defeated nation, collectively and individually, must be so impressed upon them that they will hesitate to start any new war. . . .

Too many people here and in England hold to the view that the German people as a whole are not responsible for what has taken place—that only a few Nazi leaders are responsible. That unfortunately is not based on fact. The German people as a whole must have it driven home to them that the whole nation has been engaged in a lawless conspiracy against the decencies of modern civilization.

Morgenthau's tough approach to the Germans, and particularly his idea of dismantling their industrial war-making power, had two other appeals for FDR. According to Morgenthau's calculations, it would guarantee English prosperity for twenty years after the war by eliminating German competition for coal and steel markets around the world, and it would encourage Soviet trust of the West by dispelling fears that Britain and the United States might rebuild German strength as a bulwark against the U.S.S.R. Stimson, however, raised questions about Morgenthau's plan which Roosevelt could not ignore. In written and oral arguments to the President during the first week of September, Stimson warned that the destruction of Germany's industrial capacity, and particularly of the Ruhr and the Saar, would leave thirty million Germans to starve and would deprive Europe of what had been one of its most important sources of raw materials during the previous eighty years. Despite Morgenthau's prediction that a system of international control over the Ruhr and the Saar would ultimately mean their return to Germany, Stimson urged international trusteeships for these regions which would preserve their productive capacities and speed European recovery from the war.

Characteristically, Roosevelt refused to make a clear choice between these positions. During a White House discussion with Morgenthau, Stimson, Hull, and Hopkins on September 6, the President supported deindustrialization, but proposed that it be done gradually over six months or a year. Though Morgenthau urged immediate action when they got into Germany, Roosevelt stuck to his idea of doing it over a period of time. Though he also expressed concern about the compatibility of Morgenthau's Plan with Russian desires for reparations, he accepted Morgenthau's argument that Europe did not need a strong industrial Germany, and stated his belief "in an agricultural Germany." Still, as Roosevelt prepared to leave for Quebec, he showed no interest in adopting a clear-cut policy which he could carry with him to the talks.[33]

At the Conference, however, Roosevelt pressed the case for Morgenthau's policy. The catalyst for this may have been events at Quebec, which intensified his concern to strengthen the British economy and disarm Russian suspicions toward the West. From the start of the Conference, Churchill urged the need to rebuild Britain's economic might. At the same time, Roosevelt received Harriman's telegram from Moscow on growing Soviet resistance to military and political cooperation with her Allies. According to a conversation he had with Morgenthau in Quebec, FDR believed that suspicion of American and British attitudes toward Germany motivated Soviet behavior. "Russia feared we and the British were going to try to make a soft peace with Germany and build her up as a possible future counter-weight against Russia," Morgenthau told Roosevelt. The President replied, "You are right, and I want you to read a telegram I just received from Harriman."

On September 12, after spending a day with Churchill and receiving Harriman's message, Roosevelt had called Morgenthau to Quebec to discuss British finances and postwar plans for Germany. Conferring with Morgenthau at length after his arrival on the afternoon of the 13th, he described Churchill as "very glum." The President had "excited" him, however, with the suggestion that Britain have the steel business of Europe for twenty or thirty years. Roosevelt then told Morgenthau that he had brought him to Quebec to talk to Lord Cherwell, a professor of physics and Churchill's close friend, who was at the Conference to advise on atomic energy and Lend-Lease. Roosevelt made it clear, however, that he wanted Morgenthau to discuss Germany with him. He also reported that he had asked Eden to attend the Conference, and indicated that he wanted Eden there because he expected him to join Morgenthau in advocating a tough postwar policy. Eden, Morgenthau had told the President after visiting London in August, believed "that a soft policy [toward Germany] would only rouse Russian suspicions and make postwar cooperation among the three powers more difficult." [34]

At dinner that night, the conversation between Churchill, Roosevelt, and their advisers revolved around Germany. At FDR's request, Morgenthau explained his plan for preventing another war and aiding British exports by shutting down German industry. The proposal appalled Churchill, who unleashed "the full flood of his rhetoric, sarcasm and violence," saying that he looked on Morgenthau's plan "as he would on chaining himself to a dead German." Churchill also said that simply eliminating the German arms industry would prevent another war, and he voiced skepticism about the benefits to Britain from the removal of German economic competition. Though saying little in direct reply to Churchill, Roosevelt supported Morgenthau by reminding the Prime Minister that other German industries could be converted overnight to war production. With "an absolute cleavage" of viewpoint between Churchill and the Americans after three hours of discussion, Roosevelt suggested that Cherwell and Morgenthau go into the subject on their own.

During the next two days, however, Churchill accepted Morgenthau's plan. On the morning of the 14th, at a meeting between Churchill, Roosevelt, Cherwell, and Morgenthau, the Prime Minister "seemed to accept the program designed to weaken [the] German economy," saying that he was converted to the idea of exploring the re-creation of an agricultural state such as had existed in the last quarter of the nineteenth century. On the following day he assented to a memorandum embodying Morgenthau's chief goal: the industries of the Ruhr and the Saar were to be "put out of action and closed down," with some international body assuring that "they were not started up again by some subterfuge. This programme for eliminating the war-making industries in the Ruhr and in the Saar," the document concluded, "is looking forward to converting Germany into a country primarily agricultural and pastoral in its character." [35]

Roosevelt apparently gained Churchill's backing by agreeing to his wishes on Lend-Lease. At first, he "violently opposed" the American plan for Germany, Churchill recalled in his memoirs. "But the President, with Mr. Morgenthau—from whom we had much to ask—were so insistent that in the end we agreed to consider it." Churchill also hinted that this was a quid pro quo agreement when he answered opposition from Eden: "After all, the future of my people is at stake, and when I have to choose between my people and the German people, I am going to choose my people." Though Morgenthau later objected to the idea that Churchill had accepted his plan in return for Lend-Lease commitments, arguing that Roosevelt was not to discuss Lend-Lease until the day after they had reached agreement on Germany, his memory was at fault. According to both Cherwell's and Morgenthau's records, the agreements on Germany and Lend-Lease ran parallel courses, with initial settlements on both subjects made on the morning of the 14th and final memoranda initialed at the same meeting on the 15th. [36]

Churchill's acceptance of the Morgenthau Plan may also have influenced Roosevelt's decision to occupy southwest Germany. From the moment the occupation issue arose, Roosevelt had insisted on having American forces in the northwest, where they would not become tied down in European squabbles which could agitate isolationist opinion in the United States. In February 1944, when the Combined Chiefs had reached an impasse on the subject, FDR told Churchill that he would not take responsibility for a southwestern zone because he was "absolutely unwilling to police France and possibly Italy and the Balkans as well." Churchill answered that Britain should have the northwest zone, since German naval disarmament was "a matter of peculiar interest to us," as was a continuing close liaison between the Royal Air Force and the Norwegian and Netherlands air forces. Besides, he did not think the United States would have to police France, where he expected a stable government to take hold.

But Roosevelt was not convinced. He thought Britain's special naval problem could be easily handled even if American forces were in northwest Germany, and he refused to believe that the occupation of southwest Germany would leave him free to take American forces out of

Europe at an early date. His reasons for opposing British plans, he had told Churchill on the eve of OVERLORD, were "political." " 'Do please don't' ask me to keep any American forces in France," he explained. "I just cannot do it! I would have to bring them all back home. As I suggested before, I denounce and protest the paternity of Belgium, France and Italy. You really ought to bring up and discipline your own children. In view of the fact that they may be your bulwark in future days, you should at least pay for their schooling now!" At the beginning of September, the President still had not changed his mind.

In Quebec, however, Roosevelt suddenly shifted ground. On the afternoon of September 15 he dropped his stubborn resistance to a southwestern zone of occupation for the United States and agreed that British forces should establish themselves in the northwest. His change of heart had nothing to do with long-standing complaints that American occupation of a northwest zone would compel a major shift of British and American forces at the close of the fighting. On the 14th, for example, when Leahy had told the President that they could not make such a "crossover," FDR replied, "Nonsense. It could be done." American military planners agreed. Nor had he changed his mind about France. The day before he left for Quebec he told Robert Murphy that "some time would elapse before a stable French central government is established." At the Conference, moreover, he discussed the possibility of a civil war in France, and arranged that lines of communication to the American zone would not pass through France, but through Bremerhaven, Bremen, Amsterdam, and Rotterdam, with guaranteed passage through the British zone.

At least two other considerations seem to have helped change Roosevelt's mind. One was Churchill's argument that British occupation of northwest Germany would strengthen England's position in Europe. Roosevelt told Leahy that: "After tedious argument with Prime Minister Churchill, he accepted the British contention that Northwest Germany would be of more value to the future of our friend and Ally England than to the United States of America." What FDR left unsaid, however, was his conviction that America's presence in a southwest zone bordering Austria, Czechoslovakia, and France would considerably increase the possibility of a long-term role for American ground forces in Europe. Since there is no detailed record of the conversation with Churchill that Roosevelt mentioned to Leahy, it is impossible to know the full nature of the appeal Churchill made to the President. But remarks he made to FDR, the First Lady, and Leahy at Hyde Park on September 19 offer one hint. The "only hope for a durable peace," Churchill said, "was an agreement between Great Britain and the United States to prevent international war by the use of their combined forces if necessary." He was willing "to take Russia into the agreement," he added, "if the Russians wished to join." Another compelling reason FDR apparently saw for occupying southwest Germany was Churchill's acceptance of the Morgenthau Plan. Occupation of the northwest zone would now include responsibility for deindustrializing the Ruhr and the Saar. This, Roosevelt indicated to Morgenthau, was a job he wished the British to assume.[37]

Though the agreement on occupation zones became a fixture of Anglo-American policy, the commitments on the Morgenthau Plan and Lend-Lease came unstuck. In the long run, renewed British opposition and Russian insistence on reparations from current production made Morgenthau's plan for Germany untenable. But even before these considerations made themselves felt, newspaper and Republican attacks on the Morgenthau Plan moved FDR to back away from the understanding reached at Quebec. Allegations that the Morgenthau Plan was stiffening German resistance on the Western front made Roosevelt distinctly uncomfortable, not only because he thought they might be true, but also because they might be used against him in the 1944 presidential campaign. On September 29, he released a letter to the press indicating that postwar economic planning for Germany remained unsettled, and he told Hull on the same day that "no one wants to make Germany a wholly agricultural nation again. . . . No one wants 'complete eradication of German industrial production capacity in the Ruhr and the Saar.' "

He now also gave exclusive responsibility to the State Department to "study and report upon the problem" of Germany. Four days later he told Stimson that Morgenthau had "pulled a boner," that he had "no intention of turning Germany into an agrarian state and that all he wanted was to save a portion of the proceeds of the Ruhr for use by Great Britain which was 'broke.' " When Stimson replied that the Quebec understanding promised to convert Germany into an agricultural society, and he quoted the sentences from the agreement demonstrating this, the President "said he had no idea how he could have initialed this."

In October, when bad weather, supply problems, and firmer German resistance halted the Allied advance in Western Europe and suggested that Germany would not collapse as quickly as Allied planners had believed, Roosevelt refused to make any final decisions on occupation policy. "I dislike making detailed plans for a country which we do not yet occupy," he told Hull on October 20. Occupation policy partly depends "on what we and the Allies find when we get into Germany—and we are not there yet." [38]

On Lend-Lease as well Roosevelt saw reasons to shift ground. By mid-November, he wished to act as if he had "never heard" of the Quebec agreement. Morgenthau attributed this to FDR's annoyance, during the presidential campaign, with speeches by Churchill supporting the royal families of southern Europe and with British reluctance to follow through on the Morgenthau Plan. Further, Roosevelt worried that British indiscretions about the Lend-Lease agreement might leave Americans feeling that England had gained an edge on the United States "in export trade." The fact that the war against Germany was not going to end as soon as expected also disrupted Lend-Lease plans. The agreement reached at the end of November, therefore, promised Britain only $5.5 billion in aid for the period between German and Japanese defeat, or some 20 per cent less than the British had asked.[39]

They also altered the Quebec agreement by not sending Stalin their cautionary message on "the political dangers of divergencies" in Europe. Though there is no record of why they changed their minds, Churchill's decision at the end of the month to seek a personal meeting with Stalin in Moscow shortly made a message superfluous. Probably more important, Churchill now decided to accentuate the positive. Though Soviet ambitions in southeastern and central Europe concerned him more than ever, he believed that the success of OVERLORD made this the proper time to work out an accommodation with the USSR. In a message to Stalin on September 27, he had thanked him for praising Anglo-American operations in France, assured him of his and the President's "intense conviction that on the agreement of our three nations . . . stand the hopes of the world," emphasized the need for Soviet intervention against Japan following German defeat, and asked if he might come to Moscow in October. Informing FDR of his plan, he described his objectives as, first, to clinch Soviet involvement against Japan, second, to seek a settlement on Poland, and third, to discuss Yugoslavia and Greece. He promised to keep him fully informed, welcomed Harriman's assistance, and suggested that the President send Stettinius or Marshall to represent him.

Roosevelt had mixed feelings about Churchill's plan to see Stalin. On the one hand, he was unenthusiastic about a meeting without him in which Churchill might make unacceptable commitments. On the other hand, he was sympathetic to anything that might restore the cooperative spirit of Tehran. His reply to Churchill reflected this ambivalence: he refused to underscore his commitment to the talks by sending Stettinius or Marshall, but he promised that Harriman would give any assistance Churchill wished. Eager for more than this, Churchill followed Stalin's acceptance of his proposal with a request to FDR for a message to Stalin approving the mission. He also asked for guidance on Far East war plans and the Dumbarton Oaks voting question, which "will certainly come up." On Poland, however, which would form "the bulk of our business," he asked no special instruction, since "you and I think so much alike."

Roosevelt's initial impulse was to respond with general expressions of support for the success of their meeting. An agreement on "Dumbarton" was "not a hope but a 'must' for all three of us," he answered Churchill's request for guidance. "Failure now is unthinkable." When Hopkins saw these messages, however, he persuaded Roosevelt to adopt a more cautious line which would preserve his freedom of action or shield him from commitments that might prove embarrassing to his presidential campaign. The cables FDR sent Churchill and Stalin reflected a concern not to duplicate his experience with the Morgenthau Plan. He wished Harriman to participate in the talks as his observer, he told Churchill. But the Ambassador would not be able to commit the President in advance on any issue. That would have to wait until after the presidential election when the three heads of government could meet. In the meantime, he was particularly eager that the "voting question," which was "so directly related to public opinion in the United States and . . . all the United Nations," be left until the three of them could talk. "There is in this global war literally no question, either military or political, in which the United States is not interested," he also cabled Stalin. ". . . It is my firm conviction that the solution to still unsolved questions can be found only by the three of us together." He considered the talks with Churchill, therefore, as preliminary to a Big Three conference, which he could attend any time after the election.[40]

Despite these injunctions against bilateral agreements, Roosevelt in fact was ready to support arrangements in Moscow that promoted immediate Allied cooperation and long-term possibilities for peace. This was particularly true for the Balkans. At his first discussion with Stalin on October 9, Churchill arranged a temporary spheres-of-influence agreement which gave Russia 90 per cent predominance in Roumania, 75 per cent of the say in Bulgaria, equal influence with Britain in Yugoslavia and Hungary, and a limited voice in Greece, where Britain and America were to have 90 per cent of the foreign control. After setting these percentages down on a half-sheet of paper, Churchill pushed it across the table to Stalin, who made a large tick with a blue pencil and passed it back to Churchill. "Might it not be thought rather cynical if it seemed we had disposed of these issues, so fateful to millions of people, in such an offhand manner?" Churchill asked. "Let us burn the paper." "No, you keep it," Stalin replied.

Roosevelt assented to this agreement during the next two days. Messages from Harriman and Churchill on October 10 clearly indicated that the British and Russian leaders had reached a spheres-of-influence agreement for the Balkans. "I am most pleased to know," Roosevelt answered Churchill on the 11th, "that you are reaching a meeting of your two minds as to international policies in which, because of our present and future common efforts to prevent international wars, we are all interested." "My active interest at the present time in the Balkan area," he cabled Harriman on the same day, "is that such steps as are practicable should be taken to insure against the Balkans getting us into a future international war." Though subsequent messages from Churchill and Harriman confirmed the division of the Balkans into spheres of control, Roosevelt offered no protest.[41]

On other discussions as well, Roosevelt found no reason to complain. Frank exchanges about their respective campaigns against Hitler's armies assured both sides that neither would ease the pressure on their fronts. Moreover, detailed descriptions of how the Soviets planned to fight Japan some three months after German defeat won enthusiastic support from Churchill and FDR. "You have already been informed about the obvious resolve of the Soviet government to attack Japan on the overthrow of Hitler, of their detailed study of the problem and of their readiness to begin inter-Allied preparations on a large scale," Churchill cabled Roosevelt on October 18. "When we are vexed with other matters, we must remember the supreme value of this in shortening the whole struggle." The likelihood that Soviet forces would attack the Japanese in Manchuria and free the United States from sending large American ground forces into China greatly pleased Roosevelt and his Chiefs, who promptly implemented plans to supply Soviet Far Eastern forces.[42]

Churchill's action on Poland also satisfied FDR. A communiqué saying that progress had been made and differences narrowed, Churchill advised him on the 18th, would cover over continuing differences between Moscow and the London Poles on boundaries and the make-up of the Polish government. He had not committed the President in any way on Poland, Churchill also said, and he promised that if hopes for a settlement were realized in the next fortnight, he would leave it to him to say whether the agreement should be "published or delayed." "When and if a solution is arrived at," FDR replied on October 22nd, "I should like to be consulted as to the advisibility from this point of view of delaying its publication for about two weeks. You will understand." [43]

The principal result of these talks was to strengthen Churchill's and FDR's feeling that, by contrast with others in the Soviet government, they could advance the cause of understanding with Stalin. "I felt acutely the need to see Stalin," Churchill later said of his trip to Moscow, "with whom I always considered one could talk as one human being to another." This meeting "has shown," he wrote Stalin after the conference, "that there are no matters that cannot be adjusted between us when we meet together in frank and intimate discussion." "We talked with an ease, freedom, and cordiality never before attained between our two countries," Churchill recorded in his war memoirs. "But I became ever more convinced that he was by no means alone. As I said to my colleagues at home, 'Behind the horseman sits black care.' "

Likewise, where Roosevelt could say that he "liked Stalin personally," he was "bitterly critical" of the men around him. Stalin contributed to the idea that he was more cooperative than other Soviet leaders: "The talks made it plain," he wrote FDR after Churchill departed, "that we can without undue difficulty coordinate our policies on all important issues and that even if we cannot ensure immediate solution of this or that problem, such as the Polish question, we have, nevertheless, more favourable prospects in this respect as well." It is unfair to accuse Roosevelt and Churchill of naïveté in seeing Stalin as more reasonable and cooperative than his colleagues in the Politburo, Adam Ulam, the expert on Soviet Russia, contends. No one "outside Russia realized the full extent of Stalin's omnipotence." [44]

All through 1944 Roosevelt had tried to assure that no foreign policy issue would undercut his reelection campaign. As election day approached, it was clear that attacks on the administration for selling out Poland, agreeing to spheres of influence in Europe, and committing itself to an excessively harsh postwar policy for Germany would not turn many voters against FDR. Moreover, MacArthur's successful return to the Philippines on October 20 and a decisive victory over the Japanese Navy during the following week in the battle of Leyte Gulf allowed the President to refute charges that he had starved MacArthur's forces for political reasons. "I wonder" whatever became of this suggestion, he twitted Governor Thomas E. Dewey of New York, the Republican nominee, in a speech on October 27.

Two issues had dogged Roosevelt during the campaign. First, was he healthy enough to carry the burdens of another term? Initial impressions suggested not. Having lost approximately twenty pounds since the start of the year, he appeared haggard and gaunt. In September, Robert Sherwood, who had not seen the President in eight months, "was shocked" by "the almost ravaged appearance of his face." A photograph snapped in July and used widely during the campaign showed an emaciated face with a slack, open mouth, and encouraged rumors that the President was a dying man. A nationwide radio speech from the deck of a destroyer at Bremerton, Washington, in August had added to this fear. An attack of angina pectoris, uncomfortable leg braces he had not worn in more than a year, and a strong wind coupled with a slanted deck, which unsettled his balance, made the President's delivery halting and ineffective. Many thought it the worst performance of his public career.

A series of vigorous outings in September and October, however, provided an effective answer to the warnings about his health. A speech at a Teamsters' dinner in Washington, D.C., on September 23 particularly contributed to the conviction that Roosevelt could serve another term. Considered by some the "finest speech he ever made," or at least the "greatest campaign speech of his career," the address refuted the idea that he was a feeble old man, put some needed life into the Democratic campaign, and threw Dewey onto the defensive. "These Republican leaders have not been content with attacks on me, or my wife, or on my sons," he said in the most memorable passages of that talk. "No, not content with that, they now include my little dog, Fala. Well, of course, I don't resent attacks, and my family doesn't resent attacks, but Fala *does* resent them." Recounting with mock seriousness the "concocted story" of "Republican fiction writers in Congress" that he had sent a destroyer back to the Aleutian Islands at a cost of millions of dollars to find Fala, Roosevelt objected to these "libelous statements about my dog." Dewey, who had already acquired a reputation as humorless and overbearing, the bridegroom on the wedding cake, the only man who could strut sitting down, added to this portrait when he said that the President's "snide" speech made him angry. "Even the stoniest of Republican faces around U.S. radios," *Time* magazine recorded, "cracked into a smile" over the Fala story.[45]

A second problem for Roosevelt in the campaign was to assure the backing of independent voters, especially the Willkie internationalists or liberal Republicans. FDR believed that some 20 per cent of the electorate fell into this category, and that unlike the other 80 per cent of the voters, who were already committed in roughly equal proportions to the two parties, the independents would decide the election. Willkie's decisive defeat in the Wisconsin primary in April, where he had won no delegates and finished last in every district despite being the only candidate to campaign in the state, knocked him out of the contest and left his backers up for grabs.

To win their support, Roosevelt believed it necessary to demonstrate his commitment to a strong world body free of traditional Big Power politics. His desire not to offend old-guard isolationists and his attraction to the Big Four, or Four Policemen, idea, however, made this difficult. The administration's public disclosure in the spring of its draft plan for an international organization had upset liberal internationalists. Because it lacked an international police force and left it to the Big Four to assure world peace, the plan came under liberal attack as a traditional Great Power settlement which would deny smaller nations a meaningful voice in international affairs and eventually bring on another war. The administration's plan, the *Nation* complained, "bears a striking similarity in principle to the 'new order' which the Axis has been striving to impose in Europe and Asia." In July the President added to his difficulties with the liberal internationalists when he agreed to drop Henry Wallace as a running mate. Convinced that the Vice President's outspoken liberalism "would cost the ticket a million votes" and erode bipartisan support for an international organization, FDR agreed to have Senator Harry Truman of Missouri replace Wallace as the vice-presidential nominee. A consistent supporter of the President and reliable party man who had made a national reputation through the investigation of wartime corruption and waste in military production, Truman seemed unlikely to offend either liberals or conservatives.[46]

As a counterweight to these actions, Roosevelt tried to enlist Willkie's support in his campaign. At the end of June, FDR had asked Sam Rosenman to talk to Willkie about joining in a post-election effort to set up a liberal party composed of both Democrats and Republicans. Though he assured Willkie that the plan would in no way require joint action in the current election, or a public commitment to his reelection, Roosevelt shortly invited him to confer "about the future," and word of the President's letter soon leaked to the press. To guard his independence, Willkie refused to see FDR or Dewey, and in mid-September he published an article urging all independents to support the man who espoused the most advanced view on international organization. On October 8, however, before he could decide who this was, Willkie died.

Despite his inability to draw Willkie into his camp, Roosevelt managed nevertheless to blunt Dewey's appeal to liberal internationalists. In mid-August, on the eve of the Dumbarton Oaks talks, Dewey had won widespread attention and praise for an attack on rumored plans "to subject the nations of the world, great and small, permanently to the coercive power of the four nations holding this conference." In response, Hull invited Dewey to confer with him about the future world organization "in a nonpartisan spirit." Dewey agreed to send John Foster Dulles, a prominent international lawyer and close adviser. After two days of talks in late August, Hull, with FDR's approval, persuaded the two Republicans to sign a statement removing the subject of international organization from the campaign. Though the statement allowed for "full public nonpartisan discussion of the means of attaining a lasting peace," it assured against extended debate over the nature of the new world body during the campaign and shielded the administration from continuing attacks on its affinity for Big Power control after the war.

When this agreement temporarily fell apart in October, Roosevelt outsmarted Dewey in their bid for the liberal internationalist vote. At the end of September, Senator Joseph H. Ball of Minnesota, a leading Republican proponent of a strong international organization and an early Dewey supporter, had announced that Dewey's campaign statements on world affairs had temporarily decided him against campaigning for his party's nominee. Further, on October 12 he challenged both candidates to say whether they favored joining a world body before the close of the war, opposed Senate limitations on such action, and opposed a congressional veto over using American forces to help the world body keep peace. In a major foreign-policy speech on October 18, Dewey agreed to the propositions that the country should enter a world organization without

Senate reservations before the end of the fighting, but he offered only an incomplete answer to Ball's third question: though agreeing that the world body should be able to meet aggression by armed force, he said nothing about how the United States would share in this action.

Roosevelt met the question head on. In a major campaign speech to the Foreign Policy Association in New York on October 21, FDR not only echoed Dewey's answers to the first two questions but also declared himself against final congressional control over American participation in collective-security actions. The United Nations Council, he said, "must have the power to act quickly and decisively to keep the peace by force, if necessary." Comparing the process to the policeman who would need to call a town meeting before he could arrest a felon he saw breaking into a house, the President declared: "If the world organization is to have any reality at all, our American representative must be endowed in advance by the people themselves, by constitutional means through their representatives in the Congress, with authority to act." Ball now announced himself in favor of Roosevelt's reelection, and other Willkie internationalists followed suit.[47]

By election day, most of Roosevelt's close advisers were confident of a clear-cut victory. "We are going to lick that little lying bastard," Pa Watson told Budget Director Harold Smith. "It is apparently going to be a census rather than an election and Roosevelt will win by a landslide," Hopkins cabled Lord Beaverbrook. "Otherwise I will underwrite the British National Debt, join the Presbyterian Church and subscribe to the Chicago Tribune." Roosevelt was closer to the mark when he told Smith that he thought "the race might be very close." Though winning by a wide electoral margin of 432 to 99, the President's popular majority of 3.6 million votes was the smallest since Wilson's narrow victory over Hughes in 1916. Still, Roosevelt received some 53 per cent of the popular vote and strengthened his position in the Congress, where the Democrats reestablished solid majorities in both Houses. More important, with most congressional isolationists in both parties, including Hamilton Fish of New York and Gerald Nye of South Dakota, losing their seats, the election was interpreted as a mandate for American participation in a new and stronger world league. The comparison with Wilson was irresistible. In contrast to 1918, the President would enter the peace negotiations with his domestic support intact.[48]

16

Will There Be Peace?

O F ALL THE DOUBTS about the future that concerned Roosevelt during 1944, none weighed on him more heavily than China. "How long do you think Chiang can last?" he had asked Stilwell at Cairo in December 1943. "The situation is serious and a repetition of last May's attack might overturn him," Stilwell replied. "Well, then, we should look for some other man or group of men, to carry on," the President declared. "They would probably be looking for us," Stilwell ventured. "Yes," FDR agreed, "they would come to us."

In the meantime, Roosevelt thought it best to prod Chiang along the paths best suited to American needs. It was less than easy. In response to FDR's cable from Cairo relating the change in military plans for the Far East, Chiang warned that "it would be impossible for us to hold on for six months" unless the President assisted China with a billion-dollar loan, at least a twofold increase in planes, and an expansion of Hump cargo to 20,000 tons a month. As for a decision on when to make an all-out fight in Burma, he took FDR's option of a fall campaign, and masked his continuing reluctance to fight with assurances that a full-scale amphibious landing in the south could still persuade him to move sooner.[1]

Roosevelt responded with some forthright pressure for action. Angered by Chiang's bold demand of a billion dollars to keep China in the war and by reports from Ambassador Gauss and Morgenthau that the loan was unnecessary and inadvisable and that only increased supplies to China could relieve her economic distress, Roosevelt now insisted that Chiang make an immediate all-out effort to open the Burma Road. In cables drafted in the War Department in December and January, he pressed Chiang to bring all his American-trained divisions in India and in Yunnan province in southwest China into prompt action. Though Chiang agreed to commit his India-based troops, on the condition they were not sacrificed to British interests, he refused to use the Yunnan force without an amphibious attack in the south. "If the Yunnan forces cannot be employed," Roosevelt warned in response, "it would appear that we should avoid for the present the movement of critical materials to them over the limited lines of communication and curtail the continuing build-up of stock-piles in India beyond that which will be brought to bear soon against the enemy." [2]

At the same time, Roosevelt refused Chiang's demand for a loan. On December 20, when Morgenthau recommended against it in a memorandum of "unvarnished truth" about Nationalist mishandling of earlier loans, Roosevelt decided to send Morgenthau's entire memo to Chiang. Hull discouraged the idea as likely to undermine Chinese morale further, but Roosevelt refused to back down. Though agreeing to include a proposal in the memo for a "very high-class Commission" to Chungking to discuss Chinese economic difficulties and to let Gauss soften the impact of its delivery with oral expressions of good will, he sent the full memorandum to Chiang on January 5.

Chiang refused to give ground. In "a very drastic . . . very tough" message to the President on January 16, he proposed "an out-and-out 1 billion dollar loan" to cover part of China's aid to American military forces, or direct American responsibility for the expenses of the American Army in China at the official exchange rate of 20 Chinese dollars to 1 American dollar. This was between one-sixth and one-tenth the American dollar's value on the open market in China, where it was worth between 120 and 200 Chinese dollars. Given China's sacrifices, increased American aid to Britain and Russia, and his agreement to delay the opening of the Burma Road by diverting amphibious equipment to Europe, Chiang felt free to make these demands. Should the United States Treasury reject these proposals, Chiang warned, China "would have to allow her war economy and war finances to follow the natural course of events," leaving her unable to meet the demands of the American Army in China. In effect, the United States would be hard pressed to construct seven air bases in China for sustained B-29 attacks on Japan.

Backed by the Treasury and War Departments, Roosevelt continued to resist Chiang's demands. "They [the Chinese] are just a bunch of crooks, and I won't go up [on the Hill] and ask for one nickel," Morgenthau told an aide. He wanted to "tell them to go jump in the Yangtze River . . . and we go ahead and operate on the black market." "Chiang Kai-shek . . . is holding a pistol to our head," he also said. "So the question gets down to a military question. Is this something that I have got to stomach . . . ?" Army Chiefs thought not. Stimson did not believe the Chinese would drop out of the war with victory in sight, and Marshall believed it possible to forgo China's airfields and approach Japan from the sea. Consequently, Treasury and War together drafted an unresponsive reply to Chiang. FDR made only minor revisions in the cable, but insisted that it pass muster with Hull. Under the latter's prodding, however, Roosevelt sent a more conciliatory response. Though ignoring the request for a loan and refusing to accept the official exchange rate, the President's message endorsed a Chinese proposal for discussions in Washington of "various financial and economic problems" and suggested a temporary arrangement for the expenditure of $25 million a month in China to support American forces.[3]

In his response on February 2, 1944, Chiang also evaded a showdown over these financial and economic questions but reiterated his unwillingness to send his Yunnan force to Burma without a full-scale amphibious attack. The British now also pressed the case against more than nominal action in Burma to safeguard the air route over the Hump. Churchill, who continued to see north Burma as the worst possible place to fight the Japanese, believed that "for our forces to become side-tracked and entangled there would deny us our rightful share in a Far Eastern victory." He wished instead to "break into or through the great arc of islands forming the outer fringe of the Dutch East Indies," aid the American advances on Japan from the Central and South Pacific, and ultimately recapture Singapore and Hong Kong, mainstays of the British Empire. Chiang's refusal to commit his Yunnan force in Burma persuaded Lord Louis Mountbatten, the head of a combined Southeast Asia Command since August 1943, that Churchill had the right idea. In January and February, he urged that instead of forcing a route to China through north Burma, the Allies should take a quicker, more efficient path through the East Indies and Malaya by sea.

Roosevelt saw persuasive military reasons for preserving the Burma campaign. Recent successes in the Gilbert and Marshall Islands had convinced the Joint Chiefs and the President that American forces could reach the Philippine-Formosa-China coast triangle earlier than anticipated and that this would put a premium on China-based air power. To build this to a maximum as quickly as possible, the Chiefs urged the prompt capture of Myitkyina in north Burma, which would shorten the air route into China and speed the movement of supplies for American air forces scheduled to operate there. Successful action in Burma, however, partly depended on a British offensive from Imphal, India, in the west. At a Staff conference in New Delhi on January 31, where Stilwell found "fancy charts, false figures, and dirty intentions," he countered warnings against the difficulties of a Burma campaign with a statement of its advantages compared with British plans and "a sarcastic reminder that Clive had conquered India with 123 men." "I am gravely concerned over the recent trends in strategy that favor an operation toward Sumatra and Malaya in the future rather than to face the immediate obstacles that confront us in Burma," Roosevelt cabled Churchill on February 24. Summarizing the advantages of an all-out drive in upper Burma, FDR urged Churchill's maximum support for "a vigorous and immediate campaign."

Japanese actions in February and March settled the argument. When a powerful detachment of the Japanese Fleet, including seven battle-ships, moved from the Central Pacific to Singapore, it temporarily suspended the possibility of an attack on Sumatra or "anything like it" in the Indian Ocean. More important, at the beginning of March, Japanese forces compelled British action by launching an offensive across the Burma border toward Imphal. The Japanese advance, which moved "with stunning speed and weight" and threatened to cut the Bengal and Assam Railway, the line of communications to the Hump airfields and Stilwell's forces, provoked a vigorous British response. This included requests from Mountbatten for utmost pressure on Chiang to attack from Yunnan across the Salween River toward Burma. Stilwell added his voice in a message to Marshall. "Just this once can't we get some pressure on him?" If ever he needed help, Stilwell declared, it was now.[4]

Roosevelt was quick to comply. On March 17 he advised Chiang that the situation in north Burma had reached "a very critical stage" which could be turned "to our great advantage." The dispersion of Japanese forces in Burma had weakened their defenses on the Salween and provided "a great opportunity" for Chiang's divisions to cross the river and aid Stilwell's Ledo forces to reach Myitkyina. A failure to take "aggressive action," Roosevelt warned, would "certainly" leave the enemy to "recover from his present disadvantage." The President's message crossed one from Chiang describing threats to China from Soviet forces in Outer Mongolia, Chinese Communist units in north Shensi, and Japanese divisions preparing "a large-scale offensive" along the Hankow-Peking railway line. In a reply to the President on March 27, therefore, he described the situation in China as "so grave" that it was "impossible" for his Yunnan army to take the offensive. He promised only to reinforce the Ledo troops with some of his Yunnan forces.

Continuing bad news from the Imphal front and an almost sevenfold Chinese advantage over the Japanese in men and artillery in Yunnan provoked a sharp reply from FDR. "It is inconceivable to me that your YOKE [or Yunnan] Forces . . . would be unable to advance against the Japanese *Fifty-sixth Division* in its present depleted strength. . . . Your advance to the West cannot help but succeed." If Chiang would not commit this force to action, Roosevelt told him, "our most strenuous and extensive efforts" to equip and instruct it had "not been justified." When Marshall instructed Stilwell to give no more Lend-Lease supplies unless the Y-Force moved, Chiang gave in. On April 14 his Chief of Staff pledged to advance the YOKE divisions across the Salween.[5]

Though the fighting in north Burma reached a successful climax with the capture of Myitkyina and the defeat of the Japanese drive on Imphal during the next three and a half months, difficulties over China became more intense. In April the Japanese launched a major offensive aimed at the destruction of American airfields and the stabilization of their hold on east China, particularly the lines of communication between Tientsin and Canton. Quickly scattering the Chinese defenders in Honan province, Japanese forces began their main offensive in June with a drive south from Hankow. By June 18 Changsha, the capital of Hunan province, had fallen without a fight and Hengyang, the first in a chain of American air bases to the south, was under siege. When set alongside severe economic and political deterioration in almost every part of Nationalist-controlled China, American observers anticipated a Kuomintang collapse. Characterizing the Nationalists as combining "some of the worst features of Tammany Hall and the Spanish Inquisition," journalist Theodore White questioned Nationalist ability to survive a civil war against the Communists. Worse yet, Ambassador Gauss, America's principal and most experienced representative in China, saw "nothing that I can suggest at this time that we might do." [6]

Roosevelt and his principal civil and military advisers banked their hopes on a Nationalist-Communist agreement. Most immediately, it would release a huge force to fight Japan. While Chinese resistance to Japanese advances in the spring and early summer crumbled, some 500,000 of Chiang's best trained and equipped troops blockaded a comparable Communist army in north China. Ultimately, a Nationalist-Communist agreement might also forestall a civil war which could jeopardize Soviet-American ties and defeat FDR's postwar plans for China. In February, Roosevelt had initiated steps toward a coalition by asking Chiang's permission to send American observers into north China. As John P. Davies, Jr., Stilwell's chief political adviser, suggested, an observer mission would end the isolation of the Chinese Communists, reduce their dependence on Russia, and inhibit Chiang from liquidating them in a civil war. Though the Army had an observer group ready to go by March and though Roosevelt urged the proposal on Chiang a second time, he resisted the suggestion by agreeing to have observers visit only those parts of north China under Nationalist control.

At the same time, Roosevelt and the State Department tried to ease tensions between Moscow and Chungking. Throughout the spring, FDR urged Chiang to discount suggestions that Russia and Japan had agreed to a Chinese Communist offensive against his regime, and to put "on ice" for the duration of the war conflicts with Moscow over the Outer Mongolian-Sinkiang border. In June he also had Harriman tell Stalin that Chiang was the only man who could hold China together, and that if Chiang could be persuaded to settle with the Communists, both the Nationalists and the Communists could then fight Japan. "This is easier said than done," Stalin replied. But eager to assure the survival of the Communists, who could blunt Nationalist attempts to resist Soviet border claims against China, Stalin agreed that "Chiang was the best man under the circumstances." He should come to some understanding with the Chinese Communists, who, Stalin said, were "not real Communists" but " 'margarine' Communists" and "real patriots" eager "to fight the Japs." He also counseled stronger American leadership in China, where neither Russia nor Britain could act. At the same time, Hull instructed Gauss to urge Chiang to reach an understanding with the Communists and to take steps toward "a closer understanding and cooperation with the Soviet Union." [7]

Roosevelt continued to press the case through Vice President Henry Wallace. Hoping to ease his removal from the vice presidency by having him out of the country and also hoping to disarm some of Chiang's resistance to an agreement with the Communists by sending a warm advocate of China's interests and of international cooperation, Roosevelt asked Wallace to go to China in June. Specifically, he asked him to encourage Sino-Soviet cooperation and a working arrangement between China's Nationalists and Communists that would align them against Japan. He was to advise Chiang that the President "would be happy to be called in as an arbiter between the warring factions," and "that it might be a good thing if 'he [Chiang] would call in a friend.' " He was also to tell the Generalissimo that if he "could not settle the Communist thing he, the President, might not be able to hold the Russians in line" on leaving Manchuria to the Chinese.

In four days of talks beginning on June 21, Chiang conceded little to the President's views. He disputed Roosevelt's hope that his government could achieve a settlement with the Chinese Communists, whom he characterized as " 'internationalists' subject to the orders of the Third International" and "more communistic than the Russian Communists." He warned that Chinese Communist propaganda had fooled Americans, and asserted that America's best contribution to a settlement in China would be through an attitude of "aloofness" and "coolness" toward the Communists. As for sending American observers to Communist areas and getting Communist forces fully into the fight against Japan, Chiang asked Wallace not to press the point; "please understand that the Communists are not good for the war effort against Japan," he said. Though he agreed before the end of the talks to allow American observers into the Communist-held areas and to an effort at mediation by FDR, he warned against trusting the Communists and left Wallace with little hope for "a satisfactory long-term settlement."

Chiang was more amenable to a settlement with the Soviet Union. He suggested that President Roosevelt "act as an arbiter or 'middleman' between China and the U.S.S.R.," and promised to do anything not detrimental to China's sovereignty to avoid conflict with Moscow. In fact, if the President could arrange a meeting between Chinese and Soviet representatives, Chiang promised to "go more than halfway in reaching an understanding with the U.S.S.R." A settlement with the

Soviets, Chiang hoped, would deny the Chinese Communists an important source of support. Also eager to rid himself of Stilwell and Gauss, whom he found impossible to manipulate, Chiang persuaded Wallace to urge the appointment of a Personal Representative who would give him direct access to the President on military and political matters. "With the right man to do the job," Wallace advised FDR, "it should be possible to induce the Generalissimo to reform his regime and to establish at least the semblance of a united front." Wallace suggested General Albert C. Wedemeyer, Mountbatten's American Chief of Staff, for the job.[8]

But for the moment Roosevelt was in no mood to concede anything to Chiang. At the same time that he received Wallace's reports on Chiang's resistance to closing ranks with the Communists against the Japanese, he learned that Japanese forces had captured the airfield at Hengyang. "What I am trying to find out," he told Morgenthau on June 28, is "where is the Chinese Army and why aren't they fighting because the Japanese seem to be able to push them in any direction they want to." In fact, with the Japanese offensive concentrated in east China, well removed from Chiang's strongholds to the west in Chungking and Kunming, he left the fighting to provincial or area forces and refused to move any of his Nationalist troops into the line.

At the beginning of July, therefore, when Roosevelt received a "drastic" proposal from the Joint Chiefs for saving the situation in China, he was ready to act. He agreed to make Stilwell a full General and to press Chiang into giving him command of all Chinese forces. In a cable drafted in the War Department, Roosevelt urged immediate "drastic measures" to stem the Japanese advances "which threaten not only your Government but all that the U.S. Army has been building up in China." He asked Chiang to give Stilwell "the power to coordinate all the Allied military resources in China, including the Communist forces. . . . The case of China is so desperate," he asserted, "that if radical and properly applied remedies are not immediately effected, our common cause will suffer a disastrous setback. . . . There is no intent on my part to dictate to you in matters concerning China;" he assured Chiang, "however, the future of all Asia is at stake along with the tremendous effort which America has expended in that region." The message concluded with the observation that "air power alone cannot stop a determined enemy." To assure that no one blunted the meaning of the President's cable, the senior American officer in Chungking delivered it personally to Chiang.

Roosevelt's message challenged Chiang head on. It pressed him to give military control to an American he refused to trust; it insisted on the inclusion of the Communists in the war effort, an enemy he considered even more dangerous to his survival than the Japanese; and it abandoned the air strategy he, Chennault, and the President himself had promoted as the best way to make China an effective ally against Japan. In sum, as historian Barbara Tuchman has written, it "accepted Stilwell's view of Chiang as incapable of managing his country's role in the war. It called him Peanut by implication." [9]

The message tested all the Generalissimo's well-honed powers of survival. Though Chiang had no intention of accepting Stilwell in the role FDR described or of reaching an accommodation with the Communists, he skillfully encouraged Roosevelt to think otherwise. "I fully agree with the principle of your suggestion," he answered FDR; but he insisted that carrying it out "in haste . . . would not only fail to help the present war situation here but would also arouse misunderstanding and confusion which would be detrimental to Sino-American cooperation." There would have to be "a preparatory period" before Stilwell could "have absolute command of the Chinese troops without any hindrance." This would assure against any disappointment of the President's expectations. In addition, he emphasized his hope for the dispatch of a Personal Representative who enjoyed the President's "complete confidence" and could "adjust" relations between himself and General Stilwell.

Since Chiang seemed willing to agree in principle to Stilwell's command, Roosevelt saw only a difference in timing between them. In a more agreeable message to the Generalissimo on July 13, therefore, he acknowledged that his proposal "represented a major change" and involved "many difficulties." But he urged him nevertheless to act with speed. "If disaster should overtake our combined efforts against the Japanese in China," he advised, "there will be little opportunity for the continuance of Sino-American cooperation. Therefore, some calculated political risks appear justified when dangers in the overall military situation are so serious and immediately threatening." At the same time, he accepted Chiang's suggestion for a Personal Representative, saying that he was making a search for someone with "farsighted political vision and ability to collaborate with you." But he expected this to take a while, and in the meantime he hoped Chiang would pave the way for Stilwell's assumption of command.

Chiang was unaccommodating. In a memorandum for Roosevelt on July 23, he reiterated his willingness to give Stilwell command in principle, but again insisted on the need for "a preparatory period" and now asked three limitations on Stilwell's powers: acceptance of Nationalist rule by Communist forces before they came under Stilwell's control; a clear definition of relations between himself and Stilwell; and Chinese control over all Lend-Lease supplies. Even more revealing of how little Chiang was ready to concede, he sent word through H. H. Kung, his Finance Minister who was on a mission in Washington, that Stilwell would command only those divisions already fighting the Japanese—

meaning the Y-Force and the provincial armies in east China—but not the bulk of Chiang's own troops, who were described as reserves. With Roosevelt absent from Washington for a month to confer with his Pacific commanders at Pearl Harbor, Kung did not deliver these messages until mid-August.[10]

In the meantime, FDR combined a suggestion for a Personal Representative to Chiang with another injunction to give Stilwell command. On August 4, with an answer from Chiang to the President's July 13 message still not in hand, Marshall assumed that the Generalissimo was waiting for FDR to name his Personal Representative. Convinced that the gravity of China's military condition would allow no further delay in Stilwell's appointment and that General Patrick J. Hurley, Secretary of War under Hoover and a diplomatic troubleshooter for FDR, would be a good choice as special envoy to Chungking, Marshall asked the President to put both these suggestions promptly before Chiang.

Though he had been to China in 1943 to help arrange Chiang's attendance at the Cairo Conference, Hurley was woefully ignorant of Chinese affairs. He could not even distinguish between a Chinese given name and family name: "Mrs. Hurley joins me in expressing to you and *Madame Shek* our sincere appreciation for the flowers you sent to us," Hurley had written Chiang in 1931. An impressive record of accomplishment as a conciliator, however, persuaded Roosevelt, Stimson, and Stilwell that he would make a fine choice. "It takes oil as well as vinegar to make good French dressing," Stilwell answered Marshall's suggestion of Hurley. FDR probably also liked the idea of a prominent Republican corporation lawyer sharing responsibility for prodding Chiang into an alliance with the Communists. Adding the suggestion that Donald M. Nelson, former head of the War Production Board, go along with Hurley as a means of ending a politically embarrassing feud between Nelson and his successor, Charles E. Wilson, Roosevelt asked Chiang on August 9 to take action on Stilwell's appointment before it was "too late," and to accept Hurley and Nelson as his personal envoys.[11]

Though Chiang quickly agreed to the Hurley-Nelson mission, he simply repeated his determination to precede Stilwell's appointment with "adequate preparation and thorough deliberation." But Roosevelt, who learned of Chiang's conditions when he returned to Washington on August 17, pressed Chungking harder than ever for effective military action. This was not because China's importance as a B-29 base had increased; on the contrary, the capture in July of Saipan in the Mariana Islands, from where these bombers could also strike Japan, had actually reduced China's value as an air base. Roosevelt feared that unless the Chinese continued to fight, the United States might have to follow the conquest of Japan's home islands with a mainland China campaign. He also wished to dispel the growing belief that China would not be a reliable postwar ally. "Those sections of the [American] public who think about China at all," a British Foreign Office Minute had noted in July, "are now beginning to doubt whether China will be a friendly democracy, protecting American interests in the Pacific." "In the press and everywhere else," Halifax cabled from Washington in August, "an ironical attitude to the claims of China to be a first-class power is only too observable. . . . The slump in general Chinese stock is an accomplished fact and appears to be increasing."

Roosevelt's remedy was still to give Stilwell command. "I urge that you take the necessary measures to place General Stilwell in command of the Chinese forces, under your direction, at the earliest possible date," he cabled Chiang on August 21. ". . . I am urging action in the matter . . . so strongly because . . . with further delay, it may be too late to avert a military catastrophe tragic both to China and to our Allied plans for the early overthrow of Japan." As to Chiang's conditions, which Roosevelt called "matters of detail," he rejected one and suggested dealing with the others after Stilwell received command. Stilwell's forces, he insisted, should not "be limited except by their availability to defend China and fight the Japanese. When the enemy is pressing us toward possible disaster, it appears unsound to refuse the aid of anyone who will kill Japanese." As for Stilwell's relations with Chiang and the control of Lend-Lease, Roosevelt declared that Hurley would help arrange the first and that he would soon propose a new scheme for handling the second. He asked Chiang not to wait until each detail was settled and warned that "perfection of arrangements may well have fateful consequences." [12]

During the next three and a half weeks, Roosevelt lost all patience with Chiang. In a conversation with Gauss on August 30, Chiang again rejected a compromise with the Communists, and complained that Washington's attitude only strengthened their "recalcitrance." On September 9 Gauss informed Chiang that the President and Hull urged an end to factional differences through "intelligent conciliation and cooperation" as the best way to fight the war and establish "a durable democratic peace." In a direct message, FDR reminded Chiang that he anxiously awaited "your final arrangements" on Stilwell's command.

He hoped that this would emerge from discussions Hurley, Nelson, and Stilwell began with Chiang on September 7. Though Hurley and Nelson arrived on the scene "full of P. and V.," ready "to pound the table" and demand unification in China and unification of command, they quickly found Chiang unresponsive to their pressure. Along with expressions of readiness to have Stilwell command, Chiang continued to insist on Communist recognition of his authority and full control of Lend-Lease or power to determine which Chinese troops received American arms. Worse yet, with the Y-Force in danger of defeat on the China-Burma border at Lungling, from where the Japanese could attack the Hump terminus at Kunming, Chiang threatened to move his Yunnan army back across the Salween to defend Kunming unless Chinese divisions at Myitkyina went to Lungling. "The crazy little bastard," Stilwell exploded in his diary. This would "sabotage the whole God-damn project—men, money, material, time and sweat that we have put on it for two and a half years just to help China."

Stilwell put his concerns before Marshall in a cable on September 15. "The jig is up in South China. We are getting out of Kweilin now, and will have to get out of Liuchow as soon as the Japs appear there. The disaster south of the Yangtze is largely due to lack of proper command and the usual back-seat driving from Chungking. The trouble continues to be at the top." As for the difficulties at Lungling, Stilwell attributed them to Chiang's failure to send troop replacements. The Y-Force "is now down to an effective combat strength of fourteen thousand and we are making frantic efforts to get replacements flown in." As for Chiang's threat to withdraw the Y-Force, Stilwell characterized it as "throwing away the results of all our labors. He [Chiang] will not listen to reason, merely repeating a lot of cock-eyed conceptions of his own invention. I am now convinced that he regards the South China catastrophe as of little moment, believing that the Japs will not bother him further in that area, and that he imagines he can get behind the Salween and there wait in safety for the U.S. to finish the war. Our conferences on command are dragging, and tomorrow we are going to try some plain talk with T. V. Soong, in the hope of getting to the Gmo some faint glimmer of the consequences of further delay and inaction." [13]

Stilwell's message reached Marshall and Roosevelt at the Quebec Conference, where they had persuaded the British to exploit recent successes in Burma. As described in reports to Mountbatten and Chiang, Anglo-American plans now included the continuation and expansion of the campaign in north Burma to secure the air ferry route through Myitkyina and to open overland communications between India and China. Further, Mountbatten was to help expel the Japanese from Burma as soon as possible with amphibious attacks in the Bay of Bengal. Stilwell's message, then, not only indicated little progress toward a resolution of the command problem and the crisis in east China but also raised the possibility that Chiang would ruin this Burma campaign.

Roosevelt now sent Chiang a plainspoken message "with a firecracker in every sentence."

After reading the last reports on the situation in China my Chiefs of Staff and I are convinced that you are faced in the near future with the disaster I have feared. . . . If you do not provide manpower for your divisions in north Burma, and if you fail to send reinforcements to the Salween forces and withdraw these armies, we will lose all chance of opening land communications with China and immediately jeopardize the air route over the Hump. For this you must yourself be prepared to accept the consequences and assume the personal responsibility.

I have urged time and again in recent months that you take drastic action to resist the disaster which has been moving closer to China and to you. Now, when you have not yet placed General Stilwell in command of all forces in China, we are faced with the loss of a critical area in east China with possible catastrophic consequences. . . .

The advance of our forces across the Pacific is swift. But this advance will be too late for China unless you act now and vigorously. . . .

I am certain that the only thing you can now do in an attempt to prevent the Jap from achieving his objectives in China is to reinforce your Salween armies immediately and press their offensive, while at once placing General Stilwell in unrestricted command of all your forces. The action I am asking you to take will fortify us in our decision . . . to maintain and increase our aid to you. . . . I have expressed my thoughts with complete frankness because it appears plainly evident to all of us here that all your and our efforts to save China are to be lost by further delays.

Drafted by Marshall's staff and endorsed by him, the message received Roosevelt's approval and signature and signaled his conviction that Chiang was finished. As if preparing for the inevitable controversy that would follow such an event, the message partly spoke to the issue of who was at fault. There is also an indication that Roosevelt expressed this view to Churchill. "The American illusion about China is being dispelled," Churchill wrote Field Marshal Smuts in a letter about his conversations with FDR in Quebec. "The Soong family oligarchy regime is more insecure and very likely nearing its end. Chiang . . . is in a precarious position and of course there is grotesque Chinese military diversion of effort over the Hump." [14]

Chiang, however, had greater staying power than most informed observers believed. To be sure, the President's message hit him hard. It was a virtual ultimatum, Hurley believed, and he suggested that Stilwell let him paraphrase it to Chiang. But since it had been sent in a special code that would assure delivery of a literal copy, Stilwell, who, in his biographer's words, "leapt at the chance to plunge it into the Peanut's heart," insisted on handing it directly and in full to Chiang. "The harpoon hit the little bugger right in the solar plexus, and went right through him," Stilwell gleefully recorded in his diary. "It was a clean hit, but beyond turning green and losing the power of speech, he did not bat an eye. He just said to me, 'I understand.' " A few days later Stilwell wrote his wife, "I played the avenging angel." Two stanzas from a poem he also sent her say it all.

> For all my weary battles,
> For all my hours of woe,
> At last I've had my innings
> And laid the Peanut low.

I know I've still to suffer,
And run a weary race,
But oh! the blessed pleasure!
I've wrecked the Peanut's face.[15]

Convinced that acquiescence in the President's demands would jeopardize first his military and then his political control, Chiang decided to resist the American program by ridding himself of Stilwell, the symbol and driving force behind the American call for change. By asking for Stilwell's removal, he also avoided a direct clash with Roosevelt and the possible loss of American aid. In conversations with Hurley on September 24 and in an aide-mémoire for the President sent the following day, Chiang insisted on Stilwell's recall. By delivering the President's message, Stilwell had turned him into a subordinate, Chiang complained. Were Stilwell given command, the Chinese Army might mutiny. "Stilwell had no intention of cooperating with me," Chiang advised the President, "but believed that he was in fact being appointed to command me." Though reiterating his desire to have an American officer command all forces in China, he predicted that Stilwell's appointment "would immediately cause grave dissensions in the new command, and do irreparable injury to the vital Chinese-American military cooperation." Hurley lent his support to Chiang's demands, telling FDR that the decision not to put Stilwell in command only occurred after "Stilwell, a subordinate, handed the Generalissimo your message of September 18." He also advised the President that "there can no longer be any doubt" that the two men "are incompatible." [16]

Stilwell saw more clearly what was at stake. "CKS has no intention of making further efforts to prosecute the war," he told Marshall on September 26. "Anyone who crowds him towards such action will be blocked or eliminated. . . . He believes the war in the Pacific is nearly over, and that by delaying tactics, he can throw the entire burden on us. He has no intention of instituting any real democratic reforms or of forming a united front with the Communists." "It is not a choice between throwing me out or losing CKS and possibly China," Stilwell advised Marshall in a subsequent message. "It is a case of losing China's potential effort if CKS is allowed to make rules now. . . . China is like a sick man who is telling the doctor what to do," a Chinese officer told Stilwell, "and it is now necessary for the doctor to be very firm if the patient is to be cured."

When Stilwell's analysis reached the White House, Roosevelt felt unable to adopt a firm stand. On October 1 Chiang received a telegram from Kung reporting that "Harry Hopkins had told him at a dinner party that . . . since it concerned the Sovereign Right of China, the President intended to comply with the Generalissimo's request for the recall of

General Stilwell." In a message to Chiang on October 5, Roosevelt agreed to relieve Stilwell as Chiang's Chief of Staff. But to assure the safety of the Hump route, which "is of such tremendous importance to the stability of your Government," Roosevelt urged Chiang to leave Stilwell in command of Chinese forces in Burma and Yunnan. At Marshall's suggestion, he also told Chiang that he would withdraw his proposal for an American commander of all Chinese ground forces. "The ground situation in China has so deteriorated since my original proposal," Roosevelt said, "that I now am inclined to feel that the United States Government should not assume the responsibility involved in placing an American officer in command of your ground forces throughout China." [17]

Having gained the initiative, Chiang now pressed Roosevelt to remove Stilwell entirely and put another American officer in command of China's armies. "So long as I am Head of State and Supreme Commander in China," his message to Roosevelt read, "it seems to me that there can be no question as to my right to request the recall of an officer in whom I can no longer repose confidence." Adding a tendentious indictment of Stilwell for the defeats in east China, Chiang ended with an assurance that if the President replaced Stilwell "with a qualified American officer, we can work together to reverse the present trend and achieve a vital contribution to the final victory." Hurley again endorsed the Generalissimo's requests, and warned FDR that if he sustained Stilwell "in this controversy you will lose Chiang . . . and possibly you will lose China with him." Though Roosevelt disputed Chiang's interpretation of military developments and reiterated his decision not to have an American officer command Chinese forces in China, he agreed to issue immediate instructions for Stilwell's recall. Two days later, on October 21, Stilwell left China for India and the United States.

In giving in to Chiang, Roosevelt was not disputing Stilwell's description of what his removal would mean. His acceptance of Marshall's advice against giving another American officer command of China's armies indicated that he had essentially given up on pushing the Chinese into effective military action. He now shared a belief with his Joint Chiefs that the Chinese might at best contain some Japanese forces on the mainland. As for his fear that a Chinese collapse would ultimately compel a major American ground effort in China, a fresh assurance from Stalin in September that Russia would come in against Japan relieved Roosevelt's concern; if need be, the Russians could contain and ultimately force the surrender of Japanese forces in China. Though Roosevelt now also assigned General Albert C. Wedemeyer to command American forces in China and be Chiang's new Chief of Staff, he did not ask that he be put in control of the Chinese armies, as he had for Stilwell. He also continued to increase deliveries over the Hump, and asked for the appointment of General Daniel Sultan as the new commander of Chinese forces in India and Burma. But a continuing Chinese effort in Burma and a strengthening of Kunming and Chungking defenses were the only objectives of these steps.[18]

Roosevelt's decision to accommodate Chiang rested more on political than military considerations. He believed a direct confrontation over Stilwell's appointment might precipitate Chiang's collapse. To have a part in overturning China's government would destroy all he had done to advance her emergence as an independent, sovereign state. It also promised a decisive end to his already shaky plans for bringing China into the world arena as a Great Power allied to the United States. Further, such a development in the midst of the presidential campaign might cost him the votes of liberal internationalists, who would complain of interference in another nation's sovereign affairs. It could also hurt him in the Middle West, where fears that Roosevelt wished to bring the United States government under Communist control would find confirmation in the rise of a Chinese Communist regime, the most likely successor to Chiang. Even without the election, a Chinese collapse threatened political recriminations in the United States which could weaken Roosevelt's ability to organize the peace. On a number of counts, then, it seemed better to leave Chiang in place, where he could be encouraged to compromise with the Communists or left to fall of his own accord.[19]

Roosevelt's principal interest in Chinese affairs now became the creation of a Nationalist-Communist agreement which would prevent a civil war injurious to his postwar plans. The outbreak of civil strife not only would destroy his hopes of leading China into international politics on America's side but also could bring a pro-Russian regime, Soviet control in Manchuria, and a sharp challenge to Soviet-American cooperation after the war. Churchill's conversations with Stalin in mid-October had aroused Roosevelt's concern about Soviet intentions in the Far East generally and in China specifically. During these talks, Stalin conditioned Soviet involvement in the Pacific war on the settlement of certain political questions. "The Russians would have to know what they were fighting for; they had certain claims against Japan." Once they went in, however, they would not limit their offensive to Manchuria. Japanese defeat would require the movement of Soviet forces down to the Great Wall in China and possibly even farther south. "If the Russians go in [to China]," FDR asked Harriman on November 10, "will they ever go out?" "The reports received from Moscow in October," the historian Herbert Feis concludes, "made it seem more urgent than ever that the internal division of China be composed as soon as possible."

Hurley was an enthusiastic promoter of a coalition government in China His optimism knew no bounds. A conversation with Molotov in Moscow before coming to Chungking convinced him that "the Chinese Communists are not in fact Communists . . . that Russia is not supporting the so-called Communists in China and . . . that Russia desires closer and more harmonious relations with China." By the second half of October, his conversations in Chungking had also convinced him that the Chinese Communists would "for war purposes" submit to Chiang's leadership and that Chiang in return would promise a united China ruled by democratic principles after the war. "For the first time," Hurley had cabled FDR on October 19, "it begins to look as if unification of all military forces in China is possible." "I hope present arrangements will succeed in bringing all Chinese forces together against the invaders," Roosevelt encouraged him in reply. In November, when Hurley went to Yenan to discuss unification with the Communists, Roosevelt again encouraged his efforts: "I hope that your journey will result in bringing the two antagonistic factions closer to agreement and cooperation."

In Yenan, where Hurley arrived in military uniform wearing "every campaign ribbon but Shays' rebellion" and treated his hosts to stories about the Old West and imitations of Indian war cries, he negotiated a five-point program for composing differences between the two sides. On his return to Chungking, however, he found Nationalist leaders unreceptive to an agreement that they predicted would put the government under Communist control. Believing Chiang and his associates unjustified in that opinion, Hurley pressed them to see that "a reasonable agreement with the Communists is necessary." Eager to give Hurley all possible support in this effort, Roosevelt now appointed him Ambassador to China, and asked him to tell Chiang "from me, in confidence, that a working agreement betwen the Generalissimo and the North China forces will greatly expedite the objective of throwing the Japanese out of China from my point of view and also that of the Russians. I cannot tell you more at this time but he will have to take my word for it. You can emphasize the word 'Russian' to him." Hoping to exploit Chiang's fear of the Russians, Roosevelt signaled him that the Soviets would enter the war against Japan and that a failure on his part to reach an accord with the Communists would further endanger his regime.[20]

Despite his support of Hurley's efforts, Roosevelt was highly skeptical of the results. Stilwell "was terribly distressed about the graft in China," FDR told Charles Taussig on November 13. "You have been in China long enough to know there is nothing we can do about it," he reported himself as telling Stilwell. He also recorded himself as saying that, at best, "the Chinese would not steal any more [Lend-Lease material] than they had . . . in the past." In a move even more revealing of Roosevelt's skepticism about American ability to alter Chiang's actions and save him from collapse, the White House now completed a fifty-nine-page report on "The President and U.S. Aid to China." Based on FDR's correspondence with Chiang, the document described China as on the edge of military and political collapse and blamed Chiang for having failed to follow the President's lead. Described by FDR as "excellent," the report gave him an authoritative means to meet the likely political storm that would follow Chiang's demise.[21]

Any hopes Roosevelt had that Hurley could work a change in Chinese affairs evaporated in the last six weeks of 1944. Though Hurley assured the President that his message to Chiang "was effective . . . immediately" and that both sides "seem anxious for settlement," the negotiations made no progress. Consequently, by mid-December, Roosevelt began seeking a settlement in China through an agreement with Stalin. If he could persuade Moscow to accept a coalition regime, Roosevelt believed that the Chinese Communists would also accept it, that a civil war would be averted, and that a weak, but relatively stable China would be able to lend the United States political support in postwar Pacific and even world affairs. In response to instructions from FDR, Harriman discussed the Far East with Stalin on December 14, asking specifically what political questions he wished settled before Russia fought Japan and how he viewed political developments in China. Though Stalin's remarks gave little encouragement to Roosevelt's plan, FDR believed that he could exchange territorial concessions in the Far East for Soviet support of a coalition in China.

In the seven weeks between Harriman's inquiry and a discussion of Far Eastern issues with Stalin at Yalta, Roosevelt invested considerable hope in this idea. It fueled a fresh upsurge of belief on his part that China might yet play the role of a major postwar power. In January 1945, for example, when Hurley and American military representatives reported that British, French, and Dutch authorities in the Far East were opposing a strong, unified China as contrary to their best interests in Asia, Roosevelt privately denounced this as "entirely contrary to his idea and the policy of the United States Government. Our policy," he told Stettinius, "was based on the belief that despite the temporary weakness of China and the possibility of revolutions and civil war, 450,000,000 Chinese would someday become united and modernized and would be the most important factor in the whole Far East." He thought it might be necessary to confront these Anglo-American differences over China at his next meeting with Churchill and Stalin. During the next two weeks, in fact, Stettinius raised the subject with the British Ambassador, while Roosevelt himself discussed it with Britain's Colonial Secretary, Oliver Stanley. "Winston calls the Chinese 'pig-tails' and 'Chinamen,' " FDR told him. "The Chinese don't like that. The Chinese are vigorous, able people. They may acquire Western organization and methods as quickly as did the Japanese." [22]

Clearly, Roosevelt had no illusion that a coalition regime would immediately convert China into a first-class power; this was for the distant future—twenty-five to fifty years. In the meantime, though, a coalition would allow her to move toward that goal with American support. "I take it that it is our policy to build China up," Stilwell asked Roosevelt at Cairo. "Yes. Yes," he replied. "Build her up. After this war there will be a great need of our help. They will want loans." Stilwell said that "we will need guidance on political policy on China." "Yes," Roosevelt responded. "As I was saying, the Chinese will want a lot of help from us—a lot of it."

Though Hurley and the Chinese Communists now made separate proposals for FDR's direct intervention in China's domestic politics, he resisted these suggestions as less promising than his plan for a settlement reached in conjunction with the U.S.S.R. On January 14 Hurley urged the President to win Churchill's and Stalin's agreement to immediate military and postwar political unification in China. He then wanted FDR to invite Chiang and Mao Tse-tung, Chairman of the Communist Party, to confer with him, but only on the condition that they had already reached an agreement on unification which would be promulgated when they met. In this same message, Hurley reported that Mao and Chou En-lai, the Party's Vice-Chairman, had made secret overtures through Wedemeyer for a meeting with the President in Washington.

Roosevelt ignored both proposals. Since Hurley could not demonstrate that a meeting with the President would produce an agreement between Chiang and Mao, his suggestion had no appeal to FDR. Likewise, since a conference with the two Communist leaders might make them less, rather than more, receptive to a negotiated settlement and might burden him with the domestic political onus of contributing to Chiang's collapse, he also rejected this plan. But since he was desirous as ever of having a unified, stable China linked to the United States in world affairs, Roosevelt now hoped to reach this goal through a Soviet-American accord.[23]

Despite Roosevelt's great concern about China in the winter of 1944-45, questions about American determination to continue playing a major part in world affairs worried him more. Though the defeat of isolationist Representatives and Senators in the 1944 election and strong expressions of public support for American participation in a new world league had greatly encouraged him, events in the two months after his reelection sharply challenged his hopes. On November 27, 1944, Cordell Hull retired as Secretary of State. Seventy-three-years old in the previous month and in poor health for some time, Hull no longer felt physically able to meet the heavy demands of his office. His retirement principally left a gap in the administration's relations with Congress on foreign affairs generally and on postwar planning in particular. Though Hull had played a significant part in shaping the reciprocal trade, Good Neighbor, and cautious Far Eastern policies before Pearl Harbor, his wartime actions had been largely confined to dealings with Congress on postwar affairs. But at the end of 1944, this was a matter of large concern to FDR. In Hull's place, Roosevelt appointed Undersecretary of State Edward R. Stettinius, Jr. Formerly Chairman of the Board of U.S. Steel and a prominent figure in the administration's industrial mobilization program, Stettinius appealed to FDR as someone who would not challenge his control over policy formulation or excite Republican opposition and undermine the administration's nonpartisan approach to world affairs.

The instability of mass feeling about overseas events also worried FDR. "Although a slight majority of those with opinions have faith in Russian cooperation after the war," the pollster Hadley Cantril had advised him on November 10, "sentiment here is unusually sensitive to events." Specifically, Cantril informed him that where 56 per cent of the public in June 1944 had believed Russia could be trusted to continue cooperating with the United States, that number had fallen to 47 per cent by late October.[24]

Difficulties over Poland were the source of this decline. The Soviet failure to aid the Warsaw uprising had aroused suspicions about their intentions after the war. A Polish governmental crisis in November threatened to underscore Soviet-American differences over Poland and further weaken American faith in postwar cooperation. On November 24, when Mikolajczyk failed to persuade his colleagues in the Government in Exile to reach a territorial settlement with the Russians, he resigned as Premier. The Soviets, Stettinius warned the President, "will be quick to take advantage of Mikolajczyk's resignation" to make the Lublin Committee the sole government of Poland.

Roosevelt's abiding concern was to keep the Polish issue from coming between the United States and the U.S.S.R. The President "consistently shows very little interest in Eastern European matters except as they affect sentiment in America," Harriman recorded after a conversation with FDR in late October. In another talk in November, Roosevelt told Harriman that "he wanted to have a lot to say about the settlement in the Pacific, but that he considered the European questions were so impossible that he wanted to stay out of them as far as practicable, except for the problems involving Germany." Further, when Harriman pressed him to formulate an immediate response to Soviet determination to dominate Poland, Roosevelt put him off by suggesting that Lwow might be governed by an international committee, and became annoyed when Harriman tried to bring him back to the central point. A few days later, on November 20, 1944, when former Ambassador to Poland Arthur Bliss Lane urged him to demand Russian agreement to Polish independence, Roosevelt rhetorically asked: "Do you want me to go to war with Russia?" At the same time, he responded evasively to a request from Mikolajczyk for pressure on Stalin to soften his demands on the Curzon Line.

Roosevelt strongly wished, however, to forestall Soviet recognition of the Lublin Poles. "Because of the great political implications" which recognition would have, Roosevelt cabled Stalin in mid-December, he hoped the Soviet Union would not act until they had a chance to talk again. But Stalin refused. In a lengthy response on December 27 he denounced the London Poles, depicted the Lublin Committee as representing the great majority of Poles, and insisted that it would secure Soviet Armies from an attack in the rear as they moved into Germany. "I am disturbed and deeply disappointed," Roosevelt promptly replied. He had hoped that Stalin "would realize how extremely unfortunate and even serious" such a step would be "in its effect on world opinion and enemy morale" if they were openly divided over which group legitimately represented the Poles. Frankly concluding that he saw no prospect of American recognition of the Lublin group and that he had little reason to think that it was the true representative of the Polish people, he again asked Stalin to delay recognition until they had a chance to talk. He was powerless to fulfill the President's wish, Stalin replied. The Presidium of the Supreme Soviet had already acted. "It is interesting to see that the 'Presidium of the Supreme Soviet . . . ,'" Churchill told FDR, "has now been brought up into the line." [25]

British actions now joined with Soviet policy in Poland to increase confusion and disillusionment in the United States about foreign affairs. At the beginning of December, London had tried to block the appointment of Count Carlo Sforza as Foreign Minister in the new Italian government. Though viewed by Churchill as an "intriguer and mischief-maker" who had played a leading part in bringing down Badoglio's government in June, Sforza enjoyed a reputation in the United States as a staunch anti-Fascist. British opposition to his appointment evoked widespread complaints in the American press against London's interference in Italian affairs. In response to press demands for a statement of policy on British action, the State Department reaffirmed its commitment to the solution of political problems in Italy and elsewhere "along democratic lines without influence from outside." The public interpreted the dispute as evidence that Britain remained committed to traditional sphere-of-influence diplomacy.[26]

British actions in Greece gave even stronger support to this view. In December, when a governmental crisis in Athens brought British troops into conflict with Greek Communist forces, the encounter aroused additional misgivings in the United States. Revelation of an instruction from Churchill to his commander in Athens to feel free to fire on armed opponents of British authority was particularly disturbing to Americans. As with Poland, however, British efforts to control Greek developments in themselves concerned Roosevelt less than the demoralizing effect they would have on internationalist opinion in the United States. "I regard my role in this matter as that of a loyal friend and ally whose one desire is to be of any help possible in the circumstances," he cabled Churchill in the midst of the crisis. But, he added, traditional American policies and a growing adverse reaction among the public strongly limited what he could do. It was for these reasons that he could not "take a stand along with you in the present course of events in Greece." Any attempt to do so would only injure their long-term relations. "The President's off-hand solution of the situation in Greece," Harold Ickes recorded in late December, "would be to give every Greek a rifle and then let them fight it out." [27]

Roosevelt and his principal advisers saw these Russian and British actions as reviving isolationist feelings in the United States or doubts about the value of a world league or the likelihood of sustained cooperation in world affairs. If Britain and America could not reach agreement at a civil aviation conference in Chicago, FDR had told Churchill in late November, the public and the Congress would "wonder about the chances of our two countries, let alone any others, working together to keep the peace." "Public opinion here [is] deteriorating rapidly because of Greek situation," Hopkins had cabled Churchill in mid-December. "If some bold and dramatic action is not taken soon," a member of the White House staff told Hopkins a few days later, "the reactions of the American people to the Greek, Polish and Italian situations may cause irreparable injury." "The world is fast losing faith in generalities about a bright future," geographer Isaiah Bowman advised the President at the start of the New Year.

Reluctant to confront the issue directly with Churchill, who strongly defended British policy in Italy and Greece, Roosevelt apparently used the *New York Times* to give him the message. On the basis of what Anthony Eden believed was a White House-inspired or authorized leak, the *Times* published a report in January about a stiff communication from FDR to Churchill. The message was reported as saying, "The American people are in a mood where the actions of their Allies can precipitate them into whole-hearted cooperation for the maintenance of the peace of Europe or bring about a wave of disillusionment which will make the isolation of the nineteen-twenties pale by comparison." Although Americans were more receptive now to international collaboration for world peace than at any time since 1918, the report continued, "the British have been told with force and authority that the mood can change as mercurially as the English weather if the American people once get the idea that this war . . . [is] just another struggle between rival imperialisms."

Opinion surveys reaching Roosevelt in December and January confirmed these estimates of the American mood. There was "fairly strong anti-British feeling" among leading newspaper editors in the Middle West, one report advised. These editors also believed that further developments like those in Greece would jeopardize favorable action on the world security organization and would bring "a return to a stronger isolationism than ever." Samplings of public opinion, Stettinius informed the President, demonstrated widespread resentment toward America's allies for practicing power politics, and a significant decline in confidence that the President was taking good care of the country's interests abroad. Specifically, confidence that Britain and Russia would cooperate with the United States after the war now reached its lowest point since the Moscow Conference in October 1943: 60 per cent still trusted Britain, but only 44 per cent trusted the U.S.S.R. Further, the number of Americans who believed that the nation's interests were being well taken care of had fallen from 64 per cent in June to 49 per cent in December.[28]

One of Roosevelt's principal concerns at the start of 1945 was to shore up the consensus in the United States for postwar participation in world affairs. He devoted part of his State of the Union Address in January to this goal. "In our disillusionment after the last war," he told the country, "we gave up the hope of achieving a better peace because we had not the courage to fulfill our responsibilities in an admittedly imperfect world. We must not let that happen again, or we shall follow the same tragic road again—the road to a third world war." Also urging his fellow Americans not to exaggerate current differences between the Allies or to simplify the solutions to the Greek and Polish problems, Roosevelt counseled against allowing "the many specific and immediate problems of adjustment connected with the liberation of Europe to delay the establishment of permanent machinery for the maintenance of peace."

His speech had a salutary effect on public opinion. Its "reasoned philosophy and tone of moderation . . . won praise from most commentators, including some recent critics," Stettinius told the President. Though 50 per cent of the public continued to feel that recent developments in Europe would make it more difficult for the proposed peace organization to succeed, 60 per cent of the country now endorsed participation in an international security organization even if the peace settlement did not completely satisfy American aims. This was reassuring to Roosevelt, but he believed that more stable public support for American participation abroad now depended on the results of the next Big Three talks.[29]

Roosevelt appreciated that winning agreements there that were palatable to Americans would be difficult, especially with the Russians. The decision on a conference site, for example, reminded him how unbending the Soviets could be. Roosevelt wished to meet somewhere in the Mediterranean; but Stalin, insisting that his health would not allow him to make any "big trips," urged a conference in the Soviet Union, preferably along the Black Sea coast. Roosevelt's own medical advice against flying at high altitudes, the risks attached to a voyage through the Dardanelles, reluctance to be so far from Washington with Congress in session, and "health conditions" in the Black Sea, all made FDR resistant to Stalin's proposal. But his conviction that Stalin would not leave the Soviet Union persuaded Roosevelt to meet at Yalta after his Inauguration on January 20, 1945. ARGONAUT, the name given to the men who accompanied Jason on his legendary search for the Golden Fleece on the Crimean coast, impressed Churchill as an appropriate name for the meeting. "You and I are direct descendants," Roosevelt said in agreement. When Roosevelt also told him that he would stop in Malta, Churchill burst forth: "No more let us falter! From Malta to Yalta! Let nobody alter!" [30]

At the same time, Soviet intransigence over Poland added to Roosevelt's worries about settling differences with Stalin. In a conversation with Stimson on December 31, he had remarked that "Stalin had taken Britain's desire to have a cordon sanitaire of friendly nations around it in past years as an excuse now for Russia's intention to have Czechoslovakia, Poland, and other nations whom it could control around it." Stimson answered with a warning from General John R. Deane in Moscow "that we could not gain anything at the present time by further easy concessions to Russia and . . . that we should be more vigorous on insisting upon a quid pro quo." Stimson also discussed the atomic bomb: while troubled about "the possible effect" on the Russians of remaining silent about the bomb, especially since they already knew about it, he believed it "essential not to take them into our confidence until we were sure to get a real quid pro quo from our frankness." He had no illusions about the possibility of keping such a secret permanently, but he "did not think it was yet time to share it with the Russians." Roosevelt "thought he agreed."

Roosevelt, in fact, had a complicated strategy for dealing with the Russians at Yalta. He still intended to tell Stalin nothing about the atomic bomb until the Soviets effectively demonstrated their sincere interest in postwar cooperation. Further, he intended to bargain with Stalin about the Far East and to split the differences that remained from the Dumbarton Oaks talks on the United Nations. But in Eastern Europe generally, and Poland in particular, he had little hope of deflecting Stalin from his course and was prepared to settle for agreements aimed more at satisfying American opinion than at rescuing the area from Soviet control. He indicated as much to a group of seven Senators from both parties in January. In a meeting calculated to ease congressional worries about recent developments in Europe and to answer criticism of the administration's failure to address these issues more vigorously, FDR candidly said that spheres of influence were a reality which America lacked the power to abolish. The "idea kept coming up," he explained, "because the occupying forces had the power in the areas where their arms were present and each knew that the other could not force things to an issue. He stated that the Russians had the power in Eastern Europe, that it was obviously impossible to have a break with them and that, therefore, the only practicable course was to use what influence we had to ameliorate the situation."

In the long run, he hoped this could be done through the United Nations. Was not the best course to press ahead with the Dumbarton Oaks proposals and set up that machinery as soon as possible? one Senator asked. "This was exactly the course . . . the administration was following," the President said. But before this could happen, another Senator rejoined, the Russians would settle everything by force of arms and eliminate all opposition to their plans. Roosevelt replied that "he still believed that much could be done by readjustment, if the machinery could be set up and if the Russians could be brought in and could acquire confidence in it." Roosevelt also considered the creation of a new world security organization an essential condition for sustained American participation in world affairs. Without it, American opinion would see only a return to traditional balance-of-power and sphere-of-influence diplomacy and little hope for a cooperative, peaceful world. Resurgent isolationism and a divided public seemed the likely result of such a view. To Roosevelt, then, a United Nations would not only provide a vehicle for drawing Russia into extended cooperation with the West, but would also assure an initial American involvement in postwar foreign affairs.[31]

The Conference at which Roosevelt hoped to build the foundations for a stable peace began at Yalta on February 4, 1945. Ten years of research could not have unearthed a worse place to meet, Churchill had told Hopkins eleven days before. He planned to counter the typhus and lice that thrive there by bringing an adequate supply of whiskey. Roosevelt's residence and the Conference sessions were both at Livadia Palace, a fifty-room structure built for Czar Nicholas in 1910–11 on a bluff overlooking the Black Sea. The beauty of the surroundings belied the primitive conditions under which the delegates had to live. An "acute shortage" of bathrooms and no shortage of bedbugs, which showed a total disregard for rank by biting ministers, butlers, generals, and privates led the list of complaints. Though the Soviets had made strenuous efforts to repair the extensive damage visited upon the area by the retreating Germans, they had only partly succeeded.[32]

Military conditions in Europe were a focus of discussion on the first day of the Conference. At the beginning of February, Allied forces in the West were still largely where they had been in October, on the German borders with Belgium, Luxembourg, and France. In mid-December, in a desperate attempt to reverse military developments in the West, Hitler had launched an offensive in the Ardennes forest which created a bulge in the Allied lines around the Belgian city of Bastogne. Though American forces had managed to regain all the lost ground by the time the Yalta talks began, the Allies were only then beginning an offensive that would carry them into Germany and across the Rhine. Meanwhile, on the Eastern front, Soviet armies had launched an offensive on January 12 which had gained up to 250 miles in three weeks and put the Russians only forty miles from Berlin.

Efforts by Roosevelt and Stalin to soften each other up for the coming talks on postwar affairs also marked the first day of the Yalta talks. At their initial meeting on the afternoon of February 4, Roosevelt remarked on the extensive German destruction in the Crimea and declared himself more bloodthirsty toward the Germans than ever. He hoped Stalin "would again propose a toast to the execution of 50,000 officers of the German Army." Roosevelt also told Stalin "something indiscreet": for two years the British had the idea of artifically re-creating France as a strong power that could meet a future threat on its eastern borders until Britain could assemble a strong army. "The British were a peculiar people and wished to have their cake and eat it too." At a dinner Roosevelt hosted that night for Churchill, Stalin, and the principal Big Three advisers, FDR confided to Stalin that he and Churchill called him "Uncle Joe." When Stalin seemed offended by the remark, Roosevelt explained that it was a term of endearment and one presidential aide chimed in that the term was on a level with Uncle Sam. Molotov then assured them that Stalin was only "pulling your leg. . . . All of Russia knows that you call him 'Uncle Joe.' "

Stalin played a similar game. Whereas he emphasized Soviet military advances to Churchill in their first conversation, he made much less of these in his first talk with FDR. He apparently believed that an emphasis on points of agreement rather than on Soviet power would make Roosevelt more receptive to Soviet claims. "In all probability," historian Diane Shaver Clemens contends, "Stalin played down his military hand in an effort to avert suspicion, discord, lack of co-operation, and, at worst, military retaliation." Further, when Roosevelt mentioned de Gaulle in this first talk, Stalin belittled him as not very complicated, unrealistic, and deceitful. Though he had recently agreed to a Franco-Russian alliance and praised de Gaulle as a determined and effective negotiator, Stalin now subscribed to the President's known view of de Gaulle and the French.[33]

On the second day of the Conference, attention turned to the treatment of Germany. Roosevelt's comments reflected a shift in his position on France's postwar role and his current worries about reviving American reluctance to become significantly involved in European affairs. He had already touched on these subjects in his initial talk with Stalin when he voiced regret at having accepted a south German zone of occupation for the United States. "The British seemed to think that the Americans should restore order in France and then return political control to the British," he said. The Congress and the public, he declared on the 6th, would support "reasonable measures designed to safeguard the future peace, but he did not believe that this would extend to the maintenance of an appreciable American force in Europe" for much more than two years. To help fill the power vacuum an American withdrawal would leave in controlling Germany, Roosevelt now agreed to arm eight more French divisions and to create a German occupation zone for France.

Though he had already accepted the reality of de Gaulle's power at the end of October by finally recognizing him as the provisional ruler of France, he refused to strengthen de Gaulle's position by conceding him an equal say in postwar affairs. He rejected de Gaulle's request to share in the discussions at Yalta, and he agreed with Stalin that a French occupation zone should not mean a part in the control machinery for Germany. On the next to last day of the Conference, however, after Hopkins and Harriman had persuaded him not to exclude France from the Control Council for Germany, Roosevelt announced that he had changed his mind: it would be impossible to give France an occupation zone without also making her a member of the Control Commission.[34]

At the third full scale meeting of the Conference on February 6, Roosevelt had initiated discussion on the world security organization. He at once made it clear that such an organization was essential to effective American participation abroad and to long-term peace. An international organization conforming to the Dumbarton Oaks proposals, he declared, might persuade the American public to keep troops in Europe. He did not believe in eternal peace, he added, but he thought it entirely possible to avoid another war for fifty years.

He then asked Stettinius, who had accompanied him to Yalta, to describe the American plan for resolving the deadlock over voting rights in the Security Council. The plan called for unanimity among the five permanent members of the Council or conceded a veto right to any permanent member in all decisions to preserve the peace by economic or military sanctions. It also proposed that seven out of the eleven Council votes be sufficient to bring a dispute before the Council for discussion. Any Council member who was a party to the dispute would have no vote on whether the Council would hear the issue. This whole procedure, Stettinius pointed out, would have the virtue of preserving unity among the Great Powers while also allowing smaller member states to air significant grievances in the Council. This second point, Stettinius also said, was of particular importance to the American people, who believed in "a fair hearing for all members of the organization, large and small."

Though Stalin was initially suspicious of this proposal, he agreed to it on the following day. Satisfied that it would not hurt Soviet interests to let the Council discuss questions affecting Russia, Stalin coupled acceptance of the American plan with a request that in addition to the

U.S.S.R. two or three Soviet Republics become original members of the world organization. Though the size, importance, and contribution to the war effort of the Ukrainian, White Russian, and Lithuanian Republics were emphasized, the apparent Soviet motive was to help quiet independence movements in these states. "This is not so good," Roosevelt told Stettinius when Molotov presented Stalin's request. He had been hopeful that the Soviets would abandon an idea that Americans would see as spawning Big Power control and greater influence for the Soviets than for the United States in the Assembly.

Roosevelt tried to sidestep the issue. He suggested leaving the question of United Nations membership until, or after, an organizing conference and made the proposal that the Foreign Ministers now consider when and where it would take place and who would attend. With the British strongly supporting the Soviet proposal, Roosevelt agreed to back original membership for two Soviet Republics at an organizing conference in the United States beginning April 25. When members of the American delegation, however, argued that it was unwise to give the Soviets a three-to-one advantage over the United States in the Assembly, he asked Stalin and Churchill to support two additional American votes. Possible difficulties with the Congress and the American people, he told them, impelled him to ask parity for the United States. Stalin and Churchill readily agreed.[35]

The agreement to hold a United Nations organizing conference in April also raised the subject of trusteeships. On February 9 Stettinius proposed to Eden and Molotov that the invitation to the conference include a recommendation that the Charter of the world body contain provisions relating to trusteeships and dependent areas. When the subject came before the heads of government later that day, Churchill blew up: "Under no circumstances would he ever consent to forty or fifty nations thrusting interfering fingers into the life's existence of the British Empire. As long as he was Minister, he would never yield one scrap of their heritage." Amused at Churchill's outburst, Stalin "got up from his chair, walked up and down, beamed, and at intervals broke into applause." How would Stalin feel, Churchill inquired, if it were proposed that the Crimea be internationalized for use as a summer resort? He would be glad to give it as a meeting place for the Three Powers, Stalin replied.

Stettinius's explanation of what the United States intended calmed Churchill. The proposal in no way referred to the British Empire, Stettinius assured him. Trusteeships were only intended for existing League of Nations mandates, territory detached from the enemy, and any other territory *voluntarily* put under United Nations control. It was agreed that the five permanent members of the Security Council would consult prior to the organizing conference about what to include in a United Nations Charter for dealing with this problem. This trusteeship plan, less ambitious than any Roosevelt had favored in the past, largely resulted from Churchill's resistance and the changed position of the French. De Gaulle's consolidation of power helped persuade Roosevelt that trusteeships could apply to only those three categories of territories described by Stettinius. In early January, when FDR had discussed trusteeships with Stettinius and Hopkins, the latter pointed to "a distinct difference between the Japanese-mandated islands or Japanese territory such as Korea and islands that belonged outright to allied countries such as France." Hopkins believed that "it would be difficult to apply the principle of trusteeship to territories when sovereignty was vested in a friendly allied country." Roosevelt agreed.[36]

The change in trusteeship policy found specific expression in the President's plans for Indochina. In November, when Roosevelt had learned that the British had brought French officials into South-East Asia Command (SEAC) headquarters, he cautioned American representatives in the Far East against political decisions with the French or anyone else. "We have made no final decisions on the future of Indochina," he declared. When Hurley informed him later in the month of a growing British-French-Dutch effort to reclaim their political and economic position in the Far East and asked guidance on American policy toward Indochina, Roosevelt replied that a policy "cannot be formulated until after consultation with Allies at a forthcoming Staff conference." All this was in sharp contrast to what he had previously said about the area. To be sure, he told Stalin at Yalta that he "had in mind a trusteeship for Indochina," but he also said that Britain wanted to give it back to France and de Gaulle had asked for American ships to help him reestablish French control there. Though FDR was not ready to provide the ships, it was also clear that he would not now press his plans: to do so, he told reporters off the record after Yalta, "would only make the British mad. Better to keep quiet just now."

What he left unsaid, however, was that it would also offend the French, whom he now expected to take a significant part in European affairs, and in addition it would demand an unrealizable Chinese military effort. Consequently, in mid-March, when de Gaulle asked for American help for scattered French resistance to a full-scale Japanese takeover in Indochina, Roosevelt told Taussig that he would agree to a French trusteeship there if ultimate independence were promised. On March 16 he learned from Jefferson Caffery, the American Ambassador to France, that de Gaulle had coupled a plea for American help to French forces in Indochina with a warning that a failure to help restore French power would force her to become "one of the federated states under the Russian aegis. . . . When Germany falls," de Gaulle said, "they will be on us. . . . We do not want to become Communists; we do not want to fall into the Russian orbit but we hope you do not push us into it."

Two days later Roosevelt ordered American air forces to aid the French in Indochina on the condition that such action did not interfere with operations against Japan.[37]

In backing away from international trusteeships for prewar Allied colonies, Roosevelt changed the scope but not the substance of his plans. He still believed in bringing former League mandates and detached enemy territory under United Nations civil authority and American military control. His trusteeship idea, Roosevelt told his Cabinet after returning from Yalta, was that "sovereignty would be vested in all of the United Nations . . . but that we would be requested by them to exercise complete trusteeship for the purpose of world security." Efforts by U.S. military leaders to assure full American control over some of these territories, particularly Japan's mandated islands, had little appeal for FDR. Any such action still seemed likely to encourage a scramble for national control of "dependent" areas all over the world and to discourage American faith in the value of a new world league.[38]

As with a new world body, Roosevelt believed that American receptivity to sustained involvement abroad and continued cooperation between Russia and the West partly depended on Big Three agreement about Poland. He had little expectation of winning genuine independence for the Poles, but he hoped that Stalin would accept proposals that would at least create this impression and make Poland less of an issue at home and abroad. But Stalin, who was content with the status quo—the Lublin Committee and Soviet domination—had little inclination to discuss the subject. Consequently, Roosevelt had raised it on the third day of the talks. He asserted that America's distance from Poland made him more objective about the problem. Nevertheless, he said, there were six or seven million Poles in the United States, and it would make things easier for him at home if the Soviet Government would alter the Curzon Line—specifically, giving Poland Lwow and the oil deposits in the surrounding province. He merely offered this suggestion for consideration, he quickly added, and would not insist on it. A permanent Polish government was the more important question. American opinion opposed recognition of the Lublin government as unrepresentative of the majority of Poles. Americans wished to see a government of national unity which could settle internal differences, and Roosevelt suggested the creation of a Presidential Council composed of Poland's five major parties to assume this task. Above all, the United States wanted a Poland that would be thoroughly friendly to the Soviet Union for years to come. A solution of the Polish problem would greatly help all of them keep the peace.

Despite Churchill's general endorsement of the President's views, Stalin was less than forthcoming. Poland, he declared, was "not only a question of honor for Russia, but one of life and death." Russia needed a strong, independent Poland to help protect her from another German attack. As to the Curzon Line, any retreat from this border would make him and Molotov less Russian than Curzon and Clemenceau, who had invented it. Instead, he proposed that more territory be taken from Germany by extending the Polish border to the western Neisse River. The more German territory Poland received, Stalin undoubtedly felt, the more dependent she would become on the Soviet Union to protect her from future German demands for change. Turning to the question of a Polish government, Stalin reproved Churchill for having suggested the possibility of creating a Polish government without the Poles. He was called a "dictator," he said, but he had "enough democratic feeling" to insist that the Poles play a part. But by this he meant only the Lublin or, now, Warsaw Poles. The London faction, he complained, had refused to reach an agreement with the Lublin leaders and were attacking Soviet supply lines. The Soviet Army must have peace in the rear, and the Lublin group wished to satisfy this goal. "Should we ask the Warsaw Poles to come here or perhaps come to Moscow?" he asked.

Roosevelt took up Stalin's idea. In a letter to him on the following day, FDR reiterated his need to show the American public a united front. If their differences over a Polish government continued, he said, it could "only lead our people to think there is a breach between us, which is not the case. . . . Our people at home look with a critical eye on what they consider a disagreement between us. . . . They, in effect, say that if we cannot get a meeting of minds now . . . how can we get an understanding on even more vital things in the future." Roosevelt then proposed that they bring two members of the Lublin government and two or three other representative Poles to Yalta to decide on a provisional regime.

At their meeting on the afternoon of the 7th, Stalin discounted the possibility of bringing the Poles to Yalta before the end of the Conference and suggested instead that they hear a proposal from Molotov. It asked agreement to the borders described by Stalin on the 6th, and suggested a limited reorganization of the Lublin regime: some democratic Poles from émigré circles were to join the Warsaw government; Ambassadors Harriman and Clark Kerr were to discuss the means of doing this with Molotov; the Allies were to recognize this enlarged ruling body; and the new government was to call a general election. Though Churchill objected that the Polish goose should not be stuffed "so full of German food that it got indigestion," he and the President seemed to acquiesce in the Soviet proposal on borders. On the question of a government, however, both asked for more time to consider Molotov's plan.

The differences between them on Poland came more fully into the open on the next day. Roosevelt turned aside Molotov's proposals by rejecting the western Neisse River boundary as unjustified and suggesting the creation of a provisional regime composed equally of Lublin Poles, "other democratic elements in Poland," and Polish democrats abroad. Molotov dismissed the President's plan as unacceptable to the Polish people, who would insist on keeping the current provisional government largely intact. The Conference was now at its "crucial point," Churchill declared. Nothing else they did there would overcome a failure on Poland. "We were all agreed on the necessity of free elections," Roosevelt responded, and "the only problem was how Poland was to be governed in the interval." Stalin replied with a thinly guarded appeal for autonomy in their respective spheres of influence. He saw little difference between de Gaulle and the Polish provisional government, he said. Neither held a clear-cut mandate, but he had recognized de Gaulle's rule and the Allies should do the same for the Lublin Poles. Stalin also declared that he had no intention of interfering in Greece but wanted an account of events there from Churchill. The three leaders now agreed to turn the Polish issue over to their Foreign Ministers.

Too much else was at stake for Roosevelt to allow Poland to remain a major difference between the Allies. Over the next two days, he and Stettinius took the initiative in hammering out a compromise. Instead of insisting on a new government in which the Lublin group would hold only one-third of the power, Roosevelt now agreed to a reorganization of the existing regime on a broader democratic basis with the inclusion of "other" democratic leaders within and outside of Poland. As important, he agreed to modify a proposal that the Ambassadors of the three Powers in Warsaw observe and report on the fulfillment of a pledge by this reorganized provisional government to carry out "free and unfettered elections." Giving in to the Soviet argument that this would represent an interference in Polish internal affairs, Roosevelt agreed to announce that the British and American Ambassadors would only keep their respective governments "informed about the situation in Poland." In sum, Roosevelt acknowledged that Britain and the United States would be unable to assure that either the provisional or the elected government would be a representative regime. Roosevelt appreciated this. "Mr. President," Leahy told him after looking over the final report on Poland, "this is so elastic that the Russians can stretch it all the way from Yalta to Washington without ever technically breaking it." "I know, Bill," the President replied. "I know it. But it's the best I can do for Poland at this time."

The announcement on Poland also covered over differences between Russia and her Allies on borders and made their agreement on the subject seem less fixed than it was. Unable to agree on whether Poland's western frontier should be on the Oder and the eastern or western Neisse River, the three leaders declared that after consultation with the Polish Provisional government, the western boundary would be set at a final peace conference. The Conference communiqué also stated that "the three Heads of Government consider that the Eastern frontier of Poland should follow the Curzon Line." Fearful that the Senate would see any agreement on frontiers as a breech of its treaty-making power, Roosevelt was reluctant to say anything about borders in the final Conference document. "I have no right to make an agreement on boundaries at this time," he said. "That must be done by the Senate later." When Stalin and Churchill insisted, however, that they say something about the Polish borders, Roosevelt persuaded them to state it in tentative terms. Instead of saying that "the three powers" consider the eastern boundary to be the Curzon Line and that "they agree" about putting the matter of the western frontier before a peace conference, the final communiqué spoke of "the three Heads of Government" and declared that "they feel that . . . the final delimitation of the western frontier of Poland should . . . await the peace conference." [39]

As another means of assuring domestic opinion that Britain and Russia were not creating postwar spheres of influence and also of placing a moral burden on the Soviets to act with restraint in their sphere, Roosevelt asked Churchill and Stalin to sign a Declaration on Liberated Europe. Committing themselves to assist liberated peoples in solving their political and economic problems by democratic means and, more specifically, to help these peoples establish internal peace and form democratic governments through free elections, the Declaration provoked little discussion among the Big Three. Stalin found particular appeal in a clause calling for the destruction of the "last vestiges of Nazism and Fascism" in the liberated countries. Churchill accepted the President's Declaration on the condition that a reference to the Atlantic Charter did not apply to the British Empire. He had made it plain in the House of Commons, he said, that the Charter's principles already applied to the Empire, and he added that he had given Mr. Willkie a copy of his statement. "Was that what killed him?" the President inquired. Poland would be the first test of the Declaration, Roosevelt also said. "I want this election in Poland to be the first one beyond question. It should be like Caesar's wife. I did not know her but they said she was pure." "They said that about her," Stalin replied, "but in fact she had her sins." [40]

Roosevelt also took the initiative in discussing questions about the Far East. His first concern was to assure final arrangements for Soviet entrance into the war against Japan. The knowledge that a first atomic bomb would be ready by August did not affect this goal. Only one more bomb was promised before the end of the year, and its potential strength was estimated as no more than that carried by a single flight of bombers raiding Germany. (The first bomb used over Japan was actually ten times more powerful.) In early 1945, therefore, the atomic bomb had little influence on plans for defeating Japan. "Russia's entry at as early

a date as possible consistent with her ability to engage in offensive operations," the Joint Chiefs had advised FDR in January 1945, "is necessary
to provide maximum assistance to our Pacific operations." The defeat of
Japanese forces in Manchuria, air attacks on Japan proper from eastern
Siberia, and disruption of Japanese shipping between Japan and the
Asian mainland were the gains American planners saw from Russian
participation in the war. More important, the effective execution of these
tasks seemed calculated to save many American lives in the Far East.
William Bullitt's injunction in early 1943 to limit Soviet expansion in
Europe by winning her involvement against Japan after German defeat
may have been another consideration in Roosevelt's mind.[41]

While their military chiefs worked out the details of the joint Soviet-
American effort against Japan, Roosevelt and Stalin discussed postwar
political arrangements. In a conversation with the President on February 8, Stalin had asked for a discussion of "the political conditions under
which the U.S.S.R. would enter the war." He had already heard about
these from Harriman, Roosevelt replied, and he anticipated no difficulties
whatsoever over the transfer of southern Sakhalin and the Kurile Islands
from Japan to Russia. As for a warm-water port in the Far East, the
President said he could not speak for China, but he favored Soviet use of
Darien on the Kwantung peninsula through either an outright lease or
an agreement making Dairen a free port under international control. He
preferred the latter as a way of inducing the British to do the same for
Hong Kong.

Stalin then asked for Russian use of the Manchurian railways. Again,
Roosevelt declared ignorance of Chiang's view but sympathy for the
idea if it were done by lease from China or through a Sino-Soviet commission. Unless these conditions were met, Stalin now said, he would
have difficulty explaining Soviet involvement against Japan to his people
and the Supreme Soviet. To clear all this with the Chinese, Roosevelt
replied, would risk having everything told to the whole world in twenty-
four hours. Stalin did not think it advisable to talk to the Chinese until
he could move twenty-five divisions to the Far East. In the meantime, he
wanted a written agreement to his conditions signed by the three
Powers. Roosevelt thought this possible.

A brief exchange on conditions in China suggested that Stalin would
support an agreement between the Nationalists and the Communists.
Roosevelt remarked that "for some time we had been trying to keep
China alive." Stalin answered that "China would remain alive," and
added that some new leaders were needed around Chiang. Wedemeyer
and Hurley were making some progress toward bringing the Communists
together with the Chungking government, FDR responded, though the
Kuomintang was less cooperative than the "so-called Communists."
Stalin "did not understand why they did not get together since they

should have a united front against Japan. . . . For this purpose Chiang Kai-shek should assume leadership. . . . Some years ago there had been a united front," Stalin recalled, and added that "he did not understand why it had not been maintained."

If this was all Roosevelt said to Stalin about China, it was enough to impress on him that the President wanted Soviet support for a coalition regime. Since Stalin apparently feared a Chinese civil war as likely to destroy the Communists and put the Nationalists in a position to resist Soviet claims in Manchuria and Outer Mongolia or give the Communists a victory that could also produce a challenge to Soviet border claims and to Soviet leadership of Communist movements around the world, he was entirely ready to agree. In the written statement of Soviet conditions for entering the war against Japan, they agreed to conclude "a pact of friendship and alliance" with Chiang's government to help liberate China from Japan. On February 10, after three conversations involving Harriman, Molotov, Roosevelt, and Stalin, the two sides also agreed in writing that Russia would enter the fighting against Japan two or three months after German defeat. In return, the three Allies were to preserve the status quo, a Soviet controlled regime, in Outer Mongolia, return southern Sakhalin to the Soviet Union, internationalize the port of Dairen, where preeminent Soviet interests were to be safeguarded, lease Port Arthur to the U.S.S.R. as a naval base, establish a joint Soviet-Chinese company to operate the Chinese Eastern and South Manchurian railroads, with preeminent Soviet interests again safeguarded and full Chinese sovereignty in Manchuria retained, and cede the Kurile Islands to the Soviet Union.

The terms of the agreement left unclear whether the Chinese would need to give their consent before the provisions affecting them went into effect. The initial Soviet draft simply said that "the Heads of the Three Great Powers have agreed that these claims of the Soviet Union shall be unquestionably fulfilled after Japan has been defeated." Harriman urged the President to press for a removal of this provision, but Roosevelt preferred to leave it in and add a contradictory proviso "that the agreement concerning Outer Mongolia and the ports and railroads . . . will require concurrence of Generalissimo Chiang Kai-shek." In Roosevelt's eyes, maintaining the original language had the advantage of denying Chiang an absolute veto over the understanding, a condition that would have upset the Soviets and given Chiang more control than FDR wished. At the same time, however, the additional requirement for Chiang's concurrence provided an escape clause from the agreement if military or political conditions determined that it should not be fulfilled. As to how and when Chiang learned of the understanding, the President was to inform him when Stalin gave the signal. Churchill, however, who had no part in these discussions, saw the agreement on the following day. He approved it without comment. It was "an American affair," he recalled in his war memoirs. "It was not for us to claim to shape it. . . . To us the problem was remote and secondary."

Roosevelt never explained why he entered into so controversial an understanding. Nevertheless, his motives seem reasonably clear. He apparently believed that, despite the sacrifices, Chiang would welcome an agreement that promised to help preserve the life of his regime. Chiang had made it abundantly clear that he wished an accommodation with the U.S.S.R., and he had asked FDR's help to this end. Furthermore, Roosevelt was probably confident that American opinion would consider the territorial concessions to Russia well worth a shorter war and the saving of American lives, and a small price to pay for postwar peace and stability in China. Indeed, Roosevelt apparently saw the agreement as the last best hope for preserving a weak but stable China as a cooperative ally on the world scene.[42]

Much has been made of the idea that Roosevelt was a dying man at Yalta who lacked the physical strength and mental alertness to deal effectively with Stalin. Without question, his physical condition had greatly declined by the time of the Conference. At his Inaugural on January 20, he had "seemed to tremble all over. It was not just his hands that shook," Stettinius recalled, "but his whole body as well." Frances Perkins also found him looking "very badly." His deep-gray color, expressionless eyes, and shaking hands persuaded her that he had been ill for a long time. At Yalta, moreover, Churchill's physician, Lord Moran, thought him "a very sick man. He has all the symptoms of hardening of the arteries of the brain in an advanced stage, so that I give him only a few months to live." At the same time, however, Roosevelt impressed most observers with his recuperative powers. Just before the Yalta talks, for example, Stettinius found him "cheerful, calm, and quite rested." "His appearance could change in a couple of hours from looking like a ghost to looking okay," Frances Perkins remembered.

More important, the men closest to him at Yalta thought the President performed effectively. "I always found him to be mentally alert and fully capable of dealing with each situation as it developed," Stettinius said. Even more to the point, Eden felt that the President's declining health did not alter his judgment. A review of the agreements reached at Yalta confirms his point. On all the central issues—the United Nations, Germany, Poland, Eastern Europe, and the Far East—Roosevelt largely followed through on earlier plans, and gained most of what he wished: the world body, the division of Germany, the pronouncement on Poland, and the Declaration on Liberated Europe promised to encourage American involvement abroad and possible long-term accommodation with the U.S.S.R.; similarly, the Far East agreement promised to save American lives and hold China together to play a part in helping the United States preserve postwar peace.[43]

Roosevelt's first concern at the close of the Conference was to put the best possible face on what had been done. This was not difficult, since, by and large, the mood of the American delegation was one of "supreme exultation" over what had occurred. "We really believed in our hearts that this was the dawn of the new day we had all been praying for," Hopkins later said. "The Russians had proved that they could be reasonable and farseeing and there wasn't any doubt in the minds of the President or any of us that we could live with them and get along with them peacefully for as far into the future as any of us could imagine." The Conference communiqué echoed these sentiments: the meeting in the Crimea had reaffirmed Big Three determination to maintain in peace the unity of purpose that had brought them victory in the war. The creation of the proposed international organization would "provide the greatest opportunity in all history" to secure a lasting peace.

In a personal appearance before the Congress on March 1, Roosevelt declared Yalta a huge success and asked national support for its results. It was an emotional occasion. A packed House chamber greeted him with a standing ovation, and the President begged the pardon of his audience for the unusual posture of sitting down during his speech. "I know that you will realize that it makes it a lot easier for me not to have to carry about ten pounds of steel around on the bottom of my legs; and also because of the fact that I have just completed a fourteen-thousand-mile trip." His appearance shocked those who had not seen him in a while. They noted "a decided physical deterioration": he spoke haltingly, slurring some of his words and stumbling over part of his text; his right hand trembled, and he awkwardly turned the pages of his speech with his left hand.

So far, it was a fruitful journey, he told his audience. But "the question of whether it is entirely fruitful or not lies to a great extent in your hands. For unless you here in the halls of the American Congress—with the support of the American people—concur in the general conclusions reached at Yalta, and give them your active support, the meeting will not have produced lasting results." The United States Senate and the American people would soon have to decide the fate of generations to come, he continued. "We shall have to take the responsibility for world collaboration, or we shall have to bear the responsibility for another world conflict."

He concluded with a description of the Yalta achievement. The Crimea Conference represented a successful step toward peace. "It ought to spell the end of the system of unilateral action, the exclusive alliances, the spheres of influence, the balances of power, and all the other expedients that have been tried for centuries—and have always failed. We propose to substitute for all these, a universal organization in which all peaceloving Nations will finally have a chance to join. I am confident that the Congress and the American people will accept the results of this Conference as the beginnings of a permanent structure of peace." [44]

In private, Roosevelt was less confident of the results. Adolf Berle, who was very fearful of Russian intentions, saw him just after he returned from Yalta. Roosevelt threw his arms up and said: "Adolf, I didn't say the result was good. I said it was the best I could do." He explained that the Russians had promised to reconstitute the countries they occupied by free elections. "This was only an agreement," he acknowledged. But because the Joint Chiefs were insisting on redeployment of American forces from Europe to Asia and therefore the United States would be unable to push troops into the Russian area of control, "we must rely on the Russian word." Since he had no intention of confronting Soviet power in east-central Europe, even if he had the troops, Roosevelt's comments to Berle partly sound like the answer he planned to give anti-Soviet critics if the Yalta settlement collapsed. Nevertheless, the conversation is revealing of FDR's uncertainty about the ultimate result of the Yalta talks.

There is additional evidence of this concern in what he told Sam Rosenman. While they were working on his congressional address, FDR spoke repeatedly about the Conference and expressed "doubt whether, when the chips were down, Stalin would be able to carry out and deliver what he had agreed to." Though he was not so candid with Frances Perkins, she also appreciated that his rosy descriptions of the Conference did not reveal his full view. At a Cabinet meeting after Yalta, Roosevelt described Stalin as having "something else in him besides this revolutionist, Bolshevist thing." The President thought it had something to do with his training for the "priesthood. . . . I think that something entered into his nature of the way in which a Christian gentleman should behave," FDR said. He also reported that the Russians had committed themselves to the "continuation of the war." When James Byrnes, head of the Office of War Mobilization, interrupted to observe that he did not see it "quite like that," Perkins "realized that the President was telling us what he wanted us to know, and what it was good for us to know. . . . In other words, he had to deal with his Cabinet," she recalled, "with a view to the fact that some of them would leak" Cabinet discussions to the press.

Roosevelt wanted no public expression of doubt about the Yalta accords. In December 1944, when Stettinius had pressed him to ease public concern over Soviet and British actions, he had responded "that much of this would have to wait until his return from the Big Three meeting." Now with the Yalta agreements in hand, he was intent on fostering a strong national consensus for involvement in a world body with effective means to keep the peace. He appreciated that exaggerated views of the Yalta agreements would ultimately cause some, if not considerable, disillusionment. But he believed this an acceptable price for a strong initial commitment to postwar participation abroad. For even substantial national distress over serious future differences with wartime allies seemed unlikely to reverse the country's new involvement in foreign affairs. Indeed, Roosevelt assumed that once the country entered a world league, or made an institutional commitment to political entanglements abroad, it would find it far harder to return to the isolationism of the past. The inability of domestic reactionaries to dismantle the New Deal legislation of the thirties may have encouraged him in this view.

Roosevelt's chief concern after returning to the United States was to minimize anything that might undermine support for an effective world league. He knew that the Big Three meeting had dramatically increased the number of Americans satisfied with Allied cooperation from 46 to 64 per cent and that American participation in a world body with power to assure the peace now found acceptance with over 80 per cent of the public. At the same time, however, he appreciated that only 30 per cent of the nation had some idea of what the Dumbarton Oaks proposals were, that only 32 per cent of the country thought a new world organization would be able to keep the peace for fifty years, and that 38 per cent of the public foresaw United States involvement in another world conflict in less than twenty-five years. In sum, mass enthusiasm for a new world league seemed to rest on a somewhat shaky base.[45]

Consequently, at the end of March when the Russians indicated that Ambassador Gromyko rather than Molotov would head their delegation to the United Nations Conference on International Organization in San Francisco, Roosevelt asked Stalin to send Molotov, if only for the "vital opening sessions." Since all the other sponsoring countries were sending their Foreign Ministers, Molotov's absence "will be construed all over the world as a lack of comparable interest in the great objectives of this Conference on the part of the Soviet Government." When Stalin responded that Molotov would find it "impossible" to come, Roosevelt warned of the American response. "Genuine popular support in the United States is required to carry out any government policy, foreign or domestic," he reminded Stalin. "The American people make up their own mind and no government action can change it. . . . Your message about Mr. Molotov's attendance at San Francisco made me wonder whether you give full weight to this factor." When Stalin responded by announcing that Gromyko would lead the Soviet delegation, American newspapers speculated that the administration might postpone the San Francisco Conference. Stettinius replied that the Conference would go ahead as planned.

Roosevelt's anxiety about challenging American hopes for the United Nations also registered in his reluctance to reveal the agreement to give Russia two additional Assembly votes. Though Stettinius made the voting formula for the Security Council public on March 5 and though FDR met with his San Francisco Delegation on March 13, he waited until March 23 to tell them about the Assembly arrangement. "This will *raise hell*," one delegate concluded. ". . . This effort to 'stack' the Assembly could easily dynamite San Francisco—or subsequent Senate approval of the entire treaty." When news of the "Yalta secret" leaked to the public in the following week, it provoked a storm of criticism which indicated that Roosevelt would have done better to reveal the agreement himself in early March. He managed to limit the damage, however, by having Stettinius announce that the United States would not ask for three Assembly votes, that the great suffering of the two Soviet Republics justified Stalin's request, and that there were no other secret agreements on international organization made at Yalta. Roosevelt himself tried to blunt the issue by declaring it of no "great importance." The Assembly, he told the press, was "an investigatory body only." [46]

At the same time that he worked to hold the country on a steady course toward involvement in the new world league, he also tried to assure that arrangements for China did not come unhinged. The China problem had flared again in March when Hurley and the principal American Foreign Service officers in Chungking divided on how to gain the greatest possible military effort from the Chinese. At the end of February, while Hurley and Wedemeyer were on their way back to Washington for consultations about the Nationalist-Communist negotiations, all the political officers at the Chungking embassy had advised the State Department that exclusive American aid to Chiang made him unwilling to compromise and increased the chances of a civil war which would endanger American interests. Instead, they wanted the President to inform Chiang "that military necessity requires that we supply and cooperate with the Communists and other suitable groups who can assist the war against Japan." They expected this to promote "ultimate complete unity" in China, to bring all Chinese forces into the war against Japan, and "to hold the Communists to our side rather than throw them into the arms of Russia" when the Soviets joined the fighting.

Hurley, who unalterably opposed these recommendations, received the President's support. More concerned now than ever with long-run political developments in China and the Far East than with any Chinese military effort against Japan, Roosevelt feared that outright military aid to the Communists would defeat rather than enhance the chances for a unified Chinese regime. Direct American help to the Communists would combine with the promise of Soviet arms in China to make them resistant to a compromise with Chiang. Such a step might help provoke the civil war he wished to forestall, defeat his plans for using China in a postwar security system, and open him to domestic attacks for aiding the rise of a Chinese Communist regime. It seemed much better to maintain the policy agreed upon at Yalta: reliance on Soviet force to fight the Japanese in Manchuria and intimidate Chiang into a domestic political compromise; and a Soviet treaty of alliance with Chiang to compel Communist agreement to coalition rule. At a final talk on March 24, the President instructed Hurley to return to Chungking via London and Moscow, where he was to seek reaffirmation of British and, principally, Soviet support for a unified China under Chiang's control.[47]

Roosevelt's desire for a reaffirmation of Soviet intentions toward China resulted from his growing anxiety about their willingness to follow through on the Yalta agreements for Eastern Europe. By the second week of March, Soviet actions in Roumania and Poland had greatly distressed Churchill. In Roumania they had "succeeded in establishing the rule of a Communist minority by force and misrepresentation," he complained to FDR. In Poland they were preparing the way for a totalitarian regime with liquidations and deportations and an interpretation of the Yalta agreements which barred practically all non-Lublin Poles from a part in constructing a new regime. Churchill proposed that he and the President ask Stalin to prevent a purge of non-Communists in Roumania and to fulfill the Yalta pledge to create a truly representative Polish government.

Roosevelt refused. Having for all practical purposes conceded that Eastern Europe was a Soviet sphere of control, he was reluctant to force a confrontation with Stalin over Soviet behavior there. Roumania, he told Churchill, was not a good place to judge Russian intentions. They had been "in undisputed control" there from the beginning and could make a strong case for military necessity to justify their action. As to Poland, he feared that Stalin would interpret a message from Churchill as an effort to alter the Yalta understanding to give the Lublin group the principal say in constructing a new government. At the same time, however, he believed it essential to "stand firm on the right interpretation of the Crimean decision. . . . Neither the Government nor the people of this country," he also told Churchill, "will support participation in a fraud or a mere whitewash of the Lublin government, and the solution must be as we envisaged it at Yalta." In short, the Lublin Poles would have the controlling voice in a government, but other groups would also have a say. If this did not promise a fully democratic regime for Poland, it could at least forestall a public outcry in the United States.[48]

This remained Roosevelt's principal concern. When Churchill pressed him in reply to take a strong stand on Poland through their Ambassadors, and warned that he would have "to reveal a divergence between the British and the United States Governments" unless they confronted this "utter breakdown of what was settled at Yalta," Roosevelt denied to acknowledge any divergence of policy or breakdown of the Yalta agreement until they had tried to overcome their differences with the Soviets on what the Polish understanding meant. By the end of March, however, when it became entirely clear that discussions with Molotov through the Embassies in Moscow would not resolve these differences, Churchill again suggested an approach to Stalin. "I see nothing else likely to produce good results," he cabled FDR. Moreover, "if the success of San Francisco is not to be gravely imperilled, we must both of us now make the strongest possible appeal to Stalin about Poland and if necessary about any other derogations from the harmony of the Crimea. Only so shall we have any real chance of getting the world organisation on lines which will commend themselves to our respective public opinions." Unless he got a satisfactory solution on Poland, Churchill also warned, he would have to report Anglo-American differences with Russia over Poland "openly to the House of Commons."

Churchill's appeal struck a responsive chord. He was "acutely aware of the dangers inherent in the present course of events," Roosevelt replied, "not only for the immediate issues involved and our decisions at the Crimea but also for the San Francisco conference and future world cooperation. Our peoples and indeed those of the whole world are watching with anxious hope the extent to which the decisions we reached at the Crimea are being honestly carried forward."

He echoed these concerns in a message to Stalin on March 31. The decisions they had reached at Yalta had raised worldwide hopes for postwar peace, FDR cabled. As a consequence, "their fulfillment is being followed with the closest attention. We have no right to let them be disappointed." This was particularly true for Poland, he said, which had "aroused the greatest popular interest" and was the most urgent issue before them. Unless they arranged for something more than "a thinly disguised continuation of the present Warsaw regime," the American people would "regard the Yalta agreement as having failed. . . . I wish I could convey to you," Roosevelt concluded, "how important it is for the successful development of our program of international collaboration that this Polish question be settled fairly and speedily. If this is not done all of the difficulties and dangers to Allied unity which we had so much in mind . . . at the Crimea will face us in an even more acute form."

Stalin replied on April 7 along the lines Roosevelt had anticipated. The reason for the impasse on Poland, he explained, was the effort of the American and British Ambassadors in Moscow to alter the Crimea agreement. Instead of accepting the present Polish regime as "the core of a new Government on National Unity," they were trying to create an entirely new government in which the current ruling group would play no more than a secondary role. If the Ambassadors would adhere to the provisions of the Crimea accord on Poland, the issue could be settled in a short time. "We shall have to consider most carefully the implications of Stalin's attitude and what is to be our next step," Roosevelt cabled Churchill on April 10. Still eager to assure that Churchill would not publicly agitate the issue, Roosevelt asked that they consult before anything more was said or done. At the same time, he prepared a Jefferson Day speech in which he asked the public to keep its "faith. I measure the sound, solid achievement that can be made at this time by the straight edge of your own confidence and your resolve," he declared. ". . . To all Americans who dedicate themselves with us to the making of an abiding peace, I say: The only limit to our realization of tomorrow will be our doubts of today. Let us move forward with strong and active faith." [49]

A dispute with the Russians over preliminary surrender talks with German forces in northern Italy evoked a much stronger response from FDR. In March, Allied forces in the West had driven across the Rhine, encircled the Ruhr, and reduced German strength to sixty undermanned divisions which had to contend with eighty-five superior Allied divisions backed by almost unchallenged air support. In Italy, Allied forces had advanced to a line south of Bologna. At the same time, however, Soviet forces had been stalled at the Oder River some thirty-five miles from Berlin. When Anglo-American military representatives met German officers in Switzerland to discuss arrangements for surrender talks in Italy, the Soviets asked that their representatives also take part. But fearful that the Soviets would try to delay negotiations until their final offensive in the East had achieved its tactical goals and that this would cause needless American and British losses, the Combined Chiefs denied the request. They made it clear, however, that they would welcome Soviet representatives at any later discussion in Italy of an unconditional surrender. The Soviets responded that the Allies were negotiating a German surrender in northern Italy "behind the back of the Soviet Union" and complained that this was not a case of "a misunderstanding, but something worse."

Roosevelt tried to clear the air in a message to Stalin on March 24. His assurance, however, that these were no more than preliminary discussions, which in no way violated the "agreed principle of unconditional surrender" and carried "no political implications whatever," fell on deaf ears. Stalin replied that Soviet representatives were needed in Switzerland to assure that the Germans did not use the talks to switch troops to other sectors, especially to the Soviet front. In fact, he complained, the Germans had already taken advantage of the negotiations to move three divisions from Italy to the East. Trying again to clear away the "atmosphere of regrettable apprehension and mistrust" which now surrounded the issue, Roosevelt reassured Stalin that no surrender negotiations of any kind had occurred in Switzerland and that substantive talks would take place in Italy only with Soviet representatives present. There was absolutely no intention of allowing German forces to leave the Italian front, and in fact, none had departed since the start of these talks. Stalin's information was "in error."

This did not end the clash of views. Stalin replied with accusations that astonished FDR. The President was "apparently . . . not fully informed" about the negotiations in Switzerland. They had not only taken place, Stalin asserted, they had also ended in an agreement which opened a path to the East for Anglo-American forces and promised the Germans easier armistice terms. Reflecting on the fact that Anglo-American troops were advancing rapidly against disintegrating German resistance, Stalin also complained "that the Germans on the Western front have in fact ceased the war against Britain and America. At the same time they continue the war against Russia." Repeating all his earlier assurances about the Swiss talks and adding the explanation that advances on the Western front were strictly the result of military action, Roosevelt sharply replied that "your information . . . must have come from German sources which have made persistent efforts to create dissension between us." He was astonished at Stalin's distrust of his actions and declared it potentially one of the great tragedies of history if at the moment of victory a lack of faith should prejudice the whole war effort after such colossal losses. "Frankly," he concluded, "I cannot avoid a feeling of bitter resentment toward your informers, whoever they are, for such vile misrepresentations of my actions or those of my trusted subordinates."

These exchanges convinced Roosevelt more than ever that he needed to combine accommodation with firmness in his dealings with the Soviets. Churchill agreed. "A firm and blunt stand should be made at this juncture by our two countries," he cabled FDR after reading Stalin's last message to the President. ". . . This is the best chance of saving the future. If they are ever convinced that we are afraid of them and can be bullied into submission, then indeed I should despair of our future relations with them and much else." "We must not permit anybody to entertain a false impression that we are afraid," Roosevelt replied. "Our armies will in a very few days be in a position that will permit us to become 'tougher' than has heretofore appeared advantageous to the war effort."

At the same time, Roosevelt continued to tell the Russians nothing about the atomic bomb. In mid-March he and Stimson had agreed that before the bomb was used in August he would have to decide whether to maintain an Anglo-American monopoly or introduce a system of international control. Since he had taken no step toward the latter alternative by the second week of April, it seems reasonable to conclude that he still wished to defer sharing control with the Russians until he had a stronger faith in their readiness to cooperate in other matters affecting world affairs. The bomb now probably seemed the best possible means for assuring this end.

Despite their post-Yalta difficulties, Roosevelt still believed that cooperation with Russia was within reach. Indeed, when Stalin sent him a more conciliatory response to his last message on the Swiss discussions, Roosevelt promptly thanked him and described the whole episode as a minor misunderstanding which had faded into the past. "I would minimize the general Soviet problem as much as possible," he told Churchill on April 11, "because these problems, in one form or another, seem to arise every day and most of them straighten out as in the case of the Bern meeting. We must be firm, however, and our course thus far is correct." [50]

These were Roosevelt's last messages on international affairs. In the two months after Yalta, his physical condition remained much as it had been since early in 1944. A period of hard work after returning to the United States had intensified his problems. He appeared to have lost more weight, his color was poor, and he fatigued easily. A vacation in Warm Springs, Georgia, beginning on March 29 brought a marked improvement in his condition. He regained some weight, rested well, showed better color, and was in excellent spirits. During this two-month period, as at Yalta, he remained in control of foreign affairs. Though major cables were drafted by aides, they all passed through his hands and showed a continuity with the policies he had pursued throughout the war. According to his physician, "his memory for both recent and past events was good. His behavior toward his friends and intimates was unchanged and his speech unaltered."

On April 12, 1945, the President sat perusing documents and posing for a portrait. At approximately 1:15 in the afternoon, he pressed his left hand to his temple, complained of "a terrific headache" and slumped in his chair. Dr. Howard G. Bruenn, the cardiologist who had been treating him since his hospitalization at Bethesda in March 1944, was summoned. It was quickly apparent to Bruenn that the President had suffered a massive cerebral hemorrhage. Two hours later, at 3:35 p.m., the President died. He was sixty-three years and two months old.

The news shocked and saddened people all over the world. Churchill felt as if he had been struck a physical blow; a sense of deep and irreparable loss overpowered him. In the Kremlin, Stalin greeted Harriman in silence, "holding his hand for perhaps thirty seconds before asking him to sit down." He seemed deeply distressed and questioned Harriman closely about the circumstances of the President's death. Chiang Kai-shek went into immediate mourning, leaving his breakfast meal untouched. "My Führer!" Goebbels told Hitler, "I congratulate you. Roosevelt is dead. It is written in the stars that the second half of April will be the turning point for us. This is almost Friday, April 13. It is the turning point!" In Japan, Radio Tokyo surprisingly honored "the passing of a great man" with a program of special music.[51]

Roosevelt as Foreign Policy Leader

IN THE YEARS SINCE 1945, Roosevelt has come under sharp attack for his handling of foreign affairs. To be sure, historians generally agree that he was an architect of victory in World War II, but they find little to compliment beyond that: his response to the London Economic Conference of 1933, his neutrality and peace plans of the thirties, his pre-Pearl Harbor dealings with Japan, and his wartime approach to China, France, and Russia have evoked complaints of superficiality and naïveté; his cautious reactions to the Italian conquest of Ethiopia, the demise of the Spanish Republic, Japanese expansion in China, Nazi victories from 1938 to 1941, the destruction of Europe's Jews, and apparent wartime opportunities for cementing ties with Russia, transforming China, ending colonialism, and establishing a truly effective world body have saddled him with a reputation for excessive timidity about world affairs; his indirection and guarded dealings with the public before Pearl Harbor and his secret wartime agreements have provoked charges of arbitrary leadership destructive to American democracy.

These complaints certainly have some merit. Roosevelt made his share of errors in response to foreign affairs. His acceptance of Britain's lead in dealing with the Spanish Civil War, his sanction of wiretaps and mail openings, his wartime internment of the Japanese, and his cautious response to appeals for help to Jewish victims of Nazi persecution were unnecessary and destructive compromises of legal and moral principles. Beyond these matters, however, I believe that too much has been made of Roosevelt's shortcomings and too little of the constraints under which he had to work in foreign affairs.

During the thirties, when public and congressional opinion fixed its attention on national affairs and opposed any risk of involvement in "foreign wars," Roosevelt felt compelled to rely on symbols to answer challenges and threats from abroad. His handling of the London Economic Conference, for example, was less the expression of confusion or overblown visions of curing the Depression from outside the United States than of an abortive effort to restore a measure of faith in international cooperation. Likewise, his suggestions for preserving peace during the thirties were less the product of an idealized view of world affairs than of a continuing desire to encourage leaders and peoples everywhere to work against war and, specifically, to signal aggressor nations that the United States was not indifferent to their plans.

Similarly, his acceptance of the Neutrality laws of the thirties was less an act of conviction than of realistic calculation about what he could achieve at home and abroad. Since winning congressional approval for domestic programs essential to national economic and political stability ruled out bold initiatives in foreign affairs, Roosevelt acquiesced in the widespread preference for a passive foreign policy. Instead, he aimed to meet worldwide attacks on democracy by preserving it in the United States. "You have made yourself the trustee for those in every country who seek to mend the evils of our condition by reasoned experiment within the framework of the existing social system," John Maynard Keynes, the noted economist, publicly told him in December 1933. "If you fail, rational change will be gravely prejudiced throughout the world, leaving orthodoxy and revolution to fight it out." Between 1935 and 1938, his reluctance openly to oppose aggression in Ethiopia, Spain, China, Austria, or Czechoslovakia rested not on an isolationist impulse or a desire to appease aggressors but chiefly on a determination to retain his ability to influence crucial developments at home. Roosevelt turned this influence to good account abroad. Under his leadership, a Montevideo newspaper commented, the United States had again become "the victorious emblem around which may rally the multitudes thirsting for social justice and human fraternity." "His moral authority, the degree of confidence which he inspired outside his own country," the historian Isaiah Berlin later said, ". . . has no parallel. . . . Mr. Roosevelt's example strengthened democracy everywhere." [1]

Yet Roosevelt's contribution to the survival of international democracy came not through symbolic gestures in the thirties but through substantive actions during World War II. His appreciation that effective action abroad required a reliable consensus at home and his use of dramatic events overseas to win national backing from a divided country for a series of pro-Allied steps were among the great presidential achievements of this century. In the years 1939–41 Roosevelt had to balance the country's desire to stay out of war against its contradictory impulse to assure the defeat of Nazi power. Roosevelt's solution was not to intensify the conflict by choosing one goal over the other but rather to weave the two together: the surest road to peace, he repeatedly urged the nation to believe throughout this difficult period, was material aid to the Allies. And even when he concluded that the country would eventually have to join the fighting, as I believe he did in the spring of 1941, he refused to force an unpalatable choice upon the nation by announcing for war.

Roosevelt's dissembling created an unfortunate precedent for arbitrary action in foreign affairs which subsequent Presidents have been quick to use. This consequence, however, needs to be evaluated alongside two other considerations: first, that Roosevelt's indirection forestalled a head-on clash with the Congress and majority opinion which would have weakened his ability to lead before and after Pearl Harbor; and, second, that for all his willingness to deceive the public in the interest of persuading it to go to war, he never lost sight of the fact that a national commitment to fight required events beyond his control to arrange. Indeed, what seems most striking in this period was not Roosevelt's arbitrariness in pushing the country toward war but rather his caution and restraint. For all his talk at Argentia of needing an "incident," and for all his efforts even to manufacture one in the case of the *Greer*, he refused to ask for a declaration of war until a genuine provocation from abroad made the nation ready to fight.

Did Roosevelt, then, maneuver or, at the very least, permit the country to become involved in a war with Japan as a backdoor to the European fighting? "Had FDR been determined to avoid war with the Japanese if at all possible," George Kennan has argued, "he would have conducted American policy quite differently . . . than he actually did. He would not, for example, have made an issue over Japanese policy in China, where the Japanese were preparing, anyway, to undertake a partial withdrawal . . . and where this sort of American pressure was not really essential. He would not have tried to starve the Japanese navy of oil. And he would have settled down to some hard and realistic dealings with the Japanese." [2] This picture of Roosevelt's options leaves out the domestic context in which he had to operate. The struggle against fascism in American minds was indelibly linked with China's fight against Japan. Though mindful of the advantage of concentrating American power against Berlin, Roosevelt also appreciated that opposition to Japan was an essential part of the moral imperative Americans saw for fighting. To have acquiesced in Japan's domination of China and allowed oil and other vital supplies to fuel Japan's war machine would have provoked an outcry in the United States against cynical power politics and weakened the national resolve to confront fascist power outside of the Western Hemisphere. In short, to gain a national consensus for fighting fascism overseas, Roosevelt could not discriminate between Germany and Japan; both had to be opposed at the same time.

None of this is meant to suggest that Roosevelt foresaw and accepted the surprise attack at Pearl Harbor as a necessary means of bringing a unified nation into the war. Seeing the Fleet in Hawaii as a deterrent rather than a target, lulled by the belief that the Japanese lacked the capability to strike at Pearl Harbor and by the information or "noise," as Roberta Wohlstetter calls it, indicating that an attack might come at any one of a number of points, Roosevelt, like the rest of the nation, failed to anticipate the Pearl Harbor attack. Later contentions to the contrary had less to do with the actuality of Roosevelt's actions than with isolationist efforts to justify the idea that the country had never in fact been vulnerable to attack.[3]

Historians generally give Roosevelt high marks for his direction of wartime strategy. As this and other recent studies conclude, Roosevelt was the principal architect of the basic strategic decisions that contributed so heavily to the early defeat of Germany and Japan. Commentators immediately after 1945, however, thought otherwise. Generalizing from the actualities in the last stages of the war, they described Roosevelt's thinking on wartime strategy as almost entirely a reflection of decisions reached by the Joint Chiefs. Undoubtedly for reasons of wartime unity, Roosevelt encouraged this idea, saying that he never overruled his Staff and that they had no basic differences or even minor disagreements. But the record of the years 1938–43 shows otherwise. Until the first Quebec Conference in August 1943, military historian William Emerson has written, "it is no exaggeration to say that . . . the basic decisions that molded strategy were made by the Commander-in-Chief himself, against the advice of his own chiefs and in concert with Churchill and the British chiefs." Indeed, "whenever the military advice of his chiefs clearly diverged from his own notions," Emerson also says, "Roosevelt did not hesitate to ignore or override them." In 1940, for example, when an air force planner presented detailed figures showing aid to Britain was undermining American air rearmament, "the President cut him off with a breezy 'Don't let me see that again!' " Roosevelt was rarely so blunt. With few exceptions, he masked differences with his Chiefs by having the British carry the burden of the argument. As in so many other things, this allowed him to have his way without acrimonious exchanges which could undermine his ability to lead.[4]

In his handling of major foreign policy questions as well, Roosevelt was usually his own decision-maker. Distrustful of the State Department, which he saw as conservative and rigid, he divided responsibility for foreign affairs among a variety of agencies and men. "You should go through the experience of trying to get any changes in the thinking, policy and action of the career diplomats and then you'd know what a real problem was," he once told Marriner Eccles of the Federal Reserve Board. By pitting Welles against Hull, political envoys against career diplomats, Treasury against State, Stimson against Morgenthau, and a host of other official and personal representatives against each other for influence over foreign policy, he became a court of last resort on major issues and kept control in his own hands. In 1943, for example, when George Kennan, then in charge of the American mission in Portugal, objected to Washington's method of gaining military facilities in the Azores as likely to antagonize the Portuguese government and possibly push Spain into the war on Germany's side, the State Department called him back to Washington. After a meeting with Stimson, Knox, Stettinius, and the Joint Chiefs in which he made no headway, Kennan gained access to the President, who endorsed his solution to the problem. But what about the people in the Pentagon, who seemed intent on a different course? Kennan inquired. "Oh, don't worry," said the President with a debonair wave of his cigarette holder, "about all those *people* over there."

Outwardly, Roosevelt's diplomatic appointments also suggest an *ad hoc*, disorganized approach to foreign affairs. Career diplomats, wealthy supporters of his campaign, academics, military men, journalists, and old friends made up the varied list of heads of mission abroad. But, as with major decisions on foreign policy, there was more method and purpose behind Roosevelt's selection of diplomats than meets the eye. William E. Dodd, the Jeffersonian Democrat in Berlin, signaled the President's antipathy for Nazi views and plans. Openly sympathetic to the Soviets, Bullitt and Davies had been sent to Moscow to improve relations between Russia and the United States. Nelson T. Johnson in China and Joseph C. Grew in Japan, both holdovers from the previous administration, reflected Roosevelt's desire for a continuation of the Hoover-Stimson Far Eastern policy. Joseph Kennedy, who went to London in 1938, seemed likely to keep his distance from the British government and provide critical estimates of the appeasement policy. His failure to do so disappointed and annoyed FDR. John G. Winant, a former Republican Governor of New Hampshire who succeeded Kennedy in London in 1941, reflected the President's commitment to Britain's triumph over Berlin. Standley and Harriman, both skeptics in differing degrees abovt Soviet intentions, had been sent to Moscow partly to provide a contrary perspective to the wartime euphoria about Russia. All these men were instruments of presidential purpose, expressions of Roosevelt's designs in foreign affairs.[5]

No part of Roosevelt's foreign policy has been less clearly understood than his wartime diplomacy. The portrait of him as utterly naïve or unrealistic about the Russians, for example, has been much overdrawn. Recognizing that postwar stability would require a Soviet-American accord, and that Soviet power would then extend into East-Central Europe and parts of East Asia, Roosevelt openly accepted these emerging realities in his dealings with Stalin. The suggestion that Roosevelt could have restrained this Soviet expansion through greater realism or a tougher approach to Stalin is unpersuasive. As an aftermath of World War II, George Kennan has written, no one could deny Stalin "a wide military and political *glacis* on his Western frontier . . . except at the cost of another war, which was unthinkable." Since the West could not defeat Hitler without Stalin's aid, which "placed him automatically in command of half of Europe," and since public questions about postwar

Soviet intentions would have shattered wartime unity at home and with the Russians, Roosevelt endorsed the new dimensions of Soviet power, in the hope that it would encourage future friendship with the West. As his conversation with Niels Bohr in 1944 indicated, Roosevelt also left open the question of whether he would share control of atomic power with the Russians.[6]

At the same time, however, he acted to limit the expansion of Russian power in 1945 by refusing to share the secret of the atomic bomb, agreeing to station American troops in southern Germany, endorsing Churchill's arrangements for the Balkans, working for the acquisition of American air and naval bases in the Pacific and the Atlantic, and encouraging the illusion of China as a Great Power with an eye to using her as a political counterweight to the U.S.S.R. Mindful that any emphasis on this kind of *Realpolitik* might weaken American public resolve to play an enduring role in world affairs, Roosevelt made these actions the hidden side of his diplomacy. Yet however much he kept these actions in the background, they were a significant part of his wartime Soviet policy. Hence, in the closing days of his life, when he spoke of becoming " 'tougher' [with Russia] than has heretofore appeared advantageous to the war effort," he was not suddenly departing from his conciliatory policy but rather giving emphasis to what had been there all along. Moreover, had he lived, Roosevelt would probably have moved more quickly than Truman to confront the Russians. His greater prestige and reputation as an advocate of Soviet-American friendship would have made it easier for him than for Truman to muster public support for a hard line.[7]

Did Roosevelt's equivocal wartime approach to Russia poison postwar Soviet-American relations? Many forces played a part in bringing on the Cold War, James MacGregor Burns contends, "but perhaps the most determining single factor was the gap between promise and reality that widened steadily during 1942 and 1943." Roosevelt's failure to give full rein to the policy of common goals and sacrifices by delaying a second front in France until 1944, Burns believes, aroused Soviet anger and cynicism and contributed "far more than any other factor" to the "postwar disillusionment and disunity" we call the Cold War.[8] But could Roosevelt have arranged an earlier cross-Channel attack? British opposition and want of military means, particularly landing craft, made a pre-1944 assault difficult to undertake and unlikely to succeed. Such a campaign would not only have cost more American lives, it would also have played havoc with the President's entire war strategy, undermining the nation's ability to break German and Japanese power as quickly and as inexpensively as it did.

More to the point, would an earlier, less successful or unsuccessful European attack have quieted Soviet suspicions of the West? Failure would certainly have brought forth a new round of Soviet complaints, and even a successful cross-Channel attack in 1942 or 1943 would have been no hedge against the Cold War. The Soviets, according to Adam B. Ulam, were not easily dissuaded from "their suspicions about the intentions of the Western Powers. Not the most intensive credits, not even the turning over to the Russians of sample atomic bombs could have appeased them or basically affected their policies. Suspicion was built into the Soviet system." 9

Roosevelt's thinking about China has also been imperfectly understood. Because he so often countered wartime pressures over China with glib remarks about his family ties to the China trade or exaggerated statements of China's power, Roosevelt has been described as sentimental and shallow or unrealistic about Chinese affairs. In fact, he had a good general grasp of Chinese realities, a clear conception of how he hoped to use China during and after the war, and a healthy appreciation of his limited powers to influence events there. From the beginning of American involvement in the war to the fall of 1944, when the China theater was at the bottom of the priority list, Roosevelt felt compelled to meet Chiang Kai-shek's wishes for an air campaign in China at the expense of a ground buildup and an attack in Burma. Eager to keep China going until they could make a strong effort to reopen the Burma Road and turn China into an effective base against Japan and trying to assure against serious political repercussions in the United States, Roosevelt refused to do anything that might risk a China collapse. During 1944, when it became clear that Chiang's strategy promised little Chinese help against Japan and might even lose China as a base of attack, Roosevelt pressed Chiang to give Stilwell command of all forces in China. By the fall, however, with Chiang unwilling to follow the American lead and promises of Russian help against Japan reducing the importance of effective military action by Chiang, Roosevelt gave up on expecting any significant military contribution from the Chinese.

Instead, he focused on China's postwar role. Believing that China was a valuable asset in persuading American opinion to assume a major part in world affairs and that China could be a useful balance wheel in any political test of will with the Soviets in the United Nations or in possible areas of joint occupation such as Japan and Korea, Roosevelt encouraged Great Power status for China. Since a Nationalist collapse or a civil war in China would jeopardize this plan, Roosevelt also urged the creation of a coalition regime. He appreciated that this was not easy to arrange. It was certainly clear to him that Chiang strongly opposed the idea, but he hoped that the choice between a likely collapse in a civil war against Soviet-backed Communist forces and Soviet-American support for a coalition government led by the Nationalists would persuade Chiang to pick the latter. In this, however, Roosevelt, like almost all other American political and military leaders dealing with China, mistakenly assumed that a coalition was a realizable aim. In fact, neither the United States nor the Soviet Union had the wherewithal to compel this result.

Roosevelt has been strongly criticized for uncritically backing Chiang's corrupt and doomed regime. "What should have been our aim in China," Barbara Tuchman has written, "was not to mediate or settle China's internal problem, which was utterly beyond our scope, but to preserve viable and as far as possible amicable relations with the government of China whatever it turned out to be." But Roosevelt operated under political constraints he could not easily bend or ignore. Pressure in the United States for a continued Nationalist, or at least non-Communist, government in China commanded Roosevelt's respect. As demonstrated by his concern in the fall of 1944 to prepare a defense of the administration's China policy in case of a collapse, he believed that Chiang's demise would have political consequences that could play havoc with his ability to organize the peace. Moreover, as a democratic leader concerned with checking the expansion of Soviet influence and power, he could not have welcomed the prospect of a Chinese Communist regime, however shallow, as the Soviets alleged, its Communist ties may have been. Unlike many others at the time, Roosevelt was not certain that China's Communists were simply "agrarian democrats" or "margarine" Communists. Were the Chinese Communists "real Communists" and were the Russians "bossing them?" Roosevelt asked journalist Edgar Snow in March 1945. In sum, appreciating better than either his Joint Chiefs or Stalin how little staying power Chiang might show in a civil war and determined to avoid the domestic and international problems that would flow from a Nationalist collapse, Roosevelt supported a coalition government under Chiang's control.[10]

On other major postwar questions as well, Roosevelt was more perceptive than commonly believed. His desire for a new world league with peace-keeping powers rested less on a faith in the effectiveness of Wilsonian collective security than on the belief that it was a necessary vehicle for permanently involving the United States in world affairs. Though convinced that postwar affairs would operate under a system of Great Power control, with each of the Powers holding special responsibility in their geographical spheres, Roosevelt felt compelled to obscure this idea through a United Nations organization which would satisfy widespread demand in the United States for new idealistic or universalist arrangements for assuring the peace.

His commitment to a trusteeship system for former colonies and mandates is another good example of how he used an idealistic idea to mask a concern with power. Believing that American internationalists would object to the acquisition of postwar air and naval bases for keeping the peace, Roosevelt disguised this plan by proposing that dependent territories come under the control of three or four countries designated by the United Nations. The "trustees" were to assume civil and military responsibilities for the dependent peoples until they were ready for self-rule. In this way, the United States would both secure strategic bases and assure self-determination for emerging nations around the globe.

This idea strongly influenced Roosevelt's wartime policy toward France. He opposed de Gaulle's plans for taking control in France and resurrecting the French Empire as dangerous to postwar stability in Europe and around the world. De Gaulle's assumption of power seemed likely to provoke civil strife in France, feed revolutionary movements in French African and Asian colonies longing to be free, and inhibit American or Great Power control over areas that were strategic for keeping postwar peace. Roosevelt preferred a malleable French Government ready to accept the reality of reduced French power and ultimate independence for former colonies temporarily under United Nations civil and military control.

Roosevelt's broad conception of what it would take to assure the postwar peace was fundamentally sound: a greatly expanded American role abroad, a Soviet-American accord or "peaceful coexistence," a place for a Great Power China, and an end to colonial empires have all become fixtures on the postwar world scene. But these developments emerged neither in the way nor to the extent Roosevelt had wished. His plans for a United States with substantial, but nevertheless limited, commitments abroad, an accommodation with the U.S.S.R., a stable, cooperative China, a passive France, and a smooth transition for dependent peoples from colonial to independent rule could not withstand the historical and contemporary forces ranged against them. Roosevelt was mindful of the fact that uncontrollable conditions—Soviet suspicion of the West and internal divisions in China, for example—might play havoc with his postwar plans. His decision to hold back the secret of the atomic bomb from Stalin and his preparation to meet a political storm over Chiang's collapse testify to these concerns. But his vision of what the world would need to revive and remain at peace after the war moved him to seek these ends nevertheless. That he fell short of his aims had less to do with his naïveté or idealism than with the fact that even a thoroughgoing commitment to *Realpolitik* or an exclusive reliance on power would not have significantly altered developments in Europe and Asia after the war. Russian expansion, Chinese strife, and colonial revolutions were beyond Roosevelt's power to prevent.

By contrast with these developments, external events played a central part in helping Roosevelt bring the country through the war in a mood to take a major role in overseas affairs. Much of Roosevelt's public diplomacy during the war was directed toward this goal: the portraits of an effective postwar peace-keeping body, of a friendly Soviet Union, and of a peaceful China had as much to do with creating an internationalist consensus at home as with establishing a fully effective peace system abroad. Principally influenced by Pearl Harbor, which destroyed isolationist contentions about American invulnerability to attack, and by the country's emergence as the world's foremost Power, the nation ended the war ready to shoulder substantial responsibilities in foreign affairs.

One may assume that postwar developments would not have surprised or greatly disappointed FDR. As he once told someone impatient for presidential action, Abraham Lincoln "was a sad man because he couldn't get it all at once. And nobody can. . . . You cannot, just by shouting from the housetops, get what you want all the time." [11] No doubt American willingness to play a large part in postwar international affairs would have impressed him as a major advance, while postwar world tensions would surely have stimulated him to new efforts for world peace. And no doubt, as so often during his presidency, a mixture of realism and idealism, of practical short-term goals tied to visions of long-term gains would have become the hallmark of his renewed struggle to make the world a better place in which to live.

A Note on Sources

THE STARTING POINT for any study of Franklin Roosevelt's foreign policy is the Franklin D. Roosevelt Library, Hyde Park, New York. Many of the President's significant writings and oral statements on the subject have been published in various documentary collections. I have tried as far as possible to cite the published version of these materials in my notes. As the notes demonstrate, however, the Library contains a huge body of significant unpublished manuscripts. These are broadly divided into: the Official File; the President's Personal File; the President's Secretary's File; and the Map Room Papers, which are the principal source for the war period, 1942–1945. There is also a massive alphabetical file containing correspondence from the public to the President; and there are the President's "Diaries and Itineraries," recording his daily appointments and travel schedules. These "Diaries," however, are not a complete record of the President's appointments or meetings. There are also Logs of the President's trips abroad.

The Library also contains a substantial body of valuable manuscripts for the study of foreign policy in the papers of other administration officials: Adolf A. Berle Manuscript Diary and Manuscripts; Harry Hopkins Manuscripts; John L. McCrea Manuscripts; R. Walton Moore Manuscripts; Henry Morgenthau, Jr., Farm Credit Administration Manuscript Diary; Henry Morgenthau, Jr., Manuscript Diary; Henry Morgenthau, Jr., Presidential Manuscript Diary; Harold D. Smith Manuscript Diary; Charles W. Taussig Manuscripts; and Rexford G. Tugwell Manuscript Diary.

Primary sources in other libraries and depositories used in this study are:

BRITISH PUBLIC RECORD OFFICE, LONDON, ENGLAND

Prime Minister Winston S. Churchill Manuscripts: PREMIER 3 Files: Prime Minister's Operational Files; PREMIER 4 Files: Prime Minister's Confidential Files.

Foreign Office Manuscripts: F.O. 371: Political and Diplomatic Files.

War Cabinet Documents: CAB. 65: War Cabinet Conclusions and Minutes; CAB. 66: War Cabinet Memoranda.

COLUMBIA ORAL HISTORY COLLECTIONS,
COLUMBIA UNIVERSITY, NEW YORK CITY

Thomas C. Hart, H. Kent Hewitt, Arthur Krock, Emory S. Land, Frances Perkins, William Phillips, Samuel I. Rosenman, Norman Thomas, Henry A. Wallace, James P. Warburg

HARVARD UNIVERSITY, CAMBRIDGE, MASSACHUSETTS

J. Pierrepont Moffat Manuscript Diary and Manuscripts, William Phillips Manuscript Diary, Oswald G. Villard Manuscripts

HOOVER INSTITUTION, STANFORD UNIVERSITY, STANFORD, CALIFORNIA

Raymond Moley Manuscript Diary and Manuscripts

LIBRARY OF CONGRESS, WASHINGTON, D.C.

Joseph Alsop Manuscripts, Henry H. Arnold Manuscripts, Robert W. Bingham Manuscript Diary, William Borah Manuscripts, Raymond Clapper Manuscript Diary and Manuscripts, Joseph Davies Manuscript Diary, Norman Davis Manuscripts, James Farley Manuscripts, Herbert Feis Manuscripts, Cordell Hull Manuscripts, Harold Ickes Manuscript Diary, Frank Knox Manuscripts, William D. Leahy Manuscript Diary, Breckinridge Long Manuscript Diary, George W. Norris Manuscripts

NATIONAL ARCHIVES, WASHINGTON, D.C.

Senate Foreign Relations Committee Manuscripts, File 73A-F10, Record Group 46.

State Department Manuscripts: the most significant materials for this study are published in the invaluable series, *Foreign Relations of the United States*, or are in the President's papers at Hyde Park, New York.

United States Army Manuscripts: William D. Leahy Files, Record Group 218; other significant Army Records, like the President's discussions with the Joint Chiefs, are also in the President's papers at Hyde Park, New York.

UNIVERSITY OF CALIFORNIA, BERKELEY, CALIFORNIA

Hiram W. Johnson Manuscripts

UNIVERSITY OF VIRGINIA, CHARLOTTESVILLE, VIRGINIA

Edward R. Stettinius, Jr., Manuscript Diary and Manuscripts, Edwin M. Watson Manuscripts

YALE UNIVERSITY, NEW HAVEN, CONNECTICUT

Edward M. House Manuscripts, Henry L. Stimson Manuscript Diary and Manuscripts

ABBREVIATIONS USED IN THE NOTES

AHR   American Historical Review
CAB.   British War Cabinet Documents, Public Record Office, London, England
COHC   Columbia Oral History Collections, Columbia University, New York City
FDR &   Franklin D. Roosevelt and Foreign Affairs: January 1933–January 1937. Edited by Edgar B. Nixon. 3 vols. Cambridge, Mass., 1969
FA
FDRL   Franklin D. Roosevelt Library, Hyde Park, New York
F.O.   British Foreign Office Manuscripts, Public Record Office, London, England
HAHR   The Hispanic American Historical Review
JAH   The Journal of American History
MRP   Map Room Papers, Franklin D. Roosevelt Library, Hyde Park, New York
MVHR   Mississippi Valley Historical Review
OF   Official File, Franklin D. Roosevelt Library, Hyde Park, New York
PHR   Pacific Historical Review
P.P.A.   The Public Papers and Addresses of Franklin D. Roosevelt. Edited by Samuel I. Rosenman. 13 vols. New York, 1938–1950
PPF   President's Personal File, Franklin D. Roosevelt Library, Hyde Park, New York
PREM.   Premier Files, Prime Minister Winston S. Churchill Manuscripts, Public Record Office, London, England
PSF   President's Secretary's File, Franklin D. Roosevelt Library, Hyde Park, New York

PROLOGUE

1. Frank Freidel, Franklin D. Roosevelt: The Apprenticeship (Boston, 1952), chap. 2; Rita Halle Kleeman, Gracious Lady: The Life of Sara Delano Roosevelt (New York, 1935), pp. 152–67; James MacGregor Burns, Roosevelt: The Lion and the Fox (New York, 1956), p. 5.

2. On Groton, see James McLachlan, American Boarding Schools: A Historical Study (New York, 1970), chap. 9. For Rooosevelt's experience there, see F.D.R.: His Personal Letters, edited by Elliott Roosevelt (4 vols.; New York, 1947–50), Vol. I: Early Years (New York, 1947), pp. 29–413. The best secondary accounts of the Groton years are Freidel, FDR: The Apprenticeship, chap. 3; Burns, The Lion and the Fox, pp. 10–16; Rexford G. Tugwell, The Democratic Roosevelt (Garden City, N.Y., 1957), pp. 27–38; Kenneth S. Davis, FDR: The Beckoning of Destiny, 1882–1928 (New York, 1972), pp. 101–28.

3. Freidel, FDR: The Apprenticeship, pp. 5–6; Tugwell, Democratic Roosevelt, pp. 55–6.

4. Burns, The Lion and the Fox, pp. 3–4; Tugwell, Democratic Roosevelt, pp. 24–5; Freidel, FDR: The Apprenticeship, pp. 21–3; Kleeman, Gracious Lady, chap. 9, and p. 206.

5. Freidel, FDR: The Apprenticeship, pp. 3, 6, 25–6; Kleeman, Gracious Lady, p. 222; Tugwell, Democratic Roosevelt, pp. 11–12, 27–8, 41–4.

6. F.D.R.: Personal Letters, I, 110, 230, 431; F.D.R.: His Personal Letters, Vol II: 1905–1928 (New York, 1948), p. 84; Freidel, FDR: The Apprenticeship, pp. 46, 48, 70–71, 79, 85–6; Burns, The Lion and the Fox, pp. 24–6; Tugwell, Democratic Roosevelt, pp. 41–6.

7. Freidel, FDR: The Apprenticeship, pp. 86–96, chaps. 6–7; Burns, The Lion and the Fox, pp. 29–46; Tugwell, Democratic Roosevelt, pp. 67–93.

8. Josephus Daniels, The Wilson Years: Years of Peace, 1910–1917 (Chapel Hill, N.C., 1944), p. 124; Freidel, FDR: The Apprenticeship, chap 8; Burns, The Lion and the Fox, pp. 47–50; Tugwell, Democratic Roosevelt, pp. 94–5.

9. F.D.R.: Personal Letters, Early Years, I, 4–5, 160–65, 184, 189–90, 231–3, 396–8, 470–73; Freidel, FDR: The Apprenticeship, pp 28–9, 31–2, 46–7, 49, 59–60.

10. Ibid., pp. 157–8, chap. 10; Burns, The Lion and the Fox, pp. 54–60; Tugwell, Democratic Roosevelt, pp. 105–6.

11. Freidel, FDR: The Apprenticeship, pp. 158, 172–3, chap. 13.

12. Eleanor Roosevelt, This Is My Story (New York, 1937), pp. 198–9, 232–8, 262–4, 305–6; Tugwell, Democratic Roosevelt, pp. 98–103; Burns, The Lion and the Fox, pp. 50–53; Freidel, FDR: The Apprenticeship, pp. 168–70.

13. F.D.R.: Personal Letters, 1905–1928, II, 238, 243, 256–7, 267, 270; Freidel, FDR: The Apprenticeship, chap. 14.

14. Ibid., pp. 253–62, 267, 286–92, 297–9.

15. Ibid., p. 302, chaps. 18–19.

16. Ibid., pp. 337–43; Burns, The Lion and the Fox, pp. 64–5; Tugwell, Democratic Roosevelt, pp. 106–8.

17. Freidel, FDR: The Apprenticeship, pp. 343–55, chap. 21; Burns, The Lion and the Fox, pp. 65–6; Tugwell, Democratic Roosevelt, pp. 108–9.

18. Frank Freidel, Franklin D. Roosevelt: The Ordeal (Boston, 1954), p. 52, chap. 1; Burns, The Lion and the Fox, pp. 68–9; Tugwell, Democratic Roosevelt, pp. 112–18.

19. Freidel, FDR: The Ordeal, pp. 16–19.

20. F.D.R.: Personal Letters, 1905–1928, II, 275, 313; Freidel, FDR: The Apprenticeship, pp. 265–6; Freidel, FDR: The Ordeal, chap. 4; Tugwell, Democratic Roosevelt, pp. 110–11, 119–22.

21. F.D.R.: Personal Letters, 1905–1928, II, 500–508; Freidel, FDR: The Ordeal, chap. 5; Tugwell, Democratic Roosevelt, pp. 122–9.

22. Burns, The Lion and the Fox, pp. 86–91; Freidel, FDR: The Ordeal, chap. 6; Joseph P. Lash, Eleanor and Franklin (New York, 1971), chap. 21; Elliott Roosevelt and James Brough, An Untold Story: The Roosevelts of Hyde Park (New York, 1973), pp. 91–109.

23. Freidel, FDR: The Ordeal, pp. 111–12, 115–19, chaps. 10, 12–14; Burns, The Lion and the Fox, pp. 91–9; Tugwell, Democratic Roosevelt, pp. 133–5, 144–8.

24. Freidel, *FDR: The Ordeal*, chap. 8; Roosevelt's Bok proposal, "A Plan To Preserve World Peace," is in Eleanor Roosevelt, *This I Remember* (New York, 1949), pp. 353-66.

25. "Shall We Trust Japan?," *Asia*, 23 (July 1923), 475-8, 526, 528.

26. Freidel, *FDR: The Ordeal*, pp. 237-41; Freidel, *FDR: The Apprenticeship*, chap. 16; "Our Foreign Policy: A Democratic View," *Foreign Affairs*, 6 (July 1928), 573-86.

27. Frank Freidel, *Franklin D. Roosevelt: The Triumph* (Boston, 1956), pp. 247-8.

28. *Ibid.*, pp. 248-54, 308-11; Roosevelt's speech is in the *New York Times*, Feb. 3, 1932, p. 4. On the tariff, also see *The Public Papers and Addresses of Franklin D. Roosevelt*, edited by Samuel I. Rosenman (13 vols.; New York, 1938-50), Vol. I: *The Genesis of the New Deal, 1928-1932*, pp. 723-6 (hereafter cited as *P.P.A.* with volume date).

29. *P.P.A.*: 1928-1932, pp. 756-70, 835-6; *New York Times*, Nov. 5, 1932, p. 5; Freidel, *FDR: The Triumph*, pp. 356-7; Burns, *The Lion and the Fox*, pp. 140-44; Raymond Moley, *After Seven Years* (Lincoln, Neb., 1971), pp. 45-52, 62; Frank Freidel, *Franklin D. Roosevelt: Launching the New Deal* (Boston, 1973), p. 103.

CHAPTER 1

1. Freidel, *FDR: Launching the New Deal*, pp. 102-6.

2. *P.P.A.*: 1933, p. 14.

3. On Hoover's invitation to FDR, see Robert H. Ferrell, *American Diplomacy in the Great Depression: Hoover-Stimson Foreign Policy, 1929-1933* (New Haven, 1957), chap. 7, and pp. 231-6; Arthur M. Schlesinger, Jr., *The Crisis of the Old Order, 1919-1933* (Boston, 1957), pp. 233-4, 440-43; Herbert Feis, *1933: Characters in Crisis* (Boston, 1966), chap. 3, pp. 33-4; Freidel, *FDR: Launching the New Deal*, pp. 18-23; Henry L. Stimson MS. Diary, Oct. 20, 21, Nov. 10, 13, 1932; Hoover's invitation to FDR is in *P.P.A.*: 1928-1932, pp. 873-6.

4. For the response to Hoover's invitation, see Moley, *After Seven Years*, pp. 67-72; Freidel, *FDR: Launching the New Deal*, pp. 23-30; on Moley and Tugwell, see Schlesinger, Jr., *Crisis of the Old Order*, pp. 398-401; for Roosevelt's feeling about the Hoover administration, see his Introduction to *P.P.A.*: 1933, also the note on p. 16; his letter to Hoover is in *P.P.A.*: 1928-1932, pp. 876-7.

5. Moley, *After Seven Years*, pp. 72-9; Schlesinger, Jr., *Crisis of the Old Order*, pp. 443-5; Elliot A. Rosen, "Intranationalism vs. Internationalism: The Interregnum Struggle for the Sanctity of the New Deal," *Political Science Quarterly*, 81 (June 1966), 274-80; Freidel, *FDR: Launching the New Deal*, pp. 31-6.

6. William E. Leuchtenburg, *Franklin D. Roosevelt and the New Deal, 1932-1940* (New York, 1963), chap. 2; *P.P.A.*: 1928-1932, pp. 877-84; Moley, *After Seven Years*, pp. 84-90; Rexford G. Tugwell MS. Diary: "Notes from a New Deal Diary," Dec. 20, 23, 1932; *New York Times*, Dec. 23, 1932, p. 1; Freidel, *FDR: Launching the New Deal*, pp. 36-42.

7. Feis, 1933, pp. 48-52; "We did not want the [World Economic] Conference to fail," Tugwell has written. "In fact, we felt that a great deal de-

pended on it" (Tugwell MS. Diary: "Notes from a New Deal Diary," Dec. 20, 1932); *New York Times*, Dec. 23, 1932, p. 1; Stimson MS. Diary, Dec. 22, 23, 24, 1932, and FDR to Stimson, Dec. 24, 1932, Stimson MSS; Freidel, *FDR: Launching the New Deal*, pp. 110–14.

8. For the Davis-Roosevelt relationship, see Davis to FDR, Apr. 12, 1928, July 8, Nov. 7, 1930, Feb. 25, 1931, July 4, Aug. 8, Oct. 15, Nov. 15, 18, 1932; FDR to Davis, Mar. 30, 1928, July 10, Nov. 14, 1930, Feb. 23, 1931, Aug. 22, Nov. 26, 1932, Norman Davis MSS; Tugwell MS. Diary: "Notes from a New Deal Diary," Dec. 24, 25, 26, 27, 29, 1932; Davis to Cordell Hull, Dec. 20, 1932, Davis MSS; Davis to Stimson, Dec. 28, 1932, Stimson MSS; Moley, *After Seven Years*, pp. 90–93; Freidel, *FDR: Launching the New Deal*, pp. 114–16.

9. Schlesinger, Jr., *Crisis of the Old Order*, pp. 12–15, 147, 441; Louis B. Wehle, *Hidden Threads of History: Wilson Through Roosevelt* (New York, 1953), chap. 10, esp. pp. 117–20; Orville H. Bullitt (ed.), *For the President: Personal and Secret: Correspondence Between Franklin D. Roosevelt and William C. Bullitt* (Boston, 1972), chap. 2, especially see Bullitt's cables to Wehle of Nov. 28, Dec. 2, 3, 1932, and FDR to Bullitt, Jan. 13, 1933; Freidel, *FDR: Launching the New Deal*, pp. 106–8.

10. Feis, 1933, pp. 53–63; Edgar B. Nixon (ed.), *Franklin D. Roosevelt and Foreign Affairs* (3 vols.; Cambridge, Mass., 1969), Vol. I: *January 1933– February 1934*, pp. 1–4—this three-volume collection contains the principal documents on foreign affairs in FDR's first term, 1933–37 (hereafter cited as *FDR and FA*, with the volume number); Stimson to FDR, Jan. 5, 1933, OF 20; Stimson MS. Diary, Jan. 3, 4, 5, 9, 1933; for FDR's concern about the debts, see Tugwell's comment: "F.D. tried out two ideas on me. . . . One had to do with the debts; he is evidently much worried about them. He said why not let Great Britain approach him and offer a settlement which he could make to appear reasonable? Why not start by reducing the annual payments from sixty to fifty years and make the annual meeting of these payments entirely flexible in any one year?" Tugwell MS. Diary: "Notes from a New Deal Diary," Jan. 5, 1933.

11. Freidel, *FDR: Launching the New Deal*, pp. 108–10; *Documents Diplomatiques Français*, 1932–1939 (Paris, 1966), Series I, vol. 2, 414–17.

12. Stimson MS. Diary, Jan. 15, 17, 1933, and memoranda for these dates attached to the Stimson MS. Diary; for the argument that Roosevelt did make a temporary turnabout, see Rosen, "Intranationalism vs. Internationalism," *PSQ* (June 1966), 284–92.

13. Richard E. Neustadt, *Presidential Power* (Mentor Books ed., New York, 1964), pp. 154–5; Arthur M. Schlesinger, Jr., *The Coming of the New Deal* (Boston, 1959), pp. 527–8, 583–4; Raymond Moley MS. Diary, Jan. 10, 1933; Tugwell MS. Diary: "Notes from a New Deal Diary," Jan. 17, 1933; Moley, *After Seven Years*, pp. 94–7.

14. *Ibid.*, pp. 98–101; Moley MS. Diary, Jan. 21, 1933; Stimson MS. Diary, Jan. 20, 1933; Hoover's memorandum on the conversation between himself and FDR is in Stimson's MS. Diary; "Draft of Proposed Aide Memoire for British which was rejected by Professor Moley," Jan. 20, 1933; "Copy of final Aide Memoire given to British Ambassador," Jan. 20, 1933, Stimson MSS;

Tugwell MS. Diary: "Notes from a New Deal Diary," Jan. 22, 1933; *Foreign Relations of the United States, 1933,* I (Washington, D.C., 1950), 828-9. 15. Tugwell MS. Diary: "Notes from a New Deal Diary," Jan. 23, 24, 25, 1933; *Foreign Relations, 1933,* I, 829-35, 871; *FDR and FA,* I, 5-13; *Documents on British Foreign Policy, 1919-1939,* 2nd Series, Vol. V: *1933* (London, 1956), 744-52, 769-71, cf. 772-3; on Ambassador Lindsay, see Freidel, *FDR: Launching the New Deal,* pp. 25, 107; and an unpublished manuscript, Benjamin Rhodes, "Sir Ronald Lindsay and the British View of American Politics, 1930-1939"; on the banking crisis, see Leuchtenburg, *FDR and the New Deal,* pp. 38-9; *New York Times,* Feb. 21, 1933, p. 1; cf. the Foreign Policy Association's *Foreign Policy Bulletin,* XIII (Feb. 24, 1933).

16. Schlesinger, Jr., *Crisis of the Old Order,* pp. 467-8; Schlesinger, Jr., *Coming of the New Deal,* pp. 188-94; Freidel, *FDR: Launching the New Deal,* pp. 144-7, 359-60; *The Memoirs of Cordell Hull* (2 vols.; New York, 1948), I, 155-9; Feis, *1933,* pp. 99-100; Moley, *After Seven Years,* pp. 79-81, 108-18; the memo on Moley's duties is in his papers, Box 1; for internationalist feeling that Hull's appointment would "speed action on world economics," see *New York Times,* Feb. 22, 1933, p. 1, Feb. 23, 1933, p. 16; *League of Nations Chronicle* (Mar. 1933), the editorial; cf. "Many press writers consider it extremely significant that Mr. Hull has for years strongly advocated reciprocal tariff reductions as an aid to world economic recovery" (*The Literary Digest,* 115 (Mar. 4, 1933), 8).

CHAPTER 2

1. *P.P.A.:* 1933, pp. 11-16, 61-6; Leuchtenburg, *FDR and the New Deal,* pp. 41-5; Schlesinger, Jr., *Coming of the New Deal,* chap. 1; the Lippmann quote is on p. 13; Moley's comment is in Frances Perkins, IV, 31, COHC; also see, Freidel, *FDR: Launching the New Deal,* chaps. 12-13.

2. Ferrell, *American Diplomacy in the Great Depression,* chap. 12; Robert A. Divine, *The Illusion of Neutrality* (Chicago, 1962), p. 48; *Foreign Relations, 1933,* I, 31-4, 39-41. FDR apparently had three meetings with Norman Davis about disarmament: see FDR to McIntyre, Mar. 9, 1933, OF 29; FDR, "Diary and Itineraries, 1933," Mar. 15, 16, 17, in FDRL. The press conference of March 17, 1933 is in *FDR and FA,* I, 25-6; Douglas MacArthur, *Reminiscences* (New York, 1964), p. 101.

3. *Foreign Relations, 1933,* I, 40-41, 67-8, 474-86, 489-90; *FDR and FA,* I, 24, 42; *P.P.A.:* 1933, pp. 116-18.

4. Moley, *After Seven Years,* pp. 156-61, 196-201; Moley MS. Diary, Mar. 22, Apr. 10, 17, May 6, 1933; Feis, *1933,* chap. 12; Tugwell MS. Diary: "Expanded Form, 1932-1934," pp. 21-3; "Addendum to Diary for Hundred Days," pp. 8-10; *P.P.A.:* 1933, pp. 100-101, 137-41; Hull, *Memoirs,* I, 246-9; *League of Nations Chronicle* (Apr. 1933); Schlesinger, Jr., *Coming of the New Deal,* pp. 179-205; Freidel, *FDR: Launching the New Deal,* chaps. 19 and 21.

5. See Ferrell, *American Diplomacy in the Great Depression,* chap. 13, on Hoover's Latin American policy. For the background to Roosevelt's speech, see Charles C. Griffin, "Welles to Roosevelt: A Memorandum on Inter-American Relations, 1933," *HAHR,* XXXIV (May 1954), 190-92; also see

Welles to LeHand and to FDR, Oct. 6, 1932, and draft address on Pan-American Affairs, 37/29, Moley MSS; Welles to FDR, Dec. 19, 1932, OF 470. The address itself is in *P.P.A.*: 1933, pp. 129–33.

6. Edward M. Bennett, *Recognition of Russia: An American Foreign Policy Dilemma* (Waltham, Mass., 1970), pp. 87–104; McIntyre memorandum, March 31, 1933, OF 220a; "Confidential Memorandum for the President," April 7, 1933, 37c/14; Frankfurter to Moley, Feb. 23, 1933, 37a/23, Moley MSS; Henry Morgenthau Farm Credit Administration MS. Diary, May 2, 9, 15, 1933; FDR, "Diary and Itineraries, 1933," April 14; *FDR and FA*, I, 55.

7. Tugwell, "What the World Economic Conference Can Do," New York *Herald Tribune*, Apr. 12, 1933; Tugwell MS. Diary: "The Hundred Days," April 14, 1933; *Foreign Relations*, 1933, I, 576; Schlesinger, Jr., *Coming of the New Deal*, pp. 204–6.

8. Moley, *After Seven Years*, pp. 202–7; Moley MS. Diary, Apr. 21–29, 1933; Tugwell MS. Diary: "Notes from a New Deal Diary," Apr. 26, May 3, 1933; Feis, 1933, pp. 121–2, 134–7, 142–8; James P. Warburg, Mar. 15, 30, Apr. 4, 13, 18, 21, 24, 29, 1933, COHC; *Foreign Relations*, 1933, I, 497–9, 578–80; *FDR and FA*, I, 35–9, 78–89; *P.P.A.*: 1933, pp. 147–9, 150–52, 158–9, 167; Freidel, *FDR: Launching the New Deal*, chap. 22; New York *Times*, Apr. 16, 1933, IV, 1, 3.

9. *Foreign Relations*, 1933, I, 43–54, 89–104, 106–7, 109–12, 121–6, 130–32, 138–42, 150–51, 154–8; *P.P.A.*: 1933, 185–93; Morgenthau Farm Credit Administration MS. Diary, May 15, 22, 1933; Moley MS. Diary, May 15, 1933; Alan Bullock, *Hitler: A Study in Tyranny* (New York, 1961), pp. 276–7; Freidel, *FDR: Launching the New Deal*, pp. 372–5, 377, 379–83, 399–407.

10. For evidence of this attitude and these hopes, see Ernest K. Lindley, *The Roosevelt Revolution* (New York, 1933), p. 182; Anne O'Hare McCormick, *The World at Home*, edited by M. T. Sheehan (New York, 1956), pp. 194–5; *Foreign Relations*, 1933, I, 151–3; New York *Times*, May 17, 1933, pp. 1 and 3, May 18, 1933, p. 5, May 22, 1933, p. 2, May 23, 1933, pp. 1 and 4, June 4, 1933, VI, 3; *League of Nations Chronicle* (May 1933), editorial by Clark Eichelberger; *Foreign Policy Bulletin*, XII (May 26, 1933), article by Raymond L. Buell; *FDR and FA*, I, 148, 161–2.

11. Congressman Joe H. Eagle to FDR, Apr. 24, 1933; Stephen Early, "For the Information of Senator Robinson," Apr. 28, 1933; Congressman Edward W. Pou to FDR, May 1, 1933, OF 212; *FDR and FA*, I, 93–5, 98–101, 111–12, 153–5; Freidel, *FDR: Launching the New Deal*, pp. 454, 458–9.

12. *FDR and FA*, I, 98–101, 117–18, 162–4, 170–71; *Foreign Relations*, 1933, I, 578–607, 610; Moley, *After Seven Years*, pp. 196–8.

13. MacDonald to FDR, May 25, 1933, in Moley MSS; *Foreign Relations*, 1933, I, 606–7; Moley, *After Seven Years*, pp. 215–16.

14. *Ibid.*, pp. 207–9, 406–14; Freidel, *FDR: Launching the New Deal*, pp. 460–61.

15. *Foreign Relations*, 1933, I, 607–11, 620–27. James Warburg drafted the instructions to the delegates and the resolutions on his own initiative and gave a copy of them to Moley on May 24. After FDR read them, he "expressed gratification and complimented me on the drawing of the instructions, which he said were not only just what he would have wanted me to say him-

self, but that I seemed to have stolen his language" (James Warburg, May 23–26, 1933, COHC).

16. On Roosevelt's casualness about selecting a delegation, see Schlesinger, Jr., *Coming of the New Deal*, pp. 208–9; Tugwell MS. Diary: "The World Economic Conference," p. 6; Moley, *After Seven Years*, pp. 217–18; Freidel, *FDR: Launching the New Deal*, pp. 461–2. Roosevelt tried unsuccessfully to persuade isolationist Senator Hiram Johnson to become a delegate. Johnson to Hiram Johnson, Jr., May 21, 24, 26, 1933, Johnson MSS.

17. The best accounts of these events are in Divine, *Illusion of Neutrality*, pp. 41–56; and Robert A. Divine, "Franklin D. Roosevelt and Collective Security, 1933," MVHR, XLVIII (June 1961), 42-59. I do not, however, share Divine's conclusion that Roosevelt "evidently" failed to realize that an impartial embargo invalidated the Davis pledge. Much the key to Roosevelt's thinking here, I believe, was revealed in his statement to Congressman McReynolds that while he was not happy with an impartial embargo, he nevertheless saw it as a step in the right direction. Divine cites this conversation in his article on p. 56, fn. 48. The relevant sources for these events are in *Foreign Relations, 1933*, I, 364–7, 369–78; *FDR and FA*, I, 28, 184, 198; Hull, *Memoirs*, I, 222–30; *New York Times*, May 25, 1933, p. 1, May 26, 1933, p. 3, May 30, 1933, p. 4.

18. *Foreign Relations, 1933*, I, 165–6, 396–416.

19. *FDR and FA*, I, 201–4, 210–11, 226–7, 228–35; *Foreign Relations, 1933*, I, 838–42.

20. *New York Times*, May 28, 1933, p. 1; *Foreign Relations, 1933*, I, 923–4, 629–34; Hull, *Memoirs*, I, 249–55; *FDR and FA*, I, 214–19, 237–9; Moley, *After Seven Years*, pp. 224–7; Freidel, *FDR: Launching the New Deal*, pp. 462–7.

21. *Foreign Relations, 1933*, I, 641–55; Robert W. Bingham MS. Diary, June 12, 26, 29, 1933; Fred L. Israel, *Nevada's Key Pittman* (Lincoln, Neb., 1963), pp. 89–90; Moley, *After Seven Years*, pp. 222–36; Feis, *1933*, pp. 178–87; *FDR and FA*, I, 250–51; FDR to Welles, June 24, 1933, OF 470; Schlesinger, Jr., *Coming of the New Deal*, pp. 213–17; Freidel, *FDR: Launching the New Deal*, pp. 467–9, 471–2.

22. *Foreign Relations, 1933*, I, 656–68, 671–2; Moley, *After Seven Years*, pp. 237–53; Feis, *1933*, pp. 190–94, 198–219; Hull, *Memoirs*, I, 259–61; *FDR and FA*, I, 253–4; Schlesinger, Jr., *Coming of the New Deal*, pp. 217–18; Freidel, *FDR: Launching the New Deal*, pp. 472–8.

23. *Foreign Relations, 1933*, I, 666–71, 673–4; Moley, *After Seven Years*, pp. 254–61; Moley MS. Diary, June 28–July 3, 1933; Feis, *1933*, pp. 219–33; Hull, *Memoirs*, I, 261–2, 266–9; Morgenthau Farm Credit Administration MS. Diary, June 29, 30, July 2, 1933; James A. Farley, *Jim Farley's Story* (New York, 1948), pp. 40–41; Charles Hurd, *When the New Deal Was Young and Gay* (New York, 1965), chap. 12, esp. pp. 168–9; James Warburg, June 29, July 1–3, 1933, COHC; P.P.A.: *1933*, pp. 264–6; *FDR and FA*, I, 273–9, 281–3, 298–301; Schlesinger, Jr., *Coming of the New Deal*, pp. 181–2, 219–24, 230–32; Freidel, *FDR: Launching the New Deal*, pp. 478–84, 486–9, 491–5.

24. *Foreign Relations, 1933*, I, 673, 675–98, 703–4, 734–5; Moley, *After

Seven Years, pp. 261–9; Moley MS. Diary, July 4–14, 1933; Hull, *Memoirs,* I, 262–7; Feis, *1933,* chap. 20; James Warburg, July 3, 1933, COHC; *FDR and FA,* I, 289–94, 298–301, 305–9; Schlesinger, Jr., *Coming of the New Deal,* pp. 224–30; Freidel, *FDR: Launching the New Deal,* pp. 484–5, 490–91; Robert W. Bingham MS. Diary, July 24, 1933.

25. Moley, *After Seven Years,* p. 191; Schlesinger, Jr., *Coming of the New Deal,* pp. 20–23; Tugwell, *Democratic Roosevelt,* p. 292; Morgenthau Farm Credit Administration MS. Diary, May 9, 15, 22, 1933.

CHAPTER 3

1. Freidel, *FDR: Launching the New Deal,* chap. 16; *P.P.A.: 1934,* pp. 11–12; Bryce Wood, *The Making of the Good Neighbor Policy* (New York, 1961), pp. 48–59; *Time,* XXI (May 15, 1933), 18–19.

2. *New York Times,* Aug. 20, 1933, VI, 3; *Foreign Relations of the United States, 1933,* V (Washington, D.C., 1952), 279–86, 310–11, 336–48, 352–3, 358–60; Hull, *Memoirs,* I, 312–14; Welles to FDR, May 18, 1933; FDR to Welles, June 9, 24, 1933, OF 470; *FDR and FA,* I, 218, 349–51; Wood, *Good Neighbor Policy,* pp. 59–69; E. David Cronon, "Interpreting the New Good Neighbor Policy: The Cuban Crisis of 1933," HAHR, 39 (Nov. 1959), 538–44; Irwin F. Gellman, *Roosevelt and Batista: Good Neighbor Diplomacy in Cuba, 1933–1945* (Albuquerque, N.M., 1973), chap. 2.

3. Hull, *Memoirs,* I, 308–10; Leuchtenburg, *FDR and the New Deal,* pp. 64–80; Schlesinger, Jr., *Coming of the New Deal,* pp. 64–7, chaps. 7 and 8; *FDR and FA,* I, 331–2, 373.

4. *Foreign Relations, 1933,* V, 363–5, 367–9, 371–3, 376–8, 380–90, 396–8, 402, 405–7, 410; *FDR and FA,* I, 385–92; Hull, *Memoirs,* I, 314–16; *Time,* XXII (Sept. 18, 1933), 10; Wood, *Good Neighbor Policy,* pp. 69–75; Cronon, "Interpreting the New Good Neighbor Policy," HAHR (Nov. 1959), 545–52; Gellman, *Roosevelt and Batista,* chap. 3.

5. *Time,* XXII (Sept. 18, 1933), 18; *Foreign Relations, 1933,* V, 416–18, 422–4, 433–5, 451–5, 469–74, 482, 515, 519–21, 523–6; *Foreign Relations of the United States, 1933,* IV (Washington, D.C., 1950), 40–41; *FDR and FA,* I, 409–10; Hull, *Memoirs,* I, 316–17; William Phillips MS. Diary, Nov. 6, 19, 22, 23, 1933; *P.P.A.: 1933,* pp. 499–501; Wood, *Good Neighbor Policy,* pp. 75–98; Cronon, "Interpreting the New Good Neighbor Policy," HAHR (Nov. 1959), 553–60, 564–7; Gellman, *Roosevelt and Batista,* pp. 55–72; Welles's version of these events is in Sumner Welles, *The Time for Decision* (New York, 1944), pp. 193–9.

6. *Foreign Relations, 1933,* IV, 8, 16–36; *FDR and FA,* I, 363–4, 432–3, 459–60, 469–79; J. Pierrepont Moffat MS. Diary, Sept. 22, 1933; Cronon, "Interpreting the New Good Neighbor Policy," HAHR (Nov. 1959), 557–9; Josephus Daniels to FDR, Sept. 9, 1933, OF 237; Hull to FDR, Oct. 27, 1933, PSF: Hull; William Phillips MS. Diary, Oct. 30, 1933; Hull, *Memoirs,* I, 317–19.

7. Moffat MS. Diary, July 3, 6, Aug. 16, 17, Oct. 9, 1933; *FDR and FA,* I, 281–4, 291, 317–20, 358–9, 394–5, 410–11, 421–2; Davis to Stephen Early, Sept. 5, 1933, OF 29; Robert W. Bingham MS. Diary, Sept. 6, 1933; *Foreign Relations, 1933,* I, 208–11, 245–7, 266–7, 281–6; *P.P.A.: 1933,* pp. 393–5.

8. *Foreign Relations, 1933*, I, 273–7, 289–91, 296–300; Moffat MS. Diary, Oct. 16, 24, 1933.

9. *Foreign Relations, 1933*, I, 319–21, 327–8, 330–32; FDR to Ruth Morgan, Dec. 22, 1922, PPF 919; Moffat Ms. Diary, Nov. 16, 17, Dec. 8, 1933; *FDR and FA*, I, 430, 457–8, 484–5, 558–64.

10. K. C. Blackburn to Early, Jan. 5, 8, 1934, OF 1275; R. L. Buell's comment on FDR's speech in *Foreign Policy Bulletin*, XIII (Jan. 5, 1934); *FDR and FA*, I, 589–91, 603–5, 622–6; *Foreign Relations of the United States, 1934*, I (Washington, D.C., 1951), 4, 18, 22–4, 33–8, 44–5; William Phillips MS. Diary, Jan. 31, Feb. 20, 1934; Moffat MS. Diary, Feb. 21, 22, 28, 1934; *FDR and FA*, Vol. II: *March 1934–August 1935*, pp. 3–5, 30–31; J. W. Wheeler-Bennett, *The Pipe Dream of Peace* (New York, 1935), pp. 214–18.

11. FDR Memo to Moley, Mar. 18, 1933, Moley MSS; Hiram Johnson to Hiram Johnson, Jr., April 1, 1933, Johnson MSS; *FDR and FA*, I, 539, 581–2, 598–9; Louis Howe memo, n.d., OF 202; FDR to Phillips, Jan. 2, 1934, OF 66; Resolution of Delegates to the Ninth Conference on the Cause and Cure of War, Jan. 17, 1934, OF 202a; Moffat MS. Diary, Mar. 22, 1934; D. F. Fleming, *The United States and the World Court* (Garden City, N.Y., 1945), pp. 108–16; for the hearings, see Senate Foreign Relations Committee MSS, File 73A-F10, Record Group 46, National Archives.

12. *FDR and FA*, I, 610–13, 618; Moffat MS. Diary, Feb. 15, 16, 28, 1934; William Phillips MS. Diary, Feb. 16, 1934; Divine, *Illusion of Neutrality*, pp. 58–60.

13. *FDR and FA*, I, 273–83, 298, 321, 325–8, 362–3, 382–3, 413–14, 416, 435–6, 483–4, 486, 495–7, 517–19, 521–3, 537–8; *FDR: His Personal Letters, 1928–1945* (2 vols.; New York, 1950), I, 361–2, 364–7, 371–3; *P.P.A.: 1933*, pp. 420–29; *P.P.A.: 1934*, pp. 67–76; John Morton Blum, *From the Morgenthau Diaries: Years of Crisis, 1928–1938* (Boston, 1959), pp. 61–77; Leuchtenburg, *FDR and the New Deal*, pp. 78–82; Schlesinger, Jr., *Coming of the New Deal*, pp. 233–48.

14. *FDR and FA*, I, 361, 404–6, 412–13, 420–21, 456–7, 465–6, 468–9, 512–13, 531–4; *FDR and FA*, II, 119; *The Secret Diary of Harold L. Ickes: The First Thousand Days* (New York, 1953), pp. 106–7; *Foreign Relations, 1933*, I, 842–5, 881–3, 892–3; William Phillips MS. Diary, Nov. 6, 1933.

15. For Roosevelt's attitude toward a federal role in collecting on private loans, see *FDR and FA*, I, 115–17, 151–3, 334–6, 338, 396–9, 408–9, 417–18, 462–4; *P.P.A.: 1933*, pp. 411–15; Feis, *1933*, pp. 266–78.

16. For Roosevelt's support of the Johnson bill, see *FDR and FA*, I, 514–15, 598–600, 615–16; *FDR and FA*, II, 26–7; *Foreign Relations, 1934*, I, 525–7; Hiram Johnson to FDR, Jan. 29, 1934, OF 242; Johnson to Moore, Feb. 28, 1934; Moore to Johnson, Mar. 1, 7, 1934; Moore to Hackworth, Mar. 10, 1934; Moore to Phillips, Mar. 21, 1934, Moore MSS; Hiram Johnson to Hiram Johnson, Jr., Feb. 4, 11, May 13, 1934, Johnson MSS; Bullitt to FDR, Feb. 22, 1939, PSF: France: Bullitt; J. Carl Vinson, "War Debts and Peace Legislation: The Johnson Act of 1934," *Mid-America*, 50 (July 1968), 206–22, esp. 214–15, 221.

17. Claude Swanson to FDR, Apr. 5, 1933; Early to Swanson, Apr. 22,

1933; Swanson to Early, May 9, 1933; FDR to Swanson, Aug. 19, 1933; Henry L. Roosevelt to FDR, Dec. 22, 1933, OF 18; Rev. Malcolm Peabody to FDR, Aug. 14, 1933; Carl Vinson to FDR, June 3, 1933, OF 197; Moffat MS. Diary, Dec. 8, 1933; FDR and FA, I, 68–9, 177–80, 370; FDR and FA, II, 8–11; Foreign Relations of the United States, 1933, III (Washington, D.C., 1949), 253–4, 421–8, 434–8, 458–63, 483–4; Foreign Relations of the United States: The Soviet Union, 1933–1939 (Washington, D.C., 1952), pp. 53–62; Foreign Relations, 1934, I, 217–20; George V. Fagan, "FDR and Naval Limitation," United States Naval Institute Proceedings, 81 (Apr. 1955), 411–18; Adm. Emory S. Land, pp. 124–6, COHC; Waldo H. Heinrichs, Jr., "The Role of the United States Navy," in Pearl Harbor as History: Japanese-American Relations, 1931–1941, edited by Dorothy Borg and Shumpei Okamoto (New York, 1973), pp. 207–8.

18. Moffat MS. Diary, Nov. 17, 1933; FDR and FA, I, 549–51, 627; FDR to Henry L. Roosevelt, Feb. 2, 1934, OF 18; Hull to FDR, Feb. 21, 1934, OF 404a; FDR and FA, II, 31; P.P.A.: 1934, pp. 172–3.

19. James C. Thomson, Jr., "The Role of the State Department," in Pearl Harbor as History, pp. 82, 87–8; for a detailed discussion of this policy, see Dorothy Borg, The United States and the Far Eastern Crisis of 1933–1938 (Cambridge, Mass., 1964), chaps. 1 and 2.

20. Foreign Relations, 1933, III, 260–61, 265; FDR and FA, I, 103–7, 188–9, 214.

21. Borg, U.S. and Far Eastern Crisis of 1933–1938, pp. 55–88.

CHAPTER 4

1. Leuchtenburg, FDR and the New Deal, pp. 205–6; Blum, From the Morgenthau Diaries, 1928–1938, chap. 1, and p. 54.

2. Morgenthau Farm Credit Administration MS. Diary, Sept. 26, 27, Oct. 18, 19, 1933.

3. Phillips to FDR, Oct. 19, 1933; press release, American Foundation, Oct. 30, 1933; Walter G. Hooke to McIntyre, Oct. 15, 1933; McIntyre to FDR, Oct. 30, 1933, OF 220; FDR to Bullitt, Oct. 16, 1933, OF 799; Edmund A. Walsh to McIntyre, Oct. 21, 1933; McIntyre to Walsh, Oct. 30, 1933, OF 220A; Raymond Clapper MS. Diary, Nov. 29, 1933; Moore to Bullitt, Sept. 27, 1933; Moore memoranda, Oct. 28, 30, 1933; Moore, "Notes of Conference," Oct. 30, 1933, Moore MSS; Foreign Relations: The Soviet Union, 1933–1939, pp. 6–18; FDR and FA, I, 434, n.1; Bennett, Recognition of Russia, pp. 87–114; George Q. Flynn, American Catholics and the Roosevelt Presidency, 1932–1936 (Lexington, Ky., 1968), chap. 7; Robert P. Browder, The Origins of Soviet-American Diplomacy (Princeton, 1953), chap. 5; Feis, 1933, pp. 307–16.

4. Morgenthau Farm Credit Administration MS. Diary, Oct. 23, Nov. 6, 1933; Moore, three memoranda of Nov. 9, 1933, and one of Nov. 10, 1933, Moore MSS; William Phillips MS. Diary, Nov. 10, 11, 13, 16, 1933; Foreign Relations: The Soviet Union, 1933–1939, pp. 25–37; Frances Perkins, IV, 541–9, VIII, 315, 317, COHC; Henry Wallace, II, 267–8, COHC; Bennett, Recognition of Russia, pp. 88–9, 114–38; Browder, Origins of Soviet-American Diplomacy, chap. 6, and pp. 169–75; Feis, 1933, pp. 316–28;

Peter G. Filene, *Americans and the Soviet Experiment, 1917–1933* (Cambridge, Mass., 1967), pp. 259–67, 271–6.

5. Alfred B. Rollins, Jr., *Roosevelt and Howe* (New York, 1962), pp. 399–401; Hull, *Memoirs*, I, 319–41; *Foreign Relations, 1933*, IV, 42–3, 157, 159–66, 168–9, 171, 173–4, 177–90, 192–4, 196, 199–203, 207; *FDR and FA*, I, 525, 552–3; Hull, "Some of the Results of the Montevideo Conference," Feb. 10, 1934, OF 567; Julius W. Pratt, *Cordell Hull* (2 vols.; New York, 1964), I, 152–63; *Time*, XXII (Dec. 18, 1933), 12.

6. *FDR and FA*, I, 559–60.

7. *Ibid.*, 482–3, 519–21, 541–2, 544–6; *FDR and FA*, II, 1–3, 32, 120–24, 150–55; William Phillips MS. Diary, Nov. 4, 13, Dec. 4, 11, 28, 1933, Feb. 27, 1934; FDR to Hull, Oct. 30, 1933; FDR to Phillips, Nov. 22, 1933, OF 970; "Distribution of Newspapers Expressing Opinion on Reciprocal Tariff Bill, 1934," OF 60; Hull, *Memoirs*, I, chap. 26, and p. 370; Schlesinger, Jr., *Coming of the New Deal*, pp. 83–4, 253–9; Leuchtenburg, *FDR and the New Deal*, pp. 203–5.

8. *Ibid.*, pp. 78, 93–4; "Things are going damn well at this particular time" FDR told a group of Senators on April 14, 1934, "The President's Conference with the Senators," PSF:U.S. Senate; *League of Nations Chronicle* (May 1934).

9. Robert H. Ferrell, "The Peace Movement," *Isolation and Security*, edited by Alexander DeConde (Durham, N.C., 1957), chap. 4; Laurence S. Wittner, *Rebels Against War: The American Peace Movement, 1941–1960* (New York, 1969), chap. 1; "Arms and the Men," *Fortune*, IX (Mar. 1934), 53–7, 113–26; John E. Wiltz, *In Search of Peace: The Senate Munitions Inquiry, 1934–1936* (Baton Rouge, La., 1963), chap. 1, and pp. 24–6, 32–7; Divine, *Illusion of Neutrality*, pp. 62–7; Dorothy Detzer, *Appointment on the Hill* (New York, 1948), chap. 11; Wayne S. Cole, *Senator Gerald P. Nye and American Foreign Relations* (Minneapolis, 1962), pp. 65–8.

10. Moffat MS. Diary, May 15, 18, 1934; *FDR and FA*, II, 111–12.

11. *Foreign Relations of the United States, 1934*, V (Washington, D.C. 1951), 98–107, 110, 169–75, 177, 182; Wood, *Good Neighbor Policy*, pp. 98–112; *FDR and FA*, I, 593, 663–4; *FDR and FA*, II, 21, 138–9, 156–7, 162–5, 220–21; *P.P.A.: 1934*, pp. 86–90, 270–71, 319–20, 341–4, 346–9; William Phillips MS. Diary, Jan. 14, 19, 1934; Hull to FDR, Apr. 16, 1934; Memorandum to FDR, June 26, 1934, OF 162; Dana G. Munro, "The American Withdrawal from Haiti, 1929–1934," *HAHR*, 49 (Feb. 1969), 1–26, esp. 22–5; Hull to FDR, July 28, 1934; Welles to FDR, Sept. 19, 1934, OF 159; *Time*, XXIV (July 23, 1934), 9.

12. Borg, *U.S. and Far Eastern Crisis of 1933–1938*, pp. 102–3; Heinrichs, "Role of the Navy," in Borg and Okamoto, *Pearl Harbor as History*, pp. 210–11; Robert W. Bingham MS. Diary, Feb. 20, 1934; *FDR and FA*, II, 16–19, 71–9, 88–90; William Phillips MS. Diary, Jan. 31, May 8, 24, 1934; Moffat MS. Diary, Mar. 16, May 9, 24, 1934; memorandum of conversation between FDR, Davis, and Hull, Apr. 28, 1934, Davis MSS; *Foreign Relations, 1934*, I, 222–5, 237–8; Stephen Pelz, *Race to Pearl Harbor: The Failure of the Second London Naval Conference and the Onset of World War II* (Cambridge, Mass., 1974), pp. 85–6, 117–18.

13. FDR and FA, II, 134-6, 160-62; William Phillips MS. Diary, June 26, 1934; Moffat MS. Diary, June 28, 1934; Foreign Relations, 1934, I, 266-7, 269, 272-7, 284, 289-90; Borg, U.S. and Far Eastern Crisis of 1933-1938, pp. 103-5; Pelz, Race to Pearl Harbor, pp. 119-22.

14. FDR and FA, II, 216-17, 222-3, 225-9, 248, 250-54, 258-61, 263, 273, 290-93, 309, notes 4 and 5, 322-3, 325-7; Moffat MS. Diary, Sept. 28, Oct. 3, 30, 1934; William Phillips MS. Diary, Oct. 15, Dec. 22, 1934; Foreign Relations, 1934, I, 314-15, 323-4, 355-9, 390-91, 420-21; Foreign Relations of the United States: Japan, 1931-1941, I (Washington, D.C., 1943), 269-71; Borg, U.S. and Far Eastern Crisis of 1933-1938, pp. 105-12; Pelz, Race to Pearl Harbor, chaps. 9-10.

15. Foreign Relations of the United States, 1935, I (Washington, D.C., 1952), 79-80; FDR and FA, II, 375, 439-40, 443-5, 514-16, 573; Time, XXV (Apr. 8, 1935), 38; (Apr. 15, 1935), 14.

16. Foreign Relations, 1935, I, 134-8, 144-9; Pelz, Race to Pearl Harbor, chap. 11; Heinrichs, Jr., "Role of the U.S. Navy," in Borg and Okamoto, Pearl Harbor as History, p. 215.

17. Pelz, Race to Pearl Harbor, p. 202; FDR and FA, III: September 1935-January 1937, pp. 201-2, 228-31, 248-52, 271-2, 280-81; Mabel Vernon to McIntyre, Mar. 11, 1936, OF 394; W. W. Van Kirk to FDR, Mar. 17, 1936, OF 2020.

18. FDR and FA, II, 210-14, 391; R. Walton Moore memo, Sept. 14, 1934, Moore MSS; Foreign Relations, 1934, I, 476-8, 487-8, 191-3; Wiltz, In Search of Peace, pp. 160-64; Foreign Relations: The Soviet Union, 1933-1939, pp. 140-42; Bennett, Recognition of Russia, pp. 197-9.

19. FDR and FA, II, 165-7, 172-5, 180-81, 186-7, 192, 207-9, 222-3, 232-5, 274-7, 304, 334.

20. Ibid., 255-6, 267-74, 282-6, 312-15, 319-22, 324; Rexford G. Tugwell MS. Diary: "6 March '34-31 December '34, Part II," Nov. 23-4, 26, 1934; Hull, Memoirs, I, 370-74.

21. Ibid., pp. 374-7; FDR: Personal Letters, 1928-1945, I, 518-24; FDR and FA, III, 92-4, 119-20; Power Chu, "A History of the Hull Trade Program, 1934-1939" (unpublished Ph.D. dissertation, Columbia University, 1957); William R. Allen, "Cordell Hull and the Defense of the Trade Agreements Program, 1934-1940," Isolation and Security, edited by DeConde, pp. 107-32, esp. pp. 128-32; Schlesinger, Jr., Coming of the New Deal, pp. 257-60; Leuchtenburg, FDR and the New Deal, pp. 204-5.

22. Blum, From the Morgenthau Diaries, 1928-1938, pp. 183-4, the quotes are on pp. 184 and 186; cf. Leuchtenburg, FDR and the New Deal, pp. 82-4.

23. Borg, U.S. and Far Eastern Crisis of 1933-1938, pp. 121-7; FDR and FA, II, 305-6; Morgenthau MS. Diary 3: 305; Fred I. Kent to FDR, July 24, 1935; FDR to Kent, July 26, 1935, PPF 744.

24. Borg, U.S. and Far Eastern Crisis of 1933-1938, pp. 127-37; Blum, From the Morgenthau Diaries, 1928-1938, pp. 204-28.

25. FDR and FA, II, 333, 335-43, 346-51, 353-7, 363-4; Moffat MS. Diary, Sept. 5, 14, Dec. 28, 1934; William Phillips MS. Diary, Dec. 28, 1934, Jan. 5, 9, 1935; R. Walton Moore, memo on the Court and the

League, Jan. 3, 1935, Moore MSS; Hiram Johnson to Hiram Johnson, Jr., Dec. 22, 1934, Jan. 21, 1935, Johnson MSS; Hull, *Memoirs*, I, 388.

26. Fleming, *The U.S. and the World Court*, pp. 117–37; *FDR and FA*, II, 356; *Time*, XXV (Feb. 11, 1935), 13–14; for grass roots opposition to the Court, see correspondence to Senator George W. Norris in Tray 13, Box 7, Norris MSS; also see James A. Farley to Louis Howe, Jan. 29, 1935; clippings from the St. Louis *Star-Times*, Jan. 29, 31, 1935, OF 202a; and Henry Wallace, II, 373, COHC.

27. *FDR and FA*, II, 363–4, 372–4, 376–7.

28. Hiram Johnson to Hiram Johnson, Jr., Jan. 31, 1935, Johnson MSS; *Time*, XXV (Feb. 11, 1935), 14–15; Hull, *Memoirs*, I, 389; Leuchtenburg, *FDR and the New Deal*, pp. 215–17; *FDR and FA*, II, 380–81, 386–7; William Phillips MS. Diary, Jan. 30, 31, Feb. 1, 1935; *FDR: Personal Letters, 1928–1945*, I, 449–52.

CHAPTER 5

1. *FDR and FA*, II, 437–8.

2. O. G. Villard to Hull, Apr. 22, 1935, Villard MSS; *FDR and FA*, II, 395–6; Walter W. Van Kirk to FDR, Mar. 8, 1935, OF 394; *Time*, XXV (Apr. 8, 1935), 38; (Apr. 15, 1935), 14; (Apr. 22, 1935), 30–32; Joseph P. Lash, *The Campus Strike Against War* (New York, 1935), esp. pp. 5, 17, 37–8.

3. Divine, *Illusion of Neutrality*, chap. 4; Moore to Bullitt, Apr. 18, 1935, Moore MSS; and Early to LeHand, Apr. 19, 1935, OF 1275, provide evidence on the demand for neutrality; the debate in the administration over neutrality is illustrated by Norman Davis to FDR, Feb. 23, 1934, Davis MSS; the material in boxes 3 and 12 of the R. Walton Moore MSS; and in OF 1561 of the President's papers.

4. *Foreign Relations*, 1935, I, 363–4; Morgenthau MS. Diary 4: 112; William Phillips MS. Diary, Mar. 22, 1935; FDR to Edward House, Apr. 10, 1935, House MSS.

5. Divine, *Illusion of Neutrality*, pp. 85–96; *FDR and FA*, II, 470–75; Hull, *Memoirs*, I, 406–10.

6. William Phillips MS. Diary, June 27, July 10, 1935; *FDR and FA*, II, 558–60; Hull, *Memoirs*, I, 410; Divine, *Illusion of Neutrality*, pp. 98–100; Israel, *Nevada's Pittman*, pp. 134–9; also see Wayne S. Cole, "Senator Key Pittman and American Neutrality Policies, 1933–1940," *MVHR*, XLVI (Mar. 1960), 644–62, esp. 661–2.

7. Leuchtenburg, *FDR and the New Deal*, pp. 143–62; *FDR and FA*, II, 596–72, 575–6; William Phillips MS. Diary, July 20, 1935.

8. William Phillips MS. Diary, July 17, 20, 22, 25, 26, 30, Aug. 8, 1935; Norman Davis to Phillips, July 18, 1935, Moore MSS; *FDR and FA*, II, 585–7, 594, 598–9; *Foreign Relations*, 1935, I, 343–50; Hull, *Memoirs*, I, 410–11; Divine, *Illusion of Neutrality*, pp. 100–107.

9. Hull, *Memoirs*, I, 411; *FDR and FA*, II, 553–4, 601–2; *Foreign Relations*, 1935, I, 730–33, 737–42; Department of State, press release, Oct. 2, 1935, PSF: Italy; Divine, *Illusion of Neutrality*, pp. 107–8.

10. Hull, *Memoirs*, I, 411–12; *FDR and FA*, II, 605–10, 621–2; Moore memorandum, Aug. 17, 1935, Moore MSS; J. C. Green to Moffat, Oct. 12, 1935, Moffat MSS; Divine, *Illusion of Neutrality*, pp. 94–5, 107–11.

11. Hull, *Memoirs*, I, 412–17; *FDR and FA*, II, 620–21, 623, 634–7; R. Walton Moore memorandum, Aug. 22, 1935, Moore MSS; *FDR: Personal Letters*, 1928–1945, I, 504; J. C. Green to Moffat, Oct. 12, 1935, Moffat MSS; Cole, *Nye and Foreign Relations*, pp. 105–7; Divine, *Illusion of Neutrality*, pp. 111–17.

12. Leuchtenburg, *FDR and the New Deal*, pp. 124–5; Arthur M. Schlesinger, Jr., *The Politics of Upheaval* (Boston, 1960), pp. 500–502; *FDR and FA*, III, 90; *FDR: Personal Letters*, 1928–1945, I, 506–7, 523–4; *FDR and FA*, II, 630–33.

13. Leuchtenburg, *FDR and the New Deal*, p. 170; *P.P.A.: 1935*, pp. 352–7; *FDR and FA*, III, 7, 10–11; Hoare is quoted in Brice Harris, Jr., *The United States and the Italo-Ethiopian Crisis* (Stanford, 1964), pp. 64–5; also see p. 54; *Foreign Relations, 1935*, I, 746–9, 794; *Ickes Diary: The First Thousand Days*, pp. 445–6; Robert E. Sherwood, *Roosevelt and Hopkins* (Grosset and Dunlap ed., New York, 1950), p. 79.

14. Hull, *Memoirs*, I, 428–31; Moore to Hull, Oct. 3, 1935, Moore MSS; William Phillips MS. Diary, Oct. 4, 7, 1935; *FDR and FA*, III, 15–17; *Foreign Relations, 1935*, I, 797–801; Sherwood, *Roosevelt and Hopkins*, p. 79.

15. Harris, Jr., *U.S. and Italo-Ethiopian Crisis*, chap. 6; *FDR and FA*, III, 17–19; Hull, *Memoirs*, I, 432–3.

16. "Ethiopian Mobilization Order," n.d., PSF: Italy; John P. Diggins, *Mussolini and Fascism: The View from America* (Princeton, 1972), chap. 12, esp. pp. 287–95; on Nov. 7, 1935, R. Walton Moore wrote Ambassador John Cudahy in Poland that "there has been a remarkable unanimity of approval of the course of the administration relative to the Italian-Ethiopian broil." OF 20. Roosevelt kept a close watch on national editorial opinion, which strongly supported his actions: see Blackburn to LeHand, Nov. 2, 1935, OF 1275; the mail to the State Department is described in Divine, *Illusion of Neutrality*, p. 130; the *Fortune* poll is cited in Harris, Jr., *U.S. and Italo-Ethiopian Crisis*, p. 92; for internationalist pressure and FDR's sensitivity to it, also see *FDR and FA*, III, 47–9; and *P.P.A.: 1935*, pp. 452–3; for Republican strategy, see Anthony Biddle to James Farley, Sept. 27, 1935, OF 1667; and Farley to FDR, Oct. 11, 1935, OF 547A; for black feelings, see Roi Ottley, *New World A-Coming* (Boston, 1943), pp. 109–12; and St. Clair Drake and Horace R. Cayton, *Black Metropolis* (New York, 1945), p. 403.

17. *Ickes Diary: The First Thousand Days*, p. 450; *FDR and FA*, III, 14–15; Hull, *Memoirs*, I, 431–2, 434–5; *Foreign Relations, 1935*, I, 838–9, 841–3, 845–9, 852–4.

18. R. Walton Moore memorandum: "What Is Meant by 'Arms, Ammunition and Implements of War'?," Oct. 10, 1935, Moore MSS; William Phillips MS. Diary, Oct. 11, 1935; *FDR and FA*, III, 19–20, 43; Harris, Jr., *U.S. and Italo-Ethiopian Crisis*, pp. 77–8, 70–72; Winston S. Churchill,

The Second World War: The Gathering Storm (Bantam Books ed., New York, 1961), pp. 158–9.

19. *FDR and FA*, III, 41–2; Hull, *Memoirs*, I, 435; *Foreign Relations*, 1935, I, 812–13; Harris, Jr., *U.S. and Italo-Ethiopian War*, pp. 80–83.

20. Phillips to FDR, Oct. 31, 1935, OF 547A; Feis to Hull, Nov. 7, 1935, PSF: Italy; *FDR and FA*, III, 67–9; William Phillips MS. Diary, Nov. 15, 1935; Hull, *Memoirs*, I, 435; Herbert Feis, *Three International Episodes: Seen from E.A.* (Norton ed., New York, 1966), pp. 241, 297–308; Harris, Jr., *U.S. and Italo-Ethiopian Crisis*, pp. 87–9; *Jim Farley's Story*, pp. 55–6; *Foreign Relations*, 1935, I, 819.

21. *FDR and FA*, III, 84–5, 94–6, 103–9, 121; *Foreign Relations*, 1935, I, 821–33; Hull, *Memoirs*, I, 436–41; Hull, press conference, Nov. 26, 1935, PSF: Italy; *FDR: Personal Letters, 1928–1945*, I, 529–30.

22. Harris, Jr., *U.S. and Italo-Ethiopian Crisis*, chap. 8; the quotes on public sentiment are on pp. 110–11; *Ickes Diary: The First Thousand Days*, pp. 483–4; *FDR and FA*, III, 111–12, 130.

23. *FDR and FA*, III, 122–3, 141–3, 152–6; *Ickes Diary: The First Thousand Days*, p. 494.

24. *FDR and FA*, III, 102–3; *Ickes Diary: The First Thousand Days*, p. 483; Hull, press conference, Nov. 26, 1935, PSF: Italy; Feis, *Three International Episodes*, pp. 305–8; *Foreign Relations*, 1935, I, 872–5; *Foreign Relations of the United States, 1936*, I (Washington, D.C., 1953), 165–73; the *Times* (London) quote and Laval's comment are in Harris, Jr., *U.S. and Italo-Ethiopian Crisis*, pp. 114–20.

25. *FDR and FA*, III, 143, 149–52; Moore to McIntyre, Dec. 30, 1935, OF 1561; Divine, *Illusion of Neutrality*, pp. 134–9; *New York Times*, Feb. 19, 1936, p. 18.

26. Divine, *Illusion of Neutrality*, pp. 139–50; John Bassett Moore, "That 'New Neutrality' Defined," Dec. 10, 1935, OF 1561; Borchard to Borah, Sept. 16, 1935, Feb. 22, 1936, William Borah MSS; Hiram Johnson to Hiram Johnson, Jr., Jan. 26, 1936, Johnson MSS.

27. John Norman, "Influence of Pro-Fascist Propaganda on American Neutrality, 1935–1936," in *Essays in History and International Relations*, edited by Dwight Lee and George McReynolds (Worcester, Mass. 1949), pp. 193–214; Diggins, *Mussolini and Fascism*, pp. 302–6; Divine, *Illusion of Neutrality*, pp. 150–52.

28. *FDR and FA*, III, 173–4; Divine, *Illusion of Neutrality*, pp. 152–8; Israel, *Nevada's Pittman*, pp. 145–8; Moore to Bullitt, Feb. 25, 1936; Moore to Cudahy, Mar. 3, 1936; Moore to Daniels, Mar. 5, 1936, R. Walton Moore MSS; J. C. Green to Moffat, Apr. 22, 1936, Moffat MSS; Hiram Johnson to Hiram Johnson, Jr., Jan. 26, Feb. 16, 25, 1936, Johnson MSS; *Ickes Diary: The First Thousand Days*, p. 533; William Phillips MS. Diary, Feb. 12, 18, 1936; *The New Republic*, 86 (Feb. 19, 1936), 45; *Time*, XXVII (Feb. 24, 1936), 15.

29. *FDR and FA*, III, 221–2; *Foreign Relations of the United States, 1936*, II (Washington, D.C., 1953), 109–10; *Foreign Relations, 1936*, I, 185; Harris, Jr., *U.S. and Italo-Ethiopian Crisis*, chap. 10.

CHAPTER 6

1. Postwar studies of Germany's economic preparations for war found that popular and informed opinion in the thirties greatly exaggerated the extent of German rearmament. Burton H. Klein, *Germany's Economic Preparations for War* (Cambridge, Mass., 1959), Part I. A. J. P. Taylor took this to mean that Hitler did not intend to fight a war—*The Origins of the Second World War* (New York, 1966 ed.). "But the pre-war German economy," Alan Milward contends, "was a war economy, not in the sense in which that term was used in British planning, but in an equally meaningful way. . . . German strategic and economic thinking before the war revolved around the concept of the *Blitzkreig*. . . . The concept was strategical as well as tactical. . . . It was a method of avoiding the total economic commitment of 'total war.' . . . But . . . under Blitzkreig economics Germany achieved one of the most remarkable periods of conquest in modern history" (*The German Economy at War* (London, 1965), chap. I, esp. pp. 1–8). For the letters cited, see *FDR and FA*, III, 201–2, 233–6; and *FDR: Personal Letters, 1928–1945*, I, 543, 555–6.

2. *Foreign Relations of the United States, 1935*, IV (Washington, D.C., 1952), 1–6, 113, 163, 178–9; Hull, *Memoirs*, I, 493–4; *P.P.A.: 1936*, pp. 72–4; William Phillips MS. Diary, Feb. 13, 1936.

3. The trade agreements and negotiations are described in *Foreign Relations, 1935*, IV; for the treaty negotiations with Panama, see pp. 889–910; also see Welles, *Time for Decision*, pp. 201–2; and Lester D. Langley, "Negotiating New Treaties with Panama: 1936," *HAHR*, 48 (May 1968), 220–33.

4. E. David Cronon, "American Catholics and Mexican Anticlericalism, 1933–1936," *MVHR*, 45 (Sept. 1958), 201–30; for the quotes, see pp. 209–10; also FDR to John P. Higgins, Jan. 23, 1935, OF 146; *Foreign Relations, 1935*, IV, 782–802; there is a large body of material in the Roosevelt Library illustrating this Catholic pressure on the administration: see OF 28, 146, 146A, 237; PSF: Mexico; PPF 86 and 2406; and in the Moore papers, Boxes 3, 4, 10, and 17.

5. The quotes are from Cronon, "American Catholics and Mexican Anticlericalism," *MVHR* (Sept. 1958), 217; and *Foreign Relations, 1935*, IV, 794; for Roosevelt's actions, see FDR to Hull, June 25, 1935, OF 146; McIntyre to John P. Higgins, July 2, 1935; Early to Doctor Macfarland, July 24, 1935, OF 146A; FDR to Daniels, July 12, 1935, PPF 86; *P.P.A.: 1935*, pp. 305, 410–12, 495–6; *FDR and FA*, III, 61–3, 329–30.

6. Cronon, "American Catholics and Mexican Anticlericalism," *MVHR* (Sept. 1958), 223–30; Flynn, *American Catholics and the Roosevelt Presidency*, chap. 8.

7. *FDR and FA*, III, 195, 291–4; *FDR: Personal Letters, 1928–1945*, I, 571.

8. *Foreign Relations, 1936*, I, 214–18, 228–32, 234, 244–5, 269; Arnold A. Offner, *American Appeasement: United States Foreign Policy and Germany, 1933–1938* (Cambridge, Mass., 1969), pp. 136–46. In the Rhineland crisis, Gerhard L. Weinberg explains, "Britain and France both looked to the other for reinforcement of its own weakness rather than confirmation of a

strong resolve, and both were well satisfied" (*The Foreign Policy of Hitler's Germany: Diplomatic Revolution in Europe, 1933–1936* (Chicago, 1970), chap. 10—the quote is from p. 245). *FDR and FA*, III, 261–3; *FDR: Personal Letters, 1928–1945*, I, 476–7.

9. "This was the first major campaign without Louis Howe [who died in April 1936], and FDR gathered the reins firmly into his own hands," Elliott Roosevelt has written: *FDR: Personal Letters, 1928–1945*, I, 542; for the correspondence with his envoys, see 560, 569, 574–5, 577, 585–8, 592–3; *FDR and FA*, III, 254–5; Robert Dallek, *Democrat and Diplomat: The Life of William E. Dodd* (New York, 1968), pp. 281–3.

10. Morgenthau MS. Diary, 21: 146–7, 173; 25: 150–51, 161–6, 188; *FDR and FA*, III, 308–9; Blum, *From the Morgenthau Diaries, 1928–1938*, pp. 149–55.

11. *Ibid.*, pp. 134–8, 155–73; Joel Colton, *Léon Blum: Humanist in Politics* (New York, 1966), pp. 184–8; *FDR: Personal Letters, 1928–1945*, I, 593–4; *Foreign Relations, 1936*, I, 539–41; Morgenthau MS. Diary, 33: 146–8.

12. Hugh Thomas, *The Spanish Civil War* (New York, 1961), pp. 209–36, 257–9. For the view that Blum's nonintervention policy was more the product of his own thinking than of British pressure, see Colton, *Léon Blum*, pp. 234–56, esp. pp. 241–2.

13. Richard P. Traina, *American Diplomacy and the Spanish Civil War* (Bloomington, Ind., 1968), pp. 11–13, 46–60; FDR, "Diaries and Itineraries," 1936, in the FDRL; *Foreign Relations of the United States, 1936*, II (Washington, D.C., 1953), 471, 475–6; William Phillips MS. Diary, Aug. 10, 11, 1936; *FDR and FA*, III, 374–5, 393–4; J. C. Green to Moffat, Sept. 12, 1936, Moffat MSS; Hull, *Memoirs*, I, 475–9.

14. In February 1937, 95 per cent of a sample poll expressed opposition to American involvement in another world war; Hadley Cantril (ed.), *Public Opinion, 1935–1946* (Princeton, 1951), p. 966; *FDR and FA*, III, 373–7; *Ickes Diary: The First Thousand Days*, pp. 655–6, 661.

15. *FDR and FA*, III, 377–84.

16. "It is not necessary to tell you that all the comments on the Chautauqua speech continue highly favorable," Moore wrote Bullitt, Aug. 18, 1936, Moore MSS; on reaction to the speech, also see O. G. Villard to Hull, Aug. 18, 1936; Villard to FDR, Aug. 18, 1936, Villard MSS; *Ickes Diary: The First Thousand Days*, pp. 662–3, 665, 698; Cole, *Nye and American Foreign Relations*, pp. 136–8; Mrs. Raymond Clapper to McIntyre, Aug. 19, 1936, OF 394; *New York Times*, Aug. 24, 1936, p. 1.

17. Arthur Krock, *In the Nation: 1932–1966* (New York, 1966), pp. 62–6; Arthur Krock, *Memoirs: Sixty Years on the Firing Line* (New York, 1968), pp. 183–4; Arthur Krock, pp. 39, 41–2, 89, COHC; *FDR and FA*, III, 401–2; *New York Times*, Aug. 26, 1936, p. 1; Aug. 27, 1936, p. 4; Raymond Clapper MS. Diary, Sept. 10, 1936. "This morning's paper here said he [Roosevelt] was going to call a conference for peace if he were reelected . . . just fishing for the peace women's votes," Hiram Johnson wrote his son, Aug. 26, 1936, Johnson MSS.

18. *FDR: Personal Letters, 1928–1945*, I, 605–6; *FDR and FA*, III, 373–4,

390–92, 405–8, 433–4, 455–8; *New York Times*, Aug. 26, 1936, p. 1; Dallek, *Democrat and Diplomat*, pp. 286–92.

19. *New York Times*, Aug. 31, 1936, p. 1; *FDR and FA*, III, 412–13, 424–5, 435–9; *Ickes Diary: The First Thousand Days*, p. 671; *FDR: Personal Letters, 1928–1945*, I, 614–15; Thomas, *Spanish Civil War*, pp. 260–64, 277–85, 291–3; *Foreign Relations, 1936*, II, 536–9.

20. Morgenthau MS Diary, 31: 157; *The Secret Diary of Harold L. Ickes: The Inside Struggle, 1936–1939* (New York, 1954), p. 7; Moore to Hull, Nov. 19, 1936, Moore MSS.

21. *P.P.A.: 1936*, pp. 583–4, 597–602; *FDR: Personal Letters, 1928–1945*, I, 631–5, 640; Louis Adamic, *Dinner at the White House* (New York, 1946), pp. 48–9; "The Cruise of President Franklin D. Roosevelt to South America and the Inter-American Conference for the Maintenance of Peace, Buenos Aires, Argentina, 18 November–15 December, 1936," pp. 12–14, 20–25, 30–42, in the FDRL; Adm. Emory S. Land, pp. 160–61, COHC; H. Kent Hewitt, p. 6, COHC; *FDR and FA*, III, 534. The spokesman of the Brazilian Congress hailed Roosevelt as " 'the *Man*—the fearless and generous man who is accomplishing and living the most thrilling political experience of modern times' " (Donald M. Dozer, *Are We Good Neighbors? Three Decades of Inter-American Relations, 1930–1960* (Gainesville, Fla., 1959), pp. 31–3).

22. *FDR and FA*, III, 516–21; Hull, *Memoirs*, I, chap. 35; Welles, *Time for Decision*, pp. 204–8; Beatrice B. Berle and Travis B. Jacobs (eds.), *Navigating the Rapids, 1918–1971: From the Papers of Adolf A. Berle* (New York, 1973), pp. 119–21.

23. *FDR and FA*, III, 471–7, 499–502, 526–8, 533; *FDR: Personal Letters, 1928–1945*, I, 634–5, 638, 648–9, 652–3, 656.

24. Thomas, *Spanish Civil War*, chap. 36, pp. 309–11, 315, 331–7; *FDR and FA*, III, 543–4, 562–5, 567, 592–3; *New York Times*, Dec. 23, 1936, p. 6; Dec. 30, 1936, p. 1; Jan. 3, 1937, IV, 7; Jan. 5, 1937, p. 6; Moore to Hull, Nov. 13, Dec. 9, 1936; memorandum by Sen. Key Pittman, Dec. 29, 1936, attached to FDR to Moore, Jan. 4, 1937; Moore to FDR, Jan. 5, 1937, Moore MSS; Moore press conference, n.d., "Early 1937," PSF: Spain; memoranda for Moore, Jan. 4, 5, 1937; Moore to FDR, Jan. 5, 1937, OF 1561; memorandum of Moore press conference, Jan. 5, 1937, PSF: State Dept.; Cantril (ed.), *Public Opinion, 1935–1946*, p. 807; Traina, *American Diplomacy and the Spanish Civil War*, chap. 4, pp. 171–2; Divine, *Illusion of Neutrality*, pp. 168–72.

25. William E. Leuchtenburg, "Franklin D. Roosevelt's Supreme Court 'Packing' Plan," in *Essays on the New Deal*, edited by Harold M. Hollingsworth and William F. Holmes (Austin, Texas, 1969), pp. 69–76; *P.P.A.: 1936*, pp. 235–6, 609, 634–5, 640–42; *FDR: Personal Letters, 1928–1945*, I, 605–6, 625–6, 649; Raymond Clapper MS. Diary, Jan. 20, 1937; Samuel I. Rosenman, p. 154, COHC.

26. Hull, *Memoirs*, I, 506–7; *FDR and FA*, III, 578–80; *Complete Presidential Press Conferences of Franklin Delano Roosevelt* (25 vols. in 12; New York, 1972), IX, 119; *New York Times*, Jan. 31, 1937, p. 28; Mar. 21, 1937, IV, 6; Moore to McIntyre, Jan. 30, 1937, PPF 745; Moore to FDR, Jan. 30, Feb. 15, 1937, OF 1561; Moore to FDR, Jan. 30, 1937, Moore MSS; Divine, *Illusion of Neutrality*, pp. 173–5.

27. *FDR and FA*, III, 572–3, 586–8; Morgenthau MS. Diary, 54: 303; 55: 330; 56: 341–2; *Ickes Diary: 1936–1939*, p. 51; Moore to Hull, Jan. 25, 1937, Moore MSS.; *Foreign Relations of the United States, 1937*, I (Washington, D.C., 1954), 954–73.

28. J. W. Pickersgill, *The Mackenzie King Record*, Vol. I: 1939–1944 (Toronto, 1960), pp. 3–4; *FDR: Personal Letters, 1928–1945*, I, 664–8; Mackenzie King to FDR, Mar. 8, 1937, PSF: Canada; at the end of March, Roosevelt also discussed a possible peace conference with Lord Tweedsmuir, the Governor General of Canada, see FDR to Tweedsmuir, Feb. 20, 1937; Tweedsmuir to FDR, Apr. 8, 1937, PSF: Canda; memorandum of telephone conversation with FDR, Mar. 19, 1937, Davis MSS; Davis to FDR, Apr. 13, 1937, PSF: State Dept.; Borg, *U.S. and Far Eastern Crisis of 1933–1938*, pp. 247–8, 373–6; *Foreign Relations, 1937*, I, 98–102.

29. Moore to Hull, Jan. 25, 1937; Moore to FDR, Jan. 30, 1937; Moore to Comstock, Feb. 25, 1937, Moore MSS; Moore to FDR, Feb. 15, 1937, OF 1561. While Roosevelt wanted greater discretion in applying the neutrality law, explained Arthur Krock in the *New York Times*, Congress would not allow it (Feb. 2, 1937, p. 22). A sample poll of Jan. 18, 1937, showed 69 per cent of Americans preferring congressional to executive control over neutrality policy (Cantril (ed.), *Public Opinion, 1935–1946*, p. 966). Divine, *Illusion of Neutrality*, pp. 175–80.

30. On opposition to Roosevelt over Court "packing," see Leuchtenburg, "FDR's Court 'Packing' Plan," in *Essays on the New Deal*, pp. 76–115; Roosevelt wrote Bullitt that the newspapers were calling him "a remorseless dictator" (*FDR: Personal Letters, 1928–1945*, I, 676); Hiram Johnson to Hiram Johnson, Jr., Feb. 6, 1937, Johnson MSS; Moore to FDR, Mar. 4, 1937, OF 1561; *New York Times*, Feb. 21, 1937, pp. 1–2; FDR to Senator Robinson, Apr. 20, 1937, PSF: Neutrality; Divine, *Illusion of Neutrality*, pp. 185–99; Israel, *Nevada's Pittman*, pp. 150–54.

31. Thomas, *Spanish Civil War*, p. 380, and chap. 46; *Foreign Relations, 1937*, I, 253–4, 257–8, 268, 270–72; Cole, *Nye and American Foreign Relations*, pp. 112–14; Hull, *Memoirs*, I, 510–11.

32. Thomas, *Spanish Civil War*, chaps. 48, 51, 54, 58; F. Jay Taylor, *The United States and the Spanish Civil War* (New York, 1956), pp. 88–92, 124–6; Jerry J. O'Connell to FDR, June 23, 1937, OF 422C.

33. Hull, *Memoirs*, I, 511; Taylor, *U.S. and the Spanish Civil War*, pp. 129–31; memo on Norman Thomas, June 9, 1937; Thomas to FDR, Aug. 26, 1937, OF 422C; FDR, "Diaries and Itineraries," June 29, 1937, in FDRL. "I got the distinct impression," Norman Thomas later said, ". . . that Roosevelt was primarily influenced by his feeling that he had to have the support of the Church on any move as great as this, because it was so necessary for political strength at home. I can't prove it, but I got that impression when I talked to Mr. Roosevelt" (Norman Thomas, Part II, 23, 129–30, 133, 138–9, COHC); for Catholic opinion, see Taylor, *U.S. and the Spanish Civil War*, chap. 7; and Allen Guttman, *The Wound in the Heart: America and the Spanish Civil War* (Glencoe, Ill., 1962), chap. 3.

34. FDR to Hull, June 29, 1937, OF 1561; *Foreign Relations, 1937*, I, 344–7, 353–5; Hull, *Memoirs*, I, 511–13.

CHAPTER 7

1. *Foreign Relations*, 1937, I, 98–101, 655–7, 662–4, 674–87; *FDR: Personal Letters, 1928–1945*, I, 680–81; Borg, *U.S. and Far Eastern Crisis of 1933–1938*, pp. 373–7; Robert Bingham to FDR, July 1, 1937; FDR to Bingham, July 16, 1937, PSF: Great Britain; *Complete Press Conferences*, IX, 393; X, 42–3; Joseph E. Davies, *Mission to Moscow* (New York, 1941), pp. 141–2, 158–9; Joseph Davies to FDR, June 10, 26, 1937, PSF: Russia; Winston S. Churchill, *The Second World War: The Gathering Storm* (Boston, 1961 ed.), pp. 197–9; FDR to van Zeeland, July 6, 1937, OF 14; Daniel Yergin, *Shattered Peace: The Origins of the Cold War and the National Security State* (Boston, 1977), pp. 32–5; Martin Weil, *A Pretty Good Club: The Founding Fathers of the U.S. Foreign Service* (New York, 1978), pp. 92–3.

2. Borg, *U.S. and Far Eastern Crisis of 1933–1938*, pp. 276–91; *Foreign Relations*, 1937, I, 113, 697ff.; Hull, *Memoirs*, I, 534–7; *FDR: Personal Letters 1928–1945*, I, 699–701.

3. Borg, *U.S. and Far Eastern Crisis of 1933–1938*, pp. 318–34; *Ickes Diary: 1936–1939*, pp. 185–6, 192–3, 198–9; *Complete Press Conferences*, X, 162–5, 196–7; *New York Times*, Sept. 1, 1937, p. 3; Sept. 2, 1937, p. 1; Sept. 3, 1937, p. 1; Sept. 4, 1937, p. 1; Sept. 5, 1937, p. 1; J. G. Scripps to FDR, Sept. 1, 1937; James Roosevelt to Early, Sept. 3, 1937, OF 150C, indicates FDR's awareness of the Gallup poll; William D. Leahy MS. Diary, Aug. 29–Sept. 2, 1937.

4. Borg, *U.S. and Far Eastern Crisis of 1933–1938*, pp. 336–46; *Complete Press Conferences*, X, 166–7; *Ickes Diary: 1936–1939*, p. 199; Key Pittman, "The Neutrality Act and the Far Eastern Crisis," Aug. 23, 1937, OF 1561.

5. Borg, *U.S. and Far Eastern Crisis of 1933–1938*, pp. 346–54; Hull, *Memoirs*, I, 556–8. For the debate inside the administration on whether to invoke the neutrality law, see Moffat MS. Diary, Aug. 16, Sept. 7, 14, 1937; Pittman to Hull, Aug. 26, 1937, OF 150C; Raymond Clapper MS. Diary, September 3, 1937; Morgenthau MS. Diary, 87: 274. For the pressure from the Chinese against invoking the law, see *Foreign Relations of the United States*, 1937, III (Washington, D.C., 1954), 516–17, 531–2; *Foreign Relations of the United States*, 1937, IV (Washington, D.C., 1954), 456–8; James Moffett memorandum, September 19, 1937, OF 150. For public and congressional feeling on the issue, see Official Files 150C and 1561 for August and September, 1937. Roosevelt's statement is in *Foreign Relations: Japan, 1931–1941*, II, 201.

6. Borg, *U.S. and Far Eastern Crisis, 1933–1938*, chap. 10; Bradford A. Lee, *Britain and the Sino-Japanese War, 1937–1939* (Stanford, 1973), chap. 2, esp. pp. 45–6.

7. Leuchtenburg, *FDR and the New Deal*, pp. 238–44. ". . . The first thing he [Hull] said to me was that the President must do something about Black. He said the Supreme Court and the sitdown strikes are bothering the people most. I sounded him out to see whether he was behind the idea that the President has . . . to send a message to the 55 nations and offer his services as a clearing house. Cordell is against it" (Morgenthau MS. Diary, 88: 253; 89: 52).

8. Hull, *Memoirs*, I, 544; Eichelberger to McIntyre, June 16, 1937, OF 394; FDR, "Diary and Itineraries," July 8, 1937, FDRL; Eichelberger to FDR, July 16, 1937, PPF 3833; *Ickes Diary: 1936–1939*, p. 213.

9. *P.P.A.*: 1937, pp. 406–11; the drafting of the speech is closely described in Dorothy Borg, "Notes on Roosevelt's 'Quarantine Speech,' " *Political Science Quarterly*, 72 (Sept. 1957), 405–33; and Borg, *U.S. and Far Eastern Crisis, 1933–1938*, pp. 380–81; the relevant documents on the drafting of the speech are: Norman Davis to FDR, Sept. 16, 1937, Davis MSS; Bishop Frank Sterrett to FDR, Sept. 18, 1937, and FDR to Sterrett, Oct. 7, 1937, OF 1820; "Material Used in Preparing Chicago Speech," 1937, Speech File 1093; William Phillips MS. Diary, Oct. 26, 1937.

10. Borg, *U.S. and Far Eastern Crisis, 1933–1938*, 381–6; *Complete Press Conferences*, X, 246–52; for the argument that Roosevelt had a specific plan in mind, see John McVickar Haight, Jr., "Franklin D. Roosevelt and a Naval Quarantine of Japan," *Pacific Historical Review*, XL (May 1971), 203–26. After the speech, some isolationists accused Roosevelt of trying to divert public attention from domestic problems by raising a war scare, see Charles A. Beard, *American Foreign Policy in the Making, 1932–1940* (New Haven, 1946), p. 187; "Last year when the Black appointment grew so hot with Ku Klux Klan charges . . . Roosevelt found himself in a nasty situation, from which there was no extrication, he made the celebrated quarantine speech in Chicago, and thus turned the discussion from Black to war" (Hiram Johnson to Hiram W. Johnson, Jr., Apr. 16, 1938); cf. Feb. 19, 1938, Johnson MSS. As his conversation with Morgenthau of September 20 suggests, however, Roosevelt believed it politically unwise to risk anything bold in foreign affairs at that time; his caution following the speech illustrates the point.

11. *Foreign Relations*, 1937, I, 665–70; Hull, *Memoirs*, I, 546–8; Moffat MS. Diary, Oct. 5, 6, 1937; *Foreign Relations: Japan*, 1931–1941, I, 396–7; *P.P.A.*: 1937, p. 437.

12. *Foreign Relations*, 1937, IV, 64–8, 85–6, 89–91, 114–15, 217–18; *Foreign Relations*, 1937, III, 600–601, 629–30, 632, 634–9; Bradford A. Lee shows that the British were not eager for sanctions, but if the Americans had this in mind, they were ready to follow: *Britain and Sino-Japanese War, 1937–1939*, chap. 3, esp. pp. 63–70; Haight, Jr., "FDR and a Naval Quarantine," *PHR*, 206–7; Borg, *U.S. and Far Eastern Crisis, 1933–1938*, chap. 14.

13. As Dorothy Borg and Travis Jacobs have shown, despite subsequent contentions by leading members of the administration that public reaction to the speech was almost uniformly hostile, the initial public response was in fact quite positive. *U.S. and Far Eastern Crisis, 1933–1938*, pp. 387–98; Jacobs, "Roosevelt's Quarantine Speech," *The Historian*, XXIV (1962), 483–502; a random sample of White House mail suggests that a majority of letter writers were happy to endorse Roosevelt's search for peace but gave little indication that they were prepared to support economic or military sanctions against Japan (PPF 200B, Boxes 82–84).

14. FDR, "Diary and Itineraries," Oct. 8, 1937, in FDRL; Norman Davis, memorandum of conversations with FDR, Oct. 20, 1937, Davis MSS; Borg, *U.S. and Far Eastern Crisis, 1933–1938*, pp. 388–9; Moffat MS. Diary, Oct. 8–10, 1937; *P.P.A.*: 1937, p. 438; *FDR: Personal Letters, 1928–1945*, I, 718–19.

For the argument that FDR's perception of public opinion rather than public feeling itself restrained him from a meaningful follow-up to his speech, see the Borg and Jacobs references above, and Michael Leigh, *Mobilizing Consent: Public Opinion and American Foreign Policy, 1937–1947* (Westport, Conn., 1976), pp. 29–41.

15. Norman Davis, memorandum of conversations with FDR, Oct. 20, 1937, Davis MSS; *Foreign Relations, 1937*, IV, 85–6; *Complete Press Conferences*, X, 275–6; White House statement, Oct. 19, 1937, PSF: Belgium; cf. "Notes of O.G.V.'s and Walter Van Kirk's Interview with FDR, Oct. 20, 1937," Villard MSS; FDR to Sumner Welles, Nov. 12, 1937, PSF: State Dept.; Stimson to FDR, Nov. 15, 1937; FDR to Stimson, Nov. 24, 1937, PPF 20; *FDR: Personal Letters, 1928–1945*, I, 729.

16. Leuchtenburg, *FDR and the New Deal*, pp. 243–51; Blum, *From the Morgenthau Diaries, 1928–1938*, pp. 390, 393–4; Borg, *U.S. and Far Eastern Crisis, 1933–1938*, pp. 437–8; for Roosevelt's stand on the neutrality law, see Villard to Florence Boeckel, Oct. 29, 1937, Villard MSS; also correspondence in OF 150C and 1561 for Oct. and Nov. 1937, as well as Moore to FDR, Nov. 6, 12, 1937; Moore to Hull, Dec. 6, 1937, Moore MSS.

17. *Foreign Relations: Japan, 1931–1941*, I, 522–3, 527, 529–30; Blum, *From the Morgenthau Diaries, 1928–1938*, pp. 485–90; Morgenthau MS. Diary, 102: 2, 103: 20–21, 59–62; Lee, *Britain and Sino-Japanese War, 1937–1939*, pp. 88–93; *Ickes Diary: 1936–1939*, pp. 273–5; Hull, *Memoirs*, I, 559–62; Borg, *U.S. and Far Eastern Crisis, 1933–1938*, pp. 486–503.

18. Public opinion is analyzed in Manny T. Koginos, *The Panay Incident: Prelude to War* (Lafayette, Ind., 1967), p. vii, chap. 2, pp. 80–83; "American Public Opinion on Far Eastern Issues, 1931–1941," p. 18; "Attitudes and Activities of the Organized 'Peace' Pressure Groups, 1920–1941," pp. 20–21, Cordell Hull MSS; "It is a wonderful opportunity for leadership of the overwhelming anti-war sentiment of the country . . ." Villard wrote Senator Robert LaFollette, Jr., Dec. 15, 1937, Villard MSS; McIntyre to Hull, Dec. 15, 1937, OF 150C; *FDR: Personal Letters, 1928–1945*, I, 733–4.

19. Ambassador Ronald Lindsay told Roosevelt that a blockade would lead to a war with Japan; he described the President's idea to the Foreign Office as "the utterances of a hare-brained statesman or an amateur strategist," Lee, *Britain and Sino-Japanese War, 1937–1939*, p. 91; Morgenthau MS. Diary, 103: 88–90; William D. Leahy MS. Diary, Dec. 17, 23, 1937; Koginos, *Panay Incident*, pp. 70–76.

20. Bullitt to FDR, Dec. 7, 1937, PSF: France; *Foreign Relations, 1937*, I, 195–202; *FDR: Personal Letters, 1928–1945*, I, 735.

21. *Foreign Relations of the United States, 1938*, I (Washington, D.C., 1955), 115–17; Sumner Welles, *Seven Decisions That Shaped History* (New York, 1950), pp. 14–27; *The Memoirs of Anthony Eden, Earl of Avon: Facing the Dictators* (Boston, 1962), pp. 622–5.

22. Borg, *U.S. and Far Eastern Crisis, 1933–1938*, pp. 504–12; William D. Leahy MS. Diary, Jan. 10, 13, 1938; *New York Times*, Jan. 14, 1938, p. 2; Koginos, *Panay Incident*, pp. 83–97, esp. pp. 95–7; Walter R. Griffin, "Louis Ludlow and the War Referendum Crusade, 1935–1941," *Indiana Magazine of History*, LXIV (Dec. 1968), 267–88; "Dem. whips called personally on

all Democratic members urging them to stand by administration—" Raymond Clapper noted in his Diary, "they have used telephone but never before in this administration have they made personal canvass" (MS. Diary, Jan. 10, 1938).

23. "It is always best and safest to count on nothing from the Americans but words," Chamberlain observed after Roosevelt's Quarantine speech, Keith Feiling, *The Life of Neville Chamberlain* (London, 1946), p. 325; Lee, *Britain and Sino-Japanese War, 1937–1939*, pp. 93–5, 102–4; *Foreign Relations of the United States, 1938*, III (Washington, D.C., 1955), 19–20; *Foreign Relations, 1938*, I, 117–22, 133–4; Welles, *Seven Decisions*, p. 22; for a summary of the controversy over what impact Roosevelt's plan might have had, see Offner, *American Appeasement*, pp. 229–32, who writes: "To judge from the fact that in January and February 1938 he [Hitler] was formally reversing German policy in the Far East in direct opposition to American and British interests, and from his impatience in the Austrian crisis and willingness to use force without assurances that he would not meet concerted opposition, one must conclude that he would not have been interested in a conference sponsored by a politically, and military, uninvolved United States"; Eden, *Facing the Dictators*, pp. 623–33.

24. Ibid., pp. 633–44; *Foreign Relations, 1938*, I, 122–5; Bullitt to FDR, Jan. 20, 1938, PSF: France; Moffat MS. Diary, Feb. 19–22, 1938.

25. FDR to Claude Bowers, Mar. 7, 1938, PSF: Spain; FDR to Hull, Jan. 21, 28, 29, 1938, PSF: Hull; Raymond Clapper MS. Diary, Feb. 20, 1938; *From the Berle Papers*, pp. 168–9; *Foreign Relations, 1938*, I, 126–30, 448–9, 456–7; Offner, *American Appeasement*, pp. 238–9; *P.P.A.: 1938*, p. 169; Hull, *Memoirs*, I, 575–8.

26. Moffat MS. Diary, Apr. 18–20, 23–24, 1938; *Complete Press Conferences*, XI, 319, 321–2, 369; *Foreign Relations, 1938*, I, 143–5, 147–8.

27. Divine, *Illusion of Neutrality*, pp. 221–2; Hull to Pittman, Feb. 24, 1938, Moore MSS; *New York Times*, Mar. 20, 1938, p. 1; Mar. 23, 1938, p. 1; Mar. 27, 1938, IV, 5; Leuchtenburg, *FDR and the New Deal*, pp. 249–50, 256–7, 277–9; the *New York Times* story of March 23 spoke of "mounting indications that any move to repeal the neutrality law would precipitate an acrimonious debate in Congress and conflicting views in the country"; the story of March 27 stated: "All sides seem to agree . . . that nothing could be accomplished by taking up the [neutrality] question at this time."

28. Taylor, *U.S. and the Spanish Civil War*, pp. 126–8, 163–4, 167–72; Traina, *American Diplomacy and the Spanish Civil War*, pp. 127–9; Thomas, *Spanish Civil War*, pp. 504–31.

29. Lash, *Eleanor and Franklin*, pp. 567–70, describes the pro-Loyalist feelings shared by the President and Mrs. Roosevelt, and FDR's sense of limits about doing something for the Republic; Bowers to James Farley, Feb. 19, 1938, Farley MSS; Bowers to FDR, Feb. 20, 1938, PSF: Spain; Moffat MS. Diary, Mar. 12, 14, 1938; for direct pressure on Roosevelt to push for a change in the embargo policy, see the Moffat Diary, Mar. 19–20, 24, 31, 1938; also Breckinridge Long MS. Diary, pp. 98–101; Donald Richberg to James Roosevelt, Mar. 28, 1938, OF 422C, as well as numerous other letters in this file for March, April, and May urging repeal of the Spanish

arms embargo; Hull to R. L. Buell, Mar. 22, 1938, in *New York Times*, Mar. 23, 1938, p. 6.

30. *P.P.A.: 1938*, pp. 221–33; Leuchtenburg, *FDR and the New Deal*, pp. 257–63, 266–9; Thomas, *Spanish Civil War*, p. 530; Paul H. Todd to James Roosevelt, Apr. 23, 1938, OF 1561; *Complete Press Conferences*, XI, 325–8, 365–8; *Foreign Relations*, 1938, I, 164, 171–2, 177; *Ickes Diary: 1936–1939*, p. 380.

31. Cole, *Nye and American Foreign Relations*, pp. 113–14; Breckinridge Long MS. Diary, pp. 101–2; Moffat MS. Diary, May 3–4, 1938; draft letter to Pittman, May 3, 4, 1938, Moore MSS; Traina, *American Diplomacy and the Spanish Civil War*, pp. 131–6, who persuasively argues that a *New York Times* story of May 5, 1938, p. 1, picturing the administration as ready to support the Nye resolution, was incorrect; for Hull's press conference, see *New York Times*, May 7, 1938, p. 1.

32. Moffat MS. Diary, May 5, 9–10, 13, 1938; *New York Times*, May 6, 1938, pp. 1, 5, May 7, 1938, p. 1, May 8, 1938, p. 37; *Ickes Diary: 1936–1939*, pp. 389–90; *Foreign Relations*, 1938, I, 184–6, 188–93, 216–19; Thomas, *Spanish Civil War*, pp. 536–7; Hull to FDR, May 11, 1938, OF 422C; Traina, *American Diplomacy and the Spanish Civil War*, pp. 136–43.

33. J. W. Wheeler-Bennett, *Munich: Prologue to Tragedy* (New York, 1964 ed.), chaps. 1–2; Bullock, *Hitler*, pp. 387–94; Offner, *American Appeasement*, pp. 245–50; *Foreign Relations*, 1938, I, 506–7, 509–15, 519–20.

34. *Ibid.*, 524–6, 528–30, 533–4, 541, 546, 549–51; *For the President: Correspondence Between FDR and Bullitt*, pp. 267–72, 276–7, 279–80; Joseph Kennedy to FDR, July 28, 1938, PSF: Great Britain; Hull, *Memoirs*, I, 586–8; A. A. Berle, Jr., to FDR, Aug. 15, 1938, PSF: Berle; *P.P.A.: 1938*, pp. 491–4; FDR to Lord Tweedsmuir, Aug. 31, 1938, PPF 3396.

35. Morgenthau MS. Diary 137: 166, 212–18, 227–30; 138: 20–21, 33–5; Blum, *From the Morgenthau Diaries, 1928–1938*, pp. 514–17; A. A. Berle, Jr., to FDR, Aug. 31, 1938, PSF: Berle; George Messersmith to LeHand, Aug. 31, 1938, PSF: Great Britain; *Foreign Relations*, 1938, I, 565–6; Moffat MS. Diary, Sept. 1, 1938.

36. William Langer and S. Everett Gleason, *The Challenge to Isolation, 1937–1940* (New York, 1964 ed.), pp. 32–3; *Documents on British Foreign Policy, 1919–1939*, 3rd Series, Vol. II: 1938 (London, 1949), p. 301; the French visitor was Senator Robert Thoumyre, a member of the French Senate and former Minister of Pensions, who saw Roosevelt on Sept. 1, 1938, FDR, "Diary and Itineraries," FDRL; on Sept. 9, Roosevelt told the press that interpretations that the United States was "allied morally with the democracies of Europe in a sort of 'Stop Hitler' movement" were "about 100% wrong," *Complete Press Conferences*, XII, 83–4; on Sept. 15, however, he wrote William Phillips that "if we get the idea that the future of our form of government is threatened by a coalition of European dictators, we might wade in with everything we have to give." He also said that if a war began, he would "strongly encourage" the country's "natural sympathy," which he believed was 90 per cent anti-German and anti-Italian (PSF: Phillips); *Ickes Diary: 1936–1939*, pp. 467–8.

37. *Ibid.*, pp. 469–70; Blum, *From the Morgenthau Diaries, 1928–1938*,

p. 519; *Documents on British Foreign Policy, 1919-1939*, 3rd Series, Vol. VII: 1939 (London, 1954), pp. 627-9; for examples of information on German military strength coming to Roosevelt, see Joseph Kennedy to FDR, n.d. (but probably Feb. 1938), OF 92; *For the President: Correspondence Between FDR and Bullitt*, pp. 256-60; Louis Johnson to McIntyre, June 23, 1938, PSF: War Department; Hugh Wilson to FDR, July 11, 1938, PSF: Wilson; also see *The Wartime Journals of Charles A. Lindbergh* (New York, 1970), pp. 69-70.

38. Wheeler-Bennett, *Munich*, chap. 3, and pp. 118-45; Bullock, *Hitler*, pp. 394-407; on the evening of Sept. 25, Roosevelt told Morgenthau that he had received no reply from London to his suggestion for an economic blockade or defensive war, Morgenthau MS. Diary, 142: 341, 347; *Ickes Diary: 1936-1939*, pp. 472-4; in a January 1939 dicsussion of German military superiority with Josephus Daniels, Roosevelt said, "that if he had been in Chamberlain's place [in September] he would have felt constrained to have made terms to prevent the war for which Germany was fully prepared," Jan. 14, 1939, PPF 86. Bullitt and Welles were the principal architects of Roosevelt's appeal: see Hull, *Memoirs*, I, 590-92; *From the Berle Papers*, pp. 186-7; Moffat MS. Diary, Sept. 24-25, 1938; memorandum of Bullitt telephone call, Sept. 23, 1938, PSF: Bullitt; *Foreign Relations*, 1938, I, 641-2, 657-8.

39. Bullock, *Hitler*, pp. 407-9; on the 26th, after he had sent his first peace appeal, Roosevelt received a noncommittal response from London to his blockade idea: Lindsay to FDR, Sept. 26, 1938, PSF: Great Britain; *Foreign Relations*, 1938, I, 669-72, 675-8, 684-5, 688; telephone conversation between Bullitt and Welles, Sept. 27, 1938, PSF: Bullitt; *Ickes Diary: 1936-1939*, pp. 476-9; *From the Berle Papers*, pp. 187-8; Wheeler-Bennett, *Munich*, pp. 157-8; Joseph Alsop and Robert Kintner, *American White Paper* (New York, 1940), pp. 8-11.

40. Bullock, *Hitler*, pp. 410-16; Churchill, *The Gathering Storm*, pp. 284-5; FDR to Mackenzie King, Oct. 11, 1938, PSF: Canada; FDR to William Phillips, Oct. 17, 1938, PSF: Phillips; Hull, *Memoirs*, I, 593-5; *Ickes Diary: 1936-1939*, pp. 479-80; Moffat MS. Diary, Sept. 28, 1938; O. G. Villard to FDR, Oct. 5, 1938, Villard MSS; Langer and Gleason, *Challenge to Isolation*, p. 34.

41. Lucy S. Dawidowicz, *The War Against the Jews, 1933-1945* (New York, 1975), p. 374; David S. Wyman, *Paper Walls: America and the Refugee Crisis, 1938-1941* (Amherst, Mass., 1968), pp. 3-22; Henry L. Feingold, *The Politics of Rescue: The Roosevelt Administration and the Holocaust, 1938-1945* (New Brunswick, N.J., 1970), chap. 1, esp. pp. 13-16, 19.

42. Morgenthau MS. Diary, 115: 380; 116: 264ff.; Moffat MS. Diary, Mar. 19, 21, 1938; *Complete Press Conferences*, XI, 248-50; *Foreign Relations*, 1938, I, 740-41, 791-2, 794-5; Wyman, *Paper Walls*, pp. 5, 221, and chap. 3; Feingold, *Politics of Rescue*, chap. 2, esp. pp. 32-3.

43. Leuchtenburg, *FDR and the New Deal*, pp. 285-6; Moffat MS. Diary, Nov. 14-15, 1938; *Complete Press Conferences*, XII, 227-9, 238-41; "When Roosevelt refused in late 1938 to expel 15,000 refugees who were in the United States on visitors' visas," David Wyman writes, "he was treading the outer limits of Congressional toleration" (*Paper Walls*, pp. 210-11); Wyman

also points out that "increasing the quotas for adults never was a possibility in the face of restrictionist strength" (p. 9); Feingold, *Politics of Rescue,* pp. 38 and 42.

CHAPTER 8

1. Feiling, *Chamberlain,* pp. 378–82; *FDR: Personal Letters, 1928–1945,* II, 816–17; cf. p. 818; *Foreign Relations, 1938,* I, 791, 704–7, 711–12; Bullock, *Hitler,* pp. 418–19; " 'Neville had his choice between war and dishonor and damn near chose both,' " Bowers quoted an English friend as saying, Oct. 3, 1938, PSF: Spain; cf. Anthony Biddle, Jr., to FDR, Oct. 6, 1938, PSF: Germany. Langer and Gleason, *Challenge to Isolation,* pp. 36–7, 54–5; *New York Times,* Oct. 12, 1938, p. 1.

2. John McVickar Haight, Jr., *American Aid to France, 1938–1940* (New York, 1970), chaps. 1–2; *For the President: Correspondence Between FDR and Bullitt,* pp. 297–300; *Complete Press Conferences,* XII, 155–8; *New York Times,* Oct. 15, 1938, p. 1; Morgenthau MS. Diary, 146: 279; 147: 185; Lord Elibank, "Franklin Roosevelt: Friend of Britain," *Contemporary Review,* 187 (June 1955), 364–7; a series of public opinion polls in 1938 revealed that between 65 and 90 per cent of those questioned favored strengthening the navy, army, and air force, see *The Gallup Poll: Public Opinion, 1935–1971,* edited by George H. Gallup (3 vols.; New York, 1972), Vol. I: 1935–1948, polls of Jan. 12, Mar. 13, Oct. 16, Dec. 28, 1938.

3. Morgenthau MS. Diary, 146: 281–2, 288–90, 293; 147: 39–44; 150: 337–42; Blum, *From the Morgenthau Diaries: Years of Urgency, 1938–1941* (Boston, 1965), pp. 46–9; Haight, Jr., *Aid to France,* pp. 48–65; Mark S. Watson, *United States Army in World War II: Chief of Staff: Prewar Plans and Preparations* (Washington, D.C., 1950), pp. 130–43; H. H. Arnold, *Global Mission* (New York, 1949), pp. 171–80; Forrest C. Pogue, *George C. Marshall: Education of a General* (New York, 1963), pp. 322–3, 334–5. In 1938, Germany produced only 3,350 combat planes, and her total aircraft production in 1939 was only a few hundred greater than Britain's. At the outbreak of the war in Sept. 1939 the British and the French had approximately the same number of war planes as Germany. See *New York Times,* May 9, 1948, p. 16; Klein, *Germany's Preparations for War,* pp. 19, 101–2, 177.

4. Haight, Jr., *Aid to France,* chap. 4, pp. 130–31; Blum, *From the Morgenthau Diaries, 1938–1941,* pp. 64–78, which neatly summarizes the extensive material in volumes 158, 172, and 173 of the Morgenthau MS. Diary; for Roosevelt's understanding of what the French orders meant to American aircraft production, see Morgenthau MS. Diary, 173: 183.

5. Alton Frye, *Nazi Germany and the American Hemisphere, 1933–1941* (New Haven, 1967); Haight, Jr., *Aid to France,* p. 55; Stetson Conn and Byron Fairchild, *United States Army in World War II: The Western Hemisphere: The Framework of Hemisphere Defense* (Washington, D.C., 1960), pp. 3–5; *Complete Press Conferences,* XII, 229–31; some of the backdrop to Roosevelt's concern about Latin America can be found in: McIntyre to FDR, Jan. 22, 1938, OF 2875; Louis Johnson to FDR, Mar. 12, 1938, PSF: War Department; Welles to FDR, Sept. 30, 1938, PSF: Hugh Wilson; FDR to

Louis Johnson and Charles Edison, Nov. 2, 1938, OF 2955; Welles to FDR, Nov. 17, 1938, PSF: Welles; Breckinridge Long to FDR, Nov. 18, 1938, PSF: South America.

6. E. David Cronon, *Josephus Daniels in Mexico* (Madison, Wis., 1960), chaps. 7–9; Wood, *Good Neighbor Policy*, chaps. 8–9; Blum, *From the Morgenthau Diaries, 1928–1938*, pp. 493–7.

7. Langer and Gleason, *Challenge to Isolation*, pp. 40–41; Watson, *Prewar Plans and Preparations*, pp. 86–7, 89–91, 94–8, 103–4; Conn and Fairchild, *Framework of Hemisphere Defense*, pp. 5–10, 172–5.

8. Hull, *Memoirs*, I, chap. 42; *From the Berle Papers*, pp. 191–3; *Foreign Relations of the United States*, 1938, V (Washington, D.C., 1955), 80–88; Langer and Gleason, *Challenge to Isolation*, pp. 41–2; FDR to Alfred Landon, Dec. 29, 1938, OF 567; Morgenthau MS. Diary, 161: 34–40.

9. Thomas, *Spanish Civil War*, pp. 541–68; *From the Berle Papers*, pp. 190–91; "Proposed telegram from the Lima Conference to the Spanish Government and to General Franco," Nov. 19, 1938, Adolf A. Berle MSS; *Foreign Relations*, 1938, I, 238–9, 246–7, 255, 260–61; Traina, *American Diplomacy and the Spanish Civil War*, pp. 150–52, 196–201.

10. Moffat MS. Diary, Nov. 19, 1938; Ickes to FDR, Nov. 23, 1938; Welles to FDR, Nov. 25, 30, 1938; FDR to Attorney General, Nov. 28, 1938; memorandum for the Attorney General, Dec. 5, 1938; FDR to Welles, Dec. 21, 1938, PSF: Spain; Traina, *American Diplomacy and the Spanish Civil War*, pp. 213–15.

11. FDR, "Diary and Itineraries," Dec. 15, 1938, FDRL; Welles to FDR, Dec. 22, 1938, PSF: Welles; Thomas, *Spanish Civil War*, pp. 569–73; *P.P.A.*: 1939, pp. 1–4.

12. Pittman to FDR, Jan. 11, 1939, PPF 745; Traina, *American Diplomacy and the Spanish Civil War*, pp. 203–20; Moffat MS. Diary, Jan. 19–20, 23, 1939; Stimson to Hull, Jan. 18, 1939, PSF: Spain; Moore to Hull, Jan. 23, 1939, Moore MSS; FDR to Bowers, Jan. 26, 1939, PPF 730; Welles to McIntyre, Jan. 30, 1939, OF 422; *Ickes Diary: 1936–1939*, pp. 562, 566, 569–70; Leuchtenburg, *FDR and the New Deal*, pp. 271–4. Roosevelt's unwillingness to "tamper" with the Spanish embargo has been attributed exclusively or principally to fear of offending Catholic opinion. The argument is well summarized in J. David Valaik, "Catholics, Neutrality, and the Spanish Embargo, 1937–1939," *JAH*, LIV (June 1967), 73–85, esp. 83. I believe FDR saw the issue as more complicated than this: he thought about not only Catholic reaction but also congressional resistance to doing anything, the likely impact on general neutrality revision, and whether repeal would actually make a difference. Hugh Thomas thinks that by January it was already too late (*Spanish Civil War*, p. 574). " 'You have been right all along' " FDR told Bowers (Bowers to Farley, May 17, 1939, Farley MSS).

13. Moffat MS. Diary, Jan. 20, 1939; Taylor, *U.S. and the Spanish Civil War*, chap. 9, esp. p. 200; Thomas, *Spanish Civil War*, chap. 73; Traina, *American Diplomacy and the Spanish Civil War*, pp. 220–22.

14. Pittman to Moore, Oct. 13, 1939; "Proposed Changes in Neutrality Act of May 1, 1937," Oct. 28, 1938; Moore to Hull, Nov. 7, 1938; Moore to

Senator Elbert Thomas, Nov. 29, 1938, Moore MSS; Moffat MS. Diary, Oct. 18, Nov. 7, 1938; Pittman to FDR, Jan. 11, 1939, PPF 745; Divine, *Illusion of Neutrality*, pp. 234-6.

15. The White House transcript of the President's conference with the Senators does not record him as mentioning the Rhine, but his statements added up to the same thing. The transcript is in PPF 1-P. Alsop and Kintner, *American White Paper*, pp. 30-32; Basil Rauch, *Roosevelt: From Munich to Pearl Harbor* (New York, 1950), pp. 112-14; Langer and Gleason, *Challenge to Isolation*, pp. 48-50; *Complete Press Conferences*, XIII, 112-18, 173-4; Hiram Johnson to Hiram Johnson, Jr., Feb. 4, 11, 1939, Johnson MSS; Villard to William Allen White, Feb. 13, 1939, Villard MSS; *FDR: Personal Letters*, 1928-1945, II, 862; Divine, *Illusion of Neutrality*, pp. 239-41.

16. *For the President: Correspondence Between FDR and Bullitt*, pp. 305-7; *Foreign Relations of the United States, 1939*, I (Washington, D.C., 1956), 13-17, 24-7; Bullitt to FDR, Feb. 3, 1939, PSF: Bullitt; Hull to FDR, Feb. 21, 1939, PSF: Kennedy; Langer and Gleason, *Challenge to Isolation*, pp. 57-9; *FDR: Personal Letters*, 1928-1945, II, 862-3.

17. Bullock, *Hitler*, pp. 422-35; Langer and Gleason, *Challenge to Isolation*, pp. 62-75; *From the Berle Papers*, pp. 199-202; *Ickes Diary: 1936-1939*, pp. 596-7; Blum, *From the Morgenthau Diaries, 1938-1941*, pp. 78-82; Tom Connally and Alfred Steinberg, *My Name Is Tom Connally* (New York, 1954), p. 226; *Foreign Relations, 1939*, I, 49-50, 56; Moffat MS. Diary, Mar. 15, 17, 1939; *Complete Press Conferences*, XIII, 204-5.

18. Carlton Savage to Moore, Feb. 24, 1939; Moore to Hull, Feb. 24, 1939, Moore MSS; Moore to FDR, Mar. 18, 1939, PSF: Neutrality; Divine, *Illusion of Neutrality*, pp. 241-6; Morgenthau MS. Diary, 165:134; Cantril (ed.), *Public Opinion, 1935-1946*, p. 1157; Langer and Gleason, *Challenge to Isolation*, pp. 77-8; Welles to FDR, Mar. 23, 1939, PSF: Italy; *FDR: Personal Letters*, 1928-1945, II, 873; Welles to Early and FDR, Mar. 29, 1939, PSF: Welles; Hull, *Memoirs*, I, 641; *New York Times*, Mar. 30, 1939, p. 8.

19. "Never in my life have I seen things moving in the world with more cross currents or greater velocity," FDR wrote a friend on March 25 (*FDR: Personal Letters*, 1928-1945, II, 872); Bullock, *Hitler*, pp. 435-45; *Foreign Relations, 1939*, I, 101-2, 104-5, 115, 120, 123, 125-7, 130; message for the President, Mar. 29, 1939; Halifax to FDR, Apr. 5, 1939, PSF: Great Britain; *From the Berle Papers*, pp. 210-11.

20. *Complete Press Conferences*, XIII, 259-62, 266-8; *From the Berle Papers*, pp. 211-13; Moffat MS. Diary, Apr. 15-16, 1939; *P.P.A.: 1939*, pp. 195-9, 201-5; Morgenthau Presidential MS. Diary, 1: 59, 81; Henry Wallace, III, 515-16, 552, COHC; Hull, *Memoirs*, I, 620; FDR to MacKenzie King, Apr. 16, 1939, PSF: Canada; Langer and Gleason, *Challenge to Isolation*, pp. 82-5.

21. *Ibid.*, pp. 85-90; *Foreign Relations, 1939*, I, 134-5, 137-40, 142-3, 159, 162; Williams Phillips MS. Diary, Apr. 18, 1939; Phillips to FDR, Apr. 20, 1939, PSF: Phillips; *From the Berle Papers*, pp. 213-16; Bullock, *Hitler*, pp. 446-50; Hiram Johnson to Hiram Johnson, Jr., Apr. 29, 1939, Johnson MSS; Leuchtenburg, *FDR and the New Deal*, p. 289; for the administration's concern with answering isolationist attacks on the Preisdent's

foreign policy, see "Reasons in Favor of Making Speech Dated 4-20-39 on the General Question of the War Situation"; and Berle to FDR, Apr. 24, 1939, Speech Material File, FDRL.

22. Divine, *Illusion of Neutrality*, pp. 246–57; "Neutrality Legislation," Apr. 7, 1939; Moore to Hull, Apr. 14, 1939, Moore MSS; Hiram Johnson to Hiram Johnson, Jr., Apr. 8, 21, 1939, Johnson MSS; *Complete Press Conferences*, XIII, 319; Moffat MS. Diary, Apr. 7, May 3, 1939.

23. One Washington observer told Moffat "that were any other President in the White House, it [the neutrality law] would be repealed in twenty-four hours, but that the Republicans avowedly—and half the Democrats secretly—believed that he [FDR] was trying to line us up with England and France in war and that there must be never ending vigilance in Congress to prevent this" (Moffat MS. Diary, May 2, 1939); also see entries for May 8, 16–18, 1939; Adolf A. Berle MS. Diary, May 8, 1939; Alsop and Kintner, *American White Paper*, pp. 39–43; Hull, *Memoirs*, I, 641–3; Langer and Gleason, *Challenge to Isolation*, pp. 79, 81, 136–8; Divine, *Illusion of Neutrality*, pp. 257–62; Cantril (ed.), *Public Opinion, 1935–1946*, p. 1157; *The Gallup Poll: 1935–48*, polls of Apr. 9, 14, 1939; *Foreign Relations, 1939*, I, 184–5, 656–7; Moore to FDR, May 12, 1939, Moore MSS.

24. Hull, *Memoirs*, I, 643–5; *From the Berle Papers*, pp. 223–5; Moore to FDR, May 19, 1939; FDR to Moore, June 7 ,1939, PSF: Neutrality; Feis to Bullitt, May 24, 1939, Herbert Feis MSS; Moffat MS. Diary, June 9, 1939; Langer and Gleason, *Challenge to Isolation*, pp. 138–40; Divine, *Illusion of Neutrality*, pp. 263–7.

25. Moffat MS. Diary, May 25, 31, June 6, 1939; Hull, *Memoirs*, I, 645–6; Watson to FDR, June 7, 1939, Edwin M. Watson MSS; *From the Berle Papers*, pp. 226–7, 229, 231; Hiram Johnson to Hiram Johnson, Jr., July 2, 1939, Johnson MSS; Divine, *Illusion of Neutrality*, pp. 267–73.

26. Caroline O'Day to FDR, July 7, 1939, PSF: Congress; *New York Times*, July 20, 1939, p. 18; Francis O. Wilcox, "The Neutrality Fight in Congress: 1939," *American Political Science Review*, XXXIII (Oct. 1939), 818–25; Langer and Gleason, *Challenge to Isolation*, 145–6; Divine, *Illusion of Neutrality*, pp. 273–4, 282–5; Hiram Johnson to Hiram Johnosn, Jr., June 3, 10, 17, 1939, Johnson MSS.

27. *FDR: Personal Letters, 1928–1945*, II, 899–901; *Complete Press Conferences*, XIV, 3–4; Hull, *Memoirs*, I, 646–8; *Foreign Relations, 1939*, I, 662–8; *Ickes Diary: 1936–1939*, p. 676.

28. *FDR: Personal Letters, 1928–1945*, II, 898, 902; Watson to FDR, June 29, 1939, Edwin M. Watson MSS; Israel, *Nevada's Pittman*, pp. 166–7.

29. Divine, *Illusion of Neutrality*, pp. 276–80; Hiram Johnson to Hiram Johnson, Jr., July 8, 16, 22, 1939, Johnson MSS; Morgenthau Presidential MS. Diary, 1: 157; *P.P.A.: 1939*, pp. 381–7.

30. Alsop and Kintner, *American White Paper*, pp. 44–6; a poll of May 19, 1939, indicated that 68 per cent of the public shared Borah's belief that there would be no war in 1939, *The Gallup Poll: 1935–1948*; Hull, *Memoirs*, I, 649–53; Langer and Gleason, *Challenge to Isolation*, pp. 143–5; *P.P.A.: 1939*, pp. 387–8; *Complete Press Conferences*, XIV, 85–6.

31. Langer and Gleason, *Challenge to Isolation*, pp. 146–7; Gerhard Wein-

berg, "Hitler's Image of the United States," *AHR*, LXIX (July 1964), 1010–13; Weinberg, *Foreign Policy of Hitler's Germany, 1933–1936*, pp. 21–2; Saul Friedlander, *Prelude to Downfall: Hitler and the United States, 1939–1941* (New York, 1967), pp. 15–26; Bullock, *Hitler*, pp. 451–68.

32. Hull, *Memoirs*, I, 569–70; FDR to Rockwell Kent, Oct. 21, 1938, OF 1561; *Foreign Relations: Japan, 1931–1941*, I, 477–83, 564ff., 760ff., 801–26; Langer and Gleason, *Challenge to Isolation*, pp. 42–5; Lee, *Britain and Sino-Japanese War, 1937–1939*, chap. 6.

33. Blum, *From the Morgenthau Diaries, 1938–1941*, pp. 58–64; Morgenthau MS. Diary, 143: 152–3; 146: 105–7; 153: 366–9; Chiang Kai-shek to FDR, Oct. 16, 1938; FDR to Chiang, Nov. 10, 1938; H. H. Kung to FDR, Nov. 9, 1938, PSF: China; for the argument that the loan represented the first in a series of steps between 1938 and 1941 to restrain Japan, see Frederick C. Adams, "The Road to Pearl Harbor: A Reexamination of American Far Eastern Policy, July 1937–December 1938," *JAH*, LVIII (June 1971), 73–92.

34. Cantril (ed.), *Public Opinion, 1935–1946*, p. 1156; Donald J. Friedman, *The Road from Isolation: The Campaign of the American Committee for Non-Participation in Japanese Aggression, 1938–1941* (Cambridge, Mass., 1968); Warren I. Cohen, "The Role of Private Groups in the United States," in Borg and Okamoto, *Pearl Harbor as History*, pp. 432–42; Hull, *Memoirs*, I, 570–71, 627–30; Herbert Feis, *The Road to Pearl Harbor* (New York, 1964 ed.), pp. 17–21; Langer and Gleason, *Challenge to Isolation*, pp. 52–3, 102–5, 147–50; Moffat MS. Diary, Apr. 15–16, 1939; Morgenthau Presidential MS. Diary, 1: 81.

35. Lee, *Britain and Sino-Japanese War, 1937–1939*, chap. 7.

36. Hull, *Memoirs*, I, 630–35; *From the Berle Papers*, pp. 228–30; *FDR: Personal Letters, 1928–1945*, II, 903–4; Langer and Gleason, *Challenge to Isolation*, pp. 150–56.

37. Cantril (ed.), *Public Opinion, 1935–1946*, p. 1157; *The Gallup Poll: 1935–1948*, polls of June 16 and Aug. 30, 1939; Wayne S. Cole, "The Role of the United States Congress and Political Parties," in Borg and Okamoto, *Pearl Harbor as History*, pp. 315–19; Borah to C. W. Johnson, June 16, 1939, Borah MSS; Morgenthau Presidential MS. Diary, 1: 126; Moore to Hull, July 18, 1939, Moore MSS; Moffat MS. Diary, July 26, 1939; *From the Berle Papers*, pp. 231–2; Hull, *Memoirs*, I, 635–40; Feis, *Road to Pearl Harbor*, pp. 21–4; Langer and Gleason, *Challenge to Isolation*, pp. 157–9; Lee, *Britain and Sino-Japanese War, 1937–1939*, pp. 196–204.

38. *Foreign Relations*, 1939, I, 200–205, 293–4, 296–9; *From the Berle Papers*, pp. 235, 241; Bullock, *Hitler*, pp. 468–70; Langer and Gleason, *Challenge to Isolation*, pp. 160–74, 181–5.

39. *Foreign Relations*, 1939, I, 351–2; 356, 360–63, 368, 382; Phillips to FDR, Aug. 25, 1939, PSF: Italy; William Phillips, pp. 125–6, COHC; *From the Berle Papers*, pp. 235–6, 242–3; Moffat MS. Diary, Aug. 24, 1939; Langer and Gleason, *Challenge to Isolation*, pp. 185–92.

40. "In the Event of a European War," n.d., 1939, PSF: Neutrality; *Foreign Relations*, 1939, I, 211, 368–9, 350, 355–6; Moffat MS. Diary, Aug. 24, 1939; *From the Berle Papers*, pp. 243–4.

41. Louis Johnson to FDR, Aug. 22, 1939, PSF: War Department; Morgenthau MS. Diary, 206: 180, 400; Morgenthau Presidential MS. Diary 2: 272, 277; Moffat MS. Diary, Aug. 26–27, Sept. 1, 1939; *From the Berle Papers*, pp. 237–8, 240, 242, 244–50; *FDR: Personal Letters, 1928–1945*, II, 915–16; Alsop and Kintner, *American White Paper*, pp. 58–68.

CHAPTER 9

1. Hull, *Memoirs*, I, 674–5; *P.P.A.: 1939*, pp. 460–78; Morgenthau MS. Diary, 206: 400–401; *From the Berle Papers*, pp. 244–5.

2. H. S. Houston to "Missy" LeHand, July 17, 1939; FDR to "Missy," July 20, 1939, OF 1561; *Complete Press Conferences*, XIV, 38–42, 85–6, 109–10, 128; *From the Berle Papers*, p. 244; Frederick J. Libby to FDR, Aug. 29, 1939; FDR to Libby, Sept. 12, 1939, PPF 87, and OF 1561.

3. For expressions of congressional sentiment, see the correspondence to FDR for August and September in OF 419a, 1561, and PF 4694, 4057; also see Early to FDR, Sept. 7, 1939, PSF: Early; Moore to FDR, Sept. 8, 1939, Moore MSS; Watson to FDR, Sept. 9, 1939, PSF: Watson; Feis to Bullitt, Sept. 9, 1939, Feis MSS; Johnson to Watson, Sept. 11, 1939, PSF: War Dept.: Louis Johnson; *FDR: Personal Letters, 1928–1945*, II, 919.

4. Langer and Gleason, *Challenge to Isolation*, pp. 219–20, 236; *Ickes Diary: 1936–1939*, p. 720; *For the President: Correspondence Between FDR and Bullitt*, pp. 368–72; Kennedy to FDR, Sept. 10, 1939, PSF: Joseph Kennedy; FDR to John N. Garner and congressional leaders, Sept. 13, 1939, OF 419a.

5. Watson to FDR, Sept. 13, 1939, OF 1561; Early to Bernard Baruch, Sept. 14, 1939, PPF 88; Louis Johnson, "Memorandum," Sept. 18, 1939, PSF: Senate; "Memorandum for the President," Sept. 21, 1939, Moore MSS; Moffat MS. Diary, Sept. 16–17, 1939; Divine, *Illusion of Neutrality*, pp. 297–9; *Wartime Journals of Lindbergh*, pp. 254–60; "Memorandum: Re: Neutrality Act," Sept. 15, 1939, PSF: Neutrality.

6. Langer and Gleason, *Challenge to Isolation*, pp. 201–2; *The Gallup Poll: 1935–1948*, poll of Sept. 3, 1939; Cantril (ed.), *Public Opinion, 1935–1946*, pp. 1075, 1157–8, 1185; Robert Sherrod to Early, Sept. 19, 1939, with the *Fortune* survey attached, PPF 1820 "Neutrality, 1939"; *The Secret Diary of Harold Ickes: The Lowering Clouds, 1939–1941* (New York, 1954), pp. 36–7; Watson to FDR, Sept. 20, 1939, with Vanderbilt's report attached, PPF 104; in a poll of Oct. 24, 1939, 56 per cent expressed themselves in favor of changing the neutrality law so that England and France or any other nation could buy war materials in the United States. Fifty-seven per cent of this group favored the policy because it would either improve American business or keep the country out of war; only 33 per cent saw it as a means to help England and France or to defend democracy (Cantril (ed.), *Public Opinion, 1935–1946*, p. 1158).

7. *Ickes Diary: 1939–1941*, pp. 7–8; *FDR: Personal Letters, 1928–1945*, II, 921; Sen. Pat Harrison to FDR, Sept. 18, 1939, PSF: Neutrality; *P.P.A.: 1939*, pp. 512–22.

8. Watson to Hull, Sept. 4, 1939, PSF: Hull; Morgenthau MS. Diary, 206: 317–18, 429–30; 209: 107–8, 145, 152–3, 257; 214: 185–8; Morgenthau

Presidential MS. Diary, 2: 270, 278, 334, 351; FDR to Welles, Sept. 7, 1939, PSF: Welles; Tully to Morgenthau, Sept. 19, 1939; Morgenthau to Tully, Sept. 20, 1939, PSF: Morgenthau; Bullitt to FDR, Oct. 4, 1939, PSF: Bullitt; Hull to FDR, Oct. 5, 1939, PSF: Safe File: Lord Lothian; "French Purchases in the United States," Oct. 9, 1939, PSF: Safe File: France; Hull, *Memoirs*, I, 679–81, 684; Langer and Gleason, *Challenge to Isolation*, pp. 282–3; *FDR: Personal Letters, 1928–1945*, II, 919; *Roosevelt and Churchill: Their Secret Wartime Correspondence*, edited by Francis L. Loewenheim, Harold D. Langley, and Manfred Jonas (New York, 1975), p. 89.

9. Tweedsmuir to FDR, Sept. 8, 1939; FDR to Hull, Sept. 16, 1939; Hull to FDR, Sept. 19, 1939; FDR to Tweedsmuir, Oct. 5, 1939, PSF: Canada; Watson, *Prewar Plans and Preparations*, pp. 156–63; Morgenthau MS. Diary, 209: 393–4; 212: 216A–J; Langer and Gleason, *Challenge to Isolation*, pp. 269–72; *FDR: Personal Letters, 1928–1945*, II, 933.

10. FDR conference with Democratic and Republican leaders, Sept. 20, 1939, OF 1561; Moffat MS. Diary, Sept. 20–22, 1939; Joseph C. Green memo, Sept. 19, 1939; memo on likely Senate vote, Sept. 25, 1939, Moore MSS; *Washington Post* memo, n.d., but probably Sept. 22, 1939, PPF 1820 "Neutrality 1939"; Watson to FDR, Sept. 21, 1939, PSF: Watson; Hiram Johnson to Hiram Johnson, Jr., Sept. 24, 1939, Johnson MSS; *Complete Press Conferences*, XIV, 185; *FDR: Personal Letters, 1928–1945*, II, 932–3; *Ickes Diary: 1939–1941*, pp. 28–9; Divine, *Illusion of Neutrality*, pp. 300–307; *P.P.A.: 1939*, pp. 556–7.

11. *FDR: Personal Letters, 1928–1945*, II, 924–6, 929–30, 946–7; *Complete Press Conferences*, XIV, 211–13, 216; Watson to FDR, Sept. 21, 1939, PPF 1820, "Neutrality 1939"; *P.P.A.: 1939*, pp. 514–16; *Ickes Diary: 1939–1941*, pp. 38, 43, 51; Ickes to FDR, Oct. 16, 1939; Watson to FDR, Oct. 18, 19, 1939, PSF: Neutrality; file memo, Oct. 26, 1939, and Early to Sol Bloom, Oct. 26, 1939, OF 857; Divine, *Illusion of Neutrality*, pp. 273–4, 325–31.

12. Hull, *Memoirs*, I, 688–90; Alsop and Kintner, *American White Paper*, pp. 60-62, 68–9; *From the Berle Papers*, pp. 245–6, 248–50, 252–3; Berle, "Memo for the President," Sept. 2, 1939; Welles to FDR, Sept. 5, 1939, PSF: State Dept.; *Foreign Relations of the United States, 1939*, V (Washington, D.C., 1957), 15–18, 20–21, 25–6, 28–36, 42–53, 85ff.; Wood, *Good Neighbor Policy*, chaps. 12–13; Welles, *Time for Decision*, pp. 210–14; Langer and Gleason, *Challenge to Isolation*, pp. 206–12, 215.

13. *Ibid.*, pp. 209–10, 212–18, 281–3, 355–6; Blum, *From the Morgenthau Diaries, 1938–1941*, pp. 50–58; Morgenthau MS. Diary, 216: 385–91; *From the Berle Papers*, pp. 260–61; *FDR: Personal Letters, 1928–1945*, II, 936–7; Hull, *Memoirs*, I, 690–92; Friedlander, *Prelude to Downfall*, pp. 56–65.

14. *Foreign Relations, 1939*, I, 421–4, 499–509, 521; *From the Berle Papers*, pp. 256–7, 264–6; memorandum for the President, Sept. 18, 1939, PSF: Berle; memorandum for the President, Sept. 22, 1939, Berle MSS; Berle MS. Diary, Sept. 15, 22, Oct. 6, 12, 1939; Nancy H. Hooker (ed.), *The Moffat Papers* (Cambridge, Mass., 1956), pp. 272–6; Kennedy to FDR, Sept. 30, 1939, PSF: Kennedy; Blum, *From the Morgenthau Diaries, 1938–1941*, p. 102; Joseph Davies to FDR, Oct. 7, 1939, PSF: Davies; *FDR:*

Personal Letters, 1928–1945, II, 938–9; Langer and Gleason, *Challenge to Isolation,* pp. 246–59.

15. Hull, *Memoirs,* I, 685, 701–6; *Foreign Relations, 1939,* I, 959–61, 965–7, 975, 1003–4; *The Moffat Papers,* pp. 269–71, 279; *From the Berle Papers,* pp. 255, 263–5, 273; Langer and Gleason, *Challenge to Isolation,* pp. 318–29, 265–6.

16. *FDR: Personal Letters, 1928–1945,* II, 961, 974, 972; Hull, *Memoirs,* I, 706–9; *The Moffat Papers,* pp. 280–81; *From the Berle Papers,* pp. 273–5; Morgenthau MS. Diary, 226: 261; *Ickes Diary: 1939–1941,* p. 75; Robert Sobel, *The Origins of Interventionism: The U.S. and the Russo-Finnish War* (New York, 1960), pp. 91–4; Langer and Gleason, *Challenge to Isolation,* pp. 329–32; Blum, *From the Morgenthau Diaries, 1938–1941,* pp. 125–30.

17. Langer and Gleason, *Challenge to Isolation,* pp. 334–5, 338–9; Forrest C. Pogue, *George C. Marshall: Ordeal and Hope, 1939–1942* (London, 1968 ed.), pp. 6–7, 10–11, 16–17; *FDR: Personal Letters, 1928–1945,* II, 964–5, 968, 975; FDR to Hull, Jan. 2, 1940, OF 434; Moffat MS. Diary, Jan. 5, 15, 30, 1940; Cantril (ed.), *Public Opinion, 1935–1946,* p. 1159; Sobel, *Origins of Interventionism,* pp. 115–17.

18. Morgenthau to FDR, Jan. 10, 1940, PSF: Morgenthau; Morgenthau Presidential MS. Diary, 2: 416; *P.P.A.: 1940,* pp. 49–51.

19. Moffat MS. Diary, Jan. 16, 18, 22, 1940; Henry Wallace, IV, 676, COHC; *Ickes Diary: 1939–1941,* p. 112; *P.P.A.: 1940,* pp. 92–3; Charles E. Bohlen, *The Transformation of American Foreign Policy* (New York, 1969), p. 63; Langer and Gleason, *Challenge to Isolation,* pp. 336–8, 340.

20. *Ibid.,* pp. 232–4; Hull to Emory S. Land, Nov. 6, 1939; "Draft from Welles, Nov. 1939," PSF: Neutrality; Watson to FDR, Nov. 9, 1939, Watson MSS; memorandum for Watson, Nov. 9, 1939, PSF: Congress; Watson to FDR, Nov. 13, 1939, PSF: Hull; *From the Berle Papers,* pp. 268–9; *FDR: Personal Letters, 1928–1945,* II, 953–4.

21. Langer and Gleason, *Challenge to Isolation,* pp. 288–91; H. Duncan Hall, *North American Supply* (London, 1955), chaps. 3–4; Blum, *From the Morgenthau Diaries, 1938–1941,* pp. 101–22; *FDR: Personal Letters, 1928–1945,* II, 959–60; Henry Wallace, V, 1056, COHC; Haight, *American Aid to France, 1938–40,* chaps. 7–8.

22. *For the President: Correspondence Between FDR and Bullitt,* pp. 379–80, 390–92; Kennedy to FDR, Nov. 3, 1939, PSF: Kennedy; Morgenthau MS. Diary, 230: 3–6; *From the Berle Papers,* pp. 254–8, 273, 276; Adolf A. Berle MS. Diary, Dec. 26, 1939: "Three Fallacies: 'Isolation,'" Nov. 8, 1939, PSF: Neutrality.

23. *FDR: Personal Letters, 1928–1945,* II, 965, 967–8; "President wants China to continue to play with Russia. To keep Russia and Japan apart," Morgenthau recorded after a Cabinet meeting on December 19, 1939, MS. Diary, 230: 408; Watson to FDR, Jan. 15, 1940, PSF: State Dept.; Hull to FDR, Jan. 15, 1940, PSF: Hull; *From the Berle Papers,* pp. 284–5; *P.P.A.: 1940,* pp. 1–6.

24. *From the Berle Papers,* pp. 275–9; Berle MS. Diary, Dec. 26, 1939; Langer and Gleason, *Challenge to Isolation,* pp. 346–50; *P.P.A.: 1939,* pp. 606–8.

25. Kennedy to FDR, Nov. 3, 1939, PSF: Kennedy; Alsop and Kintner, *American White Paper*, pp. 85–6; Welles, *Time for Decision*, p. 73; James D. Mooney to FDR, Mar. 15, 1940, with messages of Mar. 11, 12, 13, 14, 15, 1940, PSF: Safe: Italy; FDR to Capt. Callaghan, Mar. 25, 1940, PSF: Safe: Germany; *From the Berle Papers*, pp. 280–81, 283–4, 287–8; Berle MS. Diary, Dec. 26, 1939, Feb. 2, 1940; memorandum for the President, Jan. 10, 1940; Welles to FDR, Jan. 12, 1940, PSF: Welles; *Foreign Relations of the United States, 1940*, I (Washington, D.C., 1959), 117–22; Langer and Gleason, *Challenge to Isolation*, pp. 343–5, 350–54.

26. On the origins and purposes of the Welles mission, see Raymond Clapper MS. Diary, Feb. 12, 1940; Berle MS. Diary, Feb. 13, 1940; Alsop and Kintner, *American White Paper*, p. 86; *From the Berle Papers*, pp. 284–5; 290–91; Fred L. Israel (ed.), *The War Diary of Breckinridge Long* (Lincoln, Neb., 1966), p. 64; *Foreign Relations, 1940*, I, 1–4, 117–19; Hull, *Memoirs*, I, 737–8; Langer and Gleason, *Challenge to Isolation*, pp. 361–3; Stanley E. Hilton, "The Welles Mission to Europe, February–March 1940: Illusion or Realism?", *JAH*, LVIII (June 1971), 93–120. For the argument that the Welles mission was an attempt at appeasement, see Arnold A. Offner, "Appeasement Revisited: The United States, Great Britain, and Germany, 1933–1940," *JAH*, LXIV (Sept. 1977), 384–93. On FDR's plans for 1940, see Burns, *The Lion and the Fox*, pp. 408–18, 532–3; Leuchtenburg, *FDR and the New Deal*, pp. 314–15; ". . . It has gotten so far that it is a game with me," FDR told Morgenthau about the third-term issue on January 24, 1940. "They ask me a lot of questions, and I really enjoy trying to avoid them. . . . I do not want to run unless between now and the convention things get very much worse in Europe. . . ." (Presidential MS. Diary, 2: 419–20). FDR's comment to Bullitt is in Henry Wallace, V, 925, COHC.

27. Hull, *Memoirs*, I, 739–40; Berle MS. Diary, Mar. 13, 1940; *P.P.A.: 1940*, pp. 102–4; *Foreign Relations, 1940*, I, 18–19.

28. *Ibid.*, pp. 21ff.; CAB.65, W.M. 67 (40) 7, Mar. 13, 1940; Sir Llewellyn Woodward, *British Foreign Policy in the Second World War* (4 vols.; 1970–75), I, 164–71; *The Moffat Papers*, pp. 296–8; Langer and Gleason, *Challenge to Isolation*, pp. 363–75.

29. Blum, *From the Morgenthau Diaries, 1938–1941*, pp. 133–5; *Complete Press Conferences*, XV, 242, 264–6, 273–83; *P.P.A.: 1940*, pp. 130–32, 161.

30. Langer and Gleason, *Challenge to Isolation*, pp. 419–26, 429–35; *Complete Press Conferences*, XV, 249–52, 279–80; Hull to FDR, n.d., but probably April 21, 1940, PSF: Canada; Pickersgill, *The Mackenzie King Record, 1939–1944*, pp. 106–7; *From the Berle Papers*, pp. 304–9; *For the President: Correspondence Between FDR and Bullitt*, pp. 411–12.

31. Morgenthau Presidential MS. Diary, 2: 469, 471; Langer and Gleason, *Challenge to Isolation*, pp. 438–44, 450–52; Hull, *Memoirs*, I, 277–80; Moffat MS. Diary, Apr. 29–30, May 14, 1940; William Phillips MS. Diary, Apr. 30, May 1, 1940; *Peace and War: United States Foreign Policy, 1931–1941* (Washington, D.C., 1943), pp. 519–22, 526, 536.

32. FDR to Capt. Callaghan, May 9, 1940, PSF: Navy; Moffat MS. Diary, May 9, 1940; Watson, *Prewar Plans and Preparations*, pp. 156–68;

Blum, *From the Morgenthau Diaries, 1938–1941*, pp. 138–44; Morgenthau Presidential MS. Diary, 2: 531–4; Johnson to FDR, May 15, 1940, PSF: War Dept.: Louis Johnson; *P.P.A.: 1940*, pp. 198–204; Langer and Gleason, *Challenge to Isolation*, pp. 469–74.

33. *For the President: Correspondence Between FDR and Bullitt*, pp. 415–20; Winston S. Churchill, *The Second World War: Their Finest Hour* (Bantam Books ed., New York, 1962), pp. 19–22; *Roosevelt and Churchill: Secret Wartime Correspondence*, pp. 94–6.

34. Blum, *From the Morgenthau Diaries, 1938–1941*, pp. 149–52; Pogue, *Marshall: 1939–1942*, pp. 49–51; Morgenthau to FDR, May 25, 1940, PSF: Morgenthau; Langer and Gleason, *Challenge to Isolation*, pp. 446–9, 487–93; *Foreign Relations*, 1940, I, 227–30, 232; *Roosevelt and Churchill: Secret Wartime Correspondence*, pp. 96–7; *For the President: Correspondence Between FDR and Bullitt*, pp. 430–32.

35. Langer and Gleason, *Challenge to Isolation*, pp. 458–66; William Phillips MS. Diary, May 27, 1940; *Peace and War, 1931–1941*, pp. 536–40, 544; *Foreign Relations*, 1940, I, 234, 236–7.

36. Watson, *Prewar Plans and Preparations*, pp. 168–71; Langer and Gleason, *Challenge to Isolation*, pp. 475–6; "Memorandum for the President," May 21, 1940, PSF: Navy; *P.P.A.: 1940*, pp. 250–53.

37. Henry Cabot Lodge to the Editor, *Boston Globe*, May 20, 1940, PSF: Senate; *Ickes Diary: 1939–1941*, pp. 181–4, 193–5; *FDR: Personal Letters, 1928–1945*, II, 1026–7, 1033–4; *P.P.A.: 1940*, pp. 230–40; *Complete Press Conferences*, XV, 355–7, 359–62, 367–71; Early to FDR, May 23, 1940; FDR to Early, May 28, 1940, PSF: Executive Office: Early; Langer and Gleason, *Challenge to Isolation*, pp. 476–80.

38. United States Senate, *Final Report of the Select Committee to Study Governmental Operations with Respect to Intelligence Activities*, Book III (Washington, D.C., 1976), pp. 277–81, 561–5; Joseph P. Lash, *Roosevelt and Churchill, 1939–1941* (New York, 1976), pp. 137–40; FDR to the Attorney General, May 21, 1940, PSF: Justice: Robert Jackson; FDR to the Attorney General, May 20, 1940, Watson MSS. An inquiry to the FBI under the Freedom of Information Act for copies of papers in J. Edgar Hoover's "Official and Confidential" files describing FDR's dealings with Hoover on these and other matters produced seventeen pages of unrevealing material.

39. Early to J. Edgar Hoover, May 18, 1940; Hoover to Early, May 25, 1940, PPF 200; United States Senate, 94th Congress, First Session, *Hearings before the Select Committee to Study Governmental Operations with Respect to Intelligence Activities*, VI (Washington, D.C., 1976), 452–4; *Wartime Journals of Lindbergh*, pp. 347–50; Wayne S. Cole, *Charles A. Lindbergh and the Battle Against American Intervention in World War II* (New York, 1974), pp. 87–91, 157; FDR to Stimson, May 21, 1940, PSF: Stimson; *P.P.A.: 1940*, pp. 238–9.

40. Berle MS. Diary, Sept. 22, 1939, Apr. 2, 1940; Daladier to FDR, Apr. 4, 1940, PSF: France: Bullitt; Welles to FDR, Apr. 12, 1940, PSF: Welles; Frye, *Nazi Germany and the American Hemisphere*, chap. 9; Ladislas Farago, *The Game of the Foxes* (Bantam Books ed., New York, 1973),

chaps. 33–34; J. Edgar Hoover to Edwin M. Watson, June 3, 1940, OF 10B; *Complete Press Conferences*, XV, 483–4.

41. Farago, *Game of the Foxes*, argues the case for extensive Nazi espionage and sabotage in the United States; chapter 4 describes how the Nazis stole part of the plans for the Norden bombsight; for a critique of Farago's argument and the fact that the Nazis did not use the bombsight, see A. J. P. Taylor's review in *The New York Review of Books*, 18 (Feb. 10, 1972), p. 14; cf. Hugh Trevor-Roper's review in *The New York Times Book Review*, Jan. 30, 1972, p. 1; and see especially Louis De Jong, *The German Fifth Column in the Second World War* (Chicago, 1956), particularly chaps. 6, 12, and 15.

42. Langer and Gleason, *Challenge to Isolation*, pp. 511–12; Blum, *From the Morgenthau Diaries, 1938–1941*, pp. 152–5; Morgenthau to Watson, June 5, 1940; FDR to Morgenthau, June 6, 1940, PSF: Morgenthau; Hadley Cantril, "America Faces the War: A Study in Public Opinion," *Public Opinion Quarterly*, 4 (Sept. 1940), 387, 391–2, 397; Cantril (ed.), *Public Opinion, 1935–46*, p. 1159.

43. Leuchtenburg, *FDR and the New Deal*, pp. 315–16; for the view that FDR lagged behind public opinion, see Langer and Gleason, *Challenge to Isolation*, pp. 504–5; on the trends in domestic feeling, see Cantril "America Faces the War," *Public Opinion Quarterly* (Sept. 1940), 396–7; Hadley Cantril to James W. Young, "America Faces the War—the reaction of public opinion," n.d., but probably Nov. 1940, pp. 5–6, 11, in OF 857; Cantril (ed.), *Public Opinion, 1935–46*, p. 1159; Haight, *American Aid to France*, pp. 250–53; *FDR: Personal Letters, 1928–1945*, II, 1037–8.

44. Langer and Gleason, *Challenge to Isolation*, pp. 505, 513–17; *Complete Press Conferences*, XV, 542–8; *The Moffat Papers*, pp. 310–12; P.P.A.: 1940, pp. 259–64.

45. *Foreign Relations, 1940*, I, 245–6; *Roosevelt and Churchill: Secret Wartime Correspondence*, pp. 98–100; Churchill, *Their Finest Hour*, pp. 130–36, 153–4.

46. Langer and Gleason, *Challenge to Isolation*, pp. 518–22; FDR to Churchill, June 13, 1940, MRP; *Foreign Relations, 1940*, I, 247–57; *Roosevelt and Churchill: Secret Wartime Correspondence*, pp. 104–6; Churchill, *Their Finest Hour*, pp. 154–63.

47. There is a full discussion of this issue in chapter 16 of Langer and Gleason.

48. Cantril "America Faces the War," *Public Opinion Quarterly* (Sept. 1940), 390, 396–7; Cantril, "America Faces the War—the reaction of public opinion," pp. 4–6, 9–10 in OF 857; C. B. Yorke to Early, June 21, 1940, OF 3618 gave the White House a *Fortune* survey showing 67.5 per cent of the public favoring "active aid to the Allies"; Cole, *Lindbergh and the Battle Against Intervention*, p. 157; *Wartime Journals of Lindbergh*, pp. 356–8; Langer and Gleason, *Challenge to Isolation*, pp. 566–9, 509–11, 521–2; Blum, *From the Morgenthau Diaries, 1938–1941*, pp. 159–69; Max Freedman (ed.), *Roosevelt and Frankfurter: Their Correspondence, 1928–1945* (Boston, 1967), pp. 523–30; *FDR: Personal Letters, 1928–1945*, II, 1041–4; Harold D. Smith MS. Diary, Nov. 13, 1939; Knox to FDR, Dec. 15,

1939; Knox to Mrs. Knox, June 11, 1940, Knox MSS; Frances Perkins, VII, 639–40, COHC; Lash, *Roosevelt and Churchill, 1939–1941*, pp. 170–71.

CHAPTER 10

1. Welles to FDR, Apr. 29, 1940, PSF: State Dept.; E. C. Wilson to Hull, May 15, 1940; FDR to Welles, May 20, June 13, 14, July 16, 1940; Welles to FDR, May 20, 24, 25, June 13, 14, 1940, PSF: Welles; Bowers to FDR, May 14, 25, June 1, 7, 19, 1940; FDR to Bowers, May 24, June 3, 25, July 1, 1940, PSF: Chile; Harold Stark to FDR, June 18, 1940, PSF: Navy; Daniels to FDR, June 28, 1940, PSF: Mexico; Conn and Fairchild, *Framework of Hemisphere Defense*, pp. 31–4.

2. *Foreign Relations of the United States, 1940*, V (Washington, D.C., 1961), 6–8, 11–21; Welles to FDR, June 1, 3, 1940; FDR to Stark, June 1, 5, 1940; FDR to Welles, June 3, 1940, PSF: Welles; Conn and Fairchild, *Framework of Hemisphere Defense*, pp. 175–9, 208–13; Langer and Gleason, *Challenge to Isolation*, pp. 610–22.

3. *From the Berle Papers*, pp. 324–6, 328; Berle MS. Diary, May 24, 1940; Berle to FDR, July 15, 18, 1940; Welles to FDR, July 19, 1940, PSF: Berle; *P.P.A.: 1940*, pp. 273–4, 303–5; Langer and Gleason, *Challenge to Isolation*, pp. 629–37.

4. Harold D. Smith to FDR, Mar. 20, 1940, PSF: State Dept.; Conn and Fairchild, *Framework of Hemisphere Defense*, pp. 34–9; Langer and Gleason, *Challenge to Isolation*, pp. 622–9.

5. *Foreign Relations, 1940*, V, 180–81, 189, 200–201, 212–21, 239–42, 252–6; Hull, *Memoirs*, I, chap. 59; *From the Berle Papers*, pp. 328–31; Berle MS. Diary, Aug. 2, 1940; Langer and Gleason, *Challenge to Isolation*, pp. 688–99; Frye, *Nazi Germany and the American Hemisphere*, pp. 163–7, 193.

6. Conn and Fairchild, *Framework of Hemisphere Defense*, pp. 68–72, 214; Frye, *Nazi Germany and the American Hemisphere*, pp. 168–94, provides an excellent statement of the case for meeting a German threat; for a different view, see Bruce M. Russett, *No Clear and Present Danger: A Skeptical View of the U.S. Entry into World War II* (New York, 1972), pp. 34–7.

7. Waldo H. Heinrichs, Jr., *American Ambassador: Joseph C. Grew* (Boston, 1966), pp. 289–95; Hull, *Memoirs*, I, 717–23; Joseph C. Grew, *Ten Years in Japan* (New York, 1944), pp. 294–97; Langer and Gleason, *Challenge to Isolation*, pp. 291–301.

8. *Ibid.*, pp. 301–11, 576–9; Hull, *Memoirs*, I, 722–30; *Foreign Relations of the United States, 1939*, III (Washington, D.C., 1955), 687–91, 712–13; *Foreign Relations of the United States, 1940*, IV (Washington, D.C., 1960), 278–9; Blum, *From the Morgenthau Diaries, 1938–1941*, p. 127; *Ickes Diary: 1939–1941*, pp. 96, 132; James C. Thomson, Jr., "Role of the State Department," in Borg and Okamoto, *Pearl Harbor as History*, p. 99; Cantril (ed.), *Public Opinion, 1935–1946*, p. 1159; Heinrichs, Jr., *American Ambassador*, pp. 290, 295–301; Morgenthau MS. Diary, 231: 210–11; *FDR: Personal Letters, 1928–1945*, II, 945, 961, 969.

9. Langer and Gleason, *Challenge to Isolation*, pp. 579–95; *Foreign Relations, 1940*, IV, 647–8; Hull, *Memoirs*, I, 724, 888–95; *Complete Press Con-*

ferences, XV, 260; Callaghan to FDR, Apr. 17, 1940, PSF: Navy; Moffat MS. Diary, Apr. 17, 1940; Lord Lothian memo for FDR, May 12, 1940, PSF: Great Britain; Morgenthau Presidential MS. Diary, 3: 568.

10. Feis, *Road to Pearl Harbor*, pp. 66-71; Langer and Gleason, *Challenge to Isolation*, pp. 595-606, 719-20; Hull, *Memoirs*, I, 896-9.

11. Blum, *From the Morgenthau Diaries, 1938-1941*, pp. 348-51; Stimson MS. Diary, July 18, 19, 1940; Washington Committee for Non-Participation in Japanese Aggression to FDR, July 10, 1940, OF 197A; Lauchlin Currie to FDR, July 16, 1940, PSF: Currie; Callaghan to FDR, July 18, 1940, PSF: Navy; Feis, *Road to Pearl Harbor*, pp. 88-90; Langer and Gleason, *Challenge to Isolation*, pp. 721-2; *FDR: Personal Letters, 1928-1945*, II, 1046-8.

12. Blum, *From the Morgenthau Diaries, 1938-1941*, pp. 351-4; Feis, *Road to Pearl Harbor*, pp. 90-93; Langer and Gleason, *Challenge to Isolation*, p. 722; *Complete Press Conferences*, XVI, 62-3; Stimson MS. Diary, July 26, 1940; Irvine H. Anderson, Jr., *The Standard-Vacuum Oil Company and United States East Asian Policy, 1933-1941* (Princeton, 1975), pp. 129-35, argues persuasively that Roosevelt never intended to adopt a full-scale embargo and that the final Order reflected his real intentions.

13. Feis, *Road to Pearl Harbor*, pp. 76-87, 93-100; William L. Langer and S. Everett Gleason, *The Undeclared War, 1940-1941* (New York, 1953), pp. 4-13, 20; Morgenthau Presidential MS. Diary, 3: 644; Anderson, Jr., *Standard-Vacuum Oil Company*, pp. 135-55.

14. Feis, *Road to Pearl Harbor*, pp. 101-6; Langer and Gleason, *Undeclared War*, pp. 9-21; Blum, *From the Morgenthau Diaries, 1938-1941*, pp. 354-61; *Ickes Diary: 1939-1941*, pp. 322, 330; Stimson MS. Diary, Sept. 24, 1940.

15. Feis, *Road to Pearl Harbor*, pp. 110-28; Langer and Gleason, *Undeclared War*, pp. 21-46; Stimson MS. Diary, Sept. 19, 26, 27, Oct. 4, 8, 12, 1940, and letter to FDR, Oct. 12. 1940; Blum, *From the Morgenthau Diaries, 1938-1941*, pp. 361-2; *Ickes Diary: 1939-1941*, pp. 339, 346-7; *Roosevelt and Churchill: Secret Wartime Correspondence*, pp. 115-16; Watson, *Prewar Plans and Preparations*, pp. 117-18; *P.P.A.: 1940*, p. 466; Anderson, Jr., *Standard-Vacuum Oil Company*, p. 153; *War Diary of Breckinridge Long, 1939-1944*, pp. 137-40.

16. Watson, *Prewar Plans and Preparations*, pp. 109-13; Conn and Fairchild, *Framework of Hemisphere Defense*, pp. 36-40, 52; Langer and Gleason, *Challenge to Isolation*, pp. 559, 568-9.

17. Morgenthau Presidential MS. Diary, 3: 586-9; King George to FDR, June 26, 1940; FDR to King George, July 15, 1940, PSF: Great Britain; Ickes to FDR, June 28, 1940; FDR to Ickes, July 6, 1940, OF 4044; *Ickes Diary: 1939-1941*, p. 233; *Jim Farley's Story*, p. 253; Ben Cohen to FDR, July 19, 1940, PSF: Great Britain: Destroyers for Bases; *FDR: Personal Letters, 1928-1945*, II, 1048-9.

18. The British War Cabinet discussed the possibility of exchanging bases for American aid in May: CAB. 65, 141(40) 7, May 27, 1940; 146(40) 14, May 29, 1940; Woodward, *British Foreign Policy*, I, 340-42; *Roosevelt and Churchill: Secret Wartime Correspondence*, pp. 107-8; Mark L. Chadwin, *The Warhawks* (New York, 1970 ed.), pp. 74-89; *FDR: Personal Letters,*

1928-1945, II, 1050-52, contains Roosevelt's own notes on the Aug. 2 Cabinet meeting; *Ickes Diary: 1939-1941*, pp. 282-4, 291-3; Blum, *From the Morgenthau Diaries, 1938-1941*, pp. 177-9; Churchill, *Their Finest Hour*, pp. 345-9; Stimson MS. Diary, Aug. 2, 3, 8, 12, 1940; Langer and Gleason, *Challenge to Isolation*, pp. 742-57.

19. Blum, *From the Morgenthau Diaries, 1938-1941*, pp. 179-81; Morgenthau Presidential MS. Diary, 3: 635; Stimson MS. Diary, Aug. 13, 15, 1940; Ben Cohen to Missy LeHand, Aug. 12, 1940, PSF: Navy: Destroyers for Bases; *Roosevelt and Churchill: Secret Wartime Correspondence*, pp. 108-10; Churchill, *Their Finest Hour*, pp. 273-91, especially pp. 290-91 for statistics on the intensity of the fighting, and pp. 346-7 for Churchill's view of the deal; also see CAB. 65, 277(40) 1, Aug. 14, 1940; Langer and Gleason, *Challenge to Isolation*, pp. 757-60.

20. Ulric Bell to FDR, n.d., but apparently Aug. 3, 1940, PSF: Navy: Destroyers for Bases; memo, 1940 Election, n.d., Harry Hopkins MSS; Burns, *The Lion and the Fox*, pp. 431-2; on the staff conversations, see Watson, *Prewar Plans and Preparations*, pp. 113-14; Welles to FDR, July 20, 1940, OF 48; FDR to Churchill, n.d., but probably early Aug. 1940, PSF: Great Britain: Churchill; *Complete Press Conferences*, XVI, 123; Stimson MS. Diary, Aug. 17, 1940; Langer and Gleason, *Challenge to Isolation*, pp. 702-7, 765; Grace Tully, *FDR: My Boss* (Chicago, 1949), p. 244; *FDR: Personal Letters*, 1928-1945, II, 1056.

21. *Complete Press Conferences*, XVI, 123-7; Blum, *From the Morgenthau Diaries, 1938-1941*, p. 181; Churchill, *Their Finest Hour*, pp. 350-51; Langer and Gleason, *Challenge to Isolation*, pp. 761-2, 764-5; for the legal actions supporting the exchange, see Attorney General Jackson to Knox, Aug. 17, 1940; Stark to FDR, Aug. 21, 1940; Jackson to FDR, Aug. 27, 1940, PSF: Navy: Destroyers for Bases; Stimson MS. Diary, Aug. 21, 1940; *FDR: Personal Letters*, 1928-1945, II, 1056-7.

22. Welles to FDR, Aug. 19, 1940, PSF: Navy: Destroyers for Bases; Churchill, *Their Finest Hour*, pp. 290-91, 350-54; *Roosevelt and Churchill: Secret Wartime Correspondence*, pp. 111-14; Hull, *Memoirs*, I, 834-43; Stimson MS. Diary, Aug. 23, 25, 27, 1940; CAB. 65, 236(40) 6, Aug. 29, 1940; *Complete Press Conferences*, XVI, 173-85.

23. Langer and Gleason, *Challenge to Isolation*, pp. 770-76; Leuchtenburg, *FDR and the New Deal*, pp. 305-6; Ickes told FDR on Sept. 3 "that if I were running against him for President, I would have set out to take away from him leadership in the foreign situation. . . . Willkie overlooked the best chance that he had by being content merely to 'me too' the President on his foreign policies. . . ." (*Ickes Diary: 1939-1941*, p. 312); Chadwin, *The Warhawks*, pp. 89-108.

24. Langer and Gleason, *Challenge to Isolation*, pp. 507-8, 680-81; *FDR: Personal Letters*, 1928-1945, II, 1026; Stimson MS. Diary, June 25, July 16, 31, Aug. 1, 2, 1940; FDR to Stimson, June 26, 1940, PPF 20; Watson, *Prewar Plans and Preparations*, pp. 112-13, 183-96; Pogue, *Marshall, 1939-1942*, pp. 56-62; for opinion polls coming to the President, see Eugene Meyer to Early, May 30, 1940, OF 857; "Public Opinion News Service," clipping, June 23, 1940, OF 1413 Miscl.; *P.P.A.: 1940*, pp. 290, 295-7, 313-14, 317-

21; FDR to Senator Donahey, Aug. 3, 1940; FDR to Eleanor Roosevelt, Aug. 5, 1940, OF 1413 Miscl.

25. Leuchtenburg, *FDR and the New Deal*, pp. 307–8; Hiram Johnson to Hiram Johnson, Jr., Aug. 31, 1940, Johnson MSS; Stimson MS. Diary, Aug. 22, 1940; Senator Donahey to FDR, Aug. 1, 1940; "Mothers of America," Aug. 17, 1940, OF 1413 Miscl.; *FDR: Personal Letters, 1928–1945*, II, 1055, 1058–9.

26. Stimson MS. Diary, Aug. 23, 1940; *Complete Press Conferences*, XVI, 143–7; ". . . Willkie . . . raised hell with us here by adopting the Roosevelt foreign policy and being for conscription," Hiram Johnson wrote his son. "He really broke the back of the opposition to the conscription law. . . ." (Aug. 30, 1940, Johnson MSS); Langer and Gleason, *Challenge to Isolation*, pp. 681–3.

27. Sherwood, *Roosevelt and Hopkins*, pp. 184–90; Burns, *The Lion and the Fox*, pp. 442–8; James Rowe to FDR, Oct. 7, 1940, OF 1413; FDR to Watson, Oct. 4, 1940; Watson to FDR, Oct. 8, 1940; Rowe to FDR, Oct. 14, 1940; Lowell Mellett to FDR, Oct. 12, 1940; FDR to Watson, Oct. 15, 1940, PSF: War Dept.: Draft; *P.P.A.*: 1940, pp. 473–5, 486–8, 507–9, 510–14; cf. *FDR: Personal Letters, 1928–1945*, II, 1073–4; the most detailed account of the campaign is in Warren Moscow, *Roosevelt and Willkie* (Englewood Cliffs, N.J., 1968).

28. Cantril (ed.), *Public Opinion, 1935–1946*, pp. 601–2; Roosevelt's concern with the polls is revealed in *Ickes Diary: 1939–1941*, pp. 344–5; also see Rowe to FDR, Oct. 3, 1940, PSF: Rowe; Eicher to FDR, Oct. 9, 1940, PSF: Public Opinion Polls; Sherwood, *Roosevelt and Hopkins*, pp. 190–91; Burns, *The Lion and the Fox*, pp. 448–9; Leuchtenburg, *FDR and the New Deal*, pp. 320–21; when asked by Rosenman why he did not include the qualifying phrase about an attack, Roosevelt answered that it wasn't necessary since an attack would mean that it wasn't a foreign war. This hardly explains why he had felt compelled to use the phrase consistently in earlier speeches. Sherwood believed that these blanket assurances "left a smear on his [FDR's] record which only the accomplishments of the next five years could remove" (p. 201).

29. See, for example, numerous letters to Senator George Norris urging him to keep the Congress in session to prevent Roosevelt from taking the country into war and becoming a dictator, Tray 34, Box 9, Norris MSS; Burns, *The Lion and the Fox*, pp. 454–5; Leuchtenburg, *FDR and the New Deal*, pp. 321–2; Cantril (ed.), *Public Opinion, 1935–1946*, pp. 618, 620; what is most striking about the war issue in the election is its limited impact on the overall result. A November 1940 poll, for example, showed that the electorate saw foreign policy as a comparatively uncontroversial issue between FDR and Willkie—see poll 85 on pp. 619–20 of Cantril; also see the discussion of this point in Warren F. Kimball, *The Most Unsordid Act: Lend-Lease, 1939–1941* (Baltimore, 1969), p. 78; for FDR's and Churchill's reactions, see James MacGregor Burns, *Roosevelt: The Soldier of Freedom* (New York, 1970), pp. 3–4, 9–10.

30. Langer and Gleason, *Undeclared War*, pp. 64–79, 85–95; *Roosevelt*

and Churchill: Secret Wartime Correspondence, pp. 114–17; *Peace and War*, 1931–1941, pp. 580–81; *FDR: Personal Letters*, 1928–1945, II, 1079–81.

31. Langer and Gleason, *Undeclared War*, pp. 184–9; Blum, *From the Morgenthau Diaries*, 1938–1941, pp. 188–95; *P.P.A.: 1940*, pp. 519–20.

32. Watson, *Prewar Plans and Preparations*, pp. 306–8; Stimson MS. Diary, Nov. 7, 8, 12, 1940; *Complete Press Conferences*, XVI, 304–6; Blum, *From the Morgenthau Diaries*, 1938–1941, pp. 200–201; Langer and Gleason, *Undeclared War*, pp. 215–19.

33. For the background on Lend-Lease, see Kimball, *Most Unsordid Act*, chaps. 1–3; on Lothian's calculated remark, see pp. 96–7; *Ickes Diary: 1939–1941*, p. 367; Blum, *From the Morgenthau Diaries*, 1938–1941, pp. 199–202; *Complete Press Conferences*, XVI, 324; Morgenthau Presidential MS. Diary, 3: 719–21; Morgenthau MS. Diary, 334: 1–3; Langer and Gleason, *Undeclared War*, pp. 225–8; the most comprehensive discussion of these events is in Kimball, pp. 97–104.

34. A November 30 poll showed 88 per cent opposed to entering the war; polls of November 19 and December 11 showed between 37 and 40 per cent against helping England win at the risk of war, while another poll of December 11 indicated that 78 per cent wanted the United States to do everything possible to help England except go to war: Cantril (ed.), *Public Opinion*, 1935–1946, pp. 971–3; Cantril analyzed some of this data for the White House in "America Faces the War—the reaction of public opinion," n.d., but apparently Dec. 1940, OF 857; on FDR's concern to avoid a repetition of Wilson's mistakes, see Sherwood, *Roosevelt and Hopkins*, p. 227.

35. Churchill, *Their Finest Hour*, pp. 475–82, reproduces the letter in full; Blum, *From the Morgenthau Diaries*, 1938–1941, pp. 206–7; Kimball, *Most Unsordid Act*, pp. 105–14.

36. Sherwood, *Roosevelt and Hopkins*, pp. 222–5; Blum, *From the Morgenthau Diaries*, 1938–1941, pp. 207–9; *Complete Press Conferences*, XVI, 350–60; Kimball, *Most Unsordid Act*, pp. 119–27.

37. Langer and Gleason, *Undeclared War*, pp. 180–84, 220–21, 240–44.

38. Sherwood, *Roosevelt and Hopkins*, pp. 225–8; *P.P.A.: 1940*, pp. 633–44; Kimball, *Most Unsordid Act*, pp. 127–9; Cantril (ed.), *Public Opinion*, 1935–1946, p. 588.

39. Blum, *From the Morgenthau Diaries*, 1938–1941, pp. 210–17; Kimball, *Most Unsordid Act*, pp. 131ff., contains a detailed discussion of the drafting of the bill; *P.P.A.: 1940*, pp. 663–70, 672.

40. *Foreign Relations of the United States*, 1941, III (Washington, D.C., 1956), on the origins of the H.R. 1776 designation, see Kimball, *Most Unsordid Act*, pp. 151–3; for the bill itself, see pp. 243–6; Roosevelt's efforts are described on pp. 153ff.; also Blum, *From the Morgenthau Diaries*, 1938–1941, pp. 217–24; Langer and Gleason, *Undeclared War*, pp. 260–64; *FDR: Personal Letters*, 1928–1945, II, 1103–5.

41. *Ibid.*, pp. 1107, 1114, 1122; "Résumé of Situation Relative to Bill 1776," Jan. 22, 1941, PSF: Stimson; Sherwood, *Roosevelt and Hopkins*, pp. 242–3, quoting messages from Hopkins, who was in England, to FDR urging prompt action; on America First opposition, see memo, Jan. 16, 1941, PSF:

Willkie; Wayne S. Cole, *America First: The Battle Against Intervention, 1940–1941* (Madison, Wis., 1953), pp. 42–9; Kimball, *Most Unsordid Act*, pp. 154–5; *Complete Press Conferences*, XVII, 76–7, 82–3, 86.

42. Kimball, *Most Unsordid Act*, pp. 179, 196ff.; Sherwood, *Roosevelt and Hopkins*, pp. 260–62; Winston S. Churchill, *The Second World War: The Grand Alliance* (Bantam Books ed., New York, 1962), pp. 22–4, 107; Langer and Gleason, *Undeclared War*, p. 280; *P.P.A.: 1941*, pp. 61–3.

43. *Ickes Diary: 1939–1941*, pp. 393–4, 470; Stimson MS Diary, Dec. 19, 1940, Apr. 10, 1941; "Résumé of Situation Relative to Bill 1776," Jan. 22, 1941, PSF: Lend-Lease; *Complete Press Conferences*, XVII, 86–7; Knox to FDR, Mar. 20, 1941, PSF: Safe: Navy; Conn and Fairchild, *Framework of Hemisphere Defense*, pp. 101–8; *Roosevelt and Churchill: Secret Wartime Correspondence*, pp. 135–8; Knox to FDR, Mar. 21, 1941; FDR to Knox, Apr. 1, 1941, PSF: Navy; Blum, *From the Morgenthau Diaries, 1938–1941*, pp. 251–2; *P.P.A.: 1941*, pp. 94–7, 111–12; Langer and Gleason, *Undeclared War*, pp. 421–35.

44. Morgenthau Presidential MS. Diary, 4: 860–61; on public feeling toward Lend-Lease and editorial opinion on "convoying," see Alan Barth to Morgenthau, "Lend-Lease Hopes and Fears," Apr. 4, 1941, PSF: Morgenthau, one of several studies on public and editorial opinion Barth did for Morgenthau, who passed them on to FDR; *Ickes Diary: 1939–41*, p. 473; Stimson MS. Diary, Apr. 4, 1941; Cantril (ed.), *Public Opinion, 1935–1946*, p. 1127; on the anti-escorting or Tobey Resolution, see Langer and Gleason, *Undeclared War*, pp. 443–4; a mid-April poll of Congress asking, "Do you approve American convoys to England if believed necessary to prevent British defeat by Hitler?," showed 80 per cent opposed (Otis T. Wingo to Early, Apr. 22, 1941, OF 857).

45. Harold D. Smith MS. Diary, Apr. 11, 1941; *Roosevelt and Churchill: Secret Wartime Correspondence*, p. 138; Blum, *From the Morgenthau Diaries, 1938–1941*, p. 252; Stimson MS. Diary, Apr. 15, 1941; Hull, *Memoirs*, II, 941–2; Knox to FDR, Apr. 19, 1941, PSF: Knox; *FDR: Personal Letters, 1928–1945*, II, 1144–5; *Complete Press Conferences*, XVII, 284–91.

46. These events are described in chaps. 3, 4, 12, and 13 of Langer and Gleason, *Undeclared War*; and in Churchill, *Their Finest Hour*, Book II, and *The Grand Alliance*, Book I.

47. Churchill to FDR, Apr. 24, 1941, in Churchill, *The Grand Alliance*, pp. 120–21; and Apr. 29, 1941, which is in Churchill's papers, PREM. 3, 187; FDR to Churchill, May 1, 1941, MRP; Churchill's feeling is described on p. 198 of *The Grand Alliance*, where he reproduces part of his response of May 3 to FDR; the entire letter is in the Map Room Papers; FDR's reply of May 4 is published in *FDR: Personal Letters, 1928–1945*, II, 1148–50.

48. Stimson MS. Diary, Apr. 15, 21, 22, 24, 25, 29, May 5–12, 1941; *Ickes Diary: 1939–1941*, pp. 503, 508–14; Stimson to FDR, May 5, 1941, PPF 20; Stimson to Hopkins, May 9, 1941, PSF: Stimson; ". . . United support can best be enlisted . . . through having action forced by them [the American people], rather than upon them. . . . It would appear to be preferable to have the people push the President into danger than to have

them pulled into it by him," Barth told Morgenthau in his analysis of opinion of May 9, 1941 (PSF: Morgenthau); Morgenthau sent the report to FDR "for your information"; for Roosevelt's attitude, see Josiah Bailey to FDR, May 10, 1941, PSF: Senate; *FDR: Personal Letters, 1928-1945*, II, 1154-7; Morgenthau MS. Diary, 397: 301A-B.

49. On the discussions with Japan, see Hull, *Memoirs*, II, chap. 71, and pp. 1000-1001; on Vichy, see William L. Langer, *Our Vichy Gamble* (New York, 1947), pp. 147ff.; Langer and Gleason, *Undeclared War*, pp. 497-510; Robert O. Paxton, *Vichy France* (New York, 1972), pp. 109ff.; on the decision to move the Fleet, see Stimson MS. Diary, May 13, 14, 1941; Conn and Fairchild, *Framework of Hemisphere Defense*, pp. 109-10; on Roosevelt's actions, see Welles to FDR, May 20, 1941, PSF: Welles; Morgenthau Presidential MS. Diary, 4: 930-31; *FDR: Personal Letters, 1928-1945*, II, 1159.

50. Blum, *From the Morgenthau Diaries, 1938-1941*, p. 254; *Ickes Diary: 1939-1941*, p. 523; Ickes to FDR, May 24, 1941, PSF: Ickes; Stimson MS. Diary, May 23, 1941; Churchill discusses Crete and the *Bismarck* in chaps. 16 and 17, Book I, *The Grand Alliance*; he discussed both subjects in a message to FDR of May 23, 1941, which appears on pp. 247-8, 260; see Sherwood, *Roosevelt and Hopkins*, pp. 294-8, on FDR's remark about the *Bismarck*, and preparation of his speech; Samuel I. Rosenman, *Working with Roosevelt* (New York, 1952), pp. 279-87; Berle MS. Diary, May 26, 1941; *P.P.A.: 1941*, pp. 181-95.

51. *From the Berle Papers*, pp. 369-70; *Complete Press Conferences*, XVII, 362-70; "an unqualified national emergency was being proclaimed primarily for its psychological effect in impressing upon the country the threat of aggression and the need for strengthening our defenses in all respects," the Attorney General told a Treasury Department official (Morgenthau MS. Diary, 402: 177).

52. Stimson MS. Diary, May 27, 29, 1941; *Ickes Diary: 1939-1941*, pp. 526-7; Sherwood, *Roosevelt and Hopkins*, pp. 298-9; Cantril (ed.), *Public Opinion, 1935-1946*, pp. 1128, 972; *FDR: Personal Letters, 1928-1945*, II, 1158; Hadley Cantril to Mrs. Rosenberg, n.d., but clearly late May, providing information on polling done between May 7 and 17, 1941, PSF: Public Opinion Polls; Langer and Gleason, *Undeclared War*, pp. 441-4, 461-3; Burns, *Roosevelt: Soldier of Freedom*, pp. 65-6, 84-92, 98-101, are critical of Roosevelt's failure to offer stronger leadership.

53. "I hope you will like the speech tonight," FDR cabled Churchill on May 27. "It goes farther than I thought was possible even two weeks ago and I like to hope that it will receive general approval from the fairly large element which has been confused by details and unable hitherto to see the simple facts." (MRP). Cantril to Mrs. Rosenberg, "As of late May 1941"; Cantril, "Interviewing done between July 11th and July 19th, 1941," items 8 and 10, PSF: Public Opinion Polls; Morgenthau to FDR, May 23, 1941, enclosing an analysis of opinion by Barth, "Waiting for the President," which concluded: "The signs indicate that the American people are now ready to follow any course which the President may recommend to them. But they want to make the choices themselves. They are willing to be led, but not thrust into danger" (PSF: Morgenthau). After reading the results of Ameri-

can public opinion polls, one British Foreign Office official concluded that "in their desire to avoid war many Americans are deliberately avoiding the issue by failing to draw obvious conclusions from the available evidence" about Britain's critical situation, F.O. 371/26171/A3131/44/45, Apr. 23, 1941.

54. Sherwood, *Roosevelt and Hopkins*, p. 299; *P.P.A.: 1941*, pp. 227-30; Langer and Gleason, *Undeclared War*, pp. 335-45, 514-21, 524-32; Churchill, *The Grand Alliance*, pp. 312-15.

CHAPTER 11

1. *Foreign Relations, 1940*, IV, 428-30, 672-82, 688-92; Langer and Gleason, *Undeclared War*, pp. 292-8.

2. *Foreign Relations, 1940*, IV, 693-4, 698-700, 702-3; *FDR: Personal Letters, 1928-1945*, II, 1085; Blum, *From the Morgenthau Diaries, 1938-1941*, pp. 363-8; the abortive plan to bomb Japan is described in Michael Schaller, "American Air Strategy in China, 1939-1941: The Origins of Clandestine Air Warfare," *American Quarterly*, XXVIII (Spring 1976), 3-12; Callaghan to FDR, Dec. 17, 1940, PSF: Navy; Langer and Gleason, *Undeclared War*, pp. 298-304.

3. Stimson MS. Diary, Nov. 29, 1941; R. J. C. Butow, *The John Doe Associates: Backdoor Diplomacy for Peace, 1941* (Stanford, 1974), pp. 8-10, chaps. 1-2; Hull, *Memoirs*, I, 914-15; Langer and Gleason, *Undeclared War*, pp. 306-9, 320; *FDR: Personal Letters, 1928-1945*, II, 1093-5.

4. Stimson MS. Diary, Feb. 4, 8, 10, 1941; U.S. Congress, 79th Congress, First Session, *Pearl Harbor Attack Hearings* (Washington, D.C., 1946), Pt. 16, 2147-8, 2150-51; Pt. 19, 3442-4; Pt. 20, 4293-6; *Complete Press Conferences*, XVII, 126-7; *Foreign Relations: Japan, 1931-1941*, II, 387-9; *From the Berle Papers*, pp. 359-60.

5. *Pearl Harbor Attack Hearings*, Pt. 19, 3445-51; *Roosevelt and Churchill: Secret Wartime Correspondence*, pp. 129-30; Churchill, *The Grand Alliance*, pp. 148-51; Lowell Mellett to FDR, Feb. 15, 1941, PSF: Public Opinion Polls; Langer and Gleason, *Undeclared War*, pp. 319-31.

6. *Foreign Relations: Japan, 1931-1941*, II, pp. 389ff.; Hull, *Memoirs*, II, 988ff.; Butow, *John Doe Associates*, chaps, 3-4, 12-15, provides an excellent analysis of these discussions; there is a briefer, but less penetrating discussion of these talks in Langer and Gleason, *Undeclared War*, chap 15—the naval actions are described on pp. 485-7; Lauchlin Currie to FDR, Apr. 12, 1941, PSF: Currie.

7. Evans Carlson to FDR, Jan. 13, 1941; Chiang Kai-shek to FDR, Feb. 26, 1941; FDR to Chiang, Apr. 9, 1941; Welles to FDR, Apr. 12, 1941; Currie to FDR, May 9, 1941; FDR to Currie, May 15, 1941, PSF: China; Currie to FDR, Jan. 18, Mar. 12, 1941, PSF: Executive Offices: Currie; Carlson to LeHand, Feb. 21, 1941, PSF: State Dept.; Currie to FDR, Apr. 15, 1941; FDR to Currie, Apr. 30, 1941, OF 150; Stimson MS. Diary, Mar. 27, 1941; Philip Young to Harry Hopkins, Apr. 21, 1941; Currie to Hopkins, Apr. 25, 1941, Hopkins MSS; *Pearl Harbor Attack Hearings*, Pt. 19, 3489-95; Blum, *From the Morgenthau Diaries, 1938-1941*, pp. 370-72; Langer and Gleason, *Undeclared War*, pp. 488-93.

8. The several exchanges between FDR and Ickes over embargoing oil are printed in *Ickes Diary: 1939–1941*, pp. 552–60, 564–8; for this explanation of Japanese behavior, see Robert J. C. Butow, "The Hull-Nomura Conversations: A Fundamental Misconception," *AHR*, LXV (July 1960), 822–36; for a more general discussion of the difficulties caused by American and Japanese amateurs in these 1941 talks, see Butow, *The John Doe Associates*, "Epilogue: In the Fullness of Time."

9. *Pearl Harbor Attack Hearings*, Pt. 12, 1–2; Pt. 14, 1396–8; Pt. 19, 3496–8; Pt. 20, 4363; Stimson MS. Diary, July 5, 1941; *Foreign Relations of the United States, 1941*, IV (Washington, D.C., 1956), 289–90, 298–303; Blum, *From the Morgenthau Diaries, 1938–1941*, pp. 377–9; *Ickes Diary: 1939–1941*, pp. 583–4, 588; Frances Perkins, VIII, 5, COHC; Robert P. Patterson to Stimson, July 18, 1941, Stimson MSS; *Foreign Relations: Japan, 1931–1941*, II, 264–5, 527–30; FDR to Hopkins, July 26, 1941, PSF: Safe: Hopkins; Hopkins to Churchill, July 27, 1941, PREM. 3, 156/1; Langer and Gleason, *Undeclared War*, chap. 20.

10. *Foreign Relations: Japan, 1931–1941*, II, 266–7, 534–7, 546–50; Anderson, Jr., *Standard-Vacuum Oil Company*, pp. 174ff.; FDR to Hopkins, July 26, 1941, PSF: Safe: Hopkins; *Pearl Harbor Attack Hearings*, Pt. 20, 3998–4000; Stimson MS. Diary, Aug. 8, 9, 1941; Halifax to Churchill, Aug. 6, 1941, PREM. 4, 27/9.

11. *Roosevelt and Churchill: Secret Wartime Correspondence*, p. 143; Churchill to FDR, June 14, 1941, MRP; Hull, *Memoirs*, II, 946–7; Sherwood, *Roosevelt and Hopkins*, pp. 290–91, 308, 310–11; *P.P.A.: 1941*, pp. 255–63; Langer and Gleason, *Undeclared War*, pp. 452–3, 522–4, 575–80, which provides an excellent detailed account of these events; Churchill's description of how he wished to use the American occupation of Iceland is in a note to Eden, July 7, 1941, PREM. 3, 230/1, where he also explained: "Once the American Congress has received the news we should make the most of the event that our Ministry of Information can manage. . . . We should . . . exploit it round the world."

12. Langer and Gleason, *Undeclared War*, pp. 570–74; Pogue, *Marshall, 1939–1942*, pp. 145–54; Alan Barth to Ferdinand Kuhn, Jr., July 11, 18, 1941, PSF: Treasury: Morgenthau; Marshall to FDR, July 16, 1941; LaGuardia to FDR, July 17, 1941; Patterson to FDR, July 17, 1941, OF 1413; FDR to Stimson, July 18, 1941, PPF 20; Stimson MS. Diary, July 21, 1941; *P.P.A.: 1941*, pp. 272–7; FDR to Early, Aug. 7, 1941, PSF: Confidential File: State Dept.; FDR to Hopkins, June 12, 1941, Hopkins MSS.

13. The best accounts of aid to Russia are: Raymond H. Dawson, *The Decision To Aid Russia, 1941: Foreign Policy and Domestic Politics* (Chapel Hill, N.C., 1959), chaps. 4–6; George C. Herring, Jr., *Aid to Russia, 1941–1946* (New York, 1973), chap. 1; the sources for the details I have described are: Churchill, *The Grand Alliance*, pp. 314–15; *Complete Press Conferences*, XVII, 409–10; Sherwood, *Roosevelt and Hopkins*, pp. 303–8; for FDR's fear that the Russians might "fail to hold out through the summer," see *FDR: Personal Letters, 1928–1945*, II, 1179; Hadley Cantril to Anna Rosenberg, July 3, 1941, PSF: Public Opinion Polls; Alan Barth to Ferdinand Kuhn, Jr., July 24, 1941, PSF: Treasury: Morgenthau.

14. Again, these events are described in Dawson and in Herring, Jr., chaps. cited in note 13 above; the quotes are from: *FDR: Personal Letters, 1928–1945*, II, 1177, 1189, 1195–6; *Foreign Relations of the United States, 1941*, I (Washington, D.C., 1958), 788–9; Leuchtenburg, *FDR and the New Deal*, pp. 120–21; Burns, *Roosevelt: Soldier of Freedom*, pp. 8, 60; Sherwood, *Roosevelt and Hopkins*, pp. 92–3, 317–18, 321–2; Blum, *From the Morgenthau Diaries, 1938–1941*, pp. 263–5; *Ikces Diary: 1939–1941*, pp. 577–8, 592–3.

15. *Foreign Relations, 1941*, I, 341; Theodore A. Wilson, *The First Summit: Roosevelt and Churchill at Placentia Bay, 1941* (Boston, 1969), chap. 2, which describes the origins of the meeting. I am convinced that FDR had a clear idea of what he wanted from the Conference; Wilson believes that the President's purpose was "not entirely clear," (p. 264); *Complete Press Conferences*, XVIII, 79.

16. Berle to FDR, June 21, July 8, 9, 1941; FDR to Berle, June 26, 1941, PSF: State Dept.; FDR draft telegram to Churchill, July 11, 1941; FDR to Welles, July 12, 1941; Welles to FDR, July 13, 1941, PSF: Churchill; the final telegram to Churchill is in *Foreign Relations, 1941*, I, 342; *From the Berle Papers*, pp. 372–3; Sherwood, *Roosevelt and Hopkins*, pp. 308–11; Lash, *Roosevelt and Churchill, 1939–1941*, pp. 391–4.

17. According to Sherwood, Hopkins discussed this with Churchill on the way to the Conference, *Roosevelt and Hopkins*, pp. 349–50; Churchill, *The Grand Alliance*, pp. 366–9, 372–3; Wilson, *The First Summit*, chap. 9; *Foreign Relations, 1941*, I, 351–4, 360–69.

18. *Ibid.*, pp. 343–5; *Complete Press Conferences*, XVIII, 77; Churchill, *The Grand Alliance*, pp. 364–5; *Roosevelt and Frankfurter: Correspondence, 1928–1945*, pp. 612–13; Wilson, *The First Summit*, pp. 229–30, 264–7; *P.P.A.: 1941*, pp. 333–4; for a typical isolationist reaction to the Conference, see Hiram W. Johnson to H.W.J., Jr., Aug. 17, 1941, Johnson MSS; editorial reaction is surveyed in Alan Barth to Ferdinand Kuhn, Jr., Aug. 22, 1941, PSF: Treasury: Morgenthau; the generally favorable response to the meeting is described in Langer and Gleason, *Undeclared War*, pp. 688–91.

19. By the end of July, members of the British Foreign Office believed this to be true: F.O. Minute: "U.S. and the War," July 25, 1941, F.O.371/26172/A6153/44/45; and /26173/A8892/44/45; see Wilson, *The First Summit*, pp. 103–7, for Churchill's discussion of American intervention on the first evening; Churchill's comment to FDR's "circle" is in *The Grand Alliance*, p. 500; Churchill's description of FDR's response is in CAB. 65, 84 (41), Aug. 19, 1941.

20. *Foreign Relations, 1941*, I, 356–7; Churchill, *The Grand Alliance*, pp. 370–71; Wilson, *The First Summit*, pp. 88, 149–50, 160–63, 254.

21. Sherwood, *Roosevelt and Hopkins*, pp. 308, 370; Arnold, *Global Mission*, p. 250; Wilson, *The First Summit*, pp. 69–70, 141–5, 171; CAB. 65, 84 (41), Aug. 19, 1941.

22. *P.P.A.: 1941*, p. 257; *Complete Press Conferences*, XVIII, 38–9; Stimson MS. Diary, July 21, 1941; FDR to Mrs. Ogden Reid, quoted in Wilson, *The First Summit*, p. 22.

23. FDR's concern to assure his legal right to escort is demonstrated by Green H. Hackworth to FDR, Aug. 21, 1941, PSF: Navy; Sherwood, *Roosevelt and Hopkins*, pp. 369–70, 373–4; *P.P.A.: 1941*, pp. 365–9.

24. J. R. Beardall to FDR, Sept. 9, 1941; "Suggested Statements on the *Greer* Incident for Use by the President," Sept. 9, 1941, PSF: Safe: Navy—the first document provided FDR with an account of what actually happened, and the second document became the basis for the President's less than candid picture of events as described in his speech; *P.P.A.: 1941*, pp. 384–92.

25. Lash, *Roosevelt and Churchill, 1939–1941*, pp. 417–21; for FDR's effort to blunt the congressional inquiry, see his memo to Admiral Stark, Sept. 18, 1941, PSF: Knox; in a poll of Aug. 19, 1941, for example, 69 per cent expressed the belief that Britain would win the war, only 6 per cent thought Germany would win, Cantril (ed.), *Public Opinion, 1935–1946*, p. 1187; on public approval of FDR's escorting policy, see p. 1128; for the growing hope that aid to Russia would save America from sending troops abroad, see Dawson, *Decision To Aid Russia, 1941*, pp. 186–7, 228–9; Halifax to Churchill, Oct. 11, 1941, PREM. 4, 27/9.

26. Fulbright quote is from Lash, *Roosevelt and Churchill, 1939–1941*, p. 421; J. Edgar Hoover to Berle, Sept. 3, 1941, Berle MS. Diary; for FDR's difficulties with the Congress, see FDR to Sen. D. Worth Clark, Aug. 1, 1941, PSF: Welles; Rosenman to FDR, Aug. 22, 1941, PSF: Rosenman; memo on Rep. Stephen A. Day, Aug. 22, 1941, OF 220a; Gen. J. H. Burns to Early, Aug. 25, 1941; Sen. Charles Tobey to FDR, Aug. 29, 1941; Early to Tobey, Sept. 4, 1941; Hopkins to Early, Sept. 5, 1941, OF 4193; FDR to McIntyre, Sept. 6, 1941, PSF: McIntyre; *P.P.A.: 1941*, pp. 264–6; H. Montgomery Hyde, *The Quiet Canadian: The Secret Service Story of Sir William Stephenson* (London, 1962), pp. 24–30, 47, 50–59, 151–6; for example of this cooperation between Donovan and the British, see Berle MS. Diary, Sept, 27, 1941; FDR to Donovan, Oct. 13, 1941, PSF: Donovan; FDR to Churchill, Oct. 24, 1941, OF 4485.

27. Welles to FDR, July 9, 1941; FDR to Sens. George and Connally, July 11, 1941, PSF: Welles; Berle to FDR, Sept. 15, 1941, Berle MSS; FDR to Sen. Connally, Sept. 26, 1941, PSF: Senate; *Roosevelt and Churchill: Secret Wartime Correspondence*, pp. 155–6, 159–60; *P.P.A.: 1941*, pp. 406–11.

28. Alan Barth to Ferdinand Kuhn, Jr., Oct. 3, 24, 1941, PSF: Treasury: Morgenthau; *P.P.A.: 1941*, pp. 408–9, 438–44, 487–90; memo to Gen. Watson, Oct. 11, 1941; memo to FDR, Oct. 18, 1941, OF 1561; memo to FDR, Nov. 1, 1941, OF 857; Langer and Gleason, *Undeclared War*, pp. 750–60; Hiram Johnson to H.W.J., Jr., Nov. 8, 16, 1941, Johnson MSS; Adm. Stark to FDR, Aug. 28, 1941, PSF: Navy; Mothers of America to FDR, Nov. 15, 1941, OF 1561; Burns, *Roosevelt: Soldier of Freedom*, pp. 147–8.

29. Sherwood, *Roosevelt and Hopkins*, pp. 327ff.; *Foreign Relations, 1941*, I, 802–15; on Stalin's estimate, see Adam B. Ulam, *Expansion and Coexistence: The History of Soviet Foreign Policy, 1917–1967* (New York, 1968), pp. 319–20.

30. W. Averell Harriman and Elie Abel, *Special Envoy to Churchill and Stalin, 1941–1946* (New York, 1975), p. 74; Churchill, *The Grand Alliance*, p. 377; *Foreign Relations, 1941*, I, 819, 822–3, 826; Watson, *Prewar Plans and Preparations*, pp. 329, 361–2; Pogue, *Marshall, 1939–1942*, pp. 74–9; Stimson MS. Diary, Aug. 4, 5, 1941; Dawson, *Decision To Aid Russia, 1941*, pp. 209–12.

31. Alexander Werth, *Russia at War, 1941–1945* (New York, 1965 ed.),

chaps. 7 and 8; *Stalin's Correspondence with Churchill, Attlee, Roosevelt and Truman, 1941–1945* (2 vols.; Moscow, 1957), I, 20–22; Churchill, *The Grand Alliance*, pp. 384–8.

32. *Foreign Relations, 1941*, I, 829–30; Churchill, *The Grand Alliance*, pp. 382–3, 395–6; Harriman, *Special Envoy, 1941–1946*, pp. 77–9; Dawson, *Decision To Aid Russia, 1941*, pp. 212–16; FDR's direct involvement in these questions of supply allocation is illustrated in a series of cables between him and Harriman on Sept. 18, 19, 20, 1941, PSF: Safe: Russia; Harry C. Thompson and Linda Mayo, *United States Army in World War II: The Ordnance Department—Procurement and Supply* (Washington, D.C., 1960), p. 232, for the quote on tank production; cf. Robert P. Patterson to FDR, Sept. 19, 1941, PSF: Safe: War Dept.; *Roosevelt and Churchill: Secret Wartime Correspondence*, pp. 157–8; Hopkins to Churchill, Sept. 29, 1941, Hopkins MSS.

33. William H. Standley and Arthur A. Ageton, *Admiral Ambassador to Russia* (Chicago, 1955), p. 63; Harriman, *Special Envoy, 1941–1946*, pp. 90–92; on Stalin's attitude, see Ulam, *Expansion and Coexistence*, pp. 329–33; William C. Bullitt, "How We Won the War and Lost the Peace," *Life*, XXV (Aug. 30, 1948), 83–97; Herring, Jr., *Aid to Russia, 1941–1946*, chap. 2, provides a good analysis of FDR's attitude, though I believe that Roosevelt's uncertainty about his ability to deliver promised aid deserves more emphasis than it has been given; Hopkins to Churchill, Sept. 29, 1941, Hopkins MSS; *Foreign Relations, 1941*, I, 842; FDR to Churchill, Oct. 8, 1941, MRP.

34. Dawson, *Decision To Aid Russia, 1941*, chap. 9; *Foreign Relations, 1941*, I, 832–4; Myron Taylor (telephone message) to FDR, Aug. 30, 1941; FDR to Taylor, Sept. 1, 1941, PSF: Italy; *FDR: Personal Letters, 1928–1945*, II, 1204–5; Harriman, *Special Envoy, 1941–1946*, p. 88.

35. James Rowe, Jr., to FDR, Sept. 16, 1941, PSF: Rowe; FDR to Senator James M. Mead, Oct. 9, 1941, PSF: Senate; *Complete Press Conferences*, XVIII, 187–8; Dawson, *Decision To Aid Russia, 1941*, pp. 258ff.; *Foreign Relations, 1941*, I, 1000–1003; Harriman, *Special Envoy, 1941–1946*, pp. 103–4; *P.P.A.: 1941*, p. 440.

36. Alan Barth to Ferdinand Kuhn, Jr., Oct. 3, 1941, PSF: Treasury: Morgenthau; cf. Oscar Cox to Hopkins, Oct. 30, 1941, Hopkins MSS; George F. Kennan, *Memoirs, 1925–1950* (Boston, 1967), pp. 139–40; it is striking that Roosevelt's efforts to defuse the religious issue extended beyond his victory in the Congress to assure Lend-Lease aid for Russia.

37. Dawson, *Decision To Aid Russia, 1941*, pp. 238–40, 269ff.; Herring, Jr., *Aid to Russia, 1941–1946*, pp. 19–23, 42–6; *From the Morgenthau Diaries, 1938–1941*, pp. 267–71; *Ickes Diary: 1939–1941*, p. 620; *Foreign Relations, 1941*, I, 849–52, 857.

38. *Ibid.*, 346–9, 354–60; John H. Whitney to William Donovan, Nov. 13, 1941, reporting a conversation with Churchill, in Lash, *Roosevelt and Churchill, 1939–1941*, p. 464; War Cabinet Memorandum, Aug. 20, 1941, PREM. 3, 485/7; Churchill, *The Grand Alliance*, pp. 371–3, 377, 379.

39. Hull, *Memoirs*, II, 1016–20; *Foreign Relations: Japan, 1931–1941*, II, 553–9; *Foreign Relations, 1941*, IV, 374–6, 378–80; *Pearl Harbor Attack Hearings*, Pt. 15, 1682; Pt. 17, 2749–55.

40. Stimson MS. Diary, Aug. 18, 1941; Halifax to Foreign Office, Aug. 18, 1941, quoted in Lash, *Roosevelt and Churchill, 1939–1941*, p. 410; *Foreign Relations: Japan, 1931–1941*, II, 568ff.; Hull, *Memoirs*, II, 1020–27; Wallace to FDR, Aug. 29, 1941, PSF: Wallace; *Pearl Harbor Attack Hearings*, Pt. 17, 2794–5; Langer and Gleason, *Undeclared War*, pp. 698–705.

41. Robert J. C. Butow, *Tojo and the Coming of the War* (Princeton, 1961), pp. 242ff.; Butow believes that after the decisions of Sept. 3–6, "war was inevitable unless the United States accepted Japan's terms or the monopoly of decision-making held by the Supreme Command was broken" (p. 255); Japan's conditions are described in Langer and Gleason, *Undeclared War*, pp. 715, 718; they describe the impact of these talks on China on pp. 710–13; *Foreign Relations: Japan, 1931–1941*, II, 631ff.; Hull, *Memoirs*, II, 1028–33; Alan Barth to Ferdinand Kuhn, Jr., Sept. 12, 1941, PSF: Treasury: Morgenthau, provided FDR with a review of editorial opinion on Japan; Cantril to Mrs. Rosenberg, Sept. 13, 1941, PSF: Public Opinion Polls; T. V. Soong to Col. William Donovan, Aug. 16, 1941; James Roosevelt to Hopkins, Aug. 22, 1941; Hopkins to Sir Archibald Sinclair, Sept. 2, 1941; Hopkins to Lauchlin Currie, Sept. 2, 1941; Currie to FDR, Sept. 13, 1941, PSF: Currie; for the argument that America's China policy forced a war with Japan which could have been avoided through a modus vivendi that Tokyo and the American public would have accepted, see Paul W. Schroeder, *The Axis Alliance and Japanese-American Relations, 1941* (Ithaca, N.Y., 1958), chap 9 esp.; as my narrative suggests, I find this conclusion unpersuasive.

42. *FDR: Personal Letters, 1928–1945*, II, 1217; Ronald Campbell to Foreign Office, Oct. 6, 1941, quoted in Lash, *Roosevelt and Churchill, 1939–1941*, p. 414; Stimson MS. Diary, Sept. 12, 1941; Halifax to Churchill, Oct. 11, 1941, PREM. 4, 27/9.

43. Butow, *Tojo and the Coming of the War*, chap. 10; *Roosevelt and Churchill: Secret Wartime Correspondence*, p. 162; *Pearl Harbor Attack Hearings*, Pt. 14, 1402; Stimson MS. Diary, Oct. 16, 1941.

44. Churchill to FDR, Oct. 20, 1941, PSF: Churchill; *Pearl Harbor Attack Hearings*, Pt. 14, 1078–80; Pt. 15, 1476–81; Churchill, *The Grand Alliance*, pp. 496–500.

45. *Pearl Harbor Attack Hearings*, Pt. 14, 1061–2, 1077; *Roosevelt and Churchill: Secret Wartime Correspondence*, pp. 163–4.

46. Stimson MS. Diary, Nov. 6, 7, 1941; Frances Perkins, VIII, 42, 46, COHC; *Pearl Harbor Attack Hearings*, Pt. 12, 92–100; Hull, *Memoirs*, II, 1056–62; *Foreign Relations: Japan, 1931–1941*, II, 715–19.

47. *Pearl Harbor Attack Hearings*, Pt. 12, 125–6, 130–31, 150–55; *Foreign Relations: Japan, 1931–1941*, II, 738ff.; *Foreign Relations, 1941*, IV, 606ff.; *FDR: Personal Letters, 1928–1945*, II, 1245–6; Langer and Gleason, *Undeclared War*, pp. 871–3.

48. *Pearl Harbor Attack Hearings*, Pt. 12, 165, 172; *FDR: Personal Letters, 1928–1945*, II, 1246; Stimson MS Diary, Nov. 25, 26, 1941; "Notes on conversation . . . Feb. 4, 1945, between the Prime Minister, the President and Marshall Stalin," F.O.371/47881/N2611/165/G; *Foreign Relations, 1941*, IV, 650–67; Hull *Memoirs*, II, 1071–81; Blum, *From the Morgenthau Diaries, 1938–1941*, pp. 383–91; *Ickes Diary: 1939–1941*, pp. 654–5.

49. *Foreign Relations: Japan,* 1931–1941, II, 764–70; Stimson MS. Diary, Nov. 27, 28, 1941; *Pearl Harbor Attack Hearings,* Pt. 11, 5422–4; Langer and Gleason, *Undeclared War,* pp. 911–14.

50. Foreign Office to Halifax, Nov. 29, 1941; Halifax to Foreign Office, Dec. 1, 4, 1941, PREM. 3 156/5; *Roosevelt and Churchill: Secret Wartime Correspondence,* pp. 167–8; Sir Llewellyn Woodward, *British Foreign Policy in the Second World War,* Vol. II (London, 1971), pp. 170–74; Lash, *Roosevelt and Churchill,* 1939–1941, pp. 476–7, 482–6; *From the Morgenthau Diaries,* 1938–1941, p. 392; *Foreign Relations: Japan,* 1931–1941, II, 778–86.

51. *Pearl Harbor Attack Hearings,* Pt. 10, 4661–3; Pt. 11, 5421; "Trial Tabulations on the Far Eastern Situation," Dec. 5, 1941; Elmo Roper, "After the War: Portrait of Gloom," Nov. 12, 1941; Cantril to Mrs. Rosenberg, Nov. 17, 1941, PSF: Public Opinion Polls; Alan Barth to Ferdinand Kuhn, Jr., Dec. 5, 1941, PSF: Treasury: Morgenthau; Ickes to FDR, Nov. 25, 1941, attaching Douglas's report, PSF: Ickes; Sherwood, *Roosevelt and Hopkins,* pp. 429–30.

52. A. Russell Buchanan, *The United States and World War II* (2 vols.; New York, 1964), I, 72–6; Sherwood, *Roosevelt and Hopkins,* pp. 428, 431; Eleanor Roosevelt, *This I Remember,* p. 233; Frances Perkins, VIII, 69, 87–8, COHC; Churchill, *The Grand Alliance,* pp. 510–12.

53. Sherwood, *Roosevelt and Hopkins,* pp. 432–4, 441; Stimson MS. Diary, Dec. 7, 1941; Roosevelt satisfied Hull's demand for a full review of Japanese-American relations in a message to Congress on Dec. 15, 1941, P.P.A.: 1941, pp. 539ff.; the President's war message is on pp. 514–15; *Foreign Relations,* 1941, IV, 732–3; acting before FDR's cable arrived, Churchill received a war declaration from Parliament several hours before the U.S. declared war: Burns, *Roosevelt: Soldier of Freedom,* pp. 171–2; Halifax to Churchill, Dec. 9, 1941, PREM. 4, 27/9; Langer and Gleason, *Undeclared War,* pp. 937–41.

54. This "revisionist" argument is stated in Charles A. Beard, *President Roosevelt and the Coming of the War,* 1941 (New Haven, 1948); Charles C. Tansill, *Back Door to War: The Roosevelt Foreign Policy,* 1933–1941 (Chicago, 1952); Rear Adm. Robert A. Theobald, *The Final Secret of Pearl Harbor* (New York, 1954); Roberta Wohlstetter's analysis is in *Pearl Harbor: Warning and Decision* (Stanford, 1962); the beliefs of the isolationists are described in Manfred Jonas, *Isolationism in America,* 1935–1941 (Ithaca, N.Y., 1966).

CHAPTER 12

1. P.P.A.: 1941, pp. 522–4, 527, 530–31, 533–4, 544–57, 558–62.

2. *Foreign Relations of the United States: Conferences at Washington,* 1941–1942, and Casablanca, 1943 (Washington, D.C., 1968), pp. 5, 7–8; Halifax to Churchill, Dec. 9, 1941, PREM. 4, 27/9; Arthur Bryant, *The Turn of the Tide: A History of the War Years Based on the Diaries of Field-Marshall Lord Alanbrooke, Chief of the Imperial General Staff* (New York, 1957), p. 225.

3. Churchill's agenda for the meeting, and Roosevelt's interest in a Declaration are in *Foreign Relations: Conferences at Washington and Casablanca,*

pp. 37, 11-12, 39-40, 59-60; *Foreign Relations of the United States, 1942,* I (Washington, D.C., 1960), 1-12; Hull, *Memoirs,* II, 1114-19; Churchill, *The Grand Alliance,* p. 561.

4. *Foreign Relations: Conferences at Washington and Casablanca,* pp. 364-6, 369-70, 112; Sherwood, *Roosevelt and Hopkins,* pp. 446-9, 453; Adamic, *Dinner at the White House,* p. 60; Churchill, *The Grand Alliance,* pp. 574-5; *From the Berle Papers,* p. 394.

5. *Foreign Relations: Conferences at Washington and Casablanca,* pp. 366, 369; Gary R. Hess, *America Encounters India, 1941-1947* (Baltimore, Md., 1971), pp. 33-4; Churchill, *The Grand Alliance,* pp. 583-4; Winston S. Churchill, *The Second World War: The Hinge of Fate* (Bantam Books ed., New York, 1962), p. 181.

6. Stimson MS. Diary, Dec. 15, 1941; see FDR to Rep. Andrew J. May, Dec. 16, 1941, OF 1413, for FDR's response to the committee's action; see Hull, *Memoirs,* II, 1116, for the conclusion that America was entering into an alliance; Churchill, *The Grand Alliance,* pp. 575, 577; Eden to Churchill, Feb. 6, 1942, F.O. 371/30655/A1293/60/45; Churchill to Eden, Feb. 22, 1942, F.O. 371/30655/A1874/60/45; *Foreign Relations, 1942,* I, 25-6.

7. Churchill, *The Grand Alliance,* pp. 542, 559-60; Lash, *Roosevelt and Churchill, 1939-1941,* pp. 51, 126-7; Richard W. Steele, *The First Offensive, 1942: Roosevelt, Marshall, and the Making of American Strategy* (Bloomington, Ind., 1973), pp. 42-5, 53-9, 64-5; *Foreign Relations: Conferences at Washington and Casablanca,* pp. 69-74, 78, 130.

8. Pogue, *Marshall, 1939-1942,* pp. 10-16, 22-4; Steele, *First Offensive, 1942,* pp. 60-64, 69-72; *Foreign Relations: Conferences at Washington and Casablanca,* pp. 130, 162, 195, 267-8.

9. Steele, *First Offensive, 1942,* pp. 60-61, 67-8, 73-80; Theodore H. White (ed.), *The Stilwell Papers* (New York, 1948), pp. 16, 23, 25.

10. *Foreign Relations: Conferences at Washington and Casablanca,* pp. 59-60, 92-3, 102-5, 108-10, 128; Churchill, *The Grand Alliance,* pp. 567-71, 577-9; Sherwood, *Roosevelt and Hopkins,* pp. 455-8, 466-70; *Churchill: Taken from the Diaries of Lord Moran* (Boston, 1966), pp. 21-4.

11. Churchill, *The Grand Alliance,* pp. 558-9, 577; CAB. 66, 8 (42) 1, Sec.'s File, Jan. 17, 1942; Sherwood, *Roosevelt and Hopkins,* p. 478.

12. Adamic, *Dinner at the White House,* pp. 31-2, 38-9, 64-8, 73.

13. Sherwood, *Roosevelt and Hopkins,* pp. 506-7; Hull to FDR, Dec. 30, 1941, PSF: Safe: Great Britain; *Roosevelt and Churchill: Secret Wartime Correspondence,* pp. 174-9.

14. Hess, *America Encounters India,* pp. 35-40; *Foreign Relations, 1942,* I, 602-8, 612, 615-16; David K. Niles to Grace Tully, Feb. 18, 1942; FDR to Sen. Robert La Follette, Feb. 20, 1942, PSF: Senate.

15. Churchill, *Hinge of Fate,* pp. 185-6; Sherwood, *Roosevelt and Hopkins,* p. 512; Hess, *America Encounters India,* pp. 42-50; *Foreign Relations, 1942,* I, 631-4.

16. Barbara W. Tuchman, *Stilwell and the American Experience in China, 1911-1945* (New York, 1970), p. 258; FDR, memo, Feb. 15, 1942, with undated note from Churchill to FDR attached, PSF: Churchill; *Roosevelt and Churchill: Secret Wartime Correspondence,* p. 206.

17. *Foreign Relations*, 1942, I, 634–7, 648–50; Sherwood, *Roosevelt and Hopkins*, pp. 530–31; Churchill, *Hinge of Fate*, pp. 190–91; Hess, *America Encounters India*, pp. 55–8.

18. Herbert Feis, *The China Tangle: The American Effort in China from Pearl Harbor to the Marshall Mission* (Princeton, 1953), pp. 3–16; Tuchman, *Stilwell and China*, pp. 233ff.; *Foreign Relations of the United States, 1942*, IV (Washington, D.C., 1961), 736ff.; *Foreign Relations of the United States: China, 1942* (Washington, D.C., 1956), pp. 2–3, 5; *Foreign Relations: Conferences at Washington and Casablanca*, pp. 128, 134, 149, 154, 271–3, 284–5, 303–4; Lauchlin Currie to FDR, Dec. 13, 27, 1941; Jan. 24, 1942; Gen. Marshall to Gen. Wavell, Jan. 22, 1942, PSF: Safe: China; *The Stilwell Papers*, pp. 25–6; Churchill, *Hinge of Fate*, pp. 116–17.

19. Tuchman, *Stilwell and China*, pp. 250–51, 238; Cantril (ed.), *Public Opinion, 1935–1946*, pp. 369, 559, 911; cf. Harold R. Isaacs, *Scratches on Our Mind: American Images of China and India* (New York, 1958), 164–89; A. T. Steele, *The American People and China* (New York, 1966), pp. 22–3; and a British Foreign Office report of May 11, 1942, the "USA and Her Allies," which showed Britain "a shade less well thought of than Russia by Americans," except on the matter of postwar cooperation. "But even on that score we lag behind China!" (F.O. 371/30724/A4694/G45); *Foreign Relations: Conferences at Washington and Casablanca*, p. 284, n. 1.

20. *The Stilwell Papers*, p. 36; for a different emphasis to the encounter from the one I give, see Feis, *The China Tangle*, pp. 16–17; and Tuchman, *Stilwell and China*, pp. 249–50.

21. Feis, *The China Tangle*, pp. 17–23; Tuchman, *Stilwell and China*, pp. 251–2, 246–7; John Morton Blum, *From the Morgenthau Diaries: Years of War, 1941–1945* (Boston, 1967), pp. 87–102; Frank Knox to Mrs. Knox, Feb. 3, 1942, Knox MSS; Harold Ickes MS. Diary, May 22, 1942; Sherwood, *Roosevelt and Hopkins*, pp. 513–14; Stimson MS. Diary, Jan. 30, 1942; *Foreign Relations: China, 1942*, pp. 419ff., and p. 13.

22. For a description of Japan's early military victories, see Louis Morton, *United States Army in World War II: The War in the Pacific: Strategy and Command: The First Two Years* (Washington, D.C., 1962), Part Two; Churchill, *Hinge of Fate*, pp. 53–4, 57–62; FDR to Churchill, Jan. 31, 1942, MRP.

23. On public sentiment in early 1942, see Steele, *The First Offensive, 1942*, pp. 46–53, 81–93; *Complete Presidential Press Conferences*, XIX, 129–30; Cantril (ed.), *Public Opinion, 1935–1946*, p. 1174; *Roosevelt and Churchill: Secret Wartime Correspondence*, pp. 179–81; P.P.A.: 1942, pp. 105–16.

24. Steele, *The First Offensive, 1942*, pp. 86–90; Cantril (ed.), *Public Opinion, 1935–1946*, pp. 1175–6; P.P.A.: 1942, pp. 161–2; *Complete Presidential Press Conferences*, XIX, 205–7, 210–17; *FDR: Personal Letters, 1928–1945*, II, 1292–5, 1298–1301.

25. Pogue, *Marshall, 1939–1942*, pp. 248–51; Morton, *War in the Pacific: First Two Years*, pp. 269–74; P.P.A.: 1942, 213–16; White House Conference, Jan. 28, 1942, H. H. Arnold MSS; H. H. Arnold to FDR, May 3, 1942, PSF: Safe: Japan.

26. Stetson Conn, "The Decision To Evacuate the Japanese from the Pacific Coast (1942)," in *Command Decisions*, edited by Kent Roberts Greenfield (New York, 1959), pp. 88–109; Roger Daniels, *Concentration Camps USA: Japanese Americans and World War II* (New York, 1971); Francis Biddle, *In Brief Authority* (New York, 1962), pp. 212–26, 235–8; Burns, *Roosevelt: Soldier of Freedom*, pp. 213–17, 266–8, 463–4, 606; *Roosevelt and Churchill: Secret Wartime Correspondence*, pp. 194–5; FDR to J. Edgar Hoover, Apr. 3, 1942, PSF: Justice: Hoover; John Franklin Carter, reports on telephone conversations, June 10, 23, 1942; FDR to Carter, June 24, 1942, PSF: John Franklin Carter; Nazi and Japanese information on American ship movements after Pearl Harbor came from Spanish diplomats and journalists in the United States. They "mixed in coded and secret information with their dispatches to Spain." (*Los Angeles Times*, Sept. 11, 1978, p. 5). Morgenthau Presidential MS. Diary, 5: 1093; Harold Ickes MS. Diary, Feb. 1, Mar. 1, 1942.

27. Churchill, *Hinge of Fate*, pp. 164–74; *Roosevelt and Churchill: Secret Wartime Correspondence*, pp. 184–90; Stimson MS. Diary, Feb. 24, Mar. 5, 6, 7, 8, 1942; Alfred D. Chandler (ed.), *The Papers of Dwight D. Eisenhower: The War Years* (5 vols., Baltimore, 1970), I, 145–55, 169–71; Maurice Matloff and Edwin M. Snell, *United States Army in World War II: Strategic Planning for Coalition Warfare, 1941–1942* (Washington, D.C., 1953), pp. 165–7; Steele, *The First Offensive, 1942*, pp. 100–106.

28. *The Memoirs of Anthony Eden, Earl of Avon: The Reckoning* (Boston, 1965), pp. 335ff.; Woodward, *British Foreign Policy*, II, 220ff.; Churchill, *The Grand Alliance*, pp. 584–6; Halifax to Churchill, Jan. 11, 1942, PREM. 4, 27/9; CAB. 66, "Policy Towards Russia," Jan. 28, 1942, W.P. (42) 48; and Feb. 24, 1942, W. P. (42) 96; British Foreign Office, *Aide Mémoire*, Feb. 25, 1942, PSF: Safe: Gt. Brit.; *Roosevelt and Churchill: Secret Wartime Correspondence*, pp. 186–7, 195–6; Raymond Clapper MS. Diary, June 5, 1942; Blum, *From the Morgenthau Diaries, 1941–1945*, pp. 81–2; *Foreign Relations of the United States, 1942*, III (Washington, D.C., 1961), 494ff.; Herbert Feis, *Churchill-Roosevelt-Stalin: The War They Waged and the Peace They Sought* (Princeton, 1967 ed.), pp. 26–8, 58–60.

29. Matloff and Snell, *Strategic Planning, 1941–1942*, pp. 174–90; Sherwood, *Roosevelt and Hopkins*, pp. 518ff.; Stimson MS. Diary, Mar. 20, 25, Apr. 1, 1942; *Eisenhower Papers: The War Years*, I, 205–8; Marshall and King to FDR, n.d., but apparently Apr. 2, 1942, PSF: Safe: Marshall; Pogue, *Marshall, 1939–1942*, chap. 14; Steele, *The First Offensive, 1942*, pp. 107–21; Churchill, *Hinge of Fate*, pp. 273–83; memorandum, April 15, 1942, PREM. 3, 333/6.

30. Sherwood, *Roosevelt and Hopkins*, pp. 527–8; FDR to Hopkins, Apr. 14, 1942, MRP; *Stalin's Correspondence, 1941–1945*, II, 22–4; Churchill, *Hinge of Fate*, pp. 280, 288, 226–8.

31. Woodward, *British Foreign Policy*, II, 247–57; Churchill, *Hinge of Fate*, pp. 289–92, 295–6; *Foreign Relations, 1942*, III, 557–61, 564–5; Churchill to FDR, June 4, 1942, MRP, describes Winant's "invaluable" contribution in helping us to secure a treaty which "fulfilled our own ideas."

32. Eleanor Roosevelt, *This I Remember*, pp. 250–51; Churchill, *Hinge of*

Fate, p. 293; Sherwood, *Roosevelt and Hopkins*, pp. 556ff.; *Foreign Relations, 1942*, III, 566ff.; for FDR's comment about reckoning with military advisers, see "Molotov Conversations, May 29, 1942, 7:40 PM," Hopkins MSS; cf. Roosevelt's comment of May 6, 1942, to Stimson and the Chiefs: "I have been disturbed by American and British naval objections to operations in the European Theatre prior to 1943. I regard it as essential that active operations be conducted in 1942," (PSF: Marshall); *Roosevelt and Churchill: Secret Wartime Correspondence*, pp. 217–18.

33. Sherwood, *Roosevelt and Hopkins*, pp. 580–83; Churchill, *Hinge of Fate*, pp. 297, 300–301, 325–6; J. M. A. Gwyer and J. R. M. Butler, *History of the Second World War: Grand Strategy*, vol. III, June 1941–August 1942 (London, 1964), Part II, 596–7; Woodward, *British Foreign Policy*, II, 257–60; *Foreign Relations: Conferences at Washington and Casablanca*, pp. 419–20.

34. H. H. Arnold, notes on June 17 meeting at the White House, Arnold MSS; *Foreign Relations: Conferences at Washington and Casablanca*, pp. 421ff., 455ff.; Matloff and Snell, *Strategic Planning, 1941–1942*, pp. 234–44; Churchill, *Hinge of Fate*, pp. 327–8, 331–9; Pogue, *Marshall, 1939–1942*, pp. 328–36; Steele, *The First Offensive, 1942*, pp. 149–58; CAB. 65, W.M. (42) 82nd Conclusion, Minute 1, June 27, 1942.

35. Churchill, *Hinge of Fate*, pp. 340–55, 376–8, 381–4; *Churchill: From the Diaries of Lord Moran*, p. 51; *Roosevelt and Churchill: Secret Wartime Correspondence*, pp. 222, 224–5; Matloff and Snell, *Strategic Planning, 1941–1942*, pp. 266–78; Stimson MS. Diary, July 10, 12, 15, 1942; FDR to Marshall, July ?, 1942, John L. McCrea MSS; Sherwood, *Roosevelt and Hopkins*, pp. 600–605; Pogue, *Marshall, 1939–1942*, pp. 340–42; Steele, *The First Offensive, 1942*, pp. 158–65.

36. Pogue, *Marshall, 1939–1942*, pp. 342–9; Sherwood, *Roosevelt and Hopkins*, pp. 606–12; Matloff and Snell, *Strategic Planning, 1941–1942*, pp. 278–84; Steele, *The First Offensive, 1942*, pp. 167–79; FDR to Hopkins, Marshall, and King, July 24, and n.d., but apparently July 25, 1942; FDR, memorandum, July 29, 1942, PSF: Safe: Marshall; Stimson MS Diary, July 23, 25, 27, 1942; Bryant, *Turn of the Tide*, pp. 341–7; Gwyer and Butler, *Grand Strategy*, III, Part II, 632–6; *Roosevelt and Churchill: Secret Wartime Correspondence*, p. 227.

37. Churchill, *Hinge of Fate*, pp. 230–39; *Stalin's Correspondence, 1941–1945*, I, 52–6; Churchill to FDR, July 14, 16, 17, 1942, MRP; *Roosevelt and Churchill: Secret Wartime Correspondence*, pp. 224–5, 227–9; Woodward, *British Foreign Policy*, II, 257–64; Herring, Jr., *Aid to Russia*, pp. 65–8.

38. Churchill, *Hinge of Fate*, pp. 393–5, 411ff.; Harriman, *Special Envoy, 1941–1946*, pp. 151ff.; Woodward, *British Foreign Policy*, II, 265–72; Ulam, *Expansion and Coexistence*, pp. 336–7; *Roosevelt and Churchill: Secret Wartime Correspondence*, pp. 234–40; *Stalin's Correspondence, 1941–1945*, II, 33; Feis, *Churchill-Roosevelt-Stalin*, pp. 73–80.

39. Churchill, *Hinge of Fate*, pp. 239–40, 489–98, 500–505; *Roosevelt and Churchill: Secret Wartime Correspondence*, pp. 250, 252–9, 261–2; Churchill to FDR, Sept. 14, 1942; FDR to Churchill, Oct. 7, 1942, MRP; Hopkins to FDR, Sept. 22, 1942; Hopkins to Churchill, Sept. 22, 1942,

MRP; *Stalin's Correspondence, 1941–1945*, II, 35–8; Standley and Ageton, *Admiral Ambassador to Russia*, chap. 18; Feis, *Churchill-Roosevelt-Stalin*, pp. 80–87; *Foreign Relations, 1942*, III, 460, 730–31.

40. Morton, *War in the Pacific: First Two Years*, chaps. 15–16; Pogue, *Marshall, 1939–1942*, chap. 17.

41. *Stilwell Papers*, chap. 3; Charles F. Romanus and Riley Sunderland, *United States Army in World War II: Stilwell's Mission to China* (Washington, D.C., 1953), chaps. 3–4; Tuchman, *Stilwell and China*, chap. 11; Robert Hotz (ed.), *Way of a Fighter: The Memoirs of Claire Lee Chenault* (New York, 1949), p. 159.

42. Pogue, *Marshall, 1939–1942*, pp. 363–4; *Foreign Relations: China, 1942*, pp. 27, 33–4, 44–6, 57; Matloff and Snell, *Strategic Planning, 1941–1942*, pp. 227–9; FDR to Arnold, May 5, 1942; FDR to Chiang, May 7, 1942, PSF: Safe: Chiang; *P.P.A.: 1942*, pp. 229–30; *FDR: Personal Letters, 1928–1945*, II, 1329–30.

43. Romanus and Sunderland, *Stilwell's Mission to China*, pp. 157ff.; Tuchman, *Stilwell and China*, pp. 303, 307–8, 311–13, 317; *Foreign Relations: China, 1942*, pp. 61–2, 89, 95–6; Pogue, *Marshall, 1939–1942*, pp. 365–6; *Stilwell Papers*, pp. 118ff.; Feis, *China Tangle*, pp. 42–4; Chiang to FDR, July 5, 1942; FDR to Chiang, July 14, 1942; Lauchlin Currie to FDR, July 28, 1942; FDR to Currie, July 28, 1942, MRP.

44. Pogue, *Marshall, 1939–1942*, pp. 366–71; Tuchman, *Stilwell and China*, pp. 313–25, 341–5; Feis, *China Tangle*, pp. 45–51; *Stilwell Papers*, pp. 152, 166–8, 171; *Foreign Relations: China, 1942*, pp. 96, 119–22; Combined Chiefs of Staff, 101, "The Situation in China," Aug. 23, 1942; cf. FDR to Willkie, Sept. 15, 1942; FDR to Chiang, Oct. 10, 1942, MRP; FDR to Currie, Sept. 15, 1942, OF 150; Currie to FDR, Oct. 1, 1942, PSF: China; *FDR: Personal Letters, 1928–1945*, II, 1350.

45. *P.P.A.: 1942*, pp. 258–9, 287–9, 328, 347–54 are some examples; the Gallup poll is cited in Raymond Clapper MS. Diary, Sept. 10, 1942; Robert Divine, *Second Chance: The Triumph of Internationalism in America During World War II* (New York, 1967), p. 69; John Morton Blum (ed.), *The Price of Vision: The Diary of Henry A. Wallace, 1942–1946* (Boston, 1973), pp. 104, 128–9; Hadley Cantril to FDR, Sept. 14, 1942; James Rowe, Jr., to FDR, Oct. 14, 1942, OF 857; Burns, *Roosevelt: Soldier of Freedom*, pp. 271–3, 280.

46. Divine, *Second Chance*, pp. 49, 60–61, 64–9; *The Wallace Diary, 1942–1946*, pp. 28–31, 76–7, 79, 81, 83, 122, 635–40; Hull, *Memoirs*, II, 1177–9; *War Diary of Breckinridge Long*, pp. 217, 278; Welles, *Seven Decisions*, chap. 5; CAB. 66, "Mr. Richard Law's Visit to the United States," Oct. 26, 1942, W.P. (42) 492; *Foreign Relations, 1942*, III, 573; Chungking Embassy to Foreign Office, Aug. 1, 1942, F.O. 371/31627/F5456/54/10; Washington Embassy to Foreign Office, Aug. 13, 1942, F.O. 371/31627/ F5716/54/10.

47. CAB. 66, "Mr. Richard Law's Visit to the United States," Oct. 26, 1942, W.P. (42) 492; *Foreign Relations, 1942*, I, 677–8, 695–706; Divine, *Second Chance*, pp. 71–3; *The Wallace Diary, 1942–1946*, p. 128.

48. Burns, *Roosevelt: Soldier of Freedom*, chap. 8; *Complete Presidential*

Press Conferences, XIX, 202; XX, 65, 113; Frances Perkins, VIII, 153, 155–6, COHC; *The Wallace Diary, 1942–1946*, pp. 76, 116; *P.P.A.: 1942*, pp. 356ff., 422; *FDR: Personal Letters, 1928–1945*, II, 1359; David K. Niles to Hopkins, Dec. 16, 1942, Hopkins MSS, analyzes the election results.

CHAPTER 13

1. *Roosevelt and Churchill: Secret Wartime Correspondence*, pp. 243–4; Churchill, *Hinge of Fate*, p. 497; the preparations for and anxieties over the attack are described in George F. Howe, *United States Army in World War II: Northwest Africa: Seizing the Initiative in the West* (Washington, D.C., 1957), chaps. 2–4; also see Sherwood, *Roosevelt and Hopkins*, pp. 644–5, 648; and Burns, *Roosevelt: Soldier of Freedom*, pp. 285–92; for Roosevelt's anxiety about keeping the operation secret, also see FDR to Secs. of the Treasury, War, and Navy, Oct. 5, 1942; Grace Tully to FDR, Oct. 7, 1942, PSF: Safe: Misc.; his behavior on the day of the invasion is described in Grace Tully, *FDR: My Boss*, pp. 263–4; *FDR: Personal Letters, 1928–1945*, II, 1362–3.

2. The best description of the Vichy policy is still Langer, *Our Vichy Gamble, passim*; Robert Murphy, *Diplomat Among Warriors* (Garden City, N.Y., 1964), pp. 101–2.

3. *Roosevelt and Churchill: Secret Wartime Correspondence*, pp. 247–8, also see pp. 243–6; for FDR's sources of information, see Langer, *Our Vichy Gamble*, pp. 311–13; Murphy, *Diplomat Among Warriors*, p. 101; Hadley Cantril, "Evaluating the Probable Reactions to the Landing in North Africa in 1942: A Case Study," *Public Opinion Quarterly*, 29 (Fall 1965), 400–410; for FDR's directive implementing this policy, see *Foreign Relations of the United States, 1942*, II (Washington, D.C., 1962), 379–80; and FDR to Leahy, Sept. 22, 1942, MRP.

4. Langer, *Our Vichy Gamble*, pp. 289–90, 295, 297–8, describes the British experience with and reservations about the Free French; de Gaulle later asserted that by the end of July he foresaw the North African attack: *The War Memoirs of Charles de Gaulle: Unity, 1942–1944* (New York, 1959), p. 13; the encounter with de Gaulle is described in Pogue, *Marshall, 1939–1942*, pp. 413–14, and in Mark W. Clark, *Calculated Risk* (New York, 1950), pp. 36–7; *Roosevelt and Churchill: Secret Wartime Correspondence*, p. 252; for Churchill's agreement with this conclusion, see pp. 249, 251; cf. "File Memo," Aug. 8, 1942, PSF: War: Marshall; the exchange on when to tell de Gaulle is in Churchill, *Hinge of Fate*, pp. 525–6; also see Woodward, *British Foreign Policy*, II, 351ff.

5. *P.P.A.: 1942*, pp. 451–7; on arrangements with the French, see *Foreign Relations, 1942*, II, 379ff.; Murphy, *Diplomat Among Warriors*, pp. 109ff.; for a detailed discussion of the fighting, see Howe, *Northwest Africa: Seizing the Initiative*, pp. 89ff.; on the political developments, see Langer, *Our Vichy Gamble*, pp. 342ff.; later suggestions that a deal had been arranged with Darlan beforehand are described in Sherwood, *Roosevelt and Hopkins*, pp. 648–9; they are refuted by a conversation FDR had with Morgenthau on Nov. 12, recorded in Presidential MS. Diary, 5: 1192.

6. Sherwood, *Roosevelt and Hopkins*, p. 651; *Foreign Relations, 1942*, II, 445–7, contains the Foreign Office and Churchill messages; Blum, *From the*

Morgenthau Diaries, 1941–1945, p. 150, also see pp. 147–52; *The Eisenhower Papers: The War Years,* II, 707–10.

7. P.P.A.: 1942, pp. 479–80; Ickes MS. Diary, Nov. 22, 1942; Sherwood, *Roosevelt and Hopkins,* pp. 651–4, describes FDR's response to Eisenhower; *Complete Presidential Press Conferences,* XX, 244–7; cf. *The Wallace Diary, 1942–1946,* p. 134; and Churchill, *Hinge of Fate,* pp. 550–52; Rosenman, *Working with Roosevelt,* pp. 363–4; a State Department memorandum on this meeting does not describe the President's outburst, but suggests that it was a disagreeable encounter, *Foreign Relations, 1942,* II, 546–7; FDR's comments are quoted in *War Memoirs of de Gaulle: 1942–1944,* p. 53.

8. Langer, *Our Vichy Gamble,* pp. 374–81; Churchill, *Hinge of Fate,* pp. 554–60, which includes Darlan's complaint, Churchill's expression of concern to FDR, and his views on de Gaulle's visit and Darlan's assassination; the *Herald Tribune* quote is in Peter Tompkins, *The Murder of Admiral Darlan* (New York, 1965), pp. 239–40; for the difficulties with Darlan, see FDR to Winant, Nov. 28, 1942; Winant to FDR, Dec. 3, 1942, including Darlan's statement; FDR to Marshall, Dec. 5, 1942, MRP; and *The Eisenhower Papers: The War Years,* II, 737–9, 817–18, 820–22; *Foreign Relations, 1942,* II, 482–3, contains FDR's statement as well as Darlan's; for the de Gaulle visit, see pp. 546, 548, 555.

9. *Roosevelt and Churchill: Secret Wartime Correspondence,* p. 278; Churchill to FDR, Nov. 13, 18, 1942, MRP; *The Eisenhower Papers: The War Years,* I, 570–72; Churchill to FDR, Sept. 22, 1942, MRP; Churchill, *Hinge of Fate,* pp. 566–7; Matloff and Snell, *Strategic Planning, 1941–1942,* pp. 307–8, 322–7.

10. *Foreign Relations: Conferences at Washington and Casablanca,* pp. 488–91, 494–6, reproduces all the FDR-Churchill exchanges, except for Churchill to FDR, Nov. 25, 1942, which is in the MRP; FDR's message to Stalin is in *Stalin's Correspondence, 1941–1945,* II, 42; Churchill's invitation to Stalin is in Vol. 1, 81.

11. These exchanges with Stalin are in *Stalin's Correspondence, 1941–1945,* II, 43–4; and I, 80, 82; the English translation of Stalin's first reply to FDR with the phrase "now so hot. . . ." is in *Foreign Relations, 1942,* III, 666; Churchill to FDR, Dec. 10, 1942, MRP; *Foreign Relations: Conferences at Washington and Casablanca,* pp. 497–8.

12. Sherwod, *Roosevelt and Hopkins,* pp. 668–73; Burns, *Roosevelt: Soldier of Freedom,* pp. 316–17; *Foreign Relations: Conferences at Washington and Casablanca,* pp. 498–505; Harriman, *Special Envoy, 1941–1946,* pp. 179–81.

13. "Meetings of FDR with the J.C.S., 1942–1945," Nov. 25, 1942; also see the meeting of Dec. 10, 1942, MRP; the Jan. 7 meeting is in *Foreign Relations: Conferences at Washington and Casablanca,* pp. 505ff.; Bryant, *Turn of the Tide,* pp. 441–2; for FDR's suggestion to Stalin that Marshall come to Moscow, see *Foreign Relations of the United States, 1943,* III (Washington, D.C., 1963), 616, 620–21; for Marshall's differences with FDR, also see Forrest C. Pogue, *George C. Marshall: Organizer of Victory, 1943–1945* (New York, 1973), chap. 1.

14. Bryant, *Turn of the Tide,* pp. 443–5; *Foreign Relations: Conferences at Washington and Casablanca,* pp. 559–60, 570–73, 594–7, 630–32; Maurice

Matloff, *United States Army in World War II: Strategic Planning for Coalition Warfare, 1943–1944* (Washington, D.C., 1959), pp. 21–7; Pogue, *Marshall: 1943–1945*, pp. 31–2; Churchill, *Hinge of Fate*, p. 588.

15. *Foreign Relations: Conferences at Washington and Casablanca*, pp. 581–3, 597, 602–4, 617–22, 629, 707ff., 791ff.; Matloff, *Strategic Planning, 1943–1944*, pp. 30–37; Pogue, *Marshall: 1943–1945*, pp. 21–3, 26–31.

16. Sherwood, *Roosevelt and Hopkins*, pp. 655–6; Divine, *Second Chance*, pp. 75–6, 85–6; *FDR: Personal Letters, 1928–1945*, II, 1366–7, 1371–2, 1382; Pickersgill, *The Mackenzie King Record, 1939–1944*, pp. 429–36; *P.P.A.: 1943*, pp. 30–34.

17. Harley Notter, *Postwar Foreign Policy Preparation, 1939–1945* (Washington, D.C., 1949), pp. 124–7; Raymond G. O'Connor, *Diplomacy for Victory: FDR and Unconditional Surrender* (New York, 1971), pp. 37–8; Pickersgill, *The Mackenzie King Record, 1939–1944*, p. 433; *Foreign Relations: Conferences at Washington and Casablanca*, pp. 506, 496–7, 499, 503; Harriman, *Special Envoy, 1941–1946*, pp. 177–8; Hull, *Memoirs*, II, 1570–71.

18. *Foreign Relations: Conferences at Washington and Casablanca*, pp. 635, 726–9, 833–7, 847–9; Churchill, *Hinge of Fate*, pp. 595–600; Sherwood, *Roosevelt and Hopkins*, pp. 695–6; Hull, *Memoirs*, II, 1570; the date on Churchill's message to the War Cabinet about the doctrine is Jan. 19, not Jan. 20, as indicated in *Hinge of Fate*, the document is in PREM. 3, 197/2; Churchill himself leaves open the possibility that there was a further discussion with FDR about the doctrine after Jan. 21: "I do not remember," he wrote in *Hinge of Fate*, p. 596, "nor have I any record, of anything that passed between the President and me on the subject after I received the Cabinet message, and it is quite possible that in the pressure of business . . . the matter was not further referred to between us." A search of Churchill's papers bears out his statement about the existence of any further record. There are, however, two notes, "Note by the PM," Jan. 10, 1944, and P.M. to Cadogan, Apr. 19, 1944, in PREM. 3, 197/2, which further illustrate his difference with the President on the issue: "The matter is on the President," he wrote in the second of these. "He announced it at Casablanca without any consultation. I backed him up in general terms. Subsequent correspondence with the President has shown him very much disinclined to remodel his statements now." In September 1943, when the State Department planned to publish the notes of the conversations between Wilson, Lloyd George, and Clemenceau in Paris in 1919, Roosevelt objected "(a) because Lloyd George is still alive and (b) because notes of these conversations ought not to have been taken down anyway" (*Foreign Relations of the United States: Conferences at Washington and Quebec, 1943* (Washington, D.C., 1970), p. 1334); Paul Kecskemeti, *Strategic Surrender: The Politics of Victory and Defeat* (Stanford, 1958); for a contrary view, see Anne Armstrong, *Unconditional Surrender: The Impact of the Casablanca Policy upon World War II* (New Brunswick, N.J., 1961).

19. *Roosevelt and Churchill: Secret Wartime Correspondence*, pp. 278–9; Sherwood, *Roosevelt and Hopkins*, pp. 675–6; *Foreign Relations of the United States, 1943*, II (Washington, D.C., 1964), 23–4; *Foreign Relations: Conferences at Washington and Casablanca*, pp. 513–14.

20. *Foreign Relations, 1943*, II, 24ff., describes British-American difficulties with the French on the eve of the Casablanca conference; Murphy, *Diplomat Among Warriors*, pp. 169-72; Harold Macmillan, *The Blast of War, 1939-1945* (London, 1967), pp. 239-49; *Foreign Relations: Conferences at Washington and Casablanca*, pp. 609-12, 809ff.; Eden, *The Reckoning*, pp. 416-21; Churchill, *Hinge of Fate*, pp. 591-2; *War Memoirs of de Gaulle: 1942-1944*, pp. 78-84.

21. *Ibid.*, pp. 84-9; *Foreign Relations: Conferences at Washington and Casablanca*, pp. 692-6; *Foreign Relations, 1942*, III, 568-9; Sherwood, *Roosevelt and Hopkins*, p. 685; Murphy, *Diplomat Among Warriors*, pp. 168, 172-3.

22. *War Memoirs of de Gaulle: 1942-1944*, pp. 89-95; Murphy, *Diplomat Among Warriors*, pp. 173-5; Macmillan, *Blast of War, 1939-1945*, pp. 249-54; *Foreign Relations: Conferences at Washington and Casablanca*, pp. 705-7, 722-5, 822-3; Sherwood, *Roosevelt and Hopkins*, pp. 691-3.

23. *Foreign Relations: Conferences at Washington and Casablanca*, pp. 823-8; *Foreign Relations, 1943*, II, 47-51; Sherwood, *Roosevelt and Hopkins*, p. 686; Hull, *Memoirs*, II, 1207-10; *P.P.A.: 1943*, pp. 83-6; for a different view of Roosevelt's understanding of French affairs after Casablanca, see Murphy, *Diplomat Among Warriors*, pp. 175-6; and Macmillan, *Blast of War, 1939-1945*, pp. 254-5.

24. For work on the message, see *Foreign Relations: Conferences at Washington and Casablanca*, pp. 732, 782-4, 803-7; Churchill to Deputy Prime Minister, Jan. 26, 1943, PREM. 3, 420/3; Standley, *Admiral Ambassador to Russia*, pp. 327-8; *Stalin's Correspondence, 1941-1945*, II, 52-3.

25. Churchill to Hopkins, Feb. 13, 1943; Churchill to FDR, Feb. 3, 1943; FDR to Churchill, Feb. 5, 1943; see Admiral King's comment of Feb. 4 attached to FDR's reply to Churchill, describing the Prime Minister's message as promising *"much more* than can be done," MRP.

26. *Stalin's Correspondence, 1941-1945*, II, 55-7; I, 99-103, 105-6; or Churchill, *Hinge of Fate*, pp. 649-53; on the fighting in Russia, see Werth, *Russia at War, 1941-1945*, pp. 580-81.

27. Churchill, *Hinge of Fate*, pp. 655-9; Harriman to Hopkins, Feb. 28, Mar. 14, 1943, MRP; Churchill to FDR, Mar. 18, 25, 1943, and memo, "Reference the President's Personal Message to the Prime Minister No. 263 of Mar. 20," attached to the March 25 cable; FDR to Churchill, Mar. 20, 28, 1943, MRP; *Stalin's Correspondence, 1941-1945*, I, 98-9, 105, 107-17; Churchill to FDR, Apr. 2, 1943; FDR to Churchill, Apr. 3, 1943, MRP.

28. Stimson MS. Diary, Dec. 11, 1942; Romanus and Sunderland, *Stilwell's Mission to China*, pp. 245-50; also see Chiang to FDR, Nov. 14, 1942; and FDR to Chiang, Dec. 2, 1942, MRP.

29. Romanus and Sunderland, *Stilwell's Mission to China*, pp. 254-61; except for Chiang's Jan. 8, 1943, cable to FDR, which is on pp. 259-60 of Romanus and Sunderland, the messages between Chiang, Roosevelt, and Churchill are in *Foreign Relations: Conferences at Washington and Casablanca*, pp. 515-18; Stilwell's comments are in a cable to the War Dept. of Jan. 9, 1943, in the MRP.

30. Chennault's letter is in his memoirs, *Way of a Fighter*, pp. 212-16;

for the rest, see Romanus and Sunderland, *Stilwell's Mission to China*, pp. 250-54, 261, 277.

31. *Foreign Relations: Conferences at Washington and Casablanca*, pp. 540-41, 550, 554-5, 561-2, 590-91, 597, 600-603, 612-22, 630, 673, 718-19, 797-8, 801-2, 807-8.

32. Arnold, *Global Mission*, pp. 399, 407ff.; Chiang to FDR, Feb. 7, 1943, MRP; Romanus and Sunderland, *Stilwell's Mission to China*, pp. 269-78; Tuchman, *Stilwell and China*, pp. 355-8.

33. The FDR to Chiang message of March 8 is dated Mar. 3, 1943, in the MRP; FDR to Marshall, Mar. 8, 1943, MRP; also see Romanus and Sunderland, *Stilwell's Mission to China*, pp. 278-83.

34. For Madame Chiang's visit, see Tuchman, *Stilwell and China*, pp. 349-53; also see Raymond Clapper MS. Diary, Feb. 11, 1943; Sherwood, *Roosevelt and Hopkins*, pp. 61-6; *Complete Presidential Press Conferences*, XXI, 157-67; Blum, *From the Morgenthau Diaries, 1941-1945*, pp. 102-6; Eleanor Roosevelt, *This I Remember*, pp. 282-7; Lash, *Eleanor and Franklin*, pp. 675-81.

35. FDR to Marshall, Mar. 8, 1943, MRP; for these reports on conditions in China, see *Foreign Relations of the United States: China, 1943* (Washington, D.C., 1957), pp. 4-10, 25-9, 31-2; for FDR's apprehensions, see *Foreign Relations: Conferences at Washington and Casablanca*, pp. 597, 630, 718; P.P.A.: 1943, p. 79; *Complete Presidential Press Conferences*, XXI, 164-6. Also see Joseph Alsop to Hopkins, Mar. 1, 26, 1943, Alsop MSS.

36. *Foreign Relations: China, 1942*, pp. 268ff.; Feis, *China Tangle*, pp. 61-2; Churchill, *Hinge of Fate*, p. 488; Eden to Churchill, Mar. 17, 1943; Cadogan memo, Mar. 22, 1943; Churchill to Cadogan, Mar. 22, 1943, PREM. 4, 28/9; *Foreign Relations, 1943*, III, 33, 35-7, 39; Eden, *The Reckoning*, pp. 435-9; Churchill to Eden, Mar. 30, 1943, PREM. 4, 30/3.

37. *Foreign Relations: China, 1942*, pp. 185-7; *Foreign Relations, 1943*, III, 39; CAB. 65, W.M. (43), 53rd Conclusion, Minute 2, Apr. 13, 1943.

38. Tuchman, *Stilwell and China*, pp. 349-50; Sir Llewellyn Woodward, *British Foreign Policy in the Second World War*, Vol. IV (London, 1975), 518-21; *Complete Presidential Press Conferences*, XXI, 157-8; Eden to Churchill, Mar. 29, 1943, PREM. 4, 30/3; Eden, *The Reckoning*, p. 437.

39. For FDR's view of how shipping limits would affect ANAKIM, see Eden, *The Reckoning*, pp. 439-40; cf. Marshall to FDR, Apr. 3, 1943; and "Meetings of FDR with the J.C.S., 1942-1945," Apr. 6, 1943, MRP; Romanus and Sunderland, *Stilwell's Mission to China*, pp. 283-8, 317-20; FDR to Chiang, Mar. 31, Apr. 14, 1943; Marshall to FDR, Apr. 12, 1943; Chiang to FDR, Apr. 29, 1943, MRP.

40. Romanus and Sunderland, *Stilwell's Mission to China*, pp. 320-25; William D. Leahy, *I Was There* (New York, 1950), pp. 156-7.

41. *Foreign Relations: Conferences at Washington and Quebec, 1943*, pp. 11-17; "Handed to Mr. Eden by the President," Mar. 29, 1943, PREM. 3, 333/12; "Meetings of FDR with the J.C.S., 1942-1945," Apr. 6, 1943, MRP; *Roosevelt and Churchill: Secret Wartime Correspondence*, pp. 324-5; Bryant, *Turn of the Tide*, pp. 491-5; CAB. 65, W.M. (43) 62nd Conclusions, Apr. 29, 1943.

42. J.C.S. Memorandum for FDR, May 8, 1943, MRP; Churchill, *Hinge*

of Fate, pp. 681–5; Foreign Relations: Conferences at Washington and Quebec, 1943, pp. 24–9; Michael Howard, History of the Second World War: Grand Strategy, Vol. IV: August 1942–September 1943 (London, 1972), chap. 22, esp. pp. 419, 427–8; Bryant, Turn of the Tide, p. 494.

43. For FDR's concern about operations in Italy and eagerness for a build up in Britain, see Stimson MS. Diary, May 3, 1943; Matloff, Strategic Planning, 1943–1944, pp. 120–28; Leahy, I Was There, pp. 157–8; Foreign Relations: Conferences at Washington and Quebec, 1943, pp. 29–30, 32.

44. Churchill, Hinge of Fate, pp. 695, 701–4; Foreign Relations: Conferences at Washington and Quebec, 1943, pp. 121–3, 197–8; Matloff, Strategic Planning, 1943–1944, pp. 128–35; Stimson MS. Diary, May 17, 19, 1943; Pogue, Marshall: 1943–1945, pp. 212–13.

45. Foreign Relations: Conferences at Washington and Casablanca, 1943, pp. 31–2, 66–77, 87–91, 288–9, 295–8, 236, 134–41; Churchill, Hinge of Fate, p. 683; Romanus and Sunderland, Stilwell's Mission to China, pp. 326–33.

46. CAB. 65, 81 (43), June 5, 1943; Foreign Relations: Conferences at Washington and Quebec, 1943, pp. 67, 135, 137–8, 140–41, 76, 297–8, 369, 378–9; Churchill, Hinge of Fate, pp. 692–3; also see Howard, Grand Strategy, Aug. 1942–Sept. 1943, IV, 437–47.

47. Woodward, British Foreign Policy, II, 618–25; For the President: Correspondence between FDR and Bullitt, pp. 575–94; Foreign Relations, 1943, III, 13–15, 25, 35; Eden, The Reckoning, p. 432.

48. Woodward, British Foreign Policy, II, 625–35; Churchill, Hinge of Fate, pp. 659–62; Foreign Relations, 1943, III, 374ff.; Stalin's Correspondence, 1941–1945, I, 120–25, 127–8; II, 60–62; Roosevelt and Churchill: Secret Wartime Correspondence, pp. 328–30.

49. Foreign Relations, 1943, III, 646; Joseph Davies MS. Diary, Apr. 12, 19, 29, 1943; Stalin's Correspondence, 1941–1945, II, 63–4; Roosevelt and Churchill: Secret Wartime Correspondence, pp. 347–8.

50. Foreign Relations: Conferences at Washington and Quebec, 1943, pp. 204, 213–14, 382–7; Churchill, Hinge of Fate, pp. 704–7; Burns, Roosevelt: Soldier of Freedom, pp. 370–71.

51. Ibid., p. 371; Joseph Davies MS. Diary, June 3, 1943; Foreign Relations, 1943, III, 650–55, 657–60; Stalin's Correspondence, 1941–1945, II, 66–71.

52. Roosevelt and Churchill: Secret Wartime Correspondence, pp. 340–41; Foreign Relations of the United States: Conferences at Cairo and Tehran, 1943 (Washington. D.C., 1961), pp. 9–11; Stalin's Correspondence, 1941–1945, I, 133–5; II, 72; Harriman, Special Envoy, 1941–1946, pp. 216–18.

53. Stalin's Correspondence, 1941–1945, I, 136–8, 140–41; Woodward, British Foreign Policy, II, 553–62; Foreign Relations: Conferences at Cairo and Tehran, 1943, pp. 11–13; Pickersgill, The Mackenzie King Record, 1939–1944, pp. 513–14, demonstrates FDR's concern about Churchill's response to his exclusion.

CHAPTER 14

1. Foreign Relations, 1943, II, 110ff.; FDR to Eisenhower, June 17, 1943, MRP, supplementing the message on pp. 156–7; Foreign Relations: Conferences at Washington and Quebec, 1943, p. 324; Arthur L. Funk,

Charles De Gaulle: The Crucial Years, 1943–1944 (Norman, Okla., 1959), pp. 116–45; *Roosevelt and Churchill: Secret Wartime Correspondence,* pp. 344–7.

2. *Ibid.;* Foreign Relations, 1943, II, 160–62, 171–7, 181–4; *Stalin's Correspondence,* 1941–1945, I, 135–6, 139–40; FDR to Churchill, July 8, 1943; FDR to Eisenhower and Murphy, July 8, 1943, MRP; also see *Foreign Relations: Conferences at Washington and Quebec,* 1943, pp. 661–71.

3. *Ibid.,* pp. 668, 916–17, 919–20, 934, 953, 1101–11, 1169–71; Eden, *The Reckoning,* pp. 466–8; Hull, *Memoirs,* II, 1232–3, 1241–2; Winston S. Churchill, *The Second World War: Closing the Ring* (Bantam Books ed., New York, 1962), pp. 77, 80.

4. Matloff, *Strategic Planning,* 1943–1944, pp. 152–63, 174–5; Albert N. Garland and Howard M. Smyth, *United States Army in World War II: Sicily and the Surrender of Italy* (Washington, D.C., 1965), pp. 23–5, 239–44, 258–69; *Foreign Relations: Conferences at Washington and Quebec,* 1943, pp. 444–52, 467–79; Churchill, *Hinge of Fate,* pp. 706ff.; *Closing the Ring,* pp. 21ff.; "The Next Conference," July 15, 1943, PREM. 3, 366/1; Churchill to FDR, July 17, 1943; FDR to Churchill, July 19, 1943, MRP; FDR's message to Churchill about Portugal, and their exchanges of July 26 and 30, 1943, are in *Foreign Relations,* 1943, II, 535–6, 332–5, 337–9.

5. *Stalin's Correspondence,* 1941–1945, II, 77–9; Halifax to Churchill, July 8, 1943, PREM. 3, 366/11: There is no exact record of when Roosevelt received Stalin's cable, but it was sent through the Soviet Embassy in Washington, which, judging by other messages, would have got it to Washington by the 9th. An FDR letter dated the 10th, but apparently dictated on the 9th, suggests that he had Stalin's cable on the 9th, *FDR: Personal Letters,* 1928–1945, II, 1438; for the "run-around" comment, see "Roosevelt Off-the-Record," Sept. 15, 1943, Raymond Clapper MSS; *Foreign Relations: Conferences at Washington and Quebec,* 1943, 482–3, 496–502.

6. *Foreign Relations,* 1943, II, 332; *P.P.A.: 1943,* pp. 326–8; Burns, *Roosevelt: Soldier of Freedom,* pp. 383–4; *Complete Presidential Press Conferences,* XXII, 36, 49–50; *Foreign Relations: Conferences at Washington and Quebec,* 1943, p. 521.

7. *Ibid.,* pp. 403–4, 519–20, 522, 525–7; *Foreign Relations,* 1943, II, 336–7, 339; FDR to Churchill, July 29, 1943; Churchill to FDR, July 30, 1943, MRP; Garland and Smyth, *Sicily and the Surrender of Italy,* pp. 268–78.

8. *Foreign Relations: Conferences at Washington and Quebec,* 1943, pp. 527ff., see esp. 554–5, 1055–7, 1060–63, 1076–8, 1090–91, 1161–9, 1180–82, 1188–9, 1257ff.; also see Hopkins to FDR, Sept. 20, 1943, MRP; "Meetings of FDR with the J.C.S., 1942–1945," Nov. 15, 1943, MRP; Churchill, *Closing the Ring,* pp. 163–74; Feis, *Churchill-Roosevelt-Stalin,* chaps. 17 and 19; Garland and Smyth, *Sicily and the Surrender of Italy,* pp. 435ff.

9. Matloff, *Strategic Planning,* 1943–1944, pp. 210–30; *Foreign Relations: Conferences at Washington and Quebec,* 1943, pp. 894–9, 941–5, 1121–5; Pickersgill, *The Mackenzie King Record,* 1939–1944, p. 553.

10. *Stalin's Correspondence,* 1941–1945, II, 79–82; *Foreign Relations:*

Conferences at Washington and Quebec, 1943, pp. 1086–7, 965–7; Churchill, *Closing the Ring*, pp. 80–81; Feis, *Churchill-Roosevelt-Stalin*, pp. 170–73.

11. Harriman, *Special Envoy, 1941–1946*, p. 218; *Foreign Relations: Conferences at Washington and Quebec, 1943*, pp. 1211–15, 1287–90; Matloff, *Strategic Planning, 1943–1944*, pp. 249–53.

12. For this discussion of atomic-energy policy, I have relied heavily on Martin J. Sherwin, *A World Destroyed: The Atomic Bomb and the Grand Alliance* (New York, 1975), chap. 3; the documents underpinning this discussion are largely in *Foreign Relations: Conferences at Washington and Quebec, 1943*, pp. 1–11, 188, 209–11, 221–2, 630–53, 894, 1096–7, 1117–19; other documents are in PSF: Atomic Bomb, and Box 132 of the Hopkins MSS; the British materials are in PREM. 3, 139/8A; for a similar, but briefer discussion of atomic energy policy under FDR, see Barton J. Bernstein, "The Quest for Security: American Foreign Policy and International Control of Atomic Energy, 1942–1946," *JAH*, LX (March 1974), 1003–10.

13. *Foreign Relations: Conferences at Washington and Quebec, 1943*, pp. 1095–6, 1173–5, 1178–9, 1181–2, 1303–10, 1159–60; ". . . Stalin has a sense of humor," FDR told Harold Ickes. "He [Roosevelt] believes that he won't have any trouble talking with Stalin," (Ickes MS. Diary, Sept. 5, 1943); Harriman, *Special Envoy, 1941–1946*, pp. 226–8; *Stalin's Correspondence, 1941–1945*, I, 159–61.

14. Eden, *The Reckoning*, p. 467; Minute: "Foreign Ministers' Conference and Russia's Western Frontiers," Sept. 5, 1943, F.O. 371/37028/N5267/3666/38; R.I. Campbell to Foreign Office, Sept. 14, 1943, F.O. 371/37028/N5364/3666/38; *Foreign Relations of the United States, 1943*, I (Washington, D.C., 1963), 540–42.

15. Divine, *Second Chance*, chaps. 4 and 5, *passim*; in the first half of 1943, Roosevelt's fullest public expression on America's postwar role was made in Forrest Davis, "Roosevelt's World Blueprint," *Saturday Evening Post*, CCXV (Apr. 10, 1943), 20–21, 109–10; Pickersgill, *The Mackenzie King Record, 1939–1944*, p. 553.

16. *Foreign Relations: Conferences at Washington and Quebec, 1943*, pp. 681–3, 691–3, 698–708, 1337; Winant to FDR, Sept. 1, 1943, MRP; "Four Power Declaration," Sept. 4, 1943, W.P. (43) 389, CAB. 66; *Foreign Relations, 1943*, I, 534–5, 537–8, 541–2; William D. Hassett, *Off the Record with F.D.R., 1942–1945* (New Brunswick, N.J., 1958), pp. 218–19; Clark Kerr to Foreign Office, Oct. 6, 1943, with Churchill's handwritten comment at the bottom of the page, PREM. 4, 30/5.

17. *War Diary of Breckinridge Long, 1939–1944*, pp. 281, 322–5, 327–8; "Conversation with Hull," Sept. 1, 1943, Raymond Clapper MSS; Burns, *Roosevelt: Soldier of Freedom*, p. 350; *Foreign Relations, 1943*, I, 518–19, 530–31, 540.

18. *Ibid.*, 589–90, 592–5, 602–4, 635, 640–42, 656–9, 669; Feis, *Churchill-Roosevelt-Stalin*, chaps. 22 and 24, *passim*.

19. As early as February 1943, Stalin had indicated that he would ultimately fight Japan (Leahy, *I Was There*, pp. 147–8; Harriman, *Special*

Envoy, 1941–1946, p. 243); *Foreign Relations, 1943*, I, 628, 672–3, 686, 690; *Foreign Relations: Conferences at Cairo and Tehran, 1943*, pp. 71, 147, 152–5; "I probably have 'localitis,'" Gen. John R. Deane told the Joint Chiefs, "but I have been tremendously impressed with the possibilities for cooperation engendered during this conference," Oct. 30, 1943, MRP; Eden held a similar view: see Cadogan to Halifax, Nov. 4, 1943, F.O. 371/37030/ N6447/3666/38.

20. *Foreign Relations: Conferences at Cairo and Tehran, 1943*, pp. 23–5, 30–37, 43–6, 57–8, 67–8, 71–2, 79–80.

21. *Ibid.*, pp. 34, 37–40, 110–12, 41–2, 47–8, 50, 60, 64–7, 72, 79–80; also Churchill to Brigadier Hollis, Oct. 27, 1943, PREM. 3, 136/12.

22. Intelligence report, Naval Attaché, Chungking, May 21, 1943, MRP; S. K. Hornbeck to Adm. Leahy, July 2, 1943, Leahy Files, U.S. Army MSS, R.G. 218; Chennault to FDR and Hopkins, Sept. 5, 1943, in the Joseph Alsop MSS; Romanus and Sunderland, *Stilwell's Mission to China*, chap. 10, esp. p. 382 for FDR to Marshall; Feis, *China Tangle*, chap. 8; Tuchman, *Stilwell and China*, chap. 15; *Foreign Relations: Conferences at Cairo and Tehran, 1943*, pp. 13, 16–17, 30, 39–40, 47, 54–6, 59, 72–3, 77, 83, 198–9.

23. Churchill, *Closing the Ring*, pp. 279–80; *Churchill: From the Diaries of Lord Moran*, p. 140; *Foreign Relations: Conferences at Cairo and Tehran, 1943*, pp. 159–60, 312–15, 317–18, 349–50, 364–5, 889–90; Matloff, *Strategic Planning, 1943–1944*, pp. 347–52.

24. *Foreign Relations: Conferences at Cairo and Tehran, 1943*, pp. 242–3, 257–8, 263–5, 338–45, 347–9, 354–5, 366; Matloff, *Strategic Planning, 1943–1944*, p. 350; Tuchman, *Stilwell and China*, pp. 400–6.

25. *Foreign Relations: Conferences at Cairo and Tehran, 1943*, pp. 249, 334, 674–81, 705–10, 725–6, 803–4; Matloff, *Strategic Planning, 1943–1944*, pp. 339–40, 369–73; Tuchman, *Stilwell and China*, pp. 404–10; *The Stilwell Papers*, p. 251.

26. Chiang's comment to Mountbatten is in Tuchman, *Stilwell and China*, p. 404; Madame Chiang to FDR and the record of his political commitments to Chiang are in *Foreign Relations: Conferences at Cairo and Tehran, 1943*, pp. 442, 102–3, 257, 308, 322–5, 349, 366–7, 376, 387–9, 448–9, 567, 868–70, 887–8, 891; *The Stilwell Papers*, pp. 252–3; Charles W. Taussig, memo of conversation with FDR, Feb. 14, 1944, Taussig MSS; Feis, *China Tangle*, pp. 105–13; Feis, *Churchill-Roosevelt-Stalin*, pp. 251–7.

27. ". . . He had insisted on the participation of China in the 4 Power Declaration at Moscow," FDR told Stalin in Tehran, "not because he did not realize the weakness of China at present, but he was thinking farther into the future." *Foreign Relations: Conferences at Cairo and Tehran, 1943*, p. 532; for the rest, see pp. 488, 312, 485; and "Roosevelt Off-the-Record," Sept. 15, 1943; "2nd Roosevelt Private Conference," Oct. 20, 1943, Raymond Clapper MSS.

28. *The Wallace Diary, 1942–1946*, p. 107; Sherwood, *Roosevelt and Hopkins*, p. 572; *Foreign Relations, 1943*, III, 35, 37; *Foreign Relations, 1943*, I, 543; Feis, *Churchill-Roosevelt-Stalin*, pp. 214–15; "Résumé of . . . Conversations with Sumner Welles. . . ," Nov. 30, 1942; "Luncheon with

Winston Churchill . . . ," Dec. 17, 1942, Taussig MSS; Knox to FDR, Mar. 10, June 19, 1943; FDR to Knox, Mar. 12, June 12, 30, 1943; Wilson Brown to Leahy, Oct. 7, 1943, MRP; E. R. Stettinius, Jr. MS. Diary, Nov. 5, 1943; Stettinius, Jr. to Hull, Oct. 15, Nov. 5, 1943, Hull MSS; Leahy to FDR, Nov. 15, 1943, Leahy Files, U.S. Army MSS, R.G. 218.

29. Churchill, *Closing the Ring*, pp. 175ff.; Matloff, *Strategic Planning, 1943–1944*, pp. 249–58; *Foreign Relations: Conferences at Cairo and Tehran, 1943*, pp. 195, 210, 259, 265–6, 330, 333–4, 478, 480–82; Deane to Marshall, Nov. 6, 1943; Harriman to FDR, Nov. 7, 1943; Marshall to FDR, Nov. 22, 1943, MRP.

30. *Foreign Relations: Conferences at Cairo and Tehran, 1943*, pp. 483–4, 487ff.; for FDR's instructions to the Chiefs about Russia and Japan, see Matloff, *Strategic Planning, 1943–1944*, p. 357; for Brooke's response to the opening comments, see *Churchill: From the Diaries of Lord Moran*, p. 145; for Stalin's remarks at the first formal session, see "Conversation with Admiral King," Dec. 18, 1943, Clapper MSS. In his survey of the fighting fronts, Roosevelt did not mention that the solution to their problems of sea transport, or victory over the German U-boats in the battle of the Atlantic, had resulted from the use of new forms of radar and Ultra, the code name for British ability to read German radio messages. See F. W. Winterbotham, *The Ultra Secret* (New York, 1974), 13, 125–9; *Los Angeles Times*, Sept. 10, 1978, p. 1. For the Hopkins note, see Sherwood, *Roosevelt and Hopkins*, p. 780; for Brooke's remark, see CAB. 65, W.M. (43) 174th Conclusions, Dec. 22, 1943.

31. *Foreign Relations: Conferences at Cairo and Tehran, 1943*, pp. 495, 506–7, 533–52, 555–65.

32. For poll results comparing public interest in foreign and domestic affairs, see Divine, *Second Chance*, pp. 133–5; McIntyre to FDR, Sept. 24, 1943, OF 857; Rosenman to FDR, Nov. 24, 1943, OF 4351; " 'It will take all we've got to provide [postwar] relief to Europe, perhaps long-continued rationing over here,' " FDR told an English visitor to Hyde Park in November 1943. " 'It will also take all we've got to keep the public sold on the subject. . . . Yes, we've got some big problems ahead' " (R. I. Campbell to David Scott, Dec. 20, 1943, F.O. 371/38516/A7/7/G45); on his doubts about American readiness for policing, see "President's Talk to a Group of MP's . . . Dec. 6, 1943" in "Log of FDR's Trip . . . Nov.–Dec., 1943," MRP; FDR to Eichelberger, Jan. 11, 1944, OF 4725; *Foreign Relations: Conferences at Cairo and Tehran, 1943*, pp. 531–2, 253–6, 259, which also describes his views on occupation zones; on this issue, also see Leahy to FDR, "Europe-Wide Rankin," Nov. 18, 1943, MRP; Leahy to FDR, Jan. 26, 1944, indicating that the President also wanted an early withdrawal of occupation forces because they would be needed against Japan; and Leahy to Marshall, Feb. 20, 1944, reaffirming FDR's desire not to use American forces for peacekeeping in southern Europe, Leahy Files, U.S. Army MSS, R.G. 218.

33. Frances Perkins, VIII, 312, COHC; for the exchanges leading to FDR's stay in the Russian Embassy, see *Foreign Relations: Conferences at Cairo and Tehran, 1943*, pp. 310, 373–4, 397, 439–40, 461, 476; the

description of the dinner meeting is on pp. 553–5; the description of how he teased Churchill is in Frances Perkins, *The Roosevelt I Knew* (New York, 1946), pp. 83–5; on FDR's efforts to gain Stalin's trust, also see Adam B. Ulam, *The Rivals: America and Russia since World War II* (New York, 1971), pp. 14–15; Adam B. Ulam, *Stalin* (New York, 1973), pp. 587–92; Burns, *Roosevelt: Soldier of Freedom*, pp. 211–12.

34. *Foreign Relations: Conferences at Cairo and Tehran*, 1943, pp. 530–33, 595–6, 167, 197, 484–6, 509–511, 514, 554, 566–8, 594–5, 868–70; for Roosevelt's continuing desire to use his trusteeship idea to assure American control of strategic bases, see Leahy to FDR, Jan. 11, July 4, 1944; FDR to Admiral Brown, Jan. 14, 1944; FDR to JCS, July 10, 1944, Leahy Files, U.S. Army MSS, R.G. 218.

35. R. I. Campbell to David Scott, Dec. 20, 1943, F.O. 371/38516/A7/7/G45; "It was inconceivable to me that Stalin would submit to the reestablishment of effective sovereignty in Poland, Latvia, Lithuania, and Estonia," Admiral Leahy recorded in his diary on Sept. 23, 1943. "It also appeared probable that the Soviet Government, with its superior military power and its possibility of making a separate compromise peace with Germany, could force acceptance of Soviet desires in this matter upon America and Great Britain" (*I Was There*, p. 185); *Foreign Relations: Conferences at Cairo and Tehran*, 1943, pp. 381–5, 510–12, 575, 594, 596–601, 603–4, 847–8; Churchill, *Closing the Ring*, pp. 309–10, 337–40, 344–5; Ulam, *Stalin*, pp. 589–91, pictures Churchill and Roosevelt as trading away Polish rights at Tehran; Feis, *Churchill-Roosevelt-Stalin*, pp. 283–7, describes FDR as postponing the problem until "another day," and Churchill as trying to find a way to reinstate the London Poles as a negotiator and head off the creation of a puppet government by Moscow.

36. *Foreign Relations: Conferences at Cairo and Tehran*, 1943, pp. 253–4, 510–11, 513, 532–3, 553–4, 600, 602–4, 845–6, 881–4; Churchill, *Closing the Ring*, pp. 307–9, 342–4, 347–8; Feis, *Churchill-Roosevelt-Stalin*, pp. 272–5.

37. P.P.A.: 1943, pp. 553–8; *Complete Presidential Press Conferences*, XXII, 216–17; Ickes MS. Diary, Dec. 19, 1943.

38. *Churchill: From the Diaries of Lord Moran*, pp. 149–51, 155; *Foreign Relations: Conferences at Cairo and Tehran*, 1943, pp. 676–8, 706; Frances Perkins, VIII, 278,COHC; *My Name Is Tom Connally*, p. 265; Ickes MS. Diary, Dec. 19, 1943; Harold D. Smith MS. Diary, Feb. 16, 1944; P.P.A.: 1943, p. 561; Divine, *Second Chance*, pp. 192–4; Thomas M. Campbell and George C. Herring (eds.), *The Diaries of Edward R. Stettinius, Jr., 1943–1946* (New York, 1975), pp. 31–3; Stettinius MS. Diary, Mar. 17, 1944, where Stettinius reports Roosevelt as saying: " 'Woodrow Wilson said we are making the world safe for democracy, but can democracy make the world safe for it?' "

CHAPTER 15

1. Harold D. Smith MS. Diary, Feb. 16, 1944; Leahy, *I Was There*, p. 239; Burns, *Roosevelt: Soldier of Freedom*, pp. 448–50; and John Morton Blum, *V Was for Victory* (New York, 1976), pp. 246–7—both of whom

chiefly take their information on FDR's health from Howard G. Bruenn, "Clinical Notes on the Illness and Death of President Franklin D. Roosevelt," *Annals of Internal Medicine*, 72 (April 1970), 579–91; also see, Jim Bishop, *FDR's Last Year* (New York, 1974), pp. 2–12, 37–9, 70–72, 92.

2. Jerome S. Bruner, "Presenting Postwar Planning to the Public," Jan. 1943; Oscar Cox to Hopkins, Apr. 27, 1943, Hopkins MSS; James M. Barnes to FDR, Sept. 8, 1943; McIntyre to FDR, Sept. 24, 1943, OF 857; Rosenman to FDR, Nov. 24, 1943, OF 4351; "Current Opinion," Dec. 27, 1943; Rosenman to FDR, Dec. 31, 1943, PSF: Executive Office: Rosenman; Isidore Lubin to Hopkins, Jan. 6, 1944, Hopkins MSS; *Complete Presidential Press Conferences*, XXII, 245–51; *P.P.A.: 1944–45*, pp. 32–42; Burns, *Roosevelt: Soldier of Freedom*, pp. 421–7, 429–37, which includes the Senator's attack on FDR; Blum, *V Was for Victory*, pp. 247–54; Harold D. Smith MS. Diary, Feb. 16, 1944, for FDR's comment on the Congress.

3. On the refugee issue, I have relied heavily on Feingold, *Politics of Rescue*, pp. 82–89; FDR's speech is in *P.P.A.: 1939*, pp. 546–51; on British-French resistance to Roosevelt's plan, see A. A. Berle, Jr., to FDR, Oct. 23, 1939, PSF: Palestine; for the rest, see Feingold, chap. 5, and Blum, *From the Morgenthau Diaries, 1941–1945*, pp. 207–8.

4. For these details, see Feingold, *Politics of Rescue*, chap. 6 and pp. 167–74; for reports of mass destruction, see Ickes MS. Diary, Oct. 10, 1942; for the administration's announcements, see *P.P.A.: 1942*, pp. 329–30, 410; *Foreign Relations, 1942*, I, 66–71; FDR's discussion with Wallace and Rayburn is recorded in Henry Wallace, Nov. 26, 1942, X, 1995, COHC; for the talk with Morgenthau, see Morgenthau Presidential MS. Diary, 5: 1200–1201.

5. The Bermuda Conference, with Law's comment, the negotiations for the release of European Jews, and the Palestine issue are described in Feingold, *Politics of Rescue*, chaps. 7 and 8; also see Blum, *From the Morgenthau Diaries, 1941–1945*, pp. 208–20; the FDR-Hull exchange on action to follow the Bermuda talks is in *Foreign Relations, 1943*, I, 176–9; FDR's comment to the Cabinet is in Ickes MS. Diary, Dec. 19, 1943; on the question of bombing the camps, see Feingold, pp. 256–7, 292, 305.

6. For the constraints on FDR and his motives, see Feingold, *Politics of Rescue*, chap. 10; Burns, *Roosevelt: Soldier of Freedom*, pp. 395–8; Blum, *V Was for Victory*, pp. 175–7.

7. Blum, *From the Morgenthau Diaries, 1941–1945*, pp. 220–27; Feingold, *Politics of Rescue*, pp. 178–81, 239–47, and chap. 9—for the quote on Nazi determination, see p. 307.

8. Roosevelt was not alone in this concern. In May 1944 Stimson expressed the fear that the Russians might stop fighting when they had evicted the Germans and regained all their lost territory, plus the Baltic states (in Matloff, *Strategic Planning for Coalition Warfare, 1943–1944*, pp. 410–11). Buchanan, *The U.S. and World War II*, I, 181–2; on Churchill's plan for breaking the Italian stalemate and FDR's response, see pp. 413–16 of Matloff; and Churchill, *Closing the Ring*, pp. 364–74, 377–8.

9. *Ibid.*, pp. 383–4, 410–23; Matloff, *Strategic Planning, 1943–1944*, pp. 416–26; Charles B. MacDonald, *The Mighty Endeavor: American Armed*

Forces in the European Theater in World War II (New York, 1969), pp. 198–205; "Meetings of FDR with JCS, 1942–1945," Feb. 21, 1944, MRP; FDR to Churchill, Apr. 8, 16, 18, May 10, 12, 1944; Churchill to FDR, Apr. 14, 18, May 11, 1944, MRP; *Stalin's Correspondence, 1941–1945*, II, 138–41, 293.

10. The difficulties over Poland are well described in Llewellyn Woodward, *British Foreign Policy in the Second World War*, Vol. III (London, 1971), 154–65; for the documentary record, see *Foreign Relations of the United States, 1944*, III (Washington, D.C., 1965), 1216–20, 1226, 1228–30; *Stalin's Correspondence, 1941–1945*, I, 181–2, 192–7.

11. *Foreign Relations, 1944*, III, 1242–6, 1249–66; *Stalin's Correspondence, 1941–1945*, I, 207–8, 210–13; Woodward, *British Foreign Policy*, III, 165–83; Leahy described Stalin's message to Churchill as "the strongest and most undiplomatic document I had ever seen exchanged between two ostensibly friendly governments" (*I Was There*, p. 232).

12. On FDR's decision to send no message, see Leahy to FDR, Mar. 26, 1944, MRP; on the question of Polish-Americans entering a reconstituted Polish government, see *Foreign Relations, 1944*, III, 1230–32, 1398–9, 1402–3, 1405–7; for the exchanges on Poland, see two messages from Churchill to FDR on Apr. 1, 1944, and FDR's response of Apr. 5, 1944, MRP.

13. *Foreign Relations, 1944*, III, 1272–4; *Stettinius Diaries, 1943–1946*, pp. 76–7; Bishop, *FDR's Last Year*, p. 77, all describe the origins of Mikolajczyk's visit; on D-Day and after, see Buchanan, *The U.S. and World War II*, II, chaps. 17 and 18; MacDonald, *Mighty Endeavor*, chaps. 16 and 17; *Stalin's Correspondence, 1941–1945*, II, 145; FDR to Churchill, June 9, 1944, MRP; *Stettinius Diaries, 1943–1946*, pp. 79–80, contains FDR's comments to the Poles; for FDR's assurances to Stalin, see *Foreign Relations of the United States, 1944*, IV (Washington, D.C., 1966), 873–4, and III, 1276–7, 1284, 1289–90.

14. Winston S. Churchill, *The Second World War: Triumph and Tragedy* (Bantam Books ed., New York, 1962), pp. 61–6; *Foreign Relations of the United States, 1944*, V (Washington, D.C., 1965), 117–21, 124–5; FDR agreed to Churchill's proposal without consulting the State Department: see Lincoln MacVeagh to Hull, June 26, 1944; Hull to FDR, June 29, July 8, 1944, MRP.

15. Matloff, *Strategic Planning, 1943–1944*, pp. 466–75; Churchill, *Triumph and Tragedy*, pp. 49–60, 84–5, 108, 612–19; Churchill to FDR, June 25, 28, 29, July 1, 1944; FDR to Churchill, June 28, July 1, 1944; Leahy to FDR, June 30, 1944; Winant to FDR, July 3, 1944, all in MRP.

16. Funk, *De Gaulle: Crucial Years, 1943–1944*, pp. 191–8; Milton Viorst, *Hostile Allies: FDR and De Gaulle* (New York, 1965), pp. 181–2, 186–7; *Foreign Relations: Conferences at Cairo and Tehran, 1943*, pp. 189–90; *Foreign Relations, 1943*, II, 193–200; also see *FDR: Personal Letters, 1928–1945*, II, 1473–4.

17. FDR to Marshall, June 2, 1944; PSF: Safe: Marshall; FDR to Elmer Davis, June 1, 1944, PSF: OWI; *Foreign Relations, 1944*, III, 683, 692–4, 707–8; FDR to Eisenhower, May 12, 1944; Churchill to FDR, May 12, 26, 27 (2 messages), 28, June 7, 9 (2 messages), 1944; FDR to Churchill,

June 9, 12, 1944, all in MRP; Funk, *De Gaulle: Crucial Years, 1943–1944,* pp. 217–26, 237ff.; Viorst, *Hostile Allies,* pp. 189–201; the controversy over the military francs is described in Blum, *From the Morgenthau Diaries, 1941–1945,* pp. 165–77.

18. FDR to Marshall, June 2, 1944, PSF: Safe: Marshall; Stettinius MS. Diary, May 8, 1944; *Foreign Relations, 1944,* III, 707–8; for FDR's and Hull's comments to Stimson, and Marshall's feelings about de Gaulle, see Blum, *From the Morgenthau Diaries, 1941–1945,* pp. 173–4.

19. FDR to Eisenhower, June 17, 1943, MRP; *Foreign Relations, 1943,* II, 70–71, 117–18, 135, 192–3; CAB. 65, W.M. (43) 169th Conclusions, Minute 2, Dec. 13, 1943; memorandum of conversation with FDR, Feb. 14, 1944, Taussig MSS.

20. Churchill to Eden, May 21, 1944, PREM. 3, 180/7; Foreign Office to Halifax, Dec. 29, 1943; Halifax to Foreign Office, Jan. 19, 1944; "Memo to P.M.," Jan. 25, 1944, PREM. 3, 178/2, all describe FDR's views on Indochina; for his conversation with the diplomats, see Eden to Churchill, Dec. 20, 1943, PREM. 3, 178/2; the Foreign Office proposal is in "The Future of Indochina and Other French Pacific Possessions," Feb. 16, 1944, CAB. 66, W.P. (44), 11; Churchill's response to Eden is in the May 21 note; for FDR's instruction to the State Department and an excellent overall analysis of the Indochina issue, see Walter La Feber, "Roosevelt, Churchill, and Indochina: 1942–45," *AHR,* 80 (Dec. 1975), 1277–95; the British approach to the issue is well described in Christopher Thorne, "Indochina and Anglo-American Relations, 1942–1945," *PHR,* XLV (Feb. 1976), 73–96.

21. Henry L. Stimson and McGeorge Bundy, *On Active Service in Peace and War* (New York, 1948), pp. 550–51; FDR's remarks to de Gaulle are in *War Memoirs of de Gaulle: 1942–1944,* pp. 265–72; for the origins of de Gaulle's visit, see *Foreign Relations, 1944,* III, 693–4, 713, 718–19; Duff Cooper to Churchill, May 31, 1944, PREM. 3, 121/2; Winant to FDR, June 13, 1944; FDR to Winant, June 13, 1944; Marshall, King, and Arnold to FDR, June 13, 1944; FDR to Marshall, June 14, 1944, MRP; Viorst, *Hostile Allies,* pp. 207–9; for FDR's understanding of de facto recognition, see pp. 723–4 of *Foreign Relations, 1944,* III; FDR described his feelings about the de Gaulle visit in a conversation with Charles Taussig on July 13, 1944, Taussig MSS; Biddle, *In Brief Authority,* pp. 181–2.

22. *Stalin's Correspondence, 1941–1945,* I, 240–42, 244–6; II, 153–4; *Foreign Relations, 1944,* III, 1300–1301, 1305–13; Churchill to FDR, July 25, 26, Aug. 10, 11, 1944; FDR to Churchill, July 28, Aug. 3, 11, 1944, MRP; Woodward, *British Foreign Policy,* III, 191–202.

23. *Foreign Relations, 1944,* III, 1308–9, 1372–83; *Stalin's Correspondence, 1941–1945,* I, 248–9, 251–2, 254–5; Churchill, *Triumph and Tragedy,* p. 116; Woodward, *British Foreign Policy,* III, 202–12.

24. Churchill, *Triumph and Tragedy,* pp. 117–24, which contains all the relevant documents; FDR to Winant, Aug. 26, 1944, Leahy Files, U.S. Army MSS, R.G. 218, amplifies FDR's reasons for not pressing Stalin to help Warsaw; also see Woodward, *British Foreign Policy,* III, 212–21; Ulam, *Expansion and Coexistence,* pp. 361–3.

25. *Stalin's Correspondence, 1941–1945,* II, 150–51, 153, 156; Hopkins

to FDR, July 26, 1944, MRP; Harriman, *Special Envoy, 1941–1946*, pp. 340–41; Matloff, *Strategic Planning, 1943–1944*, pp. 500–501; *Foreign Relations, 1944*, IV, 988–90; "I have begun to wonder whether Stalin and the Kremlin have determined to reverse their policy of cooperation with their Western Allies . . . and to pursue a contrary course," Hull cabled Harriman on September 18, p. 991 of *Foreign Relations, 1944*, IV; Hopkins to Harriman, Sept. 11, 1944, MRP.

26. The record of the Dumbarton Oaks talks is in *Foreign Relations of the United States, 1944*, I (Washington, D.C., 1966), 713ff.; on the sixteen Soviet Republics and FDR's response, see pp. 738, 742–4, 750–51; also see *Stettinius Diaries, 1943–1946*, pp. 111–14, 116–18; *Stalin's Correspondence, 1941–1945*, II, 158–9.

27. *Foreign Relations, 1944*, I, 731, 737–8, 740–42, 744, 748, 750, 760, 766–7, 769, 775–7, 780–82, 784–9, 806–7, 814–16, 889–90; also see Stettinius to FDR, Sept. 14, 1944, MRP, reporting that the Russians would not give in on the veto question; and Stettinius MS. Diary, Sept. 17, 1944, recording a conversation with the President on how to adjourn the Conference; and Churchill to Eden, Sept. 18, 1944, PREM. 4, 30/11, reporting how FDR had decided to adjourn the talks.

28. *Foreign Relations of the United States: The Conference at Quebec, 1944* (Washington, D.C., 1972), pp. 3–15, 22, 37–8, 40–41, 237–44, 312–13; Leahy, *I Was There*, p. 236; Matloff, *Strategic Planning, 1943–1944*, pp. 508–9, 515.

29. *Foreign Relations: Quebec Conference, 1944*, pp. 314, 350, 221–4, 490–91; J. W. Pickersgill and D. F. Forster, *The Mackenzie King Record*, Vol. II: *1944–1945* (Toronto, 1968), pp. 70–71; Feis, *Churchill-Roosevelt-Stalin*, pp. 413–19, 421–5, describes the tensions over Roumania, Bulgaria, Yugoslavia, and Greece; *Foreign Relations, 1944*, V, 132–3, contains Churchill's message on Greece.

30. *Foreign Relations: Quebec Conference, 1944*, pp. 367–9, 229, 302–5, 313–14, 378–9, 429–30, 216–18, 439, 382, 490–91; *Foreign Relations, 1944*, V, 133–4.

31. *Foreign Relations: Quebec Conference, 1944*, pp. 16–19, 43, 159–60, 169–72, 177–81, 328–30, 344–8, 360–61, 363, 371–2, 395–6, 468, 296; also see Blum, *From the Morgenthau Diaries, 1941–1945*, pp. 306–14.

32. *Foreign Relations: Quebec Conference, 1944*, pp. 296, 492–3; on Bohr and his contacts with Frankfurter, Roosevelt, and Churchill, I have relied on Sherwin, *A World Destroyed*, chap. 4, which also contains the information on FDR's knowledge of Soviet espionage and Bush's summary of FDR's views. I differ with Sherwin, however, in my interpretation of Roosevelt's interview with Bohr. By contrast with my conclusion that FDR was using the interview to send a signal to the Russians about long-term possibilities for cooperation in the control of atomic energy, Sherwin believes that Roosevelt had no serious interest in Bohr's internationalist approach. South Africa's Prime Minister Jan Christian Smuts had much the same idea I believe FDR had on shared control: to prevent "the most destructive competition in the world" after the war, he urged Churchill to consider with the President "whether Stalin should be taken into the secret. There must of

course be the fullest trust and confidence between you as a condition precedent of any such disclosure," Smuts to Churchill, June 15, 1944, PREM. 3, 139/11A.

33. My account of the debate over postwar German policy prior to the Quebec meeting is based on Blum, *From the Morgenthau Diaries, 1941–1945*, pp. 327–69, which primarily rests on Morgenthau's and Stimson's MS. diaries. For a somewhat different interpretation of events surrounding the Morgenthau Plan, see Warren F. Kimball, *Swords or Ploughshares? The Morgenthau Plan for Defeated Nazi Germany, 1943–1946* (Philadelphia, 1976).

34. "One of the most important things I have to discuss with you is Stage II," Lend-Lease after German defeat, or the rebuilding of the British economy, Churchill wrote FDR on September 12, their second day in Quebec, *Foreign Relations: Quebec Conference, 1944*, p. 43; for the exchange about Russian fears, see pp. 327–8; the invitation to Morgenthau and the initial conversation are on pp. 43, 323–4; for Morgenthau's report to FDR on Eden's attitude, see Blum, *From the Morgenthau Diaries, 1941–1945*, p. 338.

35. *Foreign Relations: Quebec Conference, 1944*, pp. 324–8, 342–4, 360–62, 390, 466–7.

36. Churchill, *Triumph and Tragedy*, p. 134; *Foreign Relations: Quebec Conference, 1944*, p. 362; Blum, *From the Morgenthau Diaries, 1941–1945*, pp. 373–4; for the sequence of events, see pp. 328–30, 342–6, 348, 359–63, 390–91, 466–8 of the *Foreign Relations* volume on Quebec; also see Stettinius MS. Diary, Sept. 21, 1944, which records FDR as saying that in connection with a discussion on "the control of Germany," he "had a very frank talk with the Prime Minister on finances. . . . Apparently this was the point," Stettinius noted, "where they discussed the future of Lend-Lease. . . ."

37. *Foreign Relations, 1944*, I, 166, 180–82, 188–9, 223–4, 232, 263–4; FDR to Hull, Apr. 30, 1944, MRP; Stettinius MS. Diary, May 8, 1944; *Foreign Relations: Quebec Conference, 1944*, pp. 145–58, 385–90, 350, 365–6, 369–70, 373–4, 391–2, 476, 144–5; Pickersgill and Forster, *The Mackenzie King Record, 1944–1945*, pp. 70–71; Matloff, *Strategic Planning, 1943–1944*, p. 511, and esp., notes 9 and 11; Leahy, *I Was There*, p. 265; prior to the agreement on occupation zones, when Eden pressed FDR at Quebec to have "American troops next to France. . . . the President refused. Eden wanted to know why. The President said, 'Anthony, frankly, because they smell. You can make anything out of that you want, but that is what the American people think. There is going to be a revolution there'" (Stettinius MS. Diary, Sept. 21, 1944).

38. FDR's shift on postwar German policy is described in Blum, *From the Morgenthau Diaries, 1941–1945*, pp. 375–83; FDR to Hull, Sept. 29, 1944, PSF: Hull; *Foreign Relations, 1944*, I, 344–6, 358–9.

39. Blum, *From the Morgenthau Diaries, 1941–1945*, pp. 314–22.

40. Churchill, *Triumph and Tragedy*, pp. 179–82, 186–91; for Churchill's determination to emphasize the positive side of Soviet-Western relations, see the record of Eden's meeting with Molotov in Moscow on Oct. 9, 1944, 7 p.m., PREM. 3, 434/2; *Foreign Relations, 1944*, IV, 1002; FDR

to Churchill, Oct. 4, 1944, draft message not sent, MRP; Sherwood, *Roosevelt and Hopkins*, pp. 832–4.

41. Churchill, *Triumph and Tragedy*, pp. 196–200; *Foreign Relations, 1944*, IV, 1005–10; Feis, *Churchill-Roosevelt-Stalin*, pp. 447–51.

42. Churchill, *Triumph and Tragedy*, pp. 204–6; *Foreign Relations, 1944*, III, 1326; Feis, *Churchill-Roosevelt-Stalin*, pp. 444–7, 460–66.

43. *Foreign Relations, 1944*, III, 1322–8; Churchill, *Triumph and Tragedy*, pp. 203–6, 208–9; Feis, *Churchill-Roosevelt-Stalin*, pp. 453–9; Woodward, *British Foreign Policy*, III, 224–35.

44. Churchill, *Triumph and Tragedy*, pp. 186, 210, 206; *Foreign Relations: Quebec Conference, 1944*, p. 368; *Stalin's Correspondence, 1941–1945*, II, 165; "He and Molotov were the only members of the Soviet Government who wanted to deal 'softly' with M. Mikolajczyk," Stalin told Churchill during the Moscow talks, Woodward, *British Foreign Policy*, III, 231; Ulam, *Stalin*, p. 588.

45. Sherwood, *Roosevelt and Hopkins*, pp. 819–24; Burns, *Roosevelt: Soldier of Freedom*, chap. 17, esp. pp. 502, 507–8, 521–4, 527; *P.P.A.: 1944–45*, pp. 227–8, 284–93; Bishop, *FDR's Last Year*, pp. 146–52.

46. Sherwood, *Roosevelt and Hopkins*, pp. 822–3, relates FDR's view on the independent vote; see Burns, *Roosevelt: Soldier of Freedom*, pp. 499–500, on Willkie's defeat in Wisconsin; Divine, *Second Chance*, describes the administration's efforts to appease the isolationists and its difficulties with the liberal internationalists (chaps. 8 and 9, *passim*); the quote from the *Nation* is on p. 205 of Divine; the decision on Wallace is described in Burns, pp. 503–6; also see Cantril to FDR, May 8, 1944, OF 857, indicating that the public overwhelmingly preferred a "practical" man to a man with "the right ideals" for President; FDR's comment on Wallace is in Ickes MS. Diary, June 18, 1944.

47. See Burns, *Roosevelt: Soldier of Freedom*, pp. 510–13, on FDR's courting of Willkie; on Willkie and the Dewey-Roosevelt contest for the liberal-internationalist vote, see Divine, *Second Chance*, pp. 216–20, 236–40; Stettinius to FDR, Oct. 13, 1944, Hopkins MSS; *P.P.A.: 1944–45*, p. 350.

48. Harold D. Smith MS. Diary, Oct. 30, 1944; Hopkins to Beaverbrook, Nov. 6, 1944, MRP; on the results of the election, see Burns, *Roosevelt: Soldier of Freedom*, pp. 532–4; Divine, *Second Chance*, pp. 241–2.

CHAPTER 16

1. *The Stilwell Papers*, p. 252; Charles F. Romanus and Riley Sunderland, *United States Army in World War II: Stilwell's Command Problems* (Washington, D.C., 1956), pp. 74–7.

2. *Foreign Relations: China, 1943*, pp. 476–82, contains the reports from Gauss and Morgenthau; for the exchanges on using China's forces in Burma, see FDR to Chiang, Dec. 20, 27, 1943, Jan. 14, 1944; Chiang to FDR, Dec. 23, 1943, Jan. 10, 1944, MRP; *The Stilwell Papers*, pp. 262–6; Romanus and Sunderland, *Stilwell's Command Problems*, pp. 79–80, 297–8.

3. Blum, *From the Morgenthau Diaries, 1941–1945*, pp. 110–16; *Foreign Relations of the United States: China, 1944* (Washington, D.C., 1967), pp. 826–9, 835–9, 852, 859–62; Tuchman, *Stilwell and China*, pp. 410–14.

4. Romanus and Sunderland, *Stilwell's Command Problems*, pp. 300–301,

160–65, 172–4, 177–8, 304–5; Churchill, *Closing the Ring*, pp. 479–81, 489–93, which includes FDR's message to Churchill—the original in the MRP is dated Feb. 24; Tuchman, *Stilwell and China*, pp. 427–31, 437–9.

5. FDR to Chiang, Mar. 17, 1944, MRP; the other exchanges are reproduced in Romanus and Sunderland, *Stilwell's Command Problems*, pp. 306–10; Chiang's March 27 reply to FDR, however, is dated March 29 in the MRP; the Chinese decision to use the Y-Force is described on pp. 312–14.

6. On the Japanese offensive, see *Stilwell's Command Problems*, pp. 316–20, 322–7, 371–4; Tuchman, *Stilwell and China*, pp. 454–60, also describes the deterioration in China, including the quotes from White and Gauss; Gauss's report, however, also contained some hopeful notes: *Foreign Relations: China, 1944*, pp. 100–102.

7. Romanus and Sunderland, *Stilwell's Command Problems*, pp. 302–4; Feis, *The China Tangle*, pp. 157–9, chap. 14; for the relevant documents, see *Foreign Relations: China, 1944*, pp. 329, 348–9, 393–5, 799–800, 102–5; FDR to Chiang, Mar. 20, Apr. 8, 1944; Harriman to FDR, June 11, 1944, MRP; FDR to Chiang, Mar. 30, 1944; Chiang to FDR, Apr. 4, 1944, Leahy Files, U.S. Army MSS, R.G. 218.

8. For the origins of the Wallace mission, see *The Wallace Diary, 1942–1946*, pp. 308–9, 310–11, 315, 322, 326–7, 329, 331–3; *Foreign Relations: China, 1944*, pp. 216ff.; for Wallace's discussions with Chiang and his conclusions, see *The China White Paper: August 1949* (2 vols.; Stanford, 1967 ed.), II, 549–59; *Foreign Relations: China, 1944*, pp. 234–7.

9. Blum, *From the Morgenthau Diaries, 1941–1945*, p. 287; Romanus and Sunderland, *Stilwell's Command Problems*, pp. 379–84; FDR to Chiang, July 6, 1944, MRP; Tuchman, *Stilwell and China*, pp. 466–70.

10. Romanus and Sunderland, *Stilwell's Command Problems*, pp. 384–7, 413–15, reproduces Chiang's July 8 message in full, but not FDR to Chiang, July 13, 1944, or Chiang's memorandum of July 23, 1944, which was delivered to the White House on August 15—both are in the MRP; Tuchman, *Stilwell and China*, pp. 470–71.

11. Marshall to Leahy, Aug. 4, 1944; FDR to Chiang, Aug. 9, 1944, MRP; Russell D. Buhite, *Patrick J. Hurley and American Foreign Policy* (Ithaca, N.Y., 1973), pp. 147–50; Stilwell's comment is in Romanus and Sunderland, *Stilwell's Command Problems*, p. 416; FDR's attraction to a Republican for the assignment was not lost on Hurley: If any one tries to make a campaign issue out of Stilwell's recall, Hurley cabled FDR on November 1, "You are at liberty to say that recommendation was made by former Republican Secretary of War who is on the ground. . . . The Republican Ex-Secretary of War accepts full responsibility" (MRP).

12. Chiang's reply is in *Foreign Relations: China, 1944*, p. 141; on the meaning of Saipan's capture, see FDR to Churchill, June 19, 1944, MRP; Romanus and Sunderland, *Stilwell's Command Problems*, p. 405; the point about Japanese military success in China is made by Tuchman, *Stilwell and China*, p. 467; "American Articles on China," July 14, 1944, F.O. 371/41632/F3467/357/10; Halifax to Foreign Office, Aug. 20, 1944, F.O. 371/41632/F3976/357/10; FDR to Chiang, Aug. 21, 1944, MRP, the message was delivered on Aug. 23.

13. *China White Paper*, II, 561–4; FDR to Chiang, Sept. 9, 1944, MRP;

The Stilwell Papers, pp. 325–33; Romanus and Sunderland, *Stilwell's Command Problems*, pp. 422–39, gives a full account of the negotiations with Chiang; Stilwell's cable to Marshall is on pp. 435–6; also see Tuchman, *Stilwell and China*, pp. 481–91.

14. See *Foreign Relations: Conference at Quebec, 1944*, pp. 476–7, 479–80, 464–6, for the message to Mountbatten and the two messages to Chiang; also see pp. 376, 380–81; the "firecracker" description is in *The Stilwell Papers*, p. 333; on the drafting of FDR's message, see Romanus and Sunderland, *Stilwell's Command Problems*, pp. 441–2; Churchill to Smuts, Sept. 24, 1944, PREM. 4, 30/11.

15. On the delivery of the message, see Romanus and Sunderland, *Stilwell's Command Problems*, pp. 443–6; Tuchman, *Stilwell and China*, pp. 493–4; Feis, *The China Tangle*, p. 188, n. 6; *The Stilwell Papers*, pp. 333–4.

16. For Chiang's response, see Romanus and Sunderland, *Stilwell's Command Problems*, pp. 452–3; Tuchman, *Stilwell and China*, pp. 494–7; the full *aide-mémoire* and Hurley's comments are in Hurley to FDR, Sept. 25, 1944, MRP.

17. Stilwell to Marshall, Sept. 26, Oct. 10, 1944, MRP and Leahy Files, U.S. Army MSS, R.G. 218, indicating that both messages reached the White House; for Kung's cable to Chiang and FDR's message, see Romanus and Sunderland, *Stilwell's Command Problems*, pp. 456, 458–9; also see Hurley to FDR, Oct. 6, 1944, MRP.

18. This exchange of messages is in Romanus and Sunderland, *Stilwell's Command Problems*, pp. 460–63, 468–9; Hurley's warning is in a cable of Oct. 13, 1944, MRP; the view of the Joint Chiefs is described on pp. 457–8 of Romanus and Sunderland; for Stalin's fresh assurance, see Harriman, *Special Envoy, 1941–1946*, pp. 349–51; and FDR to Churchill, Sept. 30, 1944, MRP; for the military arrangements following Stilwell's recall, see FDR to Chiang, Oct. 18, 1944, MRP.

19. "The President . . . was greatly concerned with the outlook relative to China and . . . was apprehensive for the first time as to China holding together for the duration of the war," Stettinius recorded after a Cabinet meeting in May. He wanted Wallace to tell Chiang that he "could not let America down after America had pinned such faith and hope on China as a World Power" (*Foreign Relations: China, 1944*, p. 230); on the Communist issue, see Sherwood, *Roosevelt and Hopkins*, pp. 828–9; and Barbara Tuchman, "If Mao Had Come to Washington: An Essay in Alternatives," *Foreign Affairs*, 52 (Oct. 1972), 61–2.

20. Feis, *The China Tangle*, pp. 226–31, 210–16; Harriman, *Special Envoy, 1941–1946*, pp. 370–71; Hurley to FDR, Oct. 19, 1944; FDR to Hurley, Oct. 24, Nov. 10, 1944, MRP; Theodore H. White and Annalee Jacoby, *Thunder Out of China* (New York, 1946), p. 253; *Foreign Relations: China, 1944*, pp. 698–700, 703; Buhite, *Hurley and American Foreign Policy*, pp. 162–71.

21. Memo of conversation with FDR, Nov. 13, 1944, Taussig MSS; FDR to Admiral Brown, Dec. 4, 1944, MRP.

22. For Hurley's assurances and the course of the negotiations, see Hurley to FDR, Nov. 17, 20, 29, 1944, MRP; *Foreign Relations: China, 1944*, pp.

745–9; Buhite, *Hurley and American Foreign Policy*, pp. 171ff.; for Harriman's talk with Stalin, see *Special Envoy, 1941–1946*, pp. 371, 379–80; and pp. 737–8 of *F.R.: China, 1944*; for the reports on opposition to a unified China, see Marshall to Leahy, Dec. 30, 1944, enclosing a report from Wedemeyer of Dec. 29, 1944, Leahy Files, U.S. Army MSS., R.G. 218; Hurley to FDR, Jan 2, 1945, MRP; for the response, see Stettinius MS. Diary, Jan 2, 1945; Halifax to Foreign Office, Jan. 3, 1945, PREM. 4, 27/10; Memo of conversation between FDR and Stanley, Jan. 16, 1945, Taussig MSS.

23. *Foreign Relations of the United States: China, 1945* (Washington, D.C., 1969), pp. 172–7; Buhite, *Hurley and American Foreign Policy*, pp. 180–81, 184; Tuchman, "If Mao Had Come to Washington," *Foreign Affairs* (Oct. 1972), pp. 48–51, 54–6.

24. Donald F. Drummond, "Cordell Hull, 1933–1944," and Walter Johnson, "Edward R. Stettinius, Jr., 1944–1945," both in *An Uncertain Tradition: American Secretaries of State in the Twentieth Century*, edited by Norman A. Graebner (New York, 1961); Cantril to Tully, Nov. 10, 1944; Tully to Cantril, Dec. 13, 1944, OF 857.

25. *Foreign Relations of the United States: The Conferences at Malta and Yalta, 1945* (Washington, D.C., 1955), pp. 207–13, 216–18, 221–6; Harriman, *Special Envoy, 1941–1946*, pp. 366, 369–70; Arthur Bliss Lane, *I Saw Poland Betrayed* (Indianapolis, 1948), pp. 58–62; Feis, *Churchill-Roosevelt-Stalin*, pp. 518–21.

26. *Foreign Relations: Conferences at Malta and Yalta, 1945*, pp. 266–71; Churchill to FDR, Dec. 6, 1944; Stettinius to FDR, Dec. 6, 1944, MRP; Burns, *Roosevelt: Soldier of Freedom*, pp. 537–8.

27. *Foreign Relations, 1944*, V, 140–44, 148–51, 154–5; Churchill to Hopkins for FDR, Dec. 10, 16, 1944, MRP; Ickes MS. Diary, Dec. 24, 1944; Burns, *Roosevelt: Soldier of Freedom*, pp. 538–9.

28. *Foreign Relations of the United States, 1944*, II (Washington, D.C., 1967), 589; Hopkins to Churchill, Dec. 16, 1944, MRP; Oscar Cox to Hopkins, Dec. 19, 1944, Hopkins MSS; Bowman to FDR, Jan. 5, 1945, PSF: State Dept.; Eden to Churchill, Jan. 29, 1945, PREM. 4, 27/10, includes a copy of the *New York Times* story; there is no record of such a message from FDR to Churchill; "Memorandum for the President," Dec. 21, 30, 1944, Stettinius MS. Diary; "Memorandum for the President," Jan. 6, 16, 1945, PSF: State Dept.

29. *P.P.A.: 1944–45*, pp. 511–14; "Memorandum for the President," Jan. 12, 1945, Stettinius MS. Diary; "Memorandum for the President," Jan. 16, 1945, PSF: State Dept.; *Stettinius Diaries, 1943–1946*, pp. 207–8.

30. *Foreign Relations: Conferences at Malta and Yalta, 1945*, pp. 8–27.

31. Stimson MS. Diary, Dec. 31, 1944; *Foreign Relations: Conferences at Malta and Yalta, 1945*, pp. 447–9, contains a copy of Deane's report to Stimson which he passed along to FDR; *Stettinius Diaries, 1943–1946*, pp. 213–15, recounts FDR's meeting with the Senators.

32. *Foreign Relations: Conferences at Malta and Yalta, 1945*, pp. 39–40; Diane Shaver Clemens, *Yalta* (New York, 1970), pp. 113–17, describes the Conference site.

33. Buchanan, *The U.S. and World War II*, II, chap. 20; *Foreign Relations: Conferences at Malta and Yalta, 1945*, pp. 570–91; Edward R. Stettinius, Jr., *Roosevelt and the Russians: The Yalta Conference* (Garden City, N.Y., 1949), pp. 114–15; *Churchill: From the Diaries of Lord Moran*, pp. 239–40; Churchill, *Triumph and Tragedy*, pp. 298–9; Clemens, *Yalta*, pp. 85–95; 117–31, provides an excellent account and interpretation of these discussions.

34. *Foreign Relations: Conferences at Malta and Yalta, 1945*, pp. 572–3, 611–19, 283ff., 899–900; see *Foreign Relations, 1944*, III, 739–48, for the recognition of de Gaulle's government; Harriman, *Special Envoy, 1941–1946*, pp. 401–2, describes FDR's shift on a role for France in the Control Council.

35. *Foreign Relations: Conferences at Malta and Yalta, 1945*, pp. 660–67, 682–6, 711–15, 729, 734–8, 771–6, 966–8, 990–92; Stettinius, *Roosevelt and the Russians*, pp. 173–74, 281–3; Clemens, *Yalta*, pp. 218–40; also see Halifax to Foreign Office, Jan. 5, 1945, PREM. 4, 30/11, in which Halifax reported the President in conversation as hopeful that Stalin would "drop the idea of having all Soviet Republics represented in the Assembly. . . ."

36. *Foreign Relations: Conferences at Malta and Yalta, 1945*, pp. 810, 822, 844–5, 858–9, 935, 947, 977; Eden, *The Reckoning*, pp. 594–5; Clemens, *Yalta*, pp. 240–43; Stettinius MS. Diary, Jan. 2, 1945; also see FDR's comment on the "renaissance of the French people" in his State of the Union Message, *P.P.A.: 1944–45*, p. 515; Eden saw this as evidence of France's acceptance back into "the ranks of the influential nations" (CAB. 66, W.P. (45) 23, Jan. 11, 1945).

37. Dixon to Foreign Office, Oct. 12, 1944, PREM. 3, 180/7; *Foreign Relations, 1944*, III, 778–80; Wedemeyer to Marshall, Nov. 15, 1944; FDR to Hurley, Nov. 16, 1944, MRP; also see FDR to Sec. of Navy James Forrestal, Nov. 17, 1944, Leahy Files, U.S. Army MSS, R.G. 218; Stimson to FDR, Nov. 24, 1944; FDR to Stettinius, Nov. 24, 1944, PSF: Indochina; *Foreign Relations: Conferences at Malta and Yalta, 1945*, p. 770; *P.P.A.: 1944–45*, pp. 562–3; *Stettinius Diaries, 1943–1946*, pp. 304–5; La Feber, "Roosevelt, Churchill, and Indochina," AHR (Dec. 1975), 1290–93.

38. Walter Millis (ed.), *The Forrestal Diaries* (New York, 1951), pp. 33, 37–8, describes FDR's attitude; "Latest Opinion Trends in the U.S.A.," Mar. 24, 1945, PSF: State Dept.; Ickes to FDR in Stettinius MS. Diary, Apr. 5, 1945, describes current American opinion on trusteeships.

39. *Foreign Relations: Conferences at Malta and Yalta, 1945*, pp. 667–71, 677–81, 726–8, 709, 711, 716–21, 792–3, 776–82, 786–91, 803–7, 903, 905–7, 911, 938, 973–4; Stettinius, *Roosevelt and the Russians*, pp. 183, 270–71; Leahy, *I Was There*, pp. 315–16; Clemens, *Yalta*, chap. 5.

40. *Foreign Relations: Conferences at Malta and Yalta, 1945*, pp. 848–9, 853–4, 860–63, 873, 899, 908, 918–19, 935–6, 971–2; Clemens, *Yalta*, pp. 205–6, 262–4.

41. On the atomic bomb and military plans for the Far East, see Feis, *Churchill-Roosevelt-Stalin*, pp. 501–5; *Foreign Relations: Conferences at Malta and Yalta, 1945*, pp. 383–4, 395–400, 593–4, 698–9, 757–67, 834–41.

42. *Ibid.*, pp. 768–71, 894–7, 984; Harriman, *Special Envoy, 1941–1946*,

pp. 396–400; Feis, *Churchill-Roosevelt-Stalin*, pp. 505–17; Churchill, *Triumph and Tragedy*, pp. 333–5; Ulam, *Expansion and Coexistence*, pp. 470–76.

43. Stettinius, *Roosevelt and the Russians*, pp. 72–3; Perkins, *The Roosevelt I Knew*, pp. 391, 393; Frances Perkins, VIII, 283, COHC; *Churchill: From the Diaries of Lord Moran*, pp. 234, 239, 242; Leahy, *I Was There*, pp. 290, 313; Eden, *The Reckoning*, pp. 593–4.

44. Sherwood, *Roosevelt and Hopkins*, pp. 869–70; *Foreign Relations: Conferences at Malta and Yalta*, 1945, p. 975; Burns, *Roosevelt: Soldier of Freedom*, pp. 581–2; Rosenman, *Working with Roosevelt*, pp. 527–30; Adm. Thomas C. Hart, pp. 236–7, COHC; *P.P.A.: 1944–45*, pp. 570–86.

45. *From the Berle Papers*, pp. 476–7; Rosenman, *Working with Roosevelt*, p. 526; Frances Perkins, VIII, 315, 317, COHC; *Stettinius Diaries, 1943–1946*, pp. 207–8; "Latest Opinion Trends in the U.S.A.," Feb. 23, 1945, PSF: State Dept.; Acheson to FDR, Mar. 17, 1945; Eleanor Roosevelt to FDR, Apr. 2, 1945, OF 857; Divine, *Second Chance*, pp. 252–3.

46. *Stalin's Correspondence, 1941–1945*, II, 197, 199–200, 204; Divine, *Second Chance*, pp. 269–76; *The Private Papers of Senator Vandenberg* (Boston, 1952), pp. 156–7, 159–60; Stettinius to FDR, Apr. 2, 1945, MRP; "Latest Opinion Trends in the U.S.A.," Apr. 6, 1945, PSF: State Dept.; *P.P.A.: 1944–45*, pp. 610–11.

47. *Foreign Relations: China*, 1945, pp. 242–6; there is a persuasive analysis of this whole episode in Buhite, *Hurley and American Foreign Policy*, chap. 8; also see Tuchman, "If Mao Had Come to Washington," *Foreign Affairs* (Oct. 1972), pp. 56–63, who emphasizes FDR's failure to appreciate that the Yalta agreement with the Soviets could not block a civil war and that by siding with Hurley, Roosevelt helped transfer the principal American experts "representing nine decades of Chinese experience" out of China.

48. *Foreign Relations of the United States, 1945*, V (Washington, D.C., 1967), 505–6, 147–50, 509–10, 155–6; also see FDR's message to Churchill of March 29, 1945, on pp. 189–90, in which he emphasized that they had agreed to "somewhat more emphasis on the Lublin Poles than on the other two groups" and any attempt to evade this fact would open them to the charge of going back on the Crimean decision.

49. "I had a short talk with the President today in which he spoke about Poland," Halifax cabled London on March 14, 1945, ". . . he fully realised political difficulties that situation was creating for you in England, and he was also very conscious of his own" (PREM. 3, 569/9); *Foreign Relations, 1945*, V, 158–60, 163–5, 185–90, 209; *Stalin's Correspondence, 1941–1945*, II, 201–4, 211–13; *P.P.A.: 1944–45*, pp. 613–16.

50. Buchanan, *The U.S. and World War II*, II, chap. 21; Feis, *Churchill-Roosevelt-Stalin*, pp. 583–96; *Stalin's Correspondence, 1941–1945*, II, 296–7, 198–201, 204–10; *Foreign Relations of the United States, 1945*, III (Washington, D.C., 1968), 746–7; FDR to Churchill, Apr. 6, 1945, MRP; Stimson MS Diary, Feb. 15, Mar. 5, 15, 1945; Sherwin, *A World Destroyed*, pp. 136–40; *Foreign Relations, 1945*, V, 209–10.

51. These details are described in Bruenn, "Clinical Notes on . . . FDR,"

Annals of Internal Medicine (Apr. 1970), 589–91; Burns, *Roosevelt: Soldier of Freedom*, pp. 599–601; Bishop, *FDR's Last Year*, pp. 568ff.; Churchill, *Triumph and Tragedy*, pp. 403–4; Harriman, *Special Envoy, 1941–1946*, pp. 440–42.

EPILOGUE

1. The quotes are from Leuchtenburg, *FDR and the New Deal*, p. 337; and Nicholas Halasz, *Roosevelt Through Foreign Eyes* (Princeton, 1961), pp. 318–19.

2. Kennan's remarks are from a symposium on "World War II: 30 Years After," published in *Survey*, V. 21 (Winter–Spring 1975), 30.

3. Wohlstetter, *Pearl Harbor: Warning and Decision, passim.*

4. William Emerson, "Franklin Roosevelt as Commander-in-Chief in World War II," *Military Affairs*, XXII (Winter 1958–59), 181–207.

5. For the Eccles and Kennan exchanges, see Burns, *Roosevelt: Soldier of Freedom*, pp. 352–3.

6. Kennan's observation is in the *Survey* symposium, pp. 35–6; also see Hugh Seton-Watson's Comments on pp. 37–42.

7. Charles Bohlen also believed that Roosevelt would have moved more quickly against the Russians than Truman did (*Witness to History 1929–1969* (New York, 1973), p. 211).

8. Burns, *Roosevelt: Soldier of Freedom*, pp. 373–4.

9. Ulam, *Expansion and Coexistence*, p. 399.

10. For Barbara Tuchman's conclusion, FDR's conversation with Snow, and the belief of the Joint Chiefs, see pp. 60, 63–4 of her article, "If Mao Had Come to Washington," *Foreign Affairs* (Oct. 1972).

11. Schlesenger, Jr., *Coming of the New Deal*, pp. 529–30.

BIBLIOGRAPHY OF SELECTED BOOKS

Adamic, Louis. *Dinner at the White House*. New York, 1946.

Alsop, Joseph, and Robert Kintner. *American White Paper*. New York, 1940.

Anderson, Irvine H., Jr. *The Standard-Vacuum Oil Company and United States East Asian Policy, 1933–1941*. Princeton, N.J., 1975.

Armstrong, Anne. *Unconditional Surrender: The Impact of the Casablanca Policy upon World War II*. New Brunswick, N.J., 1961.

Arnold, Henry H. *Global Mission*. New York, 1949.

Beard, Charles A. *American Foreign Policy in the Making, 1932–1940*. New Haven, Conn., 1946.

———. *President Roosevelt and the Coming of the War, 1941*. New Haven, Conn., 1948.

Bennett, Edward M. *Recognition of Russia: An American Foreign Policy Dilemma*. Waltham, Mass., 1970.

Berle, Adolf A. See Beatrice B. Berle.

Berle, Beatrice B., and Travis B. Jacobs, eds. *Navigating the Rapids, 1918–1971: From the Papers of Adolf A. Berle*. New York, 1973.

Biddle, Francis. *In Brief Authority*. New York, 1962.

Bishop, Jim. *FDR's Last Year*. New York, 1974.

Blum, John Morton. *From the Morgenthau Diaries: Years of Crisis, 1928–1938*. Boston, 1959.

———. *From the Morgenthau Diaries: Years of Urgency, 1938–1941*. Boston, 1965.

———. *From the Morgenthau Diaries: Years of War, 1941–1945*. Boston, 1967.

———, ed. *The Price of Vision: The Diary of Henry A. Wallace, 1942–1946*. Boston, 1973.

———. *V Was for Victory*. New York, 1976.

Bohlen, Charles E. *The Transformation of American Foreign Policy*. New York, 1969.

———. *Witness to History, 1929–1969*. New York, 1973.

Borg, Dorothy. *The United States and the Far Eastern Crisis of 1933–1938*. Cambridge, Mass., 1964.

———, and Shumpei Okamoto, eds. *Pearl Harbor as History: Japanese-American Relations, 1931–1941*. New York, 1973.

Browder, Robert P. *The Origins of Soviet-American Diplomacy*. Princeton, N.J., 1953.

Bryant, Arthur. *The Turn of the Tide: A History of the War Years Based on the Diaries of Field-Marshall Lord Alanbrooke, Chief of the Imperial General Staff.* Garden City, N.Y., 1957.

Buchanan, A. Russell. *The United States and World War II.* 2 vols. New York, 1964.

Buhite, Russell D. *Patrick J. Hurley and American Foreign Policy.* Ithaca, N.Y., 1973.

Bullitt, Orville H., ed. *For the President: Personal and Secret: Correspondence between Franklin D. Roosevelt and William C. Bullitt.* Boston, 1972.

Bullitt, William. See Orville Bullitt.

Bullock, Alan. *Hitler: A Study in Tyranny.* New York, 1961.

Burns, James MacGregor. *Roosevelt: The Lion and the Fox.* New York, 1956.

――――. *Roosevelt: The Soldier of Freedom.* New York, 1970.

Butow, R. J. C. *Tojo and the Coming of the War.* Princeton, N.J., 1961.

――――. *The John Doe Associates: Backdoor Diplomacy for Peace, 1941.* Stanford, Calif., 1974.

Campbell, Thomas M., and George C. Herring, eds. *The Diaries of Edward R. Stettinius, Jr., 1943–1946.* New York, 1975.

Cantril, Hadley, ed., and Mildred Strunk, *Public Opinion, 1935–1946.* Princeton, N.J., 1951.

Chandler, Alfred D., Jr., et al., eds. *The Papers of Dwight D. Eisenhower: The War Years.* 5 vols. Baltimore, Md., 1970.

Chennault, Claire Lee. See Robert Hotz.

Churchill, Winston S. *The Second World War: The Gathering Storm.* New York, 1961 ed.

――――. *The Second World War: Their Finest Hour.* New York, 1962 ed.

――――. *The Second World War: The Grand Alliance.* New York, 1962 ed.

――――. *The Second World War: The Hinge of Fate.* New York, 1962 ed.

――――. *The Second World War: Closing the Ring.* New York, 1962 ed.

――――. *The Second World War: Triumph and Tragedy.* New York, 1962 ed.

Clark, Mark W. *Calculated Risk.* New York, 1950.

Clemens, Diane Shaver. *Yalta.* New York, 1970.

Cole, Wayne S. *America First: The Battle Against Intervention, 1940–1941.* Madison, Wis., 1953.

――――. *Senator Gerald P. Nye and American Foreign Relations.* Minneapolis, Minn., 1962.

――――. *Charles A. Lindbergh and the Battle Against American Intervention in World War II.* New York, 1974.

Colton, Joel. *Léon Blum: Humanist in Politics.* New York, 1966.

Complete Presidential Press Conferences of Franklin Delano Roosevelt. 25 vols. in 12. New York, 1972.

Conn, Stetson, and Byron Fairchild. *United States Army in World War II: The Western Hemisphere: The Framework of Hemisphere Defense.* Washington, D.C., 1960.

Connally, Tom, and Alfred Steinberg. *My Name Is Tom Connally.* New York, 1954.

Cronon, E. David. *Josephus Daniels in Mexico.* Madison, Wis., 1960.

Dallek, Robert. *Democrat and Diplomat: The Life of William E. Dodd.* New York, 1968.

Daniels, Josephus. *The Wilson Years: Years of Peace, 1910–1917.* Chapel Hill, N.C., 1944.

Daniels, Roger. *Concentration Camps USA: Japanese Americans and World War II.* New York, 1971.

Davies, Joseph E. *Mission to Moscow.* New York, 1941.

Davis, Kenneth S. *FDR: The Beckoning of Destiny, 1882–1928.* New York, 1972.

Dawidowicz, Lucy S. *The War Against the Jews, 1933–1945.* New York, 1975.

Dawson, Raymond H. *The Decision To Aid Russia, 1941: Foreign Policy and Domestic Politics.* Chapel Hill, N.C., 1959.

De Conde, Alexander, ed. *Isolation and Security.* Durham, N.C., 1957.

De Gaulle, Charles. *The War Memoirs of Charles de Gaulle: Unity, 1942–1944.* New York, 1959.

De Jong, Louis. *The German Fifth Column in the Second World War.* Chicago, 1956.

Detzer, Dorothy. *Appointment on the Hill.* New York, 1948.

Diggins, John P. *Mussolini and Fascism: The View from America.* Princeton, N.J., 1972.

Divine, Robert A. *The Illusion of Neutrality.* Chicago, 1962.

———. *Second Chance: The Triumph of Internationalism in America During World War II.* New York, 1967.

———. *Roosevelt and World War II.* Baltimore, Md., 1969.

Documents Diplomatiques Français, 1932–1939. Series I, vol. 2. Paris, 1966.

Documents on British Foreign Policy, 1919–1939. Third Series, vol. 2: 1938. London, 1949.

———. Third Series, vol. 7: 1939. London, 1954.

———. Second Series, vol. 5: 1933. London, 1956.

Dozer, Donald M. *Are We Good Neighbors? Three Decades of Inter-American Relations, 1930–1960.* Gainesville, Fla., 1959.

Drake, St. Clair, and Horace R. Cayton. *Black Metropolis.* New York, 1945.

Eden, Anthony. *The Memoirs of Anthony Eden, Earl of Avon: Facing the Dictators.* Boston, 1962.

———. *The Memoirs of Anthony Eden, Earl of Avon: The Reckoning.* Boston, 1965.

Eisenhower, Dwight D. See Alfred D. Chandler, Jr.

Farago, Ladislas. *The Game of the Foxes.* New York, 1973 ed.

Farley, James A. *Jim Farley's Story.* New York, 1948.

Feiling, Keith. *The Life of Neville Chamberlain.* London, 1946.

Feingold, Henry L. *The Politics of Rescue: The Roosevelt Administration and the Holocaust, 1938–1945.* New Brunswick, N.J., 1970.

Feis, Herbert. *The China Tangle: The American Effort in China from Pearl Harbor to the Marshall Mission.* Princeton, N.J., 1953.

———. *The Road to Pearl Harbor.* New York, 1964 ed.

———. *1933: Characters in Crisis.* Boston, 1966.

Feis, Herbert. *Three International Episodes: Seen from E.A.* New York, 1966 ed.

———. *Churchill-Roosevelt-Stalin: The War They Waged and the Peace They Sought.* Princeton, N.J., 1967 ed.

Ferrell, Robert H. *American Diplomacy in the Great Depression: Hoover-Stimson Foreign Policy, 1929–1933.* New Haven, Conn., 1957.

Filene, Peter G. *Americans and the Soviet Experiment, 1917–1933.* Cambridge, Mass., 1967.

Fleming, D. F. *The United States and the World Court.* Garden City, N.Y., 1945.

Flynn, George Q. *American Catholics and the Roosevelt Presidency, 1932–1936.* Lexington, Ky., 1968.

———. *Roosevelt and Romanism: Catholics and American Diplomacy, 1937–1945.* Westport, Conn., 1976.

Foreign Relations of the United States, see United States Department of State.

Forrestal, James. See Walter Millis.

Freedman, Max, ed. *Roosevelt and Frankfurter: Their Correspondence, 1928–1945.* Boston, 1967.

Freidel, Frank. *Franklin D. Roosevelt: The Apprenticeship.* Boston, 1952.

———. *Franklin D. Roosevelt: The Ordeal.* Boston, 1954.

———. *Franklin D. Roosevelt: The Triumph.* Boston, 1956.

———. *Franklin D. Roosevelt: Launching the New Deal.* Boston, 1973.

Friedlander, Saul. *Prelude to Downfall: Hitler and the United States, 1939–1941.* New York, 1967.

Friedman, Donald J. *The Road from Isolation: The Campaign of the American Committee for Non-Participation in Japanese Aggression, 1938–1941.* Cambridge, Mass., 1968.

Frye, Alton. *Nazi Germany and the American Hemisphere, 1933–1941.* New Haven, Conn., 1967.

Funk, Arthur L. *Charles De Gaulle: The Crucial Years, 1943–1944.* Norman, Okla., 1959.

Gaddis, John L., *The United States and the Origins of the Cold War, 1941–1947.* New York, 1972.

Gallup, George H., ed. *The Gallup Poll: Public Opinion, 1935–1971.* Vol. I: *1935–1948.* New York, 1972.

Gardner, Lloyd C. *Economic Aspects of New Deal Diplomacy.* Madison, Wis., 1964.

Garland, Albert N., and Howard M. Smyth. *United States Army in World War II: Sicily and the Surrender of Italy.* Washington, D.C., 1965.

Gellman, Irwin F. *Roosevelt and Batista: Good Neighbor Diplomacy in Cuba, 1933–1945.* Albuquerque, N.M., 1973.

Greenfield, Kent Roberts, ed. *Command Decisions.* New York, 1959.

———. *American Strategy in World War II: A Reconsideration.* Baltimore, Md., 1963.

Graebner, Norman A., ed. *An Uncertain Tradition: American Secretaries of State in the Twentieth Century.* New York, 1961.

Grew, Joseph C. *Ten Years in Japan.* New York, 1944.

Guttman, Allen. *The Wound in the Heart: America and the Spanish Civil War.* Glencoe, Ill., 1962.

Gwyer, J. M. A., and J. R. M. Butler, *History of the Second World War: Grand Strategy.* Vol. 3: *June 1941–August 1942.* London, 1964.

Haight, John McVickar, Jr. *American Aid to France, 1938–1940.* New York, 1970.

Halasz, Nicholas. *Roosevelt Through Foreign Eyes.* Princeton, N.J., 1961.

Hall, H. Duncan. *North American Supply.* London, 1955.

Harriman, W. Averell, and Elie Abel. *Special Envoy to Churchill and Stalin, 1941–1946.* New York, 1975.

Harris, Brice, Jr. *The United States and the Italo-Ethiopian Crisis.* Stanford, Calif., 1964.

Hassett, William D. *Off the Record with F.D.R., 1942–1945.* New Brunswick, N.J., 1958.

Heinrichs, Waldo H., Jr. *American Ambassador: Joseph C. Grew and the Development of the United States Diplomatic Tradition.* Boston, 1966.

Herring, George C., Jr. *Aid to Russia, 1941–1946.* New York, 1973.

Hess, Gary R. *America Encounters India, 1941–1947.* Baltimore, Md., 1971.

Hollingsworth, Harold M., and William F. Holmes, eds., *Essays on the New Deal.* Austin, Tex., 1969.

Hooker, Nancy H., ed. *The Moffat Papers.* Cambridge, Mass., 1956.

Hotz, Robert, ed. *Way of a Fighter: The Memoirs of Claire Lee Chennault.* New York, 1949.

Howard, Michael. *History of the Second World War: Grand Strategy.* Vol. 4: *August 1942–September 1943.* London, 1972.

Howe, George F. *United States Army in World War II: Northwest Africa: Seizing the Initiative in the West.* Washington, D.C., 1957.

Hull, Cordell. *The Memoirs of Cordell Hull.* 2 vols. New York, 1948.

Hurd, Charles. *When the New Deal Was Young and Gay.* New York, 1965.

Hyde, Montgomery H. *The Quiet Canadian: The Secret Service Story of Sir William Stephenson.* London, 1962.

Ickes, Harold L. *The Secret Diary of Harold L. Ickes: The First Thousand Days.* New York, 1953.

———. *The Secret Diary of Harold L. Ickes: The Inside Struggle, 1936–1939.* New York, 1954.

———. *The Secret Diary of Harold L. Ickes: The Lowering Clouds, 1939–1941.* New York, 1954.

Isaacs, Harold R. *Scratches on Our Mind: American Images of China and India.* New York, 1958.

Israel, Fred L. *Nevada's Key Pittman.* Lincoln, Neb., 1963.

———, ed. *The War Diary of Breckinridge Long.* Lincoln, Neb., 1966.

Jonas, Manfred. *Isolationism in America, 1935–1941.* Ithaca, N.Y., 1966.

Kahn, E. J., Jr. *The China Hands: America's Foreign Service Officers and What Befell Them.* New York, 1975.

Kecskemeti, Paul. *Strategic Surrender: The Politics of Victory and Defeat.* Stanford, Calif., 1958.

Kennan, George F. *Memoirs, 1925–1950*. Boston, 1967.

Kimball, Warren F. *The Most Unsordid Act: Lend Lease, 1939–1941*. Baltimore, Md., 1969.

———. *Swords or Ploughshares? The Morgenthau Plan for Defeated Nazi Germany, 1943–1946*. Philadelphia, 1976.

Kleeman, Rita Halle. *Gracious Lady: The Life of Sara Delano Roosevelt*. New York, 1935.

Klein, Burton H. *Germany's Economic Preparations for War*. Cambridge, Mass., 1959.

Koginos, Manny T. *The Panay Incident: Prelude to War*. Lafayette, Ind., 1967.

Kolko, Gabriel. *The Politics of War: The World and United States Foreign Policy, 1943–1945*. New York, 1968.

Krock, Arthur. *Memoirs: Sixty Years on the Firing Line*. New York, 1968.

Lane, Arthur Bliss. *I Saw Poland Betrayed*. Indianapolis, Ind., 1948.

Langer, William L. *Our Vichy Gamble*. New York, 1947.

———, and S. Everett Gleason. *The Challenge to Isolation, 1937–1940*. New York, 1964 ed.

———. *The Undeclared War, 1940–1941*. New York, 1953.

Lash, Joseph P. *The Campus Strike Against War*. New York, 1935.

———. *Eleanor and Franklin*. New York, 1971.

———. *Roosevelt and Churchill, 1939–1941*. New York, 1976.

Leahy, William D. *I Was There*. New York, 1950.

Lee, Bradford A. *Britain and the Sino-Japanese War, 1937–1939*. Stanford, Calif., 1973.

Lee, Dwight, and George McReynolds, eds. *Essays in History and International Relations*. Worcester, Mass., 1949.

Leigh, Michael. *Mobilizing Consent: Public Opinion and American Foreign Policy, 1937–1947*. Westport, Conn., 1976.

Leuchtenburg, William E. *Franklin D. Roosevelt and the New Deal, 1932–1940*. New York, 1963.

Lindbergh, Charles A. *The Wartime Journals of Charles A. Lindbergh*. New York, 1970.

Lindley, Ernest K. *The Roosevelt Revolution*. New York, 1933.

Loewenheim, Francis L., Harold D. Langley, and Manfred Jonas, eds. *Roosevelt and Churchill: Their Secret Wartime Correspondence*. New York, 1975.

Long, Breckinridge. See Fred L. Israel.

Louis, W. Roger. *Imperialism at Bay*. New York, 1978.

MacArthur, Douglas. *Reminiscences*. New York, 1964.

Macmillan, Harold. *The Blast of War, 1939–1945*. London, 1967.

McCormick, Anne O'Hare. *The World at Home*. Edited by M. T. Sheehan. New York, 1956.

MacDonald, Charles B. *The Mighty Endeavor: American Armed Forces in the European Theater in World War II*. New York, 1969.

McLachlan, James. *American Boarding Schools: A Historical Study*. New York, 1970.

Matloff, Maurice, and Edwin M. Snell. *United States Army in World War II: Strategic Planning for Coalition Warfare, 1941–1942.* Washington, D.C., 1953.

——. *United States Army in World War II: Strategic Planning for Coalition Warfare, 1943–1944.* Washington, D.C., 1959.

May, Ernest R., ed. *The Ultimate Decision: The President as Commander-in-Chief.* New York, 1960.

Millis, Walter, ed. *The Forrestal Diaries.* New York, 1951.

Milward, Alan. *The German Economy at War.* London, 1965.

Moffat, Jay Pierrepont. See Nancy H. Hooker.

Moley, Raymond. *After Seven Years.* Lincoln, Neb., 1971 ed.

Moran, Lord. *Churchill: Taken from the Diaries of Lord Moran.* Boston, 1966.

Morison, Samuel Eliot. *History of United States Naval Operations in World War II.* Vol. 3. Boston, 1948.

Morton, Louis. *United States Army in World War II: The War in the Pacific: Strategy and Command: The First Two Years.* Washington, D.C., 1962.

Moscow, Warren. *Roosevelt and Willkie.* Englewood Cliffs, N.J., 1968.

Murphy, Robert. *Diplomat Among Warriors.* Garden City, N.Y., 1964.

Neustadt, Richard E. *Presidential Power: The Politics of Leadership.* New York, 1960.

Nixon, Edgar B., ed. *Franklin D. Roosevelt and Foreign Affairs: January 1933–January 1937.* 3 vols. Cambridge, Mass., 1969.

Notter, Harley. *Postwar Foreign Policy Preparation, 1939–1945.* Washington, D.C., 1949.

O'Connor, Raymond G. *Diplomacy for Victory: FDR and Unconditional Surrender.* New York, 1971.

Offner, Arnold A. *American Appeasement: United States Foreign Policy and Germany, 1933–1938.* Cambridge, Mass., 1969.

Ottley, Roi. *New World A-Coming.* Boston, 1943.

Paxton, Robert O. *Vichy France.* New York, 1972.

Pelz, Stephen. *Race to Pearl Harbor: The Failure of the Second London Naval Conference and the Onset of World War II.* Cambridge, Mass., 1974.

Perkins, Frances. *The Roosevelt I Knew.* New York, 1946.

Pickersgill, J. W. *The Mackenzie King Record.* Vol. I: 1939–1944. Toronto, 1960.

——, and D. F. Forster. *The Mackenzie King Record.* Vol. II: 1944–1945. Toronto, 1968.

Pogue, Forrest C. *George C. Marshall: Education of a General.* New York, 1963.

——. *George C. Marshall: Ordeal and Hope, 1939–1942.* London, 1968 ed.

——. *George C. Marshall: Organizer of Victory, 1943–1945.* New York, 1973.

Pratt, Julius W. *Cordell Hull.* 2 vols. New York, 1964.

Rauch, Basil. *Roosevelt: From Munich to Pearl Harbor.* New York, 1950.

Rollins, Alfred B., Jr. *Roosevelt and Howe*. New York, 1962.

Romanus, Charles F., and Riley Sunderland. *United States Army in World War II: Stilwell's Mission to China*. Washington, D.C., 1953.

————, and ————. *United States Army in World War II: Stilwell's Command Problems*. Washington, D.C., 1956.

Roosevelt, Eleanor. *This Is My Story*. New York, 1937.

————. *This I Remember*. New York, 1949.

Roosevelt, Elliott, ed. *F.D.R.: His Personal Letters*. New York, 1947–50. Vol. I: *Early Years;* Vol. II: *1905–1928; 1928–1945* in 2 volumes.

————, and James Brough. *An Untold Story: The Roosevelts of Hyde Park*. New York, 1973.

Roosevelt, Franklin D. *F.D.R.: His Personal Letters*. See Elliott Roosevelt.

————. *Franklin D. Roosevelt and Foreign Affairs*. See Edgar B. Nixon.

————. *Public Papers and Addresses*. See Samuel I. Rosenman.

————. *Roosevelt and Churchill. Their Secret Wartime Correspondence*. See Francis L. Loewenheim.

————. *Roosevelt and Frankfurter*. See Max Freedman.

Rosenman, Samuel I., ed. *The Public Papers and Addresses of Franklin D. Roosevelt*. 13 vols. New York, 1938–50.

————. *Working with Roosevelt*. New York, 1952.

Russett, Bruce M. *No Clear and Present Danger: A Skeptical View of the U.S. Entry into World War II*. New York, 1972.

Schlesinger, Arthur M., Jr. *The Crisis of the Old Order, 1919–1933*. Boston, 1957.

————. *The Coming of the New Deal*. Boston, 1959.

————. *The Politics of Upheaval*. Boston, 1960.

Schroeder, Paul W. *The Axis Alliance and Japanese-American Relations, 1941*. Ithaca, N.Y., 1958.

Sherwin, Martin J. *A World Destroyed: The Atomic Bomb and the Grand Alliance*. New York, 1975.

Sherwood, Robert. *Roosevelt and Hopkins*. New York, 1950 ed.

Sobel, Robert. *The Origins of Interventionism: The U.S. and the Russo-Finnish War*. New York, 1960.

Stalin's Correspondence with Churchill, Attlee, Roosevelt and Truman, 1941–1945. 2 vols. Moscow, 1957.

Standley, William H., and Arthur A. Ageton. *Admiral Ambassador to Russia*. Chicago, 1955.

Steele, A. T. *The American People and China*. New York, 1966.

Steele, Richard W. *The First Offensive, 1942: Roosevelt, Marshall, and the Making of American Strategy*. Bloomington, Ind., 1973.

Stettinius, Edward R., Jr. *Roosevelt and the Russians: The Yalta Conference*. Garden City, N.Y., 1949.

————. See Thomas M. Campbell and George C. Herring.

Stilwell, Joseph. See Theodore H. White.

Stimson, Henry L., and McGeorge Bundy. *On Active Service in Peace and War*. New York, 1948.

Tansill, Charles C. *Back Door to War: The Roosevelt Foreign Policy, 1933–1941*. Chicago, 1952.

Taylor, A. J. P. *The Origins of the Second World War*. New York, 1966 ed.
Taylor, F. Jay. *The United States and the Spanish Civil War*. New York, 1956.
Theobald, Robert A. *The Final Secret of Pearl Harbor*. New York, 1954.
Thomas, Hugh. *The Spanish Civil War*. New York, 1961.
Thompson, Harry C., and Linda Mayo. *United States Army in World War II: The Ordnance Department-Procurement and Supply*. Washington, D.C., 1960.
Thorne, Christopher. *Allies of a Kind: The United States, Britain, and the War Against Japan, 1941–1945*. New York, 1978.
Tompkins, Peter. *The Murder of Admiral Darlan*. New York, 1965.
Traina, Richard P. *American Diplomacy and the Spanish Civil War*. Bloomington, Ind., 1968.
Tuchman, Barbara. *Stilwell and the American Experience in China, 1911–1945*. New York, 1970.
Tugwell, Rexford G. *The Democratic Roosevelt*. Garden City, N.Y., 1957.
Tully, Grace. *FDR: My Boss*. Chicago, 1949.
Ulam, Adam B. *Expansion and Coexistence: The History of Soviet Foreign Policy, 1917–1967*. New York, 1968.
———. *The Rivals: America and Russia since World War II*. New York, 1971.
———. *Stalin*. New York, 1973.
United States Congress. *Hearings before the Joint Committee on the Investigation of the Pearl Harbor Attack*. 79th Congress, 1st Session. 39 vols. Washington, D.C., 1946.
United States Department of State. *The China White Paper: August 1949*. 2 vols. Stanford, Calif., 1967 ed.
———. *Foreign Relations of the United States: Japan, 1931–1941*. 2 vols. Washington, D.C., 1943.
———. *Peace and War: United States Foreign Policy, 1931–1941*. Washington, D.C., 1943.
———. *Foreign Relations of the United States: The Soviet Union, 1933–1939*. Washington, D.C., 1952.
———. *Foreign Relations of the United States, 1933–1945*. Washington, D.C., 1950–69.
———. *Foreign Relations of the United States: China, 1942–1945*. 4 vols. Washington, D.C., 1956–1969.
———. *Foreign Relations of the United States: Conferences at Washington, 1941–1942, and Casablanca, 1943*. Washington, D.C., 1968.
———. *Foreign Relations of the United States: Conferences at Washington and Quebec, 1943*. Washington, D.C., 1970.
———. *Foreign Relations of the United States: Conferences at Cairo and Tehran, 1943*. Washington, D.C., 1961.
———. *Foreign Relations of the United States: The Conference at Quebec, 1944*. Washington, D.C., 1972.
———. *Foreign Relations of the United States: The Conferences at Malta and Yalta, 1945*. Washington, D.C., 1955.
United States Senate. *Final Report of the Select Committee To Study*

Governmental Operations with Respect to Intelligence Activities. Book 3. Washington, D.C., 1976.

———. *Hearings before the Select Committee To Study Governmental Operations with Respect to Intelligence Activities.* Vol. 6. Washington, D.C., 1976.

Vandenberg, Arthur H., Jr. *The Private Papers of Senator Vandenberg.* Boston, 1952.

Viorst, Milton. *Hostile Allies: FDR and De Gaulle.* New York, 1965.

Wallace, Henry A. See John Morton Blum.

Watson, Mark S. *United States Army in World War II: Chief of Staff: Prewar Plans and Preparations.* Washington, D.C., 1950.

Wehle, Louis B. *Hidden Threads of History: Wilson Through Roosevelt.* New York, 1953.

Weil, Martin, A *Pretty Good Club: The Founding Fathers of the U.S. Foreign Service.* New York, 1978.

Weinberg, Gerhard L. *The Foreign Policy of Hitler's Germany: Diplomatic Revolution in Europe, 1933–1936.* Chicago, 1970.

Welles, Sumner. *The Time for Decision.* New York, 1944.

———. *Seven Decisions That Shaped History.* New York, 1950.

Werth, Alexander. *Russia at War, 1941–1945.* New York, 1965 ed.

Wheeler-Bennett, J. W. *The Pipe Dream of Peace.* New York, 1935.

———. *Munich: Prologue to Tragedy.* New York, 1964 ed.

White, Theodore H., ed. *The Stilwell Papers.* New York, 1948.

———, and Annalee Jacoby. *Thunder Out of China.* New York, 1946.

Wilson, Theodore A. *The First Summit: Roosevelt and Churchill at Placentia Bay, 1941.* Boston, 1969.

Wiltz, John E. *In Search of Peace: The Senate Munitions Inquiry, 1934–1936.* Baton Rouge, La., 1963.

Winterbotham, F. W. *The Ultra Secret.* New York, 1974.

Wittner, Laurence S. *Rebels Against War: The American Peace Movement, 1941–1960.* New York, 1969.

Wohlstetter, Roberta. *Pearl Harbor: Warning and Decision.* Stanford, Calif., 1962.

Wood, Bryce. *The Making of the Good Neighbor Policy.* New York, 1961.

Woodward, Sir Llewellyn. *British Foreign Policy in the Second World War.* 4 vols. London, 1970–75.

Wyman, David S. *Paper Walls: America and the Refugee Crisis, 1938–1941.* Amherst, Mass., 1968.

Yergin, Daniel. *Shattered Peace: The Origins of the Cold War and the National Security State.* Boston, 1977.

INDEX

GAL. 29

OXFORD   (76870)   SNEType D-5919   12-19-78   182-62-6

Dallek: Franklin D. Roosevelt in Peace & War .... 8/9 Electra ....

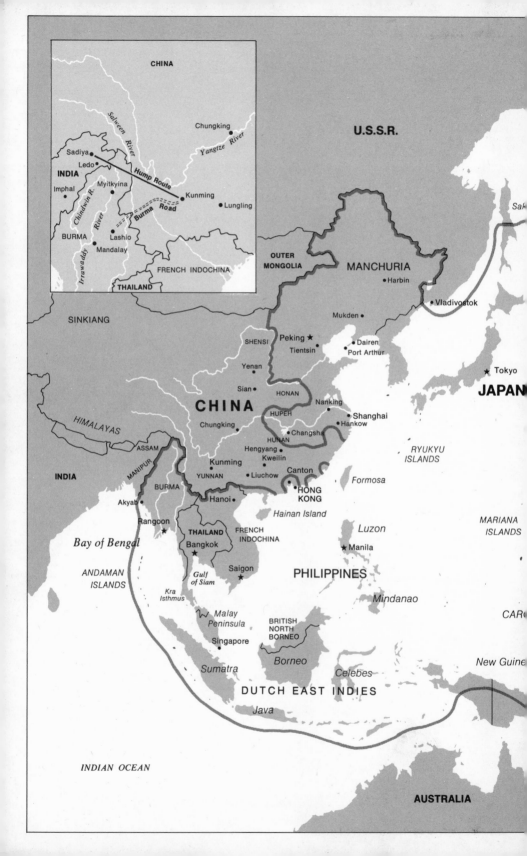